Church of the Nativity

BETHLEHEM

THE

LAND AND THE BOOK;

OR,

BIBLICAL ILLUSTRATIONS DRAWN FROM THE MANNERS AND
CUSTOMS, THE SCENES AND SCENERY OF

THE HOLY LAND.

BY

W. M. THOMSON, D.D.,
THIRTY YEARS MISSIONARY IN SYRIA AND PALESTINE.

LONDON:
DARF PUBLISHERS LIMITED
———————— 1985 ————————

First Published 1877
New Impression 1985

ISBN 1 85077 054 9

Reprinted by A. Wheaton & Co. Ltd, Exeter

CONTENTS.

LIST OF ILLUSTRATIONS.

PREFACE TO THIS EDITION.

HE work of Dr. Thomson, which the present edition is designed to make more generally known to British readers, carries us over a part of Southern Syria and over Palestine, but in a direction opposite to that pursued by most travellers. Palestine is commonly entered from the south; and Hebron, Bethlehem, and Jerusalem are among the first places visited by tourists. Dr. Thomson enters it from the north, and the places which other travellers usually visit first are kept by him to the end. In the first part of the following work the scene is laid at the foot of Lebanon, along the coast of PHŒNICIA, which, though included in the land promised to Abraham, was not, in point of fact, possessed by the Jews. From Tyre we are conducted, in the pleasant pages of Dr. Thomson, across the NORTHERN BOUNDARY OF PALESTINE; and after gazing on the snow-capped Hermon, visiting the sites of Dan, and Cæsarea Philippi, and the sources of the Jordan, we pass through UPPER GALILEE, and return to the sea at the BAY OF ACRE. There we spend some time in the survey of a neighbourhood memorable in all history, ancient and modern. Again we strike eastwards, and cross to the LAKE OF GALILEE, walking right round the shores which were so familiar to Jesus. Leaving them, we again turn westwards, till we reach the scene of his childhood, NAZARETH. From Nazareth we strike into the famous plain of ESDRAELON, survey the heights of Tabor, Hermon, and Gilboa, visit Endor and Shunem, and other places famed in Old Testament history; and crossing the Kishon and the ridge of Carmel, come again on the sea at the ruins of CÆSAREA PALESTINA.

From this ancient Roman capital of Palestine we proceed along the sea-shore, with the plain of SHARON and the mountains of Samaria on our left; leaving which we enter the plain of PHILISTIA, flanked in like manner by the mountains of Judah. From the cities of the Philistines we strike up, like Samson with the gates of Gaza on his back, to HEBRON, on the top of the great ridge that runs along central Palestine; then through the WILDERNESS OF JUDAH, to the northern edge of the DEAD SEA, JORDAN, and JERICHO. From Jericho we advance along the same wild path which was traversed by Jesus on his last journey to Jerusalem, pausing like him at BETHANY, before entering the sacred city. Having conducted us through JERUSALEM, and some of the most celebrated localities in its neighbourhood, Dr. Thomson takes his leave, after having given us an amount of information on the manners of the country, and thrown a degree of light on the meaning of Scripture, unexampled, we do not hesitate to say, in the pages of any other writer.

NOTE.

THE purposely *négligé* style in which "The Land and the Book" is thrown together, while it enlivens the narrative, and affords easy introduction to a vast variety of topics, has, nevertheless, some disadvantages. Ordinary readers will sometimes desiderate a little more plain information on the places noticed; and it will often be felt desirable to have beforehand a sort of general idea of the districts to be traversed. In republishing the work in this country, we have not thought it necessary to make any alterations on the text of the author; but we have tried to remedy the defects alluded to, by supplying—1. An occasional bird's eye view of the districts traversed; 2. Brief notices, in foot notes, regarding particular places; 3. A summary of the principal *contents*, prefixed to each chapter; and 4. Marginal notes along each page. All that has been thus supplied in the present edition (with the exception of the contents of the chapters) is distinguished from the author's text by being enclosed within brackets [].

We trust that these additions will serve to render this *unique* and truly valuable work of Bible illustration more generally useful in this country.

AUTHOR'S PREFACE.

EVERY sincere attempt to illustrate the Word of God is in itself commendable. On this fundamental fact the author rests his apology for obtruding the present work upon the notice of the public. Commentaries are daily multiplying; geographies and dictionaries, researches and travels almost innumerable, lend their aid to the student of the sacred page, and it is not proposed to add another to the long list. The author does not attempt a consecutive comment on any particular book of the Bible, but selects indiscriminately from all, such passages as contain the themes he desires to elucidate. The field is ample, and it is abundantly rich in subjects for scenic and pictorial description. Whether he has succeeded in working out his own idea or not must be left for others to determine; but if he has failed, it has not been through want of opportunity to study the originals of which his pictures are to be copies. For a quarter of a century he has resided amid the scenes and the scenery to be described, and from mid-day to midnight, in winter and in summer, has gazed upon them with a joyous enthusiasm that never tired. The first impressions, corrected and improved by subsequent study and examination, are now reproduced for the eye of the public and the heart of the pious.

The author entertains the opinion that much has been published upon Biblical illustration which recent research has shown to be incorrect or rendered superfluous; and much, also, that does not properly belong to the subject. Erudite and curious inquiries into the life and conduct of patriarchs, prophets, and kings, for example, though valuable contributions to religious knowledge, are plainly out

of place in such works; and the same remark applies to
extended critical and exegetical discussion. In these and
many other departments of Biblical literature, the student in
the heart of Germany or America, surrounded by ample
libraries, is in a better situation to carry on profitable inquiries than the pilgrim in the Holy Land, however long
his loiterings or extended his rambles. But it is far otherwise in respect to the scenes and the scenery of the Bible,
and to the living manners and customs of the East which
illustrate that blessed book. Here we need the actual observer, not the distant and secluded student. To describe
these things, and such as these, one must have seen and *felt*
them; and this the author has done through many years of
various vicissitude and adventure, and whatever of life and
truth may be in his pictures is due solely to this fact. Here
is his appropriate field, and the limit of his promise. Where
he has been he proposes to guide his reader, through that
"good land" of mountain, and vale, and lake, and river—to
the shepherd's tent, the peasant's hut, the hermit's cave, and
palace of kings, and temple of gods—to the haunts of the
living and the sepulchres of the dead—to muse on what
has been, and converse with what *is*, and learn from all
what they can teach concerning the oracles of God.

A large part of these pages was actually written in the
open country—on sea shore or sacred lake, on hill side or
mountain top, under the olive, or the oak, or the shadow
of a great rock: there the author lived, thought, felt, and
wrote; and, no doubt, place and circumstance have given
colour and character to many parts of the work. He would
not have it otherwise. That blessed Book, at once his guide,
pattern, and text, wears the same air of country life; and He
who came from heaven to earth for man's redemption loved
not the city. To the wilderness and the mountain he retired to meditate and pray. Thither he led his disciples
and the listening multitudes; and from seed-time and harvest, and flocks and shepherds, and birds and flowers, he

drew his sweetest lessons of instruction. In this identical land, amid the same scenes, has the author of this work earnestly cultivated communion and intimate correspondence with this divine Teacher, and with the internal and external life of the Book of God; and what he has found and felt he has tried to trace upon the silent page for other eyes to see and other hearts to enjoy. Whether wisely done or otherwise, herein is revealed the reason of that rural *abandon* in matter and manner with which the reader is everywhere saluted.

Though the author has had his full share of personal "experiences" during his long residence in the East, yet want of space has compelled him to omit such details, except where they serve to bring out some circumstance bearing upon the general design of the work. And the same necessity obliges him to forego, to a great extent, mere moral and devotional reflections. Many of the topics discussed not only admit of, but seem to suggest and even require them; but something *must* be left out, and, whether right or wrong, the author thought it most in accordance with the specific design of his work to omit such "meditations." And yet it is obvious that we ought not to impose silence upon the thousand witnesses to the veracity of the Bible which meet the pilgrim at every turn in his pathway. Broken columns, and prostrate temples, and cities in ruin, must bear testimony to the inspiration of prophecy; and ravens and sparrows, and cedars and brambles, and fruits and flowers, will preach sermons and utter parables, and we shall not hesitate to listen when they begin to teach.

Finally, in this connection, should any of the author's friends be disappointed in not finding more reference to the missionary operations with which he has been connected, he has no other apology to offer than *want of space*. A history of these various enterprises, American, English, Irish, and German, would require a separate work, and therefore must be omitted in this.

The "Land and the Book" is designed for general and

popular reading rather than for the professional student, and therefore it has been deemed necessary to avoid dry, textual exposition. In order to secure entire freedom in introducing into the current narrative the multifarious subjects to be illustrated, the author has adopted a modified form of dialogue, but he does not encumber his work with any complex machinery, any dramatis personæ. He is not writing a novel or a play, to teach manners and morals, or portray human character, and his travelling companion acts merely as usher, to introduce *what needs to be introduced*. It is merely a device to smooth the transition from topic to topic, and from scene to scene, as occasion may require. This, in its present application, may be *new*, but for the purpose for which it is assumed it has many and important advantages.

The "pilgrimage" is continued through so much of the Land and of the year as to allow the author to treat of those passages in the Bible which refer to such matters in their appropriate place and time ; and thus he does not speak of *harvest* in *winter*, nor of the *vintage* in *spring*, nor of *rains* and *storms* in *summer*, but of all in the seasons when they actually occur. There are also certain subjects which naturally group themselves around a few localities. For example, the battle-fields of the Bible are mainly in the southern part of Palestine, where Joshua, and Samson, and Samuel, and Saul, and David performed most of their exploits, and on the plains of Esdraelon and Hûleh. Again, the parables have all a *natural basis*, upon which they are constructed by the divine skill of Him who spoke as never man spake, and these mostly cluster about Nazareth, Gennesaret, and Capernaum.

The pictorial illustrations have been prepared with much care, and beautifully executed, and add greatly not only to the interest, but also to the real value of the work. Many of them are original, and others selected from the best existing sources, and so corrected as to be more true to nature, and more appropriate to the book. In this department the author has been largely indebted to the pencil of his son, W. H. Thomson. The maps have been compiled and drawn with exclusive reference to the present work, and embody, it is believed, all the most valuable results of recent geographical explorations in the Holy Land.

The work is supplied with two copious and carefully-prepared indexes, one of *texts*, and the other of *names* and *subjects;* and the attention of the reader is particularly directed to them, as they will greatly facilitate reference to those parts of the work where the various subjects treated of and the Scripture passages illustrated, are to be found.

And, now, with the cheerful hope and fervent prayer that our pleasant pilgrimage together through the earthly Canaan may hereafter be resumed and perpetuated in the heavenly, the author bids his courteous reader a cordial *adieu*.

INTRODUCTION.

T HE land where the Word made-flesh dwelt with men is, and must ever be, an integral part of the Divine Revelation. Her testimony is essential to the chain of evidences, her aid invaluable in exposition. Mournful deserts and mouldering ruins rebuke the pride of man and vindicate the truth of God; and yawning gulfs, from Tophet to the Sea of Death, in its sepulchre of bitumen and brimstone, warn the wicked, and prophesy of coming wrath. Even the trees of her forests speak parables, and rough brambles bear allegories; while little sparrows sing hymns to the happy, and lilies give lessons to comfort the poor. The very hills and mountains, rocks, rivers, and fountains, are symbols and pledges of things far better than themselves. In a word, Palestine is one vast tablet whereupon God's messages to men have been drawn, and graven deep in living characters by the Great Publisher of glad tidings, to be seen and read of all to the end of time.

The Land and the Book—with reverence be it said—constitute the ENTIRE and ALL-PERFECT TEXT, and should be studied together. To read the one by the light of the other has been the privilege of the author for twenty-five years; and the governing purpose in publishing is to furnish additional facilities for this delightful study to those who have not been thus favoured. The Itinerary commences with eighteen hundred and fifty-seven, but the scenes described were visited many times during the preceding quarter of a century. These almost innumerable excursions are not imaginary, but real; and the results, so far as they bear on Biblical Illustration, appear in the current narrative. The

" conversations," also, are equally genuine—are, in fact, a part of the tours—held in the open country, on horseback, or beneath the pilgrim's tent.   Each reader is at liberty to regard himself as the *compagnon de voyage;* but, in the mind of the author, his fellow-traveller is not a mythical abstraction, whose office is merely to introduce what needs to be introduced, but a true and loving brother, who thus announces his arrival, and the object of his visit to the Holy Land:—

"Ras Beirût, January 20th, 1857.

"My Dear W——, I this morning woke to find life's long dream a beautiful reality.   For twenty years and more, as you well know, a visit to Palestine has been the unattained object of my fondest aspirations; and now here am I safely landed on her sacred shore, in perfect health, and ready to prosecute our pilgrimage with cheerful courage and high hope.   The compact of our boyhood is to be realized, and I summon you to fulfil your part of it.   This land of the Bible must become familiar to me as childhood's home.   There are lessons in everything around me, I feel quite sure, and teachers on every side, did I but know their language.   You are to be my dragoman to interpret this unknown tongue of the Holy Land.   Such, you remember, is our compact.

" I am told that the necessary preparation for our travels can only be made in this city.   Come on, therefore, without delay, and let us gather together whatever will contribute to our comfort, safety, and success.   This will reach you by messenger express.   The answer, I hope, will be yourself."

This summons was neither unexpected nor reluctantly obeyed; and a few hours' ride along the shore brought the author from Sidon to Beirût, where the long-separated met in the hospitable mansion of a mutual friend.   And now, kind reader, I trust that, like ourselves, you are eager to commence this tour of the Holy Land.   But we must begin our preparations for it with " the garment of patience." Horses, and mules, and tents, and canteens, and beds, cooking apparatus, and servants to use it, with many other things, too trifling to be mentioned, yet too necessary to be omitted, cannot be secured in a day.   Meanwhile we may employ some of the hours of unavoidable delay in excursions to sites and scenes in and around our beautiful city.   Indeed, we invite you to join us in such a ramble at once through these charming suburbs.

THE LAND AND THE BOOK.

PART I.—PHŒNICIA AND LEBANON.

CHAPTER I.

BEIRUT.

January 24th, 1857

Our first walk in the Land of Promise ! [1]   To me a land of promises more Land of Promise. numerous and not less interesting than those given to the Father of the Faithful, when the Lord said, " Arise, walk through the land in the length of it and in the breadth of it; for I will give it unto thee." [2]   It is given to me also, and I mean to make it mine from Dan to Beersheba before I leave it.

Doubtless; and so every young enthusiast in trade means to make his fortune. But do you expect to gain such an inheritance as this in a few months ?   Abraham himself never set foot on one-tenth of this territory, and Moses only got a bird's-eye view of it—not a bad one, though, if the day was as intensely clear as ours is.   One seems to look quite to the bottom of heaven's profoundest azure, " where the everlasting stars abide ;" and how sharply defined is every rock and ravine, and tree and house on lofty Lebanon.   That virgin snow on its summit is thirty miles off, and yet you could almost read your own name there, if written with a bold hand on its calm, cold brow.   Through such utter transparency did the Lord show unto Moses, from the top of Mount Abarim, " all

---

[1 Beirût was included in the Land of Promise, but hardly in the land of possession, being one of the sea-ports of Phœnicia—a country that continued, after the settlement of the Israelites, to be inhabited by the remarkable people to whom it gave its name.   The great size and importance of Beirût are quite modern, attained, indeed, within the last thirty years.   They are due to its foreign commerce, there being regular steam-communication with France and Austria, and occasionally with Britain.   It is the most thriving commercial city of Syria, and is the residence of the British consul.   It is not mentioned in Scripture, at least under its present name.—ED.]

² Gen. xiii. 17.

PART
I.
_____

Views of
Palestine.

From
Lebanon.

Modes of
travelling.

the land of Gilead unto Dan, and all Naphtali, and the land of Ephraim and Manasseh, and all the land of Judah unto the utmost sea, and the south, and the plain of the valley of Jericho, the city of palm-trees, unto Zoar." [1] Nor need there have been any miracle in the matter. Though an hundred and twenty years old, "his eye was not dim, nor his natural force abated." [2] And I can guide you to many a Pisgah on Lebanon and Hermon from whence the view is far more extensive. It was through such an atmosphere as this, I suppose, that the old Phœnicians first saw Cyprus, and called it Chittim, a name afterward applied by Hebrew poets and prophets to the islands of the Mediterranean in general.

I have heard it denied, both in and out of Palestine, that Cyprus could be seen from Lebanon ; but from many a stand-point up yonder I have often beheld that favourite isle of the Paphian Venus glowing in the golden light of our summer evenings. More distinctly still is Lebanon visible from Cyprus. There is a splendid view of it from the mountain of the Cross, a few miles back of Larnica; and many years ago, when travelling through the island, I climbed, with infinite toil, the northern range of mountains to a giddy pinnacle, not far from the ruined but romantic castle of Búffavento, and from it the higher half of Lebanon looked like a huge snow-bank drifted up against the sky. Beneath my feet rolled the sparkling seas of Cilicia and Pamphylia, over which Paul sailed on his way to Rome ; while, far beyond, the glaciers of Taurus flashed back the setting sun. Through such an atmosphere, objects are visible to a distance quite incredible to the inexperienced. You will find yourself deceived in this matter a hundred times before you have travelled a week in Syria. And now we are abroad, shall we ramble on *ala bab Allâh* (towards God's gate), as our Arabs say when they neither know nor care where they are going ?

Just my case at present. Where all is new, and every prospect pleases, it matters little what path we take, and, for the moment, I am thinking of what is not seen rather than what is.

Looking for an omnibus, perhaps, or expecting the cars to overtake us ?

Not just that. I know that such things are not yet found in Syria ; but I am greatly surprised at the absence of all wheeled vehicles, and look round at every fresh noise, expecting to see a cart, or dray, or waggon of some kind or other, but am always disappointed.

And will be. There is nothing of the sort in Syria ; neither is there street or road for them in any part of the land.

How do you account for this ? It was not always so. We read of carriages and chariots at a very early age. Joseph sent waggons for the wives and little ones of his father's family.[3] Jacob's funeral was attended by chariots from Egypt to Hebron.[4] The Canaanites had chariots in the time of Joshua.[5] Judah could not drive out the inhabitants of the valley because they had chariots of iron.[6] Jaban had nine hundred,[7] and the Philistines thirty thousand (?) in the

_____

[1] Deut. xxxiv. 1–3.   [2] Deut. xxxiv. 7.   [3] Gen. xlv. 19, 21.   [4] Gen. i. 9.
[5] Josh. xvii. 16.   [6] Judges i. 19   [7] Judges iv. 13.

reign of Saul.[1] Isaiah rebuked the children of Israel because there was no end **CHAPTER**
to their chariots;[2] and thus it continued down to the time when Philip joined **I.**
himself to the chariot of the eunuch on the road to Gaza.[3] Throughout all Chariots.
this long period there were countless carriages in this country, and, of necessity,
roads for them. How is it that now there is neither the one nor the other ?

Natural enough, and very appropriate. The first inquiry of a sensible traveller in a strange land will have reference to the means of locomotion. As to
your question, however, the natives will tell you that carriage-roads cannot be
made in Syria. But this is a mistake. They might be constructed, at a Roads in
moderate expense, in nearly all parts of the country. Their total disappear- Syria.
ance can easily be explained. When the wild Arabs of the Mohammedan
desolation became masters, wheeled vehicles immediately sunk into neglect,
and even contempt. Accustomed only to the horse, the camel, and the ass,
they despised all other means of travel and transportation. Good roads were
not necessary for them, and, being neglected, they quickly disappeared from
the land, and carriages with them. Nor will they ever re-appear till some
other race than the Arab predominates, and a better than the Turk governs.
Even the Christian inhabitants of Lebanon, where good roads are most needed,
have no adequate appreciation of them, and take no pains to make them.
They drive their loaded camels, mules, and donkeys along frightful paths, and
endanger their own necks by riding over the same, from generation to generation, without dreaming of any improvement. You must educate your nerves
into indifference in this matter, and get ready as fast as possible to flounder Loaded
over all sorts of break-neck places in the course of our pilgrimage. camels.

" What man has done, man can do." I have all my life been accustomed to
the saddle, and like it; and a little danger now and then will impart additional
charms to the tour.—What tree is this which over-
shadows our path ? It is more bushy and thick-set
than the apple-tree, for which I at first mistook it,
and as we near it, I see that the leaves are longer
and of a much darker green.

That is the kharûb—the tree that bore the
husks which the swine did eat, and with which the Kharub
poor prodigal would have filled his belly.[4] The tree
"husks"—a mistranslation—are fleshy pods some- " husks."
what like those of the honey-locust-tree, from six
to ten inches long and one broad, lined inside with
a gelatinous substance, not wholly unpleasant to

the taste when thoroughly ripe. I have seen large orchards of this kharûb in
Cyprus, where it is still the food which the swine do eat. In Syria, where
we have no swine, or next to none, the pods are ground up, and a species of
molasses expressed, which is much used in making certain kinds of sweet-

---

[1] 1 Sam. xiii. 5   [2] Isaiah ii. 7.   [3] Acts viii. 28.   [4] Luke xv. 16.

meats. The tree is an evergreen, and casts a most delightful and refreshing shade to the weary traveller. In this country they do not yield large crops, but in Cyprus, Asia Minor, and the Grecian Islands, you will see full-grown trees bending under half a ton of green pods. The kharûb is often called St. John's Bread, and also Locust-tree, from a mistaken idea about the food of the Baptist in the wilderness. It is the *Ceratonia siliqua* of Linnæus.

The Syca-more.
That noble tree before us, with giant arms low down and wide open, must be the Syrian sycamore. I once heard an itinerant preacher in the "back

SYCAMORE.

woods" puzzle himself and his hearers with an elaborate criticism about the tree into which Zaccheus climbed to see the Saviour.[1] He and his audience

_____

[1] Luke xix. 4.

were familiar only with the sycamores of our flat river bottoms, tall as a steeple, and smooth as hypocrisy. "Why," said the orator, "a squirrel can't climb them." The conclusion reached was that the sycamore must have been a mulberry-tree. But nothing is easier than to climb into these sycamores; and, in fact, here is a score of boys and girls in this one; and as its giant arms stretch quite across the road, those on them can look directly down upon any crowd passing beneath. It is admirably adapted to the purpose for which Zaccheus selected it.

True; and moreover, it is generally planted by the way-side, and in the open spaces where several paths meet, just where Zaccheus found it. This

sycamore is a remarkable tree. It not only bears several crops of figs during the year, but those figs grow on short stems along the trunk and large branches, and not at the end of twigs, as in other fruit-bearing trees. The figs are small, and of a greenish-yellow colour. At Gaza and Askelon, I saw them of a purple tinge, and much larger than they are in this part of the country. They were carried to market in large quantities, and appeared to be more valued there than with us. Still they are at best very insipid, and none but the poorer classes eat them. This agrees with and explains an allusion in Amos. He had aroused the wrath of Jeroboam by the severity of his rebukes, and, being advised to flee for his life, excuses himself by a statement which implies that he belonged to the humblest class of the community: "I am no prophet, neither am I a prophet's son; but I am a herdman, and a *gatherer of sycamore fruit*." [1] None but the very poor consent to be herdmen, and only such, at this day, gather sycamore fruit, or use it.

The natives say that the sycamore bears seven crops a year. I think it is irregular in this matter. Some bear oftener than others, and the same tree yields more crops one year than another. It is easily propagated, merely by planting a stout branch in the ground, and watering it until it has struck out roots into the soil. This it does with great rapidity, and to a vast depth. It was with reference to this latter fact that our blessed Lord selected it to illustrate the power of faith: "If ye had faith as a grain of mustard-seed, ye might say unto this sycamine-tree, Be thou plucked up by the root, and be thou planted in the sea, and it should obey you." [2] Now look at this tree—its ample girth, its wide-spread arms, branching off from the parent trunk only a few feet from the ground; then examine its enormous roots—as thick, as numerous, and as wide spread into the deep soil below as the branches extend into the air above—the very best type of invincible steadfastness. What power on earth can pluck up such a tree? Heaven's thunderbolt may strike it down, the wild

Marginal notes: CHAPTER I. Adapted for climbing. Figs. Number of crops. Its steadfastness.

---

[1] Amos vii. 14. [2] Luke xvii. 6.

PART
I.
tornado may tear it to fragments, but nothing short of miraculous power can fairly pluck it up by the roots.

Illustra-
tion of
power of
faith.
I have but faint ideas of a faith that could pluck up and plant in the sea such a tree as that ; and these facts certainly add great emphasis to the " parable." You are doubtless aware, however, that other critics besides our orator of the back-woods maintain that the sycamore of the New Testament is actually the mulberry-tree, and others that the sycamine of this passage and the sycamore are different trees ; and there is a slight difference in the Greek.

I know it ; but the word *sycamine* seems to be derived from the Hebrew name for sycamore, and I know no reason why their identity should be questioned. As to the mulberry, it is yet to be shown that it was then known in Palestine, although our translators have mentioned it in one or two places ; and, further, the mulberry is more easily plucked up by the roots than any other tree of the same size in the country, and the thing is oftener done. Hundreds of them are plucked up every year in this vicinity, and brought to the city for firewood. It is not to be supposed that He who spake as man never spake would select this tree, with its short, feeble roots, to illustrate the irresistible power of faith.

Wood of
sycamore.
The wood of the sycamore is soft and of very little value. This is implied in various places in the Bible. Thus in Isaiah, " The people say in pride and stoutness of heart, ... the sycamores are cut down, but we will change them to cedars." [1] And so, in the days of Solomon, when even silver was nothing accounted of, " he made cedars to be in Jerusalem as the sycamore-trees that are in the vale, for abundance." [2] It is a tender tree, flourishes immensely in sandy plains and warm vales, but cannot bear the hard, cold mountain. A sharp frost will kill them ; and this agrees with the fact that they were killed by it in Egypt. Among the wonders wrought in the field of Zoan, David says, " He destroyed their vines with hail, and their sycamores with frost." [3] Certainly, a frost keen enough to kill the sycamore would be one of the greatest " wonders " that could happen at the present day in this same field of Zoan.

We shall not reach the city to-day if we stop at every tree and shrub that is strange, Oriental, or Biblical.

Very likely. Here, for example, are the almond, the olive, the fig, and the pomegranate, all together ; but we shall meet them everywhere in our pilgrimage, and can afford to pass them by at present. And, besides, we have before us a more interesting study—a scene not witnessed in all places in such perfection. See those men on that elevated terrace. One has spread his cloak, others their Persian rugs toward the south. They are Moslems preparing to say prayers—*perform* them rather, in this most public place, and in the midst of all this noise and confusion.

Moslem
prayers.

Let us stop and watch the ceremony as it goes on. That man next us raises his open hands till the thumbs touch the ears, exclaiming aloud, *Allah-hû-*

[1] Isaiah ix. 10.   [2] 1 Kings x. 27.   [3] Psalm lxxviii. 43, 47

akbar—"God is great." After uttering mentally a few short petitions, the CHAPTER I. hands are brought down, and folded together near the girdle, while he recites the first chapter of the Koran, and two or three other brief passages from the same book. And now he bends forward, rests his hands upon his knees, and repeats three times a formula of praise to "God most great." Then, standing erect, he cries *Allah-hû-akbar*, as at the beginning. Then see him drop upon his knees, and bend forward until his nose and forehead touch the ground, directly between his expanded hands. This he repeats three times, muttering Repetitions in prayer. all the while the same short formulas of prayer and praise. The next move will bring him to his knees, and then, settling back upon his heels, he will mumble over various small petitions, with sundry grunts and exclamations, according to taste and habit. He has now gone through one regular Rek'āh; and, standing up as at the first, and on exactly the same spot, he will perform a second, and even a third, if specially devout, with precisely the same genuflections.

They seem to be wholly absorbed in their devotions, and manifest a power of isolation and abstraction quite surprising.

That is the result of habit and education; small children imitate it to perfection. There is certainly an air of great solemnity in their mode of worship, Air of solemnity. and, when performed by a large assembly in the mosques, or by a detachment of soldiers in concert, guided in their genuflections by an imaum or dervish, who sings the service, it is quite impressive. I have seen it admirably enacted by moonlight on the wild banks of the Orontes, in the plain of Hamath, and the scene was something more than romantic. But, alas! it was by as villanous a set of robbers as could be found even in that lawless region.

You think, then, that this solemn ceremony is mere hollow-hearted hypocrisy?

Not exactly that; at least not necessarily so, nor in all cases. I would be A man of prayers suspected glad to believe there was ordinarily any corresponding moral and religious feeling connected with this exterior manifestation of devotion. The Moslems themselves, however, have no such idea. They are rather afraid of any one who is especially given to prayer—their prayers, I mean. They have a proverb to this effect: "If your neighbour has made the pilgrimage to Mecca once, watch him; if twice, avoid his society; if three times, move into another street." And, certainly, no one acquainted with the people will feel his confidence in an individual increased by the fact that he is particularly devout.

What opposite conclusions different persons can and do draw from the same premises! One who looks merely at the surface, or who is very charitable, or very indifferent, may connect this out-of-door formal praying toward Mecca with the venerable custom of the pious Israelite turning toward the temple in Jerusalem, when, like Daniel in Babylon, he made his supplications unto his God.[1] I think it probable that Mohammed, or the Arabs before him, borrowed

---

[1] Dan. vi. 10, 11,

PART
I.
this custom from the Jews ; and, to this extent, there is a relation between them. But the enlightened Christian, who has learned that neither in this mountain, nor yet at Jerusalem, shall men worship the Father, who is a spirit, and must be worshipped in spirit and in truth[1]—such a one, I say, will be reminded rather of those who loved to pray standing in the synagogues and in the corners of the streets, that they might be seen of men. And they will

Our Lord's cautions.
remember with solemnity the admonition of our Lord, "When thou prayest, thou shalt not be as the hypocrites are"[2]—either as to place, attitude, motive, or form —in public to be seen of men, using vain repetitions[3] as these men before us do. They are obliged to repeat some expressions thirty times ; others many hundred times. Would that these remarks did not apply to nominal Christians in this land as well as to Moslems ! But here we are at the gate of the city.

City gates.
Stop a moment. A city gate is a novelty to me, and I must examine in detail an apparatus so often mentioned in the Bible.

Well, what is there in a mere gate to attract attention ?

Very little, perhaps, to one who has passed in and out daily for twenty years ; but a hundred Biblical incidents connect themselves in my mind with gates. Almost every city and town of ancient celebrity had them, and they were places of very great importance.

They were, indeed ; and, although customs have changed in this respect, there is still enough remaining in this country to remind one of those olden times when nearly every public transaction took place at or near the city gates. Beirût has burst her shell by the force of sudden expansion, and will soon have neither wall nor gates ; but nearly every other city in Syria and Palestine is still protected by these venerable safeguards.

Refer-
ences in
Scripture.
And thus it was in ancient days. I remember that righteous Lot, intent on deeds of hospitality, sat in the gate of Sodom toward the close of day, somewhat as these Arabs are now seated, I suppose, and thereby he obtained the privilege of entertaining unawares those angels who saved him from the destruction of that wicked city.[4] It was at the gate of Kirjath Arba (which is Hebron) that Abraham completed the contract for the cave of Machpelah, " in the presence of the children of Heth, before all that went in at the gate of the city." [5] It was at the same place that Hamor and Shechem negotiated that fatal treaty with all that went in at the gate of the city,[6] which gave opportunity to those fierce and treacherous brethren, Simeon and Levi, with instruments of cruelty to work out their revenge. " Cursed be their anger, for it was fierce ; and their wrath, for it was cruel." [7]

Since this very unpretending entrance to Beirût is leading into a long discussion, let us prepare ourselves a seat, as Job did when he went out to the gate,[8] and then we can talk at our leisure, and our ease as well. You observe

---

[1] John iv. 21, 24.   [2] Matt. vi. 5.   [3] Matt. vi. 7.   [4] Gen. xix. 1, and Heb. xiii. 2.
[5] Gen. xxiii. 18.   [6] Gen. xxxiv. 20, 24.   [7] Gen. xlix. 5, 7.   [8] Job xxix. 7.

that the gateway is vaulted, shady, and cool. This is one reason why people delight to assemble about it. Again, the curious and vain resort thither

GATE OF CITY.

to see and be seen. Some go to meet their associates; others, to watch for returning friends, or to accompany those about to depart; while many gather there to hear the news, and to engage in trade and traffic. I have seen in certain places—Joppa, for example—the kâdy and his court sitting at the entrance of the gate, hearing and adjudicating all sorts of causes in the audience of all that went in and out thereat. Throughout sacred history, prophecy, and poetry, the gate is celebrated by numberless interesting incidents and allusions. It would require a little volume to notice and explain them all; but here we have the thing itself, with the void place about it,[1] like that where Boaz made the elders of Bethlehem sit while he contracted for Ruth, the fair

Holding courts.

---

[1] 1 Kings xxii. 10.

PART
I.

Moabitess;[1] where Eli sat trembling for the ark of God, and fell back and broke his neck when tidings of its capture came.[2] And here are the two leaves of the gate, and the bars, and the bolts, like those of Gaza, which Samson tore from their sockets, and on his shoulders carried up to the top of a hill that is before Hebron.[3] And over this gate is a chamber, like that to which David went and wept; "and, as he went, thus he said, O my son Absalom! my son, my son Absalom! would to God I had died for thee, O Absalom! my son, my son!"[4]

Public proclamations.

It is not difficult to comprehend why public proclamations were made in the gates, and why prophets so often pronounced their messages there. We read of the "gates of righteousness," because justice and judgment were there decreed and executed;[5] and so, likewise, the prophets denounced the oppression of the poor in the gate, where corrupt judges sell justice to the highest bidder: "They afflict the just, they take a bribe, they turn aside the poor in the gate from their right;" and to this refers the exhortation to "hate the evil, love the good, and establish judgment in the gate."[6]

Fortifications.

Again, gates were fortified in the strongest possible manner. In them the people trusted for safety, and they naturally became the synonym for strength and power. "Thou shalt call thy walls Salvation, and thy gates Praise."[7] Hence the prophets delighted to personify them. In times of calamity they languish and lament, mourn and howl; they sing, shout, and rejoice in prosperity. The Lord loveth the gates of Zion; and David exclaims, "Lift up your heads, O ye gates, and be ye lifted up, ye everlasting doors, and the King of Glory shall come in."[8] And remembering that all, both great and small, must enter by them, it is not far-fetched or unnatural to speak of the gates of death. And who has not felt the solemn admonition, "Strive to enter in at the strait gate," and shuddered lest he should be swept along by the thoughtless crowd through the wide gate that leadeth to destruction? I have seen these strait gates and narrow ways, "with here and there a traveller." They are in retired corners, and must be sought for, and are opened only to those who knock; and when the sun goes down, and the night comes on, they are shut and locked. It is then too late.[9]

I see we shall never get into the city, if we sit here conversing about gates until the subject is exhausted.

Names of gates.

Move on, then; but allow me to remark, as we enter, that gates have the same kind of names now as in ancient times, generally derived from some accidental circumstance connected with them. One is *Bab el Bahar*, because it leads to the *sea*. That near which the tanners carry on their business is *Bab el Dubbâgâ*. This one is *Bab es Shurraiyeh*, because the governor's palace is near it. And thus, too, the streets and different quarters of the city derive their names. Those who follow the same trade congregate in the same

1 Ruth iv. 1, 2.   2 1 Sam. iv. 18.   5 Judges xvi. 3.   4 2 Sam. xviii. 33.
5 Deut. xxi. 19, and xxii. 24.   6 Amos v. 12, 15.   7 Isaiah lx. 18.
8 Ps. xxiv. 7.   9 Luke xiii. 24, 25, and Matt. vii. 13.

street. This is sadlers', the next blacksmiths' street, and so on to the end of
the list.

Here is something new, I'll engage; sufficiently Oriental, also, though "not
according to Scripture." This old man sitting by the mosque is a letter-writer.
He has his paper near him, and his scissors to trim it to the required shape
and size. He has taken the inkhorn, or what answers to that very ancient
article of the "scribes," from his girdle, and is now pointing one of those
"reeds" which prophets and scribes so often mention. All this seems Biblical
enough. But here comes a woman, veiled from head to foot, and takes her

LETTER-WRITER.

station by his side. See, she is whispering from behind her veil the desired
message. That is sufficient; the *salams*, love, etc., etc., go in according to
rule, and to all alike.

Why, this is a sort of Moslem confessional, and that fellow's head must be
crammed with the secrets and the scandal of half the city.

No matter; I suppose, like other confessors, he keeps dark, and may be
trusted. Still, this letter-writing would not be a very thriving business in our
country.

How every circumstance and incident carries one back to ages remote and

PART I.

Veils.

primitive! This veil reminds me of Rebekah and her meeting with Isaac. But I see here and there a woman without it.

Yes; but they are peasants from the country, or else Rebekah's fair daughters who now utterly refuse to follow her modest example. *She* put on a veil before her betrothed husband; *these* resolutely assert their "rights," and their pretty pale faces are everywhere seen unveiled. They have, however,

Women's hair concealed.

certain laws of modesty, which are most rigidly enforced. For example, a Jewish matron must on no account allow her own hair to be seen. Hence, no matter how luxuriant and beautiful, it is carefully concealed under their curious head-dresses; and what appears to be hair is either silk imitation, or it is borrowed. Then, by a strange perversity of manners, or silly antagonism to Christianity, the men take pride in cultivating and exhibiting long, curling locks. There go several of these Jew dandies at this moment, with their cherished locks flowing round their ears and necks in pretty curls.

Talking of Jews and Jewesses, and veils and hair, reminds me of that difficult passage in Paul's letter to the Corinthians.[1] Do the customs of the East in such matters throw any light upon it?

Paul's counsels to the Corinthians.

I will state facts; you must judge for yourself how far they elucidate what is obscure. The words "praying and prophesying" include all the ordinary parts and acts of *public* worship. The language of Paul implies that, *in these countries* and *at that time*, the laws of modesty and propriety required the women to appear in their assemblies with their heads covered and their faces veiled. The men, on the contrary, should be uncovered. It is remarkable that in their synagogues the men in our day keep on their hats or other head-dresses, and those who read the service throw a large veil over the head and shoulders, as if in direct and intentional contradiction to the Apostle. The women, if present at all, are unveiled. Now, if these are original Jewish habits and practices, it is plain that the Christian Church, from the very first, established new customs in these respects. It is supposed that the men are required to worship with heads uncovered, as a tacit acknowledgment of Christ's divine presence among them; and a relic of this form of reverence may still be seen in Oriental churches, where all stand uncovered when the gospel, which contains the words of Christ, is read. Or these directions of the Apostle may merely be part and parcel of those modifications and adaptations by which the gospel was (as Paul says of himself) to become all things to all men for their salvation. The mixture of Oriental Christians with heathen Greeks, Romans, and other Occidental tribes, in their worshipping assemblies, would doubtless render necessary a careful compliance, on the part of the women, with *their* ideas of feminine modesty and propriety. And the farther eastward the gospel spread, such compliance would become more and more important. At the present day, the missionary finds it strictly necessary, in many places, not only that the women should be veiled, but also that there should be a

[1] 1 Cor. xi. 3–15.

separate apartment for them screened from the gaze of the men. The Apostle *CHAPTER* rebukes severely any approach toward immodesty. If the woman is deter-*I.* mined to sit in the midst of such mixed assemblies, with a bold and impudent face, aping the men, then let her head be shorn or shaved like that of the men. What *that* means at this day you can easily see by looking into this barber's shop over the way.

Well, that is strange enough; he has actually shaved the entire head bare *Shaving* as the palm of my hand. It is a hideous operation, and verily it would be a *the head.* shame for a woman to be shorn or shaven. But what do you make of the tenth verse of this remarkable passage?

The word translated "power" is perhaps a mere symbolic title of the veil *"Power"* itself; nor is the figure altogether strange or unintelligible to an Oriental. The *on the* veil is, in fact, the beautiful lady's strength and defence. Modestly veiled, *head.* she appears anywhere and everywhere in perfect safety. She is held inviolate by a sensitive and most jealous public sentiment, and no man insults her but at the risk of being torn in pieces by an infuriated mob; but without the veil she is a weak, helpless thing, at the mercy of every brute who may choose to abuse her. The veil is, therefore, the virtuous woman's "power," and when-ever she appears in public she ought to have this "*power*" on her head;"—in church, "because of the angels;" that is, the messengers and ministers, as I *"The an-* suppose. The women must be modestly veiled, because they are to sit in the *gels."* presence and full view of the ministers, comparatively strangers to them, and many of them evangelists from foreign nations. Doddridge thinks it indecent to suppose that the ladies must be veiled, lest by their attractions they disturb the minds of the ministers. Such an idea could only be entertained by one ignorant of the power of Oriental customs in these matters. The oldest and most eminently modest native preacher that I am acquainted with, objected not only to the ladies appearing unveiled (and for the very reason alluded to), but he would not have even their *voices heard* in the singing of the church, because in this country they never sing but in strains designed and adapted to excite emotions which should be utterly banished from the place of prayer. Put the case thus : A pious and modest Oriental preacher (who perhaps has rarely looked upon the face of any woman except those of his nearest relations), when he rises to preach, finds himself confronted by the beauty and fashion of the city in their best attire,—is it strange that he should be confused and dis-turbed? And, moreover, the veil is as necessary for the modest female, who desires to worship in purity and peace, as it is for the "angel." Secluded by the rigid laws of Eastern society from familiar association with all men except near relatives, so that she would be overwhelmed with confusion should her veil fall in the presence of a stranger, it is no reflection upon her purity of mind, but the contrary, that she cannot appear unveiled before the "angel" with that entire composure which becomes the house of God. Such will wear the veil from choice. Change the state of society (and in many places it is being changed), educate the females (and the males too), let the community be

PART
I.

pure from Moslem and heathen mixtures, and trained to free and becoming social intercourse, and then neither men nor women will think of veils and screens, nor need these apostolic directions in their exact letter. Their spirit, however, will always be obligatory in every country and all states of society; and a little more modesty in female attire would be a very happy improvement in many a Western congregation. But it is time we turn our steps homeward. The muezzin calls to sunset prayers from this tall minaret, and dinner will be waiting. As in ancient times, men now eat when the day's work is done.

Narrow
streets.

"Seeing is believing," says the proverb, and it is *understanding* also. I have read all my life about crooked, narrow streets, with the gutters in the middle, and no side walks, but I never understood till now. How are we to get past this line of loaded camels? Well, by bowing the head, creeping under, and dodging from side to side, we have accomplished that feat; but here is a string of donkeys carrying brush and water; their bundles actually sweep both sides of the street, and the ground too; there can be no creeping *under* this time.

True; but here is a recess in the wall into which we can step until they have passed by.

What is that fellow shouting all the while at the top of his voice?

Warning.

He cries *Daharak! wûshhak! daharak! wûshhak!* "your back! your face! your back! your face!" to warn all concerned to look sharply before and behind, or they may be run over, crushed against the wall, or have their clothes and faces torn by this brush; a very necessary admonition.

Streets.

That I perceive well enough; but are all Oriental cities built after this fashion—streets eight feet wide, houses sixty feet high, with dead stone walls without ornament or relief of any kind? They are sad and sombre at best, and must be particularly so at night. Already the shades of evening fall heavily along these gloomy avenues, and I see no provision for lighting them.

Their
darkness
at night.

There is none; and you observe that the shopkeepers are already shutting up, and leaving for home. Henceforward until morning the streets are deserted and silent, with only here and there a company returning from a visit, with a servant bearing a lantern before them. The city-guard creeps softly about in utter darkness, and apprehends all found walking the streets without a light. Remember, and act accordingly, or you may get locked up in quarters not very comfortable. Beirût is gradually departing from some of these customs, but enough remain to afford a type of all you will see elsewhere, except at Damascus. The style of that city is wholly different, and carries one back as by enchantment to the age of the Califs and the fantastic creations of the "Thousand Nights."

CHAPTER II.

BEIRUT—Continued.

Beauty of Beirût.
View from the Roadstead.
Not mentioned in Scripture.
Its history.

Earthquake of A.D. 551.
St. George and the Dragon.
Present condition.
Antiquities.

January 25th.

How is it that you never told me in any of your letters that Beriût is such a Beirût. beautiful place?

I did; but you could not understand, and no wonder. Neither pen nor pencil can do justice to Beirût. Things hereabouts are on a scale so vast, and there is such an infinite variety in the details, that it is almost impossible to select, group together, and condense into reasonable limits enough to give an adequate idea of the whole.

That I can readily believe; and yet I am unwilling to pass away from Beirût without imprinting on memory's tablet a fairer, truer copy of her charming scenery than I have yet obtained.

Follow me, then, to the terrace of our house. It commands the whole View from prospect. The city and suburbs, as you perceive, are situated on the northern a terrace. slopes of a triangular plain, whose *base line* is the shore, from Ras Beirût to Nahr Yâbis, some six miles toward Sidon. The *perpendicular* runs in eastward from the Ras about five miles to the foot of Lebanon, at the bottom of St. George's Bay. The *hypothenuse* is the irregular line of the mountains. The whole plain is a projection *seaward* from the general direction of the coast, and along the base of the hills it is so low as to appear like an island to one sailing up from Sidon. The surface rises gradually from the south to the immediate vicinity of the city, where it is about three hundred feet above the sea. Thence it falls rapidly down toward the roadstead on the north, by abrupt, irregular, and winding terraces. It is this feature that imparts such variety and beauty to the environs of Beirût. The substratum of this plain is everywhere a white marl, passing into compact limestone, and enclosing nodules of flint and thin seams of chert, similar to the adjoining hills of Lebanon. Upon Composithis rests a very large formation of arenaceous, unstratified stone, easily tion of wrought, and hence used from time immemorial for building. It is mixed with rocks. comminuted shells and corals, is very porous, and absorbs water with great rapidity, which renders the houses damp in winter. This, indeed, is almost the only defect in this otherwise admirable building stone. The quarries are to the south-west of the city, and from them a broad belt of loose, movable sand stretches inward from the shore, quite down to the point at Nahr

3

PART
I.

Groves
and
forests.

Yâbis. The south-eastern part of the plain is one dense olive grove, the largest and most productive in Syria. In the centre are beautiful pine forests, planted, or rather sowed, by successive governors at different times, from the famous Druse chief, Fakhr ed Dîn to Wamic Pasha, the present representative of the Sublime Porte at Beirût. There are a few orange and lemon gardens, where they can be irrigated. Figs, almonds, and apricots abound, and in certain parts

> "The palm-tree rears his stately head on high
> And spreads his feathery plume along the sky;"

while the mulberry, melia, kharûb, sycamore, prickly oak, and many a tree and shrub of humbler name, cast abroad their grateful shade, and draw their green mantles over our lovely suburbs. Seen from any point, Beirût is charming. Many, however, are best pleased with the view from the roadstead north of the city.

View from
the road-
stead.

I am one of those. As our steamer came bravely into harbour at early dawn, the scenery was beautiful, and even sublime. Good old Lebanon, with a diadem of stars around his snowy turban, looked for all the world like some august monarch of the universe, with his head in heaven and his feet upon the sea, and I could and did salute him with profound respect;—laugh at me if you please, but I could not help it. And as morning grew into bright and glorious day, what a charming panorama was revealed all around the city !

Environs.

The deep Bay of St. George sweeping around the base of the hills ; the mountains of Metn and the Kesrawan on the east and north-east, rugged, steep, and lofty, shaded with pine forests, and dotted with villages, churches, and convents ; the wild gorge of the Dog River, with snowy Sunnîn beyond and above ; the sandy ridge of Brumanah, and Deir el Kŭlâh, with the deep ravine of Nahr Beirût; the hills of El Ghŭrb, bold and bright against the southern sky, from Aleih to Abeîh, with hamlets, and factories, and orchards peeping over the smiling suburbs ; and the city itself, with white houses seated seaward on overhanging cliffs, or grouped on showy terraces and commanding hill-tops, or stowed away along retiring glens, half revealed, now quite concealed by crowding mulberry and parasol China trees, and waving festoons of vines and cunning creepers of many colours—this, this is Beirût, with the glorious Mediterranean all around, and ships and boats of various nations and picturesque patterns sailing or at rest. You will travel far ere you find a prospect of equal variety, beauty, and magnificence.

Is Beirût mentioned in the Bible ?

Beirût not
in Bible.

I think not. It is possible that the Berothai of 2 Samuel viii. 8, from which David took exceeding much brass, was Beirût, though that city *seems* to have been situated to the east or south-east of Hamath ; still, since Hadadezer was either king of Damascus, or in close alliance with it, Berothai may have been her sea-port, as Beirût is now ; and after David had conquered

Damascus, he might naturally enough cross over Lebanon to her sea-port, CHAPTER
where so much of her wealth would be collected. It is not at all likely that II.
the Berothah mentioned in Ezekiel, xlvii. 16, as one of the points in the
northern boundary of the land of Israel, was our city; and from the similarity
of names, and the apparent geographical position of both, we can scarcely
doubt but that Ezekiel's Berothah and Samuel's Berothai were identical, and,
of course, that neither of them was Beirût.

Dr. Wilson suggests that our city derived its name from Berûth, the wife Conjec-
of Elion, who dwelt at Byblus (Jebail); and if the chronicle of Sanchoniatho tures.
could be depended upon, I should have little hesitation in adopting the idea.
This would give it a very high antiquity. This much is certain, that at the
time when the fragments of Sanchoniatho were forged, if they are a fabrication,
Beirût was an important city, for it is repeatedly mentioned in them. Bochart
and others are of opinion that the Baal-berith of Judges viii. 33 was the god
Baal of the city of Berith, or Beirût. Nor is this supposition too far-fetched
to merit consideration; for we know, not merely from these fragments of Sanchoniatho, but from other ancient authors, that the chief seat of Baal worship
was in the regions around Byblus and Beirût. Intelligent natives say that the
name is derived from *beer*, the word for *well* in nearly all the Shemitic dialects.
Beirût would then be "the city of wells;" and such it pre-eminently is. Almost
every house has one. They vary in depth from twenty to one hundred and fifty
feet, according to position.

After all that can be said, or even surmised, the student of our city's ancient Admirable
story is surprised and disappointed to find her origin enveloped in such situation.
utter obscurity, and sighs for records which must once have existed, but are
now for ever lost. It is not to be believed that a spot so admirably adapted for
a great city should have been neglected by the Phœnicians. Every foot of this
densely crowded coast, and especially every available sea-port, was appropriated
by that enterprising people. And this is decidedly the most beautiful and
healthy locality at the head of the Mediterranean. The roadstead, it is true,
is better adapted to modern shipping than to that of ancient times; but still
there are small inlets and sheltered coves too valuable to be overlooked on a
coast where there are no good harbours. We may safely conclude, therefore,
that it was occupied at a very early day by a colony, probably from Sidon, with
which it has ever been closely connected. Accordingly, the earliest mention of
Beirût by Greek and Latin geographers and historians implies that it was then,
and had been previously, a place of importance. And this position it maintains ever after, as may be gathered from Strabo, Ptolemy, Pliny, Josephus,
and other authors, both heathen and Christian. It became a Roman colony in A Roman
the reign of Augustus, and had Julia Felix added to its name. Agrippa colony.
adorned and beautified it with colonnades, porticos, theatres, baths, and other
public buildings; and their remains are scattered over the gardens, and entombed beneath the rubbish of the ancient city. The number of large columns
of both grey and red granite built into the quay is surprising; but a far greater

PART
I.

number lie at the bottom of the sea in front of the town. In 1839-40, Mahmûd Bey, governor of Beirût, built a break-water entirely of these columns, fished up from the floor of the harbour. The unparalleled storm at the close of 1840 overturned this wall of columns, and spread them out again where they had been before. Probably this was only the repetition of a former attempt to protect the quay of Beirût, when these columns were gathered from the ruins of the city and cast into the sea for that purpose. It is otherwise difficult to

Ruins of
columns.

account for their being there at all. There is a tradition that Fakhr ed Dîn filled up the harbour to prevent the landing of pirates ; but, if there is any foundation for the report, his work is probably to be found in the heaps of rubbish directly in front of the landing.

Theatres.

It was in the theatres of Agrippa, I suppose, that Titus celebrated his own victories over Jerusalem, and his father's birth-day, by gladiatorial shows, in which the miserable captives of Zion perished in great numbers, fighting with wild beasts and with one another, as Josephus informs us in the seventh book of his " Wars."

Planting
of Christi-
anity.

Though the apostles seem never to have visited Beirût—a fact somewhat remarkable—yet Christianity was early planted here, and so flourished that it soon became the seat of a bishopric. Under the Christian emperors, it continued to prosper down to the reign of Justinian. It was then one of the most celebrated seats of learning in the empire, and its law school was frequented by youth from the first families in the state.   Then, as now, it was the most beautiful city on this coast.   But its decline commenced under this reign.   On

Earth-
quake.

the 9th of July, A.D. 551, one of those awful earthquakes, which repeatedly shook the whole Roman world in the time of Justinian, seems to have entirely destroyed Beirût,—overthrew her colleges, churches, temples, theatres, and palaces, and buried multitudes of all classes beneath the ruins ; and, although the city was rebuilt, it never regained its former magnificence. You can scarcely walk through a garden, or dig a foundation for a house, without coming upon the memorials of this dreadful calamity. It is amazing to see how deeply some of these ruins are entombed, suggesting the idea that the very terraces on which these costly structures stood were upheaved and precipitated on those below. And this corresponds with the history of that fearful time. We are told that " enormous chasms were opened, huge and heavy bodies were discharged into the air, the sea alternately advanced and retreated beyond its ordinary bounds," and a *mountain* was torn from yonder bold promontory (then called Theoprosopon, and now Ras es Shukkah), and cast into the sea, where it formed a mole for the harbour of Butrône. Perhaps the Arabic name, Ras es Shukkah—" the cape that was split open "—may be a memento and witness to this catastrophe.

Troubles
in middle
ages.

During the middle ages, Beirût shared in all the troubles and revolutions which accompanied and grew out of the triumph of Mohammedanism, including the crusades of the eleventh, twelfth, and thirteenth centuries. It was taken by Baldwin in 1110, and, during the two hundred years of Frank rule on

this coast, it was several times captured and recaptured by Saracen and Chris- CHAPTER
tian. Since the close of the thirteenth century, few signal events have II.
happened to vary the monotony of her story. But we must not forget to mention that exploit which was considered her greatest glory in the days of legendary lore. It was here that St. George killed the dragon ; exactly when, or St. George
what particular dragon I know not, but he *must* have killed him, for he has here
never been seen since that time, and all agree that he is dead. If you doubt, killed the
I refer you to the deep bay down yonder, which owes its name to this contest dragon!
on its shore. I can show you the well into which the victorious saint cast the
horrid monster, and the spot where he washed his bloody hands after this
dirty work was done. Not every legend of those days of facile faith is so
strongly attested. In the eighth century, also, an illustrious miracle spread the
name and fame of our good city far and wide. Some image-hating Hebrews,
in scorn and mockery, attempted to go through the acts of the Crucifixion upon
a very holy image and cross ; when, as they thrust a spear into the side, to
their confusion and horror, a large quantity of blood and water gushed forth.
The thing is at least possible, and without resorting to supernatural interfer-
ence. A little manœuvring, or a little money, could set either real or spurious
Jews at work in the exact way to bring on the catastrophe. But let that pass;
Beirût has no need of such doubtful claims to immortality. Judging from the
scanty and indefinite notices by the pilgrims of the mediæval ages, the number
of her inhabitants varied from 5000 to 10,000, engaged in commerce, and in
growing silk and oil, which for several centuries have continued to be the staple
productions of this neighbourhood.

Within the last thirty years our city has rapidly increased in population, Recent
commerce, and wealth. When Mohammed Aly wrested Syria from the Sultan progress.
in 1830–31, he made Beirût the grand quarantine station on this coast, and
obliged all ships to come to her port. European merchants had already
selected it for the seat of their operations, and, as the foreign consuls settled in
this city, the government was led to make it the capital of the country. Thirty
years ago the population was 5000, and the shops and markets were dependent
for supplies on Sidon; now there are not less than 40,000 inhabitants, and Popula-
Sidon is wholly dependent on Beirût. Thirty years ago there was scarcely a tion.
decent house outside of the walls; now two-thirds of the population reside in
the gardens, and hundreds of convenient dwellings, and not a few large and
noble mansions, adorn the charming suburbs. No city in Syria, perhaps none
in the Turkish empire, has had so rapid an expansion. And it must continue
to grow and prosper, with but one proviso to cast a shade of doubt upon her
bright future. Should a railroad ever connect the head of this sea with the
Euphrates and the Persian Gulf, that will infallibly dictate where the
emporium of Syria is to be. If Beirût can attract this mighty line of trade and
travel to her door, she will quickly take rank among the great cities of the
world; if she will not, or cannot, then must she wane before some other rising
queen of the East.

Are there any antiquities about Beirût which merit attention ?

Very few. We have columns and sarcophagi in abundance, and some of them have inscriptions which tell their own story. An ancient aqueduct has lately been discovered, cut through the rock, and passing beneath the city at Bab Yacōb. It must either have had a more permanent supply than the present, which fails in dry weather, when it is most needed, or have been connected with the great canal which brought water from Lebanon to ancient Berytus.

Are the existing remains of this ancient work extensive ?

More so than travellers, or even natives, are aware of. On the top of that dark, sandy ridge of Lebanon, to the north-east of Brŭmmanah, is a fountain of delicious water. It was conducted in stone tubes along the ridge south-west for six or eight miles to the temple that occupied the place of Deir el Kŭlah. From thence it descended the steep mountain, about fifteen hundred feet, in a direction nearly west, where it was carried over the river of Beirût on a series of lofty arches. The highest tier numbers twenty-five, and the canal upon them was one hundred and sixty feet above the bed of the river. The next tier below has fifteen arches; the third has only three, and the lowest two. The wall is twenty feet broad, and is built of well-cut stone—altogether a very imposing structure. Though carried over the river at so great an elevation, the canal meets, on the Beirût or west side, with perpendicular cliffs, and passes directly through them by a tunnel cut in the solid rock. I once crept into it for thirty or forty feet, beyond which it is choked up with rubbish. Descending to the margin of the plain, the canal was led along the base of the hills southward, past the Khan es Shîâhh, and thence westward to the vicinity of Beirût, and the water was distributed by many pipes to various parts of the city. As the plain west of Es Shîâhh is very low, the canal had to be elevated by a long line of arches, erected upon an immense wall. This was built solid throughout, of large, accurately cut stone, after the Roman style, and about forty feet broad. No traces of the arches remain, except masses of tufaceous deposit formed by the trickling of the water through the aqueduct, as is seen along the ancient canals of Tyre and Acre. The wall itself, however, was nearly entire when I first came to this country; but the rapid growth of Beirût created such a demand for building-stone that the greater part of it has been quarried and brought to the city. In this process, palm and olive trees, which had grown old upon the top, have been undermined and thrown away; and where the work of quarrying has been completed, the ground has been levelled, and orchards of mulberry-trees are now flourishing. What a pity ! Beirût now greatly needs just the supply of water which this noble canal once brought to it, and a moderate expense would have restored it to its former use. But this is only one of a thousand of Syria's sad desolations. The Arabs, as a matter of course, ascribe this aqueduct to Zobeîda, a sort of Moslem St. Helena, according to popular legends, but, in historic truth, the wife of Haroun er Raschîd. It is quite impossible to ascertain who constructed it ; but, whether made by Phœnicians, Greeks, or Romans, it was an admirable work, and a great blessing to Beirût. The entire length cannot be less than twenty miles, and the starting-point is at least two thousand feet above the sea.

CHAPTER III.

CHAPTER III.

CHAPTER III.

BEIRUT—Continued.

| Roofs of Houses—Battlements. | Worship on House-tops. |
| Proclamations from House-tops. | The Sparrow on the House-top. |

January 26th.

THE roofs of these houses afford such a delightful promenade, and the prospect is so beautiful, that I can scarcely keep away from them, day or night. So absorbed was I just now in gazing about, that, if it had not been for the parapet, I should have walked quite off, and then have found myself on the ground with a broken limb or neck, I suppose. As it was, I made a desperate stumble, and was excessively frightened. *Roofs of houses.*

A very practical illustration, that, of the wisdom and humanity of the command in Deut. xxii. 8: "When thou buildest a new house, then thou shalt make a battlement for thy roof, that thou bring not blood upon thine house if any man fall from thence." This ordinance ought still to be enforced by law wherever the roofs are flat, and resorted to for business, relaxation, or for sleeping. In Syrian cities the roofs are a great comfort. The ordinary houses have no other place where the inmates can either see the sun, " smell the air," dry their clothes, set out their flower-pots, or do numberless other things essential to their health and comfort. This is particularly true within the city walls; but even in villages the roof is very useful. There the farmer suns his wheat for the mill, and the flour when brought home, and dries his figs, raisins, etc., etc., in safety both from animals and from thieves. *Need of battlements.*

During a large part of the year the roof is the most agreeable place about the establishment, especially in the morning and evening. There multitudes sleep during the summer, in all places where malaria does not render it dangerous. This custom is very ancient. Though according to our translation of 1st Samuel ix. 25, 26, Samuel calls Saul *to* the top of the house, that he might send him away, instead of *from* it, yet, taking the whole passage together, there can be no doubt but that the process should be reversed. The Arabic has it thus :—" And Samuel conversed with Saul upon the top of the house, and spread his bed for him, and he slept on the roof ; and very early in the morning Samuel called Saul *from* the top of the house," etc., etc. This is natural, and doubtless the correct history of the case. Saul, young, vigorous, but weary with his long search, would desire no better place to sleep than on the roof. *Morning and evening on the roof.*

ROOFS OF HOUSES—BATTLEMENTS.

But there should always be battlements, and commissioners should be ap- CHAPTER III.
pointed to see that they are kept in proper repair. The Moslems generally
build very high parapets, in order to screen their women from observation; but
the Christians are very negligent, and often bring blood upon their houses by a
sinful disregard of this law of Moses.

Your remark about the Moslems suggests the thought that if Uriah's house
had been thus protected, David might have been saved from a long series of
dismal crimes, and Israel from dreadful calamity.

True; but then the roof of David's palace was probably so high that he could King David's roof.
look directly down into the courts of the neighbouring houses. There are such
in all cities, and you can scarcely commit a greater offence than to frequent a
terrace which thus commands the interior of your neighbour's dwelling.

Isaiah has a reference to the house-tops in the 22nd chapter, which I do not
quite understand. He says, verse 1st, "What aileth thee now, that thou art
wholly gone up to the house-tops?" For what purpose did the inhabitants of
Jerusalem thus go thither?

This is a remarkable passage. Verse 2d goes on to say, "Thou art full of Passage in Isaiah explained.
stirs, a tumultuous city, a joyous city;" from which one might suppose that the
people had gone to the roofs to eat, drink, clap hands, and sing, as the Arabs
at this day delight to do in the mild summer evenings. But, from verses 4th
and 5th, it is plain that it was a time of trouble, and of treading down, and of
perplexity; which naturally suggests the idea that the inhabitants had rushed
to the tops of the houses to get a sight of those chariots and horsemen of Elam The roof favourable for a view.
and Kir, with whom their choice valleys were full, and who were thundering
against the gates of the city. And, as Oriental houses generally have no windows
looking outward into the streets, or, if there are such, they are closely latticed,
there is no place but the roofs from whence one can obtain a view of what is
going on without. Hence, when anything extraordinary occurs in the streets,
all classes rush to the roof and look over the battlements. The inhabitants of
Jerusalem, at the time of this Persian invasion, were probably seized with
frenzy and madness, as they were long after, at the siege of Titus. According to Josephus, some revelled in drunken feasts, and kept the city in alarm
by their stirs and tumults; some were engaged in plunder and murder, when
the slain were not dead in battle; some wept bitterly, like Isaiah, and refused
to be comforted " because of the spoiling of the daughter of my people;" in a
word, it was a day of universal and utter confusion. Nobody could sit still, but
all hurried to the house-tops, either to join in untimely riots of fanaticism and
drunken despair, or to watch with fear and trembling the dreadful assault upon
their walls and gates; no wonder they had wholly gone up to the house-tops.

Was it customary in the time of our Saviour to make public proclamations
from the tops of the houses?

Such an inference may fairly be drawn from Matthew x. 27, and Luke xii. Proclama-
3. Our Lord spent most of his life in villages, and accordingly the reference tions from the roof.
here is to a custom observed only in such places, never in cities. At the pre-

sent day, local governors in country districts cause their commands thus to be published. Their proclamations are generally made in the evening, after the people have returned from their labours in the field. The public crier ascends the highest roof at hand, and lifts up his voice in a long-drawn call upon all faithful subjects to give ear and obey. He then proceeds to announce, in a set form, the will of their master, and demand obedience thereto.

It is plain that the roofs were resorted to for worship, both true and idolatrous. We read in Zeph. i. 5, of those who worshipped the host of heaven on the house-tops; and from Acts x. 9, we learn that Peter at Joppa went up to the roof to pray about the sixth hour.

Worship.
All this is very natural. The Sabeans of Chaldea and Persia could find no more appropriate place for the performance of their idolatrous worship of the heavenly bodies than these open terraces, with the stars shining down upon them so kindly. And, as very few Oriental dwellings have closets into which the devout can retire for prayer, I suppose Peter was obliged to resort to the roof of Simon's house for this purpose; and when surrounded with battlements, and shaded by vines trained over them, they afford a very agreeable retreat, even at the sixth hour of the day—the time when Peter was favoured

TERRACE WITH VINES.

with that singular vision by which the kingdom of heaven was thrown open to the Gentile world.

Our Lord says, "Let him that is on the house-top not come down to take any-thing out of his house."[1] Is it a correct inference from this that the stairway landed on the outside of the house ?

Outside of the house, but within the exterior court. It would not be either agreeable or safe to have the stairs land outside the enclosure altogether, and it is rarely done, except in mountain villages, and where roofs are but little used. They not unfrequently end in the *lewan,* but more commonly in some part of the lower court. The urgency of the flight recommended by our Lord is enhanced by the fact that the stairs do lead down into the court or lewan. He in effect says, Though you must pass by the very door of your room, do not enter ; escape for your life, without a moment's delay.

No traveller in Syria will long need an introduction to the sparrow on the house-top. There are countless numbers of them about you.

They are a tame, troublesome, and impertinent generation, and nestle just where you don't want them. They stop up your stove and water pipes with their rubbish, build in the windows and under the beams of the roof, and would stuff your hat full of stubble in half a day if they found it hanging in a place to suit them. They are extremely pertinacious in asserting their right of pos-session, and have not the least reverence for any place or thing. David alludes to these characteristics of the sparrow in the 84th Psalm, when he complains that they had appropriated even the altars of God for their nests. Concerning himself he says, "I watch, and am as a sparrow upon the house-top."[2] When one of them has lost its mate—a matter of every-day occurrence—he will sit on the house-top alone, and lament by the hour his sad bereavement. These birds are snared and caught in great numbers, but as they are small and not much relished for food, five sparrows may still be sold for two farthings ; and when we see their countless numbers, and the eagerness with which they are de-stroyed as a worthless nuisance, we can better appreciate the assurance that our heavenly Father, who takes care of them, so that not one can fall to the ground without his notice, will surely take care of us, who are of more value than many sparrows.[3]

CHAPTER III. The stair-way.

The spar-row on the house-top.

---

[1] Matt xxiv. 17.   [2] Psalm cii. 7.   [3] Matt. x. 29, and Luke xii. 7.

CHAPTER IV.

DOG RIVER.*

Ancient inscriptions—Caves—Natural bridge.

January 27th.

SAFELY back, and welcome! How have you enjoyed this first excursion in the East?

Scenery

Perfectly. It has been a day of unmingled pleasure; company agreeable, air soft and bland, horses lively, and the path through the mulberry orchards, and around the sandy Bay of St. George, quite delightful. Then the scenery at Dog River, what can surpass it? I was so enchanted with the grand, wild gorge, that I could scarcely tear myself away to examine the remains of antiquity for which the spot is celebrated; but I did look at them all, and at some with a feeling of awe and reverence quite new in my experience.

The old
road.

It is an assemblage of ancient mementos to be found nowhere else in a single group, so far as I know. That old road, climbing the rocky pass, along which the Phœnician, Egyptian, Persian, Babylonian, Greek, Roman, Frank, Turk, and Arab, have marched their countless hosts for four thousand years, has much to tell the student of man's past history, could we but break the seal and read the long roll of revelations. Those faintly-cut emblems of Sesostris; those stern, cold soldiers of Chaldea; those inscriptions in Persian, Greek, Latin, and Arabic,—each embodies a history of itself, or rather tells of one written elsewhere, which we long to possess. I have drawings of these figures, and copies of the inscriptions, which you may study at your leisure. They, of course, imply much more than they directly reveal.

Ancient
inscrip-
tions.

I was told that a large part of the river issues from a cave some six miles above the sea. Have you ever visited the spot?

Sources of
the river.

Several times; and it is worth the ride. The scenery also around the sources of the river, high up under Sŭnnîn, is very romantic. As this is the Lycus of the ancients, with a history and a myth of its own, we may spend a few more moments upon it without growing weary of the subject. No one who

[* The Nahr el-Kelb, or Dog River, is a romantic stream that flows from the Lebanon ridge into the sea a few miles north of Beirût. Its old Roman name was *Lycus flumen.* "The origin of the name is hid by the mists of tradition. Some tell us that in the long-past ages, a monster of the wolf species was chained by some god or demon at the river's mouth, which, when lashed to fury by the storms, awoke the echoes of far-distant Cyprus with his bark. . . . . Another story is, that the statue of a dog formerly stood on the pedestal that crowns the cliff; its mouth being wide open, strange sounds were heard to issue from it when the winds were high; these the Arabs long regarded as supernatural warnings of impending woe; but at length, on one occasion, they mustered courage, assembled in a body, and hurled the monster into the sea."— *Handbook for Syria and Palestine.*—ED.]

ASSYRIAN SCULPTURES AT THE NAHR EL KELB OR DOG RIVER.

has eyes, or deserves to have them, will pass up the river from its mouth without stopping again and again to admire the grey cliffs towering up to the sky on either side. The aqueduct will also attract attention, clinging to the perpendicular rock, and dressed out in drooping festoons of ivy, and other creepers, whose every twig and leaf sparkle with big drops of brightest crystal. Where the river turns to the south, the ravine becomes too narrow, wild, and rocky for any but a goat-path, and the road leads thence over the steep shoulder of the mountain for an hour and a half. It then descends by a very slippery track to the river, in the immediate vicinity of the caves. There are three of them, and all in the cliffs on the north side of the ravine. Out of the first rushes a large part of the river ; but without a boat it cannot be explored. A few rods farther up the valley is the second cave. It runs under the mountain in a straight line for eighty paces, and then descends into an abyss of water. Several smaller aisles lead in different directions down to the same abyss. On the west side of the main entrance is a parallel passage of about the same dimensions as the other, with which it communicates by a large door-way. This second tunnel leads round to the west, and unites with the lower cave at its mouth. Strike or jump on the floor, and you are startled by a dull hollow sound beneath, and feel inclined to walk softly over such unknown depths.

About forty rods higher up the ravine is the third and largest cave. The entrance of this is concealed by huge rocks, and a stranger might pass within a few feet of it without suspecting its existence. Creep carefully over the rocks, let yourself down some ten feet and you find a wide, low opening. Soon the passage becomes high enough to walk erect, and turns round toward the west. You must now light your torches, for the interior is utterly dark. A sort of gallery, or corridor, runs round three sides of this immense room. Descending to the lower part, you again come to the river, which crosses the cave, and disappears at the north-west corner with a loud noise. At the north-east, where it enters the room, there is a pool of water, clear and smooth as a mirror, and deliciously cool. How far it extends under the mountains I had no means of ascertaining. I fired a gun up it ; the echoes were loud and oft-repeated. This cave abounds in stalagmites and stalactites, some of which are of enormous size, reaching from the roof to the floor, and are grooved like fluted columns. They also hang like long wax candles from the roof of the interior pool. I longed for a boat, not only to gather them, but also to explore the mysteries of those dark and watery labyrinths. There is much said in the Bible about caves ; and ecclesiastical tradition has located many of the events recorded in the New Testament in these subterraneous abodes. We shall have abundant opportunities to examine them hereafter.

The river above the caves comes from two vast fountains, which burst out directly under the snow of Sŭnnîn—intensely cold—icy, in fact, even in summer, and clear as though running liquid diamonds. They, with their young rivers, bear names rather poetical—agreeable, at least, to Arab taste. The

CHAPTER IV.

Cliffs.

Aqueduct.

The caves.

The river. in the cave.

Fountains.

Natural
bridge.

northern is the Fountain of Honey (Niba el 'Asil) ; the southern is the Fountain of Milk (Niba el Lebn). Over the deep ravine of the latter stream, and not far from its birth, nature has thrown, or has left, a gigantic arch, which to this day is the bridge for the public highway, the *highest* in the land, creeping cautiously along the very uppermost shelf of Lebanon. I have visited it several times, but have mislaid my measurements, and must give you those of a friend. The arch is 90 feet thick ; the span 157 ; the breadth from 80 to 140 ; and the height on the lower side nearly 200 feet. These figures may be rather large ; but, without any exaggeration, it is a grand and impressive natural curiosity.

Let me now inform you, for your satisfaction, that while you have been enjoying Dog River, I have completed our travelling apparatus and equipage, and our departure is definitely fixed for to-morrow morning.

CHAPTER V.

BEIRUT TO THE DAMUR.*

Setting out on a journey.	Sand-deserts ; their advance.
Narrow paths and donkeys.	Khân Khûldeh—Sarcophagi.
Custom-house.	Lime-kilns ; " thorns cut up."
The palm.	Damûr.
The raven—The dove.	Great land-slip.
The olive—Oil—Grafting.	Stone-pillows.

January 28th.

Setting
out.

ARE we to have such a tedious and noisy scene every morning with the muleteers ?

I hope not. It is generally thus, however, the first day ; but after each one has ascertained his proper load, they proceed more quietly, and with greater expedition.

Now we are fairly on the road, let us remember to commit our way unto the Lord. " In all thy ways acknowledge him, and he shall direct thy paths." [1]
A travel-
ling motto. This has been my travelling motto, roving or at rest, ever since I left the banks of our own bright Ohio for this " Land of Promise."

No sentiment can be more appropriate. We shall need the admonition at every step, and the promise thereto annexed as well. But the royal preacher has given another piece of advice to travellers : " Let thine eyes look right on, and let thine eyelids look straight before thee. Turn not to the right hand or

---

[* The travellers now begin their course southward ; and their first station is the river Damûr, about ten miles from Beirût, on the way to Sidon.—ED.]

[1] Prov. iii. 6.

to the left: remove thy foot from evil." [1] Do so now, lest you commence our CHAPTER
journey with a practical "illustration," which will associate your name with   V.
Balaam and his much-abused ass. His path, like ours, " had a wall on this A walled
side and a wall on that;" the angel with drawn sword was in front, and the path—Ba-
poor beast thrust herself against the wall and crushed the prophet's foot. [2] laam.
Now this file of donkeys, with rough stone from the quarries on their backs,
completely blocks up this narrow way, and if you attempt to force your horse
past them, either on the right or the left, you will also meet with a crushed
foot.

That is a fact so obvious that the dumb ass, if it could speak with man's
voice as Balaam's did, might rebuke the madness of the attempt. But what
are we to do ?

Retreat to the next side-alley, and let them pass. These stone-carrying
donkeys are a great nuisance ; but we are free from them at last, and you will
not encounter a similar annoyance in all Syria, nor meet an equally patent
illustration of Balaam's misfortune.

I shall not soon forget it. These crooked, narrow paths through the Narrow
gardens of Beirût do indeed require one to observe the wise man's directions paths.
most closely. Only a few feet wide, with high walls on either side, and overshadowed by the rough arms and thorny palms of the prickly pear, the rider
must keep wide awake, or he will find his face transfixed with the sharp spikes
of the one, or his foot crushed against the other. I was stooping to avoid the
first, when your timely warning saved me from the second.

The almanac tells me that this is the 28th of January, and yet the air is
warm and bland as May. This old world and her ways are to me emphatically
new. Those tall pines, with their parasol canopies spread out along the sky,
are both new and beautiful ; and how surpassingly glorious and majestic does
Lebanon appear through and beyond them !

Those old trees were planted by Fakhr et Deen, and there are but few of
them left. I saw that pretty wood beneath them *sowed* by Mahmood Beg, the
governor of Beirût, twenty years ago. The smallest are only two years old.
Half a century hence, the tourist will here find the fairest grove in Syria.
This low, flat-roofed house on our right is a native khân—inn, or, if you please, A khân.
hotel—much like those of ancient times, I suppose. We shall have some
future occasion to test the accommodation which these Arab institutions offer
to man and beast. Here is the guard of the custom-house, and you may as Custom-
well return his polite salâm. These gentlemen are obliging or otherwise, house.
according to circumstances. On a former occasion, one of them seized my
bridle, and rudely demanded my passport. I replied that it was not customary
for residents in the country to carry such documents, and that I had it not
with me. This did not satisfy him. He ordered me back, swearing roundly
that he would not let the Grand Vizier himself pass without his tazcara.

---

[1] Prov. iv. 25, 27.   [2] Numb. xxii. 22-33.

PART
I.

Bullying
strangers.

After he had swaggered himself tired, I told him I had lived twenty years in this country, and knew the regulations of government better than he did ; that no order applicable to Franks was ever issued without official notice of the same being communicated to the consuls ; and that, as no such notification in regard to passports had been made, I would not conform to it except by force. If he turned me back, I should lodge a complaint against him with the consul, who would hold him responsible for all damages. He immediately lowered his tone, bade me go in peace, and say nothing more about the matter. I did so, and have never been annoyed with a similar demand from that day to this. He had mistaken me for a stranger, and expected to extort a bakshîsh.

It is nine hours, you say, from Beirût to Sidon ?

About twenty-seven miles, and takes six, eight, or ten hours, according to the rate of travel. But as our object is to study the land and its customs, or rather to peruse the Word of God by the light which these shed upon it, we shall pay very little attention to the hours, stages, and stations of ordinary tourists.

This suits the main purpose of my visit precisely. I have no great fondness for mere sight-seeing, and much prefer to gather instruction from the works and ways, the manners and customs of the living, than to grope for it amid the rotten ruins of the dead.

Road to
Damascus.

Doubtless the former is the richer field, at least in Palestine, but both should be carefully explored. In the meanwhile, turn a little to the left. The direct road to Sidon leads over a sandy desert, fatiguing to both the horse and his rider. The path we take lies along the eastern margin of it, through mulberry orchards and olive groves, with which we may hold pleasant and profitable converse as we pass. This broad track through the centre of the pine forest is the sultan's highway to Damascus. You can see it yonder to the south-east, winding up the face of Lebanon.—When but a few days old in the country, I made trial of it, and was astonished beyond measure to find that such a villanous path was a road to anywhere, and, most of all, that it was *the* road *par excellence* between Beirût and Syria's celebrated capital.

Palm-
trees.

Look now at those stately palm-trees, which stand here and there on the plain, like military sentinels, with feathery plumes nodding gracefully on their proud heads. The stem, tall, slender, and erect as Rectitude herself, suggests to the Arab poets many a symbol for their lady-love ; and Solomon, long before them, has sung, " How fair and how pleasant art thou, O love, for delights ! this thy stature is like the palm-tree." [1]

Yes ; and Solomon's father says, "The righteous shall flourish like the palm-tree. Those that be planted in the house of the Lord shall flourish in the courts of our God. They shall bring forth fruit in old age." [2]

---

[1] Song vii. 6, 7.　　[2] Psalm xcii. 12–14.

The royal poet has derived more than one figure from the customs of men, CHAPTER and the habits of this noble tree, with which to adorn his sacred ode. The V. palm grows slowly, but steadily, from century to century, uninfluenced by The palm. those alternations of the seasons which affect other trees. It does not rejoice overmuch in winter's copious rain, nor does it droop under the drought and the burning sun of summer. Neither heavy weights which men place upon its

PALM-TREE.

head, nor the importunate urgency of the wind, can sway it aside from perfect uprightness. There it stands, looking calmly down upon the world below, and Its up- patiently yielding its large clusters of golden fruit from generation to genera- rightness. tion. They bring forth fruit in old age. The allusion to being planted in the house of the Lord is probably drawn from the custom of planting beauti- tiful and long-lived trees in the courts of temples and palaces, and in all Fruit in "high places" used for worship. This is still common ; nearly every palace, old age. and mosque, and convent in the country has such trees in the courts, and, being well protected there, they flourish exceedingly. Solomon covered all the

4

PART I.

Palm branches.

walls of the "Holy of Holies"[1] round about with palm-trees. They were thus planted, as it were, within the very house of the Lord; and their presence there was not only ornamental, but appropriate and highly suggestive; the very best emblem, not only of patience in well-doing, but of the rewards of the righteous—a fat and flourishing old age—a peaceful end—a glorious immortality. The Jews used palm branches as emblems of victory in their seasons of rejoicing;[2] and Christians do the same on Palm Sunday, in commemoration of our Saviour's triumphal entry into Jerusalem. They are often woven into an arch, and placed over the head of the bier which carries man to his "long home," and speak sweetly of victory and eternal life. We shall meet this striking and beautiful tree all along our journey, everywhere repeating, as an old friend, the same lessons of piety and encouragement.

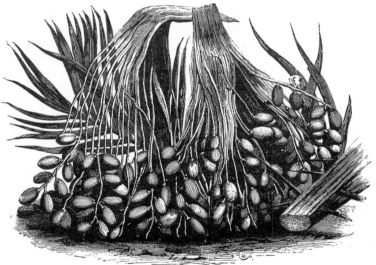

CLUSTER OF DATES.

What large black birds are those which fly furiously across the horizon, as if driven by some interior impulse of despair?

The raven.

The raven. Austere bird of ill omen! I never hear its harsh croak, or see it hurrying hither and thither, as if it could not rest, without thinking of Noah and the ark on Ararat. He sent forth this uneasy bird, which went to and fro until the waters were dried up, and never again sought safety or repose by returning to the ark. Sad emblem of those who fly from the

---

[1] 1 Kings vi. 29.　　　[2] Lev. xxiii. 40.

true Ark, and only refuge against that other deluge which shall drown the ungodly in everlasting destruction!

Olive orchards.

And now we are entering the vast olive-orchards of Shwoifat. See! our noisy approach has frightened a timid dove from the midst of that fine old tree.

The dove and the olive! another association to remind us of the ark, and the second father of mankind. Who can see the dove sitting in this tree without thinking of that evening when she returned to the ark, "and,

RAVEN.

lo! in her mouth was an olive-leaf plucked off?"[1] Mute messenger from the The dove. world below, by which Noah knew that the waters were abated from off the earth.

The olive-tree, its fruit and oil, must have been known before the deluge, but whether the dove and the branch were emblems of peace and good-will by previous custom, or whether the hint was taken from this transaction, I shall not attempt to determine. The tradition among the Greeks that the first olive-branch that reached their country was carried by a dove from Phœnicia to the temple of Jupiter in Epirus, is certainly very remarkable. The connection of the dove with the olive, however, is quite natural. These groves are their favourite resort. In them they build their nests and rear their young, and there may be heard all day long their low, soft cooing, in sweet unison with the breeze which whispers peace to the troubled and repose to the weary.

The olive branch.

DOVE.

[1] Gen. viii. 11.

PART
I.

It seems a fair deduction from the narrative in Genesis, that the flood must have risen in such a quiet way as not to destroy the trees; and must also have remained but a short time universal, else the olive would have perished.

We may at least conclude, that lands sufficiently low and warm for the olive had been for some time uncovered when the dove went forth, or it could not have found young leaves upon them. This tree does not flourish in Syria more than three thousand feet above the sea, and in the interior not so high. Indeed, it is scarcely found at all in countries adjacent to Ararat, and the dove had probably to make a long flight for its leaf, which it could easily do before "evening." And the objection to the literal meaning or strict veracity of this statement has no solid foundation, in the fact that the olive is not an inhabitant of the cold mountains of Armenia.

Habitat of the olive.

Have you ever met with any certain traces of the flood in this country?

There are myriads of fossil shells on Lebanon and elsewhere, even on the tops of the highest ranges, but no geologist would appeal to them in proof of the Noahic deluge. That was an event wholly miraculous, and the evidence of the fact is to be found in the sacred record, not in geological researches. I would by no means intimate, however, that future investigation may not uncover many well-ascertained footprints of that mighty catastrophe. But it is altogether foreign to our purpose to wander off into geological speculations, and we are not yet done with the olive-tree.

Far from it. There are many references to it in the Bible, some of which I am not able yet to appreciate. Thus Hosea says, "His beauty shall be as the olive-tree."[1] It does not strike me as very beautiful; but perhaps one's eye needs to be educated before it can distinguish properly, and decide correctly, on such questions in new and strange circumstances.

Beauty of the olive.

No doubt. To me this noble grove, spreading like a silver sea along the base of the hills, and climbing their ascending terraces, is perfectly charming; and it speaks of peace and plenty, food and gladness. The olive-tree and its fruit make the face of man to shine in more senses than one. To a stranger it is necessarily destitute of these pleasing associations; but to me it is at all times both charming and refreshing to ride through such a grove when clothed with flowers, or when bowed down with fat and oily berries.

Moses, in that last ode which he taught the children of Israel, speaks of "oil out of the flinty rock;"[2] and until now I had supposed that this tree delighted in hard, rocky soil; but this vast grove spreads over a soft and sandy plain.

Oil out of the rock.

You were not mistaken—only misled by appearances. The substratum of this plain is chalky marl, abounding in flint, and the sand is merely an intruder blown in from this desert on our right. In such soil our tree flourishes best, both in the plains and upon the mountains. It delights to insinuate its roots into the clefts of the rocks and crevices of this flinty marl; and from thence it draws its richest stores of oil. If the overlying mould is so deep that its

[1] Hos. xiv. 6.   [2] Deut. xxxii. 13.

roots cannot reach the rock beneath, I am told that the tree languishes, and its berries are small and sapless. There is, however, another explanation of this figure of Moses. In ancient times generally (and in many places at the present day) the olives were ground to a pulp in huge stone basins, by rolling a heavy stone wheel over them, and the oil was then expressed in stone presses established near by. Frequently these presses, with their floors, gutters, troughs, and cisterns, were all hewn out of solid rock, and thus it literally "poured out rivers of oil,"[1] as Job hath it in his parable. There is a ruin above Tyre, near Kânâh, called Im-il-'Awamîd, where scores of such presses are still standing, almost as perfect as they were twenty centuries ago, although every vestige of the groves which supplied the oil has long since disappeared.

I notice that the branches of some trees have been cut off, and then grafted; why is this done?

Simply because the olive, in its natural wild state, bears no berries, or but few, and these small and destitute of oil.

St. Paul has an extended reference to this matter. Stay till I turn to the passage, for there are some things in it which I have never understood. Here it is: "If some of the branches be broken off, and thou, being a *wild* olive-tree, wert graffed in among them, and with them partakest of the root and fatness of the olive-tree, boast not against the branches. But if thou boast, thou bearest not the root, but the root thee."[2] And then, in the 24th verse, "For if thou wert cut out of the olive-tree, which is wild by nature, and wert graffed, *contrary to nature*, into a good olive-tree," etc. Now here is my difficulty, and the exact point of inquiry: The olive, you say (and so says the Apostle), is wild by nature, and it must be grafted by the *good* before it will bear fruit; but here the Apostle speaks of grafting the wild into the good, not the good *upon* the wild.

True, he does; but observe, he says expressly that this is *contrary* to nature, as it really is. I have made particular inquiries on this point, and find that in the *kingdom of nature* generally, certainly in the case of the olive, the process referred to by the Apostle never succeeds. Graft the good upon the wild, and, as the Arabs say, it will *conquer* the wild; but you cannot reverse the process with success.—If you insert a *wild* graft into a good tree, *it will conquer the* good. It is only in the *kingdom of grace* that a process thus contrary to nature can be successful; and it is this circumstance which the Apostle has seized upon, and with admirable tact, to magnify the mercy shown to the Gentiles by grafting them, a wild race, *contrary to the nature* of such operations, into the good olive-tree of the Church, and causing them to flourish there, and bring forth fruit unto eternal life. The Apostle lived in the land of the olive, and was in no danger of falling into a blunder in founding his argument upon such a circumstance in its cultivation.

Grafting wild olives.

PART
I.

But have all the trees in this vast grove been reclaimed from a wild state by grafting?

The root
of the
olive.

Certainly not. The Apostle himself speaks of the *root* of the good olive,— implying that, by some means or other, it had been changed. The process by which this result is reached is quite simple. You observe certain knobs, or large warts, so to speak, on the body of this tree. Cut off one of these which has a branch growing out of it, *above* the place where it has been grafted; plant it in good soil, water it carefully, and it will strike out roots and grow. It is now a good tree from the root, and all scions taken from it are also "good by nature." But if the knob, or branch, be taken below the grafting, your tree comes wild again. The greater part of this grove is now "good" from the root. I am told, however, by olive-growers, that there is a tendency to degenerate, and that it is often a great improvement to graft even a good tree with one that is still better.

The
flower.

Job says, "He shall cast off his flower as the olive."[1] What is there in the casting off of olive-flowers which can illustrate the rejection and ruin of those who trust in vanity, for which purpose the patriarch employs the figure?

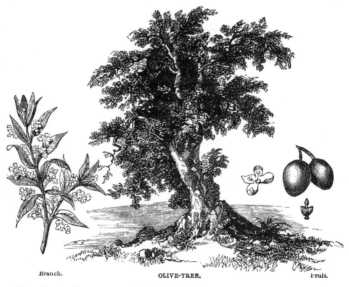

Branch.   OLIVE-TREE.   Fruit.

Abun-
dance of
flowers.

The olive is the most prodigal of all fruit-bearing trees in flowers. It literally bends under the load of them. But then not one in a hundred comes to

---

[1] Job xv. 33.

maturity. The tree casts them off by millions, as if they were of no more value than flakes of snow, which they closely resemble. So it will be with those who put their trust in vanity. Cast off, they melt away, and no one takes the trouble to ask after such empty, useless things,—just as our olive seems to throw off in contempt the myriads of flowers that signify nothing, and turns all her fatness to those which will mature into fruit. *CHAPTER V.*

This tree is of slow growth, and the husbandman must have long patience. Except under circumstances peculiarly favourable, it bears no berries until the seventh year; nor is the crop worth much until the tree is ten or fifteen years old; but then "the labour of the olive" is extremely profitable, and it will continue to yield its fruit to extreme old age, like the excellent of the earth. So long as there is a fragment remaining, though externally the tree looks dry as a post, yet does it continue to yield its load of oily berries, and for twenty generations the owners gather fruit from the faithful old patriarch. This tree also requires but little labour or care of any kind, and, if long neglected, will revive again when the ground is dug or ploughed, and begin afresh to yield as before. Vineyards forsaken die out almost immediately, and mulberry orchards neglected run rapidly to ruin; but not so the olive. I saw the desolate hills of Jebel-el-'Alâh, above Antioch, covered with these groves, although no one had paid attention to them for half a century. If the olive bore every year, its value would be incalculable; but, like most other trees, it yields only every other year. Even with this deduction, it is the most valuable species of property in the country. Large trees, in a good season, will yield from ten to fifteen gallons of oil, and an acre of them gives a crop worth at least one hundred dollars. No wonder it is so highly prized. *Slow growth.* *"Labour of the olive."*

The value of this tree is enhanced by the fact that its fruit is indispensable for the comfort, and even the existence of the mass of the community. The Biblical references to this matter are not at all exaggerated. The berry, pickled, forms the general relish to the farmer's dry bread. He goes forth to his work in the field at early dawn, or sets out on a journey, with no other provision than olives wrapped up in a quantity of his *paper-like* loaves; and with this he is contented. Then almost every kind of dish is cooked in oil, and without it the goodwife is utterly confounded; and when the oil fails, the lamp in the dwelling of the poor expires. Moreover, the entire supply of soap in this country is from the produce of the olive. Habakkuk, therefore, gives a very striking attestation of his faith in God when he says, "Although the labour of the olive should fail, yet I will rejoice in the Lord, I will joy in the God of my salvation." [1] *Its usefulness.*

Isaiah refers to the *gathering* of the olive thus: "Yet gleaning grapes shall be in it, as the shaking of an olive-tree; two or three berries in the top of the uppermost bough, four or five in the outermost fruitful branches thereof." [2] Have you noticed the circumstances alluded to by the prophet? *Gathering the olive.*

---

[1] Hab. iii. 18. [2] Isa. xvii. 6.

PART
I.

Very often ; and it is the language of familiar acquaintance with the subject. As you may never have an opportunity to watch the process, I will describe it as it occurs in such places as Hasbeiya, where I have studied it to best advantage. Early in autumn the berries begin to drop of themselves, or are shaken off by the wind. They are allowed to remain under the trees for some time, guarded by the watchman of the town—a very familiar Biblical character. Then a proclamation is made by the governor that all who have trees go out and pick what is fallen. Previous to this, not even the owners are allowed to gather olives in the groves. This proclamation is repeated once or twice, according to the season. In November comes the general and final summons, which sends forth all Hasbeiya. No olives are now safe unless the owner looks after them, for the watchmen are removed, and the orchards are alive with men, women, and children. It is a merry time, and the laugh and the song

Shaking of the olive.

echo far and wide. Everywhere the people are in the trees "shaking" them with all their might, to bring down the fruit. This is what the prophet had in mind. The effort is to make a clear sweep of all the crop ; but, in spite of shaking and beating, there is always a gleaning left—" two or three berries in the top of the uppermost boughs, four or five in the outermost fruitful branches." These are afterward gleaned up by the very poor, who have no trees of their own ;[1] and by industry they gather enough to keep a lamp in their habitation during the dismal nights of winter, and to cook their mess of pottage and bitter herbs. I have often seen these miserable outcasts gleaning among the groves, and shivering in winter's biting cold. In fact, the "shaking of the olive" is the severest operation in Syrian husbandry, particularly in such mountainous regions as Hasbeiya. When the proclamation goes forth to "shake," there can be no postponement. The rainy season has already set in ; the trees are dripping with the last shower, or bowing under a load of moist snow ; but shake, shake you must, drenching yourself and those below in an artificial storm of rain, snow, and olives. No matter how piercing the wind, how biting the frost, this work must go on from early dawn to dark night ; and then the weary labourer must carry on his aching back a heavy load of dripping berries two or three miles up the mountain to his home. To comprehend the necessity of all this, you must remember that the olive-groves are in common—not owned in common, but planted on the same general tract of land, and are without fences, walls, or hedges of any kind, mingled together like the trees in a natural forest. This tree belongs to Zeid, that to 'Abeid, as they say, and so on through the whole plantation. Such, at least, is the case with the groves we are describing. This vast orchard of Shwoifat, through which we have been riding for the last hour, has a thousand owners, and in "shaking time" every one must look sharply after his own, or he loses all. There is an utter confounding of the meum and tuum in the general conscience of olive-gatherers.

To what particular circumstance does David refer in the 128th Psalm,

---

[1] Deut. xxiv. 20.

where he says, "Thy children shall be like olive-plants round about thy CHAPTER V.
table?

Follow me into the grove, and I will show you what may have suggested the Olive plants round the table. comparison. Here we have hit upon a beautiful illustration. This aged and decayed tree is surrounded, as you see, by several young and thrifty shoots, which spring from the root of the venerable parent. They seem to uphold, protect, and embrace it. We may even fancy that they now bear that load of fruit which would otherwise be demanded of the feeble parent. Thus do good and affectionate children gather round the table of the righteous. Each contributes something to the common wealth and welfare of the whole—a beautiful sight, with which may God refresh the eyes of every friend of mine.

But here we must leave our pleasant grove for this singular sea of sand, Sea of sand. which rolls quite back to the gardens of Beirût. Geologists tell us that this sand has travelled long and far before it reached its present resting-place ;— that, in fact, its original home was in the great African desert, and, during the countless ages of the past, it has been drifted first by the wind into the sea, and then by the current along the northern coast past Egypt, and around the head of the sea, until, stopped by the Cape of Beirût, it has been thrown out by the waves on to this plain. Others say that it is the sand of the Nile transported hither by the northern current in this part of the Mediterranean. It would lead us too far from our path and our purpose to discuss these theories. My own opinion is, that we need look no farther than this immediate neighbourhood for the origin of this desert. The rock on the shore is a soft sandstone, which is continually disintegrating by the action of wind and wave. The loose sand is cast up upon the beach, and the strong south-west winds which blow across the plain are constantly spreading it inward under our very eyes. No doubt, the River Damûr, which is just ahead of us, brings down a vast amount of sand during the winter rains, which is also thrown on shore by the sea. But enough of speculation. The fact is only too certain and too sad. This sand is continually driven in upon these gardens like another deluge. Entire mulberry orchards about Beirût, with all their trees and houses, have Destruction of orchards. been thus overwhelmed since I came to the country ; and the day is not distant when it will have swept over the whole cape to the bay on the north of the city, unless its course can be arrested. I never take this ride without watching, with weary sadness, this ever-changing desert. Upon the great sandwaves, which swell up from twenty to fifty feet high, the west wind wakes up small but well-defined *wavelets*,—the counterpart in miniature of those on yonder noisy sea. Should these ripples be caught and fixed by some tranquillizing and indurating agency, we should here have a vast formation of as *wavy* sandstone as ever puzzled the student of earth's rocky mysteries.

These sandy invasions are not found to any injurious extent north of Beirût, Sand waves common in the south. but as you go south they become broader and more continuous. They spread far inland round the Bay of Acre. They begin again at Cesarea, and reach to the River 'Aujeh ; and then south of Joppa, past Askelon and Gaza, they roll in their desolating waves wider and still wider, until they subside in the great desert that lies between Arabia and Africa. Let us ride up to the crest of that bold sand-wave, and take a farewell look at this prospect, so eminently Syrian. Ibrahim Pacha told the Emeer of Shwoifat that he had three different seas beneath his feet—the blue Mediterranean, this yellow Kŭllâbât, and the silvery sea of this olive Sahrâh. Though we may not admire the poetry of the pacha, we will the scene that inspired it. All he saw is before us ; and with the noble Lebanon for background, receding and rising, range over range, up to where Sŭnnîn leans his snowy head against the marble vault of heaven. Picturesque villages by the hundred sleep at his feet, cling to his sides, hide in his bosom, or stand out in bold relief upon his ample shoulders, giving life and animation to the scene.

We will now rest and lunch at this khân Khŭldeh. It has taken three hours to reach it. Though you have but little relish for rotten ruins, there is something hereabouts will surely interest you. This broken tower, crowning the top of a half-natural, half-artificial mound, the guide-books will tell you,

A telegraphic beacon.

is one of those telegraphic beacons which St. Helen built along the road from Jerusalem to Constantinople, to convey to her royal son the very first tidings of the discovery of the true cross, for which she was then ransacking the rubbish of the Holy City. You may accept that, or else suppose that it was one of a system of watch-towers for the defence of the coast, such as are still kept up along the shores of Spain and Algiers. The hill itself, however, speaks of remote antiquity. But by far the most remarkable relics of past ages are

Ancient sarcophagi.

those sarcophagi on the side of the mountain. Their number is surprising, since for ages the inhabitants have been breaking them up for building-stone, and burning them into lime ; and still there are hundreds of them lying about on the face of the hill. They are of all sizes ; some eight feet long, and in fair proportion, the resting-place of giants ; others were made for small children. Many are hewn in the live rock ; others are single coffins cut out of separate blocks. All had heavy lids, of various shapes, approaching to that of an American coffin, but with the corners raised. They are, no doubt, very ancient. Lift the lid, and the dust within differs not from the surrounding soil from which grows the corn of the current year. And so it was twenty centuries ago, I suppose. They are without inscriptions, and have nothing about them to determine their age or origin. Here is a cherub on one, with wings expanded, as if about to fly away to the "better land ;" yonder is another with a palm branch,—emblem of immortality ; while that large one has three warlike figures, the chosen companions, perhaps, of some ancient hero. But on none of them is there a single mark or scratch which might indicate that those who made them had an alphabet. Who were they ? Certainly neither Greeks nor Romans. I find no mention of this place, unless it be the Heldua, which, according to the "Jerusalem Itinerary," was twelve miles south of Beirût. This distance, however, would take us to the next khân—Ghŭfer en Naamy ; and there was an ancient tower near it. Mark Antony spent some time at a fort

between Beirût and Sidon, called Dukekome, waiting for Cleopatra. Per- CHAPTER V.
haps this tower-crowned hill marks the spot where these mighty revellers met
and feasted. However that may be, we must now leave it. An hour's easy,
or rather uneasy, ride through the deep sand of the shore, will bring us to our
tent on the green bank of the Damûr.

Here, on the brow of this rocky hill, we have the lime-kilns you spoke of, Lime-
and men in the very act of breaking up sarcophagi to feed them. It is unpar- kilns.
donable sacrilege thus to destroy those venerable antiquities. It is outrageous
Vandalism.

Instead of hurling anathemas at these barbarians, we had better drop a tear
of compassion over such ignorance, and then see if we cannot draw some lesson
of instruction from even these destructive kilns. You see an immense quantity of this low, matted thorn-bush collected around them. That is the fuel
with which the lime is burned. And thus it was in the days of Isaiah. "The
people," says he, "shall be as the burnings of lime: *as thorns cut up shall they* Thorns cut
be burned in the fire." [1] Those people among the rocks yonder are cutting up up.
thorns with their mattocks and pruning-hooks and gathering them into bundles
to be burned in these burnings of lime. It is a curious fidelity to real life,
that, when the thorns are merely to be destroyed, they are never cut up, but
set on fire where they grow. They are only *cut up* for the lime-kiln.

And here is the Damûr, with our tent pitched among oleanders and willows
—a picturesque position for our first encampment. Permit me to introduce
you to the house of your pilgrimage. Salîm has placed your cot and luggage The tent
on the right, and mine on the left. We will pursue this arrangement hereafter, and thereby avoid much confusion.

It looks very inviting, and promises well for future comfort. The sojourn-
ing in tents, in the land where the patriarchs tabernacled so many centuries
ago, not only takes my fancy captive, but is in beautiful unison with our object.

It is. A coach or car, with its bustle and hurry, would be intolerable here;
and even a fussy, fashionable hotel would be a nuisance. Let us enjoy the
luxury of liberty, and, while dinner is preparing, take a stroll at our leisure up
this fine wady.

This name, Damûr, is it a mere variation of the Tamyras of Strabo, the The
Damura of Polybius? Damûr.

Yes, if the variation is not that of the Greek and Roman. I suspect that
Damûr is the true original. The main source of this river is near 'Ain Zehalteh, a village five hours to the east, under the lofty ridge of Lebanon. Other
streams from the mountain farther north unite with this at Jisr el Kâdy, on
the road from Beirût to Deir el Kamar. Below this the river turns westward,
and falls into the sea just south of this long, straggling village of Mûallakah.
Though not more than twenty-five miles long, yet, from the vast extent of lofty
mountains which pour their winter floods into its channel, it rises suddenly

---

[1] Isa. xxxiii. 12.

into a furious, unfordable river. Many people are carried away by it and perish at this ford. This broken bridge was built by the Emeer Beshîr Shehâb, some thirty-five years ago; but it soon gave way before the violence of the stream. From the nature of the bottom, it has always been difficult to establish a bridge at this place. The emîr erected his on the ruins of one more ancient, built probably by the Romans, and with no better success than they. The river frequently changes its channel, and the Romans constructed this heavy wall running up the stream to confine it to its proper bed; but in winter it sets all bounds at defiance. During a great flood last year it spread through these gardens of Mûallakah, tore up the mulberry-trees, and swept them off to the sea. The scenery around the head of this river is not so wild as in many other places; but the basins of the different tributaries expand on an immense scale—spreading up the declivities of Lebanon, and opening out prospects which, for depth and height, vastness and variety, are rarely surpassed. The view from Mutyar Abeih, to which I directed your eye as we came along the shore, is particularly impressive. The wady of 'Ain Zehalteh abounds in remarkable cliffs of blue argillaceous marl, which are subject to slides and avalanches on a terrific scale. The Emîr Hyder, in his "History of Lebanon," says, that about ninety-five years ago a projecting terrace at Kefr Nabrûkh, which had a small village on it, parted from the main mountain, and plunged with prodigious uproar into the wady below, carrying houses, gardens, and trees with it in horrid confusion. It completely stopped the river for seven days. Repeatedly have I stood on the awful precipice, and gazed upon the wrecks of this avalanche with terror. Few heads are steady enough for the giddy perch; and no one breathes freely there, or looks without a shudder into the gulf, which opens fifteen hundred feet directly below him. The emeer relates that one man who was on the sliding mass escaped unhurt, but was ever after a raving maniac. The catastrophe occurred during the life of the historian, and not far from his home, and we may therefore give full credit to his narrative. I have seen many similar slides on Lebanon. Indeed, they occur every winter, but rarely on so gigantic a scale, or accompanied by circumstances so romantic and tragical.

Such avalanches appear to have been known even in the days of Job, and he refers to them to illustrate the overthrow of vain man's hope and confidence. "Surely," says he, "the mountain falling cometh to nought, and the rock is removed out of his place;"[1] and he connects this with the waters which wear the stones, when, as now, they were occasioned by the great rains of winter.

They were, perhaps, more common in ancient days than at present. But there comes the call for dinner, and we must return to the tent.

What an abundant table the Lord, by the ministration of this lively cook of ours, has spread for us here in the wilderness! Neatly got up, too, and

---

nothing seems wanting. Do you know, I looked on during those days of preparation at Beirût with wonder and alarm at the hundred and one things
which you were gathering around you. I could not conceive where they were
to be stowed away, or how they were to be carried on the mules. Now I find
that everything has a place, and an office to discharge. It is said that Bonaparte never spent more than fifteen minutes at the table. However that may
be, I have no inclination to devote much time at present to this "vulgar
function of eating." Dinner over, I cannot abide the tent; for, though it has
somewhat the shape, it has none of the glory of this starry canopy above. As
to sleep, the very idea seems absurd. Could one sleep on the golden streets
of the New Jerusalem the first night? You shake your head reprovingly, and
the allusion is extravagant, but all my present surroundings seem equally so.
Boyhood's possible and impossible fancies are gathering thick about me in
living realities. I was ever given to reverie, and many a day, beneath the
leafy canopy of maple-trees on the banks of our own Ohio, have lain at ease,
and dreamed of this land of the sun, its mysteries and its miracles, and longed
to be there, and wondered if I ever should. And now I *am* here, on the shore
of this great and wide sea, with its everlasting anthem going up to the listening stars. Here am I—but you smile, and I do not choose just now to furnish food for your mirth.

Pilgrim feelings.

Better stop. Why, you have been dreaming, with that Longfellow, who

> "Used to lie
> And gaze into the summer sky,
> Where the sailing clouds went by
> Like ships upon the sea."

All this is a quarter of a century behind my experience. At that remote
date I might have understood you, but not now. From this, on, waste no more
breath in rhapsodies. A pilgrimage to Palestine has too much of the real in
it to permit us to expire in the romantic. We had better prepare to imitate
this muleteer, that we may be ready for the early dawn, and the bustle of a
new day.

The fellow is sound asleep on the bare ground, and, like Jacob at Bethel, he
has actually got a stone for his pillow.

A stone pillow.

You will often see that in this country. I have tried it myself, but could
never bring sleep and stone pillows together. I suspect Jacob was not used
to it, for he was disturbed with extraordinary dreams; but to Ahmed, with his
hard head and stuffed cap, this stone is soft as a cushion of down.

You do not mean that he will sleep all night on this sand, and with no
covering but his old cloak

Certainly; and if he were at home he would do the same, at least as to
covering. This custom of sleeping in their ordinary clothes is the basis of that
humane law of Moses for the protection of the poor: "If thou at all take thy
neighbour's raiment to pledge, thou shalt deliver it unto him by that the sun
goeth down; for that is his covering only, it is his raiment for his skin:

Sleeping in day clothes.

wherein shall he sleep?" [1] I envy him his slumbers; they are the sweet ones of the labouring man. And now come in; let us consult the "best of books," and then commend ourselves and all we love to that good Shepherd who slumbers not nor sleeps.

CHAPTER VI.

DAMUR TO NEBY YUNAS.

January 29th.

A shepherd and his flock.

WE are favoured with another bright morning, which you have been improving, as I see, by an early ramble over the hills; but come down to the river. There is something going forward worth seeing. Yon shepherd is about to lead his flock across; and—as our Lord says of the good shepherd—you observe that he goes before, and the sheep follow. Not all in the same manner, however. Some enter boldly, and come straight across. These are the loved ones of the flock, who keep hard by the footsteps of the shepherd, whether sauntering through green meadows by the still waters, feeding upon the mountains, or resting at noon beneath the shadow of great rocks. And now others enter, but in doubt and alarm. Far from their guide, they miss the ford, and are carried down the river, some more, some less; and yet, one by one, they all struggle over and make good their landing. Notice those little lambs. They refuse to enter, and must be driven into the stream by the shepherd's dog, mentioned by Job in his "parable." Poor things! how they leap, and plunge, and bleat in terror! That weak one yonder will be swept quite away, and perish in the sea. But no; the shepherd himself leaps into the stream, lifts it into his bosom, and bears it trembling to the shore. All safely over, how happy they appear! The lambs frisk and gambol about in high spirits, while the older ones gather round their faithful guide, and look up to him in subdued but expressive thankfulness.

The Shepherd of Israel.

Now, can you watch such a scene and not think of that Shepherd who leadeth Joseph like a flock; and of another river, which all his sheep must cross? He, too, goes before, and, as in the case of this flock, they who keep near him fear no evil. They hear his sweet voice saying, "When thou passest through the waters, I will be with thee; and through the floods, they shall not overflow thee." [2] With eye fastened on him, they scarcely see

---

[1] Exod. xxii. 26, 27.   [2] Isa. xliii. 3.

the stream, or feel its cold and threatening waves. The great majority, how- CHAPTER
ever, "linger, shivering on the brink, and fear to launch away." They lag VI.
behind, look down upon the dark river, and, like Peter on stormy Gennesaret
when faith failed, they begin to sink. Then they cry for help, and not in
vain. The good Shepherd hastens to their rescue; and none of all His flock
can ever perish. Even the weakest lambkins are carried safely over. I once
saw flocks crossing the Jordan " to Canaan's fair and happy land;" and there
the scene was even more striking and impressive. The river was broader, the
current stronger, and the flocks larger; while the shepherds were more picturesque and Biblical. The catastrophe, too, with which many poor sheep were
threatened—of being swept down into that mysterious Sea of Death which
swallows up the Jordan itself—was more solemn and suggestive.

But it is eight o'clock—high time to be on our way. We must be more
expeditious in the morning, or our progress will be slow indeed. The road
leads along and over this rocky headland, called Nukkâr es S'adîat; which
answers to the Platoneum mentioned by Polybius as the battle-field between
Antiochus the Great and the army of Ptolemy under Nicolaus.

It is an ugly pass to force against an enemy holding these rugged heights.
My horse can scarcely keep his feet on this detestable pavement.

Now take the advice of an old traveller, and learn to possess your soul in Bad roads
patience, even when blundering over such paths as this. Wearied, perplexed,
and disgusted, many tourists tear through this most interesting country, having
eyes that see not, ears that hear not, and hearts that cannot understand.
Better take for granted that we have gone through these annoyances from
Dan to Beersheba—have declined every case, direct and oblique, of bad roads,
bûkrah, and bukshîsh, and thrown them aside as having nothing to do with
our daily journeyings. It is only thus that one can preserve an even temper,
a joyous heart, and a mind awake to the scenes and scenery along the way.
We cannot afford to have our peace disturbed by such trifles. It would seriously interfere with the main purpose of our pilgrimage, which we must never
forget. For example, this very path, so rocky and so slippery, furnishes a
commentary on another of those humane precepts which distinguish the
Mosaic code. See those men lifting a poor donkey that has fallen under its
load. Moses says, "If thou see the ass of him that hateth thee lying under his The ass
burden, and wouldest forbear to help him, thou shalt surely help with him."[1] under his burden.
Now the people lifting this donkey are bitter enemies—Maronites and Druses
—quite recently engaged in a bloody social war, and ready to begin again on
the very first opportunity, and yet they help to lift the ass that is lying under
his burden, as though they were the very best friends in the world. We have
in this simple incident the identical occasion for the precept, and its most
literal fulfilment. Nor is this all. It is fair to infer, from the peculiar specification made by Moses, that the people in his day were divided into inimical

1 Exod. xxiii. 5.

LAB - E

PART
I.
parties and clans, just as they now are in these mountains. Moses would not have mentioned the ass of an enemy if enemies were not so common that the case specified was likely to occur. So, also, we may conclude that the donkeys were half starved, and then overloaded by their cruel masters, for such are now the conditions in which these poor slaves of all work ordinarily fall under their burdens ; and that then, as now, it required the united strength of at least two persons lifting, one on either side, to enable the ass to rise out of his painful and often dangerous predicament. The plan is to lift the beast to its feet without taking off the load, which is a tedious business. And, once more, we may infer with certainty that the roads were then as rough and slippery as this which has upset your patience and our unfortunate donkey. All these deductions I believe to be very near the truth. Manners and customs, men and things, roads and loads, continue very much what they were three thousand years ago.

The truth of that becomes more and more evident the farther we advance. Voices address the ear from all sides, and signals hang out on every hill-top to catch the eye. The stone cries out of the wall, and the beam out of the timber will answer.[1] We only need to know how to put them to the question.

Notation of time.
Without being responsible for your *accommodation* of Habakkuk, the idea is correct enough, and should be remembered and acted upon continually in our travels. Let us try the experiment with this man that comes to meet us. Ask him the time of day, and he will infallibly reply that it is about the third hour. If it were near noon he would say the sixth. Inquire the day of the week, he will tell you it is the fourth day, just as Moses wrote.[2] Question him further on the point, and he will inform you that last night and this morning make up the fourth day. They count from sunset to sunset, as Adam did, and the coming evening belongs to to-morrow. But here is something else to claim attention, whether we will or not—Arabs watering their flocks at this ancient well. They are adroit thieves and most importunate beggars. One of them stole my water-jug, from which I had just slaked his real or pretended thirst ; so let your purse lie at the bottom of your pocket, and look to your handkerchief and every loose article about you. Do you Tattooing. notice that the women are all tattooed ?

Is it that which gives such a blue tinge to their lips ?

Marks on the face, &c.
Yes ; and those marks on the forehead, chin, breast, arms, hands, and feet, are all various patterns and figures of this most ancient art. The effect is anything but agreeable to our taste. All Orientals, however, have a passion for it. Moses either instituted some such custom or appropriated one already existing to a religious purpose. He says, " And thou shalt show thy son in that day, saying, This is done because of that which the Lord did unto me when I came forth out of Egypt ; and it shall be for a sign unto thee

---

[1] Hab. ii. 11.   [2] Gen. i. 19.

upon thy hand, and for a memorial between thine eyes;" (or 16th,) " for a CHAPTER
token upon thy hand, and for frontlets between thine eyes."[1] This practice of   VI.

ARABS AT A WELL

marking religious tokens upon the hands and arms is almost universal among Process of
the Arabs, of all sects and classes.   Christian pilgrims to Jerusalem have the imprint-
operation performed there, as the most holy place known to their religion.   I ing.
have watched the process of imprinting them, and it is not a little painful.   A
number of needles are bound tightly together in the shape of the desired

---

[1] Exod. xiii. 9 and 16.

figure, or so that the figure can be marked out by them. The skin being punctured in the required pattern, certain mixtures of colouring matter are

SPECIMENS OF TATTOOING.

rubbed in, and the place bound with a tight bandage. Gunpowder, variously prepared, is very commonly employed, and it is that which gives to the tattooing of these Bedawîn its bluish tinge. Mr. Lane tells us that in Egypt smoke-black

mixed with the milk of a woman is used; and subsequently a paste of fresh-
pounded leaves of clover, or white beet, is applied, so as to give a greenish
blue colour to the marks. It is well ascertained that this tattooing prevailed
in Egypt even before the time of Moses. If he appropriated it to sacred
purposes, the patterns may have been so devised as to commemorate the
deliverance of the children of Israel from bondage. Possibly the figure of the
Paschal Lamb, whose blood on the door-posts caused the Angel of Death to
pass over their houses, was wrought into these tokens and frontlets. The
command to have the great acts of the Lord as signs upon the hand, &c.,
may appear to contradict the prohibition in Leviticus, where the people are
forbidden not only to make any cuttings for the dead, but also to print any
marks upon themselves.[1] But the direction in Exod. xiii. 9, 16, specifies
certain *purposes* for which such signs and frontlets were to be used, and this
in Leviticus mentions others for which they were made by the heathen, and
which Moses forbade the Jews to imitate. No doubt these cuttings and
prints had an idolatrous or superstitious signification, which Moses desired to
condemn. In the last song which he taught the children of Israel, he
upbraids the foolish people and unwise, because their spot was not the spot of The spot
God's children.[2] It is probable that the worshippers of the true God had of God's children.
peculiar marks to distinguish them from idolaters, which these " corrupters "
refused to wear, imprinting others used by the heathen. In the Revelation,
allusions to such religious marks are too numerous to be specified. Isaiah,
however, has a most beautiful reference to them, which we may quote, to
strengthen our trust in the watchful providence of our heavenly Father :
" Can a woman forget her sucking child, that she should not have compassion
on the son of her womb ? Yea, they may forget, yet will not I forget thee.
Behold, I have graven thee on the palms of my hands; thy walls are con- Names
tinually before me." [3] As to these Arabs, whose blue lips started us off upon graven on the hands.
this digression, we shall have many occasions to notice their strange ways and
singular customs. Those dingy brown things peeping out of the bushes on
the mountain side are their tents, and they are found spread over the whole
country, from Egypt to Mount Taurus.

Here are men on our left digging stone out of this sand-hill, and you may
be certain that they are uncovering the remains of some ancient town. The
" Jerusalem Itinerary " places Porphyreon in this neighbourhood, and I suppose
that these sand-covered ruins mark the exact site of that city. This whole
neighbourhood is now called Jîyeh. Jîyeh.

What place is this to which we are coming ?

Neby Yûnas—the prophet Jonas—or, rather, his tomb. Neby Yûnas.

Indeed ! That starts inquiries which I have long had on hand in reference
to some of the incidents in the experience of that very remarkable prophet.
Is this low building on our left the tomb ?

---

[1] Lev. xix. 28.   [2] Deut. xxxii. 5.   [3] Isa. xlix. 15, 16.

PART
I.

A khân.

The first is a khân; that south of it contains the grave, or mausoleum. It has rooms attached for the keeper, and also for the accommodation of

THE TOMB OF JONAS.

Jonah.

pilgrims—mostly Moslems and Druses—who come to discharge certain vows made to the shrine. It is in the hands of Moslems, and this crooked, club-footed anatomy, hobbling toward us for a bŭkshîsh, is the keeper. I have repeatedly spent the night here, and listened again and again to his exaggerated account of Jonah's awkward cruise with the whale. He devoutly believes that the prophet was safely landed on this sandy beach; and, for aught I know, he may be correct, though several other places claim the honour; and Josephus says he was landed on the shores of the Euxine—far enough from this, certainly.

The whale.

I care very little about these discrepancies as to the place. There are other questions, however, which I wish to have answered. The Bible says, that the Lord had prepared a great fish to swallow up the prophet;[1] but in Matthew[2] it is called a *whale* by our Saviour. Now, if I am correctly informed, there are no whales in the Mediterranean. How do you explain this ?

No whales now in the Mediterranean.

Simply by the fact that the multiplication of ships in this sea, after the time of Jonah, frightened them out of it, as other causes have driven all lions out of Palestine, where they were once numerous. It is well known that some of the best fishing stations, even in the great oceans, have been abandoned by the whales because of the multitude of whalers that visited them. This sea would, of course, be forsaken. If you could stock it thoroughly with these

---

[1] Jonah i. 17.   [2] Matt. xii. 40.

monsters to-day, there would be none left a year hence. But, up to the time of Jonah, navigation was in its infancy, ships were few and small, and they kept mostly along the shores, leaving the interior undisturbed. Whales may therefore have been common in the Mediterranean. And there are instances on record of the appearance of huge marine creatures in this sea in ancient days. Some of these may have been whales. The Hebrew word dâg, it is true, means simply *any* great fish; but nothing is gained by resorting to such a solution of the difficulty. Our Lord calls it a whale, and I am contented with his translation; and whale it was, not a shark or lamia, as some critics maintain. In a word, the whole affair was miraculous, and, as such, is taken out of the category of difficulties. If a whale had never before been in the Mediterranean, God could bring one to the exact spot needed as easily as he brought the ram to the place where Abraham was coming to sacrifice Isaac. He could also furnish the necessary capacity to accomplish the end intended. It is idle, and worse—cowardly, to withhold our faith in a Bible miracle until we can find or invent some way in which the thing might have happened *without any great* miracle after all.

Is there any gourd in this country of growth so rapid as to lay a foundation for the statement that Jonah's grew up in a night? The gourd—what was it?

Certainly not; but, without any of that anxiety about the *how* and the *possible* in miracles, we may remark that there is an economical propriety in selecting this vine rather than any other, and for several reasons. It is very commonly used for trailing over temporary arbours. It grows with extraordinary rapidity. In a few days after it has fairly begun to *run*, the whole arbour is covered. It forms a shade absolutely impenetrable to the sun's rays even at noonday. It flourishes best in the very hottest part of summer. And, lastly, when injured or cut, it withers away with equal rapidity. In selecting the gourd, therefore, there is not only an adherence to verisimilitude, which is always becoming, but there is also an economy, if we may so speak, in the expenditure of miraculous agency. The question is not about power at all. The same God who caused the gourd to grow in a night, could make a cedar do so likewise; but this would be a wide departure from the general method of miraculous interposition, which is, to employ it no further than is necessary to secure the result required. When Lazarus was to be raised, for example, Martha must guide to the tomb, some must remove the stone from the cave's mouth, and others loose the risen Lazarus from his grave-clothes. So, when Jonah was to be sheltered from the burning sun, that which was best adapted to the purpose, and which grew with the greatest rapidity, was selected to make the shade. A vine.

Is there any reason to suppose that, after all, it was not a gourd, but some other plant, that of the castor-bean, for example, as many learned critics have concluded? A castor-bean.

It would be impertinent to say or imply that there is *no* reason for this, or for any other opinion adopted by learned and impartial men, after careful ex-

amination; but their arguments do not for a moment disturb my settled conviction that it was a gourd. The cause of their mistake may probably be

Gourd.   Vine.

ARBOUR COVERED WITH GOURD AND VINE.

found in the fact that, in these modern Shemitic dialects, the word kŭr'ah—
gourd—closely resembles, both in form and sound, khŭrwah—castor-bean;
just as the *kikion*—gourd—of Jonah resembles the Egypto-Greek *kiki*—castor-
bean—according to Dioscorides. These accidental resemblances may have led
Jerome and others into the opinion that they were the same plant. But Orientals never dream of training a castor-oil plant over a booth, or planting it for
Various
transla-
tions.
a shade, and they would have but small respect for any one who did. It is in
no way adapted for that purpose, while thousands of arbours are covered with
various creepers of the general gourd family. As to ancient translations, the
Septuagint gives colocynth, a general name for gourd; and the Vulgate, castor-
bean. Augustin differed with Jerome about this vine, and even quarrelled
over it, according to a bit of patristic scandal. Let us not imitate them, for,
though I believe it was a gourd, I am quite willing that any one should adopt
that opinion which he thinks best supported.

The brief history of Jonah has always appeared to me to be encumbered CHAPTER VI.
with a large share of obscurities. For example, who were those sailors? They
were not Jews, were wholly unacquainted with the prophet, and yet they con- Jonah's sailors.
versed with him without difficulty.

In all probability they were Phœnicians, and their language was therefore
so closely related to the Hebrew that an interpreter was not needed.

Where was Tarshish, to which port or country the ship belonged or was Tarshish —where was it?
bound?

Scarcely any name in Biblical geography suggests more unanswered and
unanswerable questions than this. The Arabs believe it was Tarsus, the birth-
place of Paul, and their Bible naturally suggests this idea. In English the
name is variously written—Tarshish, Tarsis, and Tarsus. The Seventy do not
translate it always alike, and the Vulgate is still more confused. When I first
came to the East I resided some time in Joppa, and the friends with whom I
became acquainted traded largely with Tarsus. Ships, loaded with soap and Tarsus in Cilicia?
other articles, were constantly departing from "Joppa" for "Tarshish," as
they appear to have done in the days of Jonah. I had then no doubt as to
the identity of the places. Subsequent examination, however, has led me to
modify this opinion. It is true that Palestine has always traded with Asia
Minor through Tarsus; true, also, that from Tarsus to the Grecian islands the
distance is not great, and the connection by trade is natural and uninterrupted
to this day. It is not forced, therefore, to connect Tarsus and the Greek
islands together, as is frequently done in the Bible. Doubtless the first trading voyages from Phœnicia northward were along the coast, and round the
head of this sea by Tarsus, and thence westward to the islands. It was not
until after long experience in *coasting* that mariners acquired courage and
skill to strike out boldly into the shoreless ocean. It is doubtful whether they
did this in the days of Jonah, although the pilots of Hiram's ships were celebrated even in the times of David and Solomon. I am inclined to adopt the
opinion that Tarshish or Tarsis—to whatever city or country first applied—
early became a general name for large merchant ships, just as we speak of an
East Indiaman, or a whaler, or a liner. The name may have been derived first
of all from this Tarsus of Cilicia, and subsequently given to Tartessus—country Tartessus
or city, or both—in Spain, which was a colony perhaps from Tarsus. Arrian,[1] in Spain?
Diodorus,[2] and Strabo,[3] all mention such a city; and I think it probable that
Jonah meant to flee thither. Tarsus, nearly on the rout to Nineveh from
Palestine, would not have been selected by the rebellious prophet for the place
of concealment. However this may be, we must give a very wide latitude to
the expression "ships of Tarshish." They sailed everywhere;—west, along all
the shores of the Mediterranean, and out into the Atlantic; and south and
east, through the Red Sea, along the African and Arabian coasts as far as
India. From Asia Minor and from Spain they brought gold, silver, lead, tin,

---

[1] Alex. iii. 86. [2] Diod. Sic. v. 35. [3] Strab. iii. 147.

PART
I.

and iron; and from India and the East came spices, and ivory, and ebony, and apes, and peacocks, as we read in the accounts of the Jewish and Phœnician merchant navies. By the aid of this theory, we can reconcile the Biblical statements as to the time occupied by these ships of Tarshish in their expeditions—once in three years. Those trading with the far East, or with Ireland or England, might require that length of time to complete their sales and purchases, and to return home.

Apparent
piety of
the sailors.

How do you account for the very pious and becoming language used by these heathen sailors, and the humble and penitent deportment of the king of corrupt Nineveh?

There is nothing very strange in this to Orientals, or to one familiar with them. Such language is universal. No matter how profane, immoral, and even atheistical a man nay be, yet will he, on all appropriate occasions, speak of God—the one God, our God—in phrases the most proper and pious. We Americans are abashed and confounded in the presence of such holy talkers, and have not courage, or rather, have too much reverence for sacred things, to follow them in their glib and heartless verbiage. The fact is, I suppose, that Oriental nations, although they sank into various forms of idolatry, never lost the phraseology of the pure original theosophy. We are struck with this in all the Bible histories in which these people have occasion to speak of God and his attributes. The Canaanites could talk as devoutly as Abraham, and Nebuchadnezzar with as much propriety as Daniel. And the same is wonderfully true at the present day. A hard old Druse of Lebanon would edify a Payson or a Martyn. Indeed there is nothing in which modern custom corresponds more completely with the ancient than in this pious talk. There is scarcely an expression of the kind we are considering which has not its perfect parallel in the daily living language in the people around us. Place an Arab in the circumstances in which these old heathen are represented as acting and speaking, and his expressions will be so similar, even to the very words and peculiar idioms, as to suggest the idea that they have been learned from the Bible. And yet this cannot be, because the remark applies, in all its extent, to the wild Bedawîn, in whose tribe there never has been a Bible, nor a man able to read it, had there been one.

Jonah at
Nineveh.

In regard to the profound impression produced by the preaching of Jonah in Nineveh, we must suppose that he was attended by such credentials of his prophetic office and mission as commanded attention and belief. What these credentials were we do not know. Jonah was a "sign to the men of Nineveh." Perhaps he carried with him, or there had preceded him, such well-authenticated proofs of his wonderful preservation in the whale's belly as deeply alarmed the Ninevites, on whose account, in an important and portentous sense, the miracle had been wrought. Nor is it difficult to discover how such reports could have been spread abroad. The sailors of the ship could testify that they threw Jonah overboard in a tempestuous sea; very likely they saw him swallowed by the great fish. They would therefore be immensely amazed

to find him on shore, alive and well. Such a thing would now make a prodigi- CHAPTER
VI.
ous noise in the world, and the news of it would fly from city to city with incredible speed. There is no reason to doubt, therefore, that the story of the
prophet had preceded him to Nineveh, and prepared the way for the success
of his preaching.

Was that company of *horned* ladies near Neby Yûnas a party of pilgrims to   Horns—
the shrine of the prophet ?   horned
    ladies.

HORNED LADIES.

Yes ; Druse *sits* (princesses), from Deir el Kamar. It is no uncommon
thing to meet them here, either making or paying vows. The objects in view
are very various. Some, whose sorrow is like that of Samuel's mother, seek
relief from Jonah ; others vow in times of sickness, either of themselves or of
their friends, and come to fulfil them upon recovery, etc. etc.

Do you imagine that these *horns*, that stand upon their foreheads like
tent-poles for their veils, have any connection with those so often mentioned
in the Bible ?

No. These *tantours* have grown, like other horns, from small beginnings Tantours.
to their present enormous size by slow degrees, and pride is the soil that nourished them. At first they consisted merely of an apparatus designed to finish
off the head-dress, so as to raise the veil a little from the face. Specimens of
this primitive kind are still found in remote and semi-civilized districts. I
have seen them only a few inches long, made of pasteboard, and even of
common pottery. By degrees the more fashionable ladies used tin, and length-

PART
I.

ened them; then rivalry made them of silver, and still farther prolonged and ornamented them; until finally the princesses of Lebanon and Hermon sported gold horns, decked with jewels, and so long that a servant had to spread the veil over them. But the day for these most preposterous appendages to the female head is about over. After the wars between the Maronites and Druses in 1841 and 1845, the Maronite clergy thundered their excommunications against them, and very few Christians now wear them. Many even of the Druse ladies have cast them off, and the probability is that in a few years travellers will seek in vain for a horned lady.

Excom-
muni-
cated.

I do not suppose that horns like these were worn by the Jews, nor, indeed, by any nation of antiquity. So remarkable an article of dress, had it been in existence, would certainly have been noticed by authors who enter so minutely into such matters as many did. The horns in animals, where the Creator alone planted them, were their weapons of defence; and man, who lays all nature under tribute to enrich his store of images and figures, very early made it synonymous with power, and then for what that will always confer upon the possessor. To exalt the horn—an expression often occurring in the poetic and prophetic parts of the Bible—means to advance in power, honour, and dominion. To defile it in the dust, is a figure drawn from the condition of a dying ox or stag, who literally defiles his horn in dust mingled with his own blood. It is painfully significant of defeat, disgrace, and death, and for a prince like Job it was to be dishonoured and utterly overthrown.[1]

To exalt
the horn.

It is not certainly known why the corners of altars were finished off with horns. Several ideas may have been combined in this custom. These horns may have been intended to symbolize the majesty and power of the being in whose honour the altar was reared, and to whom the sacrifice was offered; or the hint may have been suggested by the horns of the victims to be slain. As altars early became sanctuaries, it was natural that the suppliant should lay hold of the horns. In fact, there was often nothing else about them which he could grasp with his hand. This natural, significant, and very expressive act is often mentioned in the Bible.

Horns of
altars.

[1] Job xvi. 15.

CHAPTER VII.

LADY HESTER STANHOPE*—SIDON.

WE have now another long, low cape, called Nukkar Jedrah, even more rocky than es S'adîat.

Are these parallel lines of rough rock, some sixteen feet apart, the curb-stones of Rome's far-famed roads ? Roman highways.

They are ; and they do not give a favourable idea of these ancient highways. But they were probably covered over with some sort of composition, not unlike the crushed rock of our modern macadamized roads. I have seen specimens of this in good preservation.

One of my fair friends in America charged me to bring her some memento from the grave of Lady Hester Stanhope. Is not her ladyship's last resting-place somewhere in this neighbourhood ?

On a mountain top, about three hours to the south-east of us ; and, as there is nothing of interest along the regular road, we can visit it, if you have no objections to a smart scramble over these hills.

Lead on. No path can be more abominable than this slippery pavement.

We must first provide for lunch. No experienced traveller in this country will forget the commissary department. I must also direct Salîm to go on to the bridge over the Owely, and there prepare dinner. We shall be ready for it about three o'clock. Now take that path up the steep face of the mountain on the left, and you will have enough to do to manage yourself and your horse without the trouble of conversation. A mountain path

Well, this is rough enough, certainly, and desolate too,—fit only for goats and their keepers. I see Arab tents, however.

Yes ; and there are villages also, hidden away in the wadies, with vine-yards, and olive-orchards, and fields for corn, which produce no mean crop.

What bird is this which abounds so much on these mountains ?

* [This eccentric lady, the niece of the celebrated William Pitt, among the brilliant society of whose house she used to move as a queen, retired after his death to Syria, took up her abode at Dahr June, and spent the latter part of her life in the strange manner described in this chapter. She died in 1839.—ED.]

PART
I.

The lap-
wing.

It is the English pewit, or lapwing, called by the natives *Now*, and *Bu-Teet*. and I know not what besides. The first name is derived from the fact that the bird appears here only in the depth of winter—*now* being a cold winter-

PEWIT.

storm. I have seen them coming down the coast in large flocks on the wings of the wild north wind. They then disperse over these mountains, and remain until early spring, when they entirely disappear. They roost on the ground wherever night overtakes them. I have frequently started them up from under the very feet of my frightened horse when riding in the dark, especially along the spurs of old Hermon, and in Wady et Teim, between the two Leba-nons. They utter a loud scream when about to fly, which sounds like a pro-longed *teet*, and hence the name *Bu-Teet*—father of *teet*. It is the *dûkephath* of Moses, translated *lapwing* in our version, and I think correctly, notwith-standing what some recent writers advance against it. It was classed by Moses among the unclean birds, and is so regarded now by the Arabs, who re-fuse to eat it. The upper parts of the body and wings are of a dull slate colour, the under parts of both are white. It has a *top-knot* on the hinder part of the head, pointing backward like a horn; and when running about on the ground, it closely resembles a young hare. The crown, or top-knot, never expands,

The hed-
hood.

like that of the *hed-hood* or *hoopoe*. This latter bird is also found in the country, and the Arabic translation of *dûkephath* is *hed-hood*, and many modern critics have adopted this opinion, but erroneously, as I think. The *hed-hood* is a small bird, *good to eat*, comparatively rare, and therefore not likely to have been mentioned at all by Moses, and still less to have been classed with the unclean. The *Bu-Teet* is large and striking, and appears in

countless numbers. There is, however, a resemblance between them, especially
in the remarkakle tuft on the head. The whole subject of Biblical ornitho-
logy, however, is obscure, and the prohibitions of Moses would now, in many

cases, be of no practical avail in reference to birds unclean, since we cannot tell to what ones he refers. But
a truce to birds. Follow me down this
winding track into the gorge below,
and be careful.

On you be the responsibility. I
have no longer any criterion by which
to judge whether a path is safe or
otherwise; and as to these little horses,
one might ride them up stairs to bed,
I presume, without hesitation, at least
on their part. But, in all seriousness,
these mountain roads are positively
barbarous. I hope you will be able

HED-HOOD.

to extract some pleasing and profitable instruction out of them, or my patience
will be again upset very soon.

Nothing easier. A whole class of Biblical figures rests on this state of Preparing
things. Isaiah says, "Prepare the way of the Lord ; cast up, cast up the high- the way.
way; gather out the stones ;"[1] and not only do modern *ways* prove the need
of such preparation, but modern customs show how, when, and why it is done.
When Ibrahim Pasha proposed to visit certain places on Lebanon, the emeers
and sheikhs sent forth a general proclamation, somewhat in the style of Isaiah's
exhortation, to all the inhabitants, to assemble along the proposed route, and
prepare the way before him. The same was done in 1845, on a grand scale,
when the present sultan visited Brusa. The stones were gathered out,
crooked places straightened, and rough ones made level and smooth. I had
the benefit of their labour a few days after his majesty's visit. From customs
like these comes the exhortation of John the Baptist, "Prepare ye the way of
the Lord, make his paths straight ;"[2] or, as it is more fully developed by the
prophet, "Make straight in the desert a highway for our God. Every valley
shall be exalted, and every mountain and hill shall be made low, and the
crooked shall be made straight, and the rough places plain."[3] The exhortation
to gather out the stones is peculiarly appropriate. These farmers do the exact
reverse—gather up the stones from their fields, and cast them into the high- Gathering
way ; and it is this barbarous custom which in many places renders the paths out the
so uncomfortable, and even dangerous.   stones.

I have been all the morning in exquisite sympathy with Job, David, Jeremiah, and other prophets and poets who complain of narrow paths. Ours has

[1] Isa. lxii. 10.   [2] Matt. iii. 8.   [3] Isa. xl. 3, 4.

PART I.

frequently been not more than a foot wide, of hard, smooth rock, and with a profound gorge yawning beneath.

Slippery places.

You will encounter many such in our rambles along the highways and by-ways of the land. A dozen "slippery places" have impressed their ugly features upon my imagination. Jeremiah says that the ways of both prophet and priest who were profane should be "as slippery ways in *the darkness*." [1]

Darkness.

This is the danger vastly aggravated, according to my experience. During the rebellion of Jerusalem in 1834, I attempted to reach the city from Lydd by ascending the mountains along secret paths in a night intensely dark. A fog also settled down upon us, and added to the gloom. My guides lost the way, and, after wandering and slipping about in the utmost danger for several hours, we were obliged to lie down upon a bare rock and wait for the morning. At such times one can appreciate those promises which insure from sliding and falling.[2] To slide and fall is, in a thousand places, certain destruction ; and no threatenings against the workers of iniquity are more terrible than that they shall be set in slippery places ; that "their feet shall slide in due time." [3] One needs a steady eye and obedient nerves to ride along the edge of yawning chasms, and listen calmly to the hard clatter of the iron upon the smooth rock. I generally dismount and walk ; but some native horsemen ride over everything. Burckhardt describes the obstinate perseverance of the old Sheikh of Kerak in this sort of desperate daring. They were descending into Wady il 'Ahsa : "It had now become dark, and this was, without exception, the most dangerous route I ever travelled in my life. The descent is steep, and there is no regular road over the smooth rocks, where the foot slips at every step. We had missed our way, and were obliged to alight from our horses after many of us had suffered severe falls. Our sheikh was the only horseman who would not alight from his mare, whose step, he declared, was as sure as his own." Very likely ; but I would rather fall from my own feet than plunge, horse and all, over some break-neck precipice. Therefore I dismount, as I do here, out of respect to this broad, slanting rock ; and you had better do the same, or we may have to pick up both horse and rider from that terrace down yonder, in no wise improved by the feat. And now we must climb once more up five hundred feet, to that castle-like enclosure around the top of this bold mountain pyramid. Safely done ; and here we stand on Dahr June, and beneath this rude and broken tomb lies buried the once lovely, and witty, and most eccentric Lady Hester Stanhope.

Dahr June.

Is it possible ? Can anything be more sad and solitary ? But perhaps it is well that it should be thus.

A melancholy change has indeed come over the scene since I first visited it. The garden, with its trellised arbours, and shaded alleys, and countless flowers, is utterly destroyed, and not one room of all her large establishment remains entire. This on the south-west corner was the apartment in which her lady-

---

[1] Jer. xxiii. 12.   [2] Prov. iii. 23 ; Jer. xxxi. 9.   [3] Deut. xxxii. 35.

ship wore out the three last dreary months of life; and this on the east of it was the open lewan, where we found the body wrapped in waxed cloths dipped in turpentine and spirits. The whole of these premises were alive with her servants and others assembled on this mournful occasion. Now not a dog, cat, or even lizard appears, to relieve the utter solitude. The tomb also is sadly changed. It was then embowered in dense shrubbery, and covered with an arbour of running roses, not a vestige of which now remains; and the stones of the vault itself are broken and displaced. There is no inscription—not a word in any language; and, unless more carefully protected than hitherto, the last resting-place of her ladyship will soon be entirely lost. The history of this place is peculiar. It belonged to a wealthy Christian of Damascus, who built the original house, to which Lady Hester added some twenty-five or thirty rooms. At his death, soon after that of Lady Hester, the property was left to an only son, who quickly spent it all by his extravagance. He then turned Moslem, and not long ago hung himself in a neighbouring house. His Moslem wife—a low, vulgar creature—fearing that the Christians would one day deprive her of the place, tore down the buildings, and sold the materials to the people of June. Thus the destruction has been intentional, rapid, and complete.

The British Consul at Beirût requested me to perform the religious services at the funeral of Lady Hester. It was an intensely hot Sabbath in June, 1839. We started on our melancholy errand at one o'clock, and reached this place about midnight. After a brief examination, the consul decided that the funeral must take place immediately. This vault in the garden was hastily opened, and the bones of General L—— or of his son, I forget which—a Frenchman who died here, and was buried in the vault by her ladyship—were taken out and placed at the head.

The body, in a plain deal box, was carried by her servants to the grave, followed by a mixed company, with torches and lanterns, to enable them to thread their way through the winding alleys of the garden. I took a wrong path, and wandered some time in the mazes of these labyrinths. When at length I entered the arbour, the first thing I saw were the bones of the general, in a ghastly heap, with the head on top, having a lighted taper stuck in either eyesocket—a hideous, grinning spectacle. It was difficult to proceed with the service under circumstances so novel and bewildering. The consul subsequently remarked that there were some curious coincidences between this and the burial of Sir John Moore, her ladyship's early love. In silence, on the lone mountain at midnight, " our lanterns dimly burning," with the flag of her country over her, " she lay like a warrior-taking his rest ;" and we left her " alone in her glory." There was but one of her own nation present, and his name was Moore.

The people of June, that village across the wady, made large profits from the liberality and extravagances of Lady Hester, and they are full of wonderful stories about her. Several of our friends in Sidon were in her service for years, and from them, and from others still more closely connected, I have had abun-

PART
I.

Her
talents.

Dress.

Spies.

Grounds.

Servants.

Death.

dant opportunity to learn the character of this strange being. On most subjects she was not merely sane, but sensible, well-informed, and extremely shrewd. She possessed extraordinary powers of conversation, and was perfectly fascinating to all with whom she chose to make herself agreeable. She was, however, whimsical, imperious, tyrannical, and, at times, revengeful in a high degree. Bold as a lion, she wore the dress of an emeer, weapons, pipe, and all; nor did she fail to rule her Albanian guards and her servants with absolute authority. She kept spies in the principal cities, and at the residences of pashas and emeers, and knew everything that was going forward in the country. Her garden of several acres was walled round like a fort; and crowning the top of this conical hill, with deep wadies on all sides, the appearance from a distance was quite imposing. But the site was badly chosen. The hill has no relative elevation above others; the prospect is not inviting; the water is distant, far below, and had to be carried up on mules. She, however, had the English taste for beautiful grounds, and spared neither time, labour, nor expense to convert this barren hill into a wilderness of shady avenues, and a paradise of sweet flowers; and she succeeded. I have rarely seen a more beautiful place.

The morning after the funeral the consul and I went round the premises and examined *thirty-five* rooms, which had been sealed up by the vice-consul of Sidon to prevent robbery. They were full of trash. One had forty or fifty oil-jars of French manufacture, old, empty, and dusty. Another was crammed with Arab saddles, moth-eaten, tattered, and torn. They had belonged to her mounted guard. Superannuated pipe-stems without bowls filled one room. Two more were devoted to medicines; and another to books and papers, mostly in boxes and ancient chests. Nothing of much value was found anywhere, and the seals were replaced to await legal action. The crowd of servants and greedy retainers had appropriated to themselves her most valuable effects. One of the wealthy citizens of Sidon is said to have obtained his money in this way. She told Mrs. T——— that once, when she was supposed to be dying of plague, she could hear her servants breaking open her chests, and ripping off the embossed covers of her cushions. "Oh! didn't I vow," said she, "that if I recovered I would make a scattering of them!" and she performed her vow to the letter. But each succeeding set, like the flies in the fable of the fox, were as greedy as their predecessors; and, as she finally died of a lingering disease, they had time enough to work their will, and nothing valuable escaped their rapacity. What a death! Without a European attendant—without a friend, male or female—alone, on the top of this bleak mountain, her lamp of life grew dimmer and more dim, until it went quite out in hopeless, rayless night. Such was the end of the once gay and brilliant niece of Pitt, presiding in the saloons of the master-spirit of Europe, and familiar with the intrigues of kings and cabinets. With Mr. Abbot and his lady she would sit out the longest night talking over those stirring times of the last century and the beginning of the present, with exhaustless spirit and keen delight. But nothing could tempt her back to England. At length, her income was greatly curtailed in order to

pay off her numerous debts.   She was furious, but unsubdued.   In her mountain nest, and all alone, she dragged out the remnant of her days in haughty
pride and stubborn independence.

    She could be extremely sarcastic, and her satire was often terrible.   Many
of her letters, and the margin of books which I purchased at the auction, are
" illuminated " with her caustic criticisms.   There was no end to her eccentricities.   In some things she was a devout believer—an unbeliever in many. Her beliefs
She read the stars, and dealt in nativities and a sort of second-sight, by which and unbe-
she pretended to foretell coming events.   She practised alchymy, and in pursuit liefs.
of this vain science was often closeted with strange companions.   She had a
mare whose back-bone sank suddenly down at the shoulders, and rose abruptly
near the hips.   This deformity her vivid imagination converted into a miraculous saddle, on which she was to ride into Jerusalem as queen by the side of
some sort of Messiah, who was to introduce a fancied millennium.   Another
mare had a part to play in this august pageant, and both were tended with
extraordinary care.   A lamp was kept burning in their very comfortable apartments, and they were served with sherbet and other delicacies.   Nothing about Whimsi-
the premises so excited my compassion as these poor pampered brutes, upon calities.
which Lady Hester had lavished her choicest affections for the last fourteen
years.   They were soon after sold at auction, when hard work and low living
quickly terminated their miserable existence.   Lady Hester was a doctor, and
most positive in her prescriptions to herself, her servants, her horses, and even
to her chickens, and often did serious mischief to all her patients.   She had
many whimsical tests of character both for man and beast, and, of course, was
often deceived by both to her cost.   But we must end these random sketches.
To draw a full-length portrait is aside from our purpose and beyond our power.
She was wholly and magnificently unique.   Now riding at the head of wild
Arabs, queen of the desert, on a visit to Palmyra; now intriguing with mad
pashas and vulgar emeers : at one time treating with contempt consuls, generals,
and nobles, bidding defiance to law, and thrashing the officers sent to her lodge;
at another, resorting to all sorts of mean shifts to elude or confound her
creditors : to-day charitable and kind to the poor; to-morrow oppressive, selfish,
and tyrannical in the extreme.   Such was Lady Hester in her mountain home
on Lebanon.   I should like to read the long, dark, interior life of such a being,
but not to live it.   Alas ! she must have drained to the dregs many a bitter
cup.   Her sturdy spirit here fought out all alone a thousand desperate battles,
and lost them all.   Let those who are tempted to revolt against society, and Her war
war with nature, God, and man, come to Dahr June—sit on the fragments of with na-
this broken tomb, amid ruins without beauty to charm or age to make vener- and man.
able—itself a ruin of yesterday, and sinking fast to hopeless oblivion.   Will
such an end pay for such a life?   But enough of Lady Hester.   Poor wandering star, struck from the bright galaxy of England's happy daughters to fall
and expire on this solitary summit of Lebanon !   I drop a tear upon thy lonely
grave, which, living, thy proud spirit would have scorned.

PART
I.

A convent.

Sowing.

"Going
forth" to
sow.

Hamlets.

The
parable
verified.

We will now pass round the head of this ravine, through June, and down those sloping hills of white marl to the River Owely. Let me call your attention to that large convent, called Deir Mukhullis, on the mountain side across the wady. It is the wealthiest establishment of the kind in this part of the country; sustains a school, not very ably conducted; and owns a printing-press, not now in operation. East of us extends the large district of the Shûf, the stronghold of the Druses. It is governed and largely owned by Saied Beg, of the Jemblât family, whose palace is at Mukhtarah.

Our path is leading us into the midst of a very lively agricultural scene; but are not these farmers too late in sowing their grain?

That depends on the nature of coming spring. If the latter part of March and the first half of April be rainy, the wheat, and especially the barley, sown now, and even weeks later, may yield a better harvest than what has been in the ground for the last month. In such seasons, the early crop grows so rank as to *lodge*, when it is entirely spoiled. If the spring, however, should be early and dry, the late sown will fail altogether. This is one of many circumstances which render the crop less certain in Palestine than in Ohio. We may now gather a harvest of our own peculiar kind from the operation going on under our eye. The parable about sowing[1] has here its illustration, even in its most minute details. "Behold, a sower *went forth* to sow." There is a nice and close adherence to actual life in this form of expression. These people have actually *come forth* all the way from June to this place. The expression implies that the sower, in the days of our Saviour, lived in a hamlet, or village, as all these farmers now do; that he did not sow near his own house, or in a garden fenced or walled, for such a field does not furnish all the basis of the parable. There are neither *roads*, nor thorns, nor stony places in such lots. He must go forth into the open country as these have done, where there are no fences; where the path passes through the cultivated land; where thorns grow in clumps all around; where the rocks peep out in places through the scanty soil; and where also, hard by, are patches extremely fertile. Now here we have the whole four within a dozen rods of us. Our horses are actually trampling down some seeds which have fallen by this wayside, and larks and sparrows are busy picking them up. That man, with his mattock, is digging about places where the rock is too near the surface for the plough; and much that is sown there will wither away, because it has no deepness of earth. And not a few seeds have fallen among this *bellan*, and will be effectually choked by this most tangled of thorn bushes. But a large portion, after all, falls into really good ground, and four months hence will exhibit every variety of crop, up to the richest and heaviest that ever rejoices the heart even of an American farmer.

Certainly nothing could be more to the point than this illustration. We doubtless are looking upon the very facts which suggested to Him who taught in

---

[1] Matt. xiii. 3–8.

parables the instructive lesson of the sower. May our hearts be like that good CHAPTER ground which brought forth fruit, some a hundred fold, some sixty fold, some VII. thirty fold ! But do you suppose that the enormous increase of a hundred fold Amount of is ever gathered by the modern farmer ? increase.

I was greatly surprised, when discussing this question on the fertile plain of Esdraelon, to hear not merely the peasants, but intelligent gentlemen, who had rented the district from government, stoutly maintain that they had themselves, and that very year, reaped more than a hundred fold from part of that plain. I could not understand it until by accident it came out that they had a peculiar mode of calculation. In sowing, they allow one third of the seed for the birds, particularly the crows, which settle down upon the fields in countless flocks. Another third is supposed to be destroyed by mice and insects, and only one third of the seed sown actually comes to maturity. Thus a man sows three bushels, and if he reap a hundred, it is a hundred fold according to his mode of calculation, but according to ours it would only be thirty-three. This latter rate is nearly the lowest mentioned in the parable as the yield of what He calls good ground, and that is really a first-rate crop for even such plains as Esdraelon, which, being directly below Nazareth, must have been perfectly familiar to our Lord ; and, as cultivation was no doubt far more careful and skilful than it is now among these stupid fellahîn, it is not at all improbable that the numbers used are in strict accordance with actual experience. Indeed, He could not have erred in this matter. We may suppose, however, that the different rates of yield had reference to various kinds of grain. Barley and wheat are sown side by side in the same field, but the former gives a much heavier crop than the latter. There is a kind of durrah—white maize—sown in this same region, which often returns several hundred fold. I have been assured by respectable farmers that they have gathered more than four hundred Four hun- fold of this corn. dred fold.

In the time of Christ the country was densely peopled, and the fields protected from the depredations of birds, mice, and insects, and also from cattle and other animals which now trample under foot so much of the grain. It would then not be necessary to sow more than one-third as much seed as at present in order to secure an equally heavy crop, and thus there might be realized, in favourable circumstances, a hundred fold. This is further confirmed Many by the fact that an extraordinary number of stalks do actually spring from a stalks single root. Here, on this plain of Sidon, I have seen more than a hundred, from one root. and each with a *head* bowing gracefully beneath the load of well-formed grains. The yield was more than a thousand fold. The supposition in the parable is history in the case of Isaac, who reaped a hundred fold in Gerar, and " in the same year." [1] There is a verbal accuracy in this statement worth noting. He received this large return the same year in which he sowed the seed. In our country—at least when I was a farmer—the seed is sown one year and the har-

---

[1] Gen. xxvi. 12.

PART I.

vest reaped the next. But these now sowing before us will reap in less than four months ; and this is the general result now, as it doubtless was in the time of the patriarchs.

Have you noticed anything in this country which may have suggested the expressions in the 126th Psalm : " They that sow in tears shall reap in joy. He that goeth forth and weepeth, bearing precious seed, shall doubtless come again with rejoicing, bringing his sheaves with him ? "

Sowing in tears.

I never saw people sowing in tears exactly, but have often known them to do it in fear and distress sufficient to draw them from any eye. In seasons of great scarcity, the poor peasants part in sorrow with every measure of precious seed cast into the ground. It is like taking bread out of the mouths of their children; and in such times many bitter tears are actually shed over it. The distress is frequently so great that government is obliged to furnish seed, or none would be sown. Ibrahim Pasha did this more than once within my remembrance, copying the example, perhaps, of his great predecessor in Egypt when the seven years' famine was ended.

The thoughts of this psalm may likewise have been suggested by the extreme danger which frequently attends the farmer in his ploughing and sowing. The calamity which fell upon the husbandmen of Job, when the oxen were ploughing, and the asses feeding beside them, and the Sabeans fell upon them and took them away, and slew the servants with the edge of the sword,[1] is often repeated in our day. To understand this, you must remember what I have just told you about the situation of the arable lands in the open country ; and here again we meet that verbal accuracy : the sower *goes forth*—that is, from the village.

Distance of fields from houses.

The people of Ibel and Khiem, in Merj 'Aiyûn, for example, have their best grain-growing fields down in the 'Ard Hûleh, six or eight miles from their homes, and just that much nearer the lawless border of the desert. When the country is disturbed, or the government weak, they cannot sow these lands

Dangers.

except at the risk of their lives. Indeed, they always *go forth* in large companies, and completely armed, ready to drop the plough and seize the musket at a moment's warning; and yet, with all this care, many sad and fatal calamities overtake the men who must thus sow in tears. And still another origin may be found for the thoughts of the psalm in the extreme difficulty of the work

Difficulties.

itself in many places. The soil is rocky, impracticable, overgrown with sharp thorns; and it costs much painful toil to break up and gather out the rocks, cut and burn the briers, and to subdue the stubborn soil, especially with their feeble oxen and insignificant ploughs. Join all these together, and the sentiment is very forcibly brought out, that he who labours hard, in cold and in rain, in fear and danger, in poverty and in want, casting his precious seed in the ground, will surely come again, at harvest-time, with rejoicing, and bearing his sheaves with him.

Does the calamity mentioned by Joel (i. 17) ever befall the farmer in these days—" The seed is rotten under their clods ? "

---

[1] Job L 14, 15.

It is certain to follow if they sow too long before the rain comes. The seed CHAPTER
VII. then rots, and the work must be done over again. The whole description of drought in this chapter is terribly graphic : " That which the palmer-worm hath Seed left hath the locust eaten, and what the locust hath left the canker-worm hath rotting. eaten, and that which the canker-worm hath left hath the caterpillar eaten. Be ashamed, O ye husbandmen; howl, O ye vine-dressers, for the wheat and for the barley, because the harvest of the field is perished. The vine is dried up ; the fig-tree languisheth ; the pomegranate-tree, the palm-tree also, and the apple-tree, even all the trees of the field, are withered. Alas for the day ! The meat is cut off before our eyes ; the seed is rotten under their clods, and the garners are laid desolate, the barns are broken down. How do the beasts groan ! the herds of cattle are perplexed because they have no pasture. Fire hath devoured the pastures of the wilderness, and the flame hath burned all the trees of the field." Such a day of destruction from the Almighty has more than once come upon this unhappy land, because of the wickedness of those that dwell therein.

But here we are upon the banks of this fine mountain stream, with the rich orchards of Sidon spread out before us. All this verdure depends upon the Orchards river, and should its fountains fail or be diverted, the whole fair scene would of Sidon. quickly vanish. But such a calamity is not likely to occur. The Owely takes The River its rise in the noble fountains of Barûk, some thirty miles to the north-east, Owely. and near those of the Damûr. Flowing at the bottom of a romantic ravine for about fifteen miles, and passing below Mukhtarah and 'Ammatûr, it unites with a branch from the south in a sweet little vale called Merj Bisry. Thence it pursues its course hither through a succession of gorges well worth visiting had we the necessary leisure. The southern branch plunges down a precipice at Jezzîn, two hundred and forty feet perpendicular—plumb as a wall. My measuring cord, held one foot in advance of the edge, did not touch the rock for more than two hundred feet. When the stream is swollen by the winter rains, it is a splendid cataract ; and there are several others almost equally grand between Jezzîn and 'Ammatûr, where rattling torrents from the heights of Lebanon leap down giddy precipices into the chasm of the main stream. Those below Jebaah es Shûf and Bathir are the most beautiful. The ride from Mukhtarah to Jezzîn is rich in the very finest scenery of this goodly mountain. The path winds along a lofty line of hanging terraces, with the Owely far below, and perpendicular cliffs towering many hundred feet above,—the favourite resort of eagles and savage beasts. To enjoy the prospect to greatest advantage, one should pass from Mezraat es Shûf down into Merj Bisry, and thence up the pine-clothed mountain toward Jebaah el Halâweh. He will thus have Pic- in view, for hours together, the river gorge in all its extent and wildness, and turesque views. also the succession of gigantic precipices by which the lofty ridge of Lebanon is reached and held up, and down which her silver streams spring joyously in bright and boisterous cascades. No one who can command the necessary time should omit this ride. True, there is nothing of historic interest along the route, but the lover of nature will not regret this ; rather would he feel it an impertinence to have man's puny structures thrust on his attention amid the infinitely grander architecture of God. At the head of the Merj Bisry, however, are the ruins of an ancient temple, with large columns, half-imbedded in rubbish, which any one who has a heart for it may examine. Those who built it probably designed to borrow solemnity and magnificence to aid their worship from this association with the handiworks of the Almighty. It was amid this

grand scenery that the celebrated Druse chief, Fakhr ed Dîn, closed his long career of rebellion against the sultan. A remarkable cliff above Merj Bisry is full of caverns, in one of which, still bearing his name, the emeer was besieged for seven years, as tradition relates. When compelled to forsake this by the poisoning of his supply of water, he took refuge in a cave under the cascade of Jezzîn. This he held until it was sapped from below. The sturdy old rebel calmly smoked his nargeleh (so the story runs) until the sapper's chisel was driven up through the rug on which he was reclining. Then he surrendered, was taken to Constantinople, and there beheaded on the 14th of March 1635— the fate of a thousand other rebels against the Grand Turk. We are reminded of the old man by this substantial bridge, of a single arch, which here spans the Owely. It was built by him, but out of materials far more ancient. Many of the stones bear the mark of the Phœnician bevel, on which I always look with the respect due to old age.

If I remember aright, Dr. Robinson identifies this river with the Bostrenus of the ancients.

And correctly enough, no doubt, though the notices of it are singularly vague and rare. How beautifully it flows beneath the bridge, and between these bushy banks ! Bridge, and stream, and khân make up a scene of beauty which the artist loves to sketch ; and in a portfolio even the old khân looks inviting. But Salîm has done well to place our dinner under these trees, and at a respectful distance from that nest of abominations. While we satisfy the demands of hunger, I will give you a chapter from my book of experiences touching this inn.

Several years ago I spent a night there. It was the 3d of December, too, and a winter-storm was coming on in all its might and majesty. Lightnings blazed along the mountain tops, and heavy thunder bellowed through the wadies of the upper Owely. As evening advanced, the wind began to sob and groan among the rocks and trees, and vast volumes of black vapour, rolling in from the sea, settled on the heights of Lebanon like " a horror of great darkness." The long-expected and much-desired rains had commenced.

When the day dawned, for want of other amusement, I watched the migration of one of those tribes of Arabs which we passed on the mountains. They were evidently fleeing from some apprehended danger. Ragged boys and girls urged forward droves of cattle, as lean as Pharaoh's types of the seven years of famine ; men, riding lank and shaggy mares, hurried onward the slow-paced camels, loaded with tent-walls and the multifarious furniture of their encampment; women staggered along with lots of children on their backs; very old people were strapped fast on the loads; and little babes up there took the pelting rain merrily as unfledged ducklings. Last of all came large flocks, with their surly canine guards and insolent shepherds. Over the bridge rushed the whole caravan, as if the avenger of blood were behind them.

A circumstance which occurred the evening before explained the reason of this hasty migration. The captain of a band of horsemen, a few miles back, called to me and inquired if my companion could read Arabic, handing to him a letter which contained an order from Saied Beg to capture all the men of a particular Arab encampment, as they were accused of robbing the house of a Maronite priest. The Arabs, however, had got the start of the officer, and by sunrise were on the south side of the Owely, and within the jurisdiction of the Governor of Sidon. I was amused with the way in which my companion re-proved the captain, and, by implication, his master. It was thoroughly Arabic —a genuine specimen, which you may preserve for future use. "Why," said he, "can't the keeper of this khân read? No! Well, that's a pity. It would A delicate rebuke. be better if every khanjy could read, and then it would not be necessary for an officer of Saied Beg to show his letters to any chance traveller that comes along. They might contain things which ought not to be published. I would advise the Beg not to rent any of these khâns to one who can't read." "Now," said I, as we rode along, " why not tell the officer himself that it was a shame for one in his station not to know how to read?" "What! would you have me insult the officer of Saied Beg? Of course that is what I meant, and he understood it; *but it would never do to come straight up to the point, and say all this to his very beard.*"

Though it rained hard, I pursued my journey to Hasbeiya, for I had no courage to repeat the experiment of the past night in this abominable hole. Our host, with his cats and kittens, his barley and straw, bread and olives, leben and oil, and every other article of his trade, shared with us, our saddles, baggage, and beds, this one low, dark vault. A few burning brands, or brands that would not burn, enabled us, with a great deal of coaxing, to boil a little water for tea, with no other penalty than that of being nearly blinded by a cloud of pungent smoke. The privacy of our apartment was further invaded by a curious bridal party, who appeared determined, bride and all, to partake A bridal party. with us in the privileges of our smoky vault. They kept up a violent row with our host until a late hour, when, buying a few cents' worth of bread, they kindled a fire in that field on the other side of the road, and, huddling round it, kept up a dismal concert of singing, shouting, and clapping hands until morning, when, cold, and wet, and woe-begone, they set off to find the bishop, not, as it now appeared, to be married, but to get unmarried! The young lady had been betrothed, *nolens volens,* to a man she abhorred, and was now, with her friends, going to get his lordship to cancel the espousals. Being a friend of emancipation in such cases, I heartily wished her success. And, now our active Salîm has got everything ready to march, let us cross the river on this

PART
I.fine bridge, and turn down to Sidon, where we shall find a home and a shelter during the storm which I see is gathering fast, and will soon burst in fury upon the coast.

Monotony
of the
road.

The ride from Beirût to Sidon is one of the most tedious and least interesting in Syria. You wade through leagues of deep sand, flounder over rocky headlands, or wind along the shore with the noisy surf dashing over the horse's heels and your own, to the discomfort of both. And to pass from one to another of these annoyances in endless succession is the traveller's only relief. The sea at your side never tires. With a monotony that varies not, wave chases wave toward the shore; then hesitate, swell up, and topple over with a heavy fall, which sends them, in quivering beds of feathery foam, to the beach. In the soft light of a midsummer moon the thing is beautiful; but utter solitude saddens, ceaseless repetition wearies, and the traveller rejoices to escape into the green alleys of old Sidon's fragrant orchards.

Sidon.

It is difficult to realize that yon little city, which we are approaching with no more reverence than if it were a village of yesterday on the banks of the Ohio, is Sidon—great Zidon of Joshua.

Ancient cities, like prophets, are not without honour except in their own country; and yet, though Sidon is my home, I never ride along this pretty beach, with the gamboling surf on one hand, tall tamarisks on the other, and the city before, without somewhat of that enthusiasm which glowed and burned within me twenty-three years ago, when first I drew near this venerable metropolis.

As we are in no hurry, let me hear something about this home of yours—this "mother of all the Phœnicians," before we enter it. She looks beautiful enough, sitting in the sea, and blushing with the warm, rosy light of the evening sun.

Story of
Sidon.

Must I begin at "the beginning?" The story is long and old, and much is forgotten or mixed with fable. It starts off in this fashion: One morning, soon after the flood—but here comes a lad with golden oranges just gathered from Sidon's luxurious gardens. Let us buy them to give relish to our dusty

Noah's
great-
grandson.

narrative. Well, the great grandson of Noah, emigrating westward when men were few and earth a wilderness, crept timidly round the low cape of Sarepta, and gazed earnestly on the plain that stretches this way along the shore. At length he moved forward, and pitched his tent on that castle-crowned *Tell*, which now overlooks the city. "Here," exclaimed the patriarch, "my wanderings cease. This mound shall be the stronghold of my future city. It meets my wants in all respects. The surface declines gently northward to the beach, where it falls back eastward, forming a little bay open to the north; and that line of low rocks, parallel with the shore, encloses a quiet basin for the ships I mean to build after the model of my grandfather's ark. That long, narrow island affords a secure retreat for the time of danger. This broad plain we will cover with orchards and gardens; and the water of yon limpid stream shall be made to visit, by a thousand rills, every tree, and shrub, and flower

SIDON.

of our new paradise. The sea will yield her varied stores in such abundance, CHAPTER
that the very art of fishing will take its name, *said*, from our metropolis; VII.
while over these eastern hills our sons will hunt the boar and fleet gazelle, or
snare the feathered fowl, to increase our stores and enrich our feasts."

The venerable patriarch did not live to see all his prophetic anticipations
realized. Sidon, however, soon grew great. Her walls towered high, and were
drawn with an ample compass, embracing an area many times larger than the
present city. Her harbour was crowded with merry mariners from every coast,
and caravans filled her magazines with the treasures and luxuries of the distant East.

None dared molest her, so that to live carelessly, after the manner of the Sidon's
Zidonians,[1] became the proverbial synonym of perfect prosperity. Even Joshua[2] glory.
ventured not to attack her; and the flying nations found a safe asylum from
his devouring sword within her gates. Her merchant ships sailed over every
sea. She built strong cities along the shore—Beirût, and Gebal, and Arvad,
and Accho, and Dor, and many more. She planted colonies in Cyprus and the
Grecian Isles, in Libya and in Spain; while by her side she nourished her fair
daughter Tyre.

Then began her long and sad decline. The streams of her prosperity were Her de-
dried up or diverted. The proud Pharaohs from the Nile—the stern Assyrian cline.
from distant Nineveh—the cruel Chaldean and Persian from Babylon—the
rough he-goat from Grecia, and the king of fierce countenance from the Tiber,
all helped to lay poor Sidon in the dust. And, long after, those locusts which
came out of the bottomless pit, with Apollyon at their head, completed the
work, during those dismal days when men sought death, but could not find it.
And yet Sidon still exists, and has always clung to life with a strange tenacity.
Her history runs parallel with the march of time, down the ceaseless current
of human generations. Not so Tyre. Long ages have rolled away since continental Tyre sunk beneath the "burden" of prophecy, and the very site where
she stood was lost; and there are men yet living who remember when the boar
was roused from his lair among the thorns and briers of even insular Tyre.
But here we are at the gate of our good city, and in a few minutes we shall be
in our own hired house, on the wall from whence you can survey at your leisure
what remains of Sidon's ruins, and that about her which never can be ruined
even by Mohammedan despotism.

---

[1] Judges xviii. 7.   [2] Josh. xi. 8.

CHAPTER VIII.

SIDON.

January 30th, 1857.

A storm.   WE were not mistaken. The storm predicted is upon us in all its majesty, and we shall not get away from Sidon until it has spent its fury.

Contrary to all my previous ideas, I find your climate extremely variable and uncertain. There seems to be no fixed time for the commencement of the winter rains, nor is it much more certain when they will cease.

Variable climate of Syria.   That is quite true. I have seen these rains begin early in November and end in February; but they are sometimes delayed until January, and prolonged into May. I was once held prisoner in a wretched khân on Lebanon for two days by a storm which commenced on the 6th of May. Fresh snow generally falls on the heights of Lebanon and Hermon in November, but I have crossed over Jebel es Sheikh late in December when there was none. It ordinarily disappears, except from sheltered ravines, early in April; and yet the mountain tops are sometimes covered with fresh snow late in May. These are, indeed, great variations, and they subject the farmer to much uncertainty and many losses. All kinds of crops, including silk, fail more frequently in Syria and Palestine than in America. This has always been the case; and the failure is also more complete and ruinous, and hence we so often read in the Bible of sore famines in this country.

May not these facts give greater point and significancy to those agricultural promises (if one may employ such language) in which regularity in the rains and certainty in the crops were guaranteed to Israel on condition of faithful obedience?

Sense of dependence on God of seasons.   No doubt; and it is worthy of remark that to this day the people of every class, faith, and character familiarly and constantly ascribe regular and abundant rains, fruitful seasons, and good harvests to the direct agency and interposition of God. This formal and devout recognition strikes a stranger from America as indicating a high degree of pious sentiment; but he soon perceives that it is merely the stereotyped idiom of daily conversation, and has very little connection with the heart. Still, this style of remark has its origin in a deep

sense of uncertainty, and of entire dependence for their daily bread upon the CHAPTER
showers of heaven, delayed nearly every year until much painful solicitude is VIII.
felt by all classes. Very often there is a universal cry, from man, beast, and
bird, and burning sky, and drooping fields, ere the Lord hears the heavens,
and they hear the earth, and the earth hears the corn, and the wine, and the
oil.[1] I have seen several instances in which Moslems, Christians, and Jews
have united in fasts, processions, and prayers in the open air, for the showers
that water the earth. On one occasion, the pasha, attended by all the principal
men of Beirût, went forth in procession, and, among other acts, the great man
held the plough with his own hands, as a public acknowledgment of dependence upon the fruits of the field, and the blessing of the Lord upon the labour
of the ox.

There is no occasion for such ceremonies at present. How long may this
wild storm last?

To judge from ordinary indications, it may continue ten days at least,
possibly twenty.

Indeed! And what may those indications be?

It is not easy to give a tangible shape to some of them, which yet have much Great
to do in producing the impression on the mind of one initiated, by long experi- rains.
ence, into the mysteries of Syrian weather. In the first place, we must not
forget that this is the time for heavy storms, especially if the season has been
hitherto warm and dry, as this has been. Great rains are now needed to start
the fountains and saturate the earth to the deepest roots of the trees. Without this no season can be truly prosperous in this country, because a large part
of the produce is gathered from the olive, the mulberry, the fig, the walnut,
the apricot, the orange, and other fruit and nut-bearing trees. Long rains are
therefore in season, and to be expected. Then this storm has obviously been
gathering for several days past, and its duration generally corresponds to the
time spent in coming on. Again, the wind is full and strong from the proper
rain quarter—the south-west—and while it holds to that point the storm will
continue. It will not clear until the wind shifts round toward the north,
which it is often slow to do, and will not now till the air becomes colder, and
Lebanon is covered deep with snow. As in ancient times, the west wind Rainy
brings rain, and the north drives it away.[2] There is also a somewhat in the winds.
thickness and colour of the clouds which speaks to the eye of experience: and
see how low they fly, tearing their garments to tatters on the rocky crags of
Jebel Rehân, and trailing their soiled skirts in the mire.

> "There's not a cloud on all the plain
> But tells of storm to come or past;
> Here, flying loosely as the mane
> Of a young war-horse in the blast;
> There, rolled in masses dark and swelling
> As proud to be the thunder's dwelling."

[1] Hosea ii. 21, 22.   Luke xii. 54; Prov. xxv. 23.

PART
I.

There will be no fair weather until they sail clear of the loftiest peaks of Lebanon. The sea, too, by its hoarse and heavy roar, warns the mariner to lower his topmasts, double his anchors, and make all tight for a long and hard gale; and even those stupid gulls, careering on the blast far inland, add their testimony to the general voice of nature. Depend upon it, we are in for a genuine winter storm, and may congratulate ourselves on having reached this snug harbour before it began. Nor need the time pass idly away. Here are books to consult; and friends, both Frank and native, from whom you can glean many a valuable hint for future use; so "wrap the garment of patience around you," and let it rain. There will be intermissions, however (for no storm in this country is without them), during which we may run about the city and its environs; and in the evenings we shall have reunions of friends, in which all sorts of subjects are discussed. You will thus be in a fine school of manners—Oriental I mean, and may learn more of the customs and ways of the people in these few days than by months of mere travel through the land.

Solace for travellers.

According to this account, Paul's euroclydon of fourteen days was no very extraordinary occurrence.

Not as to the length of the storm, certainly; nor do I understand the historian to intimate that there was anything miraculous about it. It was one, however, of extreme violence: "Neither sun nor stars appeared in many days, and all hope of being saved was taken away."[1] And yet we are not to suppose that there were no intermissions in this tempest, any more than that the people literally tarried fourteen days fasting, without taking anything. Such expressions never deceive or disturb an Oriental. They do not mean absolutely *nothing*. In our medical practice, it is almost impossible to arrive at accuracy in regard to what a patient has eaten. Both he and his friends will assure you, in the most comprehensive terms, that he has "continued fasting, having eaten nothing;" and yet, by close questioning, you find that he has loaded his stomach with trash highly injurious to him. When pressed on the point, he will merely say, "It does not deserve to be mentioned." You may take this as a general canon of interpretation, that any amount much less than usual means "nothing" in their dialect; and if you understand more by it, you are misled. In fact, their ordinary fasting is only abstaining from certain kinds of food, not from all, nor does the word convey any other idea to them.

Fasting.

The euroclydon.

In regard to Paul's euroclydon: it is no uncommon thing to encounter similar storms at this day, in the same part of the Mediterranean. I have followed nearly the exact route of his disastrous voyage, and, as our noble steamer sailed in between Catzo and Candia—the Crete of the Acts—we were met by a tremendous wind, which tried the utmost power of her engines. Slowly and laboriously she ploughed her foaming furrow through the troubled sea, close under Crete, for twenty-four hours, and then ran into the harbour of

---

* Acts xxvii. 14, 20.

Suda, which we found as quiet as a mill-pond; and, unlike Paul's Fair Havens, CHAPTER
VIII. it would be quite commodious for the entire British navy to winter in. Here we remained a "night and a day;" but, as the wind did not moderate, the captain became impatient, and sailed out in the very teeth of the gale. For a long time we made very little progress, and, as we ran under a certain island that was called Clauda, I could well understand that such a vessel as that "ship of Alexandria" must have been exceedingly tossed with the tempest. However, by the aid of steam, we were carried in four, instead of fourteen days, to that "certain island called Melita," and into the glorious harbour of Valetta, instead of being wrecked at the entrance of St. Paul's Bay. And though we were also laden with wheat, we were not obliged to cast it into the sea to "lighten the ship." I shall never forget the impressions of that voyage over the seas of Cilicia and Pamphylia, and across the "Adria," where Paul was driven up and down for fourteen days.

I no longer wonder that the people of this country believe in jan, and Ghosts. ghools, and all the exaggerated machinery of the Thousand Nights. About one o'clock I was startled out of profound sleep by the most frightful noise I

JACKALS.

ever heard. It seemed to come from this grave-yard on the east of your house, and to be very near. What on earth could have produced it?

PART
I.

A concert
of jackals.

It was nothing but a concert of jackals. You may be serenaded by them every night, but they are particularly musical in the fiercest storms.

Deliver me from their music. I was terrified. It began in a sort of solo: a low, long-drawn wail, rising, and swelling higher and higher, until it quite over-topped the wind; and just when it was about to *choke off* in utter despair, it was reinforced by many others, yelling, screaming, barking, wailing, as if a whole legion of demons were fighting among the tombs over some son of perdition that had fallen into their clutches.

Why, you have been positively startled out of all propriety by these creatures; but no wonder. What a doom is that which David pronounces upon those who seek the soul of the righteous to destroy it: "They shall fall by the sword; they shall be a portion for foxes;"[1] by which jackals are meant, as I suppose. These sinister, guilty, woe-begone brutes, when pressed with hunger, gather in gangs among the graves, and yell in rage, and fight like fiends over their midnight orgies; but on the battle-field is their great carnival. Oh! let me never even dream that any one dear to me has fallen by the sword, and lies there to be torn, and gnawed at, and dragged about by these hideous howlers.

I have been wanting to send Salîm down town on an errand, but he has been pounding at something most zealously all the morning. What is he after?

Mortar
and pestle.

MORTAR AND PESTLE.

He is braying wheat with a pestle in a mortar, to make kibby, the national dish of the Arabs, and a very good one it is. Every family has one or more of these large stone mortars, and you may hear the sound of the "braying" at all hours as you walk the streets of the city.

So I suppose Solomon means that, if we pound a fool in a mortar, among wheat, with a pestle, into a batch of kibby, yet will not his foolishness depart from him.[2]

At any rate, there is nothing else in the country so likely to suggest the proverb; and if foolishness will not depart under such discipline, the case is indeed hopeless. But our boy is braying fish, not a fool, and we shall therefore have kibbet samak, which many people are extremely fond of. It is more commonly made of mutton, mixed with fat from the large tail of the sheep. When thoroughly pounded, it is sent to the oven, and baked in a copper dish made for the purpose. It will keep good in winter for half a month, and makes a capital lunch for the road.

Seething a
kid.

While on the subject of cooking, take another favourite dish of the Arabs. They select a young kid, fat and tender, dress it carefully, and then stew it in milk, generally sour, mixed with onions and hot spices such as they relish. They call it Lebn immû—"kid in his mother's milk." The Jews, however,

---

[1] Psalm lxiii. 10.　　　　　[2] Prov. xxvii. 22.

will not eat it. They say that Moses specifically forbade it in the precept, "Thou shalt not seethe a kid in his mother's milk,"[1] which he repeated three several times, and with special emphasis. They further maintain that it is unnatural and barbarous to cook a poor kid in that from which it derives its life. This may have been one reason for the prohibition,—many of the Mosaic precepts are evidently designed to cultivate gentle and humane feelings; but "kid in his mother's milk" is a gross, unwholesome dish, calculated also to kindle up animal and ferocious passions; and on these accounts Moses may have forbidden it. Besides, it is even yet associated with immoderate feasting; and originally, I suspect, was connected with idolatrous sacrifices. A great deal of learning has been spent upon this passage by critics, to ascertain what the law-giver referred to; but after seeing the dish actually prepared, and hearing the very name given to it which Moses employs, we have the whole mystery explained. I have repeatedly tasted *Lebn immû;* and, when well prepared, it has a rich and agreeable flavour. But, though there is little of the Jew in me, yet I have some scruples about partaking of this forbidden food, just as I have in regard to any kind of dish cooked in blood. The reason assigned for the original prohibition continues in full force to this day: "But flesh with the life thereof, the blood thereof, shall ye not eat."[2] Nearly all sects of the East, Christian included, regard this reservation, in the grant to eat flesh, as strictly obligatory. The semi-barbarian Abyssinians, according to Bruce's famous story, it is true, violate the whole breadth of the precept when they cut out and devour flesh from the flanks of the *living* animal; and it is just possible that the command was aimed against some such brutal practice. However that may be, in this country, not only blood-puddings, but every preparation of blood for food, is held in utter abomination. And so, also, it is unlawful to eat animals, fowls, and birds, strangled or smothered, and cooked with the blood in them. And, in my feelings at least, the Orientals in this matter are right. Moses repeats the prohibition in these emphatic words: "Ye shall eat no manner of blood, whether it be of fowl, or of beast, in any of your dwellings."[3] And again, in chap. xvii. 10–14, it is reaffirmed in the most absolute terms, extended even to strangers, and made to include game taken in hunting. Accordingly, our hunters, when they shoot even a small bird, are careful to cut its throat, and "pour out the blood thereof." God himself declares, "I will even set my face against that soul that eateth blood, and will cut him off from among his people."

In addition to the original reason of the prohibition, that the blood is the life, it is here added, "I have given it to you upon the altar, to make an atonement for your souls." And let us not forget that the element which represents blood is still given to us in the Supper as the symbol of atonement. How often are we reminded that it is through the *blood* of atonement alone that we can receive pardon and reconciliation with God! And it seems rash, to say

Eating blood.

Atoning blood.

---

[1] Exod. xxiii. 19, and xxxiv. 26; Deut. xiv. 21.   [2] Gen. ix. 4.   [3] Lev. vii. 26.

the least, to venture needlessly upon the violation of a precept announced before the law was given, so often repeated, surrounded with so many sanctions, and suggestive of so much that should impress the heart with tenderest emotion and deepest reverence. And, finally, I believe that the apostolic council of Jerusalem solemnly reaffirms this prohibition, and with special reference to the Gentile Church.[1] For once I am an Oriental, and while I would not hastily judge him that eateth even blood, think they do better who refuse.

Sheep with large tails.
In your account of kibby you mentioned the large tails of the sheep, which reminds me of an inquiry I have to make on this subject. Russell, in his "History of Aleppo," says that these tails grow to a prodigious size—sometimes weighing fifty pounds; and that they require to be supported and defended from injury by thin boards, which have little wheels attached to them to facilitate transportation. My mother used to sing "little bo-peep," when I was a child, and of the sheep that "left their tails behind them"—a much more sensible custom than to drag them on little carriages "behind them." But, seriously, what have you to say to this strange story? I have already seen at least a thousand "tails" since landing in Beirût, and have examined them carefully, both on the living animal and when dressed for the market, and I must say that Mr. Russell's statement seems somewhat apocryphal. None that I have yet noticed would weigh more than ten pounds.

A traveller can commit no greater error than to jump to the conclusion, soon after he arrives in a country, that nothing is possible but what he has seen. As to the particular matter in hand, Russell may have copied, not from observation, but from Herodotus. The "Father of History," however, strikes off in a bolder strain than the Aleppo chaplain deemed it safe to follow.

SYRIAN SHEEP.

"In Arabia," says he, "there are two kinds of sheep. One of them is remarkable for an enormous length of tail, extending to three cubits, *if not more.*

---

[1] Acts xv. 20.

If they were permitted to trail them along the ground, they would certainly ul- CHAPTER VIII. cerate from friction. But the shepherds of the country are skilful enough to make little carriages, upon which they secure the tails of the sheep."—*Thalia*, 113.

As to the "boards" and the "carriages," I choose to say nothing, except that the thing is not absolutely impossible. But I have been to Aleppo repeatedly, and have inquired into this matter on the spot, yet could never hear of such an apparatus; nor have I found any sheep that needed, or would have known how to use such a locomotive. The rest of Mr Russell's account is sufficiently accurate, and quite credible. These tails (or, as the Bible more correctly calls them, the *rump*) of ordinary sheep in the market do not weigh more than ten or fifteen pounds—about your own estimate; but when the sheep are well fattened, they grow to an enormous size. I have seen many in Lebanon so heavy that the owners could not carry them without difficulty,—yet I never saw any that would weigh quite fifty pounds. Such a tail, however, is within the limits of possibility. The cooks use this mass of fat instead of Arab butter, and many prefer it, as it is fresh and sweet, while the other is often rancid. No doubt this is the "rump" so often mentioned in the Levitical sacrifices, which was to be taken off hard by the back-bone.[1] It is, in fact, not properly a tail, but a mass of marrow-like fat, which spreads over the whole rump of the sheep, and down the caudal extremity until near the end, which, as Russell says, turns back upon it in a kind of appendix.

The "rump."

Salîm led me through an entire street of shoe-shops this morning. Is the red leather which the shoemakers use the rams' skins dyed red,[2] which formed one of the three covers of the tabernacle?

Rams' skins dyed red.

No doubt; and there is a definiteness in the name *rams'* skins which is worth noticing. From time out of mind the southern part of Syria and Palestine has been supplied with mutton from the great plains and deserts on the north, east, and south, and the shepherds do not ordinarily bring the females to market. The vast flocks which annually come from Armenia and Northern Syria are nearly all males. The leather, therefore, is literally *rams'* skins dyed red. It is pleasant to meet such perfect accuracy in the most incidental allusions and minute details of the Mosaic record.

Yes, it is indeed satisfactory to find everything about this home of the Bible just as it should be; and the testimony seems all the stronger when the incident is so minute as to exclude the very possibility of design. Here is another illustration of the same kind. Your boy has just let down a *basket through the window* by *the wall*, to get oranges from this garden outside the city.[3] So Paul tells the Corinthians, at the close of that long list of perils and persecutions which he had encountered, that he was let down *through a window, in a basket, by the wall*, when the governor of Damascus kept the city with a garrison, desirous to apprehend him.[4]

Basket let down from window in wall.

---

[1] Exod. xxix. 22; Lev. iii. 9, and vii. 3, and ix. 19

[2] Exod. xxv. 5.

[3] Acts ix. 25.

[4] 2 Cor. xi. 33.

PART I.

Certainly the illustration is entirely to the point, and there are seventeen windows of our house on the wall of the city, from any one of which we also could easily escape, as Paul did, if the governor of Sidon should watch the gates of the city to apprehend us.

In our visit to the consul to-day, did you notice the writing over the door and all round the room ?

I did ; and it reminded me of the recommendation to the people of Israel : "These words which I command thee this day, thou shalt write them upon the posts of thy house, and on thy gates."[1] I was delighted to meet with this very ancient custom.

Writing upon walls.

Moses probably did not originate, but, as in many other cases, merely availed himself of the custom, in order to keep the precepts of the Lord ever before the eyes and in the hearts of the people. Indeed, it is certain that the Egyptians observed a similar practice from the most remote antiquity. But, whatever may be its origin, it has been perpetuated down to the present day, and among all classes in this country. The Moslems are particularly fond of it. They never set up a gate, cover a fountain, build a bridge, or erect a house, without writing on it choice sentences from the Koran, or from their best poets. Christians also do the same. The consul, as you saw, has adorned his best room with a multitude of extracts from the Psalms, written in large characters, very much involved, which is considered particularly ornamental, and is, besides, a constant puzzle to exercise the skill of the visitor. Indeed, very few can decipher these intricate mazes of Arabic caligraphy. This custom is certainly not objectionable in itself, and may be useful at all times, but it was more appropriate when books were few, and only within the reach of the learned and the wealthy. Like every other good practice, however, it could be, and was, early perverted into a hurtful superstition. These sentences were and are inscribed as charms to keep off evil spirits, and to afford protection against disease and other calamities. The same is true of the customs referred to in the 8th verse : "Thou shalt bind them for a sign upon thy hand,

Frontlets.

and they shall be as frontlets between thine eyes." These signs and frontlets, of every kind, whether engraved on signets, written on parchments and enclosed in silver cases, or simply tattooed on the hands, the forehead between the eyes, or on other parts of the body, are universally regarded as charms possessing talismanic virtues. The Moslems, Nusairîeh, and Bedawîn Arabs attach great importance to them, and never venture abroad without them. But Moses certainly did not, in any case, countenance superstition, and probably intended by these precepts to appropriate to a valuable purpose customs he could not eradicate, and ornaments which he could not induce the people to lay aside. We learn from Herodotus, and other ancient writers, that the people throughout all these countries were universally attached to such superstitions.

---

[1] Deut. vi. 9, and xi. 20

The Jews have always observed this precept, I suppose, but not always in the same way. In the times of their national prosperity, when they could act out their religion without fear of enemies, they literally engraved the "laws of the Lord" on their gates and door-posts. But for generations, no one knows how many, they have been in the habit of writing certain of these laws on small rolls of parchment, which they enclose in some sort of case, and insert into a niche made in the post, or in the plaster upon it. Even in cities like Safet and Tiberias, where the Jews are the majority, they still do the same ; and, although the parchments are not absolutely hidden, yet they are so adjusted that it was not until after many years' residence in this country that I was aware of their existence, or knew where to find them. This parchment is called medzuzah, and the passages written are generally Deuteronomy vi. 4–9, and xi. 13–30. The ceremonies accompanying the operation are different in different places, sometimes puerile, always superstitious.

Come to the kiosk, and tell me what is going forward in the street.

That is a funeral procession, which, like most other things purely Oriental, is without order—a confused medley of men and boys, in all sorts of costume, rolling on somehow or other toward the cemetery. The only thing solemn about it is the low, sad monotone in which they chant that eternal truth, "La illah illa Allah—no god but God ;" accompanied by that necessary lie, as Gibbon calls it, "W' Muhammedhū russûl Allah—and Mohammed is the prophet of God." This, and nothing else, is their funeral dirge, and they repeat it over and over until they reach the grave.

See how those women toss their arms, swing handkerchiefs, and scream, and shriek at the top of their voices ! Those are the relatives, I suppose ?

Yes, and they go before to the grave ; for it is not customary for women and men to walk together on such occasions.

But what are they about now ? They have formed a circle, like a bull-ring at a country fight, and there are two or three men inside, as if they were the combatants.

Wait a moment, and you will see what it all means. Now they begin. These two men in the centre are the choristers, and are singing one of their hymns. The whole performance is called a zikr.

How they shake their heads, and twist and jerk their bodies ! and what do they repeat with such emphasis and solemnity ?

This is but the commencement; the storm will burst out by degrees. They say nothing but "Ya-Allah ! Ya-Allah !" [1] beginning, as you see, very slowly. It will soon come—is coming faster and louder ; as they grow warm, their motions become wild and frantic ; the chant runs into a horrid, deep growl, like wild beasts, in which it is impossible to distinguish any words—merely "Allah, Allah, Allah," which they drive through their throats at a most perilous rate. This they will continue until, from sheer exhaustion, they break down.

---

[1] O God! O God!

The end.

Generally some one goes off into convulsions, and, foaming at the mouth like an epileptic, falls to the ground, when the zikr ceases. There goes one already. It is very kind and considerate in him to terminate the hideous performance so speedily. He is now supposed to be in a divine trance! There is nothing in all the customs of the East so outrageously repulsive and disgusting as this zikr. The men look like demons yelling, and stamping, and foaming around the dead. If there be demoniacal possession in our day, it is seen, beyond a doubt, in this hideous ceremony.

February 10th.

I have been down at the castle watching the waves. They come in fast and thick, hills over hills, heaving and tossing their huge volumes against the island and the rocks of the harbour with uproar prodigious—the very " noise of many waters," so often sung by Hebrew poets. Now and then one mightier than the rest rolls right over everything, thunders against the old castle, over-rides the causeway, and rushes headlong on the houses, and up the lower streets of the city. Sidon's modern mariners may well be thankful for their sheltered beach along that ancient wall, whereon to lay their tiny craft for the winter.

Ships.

The beach.

This has always been the practice, I suppose. The Phœnicians never had a harbour where ships could ride in safety during the storms of winter, and hence they drew them up on shore. They could thus dispense with harbours, and could and did build towns along the coast, wherever there was a bit of sandy beach large enough for their vessels. I counted sixteen deserted sites on the shore between Sidon and Tyre—a distance of not more than twenty miles—and not one of them ever had a harbour. When spring opens, they launch their ships, rig up and re-pitch them, and prosecute their business until the next winter, when they again dismantle and haul them on shore. Nor was this custom confined to the Phœnicians. The Greeks did the same, even with their war-ships on the coast of Troy,—which, by the way, is about as destitute of harbours as this of Syria. It is plain that Homer's heroes not only did so with their navy, but even built a fortification around their ships to protect them from the Trojans. Indeed, Sidonian ships were there to aid the beleaguered city. And it is a pleasing corroboration of the Biblical account of the ancient greatness of Sidon, to find her pre-eminent in commerce and in art at that early day. The "king of kings and fierce Achilles" were proud to wear Sidonian purple, and fight their battles in her polished armour. And Homer's heroines also arrayed themselves in gorgeous robes,—

Sidonian ships at Troy.

> " Which from soft Sidon youthful Paris bore,
> With Helen, touching on the Tyrian shore."

And from Sidon came that

> " Silver bowl, the largest of its kind,
> The pride of kings, and labour of a god."

And, if we may so judge from the story of Menelaus, in the fifteenth book of CHAPTER
the Odyssey, the Sidonians were a kind of Yankee pedlers in those olden VIII.
times :—

> " A ship of Sidon anchor'd in our port,
> Freighted with toys of every sort—
> With gold and amber chains, etc. etc.
> Each female eye the glittering links employ;
> They turn, review, and cheapen every toy."

Early mer-
chandise.

And the treacherous heroine of the story, " A fair Phœnician, tall, full-sized,
and skilled in works of elegance," was from our city :—

> " I too from glorious Sidon came,
> Famous for wealth by dyeing earn'd."

If such was Sidon's fame before Troy was burned or Homer sang, she not only
may, but must have been " great," when Joshua conquered at Merom.[1]

I have noticed every morning since coming to Sidon, that women come forth Women at
very early to visit the graves. They move about under the trees and among graves.
the tombs in the grey dawn, wrapped up from head to foot in their white
sheets, and looking for all the world like veritable ghosts. Sometimes I hear
the voice of prayer, some weep and sob, while others sing or chant in a low,
monotonous tone. The whole thing is very novel, and thus far deeply
affecting.

You do well to limit the duration of your emotion, and may safely moderate
its intensity as fast as possible. In ninety-nine cases out of a hundred, this
public manifestation is the work of that arch-tryant, custom, and nothing
more. The inquiry, What will the world say if I don't go and weep? sets all
your ghosts in motion; and, unless your sympathy is directed toward the
slave, it is merely thrown away. They themselves curse the tyrant they obey,
as bitterly as the Moslem does the fast of Ramadan, which yet he observes.
In either case, it is artificial, hypocritical, slavish. You observe that some of Weeping
these performers have tents pitched above the graves which require to be wept
over. These, however, afford but slight protection against this pitiless storm
and piercing wind. The great majority have no cover, and the mourners go
home to nurse rheumatisms and catarrhs, burn in fevers, or go blind with
ophthalmia. The real weeping is in the houses. And when you further know
that many of these mourners and chanters are hired, and weep, howl, beat
their breast, and tear the hair according to contract, your compassion will fail
fast, or take another direction, and sigh for the victims of folly and fashion.

You must not suppose, however, that there is no genuine sorrow among this
people. The voice of nature is far too strong to be stifled, even by this machinery of hypocrisy. Amid all this ostentatious parade, there are burning tears,

---

[1] [This hardly follows, as the era of Joshua was long before the siege of Troy. Joshua fought
at Merom at least 1450 years B.C. The usual date of the Trojan war is about two centuries
later.—ED.]

PART
I.

and hearts bursting in agony and despair.   Many a Mary still goes to the grave
to weep there, and true friends follow them thither with real sympathy.[1]   But

WOMEN WEEPING AT THE GRAVE.

where iron custom compels everybody to visit the bereaved, and to act well the
part of comforters and mourners according to prescribed forms, much will, of
course, be manufactured for the occasion; and so it is *ad nauseam.*   Many of
the women are admirable performers, and could put to the blush the most
accomplished actress on the European stage.   These customs date far back in
the history of earth's sorrows.   "Man is born to trouble as the sparks fly
upward."[2]   Job had his friends who came from a distance to comfort him, and
many of the expressions now detailed with a glib volubility which confounds
us simple Americans, are copied from those celebrated dialogues.   On similar
occasions lover and friend hasten from afar to mingle their condolence with
the wretched, and sometimes with no kinder feelings than those of Bildad and
his associates.

Hired
mourners.

Even the custom of hiring mourners is very ancient.   Jeremiah says, "Consider ye, and call for the mourning women, that they may come; and send for

[1] John xi. 31.   [2] Job v. 7.

cunning women, that they may come; and let them make haste, and take up a wailing for us, that our eyes may run down with tears, and our eyelids gush out with waters."[1] Every particular here alluded to is observed on funeral occasions at the present day. There are in every city and community women exceedingly cunning in this business. These are always sent for, and kept in readiness. When a fresh company of sympathizers comes in, these women "make haste" to take up a wailing, that the newly come may the more easily unite their tears with the mourners. They know the domestic history of every person, and immediately strike up an impromptu lamentation, in which they introduce the names of their relatives who have recently died, touching some tender chord in every heart; and thus each one weeps for his *own* dead, and the *performance*, which would otherwise be difficult or impossible, comes easy and natural, and even this extemporaneous, artificial sorrow, is thereby redeemed from half its hollow-heartedness and hypocrisy. There may yet be occasions, in the politer circles of European society, when such a machinery for manufacturing tears will be a great convenience.

On the whole, I do not think that the modern customs of mourning are more extravagant, even in Syria, than the ancient.

We find allusions in old authors to the custom of collecting the tears of the mourners, and preserving them in bottles. Thus David prays, "Put thou my tears into thy bottle: are they not in thy book?"[2] These lachrymatories are still found in great numbers on opening ancient tombs. A sepulchre lately discovered in one of the gardens of our city had scores of them in it. They

Tear-bottles.

TEAR-BOTTLES.

are made of thin glass, or more generally of simple pottery, often not even baked or glazed, with a slender body, a broad bottom, and a funnel-shaped top. They have nothing in them but *dust* at present. If the friends were expected to contribute their share of tears for these bottles, they would very much need cunning women to cause their eyelids to gush out with waters. These forms of ostentatious sorrow have ever been offensive to sensible people. Thus Tacitus says: "At my funeral let no tokens of sorrow be seen, no pompous mockery of woe. Crown me with chap-

[1] Jer. ix. 17. 18.   [2] Psalm lvi. 8.

PART
I.

lets, strew flowers on my grave, and let my friends erect no vain memorial to tell where my remains are lodged."

How long do these seasons of mourning continue?

There is no absolute law on the subject, and the duration and intensity of grief varies. The most bitter lamentations are for young men, and for fathers of families. These are sometimes very extravagant and greatly prolonged. That tent under our windows covers the grave of a young man, and, as you see, they are there every day, although he has been buried for several weeks. There are, however, certain days on which the regular business of mourning is renewed. A curious and rather pretty custom is very commonly practised by the Moslems, connected, however, with superstitious notions in regard to the state of the departed. On the eve preceding any great festival, the relatives, generally the women, go to the graves and fill small holes, left purposely at the head and foot of the tomb, with fresh myrtle bushes, and sometimes palm branches, which are watered daily to keep them green. Some do this every Thursday evening, because Friday is their sacred day. You had better read what Lane says on this subject at your leisure, for it would now be tedious to describe all their funeral customs, and equally useless. There is one, however, to which our Saviour alludes, that of white-washing the sepulchres, which should not pass unnoticed. I have been in places where this is repeated very often. The graves are kept clean and white as snow,—a very striking emblem of those painted hypocrites, the Pharisees, beautiful without, but full of dead men's bones and all uncleanness within. "So ye also outwardly appear righteous unto men, but within ye are full of hypocrisy and iniquity."[1]

Is there anything in modern usage which explains Deut. xxvi. 14: "I have not eaten thereof in my mourning, neither have I taken away ought thereof for any unclean use, nor given ought thereof for the dead?"

Yes; this passage is made sufficiently plain by an acquaintance with modern funeral customs. What you have just read is part of that protestation which the devout Jew was required to make at the close of the third year, "which is the year of tithing." He was to come before the Lord and say, "I have brought away the hallowed things out of my house, and also have given them unto the Levite and unto the stranger, to the fatherless and to the widow, according to all thy commandments. I have not eaten thereof in my mourning, neither have I taken away ought thereof for any unclean use, nor given ought thereof for the dead." This was the strongest possible protestation that he had dealt faithfully in the matter of tithing and consecrated things, and in charities to the poor. He had not allowed himself to divert anything to other uses, not even by the most pressing and unforeseen emergencies. It is here assumed, or rather implied, that times of mourning "for the dead" were expensive, and also that the stern law of custom obliged the bereaved to defray those expenses, however onerous. The same thing lies at the basis of that excuse for not fol-

White-
washing
sepul-
chres.

Expense
of fune-
rals.

---

[1] Matt. xxiii. 27, 28.

lowing our Saviour,—" Suffer me first to go and bury my father ;" a duty which must take precedence of all others. Such it was among most ancient nations, and such is the public sentiment at this day. Moreover, funerals are now ruinously expensive. Crowds of relatives, friends, and acquaintances assemble on these occasions. The largest gatherings ever seen on Lebanon are on these occasions. For all these guests refreshments must be provided, and not a few from a distance tarry all night, and must be entertained. Then these gatherings and feasts for the dead are repeated at stated times for forty days. The priests also, and religious functionaries of all sects, must be rewarded for their attendance at the time, and for their subsequent prayers and good offices in behalf of the dead. A young friend of mine, whose father lately died, informs me that the ecclesiastics are demanding of him twenty thousand piastres for these subsequent services. In short, many families are reduced to poverty by funerals ; and it must have been substantially so in remote ages, for the cus- toms were very similar. The temptation, therefore, to devote a part of the tithes, hallowed things, and charities, to defray those enormous, unforeseen, and providential expenses, would be very urgent ; and he who stood faithful at such times might be safely trusted on all other occasions. Hence the protestation covers the strongest case that could be selected. The words, " nor given ought thereof for the dead," are explained by a curious custom still observed with great care. On certain days after the funeral, large quantities of corn and other food are cooked in a particular manner, and sent to all the friends, however numerous, *in the name of the dead.* I have had many such presents ; but my dislike of the practice, or something else, renders these dishes peculiarly disgusting to me.

A custom prevails among the Bedawîn Arabs, and especially those around the Hûleh, which illustrates this whole subject. When one of their number dies, they immediately bring his best ox or buffalo, and slaughter it near to the body of the deceased. They then cook it all for a great feast, with burghûl, rice, and whatever else good to eat they may possess. The whole tribe, and neighbours also, assemble for the funeral, and go direct from the grave to this sacrificial feast. The vast piles of provisions quickly disappear, for the Bedawîn despatch their dinners with a rapidity that would astound a table d'hôte at a Western railway station. However, every one must partake at least of a morsel. It is a duty to the departed, and must be eaten in behalf of the dead. Even strangers passing along are constrained to come and taste of the feast. My friends of Hasbeiya inform me that this custom is so binding that it must be observed, though it consume every item of property and of provisions the man possessed, and leave the wife and children to starve. It is the feast of the dead. That the Jewish tithe-payer, when pressed even by such a stringent call as this, had left untouched the tenths which were devoted to God, was the very best proof that could be demanded or produced that he had acted honestly in this matter.

I have been sauntering through the cemeteries of Sidon. Every sect, I per-

PART
I.

Ceme-
teries.

ceive, has its separate grave-yard. That of the Moslems, under these pretty China trees, is the largest and most striking. Both they and the Christians seem to have a disposition to place the foot of the grave toward the east. Those of the Jews all turn toward Jerusalem; but the Metwalies bury as it happens, and appear to take very little care of their graves. As a general fact, I suppose the ancients expended far more upon their tombs than the moderns. Are there no old sepulchres about Sidon?

Old tombs.

Countless numbers. All those eastern hills are full of them. They are of all sizes, and the internal arrangements are very various. Most of them consist of a square or oblong room, perpendicular to the sides of which the niches for the bodies extend six or seven feet into the rock. I have counted sixteen of these in a single room; but we need not suppose that they were all hewn at the same time, or even in the same age. A family selected a *cave*, if one could be found, which they trimmed and squared, and cut in it as many niches as they expected to need. Their posterity would hew new ones as occasion required; and when the original room was full, they cut out another behind, or at the side of it, and thus went on enlarging from generation to generation, as long as the family existed.

Machpe-
lah.

This was done, as I understand the matter, in the cave of Machpelah, which Abraham purchased for a family burying-place. Jacob, when about to die in Egypt, made Joseph swear to bury him: "In my grave which I have digged for me in the land of Canaan, there shalt thou bury me." [1] Now Jacob could only dig a grave for himself in the cave of Machpelah by cutting out a separate niche. Abraham made one for Sarah, and another was prepared for himself. Isaac prepared one for himself and Rebekah, and there Jacob says he buried Leah. [2]

In some sepulchral rooms there are double tiers of niches, one above the other. This appears to have been a favourite plan with the northern Phœnicians, as you find them not far from Tortosa, Gebile, Ladakîyeh, and Seleucia. The entire system of rooms, niches, and passages, may be comprehended at

Tombs
of the
Judges.

once by an inspection of the plan of the Tombs of the Judges, near Jerusalem, which I borrow from Mr. Williams's valuable work on the Holy City. The entrance faces the west, and has a vestibule (A) thirteen feet by nine. Chamber (B), nearly twenty feet square, and eight high. The north side is seen in elevation in *Fig.* 2, and shows two tiers of niches, one over the other,—not often met with in tombs. There are seven in the lower tier, each seven feet long, twenty inches wide, and nearly three feet high. The upper tier has three arched recesses, and each recess has two niches. From this room (B) doors lead out into chambers (C and D), which have their own peculiar system of niches, or loculi, for the reception of the bodies, as appears on the plan. I have explored scores of Sepulchres at Ladakîyeh closely resembling this at Jerusalem, and there are many in the plain and on the hill sides above us here

---

[1] Gen. l. 5.   [2] Gen. xlix. 31.

at Sidon of the same general form—chambers within chambers, and each with niches for the dead, variously arrranged, according to taste or necessity. The

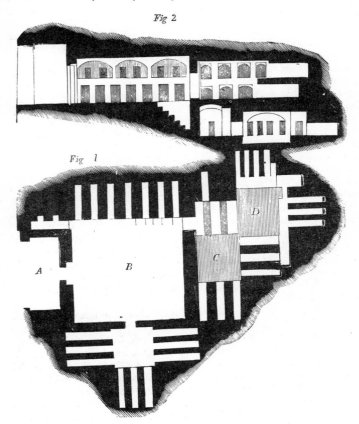

Fig 2

Fig 1

A   B   C   D

TOMBS OF THE JUDGES.

interior of not a few of those about Sidon was plastered originally, or in after ages, with a hard cement or stucco, which is still quite perfect in some of them. In one I found a Greek inscription, drawn in the stucco before it hardened. In others there were such inscriptions written on the plaster with red ink. One large one is adorned with wreaths of flowers and small birds, with palm, orange, and other trees, such as are now found in the gardens below. These would seem to prove that the orange had been cultivated at

PART
I.

Sidon from a very remote age. But I am inclined to believe that this stucco-ing, writing in Greek, and painting upon the tombs, took place long after they were first hewn in the rock, probably after the original occupants had returned to utter dust. I am confirmed in this suspicion from examining a large tomb which was uncovered last winter on the plain. The surface above it had been used from time out of mind as a summer threshing-floor. A shaft, sunk about ten feet through the soil, exposed a low door in the face of the rock opening into a room thirty feet long by twelve broad. The ceiling and walls are stuccoed and ornamented with various figures in red paint ; and a Greek inscription, written with the same paint, runs quite round the room, as a sort of ornamental border. It is much the longest inscription I have seen, and the letters are large, well formed, and as perfect as the day they were laid on. This was not the first time that this tomb had been opened, for all the antiquities it con-tained had been removed, and it was nearly full of earth, thrown there from other tombs connected with it. Something about this chamber suggested the idea that it was a kind of subterraneous oratory, and not a sepulchre,—in short, that it was one of those underground sanctuaries among the tombs, where the early Christians are said to have met for worship in times of cruel persecution. The whole area in this neighbourhood is undermined by tombs, and, if one had funds to excavate them, many curious discoveries might be made. I need hardly remind you that sepulchres hewn in the rock are mentioned in many passages in the sacred record.

CHAPTER IX.

S I D O N—*Continued.*

11*th*. We have had a delightful ramble along the aqueduct and through the vast fruit-orchards, and my respect for old Sidon has decidedly risen by the excursion. What may be the present population of the city and her gardens ?

Popula-
tion.

It is not possible to arive at perfect accuracy, as there are no statistics kept by the government. The number of inhabitants is said to be about 9000. Of these, 6800 are Moslems, including the Metāwelies, 850 Greek Catholics, 750 Maronites, 150 Greeks, and 300 Jews. These are ecclesiastical returns, and they are always under-stated, in order to diminish the taxation, which is assessed according to the people's ecclesiastical relations. The entire population is therefore not far from 10,000. This is a small figure for a city called " great"

even by Joshua. Nor is she increasing, or likely to increase much for years to CHAPTER
come. Beirût is too near, and draws everything into her all-absorbing vortex. IX.
Sidon exports tobacco, oil, fruit, and silk, but the amount is small, except in
tobacco, which is, in fact, the main dependence of her merchants. It is all
sent to Egypt.

Are there no antiquities about Sidon ?

Not many, and none very striking. She is too old. Her decline commenced Antiqui-
" before antiquity began." There are a few things, however, besides the tombs, ties.
in which her greatness was buried thousands of years ago, which are worthy
of attention. The immense stones which form the north-west angle of the
inner harbour, each one being some ten feet square, were no doubt put there
in the days of Sidon's early prosperity ; but it is surprising that the ancient
inhabitants allowed the ledge of rocks on the seaward side to be quarried
away for building-stone. This invaluable barrier has thus been so much
lowered that the sea breaks over into the harbour in every storm, not only
endangering the ships and boats, but causing a strong current to set eastward
under the arches of the causeway which leads to the castle. These arches
will, ere long, give way, as others have before, and thus the castle will be cut
off from communication with the city. This castle itself, though mostly in Castle.
ruins, has something to interest the antiquary. The oldest part is built nearly
solid, with a large number of granite columns placed at regular intervals in
the wall ;—this shows, of course, that it was not erected until after the columns
had become part of Sidon's ancient ruins ; nevertheless, it is built of very
heavy stones, having the Phœnician bevel, and probably dates back to the
beginning of our era. The slightly-pointed arch in the most ancient part does
not prove it to be modern, for I have seen this kind of arch in buildings
undoubtedly older than the Saracens ; nor do I believe that these barbarians
ever invented any arch. They found one to their taste, which they modified
and appropriated to their own structures. I called your attention to the *old* Old wall.
wall which extended along the shore north-east to the little brook Kumly ;
from thence southward it is not easy to trace it for some distance, but it kept
along the terrace which rises above the general level of the plain, and bent
round west to the sea, about twenty rods to the south of the present upper
castle. The *Tell* on which this castle stands is artificial, and, what is more
remarkable, is made up, in a great measure, of old pottery, rubbish of houses,
and thick beds of broken purpura, thrown out from Sidon's ancient manufactories of purple dye. The bluff facing the sea shows this conglomeration at
least twenty feet thick. South-east of the upper castle is a *mazar*, frequented
mostly by Jews, and called Sidône. The people do not know who he was ;
and if it were a shrine dedicated to old Sidon himself, there would be nothing
strange in the fact that the Jews frequent it. So they do Neby Seijûd yonder,
on the top of Jebel Rihân, and many other places of the same character,
although they are held by Moslems. Columns, sarcophagi, broken statuary,
and other evidences of a great city, are found everywhere in these gardens,

PART
I.

with the oldest trees growing in fertile soil many feet thick above them. These are the most remarkable remnants of Sidon's original greatness which the tooth of Time has left us. They do not contradict her ancient renown, though they throw very little light upon her history.

If the city was anciently so large, what has become of the vast amount of stone? I see nothing of it on all the plain.

Disappearance
of the
stone.

You do well to commence your study of ruined cities with this inquiry. The thing puzzled me greatly at first, but the disappearance of the stone can easily be accounted for in all cases. In fact, a large part of many old cities was built of sun-burnt brick, and these, of course, need not be sought for. In many cities the building material was a soft cretaceous stone, which crumbled back to soil almost as rapidly as sun-burnt brick. Most of the towns along the Syrian coast, however, are built of an argillaceous sandstone, mixed with comminuted shell; which, though porous and easily cut, will yet, if protected from the weather, last for ages; but, when exposed, it disintegrates rapidly, and soon melts away to dust. This process is hastened every time the ruins are *worked over* for new buildings. The stones must always be re-cut before they are put into a wall, and, after being thus reduced two or three times, they become too small for use, are thrown out into the fields, and quickly dissolve. A ruined city of this kind along the coast, or in any position from which the stone can be easily transported, is quarried over and over again until nothing remains but shapeless heaps of rubbish. Thus the stones of Sarepta, Athlîte, Cæsarea, and even of Tyre and Sidon, have recently been carried to Acre, Beirût, and Joppa, by boat, in immense quantities, and, after being cut afresh, and much reduced in size, are placed in buildings, which, in turn, will fall to ruin in a hundred years, when the same process will be repeated, until they are found no more. In other places, where the material is compact limestone, and not subject to these causes of destruction, it is broken up and burnt to lime. We saw how the sarcophagi at Khŭldeh are thus destroyed. At Kedes, an old city near the head of the Lake of Hums, I found the peasants breaking up beautiful marble columns with sledge-hammers for the same purpose. When I remonstrated with them, they replied that they had no other use for these columns, and that this had been the lime-quarry for all the region time out of mind. The whole country about that lake is volcanic, and these marble columns had been brought there from a great distance for their special accommodation. Need we wonder, therefore, at the disappearance of ruins, after the long lapse of twenty centuries of such Vandalism? I once saw the fragments of a beautiful marble statue which had been broken up for the lime-kiln! And if a sarcophagus is discovered, no matter how admirable the workmanship, you must be very expeditious if you hope to rescue it from their destructive hands. Such a one was lately uncovered here at Sidon, adorned with beautiful devices, wrought with exquisite skill. One of our friends heard of it, and went the very next morning to secure it, but too late. The owner of the ground had broken it to fragments to build into his

Marble
columns
burnt for
lime.

garden wall! You need not hesitate, therefore, about the identity of an ancient site, merely from the fact that the existing ruins do not correspond to the demands of its history.

12th. We have had another charming walk through the gardens up to Neby Yahyeh, and certainly the prospect from the Neby is exceedingly beautiful.

It is; but that from the high point two miles further south, called El Mŭnterah, is much more striking and extensive. Take your stand on the ruins of the temple which once crowned that promontory, and gaze down on plain, sea, and city, six hundred feet below, and if you are not charmed, I shall despair of satisfying your fastidious taste. But we need not lavish all our admiration on Sidon's surroundings, lovely as they certainly are. Many other spots will challenge equal admiration.

It may be so; but can anything of the kind be more rich and ravishing than those orange and lemon trees, loaded with golden fruit, single or in compact clusters, garnished with leaves of liveliest green, and spangled all over with snow-white flowers of sweetest fragrance? With a little distance to lend enchantment, Sidon's fair daughters gliding through these verdant bowers might pass for "ladies of the Hesperides," as Milton has it, set to watch these golden apples. Then those bananas, with their extraordinary leaves a dozen feet long, and drooping like great pendent ears, strike my fancy exceedingly. I cannot say that I am yet reconciled to the fruit. When green it looks like our paw-paw of Ohio, and when ripe has a sickish-sweet taste, and a doughy feel in the mouth. Miss Bremer says she thought she was biting into soap!

THE BANANA-TREE.

PART
I.

Fruits of
the Bible.

Flowers of
Sidon.

Yes; but she soon became extravagantly fond of them, and so will you. Did it ever occur to you to compare the list of modern fruits with those mentioned in the Bible ? The result will probably surprise you. In numberless places we read of grapes and figs, pomegranates, olives, dates, apples, and almonds, and these cover almost the entire list. But here, in Sidon, we have all these, and, in addition, oranges, lemons, citrons, pears, peaches, apricots, plums, quinces, bananas, prickly pears, and many smaller berries and fruits, none of which are once named in the Bible. The same superiority characterizes the modern Flora. There is no allusion to our glorious oleanders, which adorn every water-course in the land. It is doubtful whether even the rose is mentioned. The word khŭbbāzleh, translated " rose " in the Song of Solomon [1] and in Isaiah,[2] is so like our Arabic name of the malva, *khubbazy*, as to suggest the inquiry whether a beautifully flowering variety of this plant was not the " rose" of the Hebrew poets. We have them very large, double, and richly variegated. Some are perennial, and grow into a prettily shaped bush. Again, there is no mention of pinks, or geraniums, or the clematis, the ivy, the honeysuckle, or of scores of other flowers which add so much to the beauty of the hedges, and forests, and fields of Palestine. What a pity that Solomon's botany is lost, in which " he spoke of trees, from the cedar that is in Lebanon, to the hyssop that springeth out of the wall ! " [3] The cedar we know, but what is the hyssop of the royal botanist ? Mr. B——, French consul of this city, and an enthusiastic botanist, exhibited to me two varieties of hyssop ; one, called z'atar by the Arabs, having the fragrance of thyme, with a hot, pungent taste, and long, slender stems. A bunch of these would answer very well for sprinkling the paschal and sacrificial blood on the lintel and posts of the doors,[4] and over the persons and houses cleansed from the leprosy. Mr. B——, however, thinks that a very small green plant, like a moss which covers old walls in damp places, is the hyssop of Solomon. This I doubt. The other kind also springs out of walls, those of the gardens especially, and was much more likely to attract the attention of the royal student.

Native
reunions.

Visiting
customs.

I begin to understand your " reunions," and have been highly entertained by them. I am amused with that ceremonious politeness kept up between these intimate friends. When one enters the room, all rise to their feet, and stand steadfast and straight as a palm-tree to receive him. The formal salam is given and taken all round the room, with the dignity of a prince and the gravity of a court ; and when the new-comer reaches his seat, the ceremony is repeated in precisely the same words. In one of your full divans, therefore, a man gives and receives about fifty salams before he is fairly settled and at his ease. Then comes the solemnity of coffee and smoking, with a great variety of apparatus. Some use the extemporaneous cigarette, obviously a modern innovation. Others have pipes with long stems of cherry or other wood, ornamented with amber mouth-pieces. The *argeleh,* however,

---

[1] Song ii. 1.   [2] Isa. xxxv. 1.   [3] 1 Kings iv. 33.   [4] Exod. xii. 22.

with its flexible tube of various-coloured leather, seems to be the greatest
tavourite. Some of these are very elegant. The tube of the one brought to

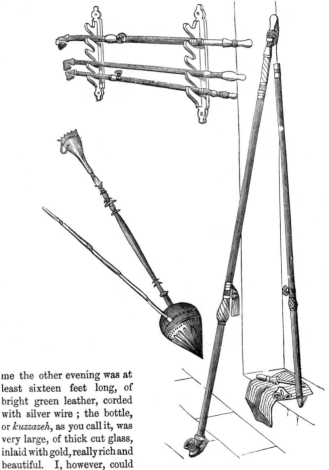

me the other evening was at least sixteen feet long, of bright green leather, corded with silver wire ; the bottle, or *kuzzazeh*, as you call it, was very large, of thick cut glass, inlaid with gold, really rich and beautiful. I, however, could produce no effect upon the water in the bottle. One needs a chest deep as a whale, and powers of suction like another maelstrom, to entice the smoke down the *tube*, *through* the water, and along the coiled sinuosities of the *snake*, or nabridj ; and yet I saw a lady make the kuzzazeh bubble like a boiling caldron without any apparent effort. The black coffee, in tiny cup, set in holders of china, brass, or silver filigree, I like well enough, but not this dreadful fumiga-

ARGELEHS.

tion. A cloud soon fills the room so dense that we can scarcely see each other, and I am driven to the open court to escape suffocation. Another thing which

FINJAN AND ZARF.

Loud
speaking. surprises me is the vehemence of the speakers. When fairly roused, all talk together at the top of their voices, and a great way above anything of the kind I have ever heard. Noticing my surprise, one said to me, "You Americans talk as if you were afraid to be heard, and we as if we feared we should not be." Indeed, it is an incessant tempest of grating gutturals, which sets one's teeth on edge ; and, in addition, head and shoulders, hands and feet, the whole

body, in fact, is wrought up into violent action to enforce the orator's meaning. CHAPTER
I wonder how you comprehend a single sentence. IX.

We are used to it; and, unless a stranger calls attention to that which has
confounded you, we never notice it. I wish you could have understood the
discussions, for they embraced some of those grand and solemn themes which
can and ought to stir the deepest fountains of feeling in the human breast.
The Arabs delight in such questions.

My two young friends, who speak English, kept me aware of the leading
topics as they came up; but it was a great annoyance not to be able to appreciate the remarks which so interested the company. We finally took a corner
to ourselves, and fell into an extended comparison between Oriental and
Western manners and customs. They maintained that we had invented and Eastern
shaped ours on purpose to contradict theirs—theirs, the original; ours, copies and West-
reversed or caricatured. Of course, the weighty questions about beards, and ners.
moustaches, and shaved heads, were duly discussed, with respect to beauty, convenience, cleanliness, and health. Escaping from this tangle of the beard, we
fell into another about long garments, and short, tight, and loose; and here
they were confident of victory. Our clothes seem to them uncomfortable and
immodest; and this is about the truth, if we must sit "asquat" on our heels,
as the Orientals do; but with chairs and sofas, their objection has but little
force, while for active life our fashion is far the best. Long, loose clothes are
ever in the way, working, walking, or riding; and I suspect that they aid materially in producing that comparative inactivity which distinguishes Orientals
from Occidentals. As to the mere matter of comeliness, we may admit their
claim to some apparent superiority. The lords of the easel and the chisel with
the sons of song in every age and country, have so decreed, and it is vain to
resist.

These matters of dress and costume have a certain Biblical interest, and Dress and
therefore form a necessary part of our study. The first garments were manu- costume.
factured by God himself, and, in addition to their primary intention, had, as I
believe, a typical significance. The skins with which the two first sinners,
penitent and reconciled, were clothed, were those of the lambs offered in sacrifice, and not obscurely symbolized the robes of righteousness purchased for
penitent believers by the sacrifice of the *Lamb* of God on Calvary. And in
many subsequent incidents and institutions, garments are invested with a
religious and typical signification. Such facts elevate the subject far above
the category of mere trivialities. But, indeed, that cannot be a matter of
indifference to the Christian student and philosopher in which all men, all
women, all children, of every age and country, have, do, and will, to the end
of time, feel a deep solicitude, and upon which is expended an infinite amount
of time, money, and labour. It would be a curious exercise of ingenuity to
trace out the very gradual development of human costume, from the first fig-
leaves and coats of skins, to the complicated toilets of a highly-civilized society.
We, however, must restrict ourselves to the Bible.

The list is not extensive until the times of the later prophets. Aprons of fig-leaves, man's first vain invention to hide the nakedness of sin—coats of skin, given in mercy by our heavenly Father—cloaks, mantles, shirts, breeches, girdles, bonnets, and sandals, invented at various dates, and most of them consecrated to religious purposes by Moses in the garments of the Hebrew priesthood—these constitute almost the entire wardrobe for the first three thousand years of man's history. The fact is, that the whole subject is much more doubtful and obscure than most people suppose. The ancient Hebrew costume is thought to have resembled, more or less closely, the Oriental dress of our day. But *which?* I would like to know. It differs more than that of Western nations. We shall select that of the Syrian Arab, which in all probability does actually approach nearest to that of the patriarchs; and with the aid of engravings, accompanied by explanations, the size and shape of the various articles, as well as

SYRIAN GENTLEMEN IN FULL DRESS.

the ordinary mode of wearing them, will be sufficiently apparent. You need not attempt to remember, or even pronounce the Arabic names; but it is difficult to talk about nameless things, and therefore we cannot dispense with these hard words.

LIST OF GARMENTS, WITH THEIR ARABIC NAMES EXPLAINED

Kŭmis, inner shirt, of cotton, linen, or silk. Those of the Bedawîn are long, loose, and made of strong cotton cloth,—the most important item in their wardrobe.

Libās, inner drawers of cotton cloth.

Shintiān, drawers, very full.

Sherwāl, very large, loose pantaloons.

Dikky, a cord or sash with which the pantaloons are gathered and tied round the waist.

Suderîyeh, an inner waistcoat, without sleeves, buttoned up to the neck.

Mintiān, an inner jacket, worn over the suderîyeh, overlapping in front,—has pockets for purse, handkerchief, &c.

Gumbāz or *Kŭftān,* long open gown of cotton or silk, overlapping in front, girded tightly above the loins by the zŭnnār.

Zŭnnār, girdle of leather, camels' hair, cotton, silk, or woollen shawls.

Sŭlta, an outer jacket worn over the gŭmbaz.

Kŭbrān, a stout, heavy jacket, with open sleeves fastened on at the shoulder by buttons.

Jibbeh, Jŭkh, Benîsh, a long loose robe or mantle, with short sleeves, very full, used in full dress.

'Aba, 'Abaiyeh, Meshleh, a strong, coarse cloak, of various forms and materials. The 'abaiyeh is often short, and richly ornamented with gold and silver thread inwoven with the cloth. The most common are made of black sackcloth, of goats' or camels' hair, very large, so that the owner wraps himself in it to sleep.

Bŭrnûs, long loose cloak of white wool, with a hood to cover the head. It is sometimes called mŭgrabîn, from the Algerîn Arabs.

DRESS OF WORKING CLASS.

PART
I.

For the *head* there is, first, the—

'Arŭkîyeh or *Takîyeh*, a cotton cap fitting closely to the head, whether shaven or not. If the head is shaved, a soft felt cap is often worn under the takîyeh.

Tarbush or *Fez*, a thick red felt cap. The best come from Algiers.

Turban, a shawl of wool, silk, or cotton, wound round the tarbush. The Turks now wear nothing but the fez, and many Arabs nothing but the tarbush, with its long tassel. Others have a small coloured handkerchief (*mandeel*) tied round the tarbush. The Bedawîn have a heavier article, woven with golden tissue, thrown over the tarbush, and confined there by a twisted rope of goats' or camels' hair, called 'Akal. This is a picturesque and very distinctive article in the costume of a genuine Arab of the Desert.

For the *feet* there is, first,—

Jerabât or *Kalsât*, socks or stockings of every variety.

Kalshîn, inner slippers of soft leather, yellow or black.

Sŭrmaiyeh, shoes, commonly of red morocco.

Bâbúje, a kind of half slipper, answering in part to the ancient sandal, which is not now used.

Jezmeh, boots of red morocco, very stout and clumsy.

There are many variations and additions to this list in different parts of the vast regions inhabited by the Arab race; they are, however, only slight departures from the general types and patterns given above, and need not be described. The Mamlûk dress is considered very graceful by Europeans. It is the official costume of the army and navy of Egypt, or was in the days of Mohammed Ali.

Mamlûk dress.

To the Biblical student, these matters are specially interesting so far only as they throw light on the sacred Scriptures; but this they do in very many passages. For example, it was the 'aba or meshleh, I suppose, with which Shem and Japheth covered the nakedness of their father.[1] It was the Jibbeh that Joseph left in the hands of that shameless wife of Potiphar, called Zuleîka, according to Moslem tradition.[2] This jibbeh may answer to the mantle which fell from Elijah, and was taken up by Elisha;[3] to the cloak in the precept, "If a man will sue thee at the law, and take away thy *coat*, let him have thy cloak also."[4] The *coat* is probably the sŭlta. It was this jibbeh that our Saviour laid aside when he washed the feet of the disciples.[5] It can be so worn, or taken off, or torn in grief or rage, as to answer every mention of it in the Bible. The same remark applies to the zŭnnâr or girdle, to the sŭrmaiyeh and bâbúj—the shoes and sandals—and, in fact, to all other articles of dress which we have described.

Different garments referred to in Bible.

By the time of Moses, the costume, I presume, had attained to about its present state among tribes purely Oriental; I mean as to pattern, not as to the number, nature, and quality of the materials. These have greatly multiplied and improved, both in variety and fineness of fabrics.

[1] Gen. ix. 23.   [2] Gen. xxxix. 12.   [3] 2 Kings ii. 8, 13
[4] Matt. v. 40.   [5] John xiii. 4.

The toilet of the ladies corresponds in most respects to that of the men,
with, of course, certain ad-
ditions. As was to be expected, it developed faster
than the other. Even during the life of Jacob there
were habits appropriate to
maids, others to married
women, and others again for
widows ; such, too, as distinguished those who were
honest, and another habit
for those who were other-
wise. This implies a great
variety in female attire ;
and thus it went on en-
larging, until their toilets
became as complicated and
mysterious in Jerusalem as
they now are in Paris or
New York. In the 3d
chapter of Isaiah we have
a catalogue, about as in-
telligible to the English
reader as the Hebrew seems
to have been to our translators : Cawls, round tires like
the moon, sweet balls, muf-
flers or spangled ornaments,
tablets or houses of the soul,[1]
etc., etc., etc. It would require half a volume to discuss these names, and then
they would be about as unintelligible as when we began.

DRESS OF SYRIAN OR EGYPTIAN LADY.

I cannot muster sufficient
.courage to enter minutely into the female costume, nor is it necessary. It
varies from that of the men mostly in the veils, which are very various, and
in the head-dress, which with the tarbush for the basis, is complicated by an
endless variety of jewels and other ornamental appendages ; these, however,
appear in the engravings, and can be better studied there than on the persons

[1] Isa. iii. 18-23

who wear them. You will not easily get permission to inspect them there. To ask it would be, in most cases, a serious insult.

Patri-
archal
dress.

HEAD-DRESS.

It is a remarkable fact, that after the first mention of coats in Genesis iii. 21, we hear no more about garments of any kind for sixteen or eighteen hundred years. Shem and Japheth, after the Deluge, had a garment so large that they laid it on each of their shoulders, in order to cover the nakedness of their drunken father without beholding his shame. Several hundred years later—in Abraham's day—we read of shoes, and of raiment presented to Rebekah ; and she covered herself with a veil when Isaac met her. Later in life, she had *goodly* raiment of her son Esau with her in the house. Then comes the coat of many colours, the occasion of sad calamities to Joseph ; Reuben, not finding the lad in the pit, *rent* his clothes—the first time this action is mentioned. Jacob also rent his; and in after ages this expression of grief becomes common, as the fabrics out of which the garments were made became of a finer texture, and more easily torn.

The ma-
terials.

The materials first used were skins of animals, and many people are clothed with them at this day. Afterward linen and woollen fabrics were invented; and coarse cloth woven from the hair of camels and goats. Silk is mentioned in Proverbs xxxi. 22, and in Ezekiel xvi. 10, 13, but I suppose hemp is

Linen—
woollen—
cotton.

meant. There is no reason to suppose that Solomon's "virtuous wife" was acquainted with silk ; nor was cotton known to the Jews until after the captivity. Possibly the mās or masi of Ezekiel was cotton. The Egyptians, and of course the Hebrews, were early skilled in embroidery with tissue of silver and gold ; and Orientals are still extravagantly fond of embroidered garments. As to *fine*-twined linen, so celebrated among the Israelites in the wilderness and elsewhere, we must understand the term relatively. All Egyptian linen is coarse, and always was to judge from the wrappings of

ancient mummies, even of kings. The favourite colours, as every reader of
the Bible knows, were blue, and purple, and scarlet; and the same taste prevails
in Syria, and in the East generally, to this day.

Let us turn philosophers in a small way while we look further into these Philoso-
Oriental manners, customs, and costumes.   Search deep enough, and I phy of
believe you will generally find that the customs of every people are the dress.
joint result of many causes acting together—a great network of necessity and
compensation. The Oriental costume, for example, is light and loose, because
the climate is warm. They do not sit on chairs, because they are hard, perpendicular, and uncomfortable, and the relaxed system in this country requires
an easier and more recumbent posture to insure rest and refreshment. Under
these circumstances tight garments are very inconvenient and incongruous.

Then, as you observe, they scrupulously drop their slippers, shoes, or boots
at the door when they enter a room, and keep on their head-dress. This
seems strange to us, but it is necessary. As they sit on the mat, rug, or divan,
with their feet under them, shoes would soil both couch and clothes, and, besides, would make a very uncomfortable seat. The demands of decency and

SHOES—BOOTS—KUBKOBS.

the calls of comfort introduced and enforced the custom of dropping the shoe Putting off
at the entrance into the sitting-room, and it was thence extended to every shoes.
place entitled to respect. From this to the idea of defilement from the shoe
was but a step, and certain to be taken. Hence the strict requisition to put
it off on entering temples and sacred places of every kind. Mohammedans
have preserved this idea in all its force, and you cannot enter any of their
mosques or holy shrines with your shoes on. This custom was probably
established in Egypt before Moses was born, and he was trained up to regard
it as obligatory. When, therefore, God appeared to him in the burning bush, Moses at
he needed only to be reminded that the place whereon he stood was holy the burn-
ground, to make the direction to put off his shoe at once intelligible and ing bush.
reasonable. And, so long as the Oriental custom of sitting on the mat or rug
is kept up, so long will it be necessary to drop the shoe at the door ; and
being necessary in *private, domestic life*, it would be disrespectful and con-
temptuous to enter holy places with them on. The custom is reasonable and
right, and we should not hesitate to conform to it. Then the people keep
their head-dress on, both because the shaven and naked rotundity requires to

be concealed, and also for the sake of health. Always covered and closely shaved, the head becomes tender, and liable to colds on the least exposure. The shaving of the head, I suppose, had reference originally to cleanliness, and to avoid scab and other cutaneous diseases, which are extremely prevalent, and difficult to subdue.

Ours, no doubt, is the highest style and the better way. It is better to keep the head clean and cool, and accustomed to bear change of temperature, with only the beautiful covering which God has spread over it. It is also best and most becoming to keep the feet covered and warm. But in this climate people do not often suffer from cold feet ; and the demands of decency are secured by strictly covering them under their loose garments. The ablutions which Mohammed required before public worship have as much reference to propriety as to spiritual or ceremonial purity. With soiled shoes or filthy feet, the performance of Mohammedan prayer, with its genuflections and prostrations, would be an exhibition of positive indecency ; and, without washing, the odour from hundreds of naked feet would be intolerable. Becomingly dressed in loose, flowing robes, and thoroughly cleansed hands, feet, and face, their prayers are not only decent, but striking and solemn. The dress of Oriental ladies is not so easily defended. It is not so full as ours,—shows more the shape of the person; and, while the face is veiled, the bosom is exposed in a way not at all in accordance with our ideas of propriety. But a general remark will help to explain the origin or basis of this seeming inconsistency. Those who set the female fashions of the East are not expected or allowed to mix in society with men, nor even to be seen by them. When they go abroad, they are closely veiled from head to foot. Their in-door dress is not contrived to meet the demands of a public exhibition. The reasons (and such there are) for thus confining the women very much to their homes, and of closely veiling them when abroad, are found in the character of Oriental people from remote ages; and the veils can never be safely abolished, nor these domestic regulations relaxed, until a pure and enlightened Christianity has prepared the way. If I had the power to remove them at once, I would not. They are a necessary compensation for true modesty in both sexes. When, therefore, you find no ladies to welcome and entertain you in your calls, and never see them in our evening gatherings, you may moderate your regret by the reflection that this is the result of a great moral necessity. The same necessity forbids a gentleman to walk arm in arm with a lady. She has no arm at liberty; and if she had, the proprieties of life would be shocked by such an action. Neither can a man in many families eat with his wife and daughters, because the meal is in the public room, and often before strange men. So, also, the ladies are accommodated in church with a part railed off, and latticed to shield them from public gaze. Moslem women never join in the prayers at the mosques.

These customs are often carried out into exaggerations and extremes by pride and jealousy, and then they are not only absurd, but barbarous. For example, a Druse sheikh, or wealthy Moslem, when he calls a physician for any of his *harem*, makes a great mystery of the matter. The poor creature is closely veiled, and if the doctor insists upon seeing her tongue, there is much cautious manœuvring to avoid exposure. I have even known cases where the tongue was thrust through a rent in the veil made for the purpose! This is sufficiently absurd, and yet I am acquainted with a sheikh who carries these jealous precautions to a still more ridiculous extreme. He never allows his women to go out of the harem (women's apartments) except at night, and not then until servants are sent ahead to clear the roads.

CHAPTER IX.

A doctor's visit.

The reluctance of even enlightened Christian men to speak of the females of their families is amusing to us, and certainly not very complimentary to the ladies. For example, according to the genuine old régime, a man, when absent from home, never writes to his wife, but to his son, if he have one, though not a month old ; and often he addresses his letter to a fictitious son, whom for the time he imagines he has, or ought to have ; and if he meets any one direct from home, he will inquire after everybody but his wife. She must not be mentioned, even though she is known to be sick. At such customs we can afford to smile, but there are others which admit of no excuse or apology. They are infamous, and degrading to the sex. The Arabs have a word— "ajellack "—by which they preface the mention of anything indelicate or unclean. Thus, ajellack a donkey, or a dog, or my shoes ; so, when compelled to speak of their women, they say, "Ajellack my woman," or simply "The woman is so and so." This is abominable, and springs from thoughts still more so. These and similar customs enable us to understand why it is that acquaintance before marriage is ordinarily out of the question. It could not be secured without revolutionizing an extended system of domestic regulations and compensations ; and, if attempted rashly, would open the door to immorality and corruption. Therefore, the present plan of arranging matters matrimonial through the intervention of friends and relatives, as it was in times most remote, must be continued, with all its evils, until a wide and general change is brought about in the condition of the women. This must be gradual, and can only be safely effected by a truly Christian education, and by a great purification and elevation of the marriage institution.

Degradation of females.

It is considered quite immodest for an unmarried lady to manifest any special regard for her future husband. The first thought seems to be that of pollution. This is a great and fatal error, fruitful in evils of many kinds. But we need not pursue this subject any further. Our object is to notice manners and customs which reveal the interior economy of Oriental society, and which, in one way or another, serve to elucidate the numerous allusions to such matters in the Bible.

The birth of a son is always a joyful event in a family, but that of a daughter is often looked upon as a calamity. The husband and father refuses to see his child, or speak to the mother ; and the friends and relatives, *particularly the females*, upbraid the innocent sufferer, and condole with the unkind husband, as if he were very badly treated. Worse than this, in those communities where

Children sons and daughters

PART
I.

divorce is permitted, this is often the only reason assigned by the brutal husband for sending away his wife. This accounts for the intense desire which many of these poor creatures manifest to become the mother of sons,—not a whit less vehement than that of Rachel, who said to Jacob, " Give me children, or else I die." [1] They also employ the same kind of means to compass their object that were used thousands of years ago. Not only do they resort to all sorts of quacks and medical empirics for relief, but make vows, as did Samuel's mother in Shiloh, when she was in bitterness of soul, and wept sore, and vowed a vow unto the Lord.[2] They also make numerous pilgrimages to such shrines as have obtained a reputation in these matters. Among Moselms, where

Polygamy.

polygamy is tolerated, and particularly in Egypt, as Lane informs us, instances are not wanting in which wives have acted as Sarah did to Abraham, and Leah and Rachel to Jacob. But these devices, which produced such great irregularities and heart-burnings in the families of the patriarchs, are equally mischievous at the present day. The circumstance mentioned in Genesis xvi. 4, which made Hagar insolent toward her mistress, has the same effect now. If the first wife has no children, the husband marries another or takes a slave ; and it not unfrequently happens that the fortunate slave, when the mother of a son, is promoted to the post of honour and authority,—which she, of course, uses with insolence toward her former mistress. The whole system is productive of evil, and that only, to the individual, the family, and the community.

Many singular customs grow out of this high appreciation of children. One is the frequency and want of modesty in talking about a subject which is banished from the list of conversable topics with us. In this country, it is now discussed just as it was in Bible days, and in exactly the same terms. Another

Assumption of son's name.

odd custom is, that the father assumes the name of his first-born son. Tannûs, the father of the infant Besharah, for example, is no longer Tannûs, but *Abu* Besharah, and this not merely in common parlance, but in legal documents and on all occasions. It is, in fact, no longer respectful to call him Tannûs. So, also, the mother is ever afterward called *Em* Besharah, "mother of Besharah." And still more absurd, when a man is married and has no son, the world gives him one by a courtesy peculiarly Oriental, and then calls him by his supposed son's name. Even unmarried men are often dignified by the honourable title of Abu somebody or other, the name bestowed being decided by that which he previously bore. Thus Elias becomes Abu Nasîf, Butrus is called Abu Salim, and so on, according to the established custom of naming first-born sons.

13*th.* I noticed that the friend at whose house we dined last evening sent a servant to call us when dinner was ready. Is this custom generally observed ?

Not very strictly among the common people, nor in cities, where Western

---

[1] Gen. xxx. 1.   [2] 1 Sam. i. 10, 11.

manners have greatly modified the Oriental; but in Lebanon it still prevails. CHAPTER If a sheikh, beg, or emeer invites, he always sends a servant to call you at the IX. proper time. This servant often repeats the very formula mentioned in Luke Calling to xiv. 17: "Tefŭddŭlû, el 'asha hâder"—"Come, for the supper is ready." a feast. The fact that this custom is mainly confined to the wealthy and to the nobility is in strict agreement with the parable, where the certain man who made the great supper, and bade many, is supposed to be of this class. It is true now, as then, that to refuse is a high insult to the maker of the feast, nor would such excuses as those in the parable be more acceptable to a Druse emeer than they were to the lord of this " great supper ;" but, however angry, very few would manifest their displeasure by sending the servants into the highwáys and hedges after the poor, the maimed, the halt, and the blind. All these characters are found in abundance in our streets, and I have known rich men who filled out the costume of the parable even in these particulars ; it was, however, as matter of ostentation, to show the extent of their benevolence, and the depth of their humility and condescension. Nevertheless, it is pleasant to find enough of the drapery of this parable still practised to show that originally it was, in all its details, in close conformity to the customs of this country.

The discussion the other evening about names interested me not a little, as illustrating ancient customs in this matter. Nearly all Bible names were Bible significant, and were conferred with reference to some circumstance connected names. with the birth of the child. Such things carry one back to the households of the patriarchs. Leah called her first-born Reuben, for she said, " The Lord hath looked upon my affliction ;" the second was named Simeon—*hearing*, for the Lord had heard her prayer ; and thus it was to the end of the list.

The customs are identical, and so are many of the names ; but the Arabs Arabian. have others to which they are very partial. The non-Christian sects often give some derivative of Hamed—*praise;* now generally in honour of Mohammed, their prophet, but not so originally. All sects join the name of God to one of his attributes, or to some other word, in order to make agreeable names for their children. Thus, Fudle Allah—God's bounty; 'Abd Allah—servant of God. So the word deen—religion—enters into many favourite names; as Hasn ed Deen—beauty of religion; Ameen ed Deen—faithful in religion; Fukhr ed Deen—glory of religion ; Sŭlah ed Deen—goodness of religion, contracted by us into Saladin, the antagonist of England's lion-hearted Richard, and the terror of Crusaders.

For daughters, the Arabs are fond of flowery and poetic names. We have Poetical all about us, among servants, washerwomen, and beggars, suns, and stars, and names of daughters. full moons, and roses, and lilies, and jessamines, and diamonds, and pearls, and every other beautiful epithet you can think of. And, as the parents assume the names of their children, we hear these poor creatures addressed continually as *The-father-of-God's-bounty* (Abu Fudle Allah), and the *Mother-of-the-Full-Moon*, etc. etc., through the whole list of poetic fancies.

Families
sleeping
together.

There are many minor matters in which the East and the West are as far apart socially as they are geographically. For example, a whole family, parents, children, and servants, sleep in the same room, and with slight change of garments, or none at all. Both these customs are alluded to in the Bible. The first in the plea of the lazy man in the parable about importunity: " My *children are with me* in bed; I cannot arise and give thee;"[1] and the second is implied in the reason assigned by Moses for the return of a garment taken in pledge from a poor man *before the sun goes down:* " It is his covering of his flesh; wherein shall he sleep ?"[2] The long, loose garments worn by this people remove, or at least mitigate, the impropriety of this practice; but with all that, it is objectionable. So, also, a whole family continue to reside under the same roof, father, sons, and grandsons, in one common household. This also is ancient; but it is very repugnant to our ideas, and has many disadvantages. Nor does the fact that they can live cheaper by such a common-stock arrangement compensate for the confusion and want of family government occasioned by the system. There never can be well-regulated households until this custom is broken up, or so modified as to call forth greater personal responsibility and independence in the younger branches of the family.

Serving
dinner.

Orientals are also far behind the day in almost every branch of domestic economy, especially in table furniture and their mode of eating. The general custom, even of the better classes, is to bring a polygonal stool, about fourteen inches high, into the common sitting-room. On this is placed a tray of basket-work or of metal, generally copper, upon which the food is arranged. The bread lies on the mat beneath the tray, and a cruse of water stands near by, from which all drink as they have need. On formal occasions, this is held in

Dishes.

SCAMLA OR TABLE.

the hand by a servant, who waits upon the guests. Around this stool and tray the guests gather, sitting on the floor. The dishes are most generally stews of rice, beans, *burgul* (cracked wheat), with soups or sauces as the case may be, in deep dishes or bowls. Some use wooden or metal spoons for their stews and thick soups, but the most common mode is to double up bits of their thin bread, spoon fashion, and dip them into the dish. There is fre-

---

[1] Luke xi. 5–8.   [2] Exod. xxii. 27.

quent reference to this custom in some of the most interesting and some of the CHAPTER
most solemn scenes of the Bible. The richer sort use silver spoons; but they   IX.
have neither knives nor forks, nor do they know how to use them. This is a Spoons.
very meagre set-out certainly; but they will tell you that it is all they want, and No knives
is every way more convenient than our custom, and immeasurably less expensive. or forks.
High tables and chairs would not only be out of place at the time, but in the way
at all times. They do not have a separate dining-room, and hence they want an
apparatus that can be easily brought in and removed, and this they have.
They all eat out of the same dish, and why not? It is within reach, and it
gives a better relish to dip their thin bread into the general hot mess, than to
take out a portion on separate plates and use spoons. As their meat is always
cut up into stews, or else cooked until it is ready to fall to pieces, knives and
forks are useless; and when they have chickens, they are easily torn to pieces
with their fingers. Nor do they see any vulgarity in this. The *very* polite *à
la mode* Oriental will tear up the best bits, and either lay them next you, or
insist on putting them into your mouth. I have had this done for me by

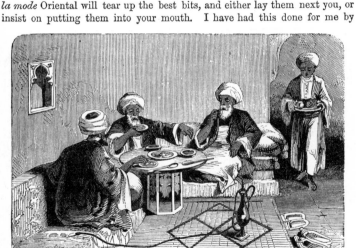

PARTY AT DINNER.

digits not particularly fair, or even clean. You observe that things correspond
with one another. And there is this great economic advantage in their way, Economy
that it demands much less labour than ours. If our system were introduced at of labour.
once, and the females of the family (who do all the work) were required to carry
it out correctly and decently, their labour would be increased tenfold. Not
only must an entirely new apparatus be procured, and kept clean and bright,
but also the table, table-linen, and chairs, and the separate room must be provided. Indeed, an entirely new and foreign department must be instituted

PART
L.

Imitation
of the
West.

and maintained under every disadvantage. Where this has been attempted in the families of native consuls, and others aping European manners, it has generally proved a miserable failure. The knives, forks, and spoons are rusty; the plates, dishes, and glasses ill-assorted, dirty, badly arranged, and not in sufficient quantity; the chairs are rickety, and the table stands on legs spasmodic and perilous. The whole thing, in short, is an uncomfortable burlesque or a provoking caricature. Then the cookery must be Frank as well as the furniture, which is worst of all. I have stood in terror before some of these compounds of dyspepsia and night-mare. No, no; let the Arabs retain their own commissary and dietetic regulations, at least until things are better prepared for a change than at present. In their own way their cooking is good, and their set-out respectable.

Washing
hands.

Of course, after such a meal as we have described, washing the hands and mouth is indispensable (it ought to be before, but is not), and the ibrîek and tûsht—their pitcher and ewer—are always brought, and the servant, with a napkin over his shoulder, pours on your hands.

Servants
to pour
water.

If there is no servant, they perform this office for each other. Great men have those about them whose special business is to pour water on their hands. Thus it was in ancient times. One of the servants said to Jehoshaphat, "Here is Elisha, the son of Shaphat, which poured water on the hands of Elijah."[1]

It was an apparatus somewhat like this tûsht and ibrîek that our Lord used at the close of his last supper with his disciples, when he girded himself with a napkin, and washed, not their hands, but their feet, and thus gave the most affecting lesson on humility the world has ever seen or heard.

There are many minor contrasts, some of which are rather amusing. When friends meet, they do not *shake* hands, but strike the tips of the fingers together, and sometimes grasp tightly the whole hand. If it is a priest, emeer, or high

WASHING HANDS.

Kissing
hands.

officer of any kind, the back of the hand must be kissed. This is strictly

[1] 2 Kings iii. 11.

enforced, and the neglect or refusal is a great offence. The clergy are particularly stringent in claiming this mark of respect. The more common mode of salutation is to raise the hand to the breast, or to the lips and forehead. Friends who have been long separated embrace, and kiss either one or both cheeks and generally each shoulder. This kissing among men strikes us as very odd, but there are numberless references to it in the Bible. The " brethren " are often enjoined by the apostles to salute one another with the kiss of brotherly love and holy charity. The women kiss each other on all occasions, and *ad nauseam;* but the different sexes are very reserved in their mutual salutations, and do not even touch each other's hands.

Arab ladies, particularly the married, are extravagantly fond of silver and gold ornaments; and they have an endless variety of chains, bracelets, anklets, necklaces, and rings. It is also quite common to see thousands of piastres, in various coins around the forehead, suspended from the neck, and covering a

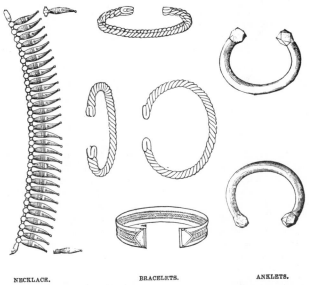

NECKLACE.　　　　　BRACELETS.　　　　　ANKLETS.

system of net-work, called sŭffa, attached to the back of the head-dress, which spreads over the shoulders, and falls down to the waist. These jewels cannot be taken for the husband's debts. A poor man often goes to prison for a few piastres, while thousands glitter and jingle on the dress of his wife. This is very provoking to the creditor, who knows that his money has been purposely attached to these inviolable ornaments, so that he may not get hold of it.

PART
I.

Fondness
of married
women
for orna-
ments.

Married women are much more eager after ornaments than unmarried. The former also adorn themselves more elaborately, and endeavour to add to their beauty by wearing gay flowers, by painting their cheeks, putting kahl around their eyes, and arching their eyebrows with the same, and by staining their hands and feet with *henna*. It is considered indelicate for the unmarried thus to deck themselves, and conveys an impression highly injurious to the girl's

NECKLACE.   EAR-DROPS.

moral character. They do not even wash their faces, or at least not openly. It is one of the strange anomalies of Oriental society that the tailors make the ladies' dresses ; but, as their garments are infinitely large, and never designed to fit, there is no measuring needed, nor trying on of garments under the hand and eye of the tailor. This, in some degree, removes the objections on the score of delicacy, but not on that of propriety and economy.

Inequality
of women.

Oriental women are never regarded or treated as equals by the men. This is seen on all occasions ; and it requires some firmness to secure to our own ladies proper respect, especially from men-servants. They pronounce women to be weak and inferior in the most absolute terms; and in accordance with this idea is their deportment toward them. Even in polite company the gentlemen must be served first. So the husband and brothers sit down and eat, and the wife, mother, and sisters wait and take what is left. If the husband or the brothers accompany their female relatives anywhere, they walk before, and the women follow at a respectful distance. It is very common to see small boys lord it over both mother and sisters in a most insolent manner, and they are encouraged to do so by the father. The evils resulting from this are incalculable. The men, however, attempt to justify their treatment of the CHAPTER women by the tyrant's plea of necessity. They are obliged to govern the IX. wives with the utmost strictness, or they would not only ruin their husbands, but themselves also. Hence they literally use the rod upon them, especially The rod. when they have, or imagine they have, cause to doubt the wife's fidelity. Instances are not rare in which the husband kills the wife outright for this cause, and no legal notice is taken of the murder; and, in general, the man relies on fear to keep the wife in subjection, and to restrain her from vice. She is confined closely, watched with jealousy, and everything valuable is kept under lock and key; necessarily so, they say, for the wife will not hesitate to rob her husband if she gets an opportunity. There are many pleasing exceptions, especially among the younger Christian families. But, on the whole, the cases are rare where the husband has not, at some time or other, resorted to the lash to enforce obedience in his rebellious household. Most Neglect of sensible men readily admit that this whole system is a miserable compensa- education. tion to mitigate evils flowing from the very great crime of neglecting the education of females; and, during the last few years, a change has taken Improve- place in public sentiment on this subject among the intelligent Christians in ment. Lebanon and the cities along the coast, and a strong desire to educate the females is fast spreading among them.

Among these minor manners and matters, we are always struck with their writing materials, and their mode of using them. They do not carry inkhorns now, as the prophets and scribes of old did, but have an apparatus consisting of a metal or ebony tube for their reed pens, with a cup or bulb of the same material, attached to the upper end, for the ink. This they thrust through the girdle, and carry with them at all times. When they are to write a letter, for example, they open the lid of the ink-bulb, draw out a long reed pen from the tube, double over the paper, and begin from the right side of the page, holding the paper in the hand without any other support. They have a stereotyped introduction, overloaded with flowers and compliments, and richly seasoned with love, no matter to whom they are writing, friend or enemy. After this rigmarole, which, if it have any mean-

Writing apparatus.

WRITING MATERIALS.

ing, is an egregious lie, they make a formal epitome of the letter which they are to answer, repeating it, word for word, as is so often done in the Bible. They date at the bottom, but rarely mention the place; and I have often been at a loss to discover who the writer was, and where to address my reply. Young men of business in the cities are adopting our mode of dating. Nearly every-

PART
I.

An open
letter.

Sandals of
females.

Sitting at
work.

Knocking.

Standing.

body wears a seal-ring, on the finger, suspended from his watch-chain, or attached to his purse, having his name engraven upon it; and this he affixes to all important letters and papers—another Biblical custom preserved in all its extent. If you wish to be very respectful, you must take a large sheet, and the lines should incline upward toward the left corner of the paper. It must be folded long, like documents on file, placed within a nicely-cut envelope made for the occasion, and the address written across the letter. It *must be sealed.* The *open* letter, therefore, or paper sent by Sanballat to Nehemiah (vi. 5) was an insult. Arabic books, both manuscript and printed, begin where ours end, their first page being our last.

The females in many places wear only sandals, which they easily drop whenever they step on a mat or rug. In other places they walk on "kŭbkobs," a wooden sandal, elevated on upright bits of board, sometimes, as in Damascus, a foot high, which make a great clattering and stamping on the pavement. These are dropped at the door of the room, and the lady descends from what seems rather a perilous elevation. The Damascus kŭbkobs are very prettily ornamented with mother-of-pearl, and the band which passes over the foot is often worked with pearls and other rich ornaments.

The people of this country *sit* at all kinds of work. The carpenter saws, planes, and hews with his hand-adze sitting on the ground or upon the plank he is planing. The washer-woman *sits* by the tub; and, in a word, no one stands where it is possible to sit. Shopkeepers always sit; and Levi *sitting* at the receipt of custom is the exact way to state the case.[1] There are no ladies' saddles in Syria, and the women ride just as do the men,—which appears to us not only ungraceful, but not even modest. Though Orientals are very jealous of their privacy, yet they never knock when about to enter your room, but walk in without warning or ceremony. It is nearly impossible to teach an Arab servant to knock at your door. They give warning at the outer gate, or entrance, either by calling or knocking. To stand and *call* is a very common and very respectful mode; and thus it was in Bible times, and to it there are many very interesting allusions. Moses commanded the holder of a pledge to stand without, and call to the owner thereof to come forth.[2] This was to avoid the insolent intrusion of cruel creditors. Peter stood knocking at the outer door,[3] and so did the three men sent to Joppa by Cornelius.[4] The idea is that the guard over your privacy is to be placed at the entrance to your premises. But this discussion of manners and customs has taken a very wide range, and grows heavy on our hands. It is a topic, however, which will be constantly suggested by what passes before our eyes, and it is well to become familiar with it at the outset.

[1] Matt. ix. 9.   [2] Deut. xxiv. 10.   [3] Acts xii. 13, 16.   [4] Acts x. 17, 18.

CHAPTER X.

FROM SIDON TO SARAFEND.*

Sea storms.	Temples—Tombs.
Gold coins—Hid Treasures.	High places—Groves.
A Phœnician sarcophagus.	Ploughing.
Inscription—Translation.	Misrule of the country.

February 14th.

"He maketh the storm a calm."—Ps. cvii. 29.

"How calm, how beautiful comes on
The stilly hour when storms are gone;
When warring winds have died away,
And clouds beneath the glancing ray
Melt off, and leave the land and sea
Sleeping in bright tranquillity!"

EVERY vestige of yesterday's commotion has disappeared, and we are riding Sea along this celebrated "coast of Tyre and Sidon," with "the body of heaven in storms his clearness like a paved work of sapphire" overhead, and the Mediterranean, but now so agitated and angry, lying at our feet gentle and calm as infancy asleep. No wonder that Hebrew poets refer to sea and storm to illustrate the might and majesty of Jehovah.

Yes; and it was this very sea that kindled their inspiration—this Mediter- Bible allu- ranean, lashed into fury by such a storm as we have witnessed, that made the sions. sweet singer of Israel exclaim, "The floods have lifted up, O Lord, the floods have lifted up their voice; the floods lift up their waves. The Lord on high is mightier than the mighty waves of the sea. Thou stillest them."[1]

David, I suppose, was no sailor, never saw the ocean, and yet his sea-storm in the 107th Psalm is unrivalled in beauty, fidelity, and spirit: "They that go down to the sea in ships, that do business in great waters; these see the works of the Lord, and his wonders in the deep. For he commandeth, and raiseth the stormy wind, which lifteth up the waves thereof. They mount up to heaven, they go down again to the depths: their soul is melted because of trouble. They reel to and fro, and stagger like a drunken man, and are at their wit's end. Then they cry unto the Lord in their trouble, and he bringeth them out of their distresses. He maketh the storm a calm, so that the waves thereof are still. Then are they glad because they be quiet; so he bringeth them unto their desired haven." And how appropriate the closing reflection:

---

* [The travellers proceed along the sea coast towards Sarafand, the representative of Zarephath or Sarepta of the Scriptures.—ED.]

[1] Ps. xciii. 3, 4.

PART
I.

"O that men would praise the Lord for his goodness, for his wonderful works to the children of men !"

It is indeed simple, natural, devout. David had witnessed the beginning, middle, and end of just such a storm as has been raging on the Mediterranean for the last fifteen days, or he would not have written this very graphic picture; and yet this is not the wildest specimen which our sea can offer. During the last days of 1840, there was one far more terrific and destructive. The British and allied fleets were then riding at anchor in the roadstead at Beirût, and the largest three-deckers were tossed about by the mighty billows like bits of cork. Many ships were thrown out on to the shore in that sort of contempt which means "there let him lie," according to Byron. The snow also came down the mountains, at that time, nearly to the shore, while now there is none on these lower ranges, though they are a thousand feet high and more.

Let me call your attention to this curious avenue of acacia-trees, the largest of the kind, I venture to say, that you have ever seen.

They are certainly remarkable specimens of vegetable architecture. Their crooked stems and muscular arms bend and twist in all directions after a fashion altogether original.

You may connect them in your memory with a circumstance which made no small stir in our good city of Sidon. About three years ago, some workmen, digging over the ground of this garden on our left, found several copper pots, which contained a large quantity of ancient gold coin. The poor fellows concealed the discovery with the greatest care, but they were wild with excitement, and, besides, there were too many of them to keep such a secret. The governor of the city heard of it, apprehended all who had not fled, and compelled them to disgorge. He recovered two of the pots, placed them beside him, and required them to refill them with coin. In this way he obtained between two and three thousand, but it is certain that there remain hundreds, if not thousands, which he could not get. The French consul told

COINS OF PHILIP AND ALEXANDER.

me that the whole number was over eight thousand. They are all coins of Alexander and his father Philip, of the most pure gold, each one worth a little more than an English sovereign. As there is no mixture of coins later than Alexander, the deposit must have been made during his reign, or immediately after. I suspect it was royal treasure, which one of Alexander's officers concealed when he heard of his unexpected death in Babylon, intending to appropriate it to himself, but, being apprehended, slain, or driven away by some of the revolutions which followed that

A storm in 1840.

Acacia-trees.

Discovery of gold coins.

event, the coin remained where he had hid it. If we remember how much CHAPTER
more valuable gold was then than now, the amount of this deposit will sur- X.
prise us, nor does it seem likely that any private man in Sidon could have Philip and
gathered what was probably at that time equivalent to forty thousand pounds, Alexander
and all of this particular coin of Philip and Alexander. The latter appears don.
as he is usually figured, and his face is too familiar to need explanation. Philip
I had not seen before, and was particularly pleased to find him associated with
the chariot and horses, of which he was so proud and so vain.

There are frequent allusions to hid treasure in the Bible. Even in Job, the Bible allu-
oldest book in the world, we read that the bitter in soul dig for death more sions to
earnestly than for hid treasures.[1] There is not another comparison within the sures.
whole compass of human actions so vivid as this. I have heard of diggers
actually fainting when they have come upon even a single coin. They become How they
positively frantic, dig all night with desperate earnestness, and continue to are dug
work till utterly exhausted. There are, at this hour, hundreds of persons thus
engaged all over the country. Not a few spend their last farthing in these
ruinous efforts. I heard a respectable man in Sidon declare that if he had
been one of those fortunate diggers in this garden, he would have killed all
the rest, and fled with the treasure out of the country. These operations are
carried on with the utmost secrecy, accompanied with charms and incantations
against the jan and other spirits which are said to keep guard over hid treasures. The belief in the existence of these guards, and of their dangerous
character, is just as prevalent now as in the time of the Thousand Nights.
Intelligent and respectable people have assured me that they have come upon Chambers.
slabs of stone, closing up doors to secret chambers, which no power on earth
could remove, because the proper pass-word or charm is lost. Others soberly
assert that they have been driven away by terrible jan, who threatened them
with instant death if they attempted to force the doors. They evidently believe what they say, and I suspect that their fears are not always imaginary.
Persons are watching their midnight labour, and when anything is found they
suddenly show themselves, dressed as ghouls or jan, and thus frighten them
out of the pit, and out of their wits as well. The wild excitement, the gloomy
darkness, and the firm faith in the existence of these creatures, render the
workmen wholly incapable of detecting the artifice. The Arabs universally
believe that the Western nations, particularly the Greeks and Mugharaby,
possess certain *daleel*, or guides, by which they discover these treasures; and
many of these vagabond Greeks cheat the ignorant and the credulous out of
large sums by contracting to lead them to the proper spot to dig; and it is
remarkable that they rarely point out a place entirely destitute of concealed
chambers and other curious indications. These, I suppose, are detected by
some peculiarity in the sounds when the surface is struck or stamped upon
above them. At any rate, they are sufficiently successful to keep up their

[1] Job iii. 21.

PART
I.
credit, although I never knew an instance where anything of value was obtained from the places indicated by these daleels. On the contrary, these deposits are always found by accident; and this is the more remarkable when it is remembered that multitudes are either secretly or openly searching for them all over the land. We shall be annoyed in all our rambles over ruins by the suspicion, almost universal among the people, that we are "seeking for hid treasures." Hence they will watch us, follow us, and, whenever a private opportunity offers, will endeavour to enter into partnership with us in the search.

Solomon's
Illustra-
tion.
Solomon has drawn a proverb from this practice : "If thou seekest her" (understanding) "as silver, and searchest for her as for hid treasure, then shalt thou understand the fear of the Lord, and find the knowledge of God."[1] Alas ! how few manifest any of this earnestness in seeking for wisdom.

Our blessed Lord also founds one of his divine parables on this same custom : "The kingdom of heaven is like unto treasure hid in a field; the which when a man hath found, he hideth, and for joy thereof goeth and selleth all that he hath, and buyeth that field."[2] Many such transactions are still negotiated in secret. It is extremely difficult, and even dangerous, to remove treasure thus discovered in another person's field; but, having purchased it, you can wait in safety, work in secret, and the coveted treasure is yours.

Hiding
treasure
in wars
and earth-
quakes.
It is not difficult to account for this hid treasure. This country has always been subject to revolutions, invasions, and calamities of various kinds, and hence a feeling of insecurity hovers over the land like a dismal spectre. The government robs, and so do the nobility and the clergy; Arabs rush in from the desert and plunder; warriors and conquerors from every part of the world sweep over the land, carrying everything away that falls into their hands. Then there are, and always have been, intestine commotions and wars, such as laid Lebanon in ruins in 1841, and again in 1845. At such times multitudes bury their gold and jewels, and in many cases the owners are killed, and no one knows where the treasure was concealed. Then, again, this country has ever been subject to earthquakes, which bury everything beneath her ruined cities.

Safed after
an earth-
quake.
On the first day of 1837, Safed was thus dashed to the ground in a moment, house upon house down the steep mountain side, and many entire families were cut off. Some were known to have had money, and it was a shocking spectacle to see hardened wretches prowling about under the ruins, amid putrefying carcases, in search of these treasures. The whole population from the surrounding villages, undeterred by the awful judgment which had laid their own buildings in heaps, and buried many of their families alive, rushed into Safed to dig out the entombed riches of the Jews; nor was the search in vain. The same shocking spectacle is witnessed in times of plague or cholera. People hide their money to keep it from those miscreants who take advantage of the general consternation to break into houses and rob. We need

---

[1] Prov. ii. 4.   [2] Matt. xiii. 44.

not be surprised, therefore, to find that this country abounds, and ever has abounded, in hid treasure. No custom can be found among any people so firmly rooted as this, of searching for hid treasure, without some real foundation for it. Lay this aside as a rule, which may be safely applied on all occasions and to all questions.

Let us turn now to something more interesting than this search after hid treasure. Yonder on our left is Mûgharet Tubloon, one of Sidon's most ancient cemeteries. The Phœnicians took immense trouble to secure their dead from being disturbed, but in vain, as we shall see. They first cut away the rock at Tubloon, so as to make a large surface perfectly level. This has long been the general threshing-floor for those who farm this beautiful plain ; beneath it, however, are countless chambers for the dead—vast catacombs, in fact, arranged after a very peculiar fashion. A square shaft was sunk through the rock, ten, twenty, or thirty feet, according to the taste or ability of the maker. From this, doors at different depths opened into halls and rooms,

around the sides of which were cut the niches for the dead. To make assurance doubly sure, some niches were sunk in the floor of the chambers, the sarcophagi there deposited, and then the whole was levelled off, and a hard stone flooring laid on above. But even these have been discovered and rifled during the long ages of earnest search for treasure.

Two years ago, on the morning of January 20th, our city was startled out of her ordinary quietude by the report that an extraordinary sarcophagus had been uncovered, which had a long inscription in an unknown character on the lid. All Sidon flocked to see it, and I among the rest, but with expectations very moderate. I had been disappointed too frequently to place much confidence on native reports. Judge, therefore, of my surprise and delight to find that this unknown character was Phœnician. I at once became as deeply excited as the gold-digger or treasure-hunter, for

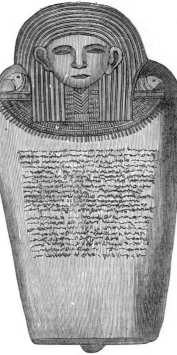

SARCOPHAGUS.

CHAPTER X.

Cemetery of Mûgharet Tubloon.

A Phœnician sarcophagus.

I had searched in vain, during twenty years, for a single word in this character.

The lid of this sarcophagus is wholly peculiar; and the upper end of it is
wrought into a human figure, with a countenance and costume every way
remarkable. It is somewhat colossal, and the features are large and prominent. The forehead is rather low; the eyes almond-shaped, but full and pro-
truding; the nose broad and flat; the lips very thick, like the Ethiopian or
Negro; the chin quite short; and the ears too large and conspicuous for
beauty. A sweet smile is spread over the countenance, and the features are
expressive, and not at all disagreeable. The whole execution is decidedly
superior to anything of the kind in this country. It *seems* to be the figure of
a female (though this is not certain); perhaps it may stand for the ideal of
Sidon's far-famed goddess, Ashtaroth. Something depends from the chin,
like a beard; but I suppose it belongs to the head-dress, which closely resembles that frequently seen on ancient Egyptian mummy-cases. On each
shoulder sits a bird, probably a dove; and the *tout ensemble* is striking and
impressive. The lid, and consequently the figure upon it, is too wide for
symmetrical beauty. It is four feet broad, and only about seven in length.
The material is blue-black basalt, intensely hard, and takes and keeps an
excellent polish. The inscription is in twenty-two long lines; and the letters,
though never cut deep, are in perfect preservation, and as easily read as the
day they were engraven. There is nothing like it in the whole compass of
Phœnician remains. I sent a copy of it to Chevalier Bunsen, who immediately
transmitted it to Professor Dietrich, then engaged in editing a new edition of
Gesenius's learned work on the Phœnician language and antiquities. This
gentleman published a translation, with an elaborate critique upon it. Other
copies were sent to France, England, and America; and the learned of every
land have tried their skill upon it.

The in-
scription.

TRANSLATION OF THE PHŒNICIAN INSCRIPTION.

A somewhat free rendering of this curious record, after the French version, runs
thus :—" In the month Bul, in the fourteenth—xiv.—of my reign, king Ashmunazer,
the king of the Sidonians, son of Tabnith, king of the Sidonians, king Ashmunazer,
king of the Sidonians, spake, saying, I am snatched away before my time, like the
flowing of a river. Then I have made a house for my funeral resting-place, and am
lying in this sarcophagus, and in this sepulchre, the place which I have built. My
prohibition to every royal person, and to every man, not to open my sepulchre, and
not to seek with me treasures—for there are no treasures with me—nor to take away
the sarcophagus of my funeral couch, nor to transfer me with my funeral couch upon
the couch of another. And if men command to do so, listen not to their opinion ;
because every royal person, and every man who shall open this funeral couch, or who
shall take away the sarcophagus of this funeral couch, or who shall transfer me with
the funeral couch, he shall have no funeral with the dead, nor be buried in a sepulchre, nor leave behind them son or posterity ; and the holy gods, with the king that
shall rule over them, shall cut off that royal person, and that man who has opened my

couch, or who has abstracted this sarcophagus; and so also the posterity of that royal person or of that man, whoever he be, nor shall his root be planted downward nor his fruit spring upward; and he shall be accursed among those living under the sun, because I am to be pitied,—snatched away before my time, like a flowing river. Then I have made this edifice for my funeral resting-place; for I am Ashmunazer, king of the Sidonians, son of Tabnith, king of the Sidonians, grandson of Ashmunazer, king of the Sidonians; and my mother, Immiastoreth, priestess of Astarte, our sovereign queen, daughter of king Ashmunazer, king of the Sidonians. It is we who have built this temple of the gods * * * in Sidon by the sea, and the heavenly powers have rendered Astarte favourable. And it is we who have erected the temple to Esmuno, and the sanctuary of Ene Dalil in the mountain. The heavenly powers have established me on the throne. And it is we who have built the temples to the gods of the Sidonians in Sidon by the sea (or maritime Sidon); the temple of Baal-Sidōn, and the temple of Astarte, the glory of Baal, lord of kings, who bestowed on us Dor and Joppa, and ample corn-lands which are at the root of Dan. Extending the power which I have founded, they added them to the bounds of the land, establishing them to the Sidonians for ever.

" My prohibition upon every royal person, and upon every man who shall open upon me, or uncover me, or shall transfer me with this funeral couch, or take away the sarcophagus of my funeral couch; lest the holy gods desert them, and cut off that royal person, or that man, whoever he may be, and their posterity for ever "·

The renderings of different *savants* in Europe and America vary largely; but the list of great names on the tablet cannot be questioned : Baal and Ashtaroth, the gods of the Zidonians in the days of Joshua; Dor, and Joppa, and Dan, cities and territories which Ashmunazer seems to have conquered. If this be correct, then we may find in these historic facts some hint to guide to the probable age of Ashmunazer. *When* was there a king of Sidon so powerful as to subdue Dor, and Joppa, and Dan? I know not; but it is plain, from the narrative of the conquest of Laish by the Danites, recorded in Judges, 18th chapter, that it then belonged to Sidon. That it ever did after that, remains to be proved. The manner in which it is described on our tablet is very accurate : "Ample corn-lands at the root of Dan." The Hûleh spreads out from the very root of Dan (Tell el Kady), the richest grain-field that I am acquainted with in any country.

Poor Ashmunazer seems to have had the utmost horror of being disturbed, and multiplied his maledictions upon whomsoever should do it. These imprecations will scarcely be visited upon Louis Napoleon, or the officers of the French corvette La Sérieuse, on board of which the sarcophagus was carried to France ; for it had been opened by some former rifler of tombs, probably in search of treasure, notwithstanding the declaration of the king that there were none with him. It is curious to notice this anxiety so early in man's history, proving that the custom of " digging for hid treasures," as Job has it, and rifling the tombs of kings for the same purpose, is extremely ancient.

Another thing interested me very much in this tablet. Many of the letters so closely resemble those of our own alphabet that one can scarcely be mistaken in tracing ours up through the Romaic and the Greek to that of Phœ-

Probable date.

Phœnician letters resemble ours.

PART
I.

Phœni-
cian let-
ters also
resemble
Hebrew.

nicia; and this accords with and confirms the ancient tradition in regard to the origin of the Greek alphabet. Still more interesting is the fact that the characters on this stone are so like the old Hebrew as to establish their close relationship, if not their actual identity. If this be so, then we have on this tablet of Ashmunazer the very alphabet that God employed to preserve and transmit to us the priceless gift of his divine law. It further appears that the language of the two peoples, as well as their alphabet, were identical. And this, too, accords with our most ancient history. In all the incidental notices of intercourse between the patriarchs and their descendants and the inhabitants of Palestine, this fact is assumed or necessarily implied. It is only in Egypt that they heard a language which they could not understand (as David has it in the 81st Psalm), and conversed through an interpreter,—a character and office never mentioned in Palestine. It is, perhaps, not necessary to suppose that either borrowed from the other, but that both inherited from their common ancestor. At any rate, it is scarcely possible that the Phœnicians could borrow their language and literature from the Hebrews. They were the more ancient people, and had attained a high civilization while the patriarchs still abode in tents and tended cattle.

Temples.

In regard to the temples mentioned by Ashmunazer, I have the idea that Baal-Sidōn was that which once covered the old mazar, or shrine now called Sidōne, a short distance south-east of the upper castle of the city. The Ene Dalil on the mountain may have been this temple of Mŭnterah on the bold promontory above the Sanîk. The position, and the apparent signification of both names would point to it. There are also traces of more than one temple at Tubloon itself,—one over the spot where the sarcophagus was found, and another farther south.

But here is one of Sidon's antiquities by the road side, which claims a passing notice. Those two mighty emperors, Septimius Severus and Pertinax Arabicus, sought to immortalize their august names by graving into this granite column the important fact that they mended this road. And this brings us to the little river Sanik, somewhat swollen by the heavy rains. I will tell you something about this river when we get settled in our tent this evening. In the meanwhile, notice its exit from the mountains a mile to the east of us, through that fine gorge, with a village in its mouth, called, by some strange whim, Durb es Sîn, or "road to China," to translate according to sound. That ruined temple on the promontory above is Mŭnterah, commanding the noble prospect I spoke of the other day. There are many tombs in the rock thereabouts, and one so large that it is still used occasionally as a church. In my rambles I once bolted into it, horse and all, and was surprised to find myself before an altar with a crucifix, an old picture of the Virgin, and a greasy earthen lamp. I subsequently learned that it was dedicated to Mary, and on a certain day of the year a great feast is celebrated at it to her honour. That large village with white domes, a little farther south, is called Gâzzîyeh, which Maundrell spells Korie. William of Tyre, and other Crusaders, make

A tomb
used as a
church

equally shrewd approximations to the reality. Those domes cover the shrines
of reputed prophets, or holy men,—a sort of patron saints very common in this
region. Each village has one or more; and, besides these, every conspicuous
hill-top has a *willy* or *mazar*, beneath a spreading oak, to which people pay
religious visits, and thither they go up to worship and to discharge vows. All
sects in the country, without exception, have a predilection for these "high
places," strong as that of the Jews in ancient times. The most pious and
zealous kings could not remove the high places from Israel; and most of them

WILLY OR MAZAR.

not only connived at, but shared in this superstition, and frequented these
shrines. They were generally surrounded with a grove, or, at least, had one

or more shade-trees planted near them; and so they have to this day. The customs are identical. There is one of these high places, with its grove of venerable oaks, on the very summit of Lebanon, east of Jezzîn. It is of an oval shape, corresponding to the top of the mountain, and the grove was planted regularly around its outer edge. When I stood within this mystic circle of mighty oaks, and looked over the vast plain of Cœle-Syria, north-east to the temple of Baalbek, and then south-west to ancient Tyre, I fancied that this had been a connecting point between the two great temples of Baal and Belus. The first rays of the "god of day" would glance from the gilded dome in Baalbek to this high place, and thence into the grand portal of Belus at Tyre. Many of these mazars, whose history no one knows, have probably come down from remote antiquity, through all the mutations of dynasties and religions, unchanged to the present hour. We can believe this the more readily, because they are now frequented by the oldest communities in the country, and those most opposed to each other. For example, Neby Seijûd, which you see crowning yon southern peak of Lebanon, is resorted to by Jews, wild Arabs of the desert, Moslems, Metâwelies, and Christians. We have, therefore, in these places not only sites of the very highest antiquity, but living examples and monuments of man's most ancient superstitions; and if this does not add to our veneration, it will much increase the interest with which we examine them. If it does not soften our condemnation, it may at least lessen our surprise.

This little brook is called Meshûn; and here the road to Hasbeiya takes off to the south-east, over those swelling hills on our left. After crossing the River Zahrany, it winds up a conical hill nine hundred feet high, to Khan Mohammed Ali, where is a fountain with a Greek inscription. Farther on are rock-tombs, and other indications of an ancient city, near the present village of Zifty. An ancient road continues due east past Deîr Zahrany and Tell Hŭbbush to the Jermŭk,—a beautiful vale which leads down to the Litany, at the ford called Tamra, seven and a half hours from Sidon. The modern road, however, passes south of this, through the long wady Kafûr to Nebatîyeh, and thence to the bridge Khŭrdîleh, below the great castle of Shŭkîf, which is about eight hours from Sidon. Beyond the Litany the road divides to various parts of Ijon,—Wady et Teim between the two Lebanons, to the Hûleh and the Hauran. In those days when Sidon possessed Dan and the fertile plains of Merom, this was an important highway, and was well kept, furnished with cisterns of water, and paved in places which required it. I trust we may be able to visit Shŭkîf on our return. It is the Castle of Bellefort or Beaufort of the Crusaders, and commands a magnificent panorama of mountains, plains, rivers, and lakes.

Our present path has brought us to a second mile-stone, with a Latin inscription, which we need not stop to copy, as it is a fragment which reveals nothing worth remembering. That pretty river before us is the flowery Zahrany, with a broken bridge of three arches embosomed in a wilderness of oleanders. We shall have something to say about this river also in the evening. In the meanwhile, we will examine that Tell, which rises like a huge hay-stack on the very margin of the sea. It is called Tell el Burak, from those very ancient cisterns east of it, in which was collected the water from fountains that rise out of the plain above it. _{CHAPTER X.}

What is that man quarrelling about with his companion? Shall I translate this last explosion of his wrath? "May God curse your grandfather, and the father of your great-grandfather! *Can't you give a man time to pray? I want to pray.*" _{Cursing and praying.}

Preposterous!

Which—the swearing, or the praying?

Both.

Both together are certainly preposterous enough; and yet this scene and language are so familiar that I should not have noticed them if you had not called my attention that way.

But what makes the man so pertinaciously resolved to pray at this hour and place?

Perhaps he has made a vow to say his prayers at this time of day, *wherever he may be,* and if he fails he must do penance or pay a piastre, which is worse. Alas! religion in the East has always been joined in fellowship with many strange and monstrous things. This man may have been prompted to get off his donkey and pray merely because it is now the 'asr—the regular hour for afternoon prayer; and this little river furnishes water for the necessary ablutions.

I am surprised to see the plain covered with men ploughing and sowing at this late season. _{Ploughing in winter.}

This is common and will continue all winter. It has always been so, I suppose. Solomon says, "The sluggard will not plough by reason of the cold,"—

PLOUGHING.

or *winter,* as the margin has it; "therefore shall he beg in harvest and have nothing."[1] Our farmers do actually plough in the severest weather. I have

---

[1] Prov. xx. 4.

PART I.

often seen them shivering with cold, and contending with wind and rain, quite enough to discourage those who are not sluggards. But time has become precious and critical, and he who expects to reap must sow, no matter how tempestuous the weather. "He that observeth the wind shall not sow; and he that regardeth the clouds shall not reap." [1] This hard necessity of winter-

Deficient imple- ments.

work is mainly owing to the wretched implements used, and to a strange deficiency in agricultural science and skill. If the farmers had good ploughs and adequate teams, they might break up and prepare their ground in fair weather, and then, when sufficient rain had fallen, they would sow the whole crop in a few days. But these men, with their frail ploughs and tiny oxen, must wait until the ground is saturated and softened, however late in the season that may be. Then they cannot sow and plough in more than half an acre per day, and few average so much, and hence the work is dragged along for months. They know nothing about the harrow, and merely plough under the seed, and leave it to take its chance. Job, however, speaks of the harrow; and, if our translation be correct, it is one of the oldest agricultural implements in the world. [2]

Manner of plough- ing.

We have another Biblical illustration before us. In 1 Kings xix. 19, we read that Elijah found Elisha, the son of Shaphat, ploughing with twelve yoke of oxen before him, and he with the twelfth. We are not to suppose that he had a team of twelve yoke of oxen before him. If you count these here at work, you find seven separate ploughs following one after another as closely as possible; and I have seen more than a dozen of them thus at work. To understand the reason of this, several things must be taken into account. First, that the arable lands of nearly all villages are cultivated in common; then, that Arab farmers delight to work together in companies, partly for mutual protection, and in part from their love of gossip; and, as they sow no more ground than they can plough during the day, one sower will answer for the entire company.

Elisha's twelve yoke of oxen.

Their little ploughs make no proper furrow, but merely root up and throw the soil on either side, and so any number may follow one another, each making its own scratch along the back of the earth; and when at the end of the field, they can return along the same line, and thus back and forth until the whole is ploughed. It was well that Elisha came the last of the twelve, for the act of Elijah would have stopped all that were in advance of him. They cannot pass one another. Such brief hints let us far into the interior of ancient manners and customs. We may fairly conclude that Elisha's plough and oxen were much like those in this field; that the people worked in com- panies as they do now, and probably for the same reasons. These reasons suggest painful thoughts about insecurity, and oppression, and robbery; about the tenure of land, the mode of raising taxes and collecting rents, and I know not what besides. Why are lands now worked in common? Because

<hr>

[1] Eccles. xi. 4. [2] Job xxxix. 10.

they belong not to the farmers, but to feudal lords, or to government, which claims a certain part of the produce. In short, a vast concatenation of causes and effects, reaching up to the remotest ages of Biblical antiquity, is suggested by the manner in which these simple ploughmen perform their labour.

To return to our Tell. It once formed the acropolis of a city whose shapeless remains are scattered over the plain. I have often seen these mounds near fountains, which they were probably designed to command. Water is of the utmost importance to the inhabitants of all towns in Syria, and their fountains must be protected at any cost. All these things, however, speak unmistakably of misrule and danger, even far beyond anything known to the present generation. Bad as the times are, the former were worse. It was infinitely worse when every hill-top was covered with a castle armed for defence, and when every farmer was at the same time a soldier — *Proofs of misrule and danger.*

This little river Burikîyeh drains the Wady Kafûr, and during heavy rains is sometimes troublesome to travellers. The Romans found it so, if we may judge from these heavy abutments of a bridge built by them, but broken by the violence of the brook long ages ago. The next stream is called el 'Akabîyeh, and is spanned by a natural bridge at its mouth. I have ridden over it, though it is not more than three feet wide in the narrowest part. The road crosses higher up. This Wady el 'Akabîyeh runs far into the interior, across the district of Shûmar into that of Shŭkîf. I once followed it to Nsar, *en route* to Safed. This Nsar was once a large town, and about it are many rock-tombs and other indications of antiquity. The country in that direction is wild and uncultivated. The inhabitants are Metāwelies, and great growers of tobacco.

One of St. Helen's towers stands on that projecting headland. It is also called 'Akabîyeh, probably from this brook. And there, by the sea-side, is our tent, pitched under the tall tamarisks of 'Ain el Kŭnterah. Near it is an apology for an inn, from which we can get barley for our horses, and eggs and lebn for ourselves ; and, what is better, there is much to interest us here-abouts, for Sarepta's ruins cover the whole plain for more than a mile to the south of our camp-ground ; but we will postpone the examination of them till to-morrow. The sun is sinking quietly to rest in the sea, beneath a glowing canopy of crimson, gold, and blue, and there will be fair weather for many days to come. Such signals never deceive, and we can discern the face of the sky as well as the Jews, and the signs of the times far better than did that wicked and adulterous generation, that did not know the day of their merciful visitation. — *Sunset and the signs of the times.*

CHAPTER XI.

NEIGHBOURHOOD OF SARAFEND.

Lebanon by moonlight.	Serpent-charmers.
Demonology—Maniacs in tombs.	Wonder-working.
Scripture expressions.	Spears through the face.
Amulets—how applied.	Mesmerism.
Anecdotes of a practitioner.	The magic mirror of ink.

OUR evening turns out as lovely as the day—quite too pleasant to be wasted in the tent. Let us take a stroll along this quiet and solitary shore.

As you please; but first wrap your cloak about you; the air is cool, and we have come from the shelter of home too recently to encounter it with safety. Let us go out to those white rocks which protect this little cove on the north.

This is indeed charming. The tired sea gently heaves its broad bosom, and the surf sobs and sighs along the shore like a vexed child sinking to sleep.

Lebanon by moonlight.

And how gloriously the full orbed moon rises over Lebanon! How many miles may those majestic mountains be from us?

The nearest, fifteen; the most distant, sixty at least; but light as are our nights, you would not see them thus distinctly were it not for their robes of fresh snow. Those mountains remind me of my promise to tell you something about the two rivers we crossed on our way from Sidon.

In the wildest of those gorges whose outlines lie in misty shadows along the south end of Lebanon, bursts out a copious spring called Neb'a et Tāsy, —Fountain of the Cup. It is the source of the Zahrany. The ancient Sidonians coveted this ice-cold water, and did actually lead it to their city, along a line of canal which might well confound the boldest engineer. A

A Sidonian watercourse.

channel was hewn in the rock, into which the new-born river was turned, and thence carried down the gorge southward until it could double the promontory of Jerju'a, after which it meandered as it could northward for eight miles, spanning deep ravines over high arches, and descending into Wady Kefrah, below Jeba'ah. Beyond this, the aqueduct was led along frightful cliffs where goats can scarcely keep their feet, for more than a mile, and thence it followed the ridge of Kefr Milky, past the village, into the wady of the Sanîk, where it was joined by another aqueduct from Neb'a er Râhib, the source of that river. The two canals were taken thence down the river, but separately, one about fifteen feet above the other. The system of arches by which these works were carried across the ravines and rivers is still almost perfect, and the cliffs to which they cling are absolutely perpendicular for miles together.

As there are no traces of arches by which the water was led across the low plain up to the city, it has been conjectured that the Sidonian engineers were acquainted, at that early age, with the principle in hydrostatics that water will rise to the level of its source. People also tell me that fragments of earthen pipes, incased in lead, have been dug up in the gardens in the probable line of these canals. These may have served to conduct the water to the city.

This great work, thus briefly described, reflects much credit not only on the ancient inhabitants of Sidon, but also on the science, skill, and courage of her engineers. The proposition to carry the water of Neb'a et Tāsy from its source, in the wild ravine of Jebel Rihan, to Sidon, would make even a New York engineer hesitate. Who constructed these canals, and when, are questions which cannot now be answered. They bear the name of Zobeida, but this affords no clue to the mystery ; the only Zobeida known to Arab history, I believe, was the wife of Haroun el Raschîd, a sort of Moslem St. Helena, author of every ancient work except those built by " Suleiman bin Daûd, upon whom be peace." It is certain, however, that this lady did not construct these aqueducts. They were broken antiquities long before she was born. Everything about them bears witness to their extreme age. Examine a specimen of the work above Kefr Milky : the cement of the canal has turned to actual stone, or has been coated with a calcareous deposit as hard, so that the whole wall looks like an unbroken crystalline rock, as compact as the mountain limestone about it. But this will not help us to a date, nor will the very ancient-shaped arches which span the ravines. At Jerjua, a village near Neb'a et Tāsy, a tombstone was lately dug up, having a figure of a boy carved upon it, with a Greek inscription by the side of him ; but it reveals nothing as to the origin of the canals.

The air grows chilly as the land-breeze reaches us from the snow-clad mountains, and we shall find the tent both safer and more comfortable.

My thoughts go back to Sidon, and the kind friends within her old walls. Your divan is now in full session.

Yes, and very likely we are the first topic discussed by every fresh arrival ; and everything which can be said about us will be repeated twenty times at least, mingled with prayers for our safety and prosperity.

I was greatly interested last night in your discussion about demonology, enchantment, charms, etc., etc. ; but, as my young dragomen were too much absorbed in it themselves to translate very adequately, I should like to go over the subject at our leisure. Indeed, I put this down on my list of subjects to study when I first decided to make this pilgrimage. The references to it in the Bible are many, and often not a little obscure. Do you find anything in the country at this day which throws light on the question of demoniac possessions ?

Nothing very decided or satisfactory ; and yet, perhaps, if we had the touchstone of a divine presence walking among us, this might bring out some very

[margin notes:] Extreme antiquity.

Enchantment and demonology.

PART
I.

wonderful developments. The basis, so to speak, of these possessions, in all their variety, is still to be met with. In Sidon there are cases of epileptic fits which, in external manifestations, closely resemble that mentioned in Mark ix. 18 ; Matt. xvii. 15 ; and Luke ix. 38. These fits have seized a young man in my own house repeatedly ; " And, lo ! the spirit taketh him, and he suddenly *crieth* out, and *foameth* at the mouth, and gnasheth with his *teeth*," and is cast down wherever he may be seized, and pineth away until you would think he was actually dead. Matthew calls him a lunatic, but according to Mark it was a dumb spirit. And there are cases in which the disease referred to accompanies, and in others it obviously occasions dumbness. I will not say that such unfortunate creatures are tormented by an evil spirit, but I am sure

Maniacs
in tombs
and caves.

that no cavilling sceptic can *prove* that they are not. The instance mentioned in Mark v. 2–16, and in Luke viii. 26–36, was most remarkable; but there are some very similar at the present day—furious and dangerous maniacs, who wander about the mountains, and sleep in tombs and caves. In their worst paroxysms they are quite unmanageable, and prodigiously strong. And this, I suppose, is about what the evangelists mean by their breaking the chains and fetters with which they had been bound. Mark and Luke certainly do not mean that no chains could hold them, but merely that those commonly used to confine such people were not sufficient for these infuriated demons. It also appears that they went naked ; for when they were healed, they were found *clothed* and in their right mind. And it is one of the most common traits in

Naked.

this madness that the victims refuse to wear clothes. I have often seen them absolutely naked in the crowded streets of Beirût and Sidon. There are also cases in which they run wildly about the country and frighten the whole neighbourhood. These poor wretches are held in the greatest reverence by Moslems, who, through some monstrous perversion of ideas, believe them to be inspired and peculiarly holy. It would certainly be rash to decide that this calamity was the work of evil spirits, and yet the manifestations are so inhuman and satanic, and the real causes so mysterious, that I am not much disposed to dispute the point with the natives of the country, who ascribe the mischief to supernatural agency.

Terms
employed
in Scrip-
ture.

But this was not exactly the subject discussed last night. The conversation was started by one of the company reading Deut. xviii. 10, 11 : " There shall not be found among you any one that useth divination, or an observer of times, or an enchanter, or a witch, or a charmer, or a consulter with familiar spirits, or a wizard, or a necromancer." His wish was to have these names in his Arabic Bible explained, many of which were unintelligible to him. Our first effort, you remember, was to affix definite ideas to the words themselves; and, with the aid of the doctor and our Syrian friend, we made quite a critical coterie in appearance, with our English, Arabic, Syriac, Vulgate, Septuagint, and Hebrew. The results, however, were not very striking or important.

Using
divination.

The first of these names we concluded was applied to any person who

prophesied or uttered oracles, the means by which he obtained them being im- CHAPTER XI.
material. The Septuagint translators seem thus to have understood it.

The second seems to look toward the clouds, and probably the professors of An observer of times.
this art dealt in lucky and unlucky days, expounded omens, and prognosticated
future occurrences mainly by observing the clouds. We have this sort of
witchcraft in abundance.

The third is rendered by the Seventy, and those who followed them, by a An enchanter.
word signifying to augur from the flight of birds ; but the Hebrew seems to
connect it with serpents. Our translation is near the truth in calling these
enchanters. Probably they employed serpents in their enchantments.

The fourth is obviously from a Hebrew root which signifies to uncover, A witch.
reveal, and may refer to furtune-tellers, revealers of stolen goods, hid treasure,
and the like. The Seventy have pharmakos, a compounder of drugs and magic
charms, but by what authority I know not.

The fifth is hobair hüber. In Arabic this would mean a repeater of news, A charmer.
and may refer to giving forth auricular responses, or to a repetition of invoca-
tions and incantations.

The sixth name in our list the Seventy seem to have thought meant ventri- A consulter with familiar spirits.
loquism ; and 'aobe may mean belly, but our English translation is probably
correct,—a consulter with familiar spirits. It is not unlikely, however, that
these diviners, by means of ventriloquism, pretended to converse with their
"familiars," and to receive audible responses from them. Even the wise So-
crates laid claim to the aid of some such spirit.

The seventh were those esteemed supernaturally wise, magicians perhaps, A wizard.
and such as performed wonderful tricks by sleight of hand, superior cunning,
or profounder insight into the mysteries of nature. And the eighth was a
necromancer, a consulter of the dead, like the witch of Endor and our modern A necromancer.
dealers in " spirit rappings."

Besides these, there are other kinds of divination, and other names employed Other terms
in the Bible, whose signification is doubtful. The magicians mentioned in
Gen. xli. 8, and Exod. vii. 11, and 22, do not appear to have belonged to any
of these classes. Probably they were originally Egyptian priests, who alone
understood the art of writing and interpreting their sacred hieroglyphics. It
is plain, however, that they professed to work wonders by their occult sciences,
of whatever sort they were. Joseph pretended to divine by the aid of his cup;[1]
and Isaiah mentions astrologers, star-gazers, and monthly prognosticators.
Daniel several times speaks of the assoppim, which the Seventy have rightly
called magi, or wise men. Our translators render it astrologers.

Well, have you been able to identify these ancient kinds of divination with
practices still found in these countries ? It occurs to me, however, that several
of them are closely related, and that it is not necessary to suppose that the
professors of these occult sciences were restricted to any one kind. On the

---

[1] Gen. xliv. 5, 15.

PART
I.

contrary, they would resort to all, or to as many as they were masters of. Thus an astrologer would not only draw his astrolabic figures and diagrams, but observe times, compound magical drugs, recite incantations, write charms, and so on, through all the labyrinths of the black art.

Common
use of
amulets.

Doubtless, for we find this true at the present day among the clumsy imitators of those ancient adepts. Perhaps the superstition most common at present is that of charms. People of every rank and station in society, and of every creed and sect, employ them for themselves, their children, their houses, their horses and cattle, and even for their fruit-trees. Amulets and charms are hung around the neck, or hid away in the bosom; they are suspended from the arch of a newly-built house; they dangle from the throat of horses and cattle; and fig and other trees have cabalistic signs drawn upon them, to guard against the evil eye.

AMULETS.

How ap-
plied.

The charms most in repute among all sects are brief sentences from their religious books, written with certain formalities, and frequently accompanied with cabalistic diagrams, drawn by those skilled in these magic mysteries. I have examined many of them. They are sewed up in small sacks, generally heart-shaped, and suspended from the tarbush of infants, round the necks of larger children, and about grown-up people according to their particular fancy.

Like nostrums in medicine, these amulets are believed to defend the wearer from sickness and accidents, from the malice of enemies, from balls in a battle,

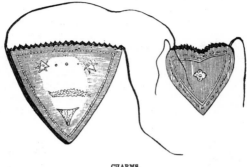

CHARMS.

from robbers by the way, from the evil eye, evil spirits, and, in short, from every species of calamity. There are some so potent that the possessor is rendered invisible to robbers, is perfectly safe in the hottest battle, and need fear neither jan, ghoul, nor devil by night or day. While I was wandering about with the Egyptian army during the revolt of Palestine against Ibrahim Pasha in 1834, I was assured by officers of respectability that Ibrahim would come in after a skirmish with the rebels, loose his girdle, and shake out the balls which had been aimed at him, beaten quite flat, but none of them had injured him. This was ascribed to the potency of the charms about his person. The Moslems generally wear portions of the Korân, which they call hejabs, or they write an endless string of the names and attributes of the Deity, or the equally numerous titles of Mohammed. These curious and absurd combinations are deposited in tin or leather cases by the poor, and in silver and gold by the wealthy. The Moslems, Druses, Metāwelies, Nusaireans, Ismailîyehs, Yezidies, Bedawîn, Nowr, Jews, and Christians, all have not only their peculiar charms, but also their separate counter-charms, to defeat and neutralize those of their enemies. Any one who has read the "Arabian Nights," with Lane's notes, will have obtained a tolerably complete acquaintance with this whole subject, and the customs are identical down to the present hour.

Another kind of charm, very common, seems designed not so much to ward In sick-off the approach of evil as to relieve from its actual presence and pressure. ness. Thus, when a person is sick, the relatives place at his head a copy of their most sacred books, Korân, Bible, Church-book, or whatever they most reverence,—a picture, image, or relic, or some treasure brought from Mecca or Jerusalem, or from the tomb of some dead saint, or the body of some living one. In the absence of Doctor V——, I was lately called to see the sick son

PART L

of one of the most respectable Moslems of Sidon. At his head was an old rotten rag, as filthy as the vilest hermit could make it. This could on no account be removed. It was part of the sheet of a very holy man now living in Joppa. It had cost several thousand piastres, and was possessed of most potent efficacy. The child, however, died, greatly to the dismay of the father. About the same time, a Christian father called me to visit his son, dangerously ill. I found a peculiarly-formed gold button placed under the lad's cap, in order to charm away the disease. He recovered, and I suppose the button will be famous a long time to come. I was once dragged in the utmost haste to see an Arab friend, said to be bleeding to death at the nose. The friends had stuck various Arabic seals about his *tarbush*, and *the blood stopped*, as they said, through their potency.

Scotch charms.

This sort of superstition is not confined to the East. Scott's fair lady of Branksome's Tower, when she drew the splinter from the breast of bold Deloraine, performed her magical rites : "And with a charm she stanched the blood." Indeed, Scott himself seems to be more than half a believer in his own prodigies; and Scotland and Ireland boast of as many, as potent, and as complicated charms as any country in the world. They are equally rich in medicinal and magical compounds. Most of them, it may be, are made and used without any definite reference to invisible beings, good or bad, but others are done with their avowed assistance. And so it is even among the Christians of this country.

The evil eye.

The belief in the malignant potency of the evil eye is very prevalent with all classes of Syrian society. So ridiculously afraid are they of this blight, that if you merely *look* at a child, especially if it be pretty, you must repeat the name of the Prophet, of God, or of the Virgin, with a brief petition for protection, or at least say Mâshallah (an exclamation of admiration or praise to God). If you extol the beauty of a horse, you must immediately spit on it; and the same is done sometimes to a child, more frequently, however, they merely blow in its face and repeat a charm. The bright red or white figures made on fig-trees are designed to attract the eye from the fruit, lest it should wither and fall. In short, against this mysterious source of evil there are countless charms and counter-charms.

Fortune-telling.

Another superstition is that of fortune-telling. This is practised mainly by female gipsies, as in other countries, and with the same fooleries. Nor need we wonder that this world-wide practice should prevail in the semicivilized East, since it is found in such countries as England, France, and America. Who has not read the story of the Empress Josephine and her fortune-telling negress ?

Detection of thieves.

There are many who pretend to discover thieves and stolen goods by incantations and other means. I spent the summer of 1835 at Brummanah, and my Moslem servant, without my knowledge, resorted to an old sheikh, with a present, to inquire after some spoons which had been stolen from my house. He made his rude diagrams in the sand, muttered his cabalistic adjurations, and engaged that the stolen property would be returned to a specified place at a given time. I have forgotten the particulars, and also the explanation by which the servant accounted for the failure of the operation without casting discredit upon the supernatural powers of the sheikh. Men who acquire a reputation for success in this business are greatly honoured, and resorted to from all quarters. One of our Protestants in Merj Aiyûn was formerly celebrated for skill in this department. Of course he has renounced all such practices now, and also denounced them, but he has often amused me with anecdotes about this trade. Once he was returning home through the Hûleh, and found a poor woman at a mill on the upper Jordan beating herself in despair because some one had stolen her meal-bag. There were Arab tents not far off, and, as Arabs are by profession thieves, he suspected that one of them had the missing bag. Calling them all before him, he told them his suspicion, and declared that he had an infallible test by which to detect the thief, and to it they must submit, or he would lodge a complaint against them with the governor. They all stoutly denied the charge, and offered to submit to his test. He then cut bits of straw, equal in number to that of the Arabs, all of the same length, and kept the measure himself, giving a bit to each of them. "Now," said he, in his most imposing manner, "keep these bits till the morning, *each one by himself;* then bring them to me, and I will measure them ; if any one of you has the bag, his stick will have grown longer *by so much.* Of course, each hid his splinter in his bosom, and in the morning one was found as much *too short* as he said it would *grow* while in possession of the thief. The credulous rascal, not doubting but that it would actually grow, had broken off just the length which he supposed had been added during the night. When thus detected, he confessed the theft, and restored the poor woman her bag.

Our friend was an adept in all sorts of divination. On a certain occasion, when travelling in Belad Beshara, he met a man on his way to consult another celebrated thief detecter. Greatly rejoiced to meet our friend, he earnestly requested him to return and spend the night at his house, in order to detect who had stolen from him a bag containing a hundred Spanish dollars. He found him living in a large house, with three brothers, all married, and he suspected that one of the wives had stolen the money. When evening was far advanced, he told his suspicion, and demanded that the women should be brought before him, each one alone. Putting on his most terrific look, he ordered each one to turn from right to left, then from left to right, to sit down, get up, stand still, etc., muttering all the while some horrible gibberish in a hollow, sepulchral voice. One of them became deadly pale, and trembled exceedingly. This he fixed on as the thief. Watching his opportunity, he gave her a significant look, and then said aloud, "I find the house very hot" (it was summer), "and I shall sleep on the terrace, under the vine-arbour." As he expected, about midnight the woman crept stealthily to him, bringing the bag of money, and begging him to keep her secret. He did so, and the next

PART
I.

morning gave the man his money, but would answer no questions as to how he got it. This man is a doctor after the Arab fashion, and often resorted to magical combinations and charms to eke out his small pharmacopœia and more scanty knowledge. He did this more especially in his treatment of maniacs, and those supposed to be bewitched; and he has had surprising success, mainly, I suppose, on the principle that "faith worketh wonders." These poor people and their friends had unbounded confidence in his ability to relieve them; hence they did just as he directed, and his general prescriptions were quite judicious.

Astrology and alchymy.

He was also an adept in astrology, so far as that very ancient science, falsely so called, is found in Arabic books. There are but few who now practise it, but I lately had a call from an old Moslem who wished to ascertain the exact latitude of Sidon, as he needed this item to complete one of his astrological combinations. There are many more who practise alchymy; indeed, not a few have spent their life and fortune in costly experiments in search of the universal *alkahest* by which all metals are to be transmuted into gold, and all diseases cured. They uniformly deal in charms and incantations.

Serpent-charmers.

One of the names in our catalogue has reference to serpents, and David, in Psalm lviii. 4, 5, speaks of serpent-charming, as does Solomon in Ecclesiastes x. 11; and Jeremiah, viii. 17; and this kind of enchantment is still practised.

I have seen many serpent-charmers who do really exercise some extraordinary power over these reptiles. They carry enormous snakes, generally black, about them, allow them to crawl all over their persons and into their bosoms, always, however, with certain precautions, either necessary or pretended to be so. They repeatedly breathe strongly into the face of the serpent, and occasionally blow spittle, or some medicated composition upon them. It is needless to describe the mountebank tricks which they perform. That which I am least able to account for is the power of detecting the presence of serpents in a house, and of enticing or "charming" them out of it. The thing is far too common to be made a matter of scepticism. The following account, by Mr. Lane, is a fair statement of this matter: "The charmer professes to discover without ocular perception (but perhaps he does so by a peculiar smell), whether there be any serpents in the house; and, if there be, to attract them to him, as the fowler, by the fascination of his voice, allures the bird into his net. As

Detecting serpents in a house.

the serpent seeks the darkest place in which to hide himself, the charmer has, in most cases, to exercise his skill in an obscure chamber, where he might easily take a serpent from his bosom, bring it to the people without the door, and affirm that he had found it in the apartment; for no one would venture to enter with him, after having been assured of the presence of one of these reptiles within. But he is often required to perform in the full light of day, surrounded by spectators; and incredulous persons have searched him beforehand, and even stripped him naked; yet his success has been complete. He assumes an air of mystery, strikes the walls with a short palm stick, whistles,

makes a clucking noise with his tongue, and spits upon the ground, and gene- CHAPTER
XI.
rally says, 'I adjure you by God, if ye be above, or if ye be below, that ye come
forth. I adjure you by the most great name: if ye be obedient, come forth; and
if ye be disobedient, die ! die ! die !' The serpent is generally dislodged by his
stick from a fissure in the wall or from the ceiling of the room. I have heard
it asserted that a serpent-charmer, before he enters a house in which he is to
try his skill, always employs a servant of that house to introduce one or more
serpents; but I have known instances in which this could not be the case, and
am inclined to believe that the dervishes above mentioned are generally
acquainted with some physical means of discovering the presence of serpents
without seeing them, and of attracting them from their lurking-places."

What these "physical means" may be is yet a secret, as also the "means"
by which persons can handle live scorpions, and can put them into their bosom
without fear or injury. I have seen this done again and again, even by small
boys. This has always excited my curiosity and astonishment, for scorpions
are the most malignant and irascible of all reptiles. The Hindoos, and after
them the Egyptians, are the most famous snake-charmers, scorpion-eaters,
etc., etc., although gipsies, Arabs, and others are occasionally found who gain
a vagabond livelihood by strolling round the country and confounding the
ignorant with these feats. In Psalm lviii. 4, 5, 6, there is evidently an allu- Scripture
sion to certain kinds of serpents which cannot be charmed: "Their poison is allusions.
like the poison of a serpent; they are like the deaf adder that stoppeth her
ear, which will not hearken to the voice of the charmer, charming never so
wisely." Jeremiah refers to the same fact: "Behold, I will send serpents, cockatrices, among you, which will not be charmed, and they shall bite you, *saith
the Lord*." [1] Such an assertion would scarcely be made in the *name of the Lord*
if the fact was not well established. So Solomon says, "Surely a serpent will
bite without enchantment." [2] Such serpents there still are, which the charmer
cannot subdue; and instances are related in which they have fallen victims
to their daring attempts to conquer these deaf and obstinate cockatrices.

There is also current an opinion that the adder will actually stop up his The adder
ear with his tail, to fortify himself against the influence of music and other stopping
charms. the ear.

Exorcism of demons and evil spirits is still practised, and with many super- Exorcis-
stitious rites and magic charms. But this is so common in all the ancient ing de-
churches that it needs no illustration. We meet with it frequently in the mons.
history of the apostles, and it would seem that the eclat of working real
miracles induced many to imitate them by exorcism and other magic operations. Thus, at Ephesus, "certain of the vagabond Jews, exorcists, took upon
them to call over them which had evil spirits the name of the Lord Jesus, saying, We adjure you by Jesus whom Paul preacheth." [3] Exorcists are still
very common, and their exploits are silly enough.

---

[1] Jer. viii. 17.   [2] Eccles. x. 11.   [3] Acts xix. 13.

The dervishes and Moslem sheikhs make some bold attempts at supernatural operations, and with singular success. Take the following: Early on
the morning of May 9th, 1837, the people of Beirût were seen hurrying along
the road toward Sidon, evidently intent upon some great affair. I soon ascertained that two celebrated pilgrims were returning from Mecca, and that the
dervishes were to perform extraordinary feats on the occasion. The whole city,
male and female, rushed along the road to meet them, accompanied with ban-
ners, drums, cymbals, and other musical instruments, singing, dancing, clapping hands, and whirling round and round like a top as they passed. In about
an hour they returned. The crowd was now immense, and the countenances
of many exhibited signs of the most intense exultation. In front of the procession came four flags of green, white, and black, the flagstaffs being surmounted with a double crescent of metal. Behind these marched a number
of dervishes from a distance, dancing with all their might, and performing
their most fanatical and fantastic pranks. They were naked to the waist,
wore a tall, conical cap of drab felt, and were the vilest and most savage-look-
ing creatures I ever saw. Two of them carried long iron spikes, the head of
which was a ball as large as an orange, and with many chains attached to it.

The sharp end of this instrument they struck with great violence into their
cheeks and *eyes*, and so deeply that it hung suspended without being held by
the hand. I know not by what trick this is performed, though I have often
seen it done, and have carefully examined the instrument. Two others had
long spindle-like spikes thrust *through the cheeks*. This was a fact, and I
saw it done by a dervish in my own house; but he had long before made holes
through his cheeks, which had healed up, like those in the ears for rings.
These his bushy beard completely concealed. After these savages came four
more flags; then two very holy dervishes, riding on small horses. They pretended to be altogether absorbed and wrapped up in devotion, prayed incessantly with their eyes closed, and took no notice of the vast and tumultuous
crowd around them. The frantic people prostrated themselves on the ground
before them, kissed their broad stirrups or the flags, but most of all the two
pilgrims, who now made their appearance, and seemed to be fagged out and
in danger of being kissed to death.

Just at the entrance into the open mdeân, south of the city, a long pavement of boys was formed in the following manner: The first lay on his face,
with his head to the south; the next with feet to the south, and so on, heads
and feet, to the end of this living corduroy causeway, the people crowding
them as close to one another as possible. A dense wall of spectators on either

side made a lane, along which the two dervishes actually *rode on top of the
boys from end to end*. I stood directly above them, and saw the operation
fairly performed, and saw the boys jump up again apparently unhurt. My
own Moslem servant was one of them, and he assured me that the sheikh's
horse was not heavier than a cat. The thing is not difficult to explain. The
boys were close together, the ground soft and sandy, the horse small, his shoes

flat and smooth, and he walked as if treading on eggs; and yet many of the CHAPTER lads, I have ascertained, were really bruised, and some seriously injured. The XI. whole scene, however, was demoniacal in the extreme. It is called Douseh, and is accompanied with a multitude of magical and supersitious ceremonies.*

There is now, or was until recently, in Cairo, a magician called 'Abd el Mesmer- Káder el Mugraby, who performed wonderful feats of magic, so like our ism. modern Mesmerism that I must ascribe to him the priority in this species of witchcraft. I have conversed with gentlemen, both English and others, who give the most extraordinary accounts of their interviews with this man. But lest they may have exaggerated, or, perhaps, might not wish to figure in such society, I will refer to Mr. Lane's book. His account is abundantly full, and undoubtedly authentic, and throws light on the matter in hand.

In preparing for the experiment of the *magic mirror of ink*, the magician The magic first asked for pen and ink, a piece of paper, and a pair of scissors; and, having mirror of ink. cut off a narrow slip of paper, wrote upon it certain forms of incantation, together with another charm, by which he professed to accomplish the experiment. He did not attempt to conceal these, but said that the object in view was accomplished through the influence of the first words—Turshoon and Turyooshoon—which were the names of two genii, his "familiar spirits." Here is the translation :—

> "Turshoon, Turyooshoon, come down,
> come down. Be present. Whither are gone
> the prince and his troops? Where are el Ahhmar,
> the prince, and his troops? Be present,
> ye servants of these names. And this is the removal, and we have removed from thee the veil, and thy sight to-day is piercing—*correct, correct.*"

Having written these, the magician cut the paper containing the forms of incantation into six strips. He then explained that the object of the latter charm was to open the boy's eyes and make him see into what is to us the invisible world.

Mr. Lane had prepared, by the magician's directions, some frankincense and The precoriander-seed, and a chafing-dish with live coals in it. These were brought paration. into the room, together with the boy, who was placed on a seat, with the magician before him. Some frankincense and coriander-seed were put into the dish, and then, taking hold of the boy's right hand, the magician drew in the palm of it a magic square, and wrote in it certain Arabic numerals. In the centre he poured a little ink, and desired the boy to look into it, and tell him if he could see his face reflected in it. The boy replied that he saw his face clearly. *The magician, holding the boy's hand all the while,* told him to continue looking intently in the ink, and not to raise his head.

* [May not this explain the allusion in Isaiah li. 23: "But I will put it " (the cup of trembling) "into the hand of them that afflict thee; which have said to thy soul, Bow down, that we may go over: and thou hast laid thy body as the ground, and as the street, to them that went over ? "—ED.]

LAB — K

He then took one of the little slips of paper inscribed with the forms of incantation, and dropped it into the chafing-dish upon the burning coals, and, as
he did this, he commenced an indistinct muttering of words, which he continued during the whole process, excepting when he had to ask the boy a question, or tell him what he was to say. The piece of paper containing the words
from the Koran he placed inside of the fore part of the boy's cap. He then
asked if he saw anything in the ink, and was answered *No;* but, in about a
minute after, the boy, trembling and affrighted, said, I see a man sweeping
the ground. When he has done sweeping, said the magician, tell me. Presently the boy said, He has done.

The magician again interrupted his muttering to ask the boy if he knew
what bairuk (flag) was; and being answered Yes, desired him to say, Bring a
flag. The boy did so, and soon after said, He has brought a flag. What
colour is it? said the magician. The boy replied *Red.* He was told to call for
another flag, which he did; and soon after said he saw another brought, and
that it was *black.* In like manner he called for a third, fourth, fifth, sixth,
and seventh, which were white, green, black, red, and blue. The magician
then asked him, How many flags have you now? Seven, answered the boy.
While this was going on, the magician put the second and third of the several
slips of paper, upon which the forms of invocation were written, into the chafing-dish, and fresh frankincense and coriander-seed having been repeatedly
added, the fumes became painful to the eyes. The boy was next desired to
say, Bring the Sultan's tent, and pitch it. This he did, and about a minute
after said, Some men have brought the tent—a large green tent; they are
pitching it; and presently added, They have set it up.

Now, said the magician, order the soldiers to come and pitch their camp
around the tent of the Sultan; which was done immediately. The magician,
putting the fourth and fifth slips into the fire, said, Tell some of the people to
bring a bull. The boy gave the order, and said, I see a bull; it is red; four
men are dragging it along. At his command they killed, cooked it, and then
ate it up before his eyes. They have done, said the lad, and are washing their
hands. The magician then told him to call for the Sultan; and, having done
so, he said, I see the Sultan riding to his tent on a bay horse, and he has
on his head a high red cap; he has alighted at his tent, and sat down in it.

Desire them to bring coffee to the Sultan, said the magician, and to form
the court. These orders were given and obeyed. The magician had put the
last of the six little strips of paper into the chafing-dish, muttering nothing
but the words of the written invocation, except on two or three occasions,
when he said, If they demand information, inform them, and be ye veracious.

Here ends the long preparation, and it certainly was magical enough. All
was now ready, and Mr. Lane proceeded to test the boy by a variety of questions, the answers to which were often strikingly correct; but he does not seem
to have been as successful that time as at some others which have been described to me. I have never heard anything like a satisfactory explanation of

this matter, and have none of my own. There are magicians in Egypt now, as there were in the days of Moses, and their achivements fill a reflecting mind with very serious thoughts. This description of Lane covers the whole series of magical forms and ceremonies practised by others, for other purposes, with but slight variations.

I asked one in Sidon whether these names, Turshoon and Turyooshoon, were known and employed by him; and he said they were. In short, this whole subject is involved in no small mystery. It exercises a prodigious influence on Oriental society, and always has, and merits a thorough examination. The boy evidently saw just such scenes as are depicted in the wildest stories *The scenes like the "Arabian Nights."* in the Thousand Nights, and I suspect that this very art was in greater perfection then than now, and that the gorgeous creations of that work were, in many cases, mere verbal pictures taken from the magic mirror of ink

But our conversation is running deep into the hours of rest, and the subject is almost boundless. We may meet with it again. Let us now seek protection from Him who slumbers not, both from actual evil and from hideous visions of the night, while we resign ourselves to "nature's sweet restorer, balmy sleep."

CHAPTER XII.

SARAFEND TO TYRE.

February 15th.

WHAT snow-capped peak is that which appears beyond these nearest mountains?

That is the very head of old Hermon. You have been out among Sarepta's *Peak of Hermon.* ruins, I perceive, for from these only is the point you mention visible. But few travellers see it, nor would you, if it had not been covered with fresh snow, and lit up by the rising sun.

These sights and names make me realize with delightful certainty that I am actually within the Holy Land.

However that may be, it is nearly certain that our blessed Lord once walked over this very plain, and gazed on those identical hills. I have the impression that it was to Sarepta he came, in the coasts of Tyre and Sidon,[1] to visit, per-

[1] Matt. xv. 21.

haps, the place where his great forerunner Elijah lived and wrought miracles; and that the woman of Canaan, whom Mark calls a Syro-phœnician,[1] belonged to the city of that poor widow with whom the prophet resided. *He* raised her son from death.[2] The Saviour delivered this one's daughter from the power of the devil.

Sarafend
—Sarepta.

This small village on the hill to our left, called Sarefend, is the modern representative of Sarepta. It seems to have been built there after the twelfth century, for at the time of the Crusades the city stood on the shore. Of course the widow's cave, and all other ancient sites now shown under the hill of Sarafend, are apocryphal.

Those who merely ride along the common road form too low an estimate of the size of the ancient city. There are two distinct groups of ruins. One on the headland, immediately west of this, 'Ain el Kŭnterah. This may have been the harbour of Sarepta; and here, I suppose, was the fortress which Phocas mentions in the twelfth century, and also the chapel erected over the reputed house of the widow. Some of those old foundations which we have just examined may mark the exact spot. Our translation makes Elijah live in

Elijah's
"loft."

a loft, but not very accurately. In Hebrew it is 'allîyeh, and this is the common Arabic word for the upper rooms of houses. This 'allîyeh is the most desirable part of the establishment, is best fitted up, and is still given to guests who are to be treated with honour. The women and servants live below, and their apartment is called ardîyeh, or ground floor,—in common parlance simple *beit* or house. The poorer sort have no 'allîyeh. We may infer several things from this *word:* that the mode of building in Elijah's time, and the custom of giving the 'allîyeh to the guest were the same as now; also, that this

HOUSE WITH AN 'ALLIYEH.

widow woman was not originally among the very poorest classes, but that her extreme destitution was owing to the dreadful famine which then prevailed.

[1] Mark vii. 26.   [2] 1 Kings xvii. 17–23.

The little chamber made for Elijah by the Shunammite[1] is also called 'allîyeh, CHAPTER and was therefore an upper room, respectable and comfortable. They are more XII. retired than the lower apartments of the house, and, of course, appropriate for the resting-place of prophets.

The main ruins of Sarepta extend southward for a mile or more, and are Ruins. very considerable. They are now being dug over, perhaps the twentieth time, for stone to build the barracks at Beirût. Observe what masses of rubbish are heaped up over the plain, among which appear broken columns, marble slabs, sarcophagi, and other relics of a flourishing and wealthy city. That dome, surmounting the tomb of Khŭdr Abu Abbas, is supposed by Dr. Robinson to be the successor of the Christian chapel built by the Crusaders; and this may be so, though Khŭdr is the Moslem name of St. George, for which somewhat fabulous saint the Mohammedans have very great respect.

One ought not to pass away from this remarkable spot without laying up in Lessons his inner heart the noble lesson taught by the widow and her barrel of meal. from In her utmost want—about to cook her last morsel and die—she yet listens to Sarepta. the call of humanity, brings water for the thirsty prophet, and shares with him her final meal. Go and do likewise. In hours of greatest darkness and destitution, share with those more needy than yourself, and let the morrow take thought for itself. Who does not often need the lesson to prompt his reluctant soul to deeds of charity, and the result to fortify his feeble faith? How many poor Gentile sinners have urged the plea of the Syro-phœnician woman for the crumbs of mercy which fall from their Lord's table,[2] and have been dismissed with the like benediction!

Lonely and lowly Sarepta! scene of stupendous miracles, fare-thee-well! The Saviour of the world has set his seal of immortality on thee. Thy name will ever teach the great truth, that the favour of our common Father above was never confined within the narrow limits of Jacob's seed; for unto no city of all the tribes of Israel was Elijah sent, but unto a poor widow within thy walls.[3] Let them of the "synagogue" be "filled with wrath," but we shall cherish thy memory all the more for the sweet lesson.

This low, flat Tell, with its ruined khan, is called Khaizeran, and so is the brawling brook south of it. The plain and rocky hill side are covered with the remains of a large place; and on the very top of that rugged promontory are ancient sarcophagi, cut in the live rock; and the base of the mountain between Quarries it and Sarafend abounds in old quarries, with their accompanying houses for the and tombs dead. This fine plain before us reaches to the cave and tombs of 'Adlûn, some three miles ahead. The ruins about the cave are identified with the Ornithon of the Greek geographers, and tesselated pavements and other remains of ancient habitations appear in many places along the shore.

I find it difficult to realize that we are passing over, and so quietly too, a region whose eventful story runs back to the earliest records of our race. Is

[1] 2 Kings iv. 10.   [2] Mark vii. 24–30.   [3] Luke iv. 25–29.

11

PART I.

there any reason to doubt that it was originally settled by the immediate descendants of Canaan ?

Origin of the Phœnicians.

Heredotus opens his celebrated History with this singular sentence : " The more learned of the Persians assert the Phœnicians to have been the original exciters of contention. This nation migrated from the borders of the Red Sea to the place of their present settlement, and soon distinguished themselves by their long and enterprising voyages," etc., etc. This assertion of the historian rests on no proof that I know of, and is not countenanced by the account of this matter found in the 10th chapter of Genesis. It is possible, however, that the grandson of Noah went first to the Red Sea, and afterward came to this coast, and thus both records may be true, but it is extremely improbable. Those who adopt the story of Herodotus generally attach little importance, I suppose, to the statement of Moses ; with us, however, it is decisive. This is a very wide subject, rather dry, too, for discussion on horseback, but it is eminently Biblical—stands connected with almost every page of the sacred records, and we must study it carefully if we would make ourselves masters of Bible history and geography ; and, since there is nothing of special importance to claim attention in this neighbourhood, we may while away the time and the road with a lesson in man's most ancient history.

Account of Josephus.

Josephus, without hesitation or qualification, asserts that Canaan, the fourth son of Ham, settled this country, and gave it his own name; and, entering into details he mentions the different sons of Canaan, and where they dwelt. Thus, Sidonius built Sidon, Amatheus founded Amath or Hamath, Arudus had the island Arudus, and Arucus built Arca. Of the remaining sons he is not so particular ; but Moses, from whom he derived his information, mentions them repeatedly—Heth, and the Jebusite, and the Amorite, the Girgashite, the Hivite, and the Sinite, and the Zemarite ; and adds that " the border of the Canaanites was from Sidon, as thou comest unto Gerar, unto Gaza, as thou goest unto Sodom, and Gomorrah, and Admah, and Zeboim, even unto Lasha."[1] The general boundaries of their country cannot be questioned, nor can we doubt that they were the first settlers after the Deluge, without disregarding the sacred record.

Sons of Ham.

The history of these various families differs widely. Those who settled in Palestine multiplied rapidly, and soon became wealthy, powerful, and extremely corrupt. They were the Hittites, Girgashites, Amorites, *Canaanites*, Perizzites, Hivites, and Jebusites—seven greater and mightier nations than the Hebrews. Their cities were " great, and fenced up to heaven."[2] " A people great and tall, the children of the Anakims, whom thou knowest, and of whom thou hast heard say, Who can stand before the children of Anak ?"[3] These were all destroyed or expelled from Canaan, and their land given to the Hebrews. The Sidonians, Arkites, Arvadites, Zimrites, Sinites, and Hamathites, whose territories lay north, and without the narrower limits of the pro-

---

[1] Gen. x. 19.   [2] Deut. vii. 1, 2.   [3] Deut. ix. 2.

mised land, long continued to flourish, and were often in alliance with the CHAPTER
XII. kings of Judah and Israel.

The exact *locale* of the Canaanitish tribes that were destroyed cannot, in Canaanite all cases, be determined. The Hittites, we know, from the history of the tribes. patriarchs, lived in the neighbourhood of Hebron.[1] The Jebusites possessed Jerusalem until the time of David;[2] and in Numbers xiii. 29, we read that the Amorites dwelt in the mountains not only of Palestine proper, but of Gilead and Bashan, east of the Jordan, while those who were called *Canaanites*, by way of eminence, occupied the sea-board and the regions near the Jordan. These *Canaanites* were probably a mixture of different tribes, who took the name of their common ancestor. The Amorites, we may suppose, became Amorites. the most numerous, powerful, and corrupt of all the race, for they are frequently made to represent the whole. Thus, in Genesis xv. 16, it is said, "The iniquity of the Amorite is not yet full;" and so in 1 Kings xxi. 26 they have the same bad eminence assigned them. Og, king of Bashan, and Sihon of Heshbon, were Amorites. They were the ruling tribe in the south-west of Judea, as we learn from Judges i. 34–36. The Amalekites dwelt in the land Amalek. of the south. There is some uncertainty about the origin of this people, although they figure long and largely in Hebrew history. It is evident that if a *tribe* of Amalekites is mentioned in Genesis xiv. 7, they could not have been descended from the grandson of Esau, the brother of Jacob. In Genesis xxxvi. 12, Moses tells us that Amalek was the son of Eliphaz by a concubine; and Josephus adds that a part of Idumea was called Amalekitis, from the descendants of this grandson of Edom. The "country of the Amalekites" which Chedorlaomer smote in the days of Abraham, I therefore take to be the district that was really inhabited by Amalek when Moses wrote, but those who dwelt there when Chedorlaomer ravaged that country were of some other race. Moses, in that passage, speaks of the *country*, not of the people. The Amalekites spread over the whole southern desert, and even into Palestine proper. They were a fierce, warlike race, and manifested the most inveterate hostility to the Jews throughout all their history; and for their ferocity and cruelty they were utterly excluded from mercy. While of Edom in general it is said, "Thou shalt not abhor an Edomite, for he is thy brother;"[3] of Amalek, the Lord said unto Moses, "Write this for a memorial in a book, and rehearse it in the ears of Joshua; for I will utterly put out the remembrance of Amalek from under heaven."[4] This terrible sentence was again repeated to Saul: "Now go and smite Amalek, and utterly destroy all that they have."[5] And Saul, in executing the command, says to the Kenites (ver. 6), "Go, depart; get you down from the Amalekites, lest I destroy you with them." Thus the land of this latter people was also forfeited to Israel, according to the promise in Genesis xv. 19, though they always continued on friendly

---

[1] Gen. xxiii. 7. [2] 2 Sam. v. 6. [3] Deut. xxiii. 7.
[4] Exod. xvii. 1 [5] 1 Sam. xv. 3.

PART
I.

terms with the Jews. Of the Kenizzites nothing is known, nor are they heard of in the subsequent history of the Bible.

Kadmon-
ites.

The Kadmonites are supposed to have resided about the head-waters of the Jordan, under Hermon. This name is still preserved among the Nusairîyeh north of Tripoli, and they have a tradition that their ancestors were expelled from Palestine by Joshua. It is curious, also, that a fragment of this strange people still cling to their original home at 'Ain-Fît, Zaora, and Ghŭjar, near the foot of Hermon. I have repeatedly travelled among them in their own mountains, and many things in their physiognomy and manners gave me the idea that they were a remnant of the most ancient inhabitants of this country. We may yet become better acquainted with them before our pilgrimage is

Rephaims.

completed. The Rephaims are often mentioned as giants and rulers among the people of the land. King Og was one of them, and so, I suppose, was Goliath. A tribe of them resided, long before, in the north of the Hauran, and were defeated and subdued by Chedorlaomer.[1] They also dwelt in the

Perizzites.

south of Judea even down to the time of David, if not later. The Perizzites seem to have been a mingled race like the *Canaanites*, and their residence was in the mountains of Judea, and northward in Ephraim as far as the plain of Esdraelon.[2] It is plain, from Joshua xi. 3, and Judges iii. 3, that the Hivites dwelt mainly along the western base of Hermon, and up the great Wady et Teim, between the two Lebanons, unto the entering in of Hamath, toward Baalbek. There is good reason to believe that, with the seven Canaanitish families condemned to extermination for their pre-eminent wickedness, there were various other tribes mingled, especially on the outskirts of the Hebrew territory: the Kadmonites and Rephaims, as we have seen, on the east; the Moabites and Arabs on the south-east; the Amalekites on the south; the Philistines from Egypt on the south-west; the Phœnicians of Sidon, Tyre, Dor, etc., on the west, and the Maacathites and Geshurites on the north; and still beyond these were the Arkites, Arvadites, Zimrites, Sinites, and Hamath-ites. These were not attacked by Joshua, and doubtless multitudes of their brethren from the south escaped and took refuge among them. Nor are there wanting faint traditions to confirm this supposition. I have visited the pri-meval seats of all these old tribes—Hamath, Sin, Zimri, Ruad, and Arca.

Tenacity
of names.

The tenacity with which these and other places cling to their ancient names is truly wonderful. One is not only surprised, but startled, to hear ignorant peasants pronounce, without an effort or a moment's hesitation, over shapeless ruins, the very names by which they were called by Moses and Abraham three or four thousand years ago.

The Phœ-
nicians
Canaan-
ites.

Do you suppose that the Phœnicians, so celebrated in ancient story, the in-ventors of commerce, of manufactures, and of letters, and the founders of so many splendid colonies, were really Canaanites, and consequently the de-scendants of Ham?

---

[1] Gen. xiv. 5.   [2] Judges i. 4; Josh. xvii. 15, 17.

I do, and that notwithstanding what has been written by learned men to prove that they came from the shores of the Red Sea, or from the Arabian, or even from the Indian Ocean. The Bible is now almost our only authority, and it is explicit. Josephus, who lived in this country nearly two thousand years ago, and had access to documents which have long since perished, does not even allude to a suspicion of such an immigration from the south; and if there are, or ever have been, cities and temples on the Persian Gulf, or along the Arabian Ocean, with names similar to those of the Phœnicians, it is much more likely that those who built them were emigrants from this country than that this country was colonized from them. It is extremely probable that the Phœnicians did establish colonies in those parts. Their general practice was to form permanent settlements wherever they carried on commerce—in the islands of the Mediterranean, in Asia Minor, in Greece, and in Spain, possibly in England, certainly at Carthage, and along the northern coast of Africa. We know also from the Bible and from other sources that they traded extensively in the Red Sea, and along the southern shores of Arabia and Africa, and are therefore quite prepared to find traces of them along those coasts. The fountain-head of the Phœnicians, however, was Sidon and her renowned daughter Tyre.

I see that the name Canaan is derived by some critics from a Hebrew root said to signify *low land;* and it is maintained that it was given to the inhabitants of this country because they dwelt on the sea-board, and not because they were descended from the son of Ham.

CHAPTER XII.

Meaning of Canaan.

Such philological criticism, when applied to questions of this kind, is far from satisfactory ; and in the present case, if it could be proved that there is such a Hebrew word, it is obvious that it could not be applied to the Canaanites with any propriety, for they resided in all parts of the land, and not merely on the shore and the low plains, and from them the whole country, though very mountainous, was called Canaan. In short, we have from the remotest antiquity, and on the very best authority, the origin of this name in that of the great ancestor of the several tribes that settled the country soon after the Deluge; and one can scarcely avoid the suspicion that it is because this authority is the Bible that certain savants have called it in question, and have rummaged among Hebrew roots and doubtful scraps of heathen authors, who knew nothing about the matter, in order to cast suspicion upon the sacred records. But here is something more interesting than dry historical discussions. Let us turn aside, and examine these gray resting-places for Phœnicia's ancient dead.

This cave, with its mouth blackened by the smoke of gipsies, is, of course, chiefly natural, though it was formerly plastered, in part at least, and fitted for a dwelling, or possibly a cistern, like those at Beit Jibrîn. The tombs were cut by quarriers who lived in the town whose ruins are scattered over the plain. These quarries extend for miles southward, and are crowded with sepulchres. The inhabitants seem to have done nothing but quarry stone for

Caves or tombs of Adlun.

PART
I.

Phœni-
cian
tombs.

other cities, and cut sepulchres for themselves. Many of these tombs are as perfect as when first made, but the doors are all gone, and the tombs empty, and were so, most likely, two thousand years ago. They are nearly all of the same pattern, having a small ante-room in front, and a door leading from that into the body of the tomb, which is about six feet square, with niches on three sides for the dead, the door occupying the fourth. Some of them are cut into the rock where it is nearly horizontal; in which case a square shaft was sunk about three feet deep, and from that a low window leads into the tomb. A deep groove ran round the face of the rock above, to turn the water away from this entrance. There are a few words of a Greek inscription over that tomb just south of this cave. The rest are absolutely destitute of architectural ornament, device, or inscription of any kind. The ancient Phœnicians delighted to cut their tombs in the perpendicular faces of the rock left in quarrying, as is seen on all this coast, and particularly at Tortosa, Ladakîyeh, and Suadea.

Did Phœnicia extend as far north as Ladakîyeh ?

Extent of
Phœnicia.

The people did, whatever may be said of the country. The Sinites settled, I suppose, along the river Sin, and doubtless they spread round the shore to Ladakîyeh, and may have even reached to the mouth of the Orontes. This would agree with Strabo. The largest extent of Phœnicia, therefore, was from the Sinites on the north to Dor on the south. Phœnicia proper, however, reached no farther northward than to the Eleutherus, the modern Nahr Kebîr, in the plain of Akkar. The width of territory belonging to these small states differed greatly. The plain of Jebilé, where the Sinites dwelt, runs far back into the interior. The Zimrites, or Zemarites, had scarcely any level land, for the mountains shut down upon the very margin of the sea. So also the Arvadites were probably confined to a narrow strip along the coast; but the Arkite had the magnificent plain of June. The plains of Tripoli, Bŭtrone, Jebail, Beirût, Sidon, and Tyre, are comparatively narrow, but that of Acre is twenty miles long, and from six to ten broad. No doubt the Phœnicians possessed also the western slopes of the mountains; and the Sidonians and Tyrians extended their territorial limits to the Ijon and the Hûleh,—perhaps still farther to the east. The average breadth of their estates, however, could not have been more than twenty miles.

Multitude
of Syrian
tribes and
sects.

Syria has always been cursed with a multiplicity of tribes and religions, which split up the country into small principalities and conflicting classes— the fruitful parent of civil war, anarchy, and all confusion. Nor has this source of mischief been materially mitigated down to the present hour. This will appear but too evident from the following statistics. The Moslems, who are the ruling class all over the country, except in Lebanon, may number

Moslems.

about 800,000

They are divided into two principal sects—the Sunites and Shïïtes.

There may be 50,000 Kurds 50,000

The Nusairîyeh occupy the mountains north of Tripoli, and may
amount to 150,000

The Ismailîyeh and Yezzîdy are too few to merit specific attention ;   CHAPTER
and the same may be said of the Nowar or gipsies, who are found   XII.
in all parts. They will not amount to more than   .   .   .   20,000

The Druses occupy the southern half of Lebanon, extend over to   Druses.
Hermon, and out into the Hauran—a few thousands reside in Jebel
el 'Alah, west of Aleppo, and on Carmel and the mountains above
Acre. They number about   100,000

The Jews are about 25,000. In Jerusalem 7000, in Damascus 5000,   Jews.
Aleppo 4000, Safed 2000, Tiberias 1500, Hebron 600, and the remainder in Beirût, Sidon, etc., etc.   25,000

The Maronites, chiefly of Lebanon, may be   .   .   .   200,000 Maronites.
The orthodox Greeks, in all parts of the country   .   .   150,000 Greeks,
Armenians 20,000, Jacobites 15,000   .   .   .   .   35,000 &c.

There are Papal offshoots from these sects, which may number 70 or
80,000   80,000

There are a few Latins in most of the large cities, and also Protestants in various parts.

This gives a total of 1,610,000 ; which, of course, is only as close an approxi- Total.
mation as the very imperfect statistics of the government and of the different sects enable us to make.*

[* In connection with the above division of the sects of Syria and Palestine, it may be useful Religious
to give a brief account of the several religious creeds. We are indebted for the information creeds.
which we here abridge to the valuable work of the Rev. J. L. Porter.

I. THE MAHOMETANS OR MOSLEMS.—Under this general head may be classed, 1. The *Sonnites*
(Sunites), traditionists, or orthodox Mahometans, who, besides the written Koran, acknowledge
the authority of the Sonna, a collection of traditional sayings and anecdotes of Mahomet. 2. The
Metawileh (sing., Mutawaly)—followers of Aly, son-in-law of Mahomet, whom they deem the
true Imam—rejecters of the Sonna—allied in faith to the Shì-ites of Persia, and very scrupulous as
to distinctions between clean and unclean. 3. The *Nusairieyeh*, or Ansairiyeh but their religion is
a secret—something, perhaps, between Mahometanism and Christianity. (See an account of
them at chap. xvi. p. 226). 4. The *Ismailîeyeh*, whose religion is also a mystery,—originally a
sect of Shì-ites, and descendants of "the Assassins" in the time of the Crusades.

II. THE DRUSES.—The origin of this sect is remarkable, and their tenets and modes of worship
are kept as secret as possible. Hâkim, an Egyptian, gave himself out to be a prophet; and
in the eleventh century, one of his followers, expelled from Egypt, took refuge at the western base
of Mount Hermon, and became the founder of the Druses. They believe in the unity of God,
and in the manifestation of God in the person of several individuals, the last of whom was
Hâkim. They believe also in the constant existence of five superior spiritual ministers, of whom
Hamza and Christ were the greatest. Their religion, they hold, shall one day be triumphant,
and Hâkim shall reign in person. The transmigration of souls is one of their tenets. They meet
in their chapels every Thursday evening, but what passes is unknown. It is believed that they
are fully more a political than a religious sect. They are very united, and very fierce in war.
They are accommodating in religion, and have even offered to become Christians, in order to
obtain the protection of this country. They are of two classes,—the 'Okkal, or initiated; and the
Juhhâl, or ignorant.

III. THE CHRISTIANS.—A full account of the native Christians will be found in Wilson's
"Lands of the Bible." They are divided into several sects : 1. The *Greeks*,—so called because
connected with the Greek or Oriental Church,—all natives of Syria. There are two patriarchates,
—Antioch and Jerusalem,—and sixteen bishoprics. The priests must be married men. 2. The
Syrians or Jacobites, a sect separated from the Greek Church on account of the Monophysite
heresy. Their service is in Syriac. Their number is very small. 3. *Maronites*. This sect

PART
I.

Desert
tribes.

Cities.

In this enumeration the Arab tribes that roam over the deserts are not included. Very little is known about their numbers, and estimates by different individuals vary surprisingly. They may be 200,000, possibly half a million. It is interesting to notice how these various populations are distributed over the country. Lebanon has about 400,000 inhabitants, gathered into more than six hundred towns, villages, and hamlets. Of the cities of Syria, Damascus is the largest, as it is the oldest—perhaps it is the most ancient city in the world that is now flourishing and populous. It numbers about 120,000. Jerusalem, the most interesting city on the globe, has only about 18,000; Aleppo has 70 or 80,000, Beirût from 40 to 50,000, Hamah 33,000, Hums 25,000, Antioch 20,000, Tripoli and Harbor 18,000, Edlip 10,000, Ladakîyeh 6000, Sidon 10,000, Tyre 3500, Acre 5000, Khaifa 3000, Nazareth 3000, Safet 4000, Tiberias 1500, Jennîn 2500, Nablus 12,000, Jaffa 11,000, Ramleh 4000, Gaza 16,000, Hebron 6000, Bethlehem 3500. In Lebanon, Zahleh is the largest, and has about 11,000 inhabitants. Deir el Kamar has 7000, Hasbeiya, in Hermon, has about 6000, and Rashaia 2500. I need scarcely remind you that the entire population is gathered into towns and villages.

Prevalent
feelings.

The various religions and sects live together, and practise their conflicting superstitions in close proximity, but the people do not coalesce into one homogeneous community, nor do they regard each other with fraternal feelings. The Sunnites excommunicate the Shiites—both hate the Druse, and all three detest the Nusairîyeh. The Maronites have no particular love for anybody, and, in turn, are disliked by all. The Greeks cannot endure the Greek Catholics—all despise the Jews. And the same remarks apply to the minor divisions of this land. There is no common bond of union. Society has no continuous strata underlying it, which can be opened and worked for the general benefit of all, but an endless number of dislocated fragments, faults, and dikes, by which the masses are tilted up in hopeless confusion, and lie at every conceivable angle of antagonism to each other. That omnific Spirit that brooded over primeval chaos can alone bring order out of such confusion, and reduce these conflicting elements to peace and concord.

Genealo-
gies lost.

Another curious fact is, that, with the exception of the Jews and Bedawîn Arabs, no one can trace back his own origin to any ancient race or nation.

originated in the Monothelitic controversy in the seventh century. Their founder was John Maron. In A.D. 1180 they renounced their heresy, and acknowledged the Pope. They are still in connection with Rome, but have service in Syriac. Their candidates for priesthood may marry before ordination. The Maronites swarm on Lebanon. There are 82 convents in Lebanon, with 2000 monks and nuns, and a revenue of £70,000 a year! The Maronites are the hereditary foes of the Druses. 4. *Greek Catholics* and *Syrian Catholics*. These are proselytes whom Romish priests and Jesuits have gained over during the last two centuries. The sect embraces a number of wealthy native Christians, and is influential in Syria.

IV. THE JEWS.—In Damascus and Aleppo many are natives, and wealthy,—Arabs in all but religion. In Palestine the Jews are all foreigners, natives of various countries.

V. THE TURKS.—These are very few in number, but occupy all the highest situations, and are the scourges of the land—ED.]

The general mass of the Moslems are the mingled descendants of the various CHAPTER
races who composed the population of the Greek empire at the time of XII.
Mohammed ; and this original confusion of races has been infinitely augmented
during the twelve centuries of their lawless occupation. In all the Christian
sects there has been the same blending of primitive races, and a large infusion
of foreign and European blood during the times of the Crusades, and subsequently, even to our day ; so that the most intelligent and learned admit that
it is absolutely impossible now to ascertain their true national origin. The
Maronites, as a body, may have descended from the ancient Syrians. The
Nusairîyeh suggest the idea that they are the miserable *debris* of the accursed
Canaanites. The Metâwelies appear to have immigrated from Persia;—they
have a decided resemblance to the Jews. The Moslems of Palestine, and
particularly from Carmel southward, have largely intermingled with the Egyptians. Perhaps some of their peculiarities of manners, countenance, and
language, may have been derived from the old Philistines, who came originally
from Egypt, as I believe, and not from Cappadocia or Cyprus. In the inhabitants of Lebanon and the plains at its base we may possibly find some traces
of the original Phœnicians. The Druses are Arabs, who came from the eastern
confines of Syria, and settled in Lebanon and Anti-Lebanon within the last
nine hundred years.

No other country in the world, I presume, has such a multiplicity of Antagon-
antagonistic races ; and herein lies the greatest obstacle to any general and ism and
disunion.
permanent amelioration and improvement in their condition, character, and
prospects. They can never form one united people, never combine for any
important religious or political purpose ; and will therefore remain weak, incapable of self-government, and exposed to the invasions and oppressions of
foreigners. Thus it has been, is now, and must long continue to be—a people
divided, meted out, and trodden down.

From these tombs of 'Adlûn to the Kasimîeh, the plain is called Abu el
Aswad, from a brook of that name which cuts through the centre of it ; or
both plain and brook derive this name (Father of Black) from the extreme
blackness of the soil. There are three paths—one along the base of the hills,
the main road through the centre of the plain, and a third by the sea-
shore. We take the latter, to avoid the mud. From the brook southward,
the regular road is now soft black mire, in the depths of which every vestige of the old Roman pavement (if there ever was one) has entirely disappeared.

Have these ruins along the shore no name ? To judge from the extent
of ground covered with foundations, fragments of Roman brick-work, tesselated pavements, and general rubbish, there must have been a large city
here.

They probably mark the site of the ancient Ornithon, though this is not The Orni-
certain. They have now no other name but that of 'Adlûn. We shall pass thon.
many other sites, for the entire coast was once a continuous village, like the

Bosphorus above Constantinople; and this renders the present utter desertion of the coast the more remarkable. From Sidon to Tyre there is not a single hamlet on the shore, and these plains are all cultivated by people who reside on the mountains.

Have the inhabitants retreated to the hills to enjoy a cooler climate, or for the sake of protection from bands of lawless soldiers passing up and down the coast?

Dangers of the sea-coast.
As far back as the time of Thucydides at least, the people in many parts of the Mediterranean were accustomed to build their towns at a considerable distance from the shore, and in strong positions, to escape the visits of pirates who then infested the sea. Any city exposed to these lawless attacks, and unable to defend itself, must of course be abandoned so long as this liability continues; but as soon as the sea is cleared of pirates, the inhabitants return and rebuild, except where some cause more permanent leads to final desertion. Such causes have long since reduced Cæsarea, Askelon, and other important places, to utter and hopeless desolation.

Change of employment.
I suppose the main reason for the total desertion of this particular coast is to be found in an entire change of employment. The Phœnicians were mariners, and hence, wherever there was a sandy beach upon which to draw up their small craft, or a sheltered cove where they could ride at anchor, there a village sprang up and flourished. Now there are no mariners,—not a boat is owned by any of these peasants; they are exclusively given to agriculture, and have no occasion to dwell near the shore. Of course it is better for them to reside on the hills, as you see they do, in those prettily-posted villages on the mountain side. That white dome south of 'Adlûn covers the tomb of a saint called Zare. A weather-beaten, surly sheikh of the village, told me that Zare was the grandson of Joshua (on whom be peace). As such, I am willing to leave him in unquestioned possession of his sepulchre and pedigree, honoured as a great saint by these semi-savage Metâwelies. It is decidedly interesting, however, to hear these austere disciples of 'Ali, as ignorant of history as the oxen they are punching along with their goads, repeat these venerable Bible names as familiar "household words."

Quick-sands.
We must take care how we cross this Abu el Asward, for there are quick-sands at its mouth. My horse once sank to his belly, and plunged desperately before he brought me to the other side. Here is a safe ford, however. Above us you see that noble arch of a Roman bridge. It is quite perfect, but the embankment on either side has long since been washed away, so that it is useless. From this on, much of the plain is impracticable marsh in winter. In the centre of it are large springs, which were once surrounded by masonry like those at Ras el 'Ain, near Tyre, and for the same purpose. The work is now broken, and indeed, most of the plain is overgrown with thorns, and abandoned to Arabs. A group of their tents spreads along the base of the hills on our left.

If those of Kedar were no more attractive than these of Abu el Asward, the

Bride in the "Song of Songs"[1] has fallen upon a very lame comparison for her charms.

Ay; but observe, it is she that is black, not the tents of Kedar, perhaps; not the curtains of Solomon, certainly. These may have been extremely beautiful. But even black tents, when new, and pitched among bushes of liveliest green, have a very "comely" appearance, especially when both are bathed in a flood of evening's golden light. And here we have started up, and sent leaping over the plain, another of Solomon's favourites. What elegant creatures those gazelles are, and how gracefully they bound! "My beloved is like a roe

GAZELLES.

or young hart: behold he cometh leaping upon the mountains, skipping upon the hills."[2] These lovely harts are very timid, and descend at night to the plains to feed among the lilies until the day break and the shadows flee away.[3] This is alluded to in the charge to the daughters of Jerusalem, "By the roes and by the hinds of the field, that ye stir not up, nor awake my love, till he please."[4] We shall meet these graceful gazelles all through Syria and Palestine, and the more you see of them the greater will be your admiration. Solo-

[1] Song i. 5.　　[2] Song ii. 8, 9.　　[3] Song ii. 17.　　[4] Song iii. 5.

PART
I.
mon is not alone in his partiality. Persian and Arab poets abound in references to them. The fair ones of these fervid sons of song are often compared to the coy gazelle that comes by night and *pastures* upon their hearts. These "cruel gazelles, with graceful gait and liquid eye," are found in other lands, and graze on other hearts besides those of Persian poets. The sacred writers frequently mention gazelles under the various names of harts, roes, and hinds. They are celebrated for their activity. Thus Jacob says of Naphtali, "He is a hind let loose;"[1] and his mountains abound in gazelles to this day. "Asahel was light of foot as a wild roe."[2] And David sings, "He maketh my feet like hinds' feet, and setteth me upon my high places."[3] I have often stopped to admire the grace, and ease, and fearless security with which these pretty animals bound along the high places of the mountains. They are amiable, affectionate, and loving, by universal testimony; and accordingly Solomon says, "Let her—the wife of thy youth—be as the loving hind and pleasant roe;"[4] and no sweeter comparison can be found. It is implied in Jeremiah iv. 5 that the hind is particularly fond of her young; for the prophet illustrates the severity of the threatened dearth and famine by declaring that the very hinds forsook their young in the field, because there was no grass. David compares his longing for the living God to the panting of the hart for the waterbrooks.[5] I have seen large flocks of these panting harts gather round the water-brooks in the great deserts of Central Syria, so subdued by thirst that you could approach quite near them before they fled. But here we are on the banks of the Kāsimîeh, and yonder, at the foot of the bridge, our lunch awaits us. This bridge, which now springs quite across the river by one bold and lofty arch, is not old, for Maundrell, in 1696, found the ancient one broken down, and he and his party had great difficulty in crossing; and so should we without a bridge.

So I should judge, for it is the largest river I have seen in this country, and appears to be full to the brim. You call it Kāsimîeh?

The Litany.
It is the ancient Leontes, and its present name, except just at this place, is Litany; apparently a corruption of the Latin—or perhaps that is merely a Latinized form of Litany. It is by far the largest stream that empties into the head of this sea, except the Orontes. Both these rise in the great plain of Cœle-Syria, and close together. The Orontes flows north, the latter south and south-west. The watershed of the valley between the two Lebanons is somewhere about Lebweh, but the farthest permanent source of the Litany is the copious 'Ain es Sultan at Baalbek. Even this is entirely used up during the season of irrigation, and not a drop of its water reaches the sea. Numerous fountains, however, rise out of the centre of the plain, and being joined, first by the strong stream of Zahleh, and afterward by the much larger one from 'Anjur (Ain Jur), the united river meanders through the lower Bŭk'ah in a south-western direction, some fifteen miles, to Jûb Jennîn. Below that it

---

[1] Gen. xlix. 21.   [2] 2 Sam. ii. 18.   [3] 2 Sam. xxii. 34.   [4] Prov. v. 19.   [5] Psalm xlii. 1, 2.

flows in a constantly narrowing vale for six or seven miles, to Jisr Kŭráone.
Not far from this bridge its volume is increased by the stream from the noble
fountains of Mushgharah. From this onward the Litany is engaged in a
furious struggle with Lebanon for a passage to the sea. It has cut out for
itself a narrow groove in the solid strata, so deep that no one at a little distance Singular chasm.
aside from it would suspect that a powerful river rushed between him and the
opposite rocks. Yet there it is at the bottom of the chasm, all in a foam of
vexation, leaping, darting, roaring along. Now it whirls round the jutting
base of some mighty cliff, so sharply that you are sure it bursts from the rock
itself. Below, it runs madly against another towering wall, from which you
see no escape; but *it* does, and, darting along the base at a terrific rate,
launches its whole force against a similar barrier, only to recoil in shattered
fragments, and shoot like an arrow down some secret pathway, quite hidden
by overhanging rocks and interlacing sycamores. After about ten miles of this
work, it does, in reality, come forth from the dark mouth of the mountain.
At a place called Kûweh—window—it has tunneled through a rock more than
ninety feet thick, and comes out quietly at the bottom of this solemn chasm.
Not long to rest, however, for immediately afterward it springs madly down
among large boulders reduced in width to half a dozen feet, but of depth unknown. The road passes over this natural bridge from Wady et Teim to
Nihah, on Lebanon. Some six or eight miles farther south, the road from
Jezzin to Hasbeiya crosses at Jisr Bûrgûs, and there the traveller has a fine
specimen of our river and its behaviour among the rocks. But you must look
upon it from the cliffs of Blāt, some five miles below, where it is eight hundred
feet beneath you, tearing at the very roots of Lebanon, and rasping out a passage for itself with mighty din and desperate haste. I have sat for hours in a
sort of dreamy ecstasy, gazing into this chasm—have let myself down from crag
to crag, until I stood all alone at the bottom—have reclined midway up its walls
upon some projecting shelf, and watched, now the timid conies creep out and
sun themselves, and now the bold eagles going and returning to their eyries in Eagles.
the cliffs. There are thousands of them, and their manœuvres, particularly
when coming home, are very entertaining. There comes a pair of them, just
visible in the blue depths of heaven. See how they sail round and round, in
ever-narrowing gyrations, as Milton's Prince of Darkness

> "Down from the ecliptic
> Threw his steep flight in many an aery wheel."

And now, right over the chasm, they poise themselves a moment; then, like a Their flight.
bolt from the clear sky, down, down they come, head foremost, with wings
collapsed; sinking far below their eyrie, they *round* to in a grand parabola,
and then, with two or three backward flaps of their huge pinions to check their
fall, like the wheels of a steam-boat reversed, they land in safety among their
clamorous children. Now take the glass, and see how they divide among
their gross and greedy chicks the prey which they have brought from far.

Come to Blāt, vain man, and answer thy Maker. "Doth the eagle mount up at thy command, and make her nest on high? She dwelleth and abideth on the

EAGLE AND NEST.

rock, upon the crag of the rock, and the strong place. From thence she seeketh the prey; her eyes behold afar off. Her young ones also suck up blood, and where the slain are, there is she." [1]

Description by Moses.

Moses, in that beautiful ode which he spake in the ears of all the congregation of Israel, refers to the habits of the eagle in a way which I have never understood: "As an eagle stirreth up her nest, fluttereth over her young, spreadeth abroad her wings, taketh them, beareth them on her wings, so the Lord did lead him." [2] Do you suppose that the parent eagle literally beareth her young on her wings?

It is not necessary to press every poetical figure into strict prosaic accuracy. The notion, however, appears to have been prevalent among the ancients, that the eagle did actually take up her yet timid young, and carry them forth to teach them how, and embolden them to try their own pinions. To this idea Moses seems to refer in Exodus xix. 4: "Ye have seen what I did unto the

_____

[1] Job xxxix. 27-30.   [2] Deut. xxxii. 11, 12.

Egyptians, and how I bore you on eagles' wings, and brought you unto myself." The fact is not impossible: the eagle is strong enough to do it, but I am not aware that such a thing has ever been witnessed. I myself, however, have seen the old eagle fly round and round the nest, and back and forth past it, while the young ones fluttered and shivered on the edge, as if eager, but afraid to launch forth from the giddy precipice. And no wonder, for the nest "is on high," and a fall from thence would end their flight for ever. If Moses was not the author of Job, they seem both to have been familiar with this bird and its habits. One allusion is very striking: "Her eyes behold afar off."[1] The power of vision in the eagle is amazing, almost incredible. No sooner does a kid fall in the wilderness among the thick bushes, than some of these keen-sighted hunters after prey notice it from their pathway in mid-heaven, and, circling round and round, they pounce down upon, and bear it away to their nest. This appears to be done purely by sight.

Descrip-tion of eagles in Job.

To what fact in the life of the eagle does the Psalmist refer in the promise to the righteous that they shall renew their youth like the eagles?[2]

Perhaps merely to his coming forth in a fresh costume and in youthful beauty after the moulting season; or it may refer to the fact that this royal bird is long-lived, and retains his vigour to extreme old age.

Renewing their youth.

But we have not yet done with our river. Turning westward, below Blât, it has cut a channel across the southern end of Lebanon, at a place called the Khŭtweh, some two hundred feet long, and so very narrow that I have sat on the west side and laid my hand on the opposite precipice, which rises at least one hundred feet perpendicular above the water. The river darts, swift as an arrow, through this groove, and, like the shuddering visitor, seems to hold its breath in terror. From this onward for a few miles the scenery is less wild, until it turns the corner south of the castle of Shŭkîf, and makes hitherward toward the sea. This last descent of eighteen or twenty miles abounds in noble scenery, but it must be seen to be appreciated. The whole length of the Litany, with its countless doublings, cannot be less than one hundred and twenty miles, and in that distance it descends full four thousand feet. European engineers have entertained the idea of carrying a railway up the Litany to the Bŭk'ah, from whence it could easily pass to Hamath, Aleppo, and the Euphrates, and also to Damascus, Palmyra, and Bagdad; but no one will dream of such an enterprise who has explored the long, wild gorge, and found out what it really is. This river is not mentioned in the Bible. Perhaps it is too far north to come in the way of Biblical narrative. It seems to have formed the northern boundary of the territory *actually subdued* by Israel, for I cannot find a single city on this side of it inhabited by either Naphtali or Asher, though David and Solomon may have held a temporary and not very well defined sway over some places farther north than even Sidon. Thus Josephus seems to imply that Arca, beyond Tripoli, was subject to Asher; but the

Proposed Litany Railway.

A bound-ary of the land of Israel.

---

[1] Job xxxix. 29.   [2] Ps. ciii. 5.

identity of the place referred to with the seat of the Arkites may well be doubted. Nor does the fact that the border of Asher reached to Zidon prove that the line of actual possession crossed the Litany, for no doubt Zidon extended her rule down to it, and thus the border would reach that of Sidon on the banks of this river. Whether the line of *permanent* possession corresponds with the utmost limits included in the original promise, is a question which we may examine at some future stage of our pilgrimage.

This khan is now much dilapidated, and was ancient two hundred and forty years ago, when Sandys passed this way. It has been a castle as well as khan, and served not merely to protect the traveller, but to command the road and the bridge over the river. In its present form it may have been built by the Crusaders, but there are traces of more ancient work about it. The name suggests, or rather coincides with, the idea that this river, with its most impracticable gorge, was the dividing line between the territory of the Jews and that of Sidon. Kasimîeh signifies *division*, or that which divides, and it appears always to have separated the governmental districts from each other,

A sort of
second
Jordan.
and does so now. There is no ascertained Jewish site in Belad es Shŭkîf, whereas Belad Besharah, on the south of the river, abounds in them. Asher and Naphtali came *to* the Kasimieh, and we can trace their actual possessions thus far, but no farther; and we have, therefore, in this river, the Divider, a sort of second Jordan to the Holy Land.

To avoid the mud in the plain, we will take down to the shore, and follow its windings to Tyre, a pleasant ride of not more than two hours. How the river meanders and doubles, as if reluctant to lose itself in the sea! Were not

Mouth of
the river.
this low plain unhealthy, there would be a large town near the mouth of the river. It is the best fishing-ground in all this part of the coast, and the markets are often supplied from here, even so far north as Beirût. The direct road to Tyre passes below some ruins on the hill side, called Mûhaibeeb, and there are many evidences thereabout of a former population thick as bees.

Farther toward the city is the fountain Babûk, which Pococke calls Bakwok, and around it are traces of an ancient city. An aqueduct once carried the water over the southern plain; but, like most other works of utility in this land, it is now destroyed. Here we have a considerable ruin on the shore, and another ahead of us, which must have been a large city. These fragments of unfortunate ships along the beach show that this celebrated mart of trade has but an insecure roadstead. The only protection for vessels, except the island itself, is that wall of rocks, which extends from the north-west corner of the island a mile or more into the sea, in a line parallel to the coast; but they are not continuous, and are too low to present any adequate obstacle to the waves during a storm. In 1834 I lay eleven days behind them in a crazy Italian brig, and found it a most insecure berth. We were often in the utmost danger of coming on shore. In ancient times, however, the smaller shipping then in use found shelter in a harbour within the city, where boats still ride in perfect safety during the wildest gales. Benjamin of Tudela, in his usual style of exaggeration, says that this was the finest harbour in the world. It was, no doubt, larger in the eleventh century, when that traveller saw it, than at present; deeper also, and much better protected; still, it must always have been too confined and shallow for any but small coasting craft. CHAPTER
XII.

Look now at Jebel es Sheikh, towering above the mountains to the north-east. This is one of the most striking and impressive views of Hermon you will ever have. You observe that the north end is much higher than the south, and the centre is lower than either. The old Sheikh, therefore, seems to have at least two heads; and this may be the reason why the name is sometimes plural, or dual, in the poetic books of the Bible. Mount
Hermon.

Who can realize that yon insignificant village is Tyre, the city that said, " I am a god; I sit in the seat of God ? " [1]

It is all that remains of her. But weep not for Tyre. This very silence and solitude are most eloquent and emphatic on themes of the last importance to the repose of Christian faith. True, indeed, the imagination is disappointed. There is nothing here of that which led Joshua to call it " the strong city" more than three thousand years ago [2]—nothing of that mighty metropolis which baffled the proud Nebuchadnezzar and all his power for thirteen years, until every head in his army was bald, and every shoulder peeled in the hard service against Tyrus [3]—nothing in this wretched roadstead and empty harbour to remind one of the times when merry mariners did sing in her markets—no visible trace of those towering ramparts which so long resisted the utmost efforts of the great Alexander. All have vanished utterly like a troubled dream. But the Christian would not have it otherwise. The very veracity of Jehovah stands pledged, or seems to be, to keep it so : " Behold, I am against thee, O Tyrus, and will cause many nations to come up against thee, as the sea causeth his waves to come up; and they shall destroy the walls of Tyrus, and break down her towers. I will also scrape her dust from her, and make her like the top of a rock. And it shall be a place for the spreading of nets in the midst of the sea, for I have spoken it, saith the Lord God." [4] As she now is, and has long been, Tyre is God's witness; but great, powerful, and populous, she would be the infidel's boast. This, however, she cannot, will not be. Tyre will never rise from her dust to falsify the voice of prophecy. Nor can I make any lamentation for her; she is a greater blessing to the world now than in the day of her highest prosperity. Tyre.

Prophe-
cies.

---

[1] Ezek. xxviii. 2.　　[2] Josh. xix. 29.　　[3] Ezek. xxix. 18.　　[4] Ezek. xxvi 3–5.

CHAPTER XIII.

T Y R E.*

February 27th.

Tyre.

WE have now been two days wandering over the ruins of Tyre, and I understand the topography of the whole neighbourhood perfectly; indeed, Dr. Robinson had made me better acquainted with this place and its surroundings than any other which we have yet visited.

Robinson's description amended.

His description, though the best we have, will nevertheless bear amendment. For example, the land does *not* project to the south of the causeway, as he represents, but it does to the north and north-west. The west end of the island is not wholly a ledge of rugged, picturesque rocks; there are a few such, however, at the south-west corner. And again, it does not correspond very closely with fact to represent this as originally a *long, narrow* island. It was scarcely a mile in length, and not much less in breadth, measuring, from the extreme angle of the island, some four hundred paces to the east of the present wall of

Robinson's description.

* [We give, abridged, Dr. Robinson's account of Tyre, referred to in the text:—"The peninsula on which Tyre, now Sûr, was built, was originally a long, narrow island, parallel to the shore, and distant from it less than half a mile. . . . The isthmus was first created by the famous causeway of Alexander the Great, [who could not take nor reach the city without connecting it in this way with the mainland]. . . . At present, the isthmus cannot be much less than half a mile in width. . . . It lies between the shore and the more northern part of the island, so that the latter, as seen from the shore, seems to project farther toward the south of the isthmus than toward the north, and forms here a larger bay, although the harbour, or rather road in which vessels lie, is that on the north. The island as such, is not more than a mile in length. The part which projects on the south beyond the isthmus, is perhaps a quarter of a mile broad, and is rocky and uneven. It is now unoccupied except by fishermen, as ' a place to spread nets upon.' The southern wall of the city runs across the island, nearly on a line with the south side of the isthmus. The present city stands upon the junction of the island and isthmus. . . . The western coast of the island is wholly a ledge of rugged, picturesque rocks. . . . The present Sûr is nothing more than a market town, hardly deserving the name of a city. Its chief export is the tobacco raised from the neighbouring hills. The houses are for the most part mere hovels. The streets are narrow lanes, crooked and filthy. Yet the many scattered palm-trees throw over the city an Oriental charm."—Vol. ii. pp. 463-467.

Tyre, as is well known, suffered two memorable sieges, one from Nebuchadnezzar, the other from Alexander the Great. It became the seat of a Christian church, then passed under Mahometan rule, and continued so till the time of the Crusades. The Christians kept possession of it for a long time, but at last, about the end of the thirteenth century, it was destroyed by the Saracens. It has never recovered from the desolation then brought upon it. Its overthrow was a special subject of prophecy.—ED.]

TYRE.

the city. To be very accurate, it is thirteen hundred and twenty-five paces CHAPTER
one way, and ten hundred and thirty-six the other. XIII.

The causeway does not " lie between the shore and the northern part of the The cause-
island," and it would not have reflected much credit upon the sagacity of Alex- way,
ander's engineers to have carried it in that direction, because the strait is
broader, and the sea deeper there than toward the south end. Alexander
would, of course, build his work where there was the least depth and shortest
distance. The point of the island which extended farthest toward the mainland lies directly east of the *fountain* nearly three hundred paces, as appears
from the remains of Tyre's most ancient wall at that place. These very interesting remains were uncovered by quarriers some three years ago, but as the
stones were too heavy for their purpose, they left them, and they are now nearly
buried again by the shifting sand. From this point the island fell back rapidly
toward the north-west, and more gradually toward the south-west. I doubt not
but that Alexander's work first touched this projecting angle. The largest
part of the causeway, however, lies to the south of it, and the wind from that
direction has there thrown up the greatest amount of sand.

There yet remains one solitary specimen of Tyre's great sea-wall, that mighty Old sea-
bulwark which no enemy could overthrow. At the extreme northern end of wall.
the island, a stone nearly seventeen feet long and six and a half thick, rests
just where Tyrian architects placed it thousands of years ago. As in every

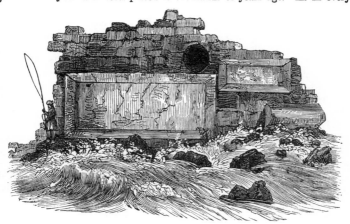

ANCIENT STONE IN WALL OF TYRE.

case that I have examined, the foundation laid for these gigantic blocks is
made with stone comparatively small. When the sea is quiet we will visit
this interesting portion of the old wall.

I do not believe that there ever was an available harbour south of the island. Harbour.

PART
I.

Not only is the water too shallow, but the south-west and west winds render it utterly unsafe to anchor there. When, therefore, authors speak of two, I suppose they must refer to the *inner* harbour and outer roadstead, both of which are on the north of the island. The natives, it is true, have a tradition that there was a harbour on the south; but their story is connected with incredible fables about a wall built by Alexander through the deep sea to Ras el Baiyod, a distance of eight or ten miles!

Granite columns.

The number of granite columns that lie in the sea, particularly on the north of the island, is surprising. The east wall of the *inner* harbour is entirely founded upon them, and they are thickly spread over the bottom of the sea on every side. I have often rowed leisurely around the island to look at them when the surface was perfectly calm, and always with astonishment. Tyre must have been a city of columns and temples par excellence. The whole north end appears to have been one vast colonnade.

The land along the western shore, and the entire south half of the island, is now given up to cultivation, pasturage, and the general cemetery of the town; and here are found the remains of those splendid edifices for which Tyre was celebrated. About three years ago, the quarriers who were digging out stone for the government barracks at Beirût uncovered a large *hajarîyeh*—floor—a few feet below the surface. Descending through rubbish some ten feet farther, they came upon a beautiful marble pavement, among a confused mass of columns of every size and variety of rock. I went down and groped about amid these prostrate columns, and found the bases of some still in their original positions,—parts of what was once a superb temple. One fragment of verd antique was particularly beautiful. In an adjoining quarry they had just turned out a marble statue of a female figure, full sized, modestly robed, and in admirable preservation. May not this be the site and the remains of the famous temple of Belus, or of Jupiter Olympus, both mentioned by Dios; or of Astarte, or Hercules, described by Menander? It is the centre and highest part of the island, and must have been very conspicuous from the sea. The mind becomes quite bewildered with the mighty revolutions and desolations which such excavations reveal. The floor above these remains is the same in kind as those now made in Tyre; but the house to which it belonged has wholly disappeared, and must have been destroyed before the city of the middle ages was built, for it is outside of the walls; and yet the ruins of this temple were then buried so deep below the surface, that the builder probably had not the slightest idea of their existence. This collection of columns and marble floors was again covered up by the quarriers in their search for available stone; and the unconscious tourist now walks heedlessly over wrecks of ancient splendour which astonished and delighted even the well-travelled "Father of History" four centuries before the birth of Christ. The entire southern half of the island is buried deep beneath just such ruins; and I hope the day is not distant when others will explore them besides poor quarriers, rummaging for building-stone at so many piastres per hundred.

Ruins of a temple.

Great antiquity.

Should any one ask incredulously, Where are the stones of ancient Tyre?— CHAPTER where, at least, the remains of those lofty towers and triple walls which so XIII. excited the wonder and admiration of the Crusaders only some seven centuries The Tyre ago?—the preceding incidents will furnish a satisfactory reply. They are of the Crusaders. found in this depth of ruins, spread over the island, and over the causeway of saders. Alexander; they are found in her choked-up harbour and at the bottom of her sea. They are at Acre, and Joppa, and Beirût, and in the *rubbish* of all those cities. In fact, the only wonder is, that so much still remains to reveal and confirm the ancient greatness of this Phœnician capital.

Do you suppose that the fountain outside of the gate has any connection with Ras el 'Ain?

The period of Tyre's greatest extent and glory was before the causeway was made, and it is not probable that an aqueduct was carried under the sea; and, besides, this fountain is not on the edge of the island nearest the mainland, as Water it would have been had such an aqueduct been constructed, but three hundred supply on paces farther west, in the interior of the original island. There is no need of the island. such a hypothesis to explain any apparent mystery about this fountain. The strata along the coast dip toward the sea, and *pass under it.* Where they terminate abruptly at the shore, innumerable streams of water run out on a level with the surface and below it. There are hundreds of such streams along this coast, and some of them very large. A little north of Ruad—the Arvad of the Bible—a fountain bursts up from the bottom of the sea, of such enormous size and power during the rainy months as to make the whole surface boil like a caldron. Now, apply this to our fountain. The strata of the plain opposite the city dip under the sea at a very small angle, and, of course, pass below the island. A shaft sunk only a few feet deep will reach a stratum that extends to the mainland, and water running beneath that stratum will pass under the island. Cut off such a stream by your shaft, and the water will rise as high as the conditions of the strata on the neighbouring plain will admit. Accordingly the people will tell you that water can be found on any part of the island by digging to the proper depth. It will generally be somewhat brackish, and this is to be expected from the close proximity to the sea. These facts explain, as I believe, how it was that the Tyrians could sustain such protracted sieges, as we know from history they repeatedly did. They appear never to have been straitened for water, because they had a supply on their own little island which the besiegers could not cut off.

Have you ever seen the shell-fish from which the far-famed Tyrian purple was obtained?

That variety of the murex from which this dye was procured is found all along Tyrian this coast, but it abounds most around the Bay of Acre. So also the Helix purple. Janthina, from which a blue, with a delicate purple or lilac tinge, may be extracted, is equally abundant. After a storm in winter you may gather thousands of them from the sandy beach south of Sidon. They are so extremely fragile that the waves soon grind them to dust. A kind of Buccinum is found here at Tyre, which has a dark crimson colouring matter about it, with a bluish livid tinge. According to ancient authors, this was used to vary the shades of the purple. Pliny says the Tyrians ground the shell in mills to get at the dye. This could not have been the only process, because the remnants of these shells found in pits along the south-eastern shore of our island were certainly broken or mashed, and not ground; and the same is true with the shells on the south of the wall at Sidon.

Sung by Homer.

This Tyrian purple was celebrated in Greece even in the remote age of Homer, who sings of

" Belts,
That, rich with Tyrian dye, refulgent glowed."

The references to these colours of red, purple, and scarlet in the Bible, are more ancient still; indeed, from Genesis to Revelation they are so numerous, and so mingled and blended together, that it is almost impossible to particularize them. Nor is it necessary; the merest child can turn to a score of them. And these colours are equally prevalent and popular at the present day among all classes of Orientals.

These and other matters, which connect the history of Tyre with that of the people of God, are invested with peculiar interest; and I have long desired to become intimately and accurately acquainted with them. I encounter a difficulty at the very beginning of her story. Isaiah calls Tyre the " daughter of Sidon;"[1] and Joshua mentions the "strong city Tyre" in describing the

Age of Tyre.

boundary of Asher;[2] from which it is certain that she was not a very young daughter even at the conquest of Canaan by the Jews. Yet Josephus, in stating the exact time in which Solomon's temple was built, says there had passed two hundred and forty years from the founding of Tyre to the building of the temple; but Joshua lived more than four hundred years before Solomon. Here is a discrepancy of more than two hundred years.

Josephus and Joshua.

There is; and it is possible that Josephus wrote four hundred and forty instead of two hundred and forty. Such errors in copying might easily occur. But Josephus lived after the beginning of the Christian era, and may have had in his mind the city that then existed, and all agree that *it* was built

"Palai Tyrus."

long after continental Tyre. This Palai Tyrus had been totally subverted for seven hundred years when the Jewish historian wrote, and he may have dropped it out of view entirely, and spoken only of that city concerning which the Roman world would feel interested. Insular Tyre was very likely not built more than two hundred and forty years before the time of Solomon. At any rate, the testimony of Joshua that there was a Tyre in his day is decisive; and if the statement of Josephus could in no way be reconciled with it, we should not hesitate which to believe. I understand him, however, to refer to different cities, and thus there is no contradiction.

---

[1] Isa. xxiii. 12.   [2] Josh. xix. 29.

Where do you find the site of continental Tyre?

It extended, I suppose, from the great fountains of Ras el 'Ain northward, included the long, low Tell Habeish as its acropolis, and in its greatest prosperity probably reached the shore opposite the island. The whole of the *Tell* is full of buried foundations. Reschid Pasha, the present grand vizier, has purchased this neighbourhood, and within two years has planted fifty thousand mulberry-trees, besides olives and fruit-trees, and seems determined to revive the place again. But the people say the enterprise must fail, because God has declared that Tyre shall never be rebuilt. Thus far the success is not very satisfactory. The mulberry-trees flourish well enough, but the place has proved so unhealthy that the peasants refuse to reside there. Last summer the pasha's agent had workmen erecting houses on Tell Habeish, and I was greatly interested to see that wherever the men dug for foundations, they came upon old works, which must have belonged to what Diodorus called Palai Tyrus in his day. Pliny says that it was thirty furlongs from insular Tyre to the south, which agrees with this locality, and with no other.

Site of Continental Tyre.

Bought by Reschid Pasha.

This was that joyous city, "whose antiquity was of ancient days," even when Isaiah sang the burden of Tyre, "the crowning city, whose merchants are princes, whose traffickers are the honourable of the earth." [1] The Lord of Hosts proposed by this utter overthrow to stain the pride of all glory, and to bring into contempt all the honourable of the earth. It is of this city that Ezekiel says, "Thou shalt be a terror, and never shalt be any more." [2] And, so far as one can judge, it will never be a city again. Alexander, as Arrian relates, scraped off the very dust of old Tyre to build his causeway, and now you can find none of the remains except by digging below the surface. Even this feeble attempt of Reschid Pasha to revive the site of old Tyre has proved a losing speculation. It is so sickly that not even a village of any size can be established there, and, should the plain become again densely peopled, the villages will be built at a distance from this fatal spot.

Never likely to be a city again.

In the prophecies relating to Tyre, there seems to be a blending together of the continental and the insular city, so that it is often difficult to distinguish which of the two is meant.

The two Tyres in prophecy

There is; but this is in entire accordance with the general method of prophetic announcements. Those of our Saviour in regard to the destruction of the city and temple of Jerusalem are mixed up with other matters connected with, or analogous to that great event, and it is impossible now to assign to each its proper part. There is, in reality, a propriety in thus joining together continental and insular Tyre. The same people—guilty of the same vices—they deserved and received the same judgments, though in different degrees and at various times. The one was totally destroyed, never to rise again; the other repeatedly overwhelmed, but again partially reviving, just as

---

[1] Isa. xxiii. 7, 8, 9. [2] Ezek. xxvii. 36.

PART
I.

the whole drift of the prophecies would lead us to expect. Indeed, it is nearly certain that the two cities were actually connected long before Alexander joined the island to the coast, and thus there would be no impropriety in speaking of them as one great whole. Josephus, in his controversy with Apion, states distinctly, on the authority of Dius, who, he says, wrote the Phœnician history accurately, that Hiram joined the temple of Jupiter Olympus, which stood before on an island by itself, to the city by raising a causeway between them. There never has been more than one island here, and the causeway must have joined that to the mainland. Thus the ancient city and the island were connected even in the time of Solomon; nor would the work be very difficult, owing to the shallowness of the water. This, with other notices of Tyre by Menander the Ephesian, render it highly probable

Ancient
extent.

that continental Tyre extended along the shore from Ras el 'Ain to the island; and this, again, agrees with the statement of Pliny, that Tyre was nineteen miles in circumference, including old Tyre, but without it about four. A line which would now include the island and Ras el 'Ain might easily be so drawn as to be nineteen miles long, while the utmost extent of the walls around the island alone would be nearly four miles, as Pliny has it.

The history of this fallen representative of ancient wealth, commerce, and civilization spreads over so many ages of stirring activity—there is so much to oe seen, and so many are the reflections suggested by what is no longer to be seen, that one becomes quite bewildered.

It is, indeed, long since Joshua divided yonder hills and valleys between Asher and Naphtali, and during a large portion of this time Tyre was the

Ancient
glory.

most splendid city, perhaps, in the world. In the days of David and Solomon she was able not merely to maintain her independence in presence of these mighty conquerors, but by her unrivalled skill in arts and architecture she became an honoured ally and necessary partner in the enterprise of building a temple for the Most High to dwell in. From this time she is associated, more or less intimately, with the history of God's chosen people for a thousand years. They had, in general, the same enemies, and, to a certain extent, shared the same fortunes. When the kings of Nineveh, or Babylon, or of Egypt came against the land of Israel, they attacked Tyre also. Yet, in spite of all her enemies, she flourished beyond a parable. The Hebrew historians, prophets, and poets constantly allude to her power, wealth, luxury, and vices; and Ezekiel seems to tax the entire geography of the known world to set forth the extent of her commerce and the multitude of her

Subse-
quent
history.

riches. It would take a volume to trace the varied fortunes of Tyre through Egyptian, Chaldean, Macedonian, Roman, Saracenic, Frank, and Turkish dynasties, down to the present wretched representative of so much greatness and glory. With but few exceptions, it is now a cluster of miserable huts, inhabited by about three thousand five hundred impoverished Metawelies and Arab Christians, destitute alike of education, of arts, and of enterprise, carrying on with Egypt a small trade in tobacco from the neighbouring hills, and

of lava mill-stones from the Hauran. This is a sorry schedule for the name of
Tyre, but it is about all she can exhibit:—

> " Dim is her glory, gone her fame,
>   Her boasted wealth has fled;
> On her proud rock, alas! her shame,
>   The fisher's net is spread.
>
> The Tyrian harp has slumbered long,
>   And Tyria's mirth is low;
> The timbrel, dulcimer, and song
>   Are hushed, or wake to woe."

It is, indeed, a fearful falling off from the catalogue in the 27th chapter of
Ezekiel. Can you follow the geography of the prophet with any degree of
certainty?

Not in all cases, but we can make a nearer approximation than might be
supposed. It well deserves a careful study; for, judged by its undoubted
antiquity, it is the most important geographical document, and by far the
most suggestive commercial tariff in existence; and now is the time, and this
the place, to examine it with pleasure and profit. Undeterred, therefore, by
its length, let us read over this 27th chapter of Ezekiel, and a few very brief
additions to the text will show how many of the countries named are now
known, and how far the commodities and the characteristics ascribed to them
still hold good. *Extent of commerce.*

" O thou that are situate at the entry of the sea"—beautifully significant of
continental and insular Tyre united—"a merchant of the people for many isles,
thus saith the Lord God: O Tyrus, thou hast said, I am of perfect beauty.
They have made all thy ship boards of fir-trees from Senir (Mount Hermon),
and of cedars from Lebanon have they made thy masts. Of the oaks of
Bashan have they made thine oars, and thy benches of ivory brought out of
the isles of Chittim (Cyprus and the Grecian islands). Fine linen, with
broidered work from Egypt, was that which thou spreadest forth to be thy
sail (and Egypt still deals largely in linen, though not remarkably 'fine');
purple and scarlet from Elishah (Greek islands and neighbouring nations) was
that which covered thee. The inhabitants of Sidon and Arvad were thy mariners (Arvad is now wholly inhabited by mariners). The ancients of Gebal
were thy calkers (and their city is still found on the shore north of Ruad; or,
if Jebeîl be meant, tar and pitch for calking is now made on the mountains
above it). They of Persia, and of Lud, and of Phut were in thine army (Phud
and Lud were in Mesopotamia[1]). Tarshish (Tarsus in Cilicia, possibly Tartessus in Spain) was thy merchant, with silver, iron, tin, and lead (and in
both these regions rich mines of these metals abounded in ancient days, and
are still found). Javan, Tubal, and Meshech (Northern Asia Minor, Georgia,
and Circassia) traded the persons of men (as they still do, or more frequently *Ezekiel xxvii.* *Ancient geography.*

---

[1] Judith ii. 23

PART
I.

the persons of women). They of the house of Togarmah (Armenia) traded in thy fairs with horses and mules (and this country is still celebrated for its horses). The men of Dedan (Ethiopia and along the Red Sea) brought thee for a present horns of ivory and ebony. Syria occupied in thy fairs with emeralds, purple, and broidered work, and fine linen, and coral, and agate. Judah and the land of Israel traded in thy market wheat of Minnith and Pannag (in the Howran[1]), and honey, and oil, and balm. Damascus was thy merchant in wine of Helbon (Aleppo, or more probably from a city some twenty miles north of Damascus) and white wool. Dan and Javan going to and fro (Arabs from the Persian Gulf) occupied in thy fairs : bright iron, cassia, and calamus. Dedan in South Arabia, and all the princes of Kedar, occupied with thee in lambs, rams, and goats (and Southern Palestine is now supplied with them from the same regions). The merchants of Sheba and Raamah occupied in thy fairs with chief of all spices, and with all precious stones and gold. (The Abyssinians claim Sheba, and Raamah was probably in the same region, where spices grow and precious stones are gathered). Haran and Canneh, Eden and Sheba, Asshur and Chilmad (which ends the list, were countries and cities along the Euphrates and Tigris), they were merchants in all sorts of things, blue cloths, broidered work, and chests of rich apparel, bound with cords, and made of cedar. The ships of Tarshish did sing of thee in thy market, and thou wast replenished, and made very glorious in the midst of the seas."

Extent
of com-
merce.

Thus extensive was the commerce of Tyre. From Abyssinia and Arabia on the south, to Armenia and Georgia on the north, and from the frontiers of India to the utmost islands of Greece, and, indeed, far beyond both, came to this little spot—the caravans by land and the ships by sea—a commerce rarely exceeded in extent and variety—a concentration of wealth and luxury which few cities of any age or country could boast. No doubt her merchants were princes, and her traffickers the honourable men of the earth. How impressive the change ! Well might the "isles shake at the sound of her fall."[2] Her present utter prostration and poverty are abundantly sufficient to meet the demands of prophecy, even without reference to continental Tyre, which has been literally wiped off the map of the earth. She has sunk down to the dust beneath the heavy "burden" of prophecy ; nor can she ever recover her ancient glory without a succession of mighty physical, moral, and political miracles, such as the world has never seen, and which we have no reason to expect.

Must we not allow a very wide application to some of Ezekiel's names, in order to compass the entire range of Tyrian commerce ?

Compre-
hensive
expres-
sions.

No doubt ; and therefore great latitude must be given westward to Elishah, Chittim, and Tarshish, and northward to Javan, Tubal, and Togarmah; to Aram, Persia, and Dedan eastward, and to Sheba and Raamah toward the south. Many of these names were probably applied in a loose way to regions

[1] Josephus v. 7, 10.   [2] Ezek. xxvi 15-21.

but little known and of vast extent. Hiram had ships that traded from Ezion-geber, at the head of the Gulf of Akabah, out into the Indian Ocean, and brought from Ophir, once in three years, almug-trees, precious stones, silver, ivory, apes, and peacocks.[1] And so, also, through Carthage and Cadiz, their commerce spread along the whole northern coast of Africa and southern shores of Europe, and even to Ireland and England. Ezekiel could not have been ignorant of this, and it is fair to explain his catalogue according to this large interpretation.

After all, the commerce of Tyre was very limited in *variety* as compared with that of modern times—neither cotton, nor silk, nor rice, nor Indian corn, nor sugar, nor coffee, nor tea, nor tobacco, nor potatoes, nor oranges, nor any of the almost countless fruits and nuts which enrich our markets of the present day. It is fair to conclude that there has been a very great advance in all the arts of life since that early day.

28th. It has taken just an hour to ride from our tent to this celebrated Ras el 'Ain.*

And, as our pace has been more rapid than usual, the distance is full thirty furlongs, and our ride has thus corroborated the statement of Strabo in regard to the central site of continental Tyre, though the whole distance from this to the island must have been occupied by the city and suburbs in the days of her greatest prosperity and largest extent.

These pools—*birkehs*, you call them—are, indeed, extraordinary structures, and appear to be very ancient.

As old, perhaps, as the pools of Solomon, in which case they may have been erected by Hiram himself, the friend and ally of the wise king. These vast masses of tufaceous deposit bear convincing evidence of extreme antiquity. They mark the line of the aqueduct which connected this lowest birkeh with the canal which led the water from the other two northward over the plain. It must have taken hundreds, if not thousands of years, to deposit such hills of tufa, and yet this canal itself has been entirely broken away for centuries, no one knows how many. The supposition that Alexander built these pools cannot be maintained with any probability. He was here too short a time, and in no mood of mind to benefit or adorn the place with such noble cisterns. They are much more ancient than his day. I have the impression that the old aqueduct, which we shall trace out on our return along the upper edge of the plain northward to that fine Tell called Mashûk, describes the circuit, in that direction, of the ancient city in its largest extent. In the meanwhile,

CHAPTER XIII.

Commerce limited compared with modern.

Ras el 'Ain.

Water pools.

---

[1] 1 Kings ix. 26-28; and x. 11, 22.

* [Ras el 'Ain, an hour's distance from Tyre, was the fountain-head of the aqueducts by which the city was anciently supplied with water. "It is a collection of large fountains, where the water gushes up in several places with great force, and in very large quantities. ... In order to raise them to a head sufficient to carry off the water by aqueducts, the ancients built around them elevated reservoirs with walls of large stores, immensely thick, and fifteen or twenty feet high. There are four of these reservoirs in all at this place."--*Robinson*, ii. 457.—ED.]

you observe that this most seaward cistern is octagonal, about eighty feet in diameter, and twenty deep. This large volume of water is now of no further use than to drive those mills attached to its walls, after which it flows down directly into the sea. Anciently, however, it was connected with the great canal which carried the water of all three birkehs to the city and over the plain. The other two cisterns are some twenty rods farther east, and close together.

These fountains rise from the bottom of this shallow vale, which descends toward the sea. The geological cause I suppose to be the obtrusion here of a thick formation of that unstratified sandstone which abounds all along this coast. The water, descending from the eastern mountains, meets at this point with this formation, and is compelled to rise to the surface to find a passage to the sea. These pools were built around the separate fountains to elevate the water sufficiently high to irrigate the plain; and it might be raised still higher, I presume, if there was any occasion to do so. These two are not so large as the one below, and the water of both is not equal to that alone. The upper of these is fifty-two feet by forty-seven, and twelve deep, and the other fifty-two by thirty-six, and sixteen deep; and the channel connecting them is forty-three feet long. The water enters the canal from the second, and is carried over the whole plain northward to Tell M'ashûk, and in ancient days to the city itself. At present, however, as there is no need of irrigation, it passes out by three separate channels, and drives as many mills. From the upper one, also, the water is let into the aqueduct, which crosses the wady southward on that row of arches. This is not a very ancient work; and, indeed, the birkeh itself seems more modern than the other two. The walls of the second birkeh vary in thickness from twenty-three to twelve feet, and much of the heavy casing-stone has been carried away. Still it will stand for thousands of years

Badness of the water. to come, if not purposely destroyed. The water is largely impregnated with lime and earthy matter, and is called thukîl (heavy) by the Arabs. It is considered unhealthy, and the locality hereabouts is so to a proverb; nevertheless, it is a beautiful place, and might be made a very paradise were it not for this single difficulty. But Eden itself, with ague and jaundice, would be a miserable abode. These fine geese and ducks, however, are more than contented with it; and to see anything so truly American, so clean, and so happy, is quite worth the ride here from the city.

Land of Cabul. Where is the district of Cabul, which Solomon gave to Hiram in return for his cedar and fir trees out of Lebanon?

The account of this matter in 1 Kings ix. 11–13 is remarkable, and reads like an addition to the history by a later hand. Solomon gave Hiram twenty cities in the land of Galilee, and as they did not please him, he called the land Cabûl *unto this day*. What day? that on which the record was made, I suppose. These twenty cities were mere villages, of course, and it is a genuine Eastern trick to dignify a small present with a pompous name. And so the remonstrance of Hiram with Solomon is very natural, " What cities are these

which thou hast given me, *my brother?*" and then he fastens upon the gift a CHAPTER
name of contempt—Cabûl, vile or displeasing; a mode of expressing and of per- XIII.
petuating dissatisfaction eminently Oriental. Josephùs says that these cities
were not far from Tyre; but this throws very little light on the locality. There
is a village in Wady Shaghûr, east of Acre, bearing this very name. This may
have been the largest, and the other nineteen were probably small places immediately adjacent to, and dependent upon it. Cabûl certainly belonged to
Galilee, and this is the only place in that district bearing that name. This
identification seems to make the dominion of Hiram extend southward at least
to Acre; nor is this unlikely, for the sea-coast was never in actual possession
of the Jews. And so Hiram must have ruled over Lebanon above Sidon, and
even much farther north; for the cedar and fir which he furnished to David
and Solomon grew on the mountains east and north-east of Sidon. We may
safely conclude that at that early day Tyre had entirely eclipsed the mother
city, if she had not actually reduced Sidon to a mere dependency of her own.

I have been out examining the remains of the cathedral mentioned by most Cathedral
visitants to Tyre. It must have been a noble edifice. Is there any reason to of Tyre.
doubt that these ruins belonged to that grand basilica built by Paulinus, and
so pompously described by Eusebius in his speech at the consecration of the
edifice?

None that I know of or can suggest. He says it was by far the most noble
in Phœnicia, and the present remains justify the assertion. The foundation of
no other ancient church in this country can compare with it. The whole consecration speech of Eusebius is well worth a careful study, not so much for its
inflated oratory, as for the light which it throws on the style of ecclesiastical
architecture at the beginning of the fourth century. " It appears to be super- Its an-
fluous," says he, " to describe the dimensions, length, and breadth of the edi- tiquity.
fice, the grandeur that surpasses description, and the dazzling aspect of works
glittering in the face of the speaker, the heights rising to the heavens," &c.
Now I wish he had performed just this superfluous work. It is not easy to
ascertain these facts at present. My measurements give for the length two
hundred and twenty-two feet, and for the breadth a hundred and twenty-nine
and a half; and by estimation from the spring of the arch at the east end, the
height to the dome must have been at least eighty feet. Native ecclesiastical
traditions assign a far greater elevation, probably suggested by the words of
Eusebius, "the height rising to the heavens." I have been gravely assured
that Cyprus could be seen from the top, which, under the most favourable circumstances, requires a stand-point not lower than eighteen hundred feet. The
tradition is therefore incredible and absurd.

Our largest dimensions I understand to include that " wider space, the outer Its size
enclosure, strengthened with a wall to compass the edifice, that it might be a
most secure bulwark to the whole work." The south and east of this outer
bulwark can still be measured quite accurately. The entrance was, of course,
from the west, and into " a large and lofty vestibule." Passing through this,

the worshipper found himself in a " quadrangular space, having four inclined
porticos, supported and adorned with pillars on every side ;" and there stood
those noble rose-granite columns, specimens of which now lie half buried beneath the ruins at the west end. I suppose others would appear if the modern
huts, and hills of rubbish which now choke up the whole area, were cleared
away. We cannot follow Eusebius through all the intricacies of an ancient
cathedral, but, having noticed so much as still remains for the tourist to
examine and compare with his description, we take our leave, commending
the oration to the study of the curious about such matters.

We may, of course, infer that Tyre early became a Christian city ?

*Church at
Tyre
founded
early.*
No doubt. Indeed, it is clear from Acts xxi. 3–7 that Paul found a considerable number of disciples here on his visit to Jerusalem from Greece. He
remained with them a week, and when he left, " they all brought us on our
way, with their wives and children, till we were out of the city, and we kneeled
down on the shore and prayed." I have often been reminded of this interesting scene when taking leave of my Tyrian friends outside of the city, on the
same sea-shore. These people of modern Phœnicia are especially given to
such external manifestations of friendship. Leaving, they accompany you ;
returning, they go forth to meet and welcome you. It is, in fact, a stringent
and tyrannical custom, the neglect of which is felt as an insult, remembered
long, and paid back with interest on the first favourable occasion.

What does " yukta ámmrû" mean ?

Hah ! what are you driving at now ?

Nothing in particular, only Salîm was dealing it out very plentifully just
now in the market. The fact is, I have, for the first time in my life, come in
personal contact with that very ancient law concerning things clean and
unclean, and have been surprised, and somewhat scandalized, to find myself
classed among the latter.

Indeed ! so you have been among the Metâwely shopkeepers ?

Yes; and a queer set they are. Walking through the market, I picked up
a specimen of dried figs to examine, when the owner shouted out something
very savage at me, which I took to mean put it back, and, in all haste, was
going to do so, to avoid a brawl in the streets, but at this he was more furi-
*"Yukta
ámmrû."*
ous than before. I looked to Salîm for an explanation, and he said, " Yukta
ámmrû !" half a dozen times, and then told me that the owner says you have
" nejest" it. " And what is that ?" " Why, only, sir, that you make it dirty
—no, not that, you make him unclean, sir." " How ! I make him unclean ?"
" Yukta ámmrû : he tink so by his religion." " Oh, I understand. According to his creed, I have defiled his figs by touching them." " Yes, sir; yukta
ámmrû !" and he kept on growling to himself as he walked the street, " You
one gentleman Amelican defile this Metâwely beast ! yukta ámmrû !"

*Profanity
of the
people.*
There, that will do. This is a favourite form of cursing, which Master
Salîm would not have used so freely if I had been present. This people are
fearfully profane. Everybody curses and swears when in a passion. No people

that I have ever known can compare with these Orientals for profaneness in CHAPTER XIII. the use of the names and attributes of God. The evil habit seems inveterate and universal. When Peter, therefore, began to curse and to swear on that dismal night of temptation,[1] we are not to suppose that it was something foreign to his former habits. He merely relapsed, under high excitement, into what, as a sailor and a fisherman, he had been accustomed to all his life. The people now use the very same sort of oaths that are mentioned and condemned by our Lord.[2] They swear by the head, by their life, by heaven, and by the Oaths. temple, or, what is in its place, the church. The forms of cursing and swearing, however, are almost infinite, and fall on the pained ear all day long.

If the laws of Moses concerning things and persons unclean were intended Cere-monial defile-ment. to keep the Jews from mingling with the surrounding nations, nothing more effectual could have been devised for this purpose. I know by experience that it even renders it very unpleasant to reside in a Metāwely village, and is an effectual barrier against forming any intimate relations with them. You never contract friendships with persons who will neither eat, drink with, nor visit you, and into whose houses you cannot enter without contracting or imparting defilement. The law must be broken down before people thus situated can either unite in religious ceremonies or contract family alliances. These Metā- The Metā-welies. welies do thus live separated, both in fact and feeling, from their neighbours, hating all, hated by all. Of course, they refuse to eat with all classes except themselves; and so it was with the Jews. Even the apostles esteemed it a thing unclean to associate or to eat with one of another nation. Peter said to Cornelius, "Ye know how that it is an unlawful thing for a man that is a Jew to keep company or come to one of another nation;"[3] and it required a voice from heaven thrice repeated to convince him that he should not call any man common or unclean. Nor did this divine vision permanently cure him of this deeply-rooted feeling, for not long after it he separated himself, and refused to eat with Gentile converts at Antioch, and was led into a guilty dissimulation in consequence, which Paul openly and sternly rebuked.[4] We need not, therefore, be surprised at the strength of this custom among these poor Metāwelies.

From whom did they derive this law?

It is impossible to ascertain. In its details it so closely resembles the Mosaic Their rules. precepts concerning ceremonial defilements, as to suggest the idea that they have borrowed it from the Jews. Their rules are almost exactly the same as those found in the 11th chapter of Leviticus, even to the breaking of earthen vessels which have become defiled. And this resemblance is carried into many other things besides clean and unclean meats, drinks, apparel, and vessels for household use. The law which obliged persons affected with loathsome diseases to dwell without the camp[5] is still in force, not merely among tent-dwelling

---

[1] Matt. xxvi. 74.   [2] Matt. v. 34–36.   [3] Acts x. 28.
[4] Gal. ii. 12, 13.   [5] Lev. xiii. 46.

PART I.

A woman separated.

Conduct of the women before and after death.

Women praying.

Arabs, but also with these people. We spent the hot summer months of 1852 in a village above Sidon. The inhabitants are nearly all Metâwelies, and very fanatical. On a rocky hill south of our house, a poor woman was thus separated, living in a booth of green branches. She was not allowed to leave her solitary shelter, and no one was permitted to visit her but the person who carried her daily allowance of food. There she passed her wretched days and nights until death delivered her from this dismal solitude. We remonstrated with the people against this barbarity, and the *men* consented to have her brought into a room hired for the purpose, where we could provide suitable food, and Dr. Van Dyck prescribe for her disease. But the *women* rose in furious clamour and rebellion against the proposal, and we were obliged to abandon it. We did this more willingly when we ascertained that the dying wretch herself would neither take the medicines nor taste our food; and yet she was being devoured by that horrid disease generated by vice and pollution. I was amazed at the barbarity and hypocrisy of the women. Sternly they passed her by, day after day, until she died; but then they assembled in troops, and screamed, and tossed their arms, and tore their hair in boisterous grief. There is a sad callousness in the composition of this people; at least they lack those beautiful traits of kindness and sympathy with the diseased and wretched which so adorn Christian countries, and fill them with hospitals, societies, and committees, to shelter, aid, and cure them. Religion makes the difference; not that the Metâwelies are without religion, and plenty of it too. While the above tragedy was slowly enacting before our eyes, the feast of Ramadan was kept in its utmost stringency, though it was blazing midsummer, and the people nearly perished with thirst. They neither ate, drank, nor smoked for more than fourteen hours of fierce sunshine, and even young children were forced to go through this long fast. There was public prayer, too, in abundance, a sort of Metâwely protracted meeting.

Even the women assembled daily at the fountains, performing their ablutions, and going through their genuflections and prostrations beneath the noble walnut-trees which adorn the hill sides of beautiful Jebaah. Nowhere else have I seen Moslem women thus pray in public, and the whole performance is immodest and disgusting. They are a sallow, forlorn, and ill-conditioned generation, every way inferior to the Christian women who dwell by their side. It is religion that makes the difference, even though the Christianity known there is little better than a caricature of the religion of Jesus.

Before leaving these Metâwelies, I must call your attention to the remarkable resemblance between them and the Jews. They have the Jewish contour and countenance, and even cultivate their love-locks after the same fashion. They are also alike in one other respect: though both are afraid to associate with you lest you contaminate and pollute them, they are both so intolerably filthy in all their habits and habitations that it is no great trial to avoid and be avoided by them.

In the 11th chapter of Leviticus and the 14th of Deuteronomy we have an extended enumeration of things clean and unclean, of what might be eaten and what not: are these laws and customs still in force in this country to any considerable extent?

Those distinctions are still kept up among various classes of people, but not exactly as Moses ordained. The camel was forbidden to the Jews, and it is still rejected by all except the wild Arabs. The cony is so rare that I have not heard of its being eaten, but suppose it would be allowed, as it resembles the rabbit, which few, except Jews, hesitate to eat. Swine are still held in abomination by Moslems, Jews, Druses, and most Orientals. Even some Christians refuse swine's flesh. Except by the Jews, there is no attention, apparently, paid now to the distinction between what has and what has not scales, but anything from the sea fit to eat is used without hesitation. The eagle, ossifrage, and osprey, vultures, hawks, kites, owls, ravens, and crows, after their kinds, are all rejected. The stork is sometimes eaten by Druses. Swans, geese, ducks, snipes, and all kinds of pigeons, doves, partridges, quails, larks, and an endless variety of small birds, are highly prized. The locust is still eaten by Bedawin Arabs; so is the snail; but I have never heard that beetles were used for food, and suppose it to be a mistranslation in Leviticus xi. 22. Bats, rats, mice, the tortoise, hedgehog, squirrels, ferrets, and lizards of all varieties, are rejected. "Whatsoever goeth upon his *paws*, among all manner of beasts that go on all four, those are unclean;" and they are generally so to this day.

Animals clean and unclean.

Modern Jewish practice.

We have one curiosity of Old Tyre yet to examine, and had better devote this fine morning to it. I wish to show you some of her most ancient walls. They lie buried beneath those sand-heaps where the causeway is joined to the island. The workmen sent to open the entrance for us say they have found the place; and while they are clearing away the sand we will trace the line of the wall from sea to sea. This large mass of old rubble-work marks the south-east angle, and from it the direction of the original wall along the margin of the island, toward the north, is easily followed to the opposite bay; and by descending into this vault we can see what sort of workmanship it was. Take off your coat, and slide down after me, crab-fashion, and with as much caution as you have at command; and now you stand beneath the most ancient vault that ever spread its arch over your head. Stop a moment until we light our tapers, for the interior is as dark as the centre of a tar-barrel.

Walls of Tyre.

We are nearly on the water-line, and are passing along the extreme eastern ledge of the island. The main wall is on our left, protected outside by this strong arched culvert, which rests against it, forming a vast vault, which probably extended the whole length of the island from south to north. In it thousands of soldiers could stand in safety and shoot through these lancet loop-holes. Here were congregated those bold Tyrians who so long and so desperately resisted the fierce Macedonian, and so often thwarted his efforts by destroying his works. Give your particular attention to the *bevel* of these great stones in the main wall. Let your eye become familiar with it, for you

How defended.

13

will learn to look with the respect due to most venerable antiquity upon every stone that has this mark upon it.

It would be easy to open a ditch along the line of this wall from south to north, and thus again make Tyre an island. Indeed, William of Tyre says that in his time this was actually done. He calls the ditch a "vallum late patens,"—something more than an ordinary fosse; and into it the sea could be introduced from both sides. I regard this section of the old wall as by far the most interesting relic of ancient Tyre.

PART II.—NORTHERN PALESTINE.

[Our travellers now cross the Scriptural boundary of the tribe of Asher, the northernmost of the twelve tribes, and enter the land of Israel. The tour through northern Palestine may be divided into two parts, in each of which the country is crossed from west to east, and from east to west.

In the first of these journeys, setting out from Tyre, we traverse the territories of Asher and Naphtali, abounding in picturesque highland scenery. Among other places we visit Dan, now Tell el Kady; Banias, anciently called Panias, and afterwards Cæsarea Philippi; and Kedesh-Naphtali, one of the cities of refuge. Few of the other places in this district are celebrated in Bible history. The chief interest of this excursion is in connection with the sources of the Jordan, which are in this district. The Jordan has several sources, the longest of its streams being the Hasbâny, but the most interesting that which gushes out of the rock at Banias. A very full account is given of the Lake Hûleh, called in the Bible the Waters of Merom, and of the country around. Leaving the Hûleh, we come by Kedesh-Naphtali, Safed, and other places, in a zigzag direction to the sea at Acre.

In the second excursion through northern Palestine, our route lies chiefly through the tribes of Zebulun, Naphtali, and Issachar. The Lake of Galilee is the great centre of interest in this excursion. Striking eastward from Acre (after visiting Carmel), we reach the Lake of Galilee by el Mughar, and traverse its whole margin. Leaving it at Magdala, we come in a south-westerly direction to Nazareth. The mountains on the east of the plain of Esdraelon, and the plain itself are then visited, and we again return to the sea at Cæsarea Palestina, once the Roman capital of Palestine, now an utter ruin.—ED.]

CHAPTER XIV.

TYRE TO KANAH.*

Boundary of tribe of Asher—and of Naphtali.	Ancient sculptures near Kanah. Kanah.
Hiram's tomb.	Sheepfolds and shepherds.
The cedars of Lebanon described.	Scripture allusions.

March 1st.

IT is delightful to be again on our journey, and the more so that the region into which we are about to penetrate is absolutely unknown to me. **Boundary of Asher.**

We are now crossing the territory of Asher toward the Kanah which belonged to that tribe; but it is not probable that the Jews ever had possession of this plain, nor even certain that Kanah itself was inhabited by them. East of it lies the country of the warlike tribe of Naphtali, where Jews always resided from the days of Joshua until several centuries after the destruction

---

* [Kanah, the name of the first place in Palestine proper of which notice is taken in this chapter, is not to be confounded with Cana of Galilee. The present Kanah was in the tribe of Asher, and is probably the Kanah mentioned by Joshua (xvi. 8), as belonging to that tribe.—ED.]

of Jerusalem; and even yet they cling to certain places in it with invincible
tenacity. How beautiful the sea, the city, and the plain, from these hills! and
as the eye runs along the sloping declivities north and south, it rests on many
a ruin which bears indubitable marks of Phœnician origin. I have wandered

Want of historic interest.
from place to place among them, hoping to find inscriptions in that ancient
language, but in vain; and since they have no historic interest, it is useless to
load the memory, or cram one's note-book with long lists of unpronounceable
names. Here, however, is something which merits attention. That singular

Hiram's tomb.
structure is called Hiram's Tomb,—upon what authority, except native tradition, I know not. But as there is nothing in the monument itself inconsis-

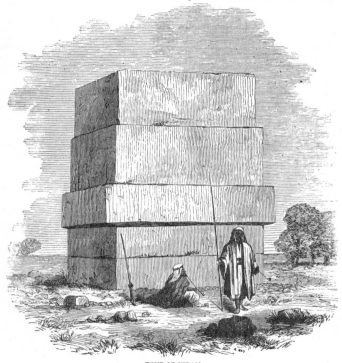

TOMB OF HIRAM.

tent with the idea that it marks the final resting-place of that ancient king
of Tyre, I am inclined to allow the claim to pass unquestioned. It bears
about it unmistakeable marks of extreme antiquity. The base consists of two
tiers of great stones, each three feet thick, thirteen feet long, and eight feet

eight inches broad. Above this is one huge stone, a little more than fifteen CHAPTER
feet long, ten broad, and three feet four inches thick. Over this is another, XIV.
twelve feet three inches long, eight broad, and six high. The top stone is a
little smaller every way, and only five feet thick. The entire height is
twenty-one feet. There is nothing like it in this country, and it may well
have stood, as it now does, ever since the days of Solomon. These large,
broken sarcophagi scattered around it are assigned by tradition to Hiram's
mother, wife, and family. Concerning them nothing need or can be said.
This whole neighbourhood abounds in Phœnician remains, and it is quite
natural that it should be so. The situation is beautiful; near enough, and
sufficiently high, to command the then glorious prospect of plain, city, and
crowded harbour; and no doubt the summer seats and summer residences of
Tyre's "merchant princes" crowned these hills. This village of Hânaweih is
built out of the ruins of such palaces, and similar remains lie scattered over all
the neighbourhood.

Are there any of the cedar-trees which Hiram transported by sea to Joppa
still found on these mountains?

I do not suppose there ever were any, for Lebanon terminates with Jebel Locality of
Rihan, far to the north-east of Tyre. These lower mountains, comprising the the cedars.
territories of Asher and Naphtali, are the favourite zone of the oak and the
terebinth. Even the pine is rarely seen, and the cedar never. It is only on
the loftier ranges of Lebanon that they flourish, and the true Biblical cedar is
now confined to a single locality.[1] Hiram, I suppose, had the control of these
mountains, and brought the cedar-tree to the coast at Tripoli, Batrone, Jebail,
or Beirût.

Have you ever visited these cedars?

Many times. They are situated high up on the western slope of Lebanon,
ten hours south-east from Tripoli. Besherrah is directly west, in the romantic gorge of the Khadîsha, two thousand feet below them, and Ehden is three
hours distant on the road to Tripoli. In no other part of Syria are the mountains so Alpine, the proportions so gigantic, the ravines so profound and awful.
You must not leave the country without visiting the cedars. There are several Romantic
routes to them, and all wild, exciting, delightful. One of the most romantic scenery of
is to climb Lebanon from Beirût quite to the base of Jebel Knîseh, then wind the neighbourhood.
northward around the heads of the stupendous gorges made by the rivers of
Beirût, Antelîas, Dog River, Nahr Ibrahim, Nahr el Jous, and the Khadîsha.
I have repeatedly followed that wildest of routes, with or without a path, as
the case might be, clinging to the shelving declivities midway to heaven, with
a billowy wilderness of rocks and ravines sinking away westward down to the
sea. The very thought of it at this minute is positively intoxicating. The

[1] Those travellers who speak of finding these cedars in abundance on other parts of Lebanon,
are simply mistaken in the tree. There are considerable groves of cedar in various places,
generally along the very highest range,—for example, north of Tomat Niha, above Barûk,
Aphcah, and other similar localities; but they are quite different from *the* cedar of Lebanon.

PART
II.
The cedar
grove.

platform where the cedars stand is more than six thousand feet above the Mediterranean, and around it are gathered the very tallest and greyest heads of Lebanon. The forest is not large—not more than five hundred trees, great and small, grouped irregularly on the sides of shallow ravines, which mark the birth-place of the Khadîsha, or Holy River.

But, though the space covered by them does not exceed half a dozen acres, yet, when fairly within the grove, and beneath the giant arms of those old patriarchs of a hundred generations, there comes a solemn hush upon the soul as if by enchantment. Precisely the same sort of magic spell settles on the spirits, no matter how often you repeat your visits. But it is most impressive in the night. Let us by all means arrange to sleep there. The universal si-

Sensation
by night.

lence is almost painful. The grey old towers of Lebanon, still as a stone, stand all around, holding up the stars of heaven to look at you; and the trees gather like phantoms about you, and wink knowingly, or seem to, and whisper among themselves you know not what. You become suspicious, nervous, until, broad awake, you find that it is nothing but the flickering of your drowsy fire, and the feeble flutter of bats among the boughs of the trees. A night among the cedars is never forgotten; the impressions, electrotyped, are hid away in the inner chamber of the soul, among her choicest treasures, to be visited a thousand times with never-failing delight.

There is a singular discrepancy in the statements of travellers with regard to the number of trees. Some mention seven, others thirteen—intending, doubtless, only those whose age and size render them Biblical, or at least historical. It is not easy, however, to draw any such line of demarcation. There is a complete gradation from small and comparatively young to the very

Number of
the trees.

oldest patriarchs of the forest. I counted four hundred and forty-three, great and small; and this cannot be far from the true number. This, however, is not uniform. Some are struck down by lightning, broken by enormous loads of snow, or torn to fragments by tempests. Even the sacrilegious axe is some-times lifted against them. But, on the other hand, young trees are constantly springing up from the roots of old ones, and from seeds of ripe cones. I have seen these infant cedars in thousands just springing from the soil; but, as the grove is wholly unprotected, and greatly frequented both by men and animals, they are quickly destroyed. This fact, however, proves that the number might be increased *ad libitum*. Beyond a doubt, the whole of these upper terraces of Lebanon might again be covered with groves of this noble tree, and furnish timber enough not only for Solomon's temple and the house of the forest of Lebanon, but for all the houses along this coast. But, unless a wiser and more provident government control the country, such a result can never be realized; and, indeed, the whole forest will slowly die out under the domin-ion of the Arab and Turk. Even in that case the tree will not be lost. It has been propagated by the nut or seed in many parks in Europe, and there are more of them within fifty miles of London than on all Lebanon.

We have seen larger trees every way, and much taller, on the banks of the

CEDARS OF LEBANON

Ohio, and the loftiest cedar might take shelter under the lowest branches of CHAPTER
California's vegetable glories.   Still, they are respectable trees.   The girth of   XIV.
the largest is more than forty-one feet ; the height of the highest may be one Size.
hundred.   These largest, however, part into two or three only a few feet from
the ground.   Their age is very uncertain, nor are they more ready to reveal it Age.
than others who have an uneasy consciousness of length of days.   Very different estimates have been made.   Some of our missionary band, who have experience in such matters, and confidence in the results, have counted the
growths (as we Western people call the annual concentric circles) for a few
inches into the trunk of the oldest cedar, and from such data carry back its
birth three thousand five hundred years.   It may be so.   They are carved
full of names and dates, going back several generations, and the growth *since*
the *earliest date* has been almost nothing.   At this rate of increase they must
have been growing ever since the flood.   But young trees enlarge far faster,
so that my confidence in estimates made from such specimens is but small.

The wood, bark, cones, and even leaves of the cedar are saturated, so to The tim-
speak, with resin.   The *heart* has the red cedar colour, but the exterior is ber.
whitish.   It is certainly a very durable wood, but is not fine grained, nor

CEDAR CONES.

sufficiently compact to take a high polish; for ordinary architectural purposes,
however, it is perhaps the best there is in the country.   There is a striking

PART
II.

The
branches.

peculiarity in the shape of this tree, which I have not seen any notice of in books of travel. The branches are thrown out horizontally from the parent trunk. These, again, part into limbs which preserve the same horizontal direction, and so on down to the minutest twigs, and even the arrangement of the clustered leaves has the same general tendency. Climb into one, and you are delighted with a succession of verdant floors spread around the trunk, and

Cones.

gradually narrowing as you ascend. The beautiful cones seem to stand upon, or rise out of this green flooring. I have gathered hundreds of these cones for friends in Europe and America; and you will see them in private cabinets more frequently than any other memento of the Holy Land.

Ancient
sculp-
tures.

We will now turn to the left, and visit some curious sculptures in the face of the rocks on the south side of this ravine which comes down from Kanah. Here they are, some twenty figures of men, women, and children, rudely carved in alto-relievo when no great progress had been made in sculpture. They may be of any supposable age, and were probably cut by Phœnician artists, before Tyre had any such masters as that Hiram who was filled with all wisdom to work all cunning work,[1] whom Solomon employed to beautify the temple of the most high God.

ANCIENT FIGURES ON ROCKS AT KANAH.

Kanah.

And that is Kanah spreading down the mountain to the east. It is a village of not more than two thousand inhabitants, and I see no evidence of antiquity about it.

That may be accounted for from the nature of the stone, a white marl, barely hard enough to be wrought, and which soon dissolves into soil when exposed to sun and rain. There is a ruin about a mile north of it, called 'Em el 'Awamid, which was built of hard rock, and there are ancient remains in abundance—foundations, columns, oil-presses, cisterns, and posts of houses scattered far and wide over the face of the mountain. There, too, are some

[1] 1 Kings vii. 14.

well-preserved specimens of Cyclopean architecture, such as I have seen nowhere else in this country. The original name is lost, and the present one,
" Mother of columns," has been given by the Arabs on account of the columns
which form so conspicuous a feature in its ruins. From the great number of
old oil-presses at this place, and others north and south, it is evident that
those now naked hills were once clothed with olive-trees. And that is probable
enough, for this chalky marl is the best of all soils for the olive. When thus
cultivated and adorned, this part of Asher must have been most beautiful. So
thought that crowning city Tyrus, and in her self-complacent vanity exclaims,
" I am of perfect beauty."

We will now pass into the wady on the east of Kanah, where the servants
are expecting us. With our wanderings and explorations, the ride from Tyre
has taken three hours, but it can easily be done in two. Though it is early in
the afternoon, we shall spend the night here, for there is no suitable place to
encamp between this and Tibnîn.

Owing to the wild wadies covered with dense forests of oak and underwood,
the country above us has ever been a favourite range for sheep and goats.
Those low, flat buildings out on the sheltered side of the valley are sheepfolds.
They are called mârâh, and, when the nights are cold, the flocks are shut up

MARAH--SHEEPFOLD.

in them, but in crdinary weather they are merely kept within the yard. This,
you observe, is defended by a wide stone wall, crowned all around with sharp

thorns, which the prowling wolf will rarely attempt to scale. The nimer, however, and fahed—the leopard and panther of this country—when pressed with hunger, will overleap this thorny hedge, and with one tremendous bound land among the frightened fold. Then is the time to try the nerve and heart of the faithful shepherd. These humble types of Him who leadeth Joseph like a flock[1] never leave their helpless charge alone, but accompany them by day, and abide with them at night. As spring advances, they will move higher up to other mârâhs and greener ranges; and in the hot months of summer they sleep with their flocks on the cool heights of the mountains, with no other protection than a stout palisade of tangled thorn-bushes. Nothing can be more romantic, Oriental, and even Biblical, than this shepherd life far away among the sublime solitudes of goodly Lebanon. We must study it in all its picturesque details. See, the flocks are returning home as the evening draws on; and how pretty the black and spotted goats, with their large, liquid eyes, and long, pendant ears—now in bold relief on the rocks, now hid among the bushes, but all the while rolling along the hill side like a column of gigantic ants! If some sharp-witted Jacob should take all the spotted, ring-streaked, and speckled of these flocks, he would certainly get the lion's share;[2] nor do I wonder that the countenance of that money-loving father-in-law of his should not be toward him as yesterday and the day before.[3] These bushy hills are the very best sheep-walks, and they are mostly abandoned to herds and flocks. They are now converging to this single point from all quarters, like the separate squadrons of an army. The shepherd walks before them, and they follow after, while the dogs, that Job talks of, bring up the rear.[4] These Oriental shepherd dogs, by the way, are not, like those in other lands, these faithful fellows, the friend and companion of their masters, and fit to figure in poetry. This would not suit Job's disparaging comparison. They are a mean, sinister, ill-conditioned generation, kept at a distance, kicked about, and half starved, with nothing noble or attractive about them. Still, they lag lazily behind the flocks, making a furious barking at any intruder among their charge, and thus give warning of approaching danger.

As you mentioned at the Damûr the other day, I notice that some of the flock keep near the shepherd, and follow whithersoever he goes, without the least hesitation, while others stray about on either side, or loiter far behind; and he often turns round and scolds them in a sharp, stern cry, or sends a stone after them. I saw him lame one just now.

Not altogether unlike the good shepherd. Indeed, I never ride over these hills, clothed with flocks, without meditating upon this delightful theme. Our Saviour says that the good shepherd, when he putteth forth his own sheep, goeth before them, and they follow.[5] This is true to the letter. They are so tame and so trained that they *follow* their keeper with the utmost docility. He leads them forth from the fold, or from their houses in the

Shepherds.
Goats.
Dogs.
Scripture allusions.

[1] Ps. lxxx. 1.   [2] Gen. xxx. 35.   [3] Gen. xxxi. 2.   [4] Job xxx. 1.   [5] John x. 4.

villages, just where he pleases. As there are many flocks in such a place as CHAPTER XIV. this, each one takes a different path, and it is his business to find pasture for them. It is necessary, therefore, that they should be taught to follow, and John, not to stray away into the unfenced fields of corn which lie so temptingly on ch. x. either side. Any one that thus wanders is sure to get into trouble. The shepherd calls sharply from time to time, to remind them of his presence. They know his voice, and follow on; but, if a stranger call, they stop short, lift up their heads in alarm, and, if it is repeated, they turn and flee, because they know not the voice of a stranger. This is not the fanciful costume of a parable; it is simple fact. I have made the experiment repeatedly. The shepherd goes before, not merely to point out the way, but to see that it is practicable and safe. He is armed in order to defend his charge; and in this he is very courageous. Many adventures with wild beasts occur not unlike Wild that recounted by David,[1] and in these very mountains; for, though there are beasts. now no lions here, there are wolves in abundance; and leopards and panthers, Leopards exceeding fierce, prowl about these wild wadies. They not unfrequently and pan-thers. attack the flock in the very presence of the shepherd, and he must be ready to do battle at a moment's warning. I have listened with intense interest to their graphic descriptions of downright and desperate fights with these savage beasts. And when the thief and the robber come (and come they do), the faithful shepherd has often to put his life in his hand to defend his flock. I have known more than one case in which he had literally to lay it down in the The good contest. A poor faithful fellow last spring, between Tiberias and Tabor, shepherd giving his instead of fleeing, actually fought three Bedawîn robbers until he was hacked life. to pieces with their khanjars, and died among the sheep he was defending.

Some sheep always keep near the shepherd, and are his special favourites. Each of them has a name, to which it answers joyfully; and the kind shepherd is ever distributing to such choice portions which he gathers for that purpose. These are the contented and happy ones. They are in no danger of getting Variety of lost or into mischief, nor do wild beasts or thieves come near them. The great character body, however, are mere worldlings, intent upon their own pleasures or selfish sheep. interests. They run from bush to bush, searching for variety or delicacies, and only now and then lift their heads to see where the shepherd is, or, rather, where the general flock is, lest they get so far away as to occasion remark in their little community, or rebuke from their keeper. Others, again, are rest-less and discontented, jumping into everybody's field, climbing into bushes, and even into leaning trees, whence they often fall and break their limbs. These cost the good shepherd incessant trouble. Then there are others incurably reckless, who stray far away, and are often utterly lost. I have repeatedly seen a silly goat or sheep running hither and thither, and bleating piteously after the lost flock, only to call forth from their dens the beasts of prey, or to bring up the lurking thief, who quickly quiets its cries in death.

[1] 1 Sam. xvii. 34–36.

PART
II.

Isaiah
xl. 11.

Isaiah has a beautiful reference to the good shepherd: "He shall feed his flock like a shepherd; he shall gather the lambs with his arm, and carry them in his bosom, and shall gently lead those that are with young."[1] Have you ever noticed these actions mentioned by the prophet?

Feeding
the flock.

Yes, in every particular. In ordinary circumstances the shepherd does not *feed* his flock, except by leading and guiding them where they may gather for themselves; but there are times when it is otherwise. Late in autumn, when the pastures are dried up, and in winter, in places covered with snow, he must furnish them food, or they die. In the vast oak woods along the eastern sides of Lebanon, between Baalbek and the cedars, there are then gathered innumerable flocks, and the shepherds are all day long in the bushy trees, cutting down the branches, upon whose green leaves and tender twigs the sheep and goats are entirely supported. The same is true in all mountain districts, and large forests are preserved on purpose. Life in these remote and wild woods is then most singular and romantic. The ring of the axe, the crash of falling trees, the shout of the shepherds, the tinkling of bells and barking of dogs, wake a thousand echoes along the deep wadies of Lebanon. I have ridden five hours at a stretch in the midst of these lively scenes, and the mere remembrance of them comes back now like distant music dying out sweetly along the solemn aisles of the wood. From early boyhood there has been within me an earnest sympathy with the mighty forest—something ever ready to sigh for such boundless continuity of shade as these wide sheep-walks

Shepherd
life in
Lebanon.

of Lebanon and Hermon afford. Can anything be more poetic than this life of the Syrian Shepherd! It ought to be religious too. Far, far away, out on the lone mountain, with the everlasting hills around, and heaven above, pure, blue, and high, and still,—there go and worship, free from the impertinence of human rhetoric, and the noisy cadences of prima donnas courting applause— in spirit and in truth worship—in solemn silence and soul-subduing solitude worship the most high God in his temple not made with hands. There

> "His varied works of wonder shine,
> And loud declare the hand divine
> That made the day, and made the night,
> And sowed the sky with diamonds bright;
> And bade old ocean in his might,
> And mountains bathed in golden light,
> The ever-present God proclaim—
> Holy and reverend be his name!"

Did you ever see a shepherd gather the lambs in his arms, and carry them in his bosom?

Carrying
the lambs
in the
bosom.

Often: and he will gently lead along the mothers, in those times when to overdrive them even for a single day would be fatal, as Jacob said to his brother when he wanted to get rid of him: "My lord knoweth that the flocks and herds with young are with me, and if men should overdrive them one day,

---

[1] Isa. xl. 11.

all the flock would die."[1] This, by the way, proves that Jacob's flight was late in the autumn, when alone the flocks are in this condition. The same is implied in his immediately building booths at Succoth for their protection during the winter.[2]

Micah, perhaps, had noticed the flocks feeding in the wilderness somewhat as you describe them along the slopes of Lebanon. He says, " Feed thy people with thy rod—the flock of thy heritage, which dwell solitarily in the wood in the midst of Carmel; let them feed in Bashan and Gilead as in the days of old."[3]

No doubt the reference is to the same thing. Large parts of Carmel, Bashan, and Gilead, are now covered with just such forests, which, at the proper season, are alive with countless flocks, which live upon the green leaves and tender branches.

How do you explain the expression, " Feed—with thy rod?"

The word signifies both to feed and to rule; and both ideas are natural. The shepherd invariably carries a staff or rod with him when he goes forth to feed his flock. It is often bent or hooked at one end, which gave rise to the shepherd's crook in the hand of the Christian bishop. With this staff he rules and guides the flock to their green pastures, and defends them from their enemies. With it, also, he corrects them when disobedient, and brings them back when wandering. This staff is associated as inseparably with the shepherd as the goad is with the ploughman. David, in the 4th verse of the 23d Psalm, has an extended reference to the shepherd and his kind offices, and among them is an allusion to this rod: " Thy rod and thy staff, they comfort me"—in every way in which these are employed by the good shepherd in the discharge of his office.

And now the lights are out in the village, the shepherds are asleep by the side of their flocks, the tinkling bell from the fold falls faintly on the still night air, and the watch-dog bays drowsily from his kennel at the gate. Good night, fair world; 'tis time to seek repose, and

> "The timely dew of sleep,
> Now falling with soft slumb'rous weight,
> Inclines our eyelids."

Let us first read, and meditate a while upon that delightful chapter in John,[4] where our blessed Saviour appropriates all these characters of a good shepherd to himself.

---

[1] Gen. xxxii. 13.   [2] Gen. xxxiii. 17.   [3] Micah vii. 14.   [4] John x. 1-29.

CHAPTER XV.

TIBNIN—HUNIN.*

Morning.
Olives and oil.
Ravines and roads.
Partridges and falcons.
Gazelles and bustards.
Tibnîn.
Messengers and mediators.
A divan.

Romantic wadies of Naphtali.
Water and water pools.
Magnificent view.
Vale of Upper Jordan.
Sources of the Jordan.
The Hûleh—Dan.
Abel-beth maachah.

March 2d.

Morning.   EITHER from association of ideas, or from the barking of dogs, the wailing of jackals, and the tinkling of bells, my head has been crowded with visions of shepherds, and flocks, and wild beasts, and wild Arabs, all night long.   Then, ere it was fully light, the reality was before me, and I have been out watching an Oriental village wake into life as the morning comes on.   There were some astir long before the dawn, loading donkeys and camels, and setting off as if going to market.   Then came ploughmen, goad in hand, and plough and yoke on the shoulder, driving their tiny oxen afield.   Later still, women and girls descended to the fountain with their "pitchers" to draw water; and as the sun rose over these dark mountains of Naphtali, the doors were thrown open, and forth from the folds poured thousands of goats, sheep, and young cattle, radiating in all directions, and spreading themselves over the hills in eager haste to crop their fragrant food while the dew lay upon it.   The whole scene has been one of entire novelty in my experience.

Here, now, is another, equally novel, perhaps, and quite as agreeable. Salîm has placed our breakfast, smoking hot, on this great rock, that the muleteers, while we enjoy it, may strike the tent and prepare for marching. In a few minutes our tabernacle will disappear from its place entirely and for ever.   It is to this that Hezekiah compares his life in the cutting off of his

Shep-
herds'
tents.

days : "Mine age is departed, and is removed from me as a shepherd's tent"[1] —suddenly and wholly, leaving not a trace behind.   And such is life at the best and longest—a pilgrimage in tents soon to be struck, folded up, and vanish away, "till the heavens be no more."

---

* [Neither Tibnîn nor Hunîn is a Scriptural name.   They are or were strong fortresses, that figure in the history of the Crusades, and in later history.   In this chapter we cross the boundary between Asher and Naphtali.   Naphtali is remarkable for striking highland and sylvan scenery.   The words of Jacob, "Naphtali is a hind let loose," have been also translated, "Naphtali is a spreading terebinth,"—quite the aspect of this district.   Though the tribe of Naphtali was not a distinguished one, its territory was the scene of some great events, such as Abraham's defeat of the Mesopotamian kings, and Joshua's defeat of the confederate Canaanites of the north.—ED.]

[1] Isa. xxxviii. 12.

We may leave the servants to pack up and pursue the regular route over that hill to the north-east on the road to Tibnîn, while we take down that wady Shimaliyeh, and thence northward to the ruins of Em el 'Awamîd. In no other place will you find such perfect specimens of ancient oil-mills and oil-presses, in a word, such a complete exhibition of what a large Phœnician agricultural village was. That road which passes over the hill to the south leads up a long ravine to Yathîr, thence into the great wady Aîûn, which it follows for many miles, past the site of Hazor, past Rumeîsh, and Kefr Bûr'îam, and Gish, to Safed and Tiberias. There are many ruins along it; indeed, every village occupies the site of an ancient town. We shall visit some of them on our return.

And this is Em el 'Awamîd—the mother of columns—and a curious place it is. But nearly all these pillars are square.

These are the upright posts of the oil-presses. You observe that they stand in pairs about two feet apart, having a deep groove in the inner faces,

ANCIENT OIL-MILLS AND PRESSES.

running from top to bottom. In this groove moved the plank on the top of the olive *cheeses*, forced down by a *beam*, as a lever, acting against this huge stone which lies on the top of the columns. Here is the stone trough into which the oil ran; and close by are two immense basins, in which the olives were ground to a pulp by the stone wheel that was rolled over them. This basin is nearly eight feet in diameter, and it must have cost no small labour to cut it out of the mountain and bring it to this spot. It is polished perfectly smooth by long use. Here is another basin, smaller and more concave. It may have served to *tread* the olives with the feet—a process not now used, but to which there is an allusion in Micah vi. 15: "Thou shalt tread the olives, but thou shalt not anoint thee with oil."

Were all these upright and prostrate columns parts of oil-presses?

Most of them. A few seem to have belonged to houses, or were the posts

PART
II.
of gateways, but the great majority were presses, and they speak of vast olive-orchards, not a trace of which now remains. When we reflect that these ruins have been broken up, and carried off to the surrounding villages from time immemorial, we may well be astonished at the number which still remain. And here let me inform you, for your guidance among ruins, that it does not follow that every village whose houses are built, in whole or in part, of large old stone, must necessarily be ancient, not even if it should itself be now a ruin. That village to the west of us is almost entirely made of such stone, *taken from here*, and it is fast falling into decay, though it may not be five hundred years old.

What a wild, broken region spreads up the mountain to the east of us!

Ravines and roads.
Those ravines are different branches of the great wady Jelo, which enters the plain of Tyre nearly opposite the city. Our road lies in the bottom of this branch from the south-east, called wady Habis, and it is time we should descend into it and prosecute our journey; and, when in, we shall not get out for two hours, but must wind about according to its own eccentricities, sometimes between cliffs perpendicular and bare, at others less precipitous, and clothed with beautiful oak woods. Here comes in the road from Kânâ, and high up the face of this rampart on our left is a tomb cut in the rock. He who made it must have been like Edom, ambitious to place his nest as high as the eagle; and yet, saith the Lord, "I will bring thee down from thence." [1] And, long ages ago, his dust was scattered in this brawling brook, and swept away to the sea of Tyre. Here is an extraordinary growth of cactus, climbing the face of the cliff for many hundred feet,—the only thing of the kind I have seen in Syria. We begin to hear the tinkling of our mule-bells, and now and then the song of the driver comes echoing down between these gigantic cliffs. And there is the sharp crack of Salîm's gun. They are evidently enjoying our romantic valley and this delicious air.

What bird is that whose call rings responsive from side to side?

The partridge.
The red-legged partridge, of which there are countless flocks in these hills and wadies of Naphtali. It is at them that Salîm is exercising his skill. Should he succeed we shall have the better dinner, for they are twice as large as our American quail, to which, in other respects, they bear a close resemblance. Hear how they cackle and call to one another directly above our heads. They are very wary, however, and often lead the vexed hunter over many a weary mile of rough mountains before he can get a shot at them.

The emeers and feudal chiefs of the country hunt them with the hawk, and keep up, with great pride, the ancient sport of falconry. The birds are generally brought from Persia and the cold mountains of Armenia, and do not thrive well in this climate. They are of two kinds, a large one for wood-cock and red-legged partridges, and a smaller for the quail.

The Beg at the castle of Tibnîn which we are now approaching, always keeps

[1] Jer. xlix. 16.

several of these large falcons on their perches in his grand reception-hall, CHAPTER
where they are tended with the utmost care. I have been out on the moun-   XV.
tains to see them hunt, and it is a most exciting scene. The emeers sit on The fal-
their horses holding the birds on their wrists, and the woods are filled with con.
their retainers, beating about and shouting, to start up and drive toward them
the poor partridges. When near enough, the falcon is launched from the
hand, and swoops down upon his victim like an eagle hasting to the prey.
After he has struck his quarry, the falcon flies a short distance, and lights on
the ground, amid the redoubled shouts of the sportsmen. The keeper darts
forward, secures both, cuts the throat of the partridge, and allows his captor
to suck its blood. This is his reward. Notwithstanding the exhilaration of
the sport, I could never endure the falcon himself. There is something almost
satanic in his eye, and in the ferocity with which he drinks the warm life-
blood of his innocent victim. I once saw some men of Tortosa catching the
Syrian quail with a small hawk. This was done on foot, each sportsman Hunting
carrying his bird on the right wrist, and beating the bushes with a stick held part-
in his left hand. These quails are less than the American; are migratory, ridges.
coming here in early spring, and passing on to the north. They hide under
the bushes, and will not rise on the wing unless forced to do so by a dog, or by
the hunter himself. I was surprised to see how quickly and surely the little
hawk seized his game. His reward, also, was merely the blood of the bird.
I do not know whether or not the Jews in ancient days were acquainted with
falconry, but David complains that Saul hunted for his blood as one doth hunt
for a partridge in the mountains ;[1] and this hunting of the same bird on these
mountains, and giving their *blood* to the hawk, reminds one of the sad complaint of the persecuted son of Jesse.

In the neighbourhood of Aleppo the smaller falcon is taught to assist the Hunting
sportsman to capture the gazelle. Neither horse nor greyhound can overtake the ga-
these fleet creatures on the open desert, and therefore the Arabs have taught zelle.
the hawk to fasten on their forehead, and blind them by incessant flapping of
their wings. Bewildered and terrified, they leap about at random, and are
easily captured. They are also trained to attack the bustard in the same The bus-
region. This bird is about as large as a turkey, and highly prized by the lovers tard.
of game; but as they keep on the vast level plains, where there is nothing to
screen the cautious hunter, it is almost impossible to get within gunshot of
them. When they rise in the air, the little falcon flies up from beneath and
fastens on one of their wings, and then both come whirling over and over to
the ground, when the hunter quickly seizes the bustard, and delivers his
brave bird from a position not particularly safe or comfortable. They will even
bring down the largest eagle in the same way; but in this desperate game
they are sometimes torn to pieces by the insulted majesty of the feathered
kingdom.

---

[1] 1 Sam. xxvi. 20.

PART
II.

Tibnin.

And now we have gained the summit of this long ravine, let me inform you that it is but one of many which cut down, in all directions, from the high plateaus of Naphtali. We shall be obliged to regulate our march in all cases according to their dictation. Yonder is Tibnîn, crowning the top of a lofty Tell, partly natural and partly artificial. It rises like a huge hay stack at least two hundred feet above all its surroundings. The present buildings are comparatively modern, but it figured in the wars of the Crusaders, by whom it was called Toron. No doubt those mailed champions of the Cross often dashed up Wady Habis in a style very different from our peaceful and pleasant saunter, and on a very different errand, for they had to encounter the victorious squadrons of the terrible Saladin. Toron is not, probably, the most ancient

The castle. name of this castle. A place so conspicuous, so strong, and so central, must have always been occupied, as it is now, by the family that governed the province around it; and there are not wanting traces of that more ancient castle. The top of the Tell is perforated like a honey-comb with old cisterns; and on the east side are heavy foundations, the stones of which have the Phœnician *bevel*. They may have been there at the time of Joshua, and Tibnîn probably represents some one of the places given to Naphtali, though what one it is impossible to determine. The Beg informed me that Jezzar Pasha of Acre destroyed this castle, broke down the wall, and filled up the ditch, which ran quite round the Tell. He did the same to Hûnîn, and, indeed, to all the castles in these mountains, and killed or expelled the native chiefs. If the *Butcher* had done nothing worse, he would have deserved praise rather than censure. After his death, however, the feudal lords returned more greedy and tyrannical than ever.

The governor.

The present head of the house of Aly es Sughîr pretends that his ancestors were made governors of Belad Bsharah by the great Saladin himself. This may be fairly doubted, though I do not know when they actually rose to power in the country.

Shall we call on this governor in the castle?

By no means. There would be no getting away until to-morrow. Two years ago I spent the night there with my family, and that will last me all my life. I had no intention of doing such a foolish thing then, but began to pitch the tents in some threshing-floors which overlook the wady on the north of the castle. The Beg had seen us pass, and despatched a messenger to invite us to

Messengers "more honourable."

his palace. I sent an apology. Then came a deputation "more honourable," his secretary and a near relative, with a note from the Beg, urging the invitation so earnestly that I felt obliged to comply. This sending honourable princes to press the request reminded me at the time of the way in which Balak overcame the real or pretended reluctance of Balaam. "He sent again princes, more, and more honourable than they; and they said to him, Let nothing, I pray thee, hinder thee from coming unto me." [1] This is a very

---

[1] Num. xxii. 15, 16.

ancient and very common custom. Everything is done by mediation. Thus CHAPTER
the centurion sent unto Jesus elders, beseeching him that he would come and XV.
heal his servant.[1] In a hundred instances I have been pressed and annoyed Mediators
by these mediating ambassadors. Their importunity takes no denial. To
save ourselves from such a siege, we will keep quite clear of the castle, and
go on about half an hour to a well at the bottom of that wady east of us,
and there take our lunch. In the meantime, I will give you an account of
that visit, as the cheapest way into the interior of a Metăwely governor's
palace.

The old Beg received me with the utmost politeness,—descended from his
divan, kissed me on both cheeks, and insisted on my sharing his elevated seat. A divan.
To the best of my knowledge, it was the first time I ever saw him, but he insisted that he had been at my house in Beirût some fifteen years before,
and that I had done him a very important service by speaking a word in his
behalf in the right quarter. It may have been so; at any rate, he was as kind
as he knew how to be—gave me a Metăwely dinner, and kept me up till late,
talking about all sorts of topics before a full divan of his relatives and retainers,
and then had my bed spread on the same divan. According to *court* etiquette
at Tibnîn, the ladies of my party had their own apartment, and, after being
served with dinner, they called on the great *sit*, or lady of the Beg, whose
apartments were in another section of the castle. It would be tedious to detail
all they saw and heard; but they were much pleased with some of the
" harem," who appeared modest, lady-like, and pretty. Others, however, were
coarse and ill-bred enough.

I was greatly disappointed in the Beg. His conversation was incessant,
loud, and often utterly absurd. We fell at last into a rambling and useless
discussion about religion, in which Mohammed's character and prophetic claims
were handled rudely enough, to the great scandal of the dervishes present; and
at midnight I was glad to break up the divan, and try to sleep—no easy task, A sleepless
or, rather, it was impossible. The visitors had filled the divan with fleas, and night—
the wind, which began to blow hard before we left our tents, proved to be one fleas.
of those siroccos which make all sorts of vermin doubly active and man excessively nervous. The whole night was passed in fruitless skirmishes with these
contemptible enemies, and the suffocating wind whistled and piped most doleful tunes through every chink and cranny of the old castle. The ladies had
fared even worse than myself, and the morning found us dejected, *headachy*,
and quite discouraged. Having with difficulty achieved a breakfast, in the
midst of confusion which reminded me of Scott's Highland stories, we took a
guide from the Beg and started for Hunîn, where we expect to get to-night.

I shall never forget the experience of that dismal night, nor the charming Romantic
ride of that day through these romantic wadies of old Naphtali. We filled our wadies of
water-bottles at these very wells where we are now quietly taking lunch, and Naphtali.

then rode over that hill east of us. Beyond it our guide turned suddenly to the left down a shallow ravine, but one that deepened every moment, until we were completely shut in between lofty walls of grey rock. Deeper and deeper into the bowels of the earth we dived for more than an hour, to where two other wadies joined ours—one from the south, the other from the east. The three in one trend off toward the north, and, under the name of Hajeîr, descend to the Litany at Jisr K'ak'aîyeh. The one from the south passes by an ancient castle called Dubay, about which nothing need be, and very little can be said. We took the eastern ravine, called Hûla (from a village at the head of it)— strange, wild, romantic. For miles the path was literally roofed over with a dense canopy of trees and bushes, forming, with the bed of the brook whose windings we had to follow, a sort of tunnel wholly peculiar. We were often obliged to lie flat on the necks of our horses, and be drawn through this verdant vault by main force. At the end of two hours we emerged from this labyrinth, and climbed a steep and lofty hill to the village of Hûla—the same name, nearly, as that of the lake below Hunîn. We intended to rest a while there; but such a mob of rude Metāwelies, of every age and sex, beset us, clamorous to see the *seigniorât*—as they call Frank ladies—that we were compelled to decamp immediately, and, after another hour's pleasant ride, we pitched our tents among the oaks, olives, and terebinths on the western margin of the vale of Hunîn.

And now, lunch over, let us ride, and to the south-east for half an hour, to avoid the wady in which our story has been entangled. We are passing through the very heart of Naphtali, wild and savage, just fitted to be the home of that warlike tribe. No European, and but very few native travellers, ever venture along this desolate road. We shall soon get down to an old guardhouse, called Beer en Nŭkkar, erected for the protection of the traveller through this dangerous district. Off yonder to the south-west is 'Ain'ata, supposed to be the Anatha or Beth-Anath given to Naphtali; and half an hour farther south is Bint Jebail—daughter of a little mountain (to translate), and the capital of this region. To the left of us, in the woods, is a ruin with columns, and foundations of old temples, called Kŭbrîkha, and the entire neighbourhood is crowded with ancient but deserted sites. A long, rocky ascent eastward now leads us to Neby Mûhaîbeeb—a celebrated saint of the Metāwelies—picturesquely perched upon a bold promontory. We pass north of it on the direct road to Mais el Jebel, which is just visible yonder to the north-east of us. Let me call your attention to this very unromantic, nonpoetic pool. Every village in this region has one or more of them for their herds and flocks. In very dry seasons they entirely fail; and there are frequent allusions to such a calamity in the Bible. It is among the threatened judgments upon unbelieving Israel that the Lord will dry up all their pools.[1]

Marginal notes: Anatha or Beth-Anath. Water-pools.

---

[1] Isa. xliii. 16.

Do the people drink this composition of nastiness?

Many do, and all use this water for culinary and other household purposes. Bad water. Nothing is more common than to see flocks and herds standing up to their bellies in these pools, and the people filling their jars in the midst of them. I have been obliged to drink it myself when of the colour of soap-suds, full of living animalculæ, and with a strong smell of the barn-yard. I once gave five piastres to get a jar of good water at this Hunîn where we are to spend the night, was cheated at last, and compelled to drink this abominable decoction. The Jews of all this region must have been supplied with water in the same way. Natural fountains are very rare, nor can wells be dug with success. The ancient inhabitants, however, depended greatly upon cisterns, and there are countless numbers of them about these old sites; but the water, even in these, is filthy and full of vermin, unless great care be taken to keep them clean and sweet.

That is quite sufficient on this topic. There seems to be a castle here. Has the place any historic name?

Not that I know of. The castle, at least in its present form, is comparatively modern. There are traces, however, of genuine antiquity about this Mais, and I doubt not there was once a Jewish town here. But we must pass on to our camp-ground at Hunîn, which is still an hour and a half to the north-east of us.

How charming these hills, clothed with evergreen oaks, terebinth, and bay trees!

This may be my twentieth visit, and yet they appear as lovely now as on the Beauty of day I first saw them. Such beauty never wearies the eye—always rejoices the the hills. heart. Let the muleteers go on and pitch the tent, while we turn up to this ruin on our right, called Mŭnârâh. Step out now upon this rocky platform, and enjoy at your leisure, and in silence, a panorama more beautiful and as vast as that which Moses saw from the top of Pisgah.

Well! I have never seen any prospect to equal that.

I presume not. The declivity sinks beneath our feet down—down, sheer down fifteen hundred feet and more, to the plain of the Hûleh; and when you can withdraw your gaze from this scene of utmost loveliness, turn to that which Magnifi- surrounds it. Lofty Lebanon stretches northward to the snowy summit of cent view. Sŭnnîn, which looks down on Cœlo-Syria and the ruins of Baalbek. Before us Hermon lifts his head to heaven in solemn and solitary majesty. Those sugar-loaf hills on that vast plateau to the east and south-east are so many landmarks in the misty and mysterious Hauran, with the Great Desert of Arabia behind and beyond. Those shadowy lines that bound the hazy horizon to the south are Gilead and Bashan, the territories of old Sihon and Og, kings of the Amorites. On our right are the mountains of the Galilees and Samaria, while behind us the hills of Naphtali and Asher sink, by successive terraces, down to the sea-coast of Acre, Tyre, and Sidon. What countless thoughts cluster around such a group of things and names as this!

Not to confuse the mind with dim distances and immeasurable magnitudes, let us study a while this noble vale beneath us. It is the basin of the Jordan,

Vale of Upper Jordan.

the birth-place of that sacred river in which the Son of God was baptized. During the rainy months of winter it receives a hundred little tributaries of those snowy ravines around the north end of Hermon. From thence it cuts its way through dark beds of lava, some twenty miles, to the great fountain of Fuarr, below Hasbeiya, which is its most distant *permanent* source. With the name of Hasbâny it passes southward to this plain and marsh of the Hûleh, receiving on its way the stream from Shib'ah, the great fountain of Sureîd, beneath Kefr Shûb'ah, and the Luisany at El Ghŭjar. Thus augmented, it penetrates the marsh about five miles, when it is joined by the Leddan, from Tell el Kady, and the Baniasy, from Banias, united a short half mile north of

the Tell called Sheikh Yusûf. Of these main branches of the Jordan, the Hasbâny is the longest by forty miles, the Leddan is much the largest, and the Baniasy the most beautiful. Besides these, a considerable stream comes from the plain of Ijon, the joint contribution of the Derdarah and Ruahîny, west of Abel. Several immense fountains also burst out along the base of this mountain on which we are standing, and send their streams through the marsh to the river and the lake. The largest are those of Blât and El Mellahah. The lake itself may be eight miles long, and six broad across the north end, but it runs to a point southward, where the Jordan leaves it. This is the Merom of

Joshua, the Samechonitis of the Greeks, the Hûleh of the Arabs. The plain and marsh above it are about ten miles square. The eastern half is sufficiently dry for cultivation, and is, in fact, the great granary of the surrounding country, and the boast of the Arabs. The climate is warm, the soil fat as that of Egypt, and the whole is irrigated by innumerable canals from the Hasbâny, the Leddan, and the Baniasy.

In the centre rises the Leddan, at the base of that circular mound, which you can trace by the line of trees around its outer margin. It marks the site of the Sidonian Laish, the Dan of the Bible. Often have I sat under its great oak, and gazed in dreamy delight upon the luxuriant plain of the Hûleh. No wonder the spies exclaimed, " We have seen the land, and, behold, it is very good: a place where there is no want of anything that is in the earth."[1]

Abraham's battle at Dan.

We have spread out before us one of the great battle-fields of the Bible—a vast theatre built by the Architect of the universe; and upon its splendid stage has many a bloody tragedy been played out in downright earnest. In the opening scene the chief actor is no less a personage than the "Father of the Faithful," scattering to the winds those hard-named confederates who conquered Sodom, and carried away righteous Lot, with his family, captive. Abraham was sitting in his tent-door, under the great oak of Mamre, when a fugitive from the vale of Siddim brought the tidings of his nephew's captivity. This was no time for rending of garments and fruitless lamentations. Arming his own servants—three hundred and eighteen—and sending a hasty summons to Mamre, and his brothers Eshcol and Aner, to join him, he set off in hot pur-

[1] Judges xviii. 9, 10.

suit. Passing Bethlehem and Salem, he swept over the mountains, and along the plains of Sychar and Esdraelon, and at the close of the fourth day (Josephus says he attacked them on the fifth night) he was probably climbing these hills of Naphtali. From these bold headlands he could see with perfect distinctness the enemy carousing in careless security around the fountain of Leddan. Having made the necessary dispositions for the attack, he waits for the veil of darkness; then, like an avalanche from the mountains, he bursts upon the sleeping host. The panic is immediate and universal, the confusion inextricable, the rout wild and ruinous. No one knows friend from foe. They trample down and slay each other, are swamped in miry canals, and entangled and torn to pieces in the thorny jungles of the Baniasy. Terror lends wings to the fugitives. They climb Castle Hill, rush along the vale of Yafûry, and, descending to the great plain by Beit Jenn, cease not their frantic flight until they reach Hobah, which is on the left hand of Damascus.[1] Abraham returns victorious to Laish, which is Dan; the captives are released, and the goods collected. None have perished; nothing is lost. In triumph, and with devout thanksgiving, he, who through faith waxed valiant in battle,[2] marches back by Jerusalem to his tent on the plain of Mamre. Thus falls the curtain on the first act.

When it is again lifted, the theatre is crowded with a mighty host—the Canaanite from the east and the west, the Amorite, the Hittite, and the Jebusite from the mountains, and the Hivite under Hermon—" much people, even as the sand that is on the sea-shore in multitude, with horses and chariots very many."[3] Far as the eye can reach, the plain is darkened by countless squadrons of the heathen. Confident in their numbers, they dream not of danger, when Joshua, with his valiant men of war, falls suddenly upon them. The mighty shout strikes terror into every heart. The shock is irresistible. Jabin, with his confederate kings, wakes only to join the universal rout. This vast theatre of plain and marsh, and valley and mountain, is covered with fugitives and their fierce pursuers. Those whose homes lay beyond the mountains to the north and east, sought them by the great wady of the Upper Jordan, now Wady et Teim; or out east of Hermon, in the Hauran, the land of Mizpeh. Those from the sea-coast of Acre and Carmel fled over these hills, and down south-west by Hazor to Misrephoth-Maim,[4] on the north border of the plain of Acre, now called Musheirifeh. Thence they dispersed to their homes along the sea-board as far south as Dor. Joshua himself chased a third division along the base of our mountain northward, past Abel-Beth-Maachah, through the plain of Ijon, down the tremendous gorge of the Litany to the ford at Tamrah, or the bridge at the Khŭtweh, and thence over the wooded spurs of Jebel Rihan toward great Zidon, behind whose lofty walls the flying host alone could find safety. Returning southward, he recrossed the Litany, stormed Hazor, the capital of King Jabin, and utterly consumed

Marginal notes: Joshua's victory over the Canaanites. Hazor.

[1] Gen. xiv. 15.   [2] Heb. xi. 34.   [3] Josh. xi. 1–5.   [4] Josh. xi. 8.

PART
II.

the city with fire.[1] The shapeless ruins may still be seen a few miles west of us, with the identical name, and having a celebrated mazar, sacred to Joshua, the son of Nun. The curtain drops over the burning capital.

The co-
lony of
Danites.

And now it rises once more, revealing a scene of dark treachery and cruel slaughter. See that band of daring Danites creeping stealthily around the reedy margin of the marsh toward Laish. Will no one sound the alarm ? Alas ! the indolent, luxurious, demoralized citizens slumber in fatal security, soothed by the murmurs of their magnificent fountain. And now the mound is gained, the walls scaled, the gates burst open, the city on fire, and men, women, and children fall in indiscriminate butchery. There is no help—no mercy. They are far from their parent city, Sidon—have no business with any-body, no friends, no allies.[2] The foul work over, the murderous band sit down in quiet possession, rebuild, and call the city Dan, after the father of their tribe. Henceforth it is famous as the boundary on the north of the Promised Land, and " from Dan to Beersheba" becomes the proverbial limit of Israel's inheritance.[3]

People of
Laish.

I read this tragedy with feelings of indignation and abhorrence. True, these Phœnician dwellers in Laish were every way ripe for destruction. *They were lazy*, dwelling carelessly, after the manner of the Zidonians, quiet and secure. *They had nothing to do.* They had no business with any one. *They had no government and no moral character.* There was no magistrate in the land that might put them to shame in anything.[4] They deserve little commisera-tion, no doubt, but then these Danites were thieves and robbers, " bitter and angry fellows," ready to run upon and murder poor Micah, whom they had plundered of his property.[5] They were also traitors to their religion and the God of their fathers. Immediately they set up the graven image stolen from Micah; and the golden calves of Dan became a snare to all Israel, until they were carried captive by Shalmaneser, and placed in Halah and in Habor, by the River Gozan.[6] Dan has ceased to be a city for ages. Not one solitary habitation is there. The fountain still pours forth its river of delicious water, but herds of black buffaloes wash and wallow in its crystal pools. You cannot even examine the site with satisfaction, so dense is the jungle of briars, thorns, and thistles which have overspread it.

Insurrec-
tion of
Sheba.

One more act, and our drama is ended " A man of Belial—Sheba, the son of Bichri—blew a trumpet, and said, To your tents, O Israel. We have no part in David, neither have we inheritance in the son of Jesse."[7] David was extremely disturbed at this rebellion of the son of Bichri, and Joab, the bloody murderer, but mighty captain, was sent in pursuit of him through all the tribes of Israel; and he came and besieged him in Abel of Beth-Maachah. There it is, on that long oval mound to the north-east of us. I have repeatedly ridden round it, and stood on the top, trying to realize the scene. Taking advantage

---

[1] Josh. xi. 13.   [2] Judges xviii. 28.   [3] 1 Sam. iii. 20.   [4] Judges xviii. 7.
[5] Judges xviii. 22-25.   [6] 2 Kings xvii. 6.   [7] 2 Sam. xx. 1.

of an oblong knoll of natural rock that rises above the surrounding plain, the CHAPTER
original inhabitants raised a high mound sufficiently large for their city. With XV.
a deep "trench" and strong wall, it must have been almost impregnable. The
country on every side is most lovely, well watered, and very fertile. The
Derdâra, from Ijon, falls from that plain by a succession of cataracts, and glides
swiftly along the western declivity of the mound, and from the neighbouring
mountain gushes out the powerful stream of Ruahîny. Such fountains and
brooks would convert any part of this country into a paradise of fruits and
flowers; and such, no doubt, was Abel, when she was called "a mother in Abel of
Israel." But the iron hoof of war tramples all in the dust. The besiegers Beth-
cast up a mount against the city, "and it stood in the trench, and all the people Maachah.
that were with Joab battered the wall, to throw it down. Then cried a wise
woman out of the city, Hear, hear; say, I pray you, unto Joab, Come near
hither, that I may speak with thee. And when he was come near unto her,
the woman said, Art thou Joab ? and he answered, I am he. Then she said,
Hear the words of thine handmaid. And he answered, I do hear. Then she
spake, saying, They were wont to speak in old times, saying, They shall surely
ask counsel at Abel, and so they ended the matter. I am one of them that
are peaceable and faithful in Israel : thou seekest to destroy a city and a
mother in Israel : why wilt thou swallow up the inheritance of the Lord ?
And Joab answered and said, Far be it, far be it from me, to swallow up or
destroy. The matter is not so; but a man of Mount Ephraim, Sheba, the son
of Bichri by name, hath lifted up his hand against the king, even against
David : deliver him only, and I will depart from the city. And the woman
said, His head shall be thrown to thee over the wall. Then the woman went
to all the people in her wisdom : and they cut off the head of Sheba the son of
Bichri, and cast it out to Joab : and he blew a trumpet, and they retired from
the city, every one to his tent, and Joab returned to Jerusalem unto the king." [1]
Thus ends the last act of our tragedy. The curtain falls, and we must retire
to our tent, as did the host of Joab.

I trust you will not be greatly scandalized, but, fascinated with the theatre
and the stage, I have been a very heedless listener to your tragedy.

I am not at all surprised. The first time I gazed upon this scene I should
have felt anything an impertinence that disturbed the pleasing trance. But
seek not a closer acquaintance. 'Tis distance lends enchantment. Abel
itself is a sad example of the utter decay and ruin that has "swallowed up the
inheritance of the Lord." The present village, far from being a mother in Present
Israel, occupies only a small portion of the mound; and wisdom and counsel village.
will be sought in vain at the hands of the peasants who lounge in rags and
filth upon the dunghills which barricade their streets and doors. And now the
green hills of Naphtali are casting their shadows over the lovely Hûleh as the sun
sinks to rest in the distant sea, and we must hasten to our camp under Hunîn.

---

[1] 2 Sam. xx. 15—22.

LAB — O

CHAPTER XVI.

HUNIN—HULEH—BANIAS.

March 3d.

Hunîn.

I HAVE been out examining this castle and its surroundings. The view from some of the towers over the Hûleh and the eastern mountains is very grand. What place do you suppose it may have been in olden time?

Many years ago I thought it might mark the site of Hazor, but since then have discovered that place, as I believe, a few miles back in the interior; and, on the whole, I have been inclined of late to identify it with Beth-Maachah. The small province of which this city was the capital is associated in the Bible with Abel, and must have extended round the head of this great marsh to the vicinity of Hunîn, for Abel is just below it. Dr. Robinson makes this Beth-Rehob; but Dan, which is Tell el Kâdy, is said to be in the valley that lieth by Beth-Rehob, and this more naturally points to Banias, as you will see hereafter. It is difficult to believe that either of the Rehobs given to Asher was at this place, for Hunîn is in the territory of Naphtali. Dan, however, and the plain around it, including Banias, seem to have belonged to Sidon, and that city, with its territory, was assigned to Asher. If Banias, therefore, is Beth-Rehob, it might have been given to Asher in the original distribution, but it never was really in their possession; for we know from Judges i. 31 that they could not subdue it. So doubtful, however, is the location of these cities, that, if Rehob be Hunîn, I should place Beth-Maachah at Banias, and *vice versa*.

Probably Beth-Maachah.

The castle.

This castle has a very imposing appearance from the plain below, owing to its position, and the round towers which defend the southern portion of it. These are, however, comparatively modern. The only part really ancient is the north end, which is about three hundred feet square, and surrounded by a fosse cut in the solid rock, forty feet wide and twenty deep. The original wall was built of large bevelled stone, after the Phœnician manner, and bound together by iron cramps, as may be seen in a few places under the modern ruins.

Late sowing.

Though we have made an early start, these farmers are in advance of us, and are actually sowing barley at this late season of the year. Will it come to perfection during the brief space that remains between this and the harvest season in this country?

It is more than possible ; but it depends entirely on the character of the coming spring. I have seen one winter, at least, when there was not enough rain to enable the farmers to sow their grain until the month of February; but then there followed an uncommonly cold and wet March. The mountains were covered, on the last day of that month, with a heavy fall of fresh snow, and by the end of April the fields were rejoicing in as rich a crop as ever gladdened the anxious husbandman. It may be thus this year, and it may not. Should the rains cease early, no reaper will fill his bosom with sheaves from these fields. These men are therefore sowing in hope in a very emphatic sense. There is, at least, an equal chance against them, and still they plough and sow on vigorously, with only this basis for their expectations.

It was upon facts such as these the wise man founded his admonition, " In the morning sow thy seed, and in the evening withhold not thine hand ; for thou knowest not whether shall prosper, either this or that, or whether they both shall be alike good." [1] Of course, the idea is, *sow early* and sow *late*, as opportunity offers or circumstances require. And the wise farmer, in this country, must thus act ; for no human sagacity, no length of experience, will enable him to determine, in any given year, that what is sown early will prosper best. If the spring be late, wet, and cold, the early grain grows too rank, *lodges*, and is blasted, while the *late sown* yields a large harvest. This farmer tells me, in answer to my question, that they will be both alike good this year, or, as he expresses it, the late will *overtake* the early. This may be so, but, as Solomon says, he does not know it.

These men seem about to realize the prophecy of Amos : " Behold, the days come, saith the Lord, that the ploughman shall overtake the reaper." [2] If I remember correctly, reaping will commence in the coming month.

Yes, in the valley of the Jordan, which is here just below us. No doubt this late ploughing and sowing suggested the terms of the prophecy, and gave an air of verisimilitude to it. So, also, the next clause in this 13th verse, " The treader of grapes shall overtake him that soweth seed," derives its significance from facts in agricultural experience. The time for the treading of grapes comes on during the dry months of autumn, and is ordinarily soon over ; but this promise implies that the vintage will be prolonged into the rainy season, when alone the husbandman can begin to sow his seed. This does not generally occur until November. In the good days of the promise, however, the vintage will be abundant and long, while the rains will be early and copious, and thus the treading of grapes will run on to the time when the fall crops are sown. This is never actually the case at present, yet, in seasons remarkably favourable, an approximation is seen sufficiently near to justify the allusion.

---

[1] Eccl. xi. 6.   [2] Amos ix. 13.

PART
II.

Times of
sowing,
reaping,
threshing,
vintage.
In Leviticus xxvi. 3, 5, there is the same promise : " If ye walk in my statutes . . . the vintage shall reach unto the sowing-time." But here the preceding parallelism is varied. Instead of " The ploughman shall overtake the reaper," it is " Your threshing shall reach unto the vintage." The *threshing* comes *between* the reaping and the treading of grapes, and the promise, therefore, covers another portion of the farmer's year. Reaping is done in April, May, and June, and the vintage is in September and October. Hence the harvest, according to the promise, is to be so heavy that it will take three or four months to tread out the grain. And here, again, actual experience suggested the costume of the prophecy. In very abundant seasons I have often seen the threshing actually prolonged until October. Take the three promises together, and they spread over the entire year of the husbandman. The ploughman will continue his work until that which was first sown is ready for the sickle ; the threshing follows the reaper, and extends to the vintage; and then the treading of grapes reaches to the time to sow for the next crop. And such is the happy nature of this climate, that the whole series of promises is even now realized in those favourable years in which " the Lord gives rain in due season."

What a splendid day, and how warm too, for the first of March !

We are favoured in that respect. I was once here with the Countess of Schlieffen and her son, when the ground was frozen hard, and flying clouds kept pelting me with sleet and snow as I rode back to Hasbeiya. Eighteen hundred and forty-nine had been swept away by a perfect deluge of rain and snow, and the new year came in clear and cold. Our German friends, who had been detained in my house for a month by sickness, had left us several days before, carrying the maid-servant on a kind of bier. As it began to rain violently soon after they started, we were quite anxious about them, and our solicitude was not relieved by the contradictory accounts brought to us by the peasants. After breakfast I set off in search of them. The Hasbâny was not fordable, and I rode to the bridge, where I had an opportunity to see the Upper Jordan rushing full and headlong over its rocky bed. The country was flooded with water, and yet the farmers were already out ploughing and sowing on the mountain declivities. The truth is, that the long, pointed share of the native plough will root through mud and water without hesitation or encumbrance, and for such soil and climate this miniature machinery is just the article wanted. Moreover, their tiny teams could manage no other. I saw a man ploughing with two donkeys, very small and poor. They looked sour and displeased, as though the yoke was degrading to their asinine sensibilities.

In three hours I reached Kûleîyeh, on the top of yon ridge that forms the western boundary of Ijon. There I found the countess and party in sad confusion. Their history, after leaving Hasbeiya, was briefly this : The men hired to carry the sick girl set down the bier in the mud, and ran away. The rain came on in torrents, and the count had to summon. in the name of the govern-

ment, the entire population of Kûleîyeh to their assistance. They finally
reached the village about dark. Here they had been detained ever since by
the storm, and in quarters as filthy and uncomfortable as even this wild
country can furnish. Not being able to procure porters, the dragoman had left,
two days before, for Safed, to hire carriers from that place. This morning,
however, twelve men had offered to take the girl to Hunîn for 300 piastres,
and the count had already set off with them, leaving his mother and Mr. Z——,
their travelling chaplain, to come on as best they could.

It was now after twelve o'clock, and but little progress had been made in prepa- Adventures and difficulties.
ration. They were surrounded by a rude mob, screaming, scolding, and quar-
relling in the wildest uproar. The countess begged me to take the direction of
matters, as she could not talk a word with the people, nor comprehend the
reason of this hubbub and delay. After a sufficient amount of rebuke and
threatening, the refractory muleteers loaded their animals, and set off—a party
of about forty, horses, mules, and donkeys, besides certain beasts so lank and
filthy that it was not easy to decide to what particular family they belonged.
I had made no arrangements to stay out over night, but could not leave the
countess in such doubtful circumstances; so away we went, scattering all about
the country in search of practicable paths, but in a general direction southward, along the ridge that divides the Litany from Ijon. Passing by Khŭreî-
beh, on the brow of that hill north of us, we came along between Deir Mimas
and Kefr Keely on the west, and that large Druse village, El Matulleh, on the
east. At the end of two hours we stopped to rest at this Neb'a eu Nihah. Our
party had taken different roads, and but few had followed our track. From
this we toiled up to Hunîn, along the wild path which we have this morning
descended. Just before reaching the castle we overtook Count William and
his party, who had been all day in making this distance of nine miles. Hunîn,
as you know, is inhabited by Metâwelies, an inhospitable and villanous set.
But the firman of the sultan, and the stringent orders of the pasha, were not
to be resisted. The sheikh gave up his own room to the countess and her sick
girl, while a poor widow vacated her habitation—about twelve feet square—for
us gentlemen. These preliminaries settled, the loads began to come in, and by
dark all had arrived except the cook and two or three companions of his. Hav- A missing cook.
ing waited until after nightfall for our missing cook and party, we then roused
the whole village to go in pursuit, when they were soon found and brought in
safely. Both they and Mr. Z—— had been stopped by Arabs, and compelled to
pay Bedawîn toll before they were allowed to pass. It was now very cold, and Bedawin toll.
utterly dark. The wind howled along the mountain tops, and tore to tatters
the ponderous clouds, which pelted us with rain and snow whenever we ventured out of our retreats. With immense noise and confusion, we got the luggage stowed in the room of the countess, and our forty animals crammed into
a large vault of the old castle, and fed, amid uproar, kicking, and fighting, in
absolute darkness. By ten o'clock the cook had prepared some sort of dinner, A night's lodging.
and we spent an hour in talking over the adventures of the day and night.

PART
II.

Then we lay down in our clothes and muddy boots, cold, wet, and without beds, and tried to sleep; but with dogs barking outside, cocks crowing overhead, fleas tickling, and other joint occupants of our twelve-foot room crawling over us, our sleep was none of the sweetest.

Morning came, however, at last. Our friends set off for Safed, and I returned to Hasbeiya. It is not easy to exaggerate the hardships and even dangers which such parties encounter at this season of the year. Tents cannot be used, and they are therefore at the mercy of these lawless peasants. The amount of money which the countess spent could not have been less than fifty dollars a day, and yet the discomforts of her situation were enough to drive any ordinary person to despair. Houses not fit to put pigs in—every door, yard full of mire and filth,—through this ineffable mixture you must flounder, and into it your luggage will be tumbled. To add to your perplexity and distress, the villagers, of every size and sex, throng you like bees, and laugh at your expense. Dogs bark, donkeys bray, mules and horses kick and break bounds; servants are chaffering, and buying any kind of eatables that turn up, and at exorbitant prices; the poor are begging, and all are demanding *bukshish* for contributing their share to the intolerable annoyance. We went through all this and more, for twelve hours at a stretch, and the marvel is that the sick girl survived at all, recovered, and returned to Germany. The countess remarked that she needed no other illustration of the admonition, "Pray ye that your flight be not in the winter." [1]

If that was Banias which you pointed out nearly due east of Hunîn, we are making a long detour to the north.

Still, there is time enough to continue in the same direction to the top of the ridge before us; and my object is to give you a near view of the great castle of Shûkîf,* and of the pretty plain of Ijon. Look, now, across the profound gorge of the Litany, and you can see that fine old fort hanging on the very edge of the precipice. I have often visited it, and have spent several nights encamped in its ample fosse. The view from the top is magnificent, and the gulf, fifteen hundred feet deep, down to the river beneath, is frightful. I never visit it without playing the boy by rolling stones from the top of the castle, and watching their gigantic leaps from point to point, until they are lost in the bushes or the river at the bottom. The castle is the most conspicuous object in this region, and we shall have it looking out upon us in all our rambles hereabouts. The Crusaders called it Bellefort, but they did not construct it. Indeed, I think it probable that a castle occupied this commanding position from remote antiquity. And here we have a fine view of the Ijon. The present name—Merj Aiyûn—is a mere variation of the Hebrew. It is about six miles long and two broad, with a regular descent southward from that great mound at the north end, called Tell Mamo, and sometimes Tell Dibbeen, from a vil-

Expense
and
misery.

Flight in
winter.

Castle of
Shûkîf.

The Ijon.

---

[1] Matt. xxiv. 20.

* [In Dr. Robinson's "Biblical Researches," vol. iii. pp. 49–53, the reader will find a full account of this remarkable place, and the glorious view obtained from it.—ED.]

lage of that name beyond it. The top of the mound is covered with the rub- CHAPTER
bish of the ancient city, which spread over the plain to the north-east for some XVI.
distance. Tradition makes this the site of Ijon, and I see no reason to ques- History of
tion the fact. It was taken by Benhadad about the year 950 before Christ, Ijon.
and again by Tiglath-Pileser some 200 years later.[1] There is a noble fountain
in the centre of the Ijon, called Derdara, and we shall cross the brook that
comes from it at the bottom of the plain.

' Let me point your eye to those white hills on the north-east. Where they
terminate in this direction are the famous Bitumen Wells. They are about three Bitumen
miles west of Hasbeiya. The rock is a chalky marl, exceedingly white. The wells.
shaft actually worked when I was last there was one hundred and sixteen feet
deep to the bitumen. The thickness of the stratum varies. In some shafts it
is fifteen feet, and in others it is not five. So, also, the quality varies. In
some places it is extremely pure, like real jet, or black amber; in others, only
a few feet distant, it is unctuous, earthy, and of the colour of iron rust. The
people that work the mine believe that new bitumen is constantly forming ; Theory of
and the fact that the entire area through which these *wells* are and have been formation
sunk from remote ages does not exceed an acre in extent, strongly confirms
the theory. The whole space must have been dug over many times, and yet
they find it as abundant and perfect as ever. It is probable, therefore, that
this mineral exists in vast quantities in the marly mountain north of the
wells, and that it exudes slowly, in the form of semi-liquid petroleum, into
this peculiar receptacle, and there, in time, hardens into bitumen. It is
difficult to account for the continued supply on any other supposition.

The Arabs on the shore of the Dead Sea have a similar theory to account
for the appearance of bitumen there. They say that it forms on the rocks in
the depths of the sea, and by earthquakes or other submarine concussions is
broken off in large masses, and rises to the surface. A few miles north of
these wells of Hasbeiya a new mine has been opened, not far from a village
called Yahmûr. The shaft is sunk through hard rock, and the bitumen is
found at different depths. It is actually semi-fluid, and exudes into the shaft
from crevices in the rock strata.

Is bitumen ever mentioned in the Bible ?

Very often, but under the name of pitch in our translation. I think it The
nearly certain that "Noah *pitched* the ark within and without" with a pre- "pitch" of
paration of bitumen, although the Hebrew word in Genesis vi. 14 is not the Scripture
ordinary Shemitic name for it. In the Septuagint, however, it is translated asphaltum. Very early after the Deluge, the immediate descendants of
Noah were acquainted with, and used bitumen to bind together the bricks in
building the Tower of Babel.[2] This is still seen in some of the ruins of old
Babylon. Some two or three hundred years later, we find that the people of
Sodom were in the habit of digging bitumen "wells" like those below

---

[1] 1 Kings xv. 20; 2 Kings xv. 2, 9.   [2] Gen. xi. 3.

PART
II.

Slime-pits.

Ark of
bulrushes.

Hasbeiya. Our translation has it "*slime-pits*,"[1] but the Hebrew is the same that our Arab friends now employ for these *wells*—biâret hŭmmar. It was probably an important article of merchandise, even at that early day, with Egypt, for the Egyptians employed it largely in embalming their dead. The mother of Moses also "daubed" her ark of bulrushes with slime and with pitch, as we have it; but in the Hebrew she *bitumed* it with bitumen, and tar or pitch.[2] This is doubly interesting, as it reveals the process by which they prepared the bitumen. The mineral, as found in this country, melts readily enough by itself; but then, when cold, it is as brittle as glass. It must be mixed with tar while melting; and in that way it forms a hard, glassy wax, perfectly impervious to water. I once covered the roof of a room that leaked like a sieve with such a preparation, spreading it on while the rain descended in torrents, and yet with perfect success. The basket of bulrushes for the infant Moses, when thoroughly bitumed, was well adapted for the object for which it was made. Our translation of this passage is deficient in clearness. The bulrush—gomeh—is the Egyptian papyrus. Taboth—ark—is the Arabic word for *coffin*. Slime and pitch are bitumen and tar. The whole was made like a coffin, to deceive the watchful officers of government with the appearance of a funeral. This, too, would appeal more tenderly to the daughter of Pharaoh, and there is a sort of typical signification in it. The saviour of Israel was laid in a coffin, and taken from a watery grave : the Saviour of the world rose from a rock-sepulchre in Jerusalem.

A cold
wind.

Travellers
chilled to
death.

This plain of Ijon has lately been rendered famous by a most extraordinary storm. It was on the 28th of December. Some friends of mine, from Hasbeiya, were coming down the hill by Kefr Keely, that village west of Matully, when one of them called their attention to tall columns of mist over the marsh of the Hûleh. They came this way very rapidly, and soon broke upon them with awful fury. Those of the party who were from Khyam, on the east side of this plain, fled homeward. My friends from H—— were driven before the blast to Khureibeh, that little hamlet just north of us, and with difficulty escaped to it. Those who attempted to reach Khyam perished in the plain, although it is not more than two miles wide, and in full view of their houses. Thus ten men died in a few minutes from the mere chill of this wonderful wind. There was no snow, no frost, and not much rain ; but the wind was perfectly awful, driving and upheaving everything before it. These cold winds draw out all animal heat with amazing rapidity. Not only were these men chilled to death almost instantly, but eighty-five head of cattle also perished before they could be brought to the village. The inhabitants have no tradition of a similar catastrophe. People often perish in snow-storms on the mountains, and on the vast desert of the Hauran ; but it was never known before that a mere wind, and that down on this low plain, could chill people to death. The storm scattered and dispersed in various direc-

[1] Gen. xiv. 10.   [2] Exod. ii. 3.

tions. It did much mischief here on the hills of Naphtali, and over yon- CHAPTER
der on the Jaulan several people perished by it, and many cattle. It was XVI.
felt along the sea-board; and I myself caught a violent cold riding from
Beirût to Sidon on that day. I examined into the accuracy of these facts on
the ground, and know them to be true. My Hasbány friend, who is a sort of
travelling merchant, sold the shrouds of the victims, and saw nine of them
buried the next morning. I have often felt the extreme power of these winds
to cool down the vital heat of the body, but never encountered anything like "An hor-
this. It reminds one of David's horrible tempests.   rible tem-
                                                                            pest."
   This Ijon is a very fertile plain, and, when clothed with golden harvests, it
must be charming. And here are the cascades you spoke of, I suppose?

   Yes; and by a singular succession of them, the stream leaps down to the
level of Abel, and is there joined by the Ruahîny, which you can see bursting
out at the base of the western mountain. Those cliffs are covered for a long
distance by the ruins of an extremely old town, for which I can get no other
name than that of the fountain. The whole distance around and south of it
is also called Ard er Ruahiny. Let us now incline to the north-east to visit
the artificial caves and tombs called Serada, which are at the southern
termination of that rock ridge of Khyam. I had another object in making
this detour. You must know that the Hûleh is my pet lake—under my
special protection. I am self-constituted cicerone, and jealous of her reputation. By right of office, I maintain that the Hûleh is unrivalled in beauty, Unri-
no matter when or from what point beheld. From the distant heights of valled
Hermon, the hills of Naphtali, the plain of Ijon, or the groves of Banias, in the Hûleh.
mid-winter or mid-summer, in the evening or in the morning—Stop just
where you are. There lies the Hûleh like a vast carpet, with patterns of
every shade, and shape, and size, thrown down in Nature's most bewitching
negligence, and laced all over with countless streams of liquid light. Those
laughing brooks of the Hûleh, in straight lines drawn and parallel, or
retreating behind clumps of nodding shrubbery, in graceful curves, to tie up
love-knots in sport; here weaving silver tissue into cunning complications,
there expanding into full-faced mirrors. The Arab tent is there, and the war-
horse, with his wild rider. The plain is clothed with flocks, and herds of
black buffalo bathe in the pools. The lake is alive with fowls, the trees with
birds, and the air with bees. At all times fair, but fairest of all in early
spring and at eventide, when golden sunlight, through many a mile of warm,
ethereal amber, fades out into the fathomless blue of heaven. Such is the
Hûleh: "Behold it is very good; a place where there is no want of anything
that is in the earth."[1]

   But here we are at the caves of Serada. They are now used to store away Caves of
grain and tibn (chaff), and to shelter the herds of these miserable Arabs. Serada.
Serada was once a large town, and inhabited by people who took a pride in

[1] Judges xviii. 10

15

PART
II.

rock tombs for their dead. They were probably Phœnicians, for their sepulchres are exactly like those of Tyre and Sidon. Besides these, there is nothing to detain us, and we may pursue our journey. It is an hour from this to the Hasbāny at El Ghŭjar, by a blind path over and among boulders of black lava. On this side of the river is the small Arab village Luisa, and below it are large

Fountains of Luisany.

fountains called Luisany, which add greatly to the size of the Hasbāny. The channel of the river is one of the curiosities of this region. During the countless ages of the past, it has cut a tortuous canal through the hard lava at least two hundred feet deep, and in many places the distance from bank to bank is not much greater.

The Hasbāny.

This, then, is the most distant branch of the Jordan. It is really a respectable stream, even here, and the only one I ever saw in such a dark volcanic gorge ; beautifully adorned, too, with oleanders, willows, and sycamores, and alive with fish. Altogether, I am not disappointed in it. Is it fact, or a mere fancy of mine, that these people of El Ghŭjar have a physiognomy quite peculiar, and so unlike the Arabs as to indicate a different origin ?

The sect Nusairîeh.

They are Nusairîeh, and there are but two other villages of them in this part of the country. The great body of this tribe reside in the mountains above Tortosa, Mulkŭb, Jebile, and Ladakîyeh. There are many of them also in Antioch, and they spread around the north-east end of the Mediterranean toward Tarsus and Adana. It is impossible to ascertain their number, but they have more than a thousand villages and hamlets, and have been estimated as high as two hundred thousand. I have repeatedly travelled among them, and coincide in the general verdict rendered against them by those best acquainted with their character. They are the most ignorant, debased, and treacherous race in the country. Their religion is a profound secret, but is believed to be more infamous than even their external morals. The skill with which they evade any approximation toward a disclosure of their religious mysteries always excited my astonishment. My party and I once stopped to rest under the shadow of a great rock between Jebile and Ladakîyeh, and while quietly taking lunch, a company of these people came up. Their sheikh, learning from the muleteers that one of us was a doctor, made very earnest and respectful application for medicine. While the hakim was preparing it, I began with the old man, gradually and very cautiously approaching the

Their religion a secret.

delicate subject of his religion. As the questions came more and more directly to the point, he grew restive, and fearing that he would decamp even without the coveted medicine, I cut right across to the matter in hand by asking him what sort of people inhabited the mountains above us.

Oh ! they are fellaheen.

I know that very well ; but what is their religion ? (This, you are already aware, is the first question in this country).

Religion ! said he ; what need have fellaheen of religion ?

Certainly, everybody has some sort of religion, and so have you, I am sure. What is it ? Whom do you follow ? What prophet do you love ?

We rather love Ali; but whom do *you* follow?

We are Christians; we love Jesus Christ, and our religion is contained in the New Testament.

Very well; we also love Jesus Christ and curse Mohammed. We and you are *one*.

No, no, you are not Christians.

Why not? We love Christ and Moses: your religion and ours are exactly the same; and, snatching up his medicine, he made off as fast as possible.

The governor of Hamath sent a horseman to guide and protect us across the wild mountains between that city and Tripoli. Our guide compelled a man from a village of this people to accompany us, and, as he could not run away, I determined to pump him about his secret faith. I gave him my horse to lead, lighted a pipe for him to smoke, and, walking by his side, made myself as agreeable as possible. We soon became quite at our ease, and talked away, without reserve, on all sorts of subjects, I approaching the ticklish point in circles, like a moth does a lighted candle. At length I told him something about my religion, that of the Druses and the Hindûs; with all which he seemed much interested. Finally, in a careless and indifferent manner, I put the question about his faith. I am a *fellah*, said he. I know you are a farmer; it was not your occupation, but your religion I asked after. Come, now, we are alone; nobody will hear us; do tell me something about your faith. *I* am a Christian. I tell you what I believe and how I worship; so will the Moslem, the Jew, the Hindû, and even the poor savage in the centre of Africa. Why will not you do the same?

We are fellaheen, that is enough. What do we want of religion?

I know you have a religion of your own, why should you keep it secret?

Do you see that white tomb on the top of that hill? It is Skeikh Ibrahîm el Hakîm. If any one has sore eyes, and visits that mazar, he will get well.

We will talk about that good doctor by-and-by, if you please; but now I want an answer to my question.

May God curse the father of that donkey!

Never mind the donkey, he will go well enough; and you should not curse the poor beast; besides you mentioned the name of God; who is he? what do you believe about him?

Is it not near noon? We have four hours yet to Hŭsn from that ridge ahead of us.

This is a specimen of a long trial, in which I was completely baffled by an ignorant fellah from the wild mountains of the Nusairîyeh.

This remarkable people have no known forms of prayer, no times or places of worship, and no acknowledged priesthood. At weddings and funerals they sometimes use Mohammedan prayers, but only when in the vicinity of Moslem towns. They practise polygamy, and marry very near relatives—the nearest of *all*, according to the reports of their neighbours. They themselves deny that a Nusairîyeh can marry his own mother. However this may be, the

Attempts to discover the secret.

General laxity of the sect.

PART
II.

marriage relation is very loose among them. I could not learn whether they believed in the immortality of the soul and a future state of rewards or not, but they hold to transmigration of souls somewhat as do the Druses. They seem to have derived some of their customs and reputed tenets from Persia. The truth probably is, that whatever of Mohammedanism has been incorporated with their original superstition was borrowed from the followers of Ali ; and they are, to this extent, a heretical set of Moslems. But many things led me, when among them, to suspect that they were fragments of Syria's most ancient inhabitants—descendants of those sons of Canaan who were in possession of Arka, Arvad, Zimra, and Sin, on the shore west of their mountains ; and of Hamath, on the east, when Abraham " came from Ur of the Chaldees." Expelled by foreign nations from their primeval seats, they retired to the inaccessible mountains, where they now live. These are so situated that they were never penetrated by any great military roads or mercantile routes, and never will be. Perhaps many of their brethren, when driven from the south by Joshua, took refuge with them. I was struck with the prevalence, all over these mountains, of names of men, and mountains, and castles, and villages, which were identical with those once common in Palestine.

Perhaps a
remnant
of the
original
Canaan-
ites.

As Christian missions are now established among them, we may hope, ere long, to be better acquainted with the origin, history, manners, customs, and religion of this remarkable people. I have seen a few books which pretended to give an account of their faith ; but the Nusairîyeh themselves would not acknowledge them. They are not to be trusted, and, besides, they throw very little light on the matter. They have countless sacred tombs called Mazars, to which they resort on various occasions ; but their ceremonies there are always performed in secret. Should any of their number divulge their mysteries, he would be assassinated without remorse, mercy, or delay. This is certain ; and this horrible fact may have given rise to the stories about the *assassins*, for it was on these mountains that those somewhat fabulous monsters are said to have resided.

But enough of the Nusairîyeh for the present. 'Ainfit and Z'aora, on the mountain south of Banias, are the only other settlements of this people in this region. What noble oak glades spread over these hills before us ! Indeed, this whole scenery is more park-like than any I have seen in Syria.

Park-like
scenery.

Or will see. The peasants of Banias, however, are cutting away these magnificent trees, and in a few years this part of the grand platform of old Panium will be stripped quite naked. You will observe that we have been riding over the ruins of the ancient city for some time, and there is its modern representative, half buried beneath shapeless ruins, which are quite overgrown with bushes, briers, and creepers. We must wade through this rattling river, and find our way to that fine old terebinth, where our tents are waiting our arrival. I, at least, am quite ready for them, and for what our good cook will spread before us.

Curiosity is an overmatch with me just now for fatigue, and even hunger.

I must look upon the birth-place of the Jordan, and have a draught of its water before night closes upon us.

That is soon done. Follow the path to that cliff, and you may have the whole fountain to yourself.

Well, have you seen and tasted ?

Is it not magnificent ? The fountain, I mean. But let us address ourselves to dinner. The new-born river will sing to us. Hark how its merry laugh floats out on the evening air, and swells up the sides of the echoing hills ! Our ride to-day has been perfectly delightful through and to scenes and sites of most romantic interest. There can be no doubt, I suppose, but that this is the source of the greater Jordan, mentioned by Josephus ; and this mass of rubbish below the cave, through which the fountain pours its hundred streams, is the debris of the temple of Panium.

Fountain of the Jordan.

Temple of Panium.

CAVE AT BANIAS.

Those Greek inscriptions on the face of the cliff confirm the fact. But we are now on ground much more sacred than mere classic association can render any place. Our blessed Lord has been here, has drunk of this same fountain, and looked upon this lovely scene. With his usual compassion, he taught the people, and healed their diseases. Eusebius says that the woman cured of an issue of blood[1] belonged to this city, and he thus writes on this subject :—

Christian legends.

[1] Luke viii. 43.

PART
II.

"They say that her house is shown in the city, and the wonderful monuments of our Saviour's benefit to her are still standing. At the gate of her house, on an elevated stone stands a brazen image of a woman on her bended knees, with her hand stretched out before her, like one entreating. Opposite to this there is another image, of a man erect, of the same material, decently clad in a mantle, and stretching out his hand to the woman. This, they say, is a statue of Christ, and it has remained even until our times, so that *we ourselves saw it* when staying in that city."[1] Who knows but that these statues are still buried under this rubbish, and may some day be brought to light. Theophanes, however, says that Julian the Apostate broke them to pieces. It would be like him, if he ever happened to see them.

Eusebius' account of Panias.

The same author thus discourses about the cave and the fountain:—"At Cæsarea Philippi, which is called Panias by the Phœnicians, they say there are springs that are shown there at the foot of the mountain called Panias, from which the Jordan rises; and that on a certain festival day there was usually a victim thrown into these, and that this, by the power of the demon, in some wonderful manner, entirely disappeared. The thing was a famous wonder to all that were there to see it. Astyrius (a pious Roman of senatorial rank) happening to be once present at these rites, and seeing the multitude astonished at the affair, pitied their delusion. Then, raising his eyes to heaven, he implored the God over all through Christ to refute the seducing demon, and to restrain the delusion of the people. As soon as he prayed, *it is said* that the victim floated on the stream, and that thus this miracle vanished, no wonder ever more occurring in this place." The latter remark is probably true, whatever we may think of the rest of the story. These passages, however, are curious as showing what the traditions concerning this place were at the close of the third century, when Eusebius visited it.

Josephus' account.

Josephus thus describes this locality in Ant., b. xv. ch. x. v. 3; he calls it Panium: "This is a very fine cave in the mountain, under which there is a great cavity in the earth, and the cavern is abrupt, and prodigiously deep, and full of still water. Over it hangs a vast mountain, and under the cavern arise the springs of the River Jordan. Herod adorned this place, *which was already* a very remarkable one, still further by the erection of this temple, which he dedicated to Cæsar." There is a close resemblance between these stories of this fountain and that of Josephus in his Wars of the Jews, book i. ch. xxi. v. 3:—"And when Cæsar had further bestowed on him (Herod) another additional country, he built there also a temple of white marble, hard by the fountains of the Jordan. The place is called Panium, where is the top of a mountain that is raised to an immense height, and at its side, beneath, or at its bottom, a dark cave opens itself, within which there is a horrible precipice that descends abruptly to a vast depth. It contains a mighty quantity of water, which is immovable; and when anybody lets down anything to measure

---

[1] Euseb., book vi., chap. xviii.

the depth of the earth beneath the water, no length of cord is sufficient to CHAPTER reach it." Making all due allowance for subsequent changes, it is still im- XVI. possible to clear our author of great exaggeration. He probably never saw Banias himself, and took the extravagant stories of others for truth.

It is evident that Banias was a remarkable place before the age of Augustus. History of Philip the Tetrarch called it Cæsarea in honour of Tiberius, and Philippi in Banias. his own, and to distinguish it from Cæsarea Palestina. Herod Agrippa beautified it, and complimented that monster Nero by giving it the name of Neroneas. But all these foreign titles soon fell off, and it resumed its old name, Banias, by which alone it is now known. For its history during the Roman empire, and under the Saracens, Crusaders, and Turks, you must consult more authors than I can now mention. Reland's "Palestina" and Robinson's "Researches" will serve as guides to the original sources of information.

Great changes have happened to the cave since these authors wrote about The cave. it. Probably the earthquake which overthrew the temple may have filled up the depths spoken of. It was here that Titus, after the destruction of Jerusalem, was feasted by Agrippa for twenty days; and in this temple he "returned public thanks to God for the good success he had in his undertakings."

If all that is recorded in the 16th and 17th of Matthew in immediate con- Scene of nection with the visit of our Saviour actually occurred in this neighbourhood, the Trans-figuration it has been the scene of some very remarkable transactions. Among them was the Transfiguration, and this Panium may have been that high mountain apart into which our Lord took Peter, James, and John, and was transfigured before them.[1] I have supposed, ever since my first visit to Tabor, that that could scarcely have been the place, for the whole summit was covered by a vast castle, which we know was occupied, if not then, yet shortly after, by soldiers. It is true that Josephus says he built the castle,—the only foundation for which assertion being that he repaired one that had been there for ages. Moreover, that locality does not suit the accounts given of events immediately connected with the Transfiguration as recorded by the Evangelists, though it must be confessed that these are not definite or very decisive. I would not, therefore, contend with those who prefer the old tradition in favour of Tabor, and yet I think it probable that it was somewhere in this direction, and see Probably no good reason why it may not have been on this lofty and lonely Panium, or not Tabor but Hermon. rather Hermon, of which it forms the southern termination.

Here also occurred that remarkable discourse with the disciples, in which Simon Peter answered our Lord's question by the solemn assertion, "Thou art the Christ, the Son of the living God;" and received in reply, "Thou art Peter, and upon this rock I will build my church."[2] Could the claims of Banias to this wonderful discourse be established, it might vastly enhance the interest of the place in the eyes of those who have made so much capital out

---

[1] Matt. xvii. 1-18.　　　　[2] Matt. xvi. 16, 17.

PART
II.

of the power of the keys here conferred. We leave the hint for those whom it more immediately concerns.

Locality famous for shrines.

There must be something about this Upper Jordan and its surroundings particularly calculated to call out and foster the religious or the superstitious propensities of our nature. Tell el Kady, four miles west, was the great seat of false worship, from the days when the Danites conquered it, and there set up their teraphim, a graven image and a molten image.[1] Long after this, Jeroboam placed golden calves in Dan; which thing became a sin, for the people went to worship before the one, even unto Dan.[2]

Worship of Pan.

Then this Banias itself was always celebrated for its worship of Pan, and as we follow up the country we meet with heathen temples all over these mountains. There are ruins of several at a place called Bustra, not far from Kefr Shûbah; another on the high point of Mûtaleîh, above Rashaiet el Fûkhâr; and one at Sed Dan, farther in the mountains. A short distance north-east of Rashaiet el Fûkhâr is the fine temple of Hibbarîyeh, with a Greek inscription, much defaced. Two miles farther north are the ruins of another, and higher up still is the temple of Ain Hershah, with Greek inscriptions. Then come those of 'Aihah, Kefr Kûk, Rakhleh, Deir 'Asheîr, Burkûsh, Bekkeh, Munseh, and several others; and across Wady et Teim, west of Rashaiet el Fokah, is the fine temple of Tilthatha, called Neby Sûfah. Certainly no part of Syria was so given to idolatry as this region round the head-waters of the Jordan. These temples fronted the east, and were probably devoted to the worship of Baal. A description of one or two will answer for all. That at Hibbarîyeh is

Neighbouring temples.

a fair specimen. It is fifty-eight feet long, thirty-one wide, and to the top of the frieze on the west side is thirty-two feet. It is built of large, well-cut stones, some of them fifteen feet long. The interior, as usual in such edifices, was divided into three parts; that of the altar at the west end, considerably raised and eleven feet deep; that of the *temple, nave*, or body of the edifice, twenty-three feet; and the portico, nearly sixteen feet, with columns in front. The temple at Rakhleh is eighty-two feet eight inches long, and fifty-seven wide. The altar is semicircular, like that of ancient churches, and with apses on either side. A double row of Ionic columns extended from the altar to the entrance. This edifice is thrown down nearly to the ground. On the south-east corner is a stone belonging to the original wall, about six feet square, and having a circular wreath on the face of it five feet in diameter. Within this is another circle four feet in diameter, and this surrounds the colossal face of an image handsomely carved in bold relief. The length of the face, from the chin to the top of the hair, is three feet four inches, the width two feet four inches. It has been purposely disfigured, but the features are still very distinct and striking. It is probably an image of the god of the temple, perhaps the face of *old Baal himself.*

An image of Baal?

The temple at Deir 'Asheîr stands upon an elevated platform, ornamented

[1] Judges xviii. 14–20.   [2] 1 Kings xii. 29, 30.

with a frieze and cornice of its own. It is one hundred and twenty-six feet CHAPTER
long, and sixty-nine wide. The length of the edifice built upon this platform   XVI.
is eighty-nine feet, the breadth about forty, and the height to the top of the
cornice fifty-four. The interior is divided like that of Hibbarîyeh. The style
of architecture resembles the Ionic, and the egg and cup, or cup and ball
ornaments occur everywhere, as at Baalbek. There are other ancient buildings at this Deir 'Asheîr, and the place is well worth a visit.

Proceeding farther north, there are remnants of small temples at various
points along the slopes of Anti-Lebanon. At Neby Sheet is the tomb of Seth, Tomb of
under a vaulted room more than one hundred feet long. The tomb is about Seth.
ten feet broad, extends the entire length of the vault, and is covered with a
green cloth. This prophet Seth is the third son of Adam, transformed into a
grand Moslem saint, with three hundred wives, and children without number.
Opposite to this tomb, on the west side of the Bŭk'ah, is that of Noah, or
Kerak. It is a little more than one hundred and thirty feet long, and even
at that accommodated the tall patriarch who stepped across the Deluge only
to the knees, the remainder being provided for by a deep pit sunk perpendicularly into the earth. But this entire system of fanes and temples received
its grandest enunciation in the wonderful structures at Baalbek, on the eastern
side of the Bŭk'ah.

Is Baalbek the Baal-gad of the Bible?   Baalbek
                                                                        or Baal
The main reasons for the support of this opinion are that the names are gad.
very similar—the first half identical in form, the other probably so in significance, and both correctly translated by Heliopolis, City of the Sun. Then,
again, the notices of it in the Bible lead us to search for Baal-gad in the direction and neighbourhood of Baalbek. In the valley of Lebanon, under Hermon, and the entrance into Hamath ;[1] these are the geographical indications.
That it is in *the* valley of Lebanon cannot be questioned ; that it is under
Hermon is equally certain ; and that it is at or on the road to the "entrance Entrance
into Hamath," my explorations in that direction have fully satisfied my own of Ha-
mind. This "entrance," so conspicuous in ancient Biblical geography, was math.
the province at the north end of the Bŭk'ah, drained by the sources of the
Orontes, *the* river of Hamath. This province was reached from the west or
sea-board by the passes over the low mountains of Akkar, at the north end of
Lebanon, which I take to be the Mount Hor of Numbers xxxiv. 7, 8. "This,"
says Moses, "shall be your north border : from the great sea ye shall point out Mount
for you Mount Hor (Heb. Hor Hahor); and from Mount Hor ye shall point out Hor—
your border unto the entrance of Hamath." Of course the *kingdom*, not the Hahor."
city of Hamath, is meant in all cases ; and the southern province of it would
be reached through the Bŭk'ah, past Baalbek, and from the sea through
Akkar, as just described. This theory ascertains the line of Israel's northern
boundary, and at the same time corroborates the idea that Baal-gad is identical

[1] Josh. xi. 17, and xiii. 5.

with Baalbek. Let any one ride from Baalbek northward to Lebweh or 'Ain, or, better still, to Kamûa Hermel, and look off toward Hamath, and he will be struck with the propriety of the phrase, "Entrance into Hamath." From this stand-point the *valley* of the Bŭk'ah opens out like a vast fan on to the great plain of northern Syria, and he is at the gate of the kingdom. Baalbek being, therefore, in the neighbourhood where we must look for Baal-gad, there seems to be no good reason to doubt their identity, for there is no rival to dispute the honour of the name and site.

Baalbek. The remains at Baalbek are adequate to meet the demands of any history, and some of them may claim an antiquity equal to anything that even Egypt can boast. The substructures of the great temple can scarcely be of a later age than that of Solomon, and *may* have supported a magnificent edifice in the time of Joshua. If we reject this identification, what other name shall we or can we give to these wonderful ruins? I can think of none; and after travelling up and down and across that whole region for twenty-five years, and studying every ancient site in it, I find no other Baal-gad, and ask for none.

How much evidence is there that Solomon erected any of these temples at Baalbek?

Solomon's connection with it. The unanimous voice of Mohammedan romance and Oriental fable. That he should have had something to do with Baal-gad is, however, not incredible. His government included the Bŭk'ah; he was given to magnificent architecture; he built with great stones, quite equal, according to Josephus, to those in the substructures at Baalbek, and not much less, according to the Bible; and, finally, there is no other prince known to history to whom the most ancient parts can be ascribed with greater plausibility. If not this very Suleyman Bin Daoud of the Moslem, their author is absolutely unknown.

It is the general opinion, I believe, that the remains there are of very different ages.

It requires no great architectural knowledge to decide that point, but just how many ages and orders can be distinguished in the wilderness of present ruins I will not undertake to determine. The most ancient, no doubt, are the foundations seen on the west and north sides of the great temple, to which the *six columns* belonged. The first tier above ground consists of stones of different lengths, but all about twelve and a half feet thick, and the same in **Colossal blocks of stone.** width. Then came over these stones more than *sixty-three* feet long,—the largest blocks, perhaps, that were ever placed in a wall by man.[1] One of this class lies in the quarry, where it can be viewed all round, and measured easily. It is *fourteen* by *seventeen*, and sixty-nine feet long! Here is a drawing of it; and remember, as you look at it, that *three* very respectable rooms

---

[1] Dr. Robinson, the greatest master of measuring tape in the world, gives the dimensions of these three stones thus: One is sixty-four feet long, another sixty-three eight inches, and the remaining one sixty-three feet; the whole, one hundred and ninety feet eight inches. The height about thirteen feet, and the thickness perhaps greater.

might be cut in it, and still leave partition walls three feet thick! How such
blocks could be transported a mile over uneven ground to the temple, and
elevated to their position on its platform, is yet an unsolved problem in the
science of mechanical forces. But there is something about them still more
wonderful. The corresponding surfaces of these enormous stones are squared

GREAT STONE IN THE QUARRY.

so truly and polished so smoothly that the *fit* is most exact. I was at first
entirely deceived, and measured two as one, making it more than a hundred
and twenty feet long. The *joint* had to be searched for, and, when found, I
could not thrust the blade of my knife between the stones. What architect of
our day could cut and bring together with greater success gigantic blocks of
marble more than sixty feet long and twelve feet square?

It is admitted, is it not, that the temple for which this foundation was laid
was never completed?

It is; but this does not prove it. That those who subsequently built upon Great
the foundation did not occupy the whole of it, is evident enough. The portion temple un-
left out is indicated by the tier of great stones on the north-west corner; but finished.
it is not certain that the remains of *the* most ancient temple were not taken,
so far as needed, for the smaller structures of succeeding architects. I suspect
that we now see the fragments of these blocks in the Grecian columns, capitals,
and cornices which encumber the platform of the present edifices. The quality
of the rock is identical, and there could be no reason why the Grecian architects should not appropriate to their use these *ruins*, just as they did so much
of the *foundation* as suited their purposes.

Are there no inscriptions to aid in determining these doubtful points? Inscrip
None older than the age of Antoninus Pius, I believe. The grand entrance tions.
to the platform of the temple was on the east side, fronting the city, and was
adorned by twelve noble columns. On the pedestals of two of these columns
are long Greek inscriptions, but they are so high in the wall that it is difficult

PART
II.

to get at them. I was twice let down by ropes from the top of the wall, and copied them with no little pain and with some peril. As they have been often printed, you can study them at your leisure, if you have a fancy for such researches. I myself do not believe that Antoninus did much more than repair, or restore temples already there, and then, like modern Arabs, write his own name and deeds upon them.

Vandalism of the Mohammedans.

During the last thirteen centuries, the Mohammedans—fanatical haters of all temples, idols, and even innocent statues—have done what they could to deface and destroy the architectural and artistic beauties of Baalbek, and they have recorded their zeal and success in numberless pompous inscriptions; none of them, however, have much historic value. By these barbarians, the entire platform, vaults, temples, and all were early converted into a strong fortress, and it is still known to them only as Kul'a et Baalbek—castle of Baalbek.

We have so many admirable drawings of these temples, and from so many different points, that I fancy myself perfectly acquainted with them.

True; but, like most other fancies, you will find very little correspondence between it and the reality, if your experience coincides with mine. As you approach from Zahleh, the columns come into view at a great distance, and appear small. Hour after hour you ride on in tedious monotony, and seem to get no nearer, the temples no larger. Half a dozen times you prick your horse into a gallop, expecting to dash right in among the columns, but hold up again to breathe your jaded nag, who has not one grain of your enthusiasm.

Emotions of the visitor.

At length, as his iron hoof clatters on the pavement at the gate, you exclaim in disappointment, almost vexation, Is *this* Baalbek? Yes, it is, sir; and now give over the rein to the groom, and yourself to two days' diligent exploration and study. You will need all that time to master the problems before you; and when you have left, you will long to return, and will do so if you can. I have repeated my visits half a dozen times, and always find something new to admire. The first impression of disappointment runs rapidly into admiration and wonder. You go to the end of a prostrate column, and are almost startled to find that, on tiptoe, and with the hand at utmost stretch, you cannot measure its diameter! You climb in between two of those standing columns, and feel instantly dwarfed into an infant. Looking up to the entablature with a shudder, you wonder how big it may be. A fragment lies at the base; you leap down and measure. It is fourteen feet thick! And such fragments and such columns are all round, and block up your way. Little by little, and with difficulty, you grasp the grand design, and, going out eastward into the centre of the broad platform, take your stand in front of the main entrance. With those six pillars to help your imagination, you reconstruct the whole noble edifice, with twenty such giants on a side! and there you may be safely left much longer than we have time to wait for you. It is growing late, and the subject tedious. If you want to study either Baalbek or Palmyra in detail, I commend you to the magnificent drawings of Wood and

Colossal remains.

Dawkins. They visited Baalbek in 1751; but, though thus old, they are far more elaborate and minute than any others. Of written descriptions there are countless numbers, but the only way to become really possessed of Baalbek is to visit, explore, and study it for yourself. Dr. Robinson's admirable chapter on Baalbek, in his last volume of "Researches," is the best and most comprehensive epitome of all that has been or can be said about these wonderful remains, and I advise you to study it attentively.

The cause of greatest perplexity arises from the many Saracenic castles and towers with which these barbarians have encumbered and disfigured every part of the grand platform. The entire length from east to west is about eight hundred and eighty feet, and the width across the central court nearly four hundred. To picture the whole magnificent group of portico, courts, towers, and temples, as they once appeared to the proud citizens of Baalbek, one should stand some little distance in front of the main entrance, and restore, in imagination, the portico, one hundred and eighty feet long, adorned by twelve splendid columns, reached by a noble flight of steps. Landing among these columns, and stopping to admire the highly ornamented pavilions at each end, the visitor passes through the deep portals into the main court of the temple, nearly four hundred feet square, and surrounded on all sides by chapels, oratories, niches, and statues, of exquisite workmanship. All these, however, will be unheeded at first, for at the south end of the vast court towers the peerless temple itself, with its statues, golden gates, and colonnades rising to the sky. This is a study by itself, and we shall let each one prosecute it as he likes. The smaller temple was an after-thought, perhaps erected from the ruins of the other; both, however, are of the same pale white limestone from the adjacent hills, which, though hard and durable, does not take a high polish. The architecture, as the drawings have taught all the world, is Corinthian, and the carving and ornamental tracing is rich and elaborate. The best specimens of this are seen in the entrance to the smaller temple. There are other remains about Baalbek which would merit and receive attention anywhere else, but in the presence of these gigantic works they are passed by unnoticed, nor can we spend time now in describing them. The visitor is surprised to see the fragments of granite columns scattered about the ruins, which must have been brought from Egypt, and transported over the mountains to this central and elevated spot by machinery, and along roads every trace of which has long since disappeared from the country.

This is quite enough about Baal-gad and ancient heathen temples; but the discussion has abundantly confirmed the remark made at the outset, that either there is something in the structure of these cliffs and valleys of old Hermon peculiarly suggestive of religious, or rather superstitious *edification*, or that there was something remarkably devotional in the character of the inhabitants of this mountain. All these temples belong to Anti-Lebanon, while Lebanon proper, though the more magnificent of the two, had scarcely any, and none that have become historic. There was a small one at Bisry, on

The temples.

Abundance of temples in Anti-Lebanon.

PART
II.

the Owely; another at Deir el Kŭlah, above Beirût; one at Fakhrah, near the natural bridge on Dog River; one at Aphcah, the source of the River Adonis; two rude oratories at Naous, above Deir Demitry; one at Nihah, facing the Buk'ah, and another on the north end of Lebanon, at a place called Deir; but none of these ever atttracted much attention, or deserved to do it, while Hermon is crowded with them. I hope we may be able to visit them hereafter, but at present I am more inclined to visit the couch and seek repose. The young Jordan will sing our lullaby.

CHAPTER XVII.

LAKE PHIALA—CASTLE OF BANIAS.

Kamûa Hermel,—a Syrian monument.
Road to Lake Phiala.
Lake Phiala—now Burket Ram.
Sacred groves—High places—Inhabited trees.

Oak or terebinth?
Oak forests.
Castle of Banias—perhaps Baal-Hermon.
Scorpions.

March 4th.

Northern boundary of land of Israel.

ACCORDING to your location of the "entrance into Hamath" in our conversation of last night, I suppose you make the northern end of the Buk'ah * the limit of Israel's inheritance in that direction?

I do not mean to be led into a discussion of this vexed question, as difficult to settle as any other boundary-line which has perplexed the politicians of Europe and America; but when I have stood at the Kamûa Hermel, and looked out northward and eastward over the vast expanded plain of Hamath, I have felt assured that I stood near that celebrated "entrance;" and a careful study of all the passages in the Bible which deal with this question has confirmed the impression made by the eye and the scene.

What is this Kamûa, which you have mentioned more than once?

Kamûa— a Syrian monument.

It is the most singular monument now standing in this part of Syria, and was probably erected by some of the Seleucidæ, kings of Antioch; but this is not certain. It seems to represent hunting scenes, and some of them were sufficiently fond of the chase to lead them to seek immortality in connection with its trophies. What else it was intended to commemorate cannot now be ascertained, for the tablets of inscription, if ever there were any, are gone. The south-west corner has fallen down, showing the fàct that the entire structure is built solid throughout. It is nearly thirty feet square, and about sixty-five high, the latter fifteen of which is a regular pyramid; the remaining

---

* [El Buk'ah, or Bukáa, is the modern name of the celebrated valley between Lebanon and Anti-Lebanon—the Cœle-Syria of ancient history.—ED.]

fifty feet is divided into two storeys, with a pedestal of three feet and a half. CHAPTER
There are square pilasters at the corners of the lower storey, and additional XVII.
ones in the centre of the upper storey. Upon a broad belt of well-smoothed
stones, near the top of the first storey, are the animals and hunting implements, drawn at about full size. The execution, though graphic and bold,
looks toward the burlesque.

From its elevated position, I saw this curious monument, when coming from
Aleppo in 1846, for a day and a half before I got to it, and wondered all the
while what it could be, as no traveller had visited it or the region about it.
Since then it has become a favourite detour from the regular route to the
cedars from Baalbek, and I would advise all who can to make it, not merely
to see the Kamûa, but also the sources of the Orontes at Lebweh, 'Ain, and
Mugharet er Rahib, near Hermel. The ride to the cedars from this fountain,
up Wady el Farr, is one of the most romantic in Syria or anywhere else. But
it is high time we were in the saddle, for we have a smart ride, and plenty to
see before us to occupy one day.

You had a long ramble this morning, or at least you forsook the pillow and
the tent at a very early hour.

I am too deeply interested in these scenes to waste the morning hours in Rambles
sleep. My first visit was to the fountain, to bathe and drink. I shall not lose through
the memory of that hour, should I live a thousand years. Then I followed
the brook, crossed over to the western side, and strolled away, I know not
how far, among those venerable oaks. Returning, I climbed to the top of the
castle on the north-west corner of the city, and looked into the wilderness of
bushes and briers that hides the brawling river at its base. Descending to
some mills I forced my way through sharp thorns to the south-west corner,
and then followed up the wall to the gate and bridge over the ravine called
Saäry, which, I suppose, formed the southern fosse of the city. From the
south-eastern corner I followed the ditch, which brought me back here to the
tent.

You have made the entire circuit of the city, which, indeed, is not great;
but as it was entirely surrounded by deep ravines, or by a ditch which could
be filled with water from the great fountain, it must have been a very strong
place. This, however, was merely the citadel: the city spread out on all sides
far beyond these narrow limits. The traces of this extension are found not
only among the oak groves on the north and west, but also south of the brook
es Saäry, and on the plain to the east, as we shall see along our road to the
Phiala.* This is the extent of our excursion for to-day.

This lake, now called Burket Ram, is two hours nearly due east, and for the

* [Lake Phiala, so called by Josephus from its resemblance to a cup, is now called Burket
Ram. "It lies," says Dr. Robinson, "at the bottom of a deep bowl, apparently an ancient
crater, not less than from 150 to 200 feet below the level of the surrounding tract. The form
is an irregular circle, the diameter of the water being a mile and perhaps more. This lake is
not mentioned in Scripture.—ED.]

first hour, to 'Ain Kŭnyeh, the ascent is quite steep, and over vast formations of trap rock, and this whole region is of the same volcanic character down to the River Jermuk, south-east of the Lake of Tiberias. This brook, es Sääry, has cut a deep channel in the trap rock, verifying the proverb of Job that the waters wear the stones,[1] even the hardest of them. The country hereabouts is very fertile, and, at the proper season, clothed with luxuriant harvests. Those olive-trees which climb the steep declivities on our left, quite up to the castle, I have seen bowing to the earth under a heavy load of oily berries, and every one is delighted with the variety and beauty of the wild flowers which in spring adorn these ravines; even now they begin to appear in profusion.

This 'Ain Kŭnyeh shows evident traces of antiquity. Is anything known in regard to its past history ?

Not that I am aware of. It was probably the country residence and health-retreat for the citizens of Cæsarea, and is, in fact, still celebrated for its good climate. There is yet another hour to the Phiala, and our path lies along the mountain side, above this noisy Sääry. This oak wood on our right extends far south, and is a favourite resort for the flocks of those Arabs which occupy the western borders of the Jaulân. It is not particularly safe to explore this neighbourhood, but I hear of no special danger at present; and the number of people from the lower villages who are out on the border of the forest burning and carrying coal, is a pretty certain indication that we can go to the lake without interruption. It is a wild and lawless region, however, and I never stay at Phiala longer than is necessary for my purpose. We must here cross the Sääry at this mazar, called Mesâdy. The brook comes down from the southern extremity of Jebel es Sheikh, and across that plain of Yafûry on our left ; so named from a saint, whose white-domed mazar is seen on the edge of it, about a mile north of Phiala. And here is the lake itself, round like a bowl, motionless as a molten mirror, but alive with frogs, ducks, and hawks. We must guide our horses carefully along the rim of this strange volcanic basin to some slope sufficiently gradual to allow us to descend to the water.

There is an air of mysterious solitude and desolation quite oppressive about this mountain lake.

Shall we ride round it ?

As you please.

How great is the circumference ?

That we shall know better after we get back. I have never made the circuit, and am not quite sure we shall find a practicable track all the way.

Large parts of its surface are covered with a sort of sea-weed, and upon it and all round the margin,

" These loud-piping frogs make the marshes to ring.

It seems to be the very metropolis of frogdom.

Yes, and upon this grass feed countless millions of leeches. The Phiala, in CHAPTER
XVII. fact, has long furnished the chief supply of that insatiable mother, whose two daughters ever cry, Give, give! Solomon says so.[1]

What are those large hawks after? They swoop down like a bolt from the Hawks. clouds, just graze the surface, and rebound, as it were, again to the sky.

Don't you see how the frogs hush their clamour and dive under when this their great enemy makes a descent in their vicinity? My muleteer shot one of them on a former visit, which fell into the lake near the shore, and he attempted to wade in for it, but got entangled in this interminable grass, and we were glad to get him back in safety. Without a boat it is impossible to explore the lake to any considerable distance from the shore.

Do you believe that this water covers the bottom of an extinct crater?

It resembles one in all respects, and is like nothing else that I know of. Singu-This Phiala has neither inlet nor outlet; that is, no stream runs into it, and larity of none leaves it. There must be large fountains, however, beneath the surface, the lake. for the evaporation in this hot climate is very rapid, and yet the lake is equally full at all times, or so nearly so as to sanction the native accounts to that effect.

What think you of the opinion of Josephus, that this is the more distant source of the fountain at Banias?

And that Philip proved the fact by casting chaff into the Phiala, which came out at Banias? I don't believe it, and I wish it were the only absurd thing to be found in his history. He thinks it worth while to mention a tradition that the fountain of Capernaum (probably that of Tabigah) comes from the Nile, because it produces fish similar to the coracinus of the lake near Alexandria. The Moslems about Tyre will assure you that Ras el'Ain comes from the same river, and there are many other such stories equally absurd. In regard to this Phiala, it is impossible, from the geological construction of Not con-this region, that its waters could flow down to Banias. Then, also, this water nected is dark-coloured and insipid, and abounds in leeches, while the Banias has Banias. none of them—is bright as sunlight, and deliciously cool and sweet. And still more to the point is the fact, that the river which gushes out at Banias would exhaust this lake in forty-eight hours. And now we have made the circuit in fifty-five minutes; the lake is, therefore, full three miles in circumference. I had judged it to be at least that, merely from appearance. Our next point is the castle of Banias, and the path leads over the mountain to the north-west. This large village on our right is Mejdel es Shems, inhabitated by Druses, a fierce, warlike race, sufficiently numerous to keep the Bedawîn Arabs at a respectful distance. We may stop in safety under these splendid oaks to rest and lunch.

This is certainly the finest grove of the kind I have seen. A solemn still- Oak ness reigns within it; and what a soft, religious light struggles down through grove.

---

[1] Prov. xxx. 15.

PART II.

the thick branches ! It is not unlikely that this was one of those "high places" of idolatry which were always accompanied with groves.

Sacred groves and high places.

It is still sacred. The mazar is in honour of one Othman el Hazûry, or Othman of Hazor, and some indistinct traces of a village between this and the castle still bear that ancient name. But this could not have been the capital of Jabin, as some have supposed. That city was given to Naphtali, and must have been situated somewhere in Upper Galilee. But your remark about the religious shade of this grove reminds me of a certain kind of superstition, as prevalent now in these parts as idolatry was in the days when those temples we spoke of yesterday were thronged with deluded worshippers. Ezekiel says, " Then shall ye know that I am the Lord, when their slain shall be among their idols round about their altars, upon every high hill, in all the *tops* of the *mountains*, and under every green tree, and under *every thick oak*, the place where they did offer sweet savour to all their idols."[1] Not only did the heathen delight to build temples and rear altars in the tops of the mountains, as these ruins testify, but they worshipped their idols under every green tree,

Inhabited trees.

and especially under thick oaks. They do so still, in a modified form. These oaks under which we now sit are believed to be inhabited by Jan and other spirits. Almost every village in these wadies and on these mountains has one or more of such thick oaks, which are sacred, from the same superstition. Many of them are believed to be meskûn (inhabited) by certain spirits called Benat Yacobe—Daughters of Jacob—a very strange and obscure notion.

Rag peace-offerings.

The common people are afraid of these inhabited trees, and when they pass them hang on the branches a rag torn from their clothes, as an acknowledgment of their presence, and a sort of peace-offering to avert their anger. I have seen scores of such thick oaks all over the country, but could never obtain an intelligible explanation of the notions or traditions upon which this widespread custom is based. It has rather seemed to me to be an indistinct relic of ancient idolatry, which the stringent laws of Mohammed banished in form, but could not entirely eradicate from the minds of the multitude. Indeed, the Moslems are as stupidly given to this superstition as any other class of the community. Connected with this notion, no doubt, is the custom of burying their holy men and so-called prophets under these trees and erecting *mazars* to them there. All non-Christian sects believe that the spirits of these saints love to return to this world, and especially to visit the place of their tombs. Nor can we restrict our remark to the heathen. It is difficult to distinguish between this and the belief or feeling which lies at the bottom of all saint-

Allusion in Isaiah.

worship. Isaiah speaks of a time when the people shall be ashamed of the oaks which they have desired.[2] May that day speedily dawn. It implies the spread of light and knowledge. No sooner is a man's mind even partially enlightened by the entrance of that word that giveth light,[3] than he becomes heartily ashamed of these oaks, and of his former fear and reverence for the

---

[1] Ezek. vi. 13.   [2] Isa. i. 29.   [3] Ps. cxix. 130

beings supposed to inhabit them. I have witnessed some ludicrous displays of CHAPTER
daring enacted about these old trees by Protestant Arabs just emancipated XVII.
from this degrading superstition; and I can point you to many respectable
people who have been all their lives long, and are still, held in bondage through
fear of these imaginary spirits.

Scarcely any tree figures more largely in Biblical narrative and poetry than
the oak, but I observe that certain modern critics contend that it is, after all,
not the oak, but the terebinth.

The criticism is not quite so sweeping as that. It is merely attempted to *Oak versus*
prove, I believe, that the Hebrew word *alah*, which, in our version, is generally *terebinth.*
rendered *oak*, should be translated terebinth. *Allon*, they say, is the true
name of the oak. It is not for us to settle such controversies, but I have not
much confidence in the results. In fact, the Hebrew writers seem to use these
names indiscriminately for the same tree, or for different varieties of it, and
that was the oak. For example, the tree in which Absalom was caught by the *Absalom's*
hair was the *alah*, not the *allon*, and yet I am persuaded it was an oak. That *oak.*
battle-field was on the mountains east of the Jordan, always celebrated for
great oaks—not for terebinths; and this is true to this day. Again: that
"wood of Ephraim," in which the battle was fought, and which devoured more
people than the sword,[1] is called *yaar* in Hebrew, *waar* in Arabic—evidently
the same word; and it signifies a wild, rocky region, overgrown with trees—
mostly oak, *never* the terebinth. There is no such thing as a terebinth *waar*
—no such thing in this country as a terebinth wood. And yet this *alah* which
caught Absalom formed part of the wood of Ephraim. *It was an oak*, I firmly
believe. There are thousands of such trees still in the same country, admirably suited to catch long-haired rebels, but no terebinths. Indeed, this latter
tree does not meet the requirements of this catastrophe at all. I see it
asserted by the advocates of this translation that the oak is not a common nor
a very striking tree in this country, implying that the terebinth is. A greater
mistake could scarcely be made. As to strength, it is simply ridiculous to
compare the terebinth with the oak; and the same in regard to size. The
terebinth under which our tent is pitched down at Banias is the largest I have
seen, and yet there are many oaks to which it is but as an infant. Still more
surprising are the statements about the extent of oak forests in this land.
Why, there are more mighty oaks here in this immediate vicinity than there
are terebinths in all Syria and Palestine together. I have travelled from end
to end of these countries, and across them in all directions, and speak with
absolute certainty.

Besides the vast groves around us, at the north of Tabor, and in Lebanon *Great ex-*
and Hermon, in Gilead and Bashan, think of the great forests, extending *tent of oak*
thirty miles at least, along the hills west of Nazareth, over Carmel, and down *forests.*
south beyond Cæsarea Palestina. To maintain, therefore, that the oak is not

---

[1] 2 Sam. xviii. 6–8.

PART
II.

a striking or abundant tree in Palestine, is a piece of critical hardihood tough as the tree itself. And, finally, the terebinth is deciduous, and therefore not a favourite shade-tree. It is *very* rarely planted in the courts of houses, or over tombs, or in the places of resort in villages. It is the beautiful evergreen oak that you find there. Beyond a doubt, the idolatrous groves so often mentioned in Hebrew history were of oak. The straggling, naked terebinth is never selected for such purposes. It sheds down no soft twilight, suggests no religious thought, awakens no superstitious fears. It takes the dense, solemn, mysterious oak to do this. I confess that I never come within such a grove even as this without being conscious of a certain indescribable spell, a sort of silly timidity, tending strongly to religious reverence. With the ignorant this might easily be deepened into downright idolatry.

Abra-
ham's oak
at Hebron.

I do not believe that Abraham's celebrated tree at Hebron was a terebinth, as many now affirm without qualification. It is *now* a very *venerable oak*, and I saw no terebinth in the neighbourhood. That there are mistakes in our translation in regard to the trees, as well as other things, I would not deny; but until we have more light on this particular matter, and more decisive, let us continue to read out bravely the good old word *oak*, and never fear the smile of overwise critics.

Approach
to Castle
of Banias.

And now we must leave this fine grove for the Castle of Banias.* Prepare for one of the roughest scrambles you have yet encountered in the East, and look well to your clothes, or they will be left streaming on the sharp thorn-bushes through which we must force our way. And now, as we ascend Castle Hill, hold a steady rein, or you will meet with something far worse than thorns.

This is, indeed, a fearful ascent, and of itself enough to confound any assailing party, without the aid of walls and bulwarks.

Those who built the castle did not think so. But all danger is past, and our path lies along this south wall to that curious and well-defended entrance.

Is it probable, or even possible, that the Crusaders erected this prodigious fortification?

Its anti-
quity.

I think not. Dr. Robinson, with whom I once visited it, decided, without hesitation, that it was ancient. These deep grooves in the *posts* of this gateway show that the door did not open and shut, but was drawn up by machinery. To such an apparatus David, perhaps, alludes in the 24th Psalm:

Lifting up
gates.

" *Lift up* your heads, O ye gates ; and be ye lifted up, ye everlasting doors; and the King of glory shall come in." [1] You will find no other good specimen of this kind of gateway in all Syria, and it is therefore the more

---

* [The Castle of Banias, more properly the castle of Subeibeh, is about an hour's ride from the town, at an elevation above it of at least 1000 feet. It resembles the Castle of Esh-Shukîf, which may indeed be seen from it. (See p. 222). Though the extreme antiquity of the castle has not been doubted, it becomes famous in history only in the time of the Crusaders. It was finally abandoned in the seventeenth century.—ED.]

[1] Ps. xxiv. 7.

worthy of special notice. It is also a tacit witness to the antiquity of these works.

Is not the entire castle too fresh, and in too high a state of preservation to accord with a very remote antiquity.

That is owing to the quality of the stone, which is very compact, and hard as adamant; it rings, when struck, like metal. Even those that have been thrown down in confusion for many centuries are as perfect as the day when they were cut from the mountains: they will last to the end of the world. But let us tie up our horses, for it will take hours to explore the place to your satisfaction. The site is admirably adapted for a castle. The ridge is high, sharp, and isolated, and at least seven hundred feet long from east to west. The two ends are much broader than the middle, and the whole summit is included within the walls. The east end is far the highest, and the fortifications there are exceedingly strong, commanding most effectually the steep declivity up which the road was cut. On the south and west the mountain sinks down steeply for a thousand feet to the plain of Banias, and on the north yawns the frightful gorge of Khushaib. It is thus unapproachable by an assailing force on all sides, and, until the invention of cannon, it could have been taken only by treachery or starvation. Nor would it have been easy to starve the place into surrender, if properly victualled. There is space sufficient for a strong garrison, and they might even raise vegetables for their table, as the shepherds grow fine crops of tobacco at present; and, though there is no fountain, these immense cisterns would afford an abundant supply of good water. The native tradition is, that the dark stairway here at the west end, down which we groped our way into the vaults beneath, was a subterranean, or, rather, submontane path to the great fountain of Banias, by which the garrison could obtain both water and provisions ; but as that is two miles distant, and a thousand feet below, the thing is scarcely credible. A respectable man of Hasbeiya, however, assured me that he once descended it a long distance, to where it was blocked up by the falling in of the roof. By my aneroid, the top of this castle is 2300 feet above the Mediterranean, being nearly the same elevation as that of Shukîf.

Is there no history of this remarkable place ?

None that reaches much further back than the time of the Crusaders. Under the name Subeîbeh it figures largely in the wars between the Saracens of Damascus and the Templars of Jerusalem; and these long Arabic inscriptions speak of repairing and rebuilding by Melek et Dâhar and others, some six or seven centuries ago ; they, however, were not the original architects of this great fortress. As it commands the pass from the Hûleh and the plains of the Jordan over Hermon to Damascus and the east, it must always have been a place of great importance. I have long suspected that this is the site of Baal-Hermon mentioned in Judges iii. 3, and 1 Chronicles v. 23. From these notices it appears that Baal-Hermon was at the south end of the general mountain of Hermon; and there is no other point in this whole region

CHAPTER XVII.

The castle

Famous in time of Crusaders

Perhaps Baal-Hermon

PART
II.

Noble
view.

Scorpions.

so important or so conspicuous as this. It is not possible, however, to identify some of these ancient sites with certainty, and this is one of the most
doubtful. By leading our horses down the terraces through this olive grove,
we shall shorten our distance to the town more than half. What a noble view
over plain, and marsh, and lake, and mountain! and how sweetly reposes the
village of Banias in this verdant and sheltered nook of Hermon! Its fifty
tottering huts, however, form a wretched representative of ancient grandeur,
and the place is now very unhealthy, especially in autumn. During the hot
months the people erect booths on their roofs, elevated on poles, to escape
from scorpions, of which there are countless numbers among the ruins. I have

had them tumble
down upon me while
sitting under the
terebinth-tree near
our tent; and I
never pitch there in
summer without
carefully turning
up every stone in
search of those
dangerous reptiles.
I should like to

SCORPION.

see one of these stinging scourges. They are not a little celebrated in the
Bible. An insolent allusion to them cost Rehoboam the loss of ten tribes.
They magnified the horrors of that "great and terrible wilderness," and are
standing types of the wicked, "whose torment is as the torment of a scorpion
when he striketh a man." [1]

Return here three months hence, and your wish can easily be gratified.
You may chance to get even more than you seek for.

Scripture
allusions.

Is there any resemblance between a scorpion and an egg, to suggest the
antithesis in our Lord's question, "If he ask an egg, will he offer him a
scorpion?" [2]

There is no imaginable likeness between an egg and the ordinary black
scorpion of this country, neither in colour nor size, nor, when the tail is
extended, in shape. But old writers speak of a *white* scorpion, and such a
one, with the tail folded up, as in specimens of fossil trilobites, would not
look unlike a small egg. Perhaps the contrast, however, refers only to the
different properties of the egg and the scorpion, which is sufficiently emphatic.

Our Lord says, "Behold, I have given you power to tread on serpents and
scorpions," etc.[3] Is this ever done now?

Catching
scorpions.

I have seen little boys draw out scorpions from their holes by thrusting in
small sticks with wax on the end, into which their claws fasten. They then

---

[1] Rev. ix. 5.   [2] Luke xi. 12.   [3] Luke x. 14.

catch them in their fingers, and stick them on to a rod of bird-lime or com- CHAPTER
mon wax, until they cover the rod with them; nor do they seem to be afraid, XVIII.
but rub their hands up and down this string of scorpions without hesitation.
We also hear of fanatics who actually crush them in their mouths and pretend
to eat them.   But it is to be remembered that the scorpion's sting is in its tail, Habits of
with which it *strikes* its victim (as is correctly implied in the quotation from scorpions.
the Revelation), and that it cannot strike *sideways*.   If, then, it be properly
held between the fingers, or so stuck into the bird-lime as not to admit its
longitudinal stroke, there is no danger; and, moreover, the boys may have
something on their hands or in the wax which " charms " or stupifies it.   The
pain from its stroke is very intense, but never fatal in Syria.   Those on the
northern coast of Africa are *said* to be larger, and the poison so virulent as
frequently to cause death.   At any rate, it is a hateful creature, crabbed and
malicious in the extreme.   I have tried the experiment of surrounding one
with a ring of fire; and, when it despaired of escape, it repeatedly struck its
own head fiercely, and soon died, either from the poison, its satanic rage, or
from the heat, I could not be certain which, perhaps from all combined.   For
a minute description of this reptile you must apply to books of natural history,
and to drawings of them, which can easily be procured.

We shall sleep all the more safely because, from hibernating instincts, they
are now buried deeply beneath the rubbish of old Banias.

CHAPTER XVIII.

TELL EL KADY—(DAN)—PLAIN OF THE HÛLEH.

March 5th.

OUR camp-ground to-night is at Kŭdes, the Kedish-Naphtali of the Jews,
and we are again favoured with a superb day.   It might have been otherwise,
as I know by sad experience, and then the ride round this marsh is gloomy
and disagreeable, as it is now bright and cheerful.

From the plateau south of the Sääry I saw the world wake up this morning Nature at
about old Hermon, and it was an hour never to be forgotten—universal nature worship.
at worship, harping on ten thousand harps the morning psalm.

Banias and her surroundings do in fact form one of nature's grandest

PART
II.

Temple of
nature.

Tell el
Kady—
Dan.

The young
Jordan.

Its lessons.

temples, in whose presence those made by men's hands are a mere impertinence. These oak glades and joyous brooks, these frisking flocks and happy
birds, all bear their parts in the service; and so, also, the mountains preach,
the hills and valleys sing, and the trees of the field clap their hands. Thus
the ancient prophets heard and interpreted the manifold utterances of nature:
"Praise the Lord from the earth, mountains, and all hills; fruitful trees, and
all cedars: beasts, and all cattle; creeping things, and flying fowl: kings of the
earth, and all people; both young men and maidens, old men and children: let
them praise the name of the Lord; for his name alone is excellent; his glory is
above the earth and heaven."[1] In these scenes and scenery of Hermon, there
is not only poetry, but solemn mystery and suggestive types, and rich spiritual
adumbrations; and he that hath an ear for such heavenly discourse may ever
hear with ravishing delight. And now we are at Tell el Kady—Hill of Dan
—the Judge—to translate both the Hebrew and the Arabic names at once.

And is this circular, semi-concave mound the site of that famous city?
How utterly desolate!

Josephus calls it the source of the Lesser Jordan, with reference to others
more distant, I suppose, for this is far the *largest* of them all.* Look southward, and you see that the river runs in a straight course through marsh, and
lakes, and sinking plain, quite down to the dark and bitter sea in which it is
finally lost. Dan and the Dead Sea—the cradle and the grave—the birth-
place and the bourne! Men build monuments and rear altars at them, and
thither go in pilgrimage from generation to generation. Thus it has been
and will ever be. It is a law of our nature. We ourselves are witnesses to
its power, drawn from the distant New World to this lonely spot, where the
young Jordan leaps into life, by an influence kindred to that which led the
ancients to build temples over it.

The young Jordan! type of this strange life of ours! Bright and beautiful
in its cradle, laughing its merry morning away through the flowery fields of
the Hûleh; plunging, with the recklessness of youth, into the tangled brakes
and muddy marshes of Merom; hurrying thence, full-grown, like earnest
manhood with its noisy and bustling activities, it subsides at length into
life's sober midday in the placid lake of Gennesaret. When it goes forth
again, it is down the inevitable proclivity of old age, sinking deeper and
deeper, in spite of doublings and windings innumerable, until finally lost
in the bitter Sea of Death—that melancholy bourne from which there is
neither escape nor return.

But surely the Jordan can teach other and happier lessons than these. It
speaks to me and to all mankind of forgiveness of sin, of regeneration by the

[1] Psalm cxlviii. 7–13.

* ["It is probably the largest fountain in Syria, and among the largest in the world; but for
grandeur and picturesque beauty, it cannot be compared to the fountain of the Abana at Fîjeh
(Damascus). Another smaller fountain springs up within the Tell, and flows off through a break
in the river on the south-west" (*Hand-Book for Syria and Palestine*, p. 436).—ED.]

CHAPTER XVIII.

Spirit of God, and of a resurrection to everlasting bliss. Must this dear type of life and immortality be swallowed up for ever by the Dead Sea?

Far from it. That is but the Jordan's highway to heaven. Purified from every gross and earthly alloy, it is called back to the skies by the all-attracting sun, emblem of that other resurrection, when Christ shall come in the clouds, and all the holy angels with him. May we be thus drawn from earth to heaven by the mighty attraction of that glorious Sun of righteousness!

More than three thousand years ago a vast and mingled host encamped on the eastern bank of this river. There was the mailed warrior with sword and shield, and the aged patriarch trembling on his staff. Anxious mothers and timid maidens were there, and helpless infants of a day old. And there, too, were flocks and herds, and all the possessions of a great nation migrating westward in search of a home. Over against them lay their promised inheritance,—

"While Jordan rolled between,"

The passage of Joshua.

full to the brim, and overflowing all its banks. Nevertheless, through it lies their road, and God commands the march. The priests take up the sacred ark, and bear it boldly down to the brink; when, lo! "the waters which came from above stood and rose up upon an heap very far from the city Adam, which is beside Zaretan; and those that came down toward the sea of the plain, even the salt sea, were cut off; and the people passed over right against Jericho."[1] And thus, too, has all-conquering faith carried ten thousand times ten thousand of God's people in triumph through the Jordan of death to the Canaan of eternal rest.

"O could we make our doubts remove—
Those gloomy doubts that rise—
And see the Canaan that we love
With unbeclouded eyes;
Not Jordan's stream, nor death's cold flood,
Should fright us from the shore."

I shall not soon forget this birth-place of the Jordan, nor the lessons which it can teach so well. But it is time we were prosecuting our long ride.

As we pass round this singular mound, you see that it resembles the rim of a crater. The fountain rises among those briers and bushes in the centre—at least that portion of it does which passes by this ancient oak, and drives these mills below it. Most of the water, however, glides through the volcanic wall, at the north-west corner of the Tell, into the pool beneath those wild fig-trees. If this be really the mouth of an extinct crater, it is probable that the water from the slopes of Hermon, following the line of the inclined strata, met, far below, this obtrusion of trap, and, being cut off by it, rose to the surface in this volcanic shaft or chimney. At any rate, it first appears in the centre of

The fountain at Dan.

[1] Josh. iii. 16.

LAB – Q

the mound, and, of course, old Dan had an inexhaustible supply of excellent water within her walls.

I see very little evidence of the ancient city, unless the houses were built out of this shapeless lava over which we have been stumbling.

No doubt they were, in the main; and as basalt never disintegrates in this climate, we have them before our eyes just as they were three thousand years ago. Limestone exposed melts back to dust in a few generations. I was once here, however, when men were quarrying well-cut limestone from the rubbish on the north side of the Tell. Dan never became an important place after Benhadad smote it, nearly a thousand years before Christ.[1] When Tiglath-Pileser took Ijon, and Abel, and all this region, some two hundred years later, this place is not even mentioned.[2] It may have sunk, by that time, to an unimportant village, known merely as a *mazar*, sacred to religious purposes.

Fall of
Dan.

The buffalo.

This pool is crowded with buffaloes; and how oddly they look, with nothing but the nose above water!

Yes; and observe that their mouths are all turned up stream toward the fountain, and on a level with the surface, as if, like Job's behemoth, they trust that they can draw up Jordan into their mouths.[3]

Do you suppose that the buffalo is the behemoth of the Bible?

Probably
the behemoth of
Job.

It is not easy to adjust Job's magnificent description in all the details to the buffalo, yet I am inclined to believe that these black, hairless brutes are the modern, though immensely belittled representatives of that chief of the ways of God, who " eateth straw like an ox, who lieth under the shady trees in the covert of the reeds and fens. The shady trees cover him with their shadow,

THE BUFFALO.

the willows of the brook compass him about." [4]   All these particulars are exact enough, and, indeed, apply to no other known animal that can be associated

---

[1] 1 Kings xv. 20.   [2] 2 Kings xv. 29.   [3] Job xl. 15–23.   [4] Job xl. 15, 21, 23.

with the Jordan. Large herds of buffaloes lie under the covert of the reeds
and willows of the many brooks which creep through this vast marsh, and we
shall see them all day, as we ride round it, wallowing in the mire like gigantic
swine. They are larger than other cattle of this region. Some of the bulls
are indeed rough and monstrous fellows, with bones black, and hard "like bars
of iron." With the aid of a little Oriental hyperbole I can work up these
buffaloes into very tolerable behemoth. And in justification of our version of
Psalm l. 10 may be cited the fact, that the general word for cattle in the
dialect of this country is behîm or behaim, evidently from the same root as the
Hebrew behemoth.

These circumstances and characteristics render it probable that these very *Habits of the buffalo.*
unpoetic animals are the identical behemoth of Job. Buffaloes are not only
larger, but far stronger than the ordinary cattle of Syria, and a yoke of them
will carry a plough through tough sward or stiff soil which utterly balks the tiny
ox. At times, too, they are unruly, and even dangerous. A friend of mine,
near this village below us, saw a cow rush at a woman, knock her over, and
then throw herself upon her with such fury that the poor creature was
instantly crushed to death. The cow had been alarmed and maddened by the
seizure of her calf; and, unless greatly provoked, they are quiet and inoffensive.

The fact that the region east of the Hûleh was the land of Uz—the home of *Land of Uz—where?*
Job—coincides, at least, with the idea that the buffalo is the behemoth of his
most ancient poem.

Is this an admitted geographical fact?

The tradition of antiquity was to that effect, and I see no reason to question
it. To ridicule the extravagant mania for pilgrimages in his time, Chrysostom
says that many people made long journeys into the Hauran to visit the dung-
hill upon which the patient patriarch sat and scratched himself with a
potsherd. This shows the opinion of that early day in regard to the land of
Uz, and modern research confirms the tradition. With a little antiquarian *Sons of Aram.*
generosity to assist me, I can locate the whole family of Aram. This Hûleh
may have derived its name from Hul, the brother of Uz. If so, then they and *Hul— Hûleh.*
their descendants must have been familiar with the reeds, and fens, and
brooks of this great marsh, the chosen resort of the buffalo, and had often seen
them, as we to-day, lying at the birth-place of the young Jordan, as if they
could draw him into their open mouths.[1]

Gether, the next brother, was probably the Gesher from whom the district *Gether— Gesher.*
immediately around the eastern side of this lake took its name. Maacah, wife
of David and mother of Absalom, was from this little kingdom, and hither
that wicked son fled after the murder of his brother.[2] As for Mash, or Mas,[3]
his name may be perpetuated in that *Mais* or Mais el Jebel, which we passed
the other day on our way to Hûnîn. It is proper to inform you, however, that
these locations are somewhat hypothetical, and even similarity of names is no

---

PART
II.

very safe basis for such theories. The word Hûleh, for example, is now applied to any low, marshy plain, like this on our left.

I thought that critics were pretty nearly agreed that the buffalo is the reem — the unicorn of the Bible?

The unicorn.

And this may be so, though I have my doubts. The description of the unicorn in the 39th chapter of Job does not suit the buffalo : " Will the unicorn be willing to serve thee, or abide by thy crib? Canst thou bind the unicorn with his band in the furrow? or will he harrow the valleys after thee? Wilt thou trust in him, because his strength is great? or wilt thou leave thy labour to him? Wilt thou believe him, that he will bring home thy seed, and gather it into thy barn?" [1] Now, it is implied by all this that the *reem* is a wild, stubborn, untameable animal, that utterly refuses the yoke and the service of man. This is inapplicable in every item to the buffalo, a patient servant of all work. Other references to the *reem* or unicorn speak of the *horn* in a way equally inapplicable to that of the buffalo. He has *two* instead of one, and they are ill-shaped, point backward and downward in an awkward manner, and are not particularly formidable as weapons, either offensive or defensive. They would hardly be selected for the poetic image of strength.

If, therefore, the reem be the buffalo, it must have been some other species than the one known in Egypt and this part of Syria. As to the *unicorn*, I think it more than doubtful whether there ever was such a beast, although there is a vague tradition of this kind among the Arabs of the Desert, and in

Probably
a species
of rhino-
ceros.

some other parts of the East, and even in Africa. It may be a species of rhinoceros. If not altogether fabulous, such reports probably refer to some animal yet unknown to modern discovery. Certainly the fierce-looking monster on Her Majesty's escutcheon was never copied from these sluggish and disgusting friends of the marsh and the mud. If the Hebrew word translated *kine* in Pharaoh's dream will include the buffaloes, I should not hesitate to render it thus, because these animals are very common in Egypt, and delight to bathe and wallow in the Nile. It would be altogether natural, therefore, that the king should see *them coming up out of the river;* and certainly, when old and lean, they are the most " ill-favoured" brutes in the world. The original word, however, is the name for ordinary cattle ; and in these hot countries all kinds delight to stand in the rivers, not only to cool themselves, but also to keep off the swarms of flies which torment them. The conditions of the dream do not require that the *kine* should be buffaloes.

You say that these different branches of the Jordan unite into one river about five miles south of us.

Union of
the Jordan
streams.

I rode from Tell el Kady to the junction with Doctor Robinson in an hour and forty minutes. If it were not too muddy, and the streams too full for a pleasant excursion, we would have included it in our programme for to-day ; instead of that, I can give you some account of that ride as we pass along. It

[1] Job xxxix, 9–12

was on the 26th of May, 1852. The first thing that struck me, on descending
south of the Tell, was, that the trap formation ceased at once, and we came
upon limestone. At that season, too, the bottom was firm and the road good,
whereas I had expected to flounder through deep mud. The time, however,
was particularly favourable ; the harvest was just ripe, and there was no irrigation. I never saw heavier crops of wheat than those on this plain, and particularly those about the site of Difneh, the ancient Daphneh of this neighbourhood, twenty minutes south of the Tell. Passing some magnificent oaks, with
countless birds' nests on the branches, we came, in fifty minutes, to Mansûra,
a mill, with magazines for grain and straw (tibn) near it. Crossing the Baniasy
at a well-wooded place called Sheikh Hazeîb, we came, in fifteen minutes, to
the main branch of the Leddan, and in ten minutes more to another branch,
with the name of Buraij. Half a mile from this all the streams unite with the
Hasbâny, a little north of Sheikh Yusuf, a large Tell on the very edge of the
marsh. Of these streams, the Leddan is far the largest; the Baniasy the most *The*
beautiful; the Hasbâny the longest. The Baniasy is *clear*, the Leddan *muddy;* *Leddan,*
Baniasy,
the Hasbâny, at the junction, muddiest of all. Thus far the branches all flow, *and Has-*
with a rapid current, in channels many feet below the surface of the plain, and *bâny.*
concealed by dense jungles of bushes and briers. After the junction, the river
meanders sluggishly through the marsh for about six or seven miles, when it
blends insensibly with the lake. All ancient maps of this region and river are
consequently incorrect.

The soil of this plain is a water deposit, like that of the Mississippi Valley *Produce*
about New Orleans, and extremely fertile. The whole country around it *of the*
plain of
depends mainly upon the harvests of the Hûleh for wheat and barley. Large *Hûleh.*
crops of Indian corn, rice, and sesamum (simsum), are also grown by the Arabs
of the Hûleh, who are all of the Ghawaraneh tribe. They are permanent
residents, though dwelling in tents. All the cultivation is done by them.
They also make large quantities of butter from their herds of buffalo, and
gather honey in abundance from their bees. The Hûleh is, in fact, a perpetual pasture-field for cattle, and flowery paradise for bees. At Mansûra and
Sheikh Hazeîb I saw hundreds of cylindrical hives of basket-work, *pitched,*
inside and out, with a composition of mud and cow-dung. They are piled tier
above tier, pyramid fashion, and roofed over with thatch, or covered with a
mat. The bees were very busy, and the whole region rang as though a score
of hives were *swarming* at once. Thus this plain still flows with milk and
honey, and well deserves the report which the Danite spies carried back to
their brethren : "A place where there is no lack of anything that is in the
earth."[1] I have the names of thirty-two Arab villages, or rather permanent *Number of*
encampments, in this flat plain, and this is not a complete list ; but, as there *villages.*
is not a *house* in any of them, and all except Difneh are unknown to history,
you can feel no interest in them.

[1] Judges xviii. 10.

PART
II.

Those white domes to the south, about three miles, are called Seîd Yehûda, and the place is worth visiting. There are three conspicuous domes over as

Seîd Ye-
hûda.

many venerated tombs. That of Seîd Yehûda is in a room about eight feet square, and is covered with a green cloth. By the Arabs he is believed to be a son of Jacob, and all sects and tribes make vows to him, and religious pilgrimages to his shrine. A few rods south of this is an oblong room, whose dome, still perfect, is the best specimen of Roman brick-work I have seen.

Ruins of
temples.

But the most remarkable remains are the ruins of ancient temples on a hill called 'Amery, about sixty rods east of these tombs. They are utterly demolished, and the columns and capitals lie scattered about the base of the hill on which they originally stood. Across a small wady directly north of them is a square building of very large well-cut stone, the object of which I was not able to make out. It may have been a temple; but if so, it was after a very antique and unique model. Farther north, on a high natural mound, are the ruins of 'Azeizat, once a very considerable place; and all about are manifest indications of a former dense population. The Baniasy meanders through the plain directly below Seîd Yehûda, and upon it are situated the Towahîn Difneh—mills of Daphneh. The site of the ancient city is farther west.

Who was this Lord Judah—for such is the signification of the name—and what place is this? That it marks some very ancient site is unquestionable;

"Judah
on Jor-
dan."

and I believe it is that "Judah on Jordan, toward the sun-rising," which Joshua mentions as the extreme north-eastern point in the boundary of Naphtali.[1] If this identification be correct, it solves one of the greatest geographical puzzles in the Bible. It always seemed to me impossible that the border of Naphtali could touch that of Judah anywhere, certainly not "upon Jordan toward the *sun-rising*." But here we have an important ancient site called *Judah, on this most eastern branch of the Jordan*, at a point which must have marked the utmost border of this tribe eastward, if we admit that it came up to it, and I see no valid objection against this admission. Naphtali possessed the western side of this plain, and, if able, would certainly have extended their border quite across it to the foot of the mountains, just where this Seîd Yehûda stands. I have great confidence in this identification, and regard it as another evidence that, as our knowledge of this country becomes more extensive and accurate, difficulty after difficulty in Biblical topography will vanish away until all are solved.

Beth-
Rehob.

Before leaving this interesting neighbourhood, I wish to call your attention to another question in Biblical geography. As stated in our conversation at Hunîn, I am inclined to place Beit Rehob in this vicinity. In Judges xviii. 28, it is said that Laish, alias Dan, alias this Tell el Kady, was *in the valley that lieth by Beth-Rehob.* Now, it is scarcely possible that Hunîn, *high on the mountains,* and many miles west of this, should be Beit Rehob. But this shallow vale, which comes down to our very feet from the mouth of Wady el 'Asil,

---

[1] Josh. xix. 84.

north-east of us, is called Rûheîb—a name having all the radicals of Rehob
in it; and upon the mountains above Banias, and near the castle, is a ruin
named Deir Rahba, which also contains the radicals of Rehob. May not
either Banias itself, or some other town in this immediate vicinity, have been
the ancient Rehob? Banias is a foreign word of Greek extraction; and it is
not improbable, to say the least, that the city, which certainly stood there
long before the Greeks entered this country, had an Aramaic name, which was
exchanged, in process of time, for the foreign one, as has happened in a few
other cases. And as Rûheîb and Rahba are found still clinging to sites both
above and below Banias, may not this have been the true seat of the old
Rehobites?

And now let us ride. It is twenty minutes to Jisr el Ghŭjar, over the Beauty of
Hasbäny. You will be struck with the picturesque beauty of the rocks, the the Hasbäny.
river, and the bridge, and wish for a drawing of them to carry home with you.
It is much more charming, however, in May, when these magnificent oleanders
are all in a glow of rosy blossoms. I have spent hours here, gazing into the
pools of the pretty Hasbäny, and watching the innocent sports of the fish, with
which it at times is over-crowded. They come up from the marshes of the
Hûleh in numbers almost incredible. But we have no time to waste on them
now. Have you any curiosity to see a real Arab village?

By all means. That is one of the *points* which I have yet to make.

Turn down, then, to the left, and we will soon reach that encampment of
Ghawaraneh, on the edge of this wet plain. You need not be alarmed by that
troop of noisy dogs charging down upon us with open mouths. Their bark is
worse than their bite—genuine Arab bluster, and nothing more.

Will these coarse mat walls and roofs shed rain and defend from cold?

Better than you imagine; still, they are a miserable abode for rational
beings. These tribes are stationary fellaheen or farmers, and are therefore
regarded with sovereign contempt by the true Bedawîn.

They are the most sinister, ill-conditioned race I have ever seen, and do not Character
of the Be-
begin to fill my *beau ideal* of the free, proud denizen of the desert. dawîn.

Like most other *beau ideals*, this in regard to tent-dwelling Arabs would
flatten down sadly by close acquaintance. Pshaw! the Bedawîn are mere
barbarians—rough when rational, and in all else coarse and vulgar.

What are these women kneading and shaking so zealously in that large black
bag, suspended from this three-legged crotch?

That is a bottle, not a bag, made by stripping off entire the skin of a young A bottle
buffalo. It is full of milk, and that is their way of churning. When the churning.
butter "has come," they take it out, boil or melt it, and then put it in *bottles*
made of goats' skins. In winter it resembles candied honey, in summer it is
mere oil. This is the only kind of butter we have.

Do you mean to say that our cooking is done with this filthy preparation?

Certainly; and this Hûleh butter is the best in the country. Some of the Butter.
farmers have learned to make our kind of butter, but it soon becomes rancid,

PART
II.
and, indeed, it is never good. I believe it was always so; and thus, too, I
suppose they made butter in olden times. Solomon says, "Surely the churning of milk bringeth forth butter, and the wringing of the nose bringeth forth
blood."[1] But the word for "churning" and "wringing" is the same in the
Hebrew. It is the *wringing* of milk that bringeth forth butter, just as these
women are squeezing and wringing this milk in the "bottle." There is no
analogy between *our* mode of *churning* and pulling a man's nose until the
blood comes, but in this Arab operation the comparison is quite natural and
emphatic. The Arabic translation of this proverb is curious, and very far
from the original: "He that wrings the *dug* violently that he may bring
out milk, brings forth butter, and he who milks harder still will bring out
blood."

Hûleh lily.

This little brook we are crossing comes from Ijon, by Abel. It is associated
in my experience with the beautiful Hûleh lily, the flower, as I believe, mentioned by our Lord in that delightful exhortation to trust in the kind care of
our heavenly Father: "Consider the lilies how they grow: they toil not, they
spin not, and yet I say unto you that Solomon in all his glory was not arrayed
like one of these."[2] This Hûleh lily is very large, and the three inner petals
meet above, and form a gorgeous canopy, such as art never approached, and
king never sat under, even in his utmost glory. And when I met this incom-
parable flower, in all its loveliness, among the oak woods around the northern
base of Tabor and on the hills of Nazareth, where our Lord spent his youth, I
felt assured that it was to this he referred. We call it Hûleh lily because it
was here that it was first discovered. Its botanical name, if it has one, I am
unacquainted with, and am not anxious to have any other than that which
connects it with this neighbourhood. I suppose, also, that it is this identical

Scripture
allusions.
flower to which Solomon refers in the Song of Songs: "I am the rose of
Sharon, and the lily of the valleys. As the lily among thorns, so is my love
among the daughters." The bride, comparing her beloved to a roe or a young
hart, sees him feeding among the lilies.[3] Our flower delights most in the valleys, but is also found on the mountains. It grows among thorns, and I have
sadly lacerated my hands in extricating it from them. Nothing can be in
higher contrast than the luxuriant, velvety softness of this lily, and the
crabbed, tangled hedge of thorns about it. Gazelles still delight to feed
among them, and you can scarcely ride through the woods north of Tabor,
where these lilies abound, without frightening them from their flowery
pasture.

Sinselet el
Hieyeh.
This long volcanic hill, running up north, is called Sinselet el Hîeyeh—chain
of the serpent—from its serpentine shape; and the brook in the wady between
it and Hunîn comes from a large fountain about two miles up it, called 'Ain
et Dahab—gold fountain. Our road now turns south between the mountains
of Kŭdes and this vast marsh which here comes up to the foot of the cliffs.

[1] Prov. xxx. 33.   [2] Luke xii. 27.   [3] Song ii. 1, 2, 16.

This fountain is called 'Adely, and a much larger one ahead of us is named Amûdîyeh, where is the village, or, rather, encampment of Boizîyeh. From this to Blâtâ is half an hour, and there we shall rest and lunch.

There are traces of large buildings about this fountain.

Yes, and a wall with a ditch was once carried from the marsh to the mountain, and thus effectually commanded the road toward the south. Here is another pool crowded with buffaloes wallowing in swinish felicity, with only the tip of the nose above the muddy water.

From our present position we can look over the entire marsh north of the lake. If you are fond of solving geological problems, you may calculate the time it has taken to fill up this spongy plain to its present level and consistency. The great fountains of Banias, Tell el Kâdy, and all the rest, are clear as crystal the year round, and would not deposit slime enough in a mulion of years to fill an acre of this ten-mile marsh. But the Sââry, the Hasbâny, the Derdara from Ijon, and many small torrents from the mountains, are quite muddy during the winter rains, and their contributions have slowly gained upon the lake through past ages, crowding it southward into narrow and till narrower limits, and the time may come when it will be entirely obliterated. The infant Jordan seems in danger of suffocation in this tangled jungle of cane and bushes. I once asked an Arab if I could not penetrate through it to the lake. Looking at me keenly to see if I were not in joke, he slowly raised both hands to his head, and swore by "the great—the Almighty," that not even a wild boar could get through. And he spoke the truth. It is an utterly impassable slough, worse than Bunyan ever dreamed of. When encamped, two years ago, at this village which we have passed, I was tempted down to the verge of the jungle by a flock of ducks. With gun in hand and eye on the game, and not upon my footsteps, I cautiously advanced, when suddenly I was in oozy mud that seemed to have no bottom. Flinging the gun back and struggling desperately, I regained the bank, and ever after kept a sharp and suspicious eye upon its treacherous depths. But this very impenetrability to man and beast makes it the favourite retreat of crows and rooks; there they breed, and thither they return at night from their rambles over the country. Upon the mountain above Hunîn I have watched them at early dawn rising in clouds from this jungle. On they came, like wild pigeons in the West, only their line was not across the horizon, but like the columns of an endless army, stretching from the Hûleh up Wady et Teim farther than the eye could follow them; the column, however, grows less and less dense by the departure in every direction of small squadrons, according to some social regulations known only to themselves, until the whole is dissipated. These birds are the plague of the farmer. They light by thousands on his fields, and devour so much of the fresh-sown seed that he is obliged to make a large allowance for their depredations. It is utterly useless to attempt to frighten them away. They rise like a cloud at the crack of your gun, wheel round and round for a few minutes, *cawing* furiously at you, and then settle down

17

PART
II.

again to their work of robbery as if nothing had happened. They fly to an immense distance in their foraging excursions. I have met them at least fifty miles from this their roosting-place. It is curious to see them in the afternoon preparing to return hither from the wadies around the north end of Hermon. They assemble in groups, caw and scream, and wheel round and round in ascending circles, until almost lost in the blue depths of the sky; then they sail in a straight line for this marsh, chattering to each other all the way. Assembled in the evening, they report the adventures of the day in noisy conclave, loud as the voice of many waters.

But, lunch over, we must be on the march, for the sun will set ere we can visit the shore of the Hûleh and return to Kŭdes, on this high mountain west of us. Do you notice anything peculiar in this clump of thorn-trees on our left?

Nothing, except that they seem to be stuffed full of dry stubble.

The field-sparrow.

That is the deserted nests of the field-sparrow. The tree is called sidr, and abounds all over Palestine, but I have nowhere seen it so large as around the Hûleh. I passed this way last year on the twenty-first of May, and these trees were covered with those birds. There were literally thousands of them, and they were holding an angry and troubled consultation as to the safest means of expelling a couple of hawks that had called there for their breakfast. I drove away their enemies, and they speedily calmed down into comparative silence, though they are never absolutely quiet except when asleep.

This white-domed mazar above us, on our right, is Neby Hûshâ—Prophet Joshua—and is a place of great resort. A little farther on, the Wady el Mûaddumîyeh comes precipitately down from the mountains. Notice the

Boulders.

immense quantity of boulders which this impetuous torrent has brought hither in the winter, and spread far and wide over the plain. We shall cross this wild wady to-morrow on our road to Safed. From this to el Mellâhah is forty minutes; there the marsh ends, and the splendid plain of the Ard el Kheît begins. We have been more than two hours coasting the west side of the marsh, and have ridden hard; it cannot, therefore, be less than ten miles long.

Fountain of el Mel-lâhah.

Here is the celebrated fountain of el Mellâhah. The water is brackish and slightly tepid, and this is the reason why it is so crowded with fish. It is only a mile from the north-west corner of the lake, and from it, in cold weather, come up an incredible number of fish. The pool is about four hundred feet in circumference, and from it the whole country round is supplied with fish. The water is led directly from the pool on to these mills, which are now the only houses in this neighbourhood, although there was once a considerable town here, as appears from the foundations of old buildings, and from the rock-tombs in these cliffs above the fountain. Let us hasten down to the shore of the lake, for time is precious, and the neighbourhood is anything but safe.

Plain of 'Ard el Kheît.

What a splendid plain! and evidently as fertile as it is beautiful.

I saw it last May covered with golden harvests ready for the sickle. There were then many tents pitched here and there for the reapers, who come from

Kŭdes and other villages on the mountains. There is not an inhabited house **CHAPTER** on all this plain, and this is entirely owing to insecurity, not insalubrity. **XVIII.** 'Ard el Kheît, as the district is called, is peculiarly exposed to incursions **Liability** from the desert east of the Jordan. I came near being plundered by Bedawîn **to plun-** from the Ghor the first time I visited the lake. **derers.**

Here we are at the shore, and, though somewhat soft, it is as well defined as that of any other lake, and there is no difficulty whatever in reaching it. There are also many fresh-water shells along the bank.

Though the reports on this subject are great exaggerations, still it is quite impossible to get to the lake except on the east side and along this south-western shore. From the utter desertion of this region, it has become the favourite resort of water-fowl, and they have it all to themselves. No boat is ever seen on the tranquil bosom of the Hûleh—no hunter disturbs them here. The plain down to the exit of the Jordan is level as a floor, and much of it is carpeted with the softest, richest sward in all the East. One feels tempted to leap from the saddle, and gambol and roll about on it like a little child. The lake ends in a triangular marsh, the largest part of which is on the eastern bank of the river. It is an impenetrable jungle of ordinary cane, mingled with that peculiar kind called babeer, from whose stems the Arabs make coarse mats **Babeer** for the walls and roofs of their huts. This cane is the prominent and distinc- **cane.** tive production of these marshes, both at the north and south end of the lake. I have seen it also on the banks of brooks in the plain of Sharon, north of Jaffa. The stalk is not round, but triangular. It grows eight or ten feet high, and ends above in a wide-spreading tuft of stems like broom-corn, shoot-ing out in every direction with surprising regularity and beauty. It imparts a

BABEER CANE.

singular appearance to the whole marsh,—as if ten thousand thousand brooms **Course of** were waving over it. Through this jungle the Jordan creeps sluggishly for **the Jor-** **dan.**

PART
II.

half a mile, and then glides tranquilly between green sloping banks for another mile to Jisr Benat Yacobe. Thence it commences its headlong race over basaltic rocks down to the Lake of Tiberias, a distance of about six miles, and the distance, according to my aneroid, is ten hundred and fifty feet. Of course it is a continued repetition of roaring rapids and leaping cataracts. I once rode, walked, and scrambled from the bridge down to the entrance into the lake—a wild, stern gorge, fit haunt for robbers, from whom it is never free.

Bridge of
Jisr Benat
Yacobe.

The bridge is concealed from our view by that projecting hill on the south corner of this plain. It is not ancient—at least not in its present form—but is a very substantial affair, having three broad arches. A guard is always stationed at it, and a few Arabs generally pitch their tents near, to profit from the passing traveller by selling eggs and lebn, and by pilfering as occasion offers. On the east of the bridge are the remains of an old khan, with a beautiful cistern of well-cut stone in the centre of the court. It had handsome basaltic columns at the corners, and was supplied with water by a canal from the mountains above. The whole road from the bridge to the khan, and thence up the eastern mountain, was once paved with large basaltic slabs. The road from Jerusalem to Damascus passes up it and out on to the wild rocky region of the Jaulān.

About a quarter of a mile south of the bridge are the ruins of a large castle,

PELICAN.

called now Kusr 'Atra. It is on the west bank, and was evidently built to command the ford at that place and above it.

Wild animals of the Hûleh.

This Hûleh—plain, marsh, lake, and surrounding mountains—is the finest hunting-ground in Syria, and mainly so because it is very rarely visited. Panthers and leopards, bears and wolves, jackals, hyenas and foxes, and many other animals, are found, great and small, while it is the very paradise of the wild boar and the fleet gazelle. As to waterfowl, it is scarcely an exaggeration to affirm that the lower end of the lake is absolutely covered with them in the winter and spring. Here only have I seen the pelican

The pelican.

of the wilderness, as David calls it.[1] I once had one of them shot just below this place, and, as it was merely

---

[1] Ps. cii. 6.

wounded in the wing, I had a good opportunity to study its character. It was CHAPTER
certainly the most sombre, austere bird I ever saw. It gave one the blues XVIII.
merely to look at it. David could find no more expressive type of solitude
and melancholy by which to illustrate his own sad state. It seemed as large Its melan-
as a half-grown donkey, and when fairly settled on its stout legs, it looked like choly.
one. The pelican is never seen but in these unfrequented solitudes, and to
this agree all the references to it in the Bible. It is sometimes called cormo-
rant in our English translation.[1]

There is an easy ascent to Safed from this plain of el Kheît. It is half an
hour to a large winter torrent called Hendâj, and forty minutes farther to
Wady el Wŭkkâs, at the foot of the mountains, where is a large Tell of the Way to
same name, more than seven hundred paces long and about one hundred feet Kŭdes.
high, with a miserable village on the east end of it. Thence the path ascends
by Kûbbaah to Ain 'Askûl and upward toward the south-west, till, at the end
of three and a half hours from el Mellahah, you are at Safed. Our present
business, however, is to reach Kŭdes yonder in that recess of the mountain to
the north-west of us. It will take an hour of busy, earnest climbing ; and the
long ride and brisk mountain air will sharpen our appetites for dinner, which
will no doubt be waiting.

It seems that we have rather suspicious neighbours ; such, at least, is the
apprehension of the muleteers. Kŭdes has, in fact, a bad reputation in more
respects than one. It is so unhealthy that the Metâwely lords of these mountains find it difficult to get people to live here and cultivate the lands. They
constantly leave, and it has then to be colonized anew. Those now here are
strangers from the French colony of Algeria. Several thousands of the Alge- French
rines, to whom the French yoke was intolerable, obtained permission to settle Algerian
in Syria, and a small body of them came here under the direction of Tamar colony.
Beg. I never saw a more forlorn band of pilgrims than they appeared to be
when they landed at Beirût, and I fear this Kŭdes will prove but a poor city
of refuge to them.

By the way, this is one of the cities of refuge. No better proof of antiquity
and past importance could be desired.

Yes, this is that Kedesh in Galilee, in Mount Naphtali, which was given to Kedesh-
the Levites of the family of Gershon,[2] and then selected to be the most north- Naphtali.
ern city of refuge.

I somewhere read, when young, that these cities were seated on commanding heights, so as to be visible at a great distance ; but this one, at least, is
hid away under the mountain, and cannot be seen until one is close upon it.

The idea, though common and even ancient, is certainly a mistake. Nablûs
and Hebron, the other two cities west of the Jordan, lie low in valleys, and it is
evident that the selection was made without reference to elevation ; they were
central, however,—this for the north, Nablûs for the middle, and Hebron for

---

[1] Isa. xxxiv. 11 ; Zeph. ii. 14.   [2] Josh. xx. 7, and xxi. 32.

PART
II.

Cities of
refuge.

the south of Palestine. A few hours' rapid flight would bring the unhappy man-slayer to one or other of these asylums. The Jewish writers affirm that it was the duty of the Sanhedrim to keep the roads to the cities of refuge in good repair, and to have guide-posts wherever needed, with the words *Refuge! Refuge!* written upon them, that there might be no mistake, no delay. If these things were not so, they ought to have been; and although we never read of any instance in which this provision for safety was embraced, yet no doubt it was; and whether or not, still, as good old Henry says, there is a great deal of excellent gospel taught or implied in this institution. The account of it is very fully given in the 35th chapter of Numbers and 19th of Deuteronomy.

Land of
fountains.

Our ride for the last two days around the sources of the Jordan has reminded me of the words of Moses to the children of Israel in regard to this country: "The Lord thy God bringeth thee into a good land; a land of brooks of water, of fountains, and depths that spring out of the valleys and hills."[1] Certainly this is a good land. I have never seen a better; and *none* where the fountains and depths that spring out of the valleys and hills are so numerous, so large, and so beautiful.

Climate.

And then remember that this is a climate almost tropical, where water is fertility and life, and the absence of it sterility and death, and the greatness of the blessing is vastly enhanced. The number of these fountains and depths is prodigious. Many of those whose united contributions make up the Jordan, we have looked into during these last few days; but the whole land is full of them;—those of the Dog River; of the River of Beirût; of the Damûr; the Owely; the Zahrany; those of the Litany at Baalbek; Zahleh, 'Ainjar, and Mushgarah; the great Ras el 'Ain at Tyre; those of Kabery and the Naamany, on the plain of Acre; and of the Kishon at Jenîn, Lejjum, and Wady Kŭsaby; of the Zerka, near Cæsarea; and those of the Aujeh at Antipatris, and the Ras in Sharon. And thus we might go all through Palestine, on both sides of the Jordan, and enumerate hundreds of them—powerful fountains—the permanent sources of every river in the country. I have visited them often, and always with admiration and astonishment. Nor need we wonder that so much is made of them in the Bible: they are the glory and the life of the land, and they abound to an extent almost incredible. Many single villages in the mountains have scores of smaller springs, which run among the valleys, and give drink to every beast of the field. Some even boast of hundreds of these little sources of fertility.

Fountains
every-
where.

Peculiari-
ties of
some.

Many of these fountains have some peculiar characteristic about them. Some are tepid, as those along the shore of Tiberias; many are slightly brackish, and not a few are remittent or wholly intermittent. Of this latter class is Neb'ah Fûârr, the source of the Sabbatic River; the Menbej, east of Beit Jenn, the head of the second river of Damascus. The main source of the Litany at 'Anjur

---

[1] Deut. viii. 7.

is a remitting fountain of a very extraordinary kind. But we must not make a pleasant subject tedious by too much detail. Enough has been said to justify the declaration of Moses that this is eminently the land of fountains.

You mentioned the Sabbatic River just now, and I should like to know something about this rather apocryphal stream.

That of the Jews is, indeed, sufficiently apocryphal, but that of Josephus is not, though the phenomenon on which it is based is somewhat exaggerated in his hands. In book seven of his "Wars," he says : "Now Titus tarried some time in Berytus, as we told you before. He then removed, and exhibited magnificent shows in all the cities of Syria through which he went, and made use of the captured Jews as public instances of the destruction of that nation. He then saw a river as he went along, of such a nature as deserves to be recorded in history. It runs *in the middle*, between Arca, belonging to Agrippa's kingdom, and Raphanea. It hath somewhat very peculiar in it ; for when it runs its current is strong and has plenty of water, after which its springs fail for six days together, and leave its channel dry, as any one may see ; after which days it runs on the seventh as it did before, and as though it had undergone no change at all. It has also been observed to keep this order perpetually and exactly, whence it is that they call it the Sabbatic River, that name being taken from the sacred seventh day of the Jews." So much for Josephus. Pliny also, in his "Natural History," very likely refers to the same river : "In Judeah rivus, Sabbatis omnibus siccatur." This makes it rest every seventh day, according to the fourth commandment. Pliny, however, knew less of the actual phenomena of the river than Josephus ; and, in order to make it a consistent Jew, required it to rest on the seventh day.

The translator of Josephus says that this famous river is extinct, and in this opinion the learned Reland concurs. Niebuhr, the celebrated Danish traveller, having discovered an independent tribe of Jews residing in Arabia, says, "The circumstances of this settlement have perhaps given rise to the fable of the Sabbatic River." What those circumstances were he does not mention, nor is it easy to understand how he could venture to write such a sentence. He may have had some fable of the Talmud in his mind at the time. I discovered this river and its source in 1840. Let us return to and examine the quotation from Josephus. From Beirût, Titus marched northward to Zeugma, on the Euphrates. On his march he saw this river running between Arca, in the kingdom of Agrippa, and Raphanea. The mention of Agrippa's kingdom probably induced most travellers to look for the Sabbatic River somewhere in the south of Palestine, where it is not to be found, although there are traces of ancient cities in that region with names similar to those of Arca and Raphanea, But the kingdom of Agrippa did actually extend, at one time, as far north, I believe, as the River Eleutherus, and therefore included Arca. At any rate, the account requires that we search for the Sabbatic River between Arca and Raphanea ; and there I found it. Arca, the capital of the Arkites, lies about half a day's ride to the north-east of Tripoli ; and between it and Hamath, on

PART
II.

the east of Jebel Akkar, is the site of Raphanea. A short distance west of Kŭlaet Hŭsn is the great convent of Mar Jirius, and in the wady below it is a fountain called Nebâ el Fûârr, which throws out, at stated intervals, an immense volume of water, quite sufficient to entitle it, in this country, to the dignified name of river. This site answers to the description of Josephus in all respects; but there are some discrepancies between the actual phenomena of this fountain and his Sabbatic River which require explanation.

Nebâ el
Fûârr.

In the first place, this Nebâ el Fûârr is now quiescent two days, and active on a part of the third. The account which the monks gave me of the matter was, that every third day St. George descends and forces out the water with great violence and loud noise, to irrigate the extensive plantations of this richest Syrian convent. The cave out of which the river flows is at the base of a hill of limestone, entangled in a vast formation of trap-rock. It was a day of rest when I examined it, but evidently a large volume of water had rushed along the bed of the river only a few hours before. Now, Josephus says that it rested six days and ran on the seventh; but Pliny makes it run six and rest on the seventh. At present it rests two days and runs on the third. These discrepancies admit of a probable explanation. Both historians appear to have depended upon report, and did not carefully examine the facts of the case for themselves. The numbers in both versions of the story were adopted in order to connect this singular phenomenon with the Sabbatic division of time, and it is not necessary to suppose that either of them was strictly accurate; if, however, we must admit that one or other was literally exact, the difference between the periods of resting and running eighteen hundred years ago and at present may still be accounted for.

Principle
of the
siphon.
Explana-
tion of the
phenome-
non

It is well known that these intermitting fountains are merely the draining of subterranean reservoirs of water, on the principle of the siphon. Let A in our diagram represent such a reservoir, filled by the veins D E F. Let S be the siphon, which, of course, must begin at the bottom of the pool, rise over the elevation at C, and end in the wady at B, lower than the bottom of the pool. Now, the condition necessary to make the stream intermit is, that the capacity of the siphon be greater than the supply from D E F. If the supply were greater, or exactly equal to this capacity, the pool would be always full, and there could be no intermission. The periods of intermission and the size of the stream depend upon the size of the pool A, the supply from D E F, and the calibre of the siphon S. If it required six days for D E F to fill the pool, and the siphon could exhaust it in one, we have the conditions required by the statement of Josephus—a river running only on the seventh day. On the other hand, if D E F fill the pool in one, and their continued supply is so nearly equal to the draining power of the siphon that it requires six days to draw off all the water, then it will run six days, according to Pliny, and rest on the seventh. The fact *now* is, that the supply ordinarily fills the reservoir in about two days and a half, and the siphon drains it off in half a day. It results, of course, that the reservoir under the mountain of Mar Jirius must be very large to contain the vast amount of water that issues at B.

FOUNTAIN OF SABBATIC RIVER.

If the account of Josephus was strictly true when he wrote, one of the following changes must have taken place during the eighteen hundred years which have since elapsed : Either the supply from D E F has increased so as to fill the pool in two days and a half instead of six, and the capacity of the siphon so enlarged as to exhaust this treble supply in half the time he mentions ; or, the supply and the siphon remaining the same, the reservoir itself must have been reduced to about one-third of its former capacity. The former supposition is not probable in itself, and is discountenanced by the fact that the amount of water was then so great that Josephus calls it a river, and it can only obtain that title now by courtesy. But we can readily admit that the pool may have become partly filled up by the falling in of its superincumbent roof of rock.

Change since time of Josephus and Pliny

If Pliny was correct, then either the supply must be greatly diminished, or the reservoir much enlarged ; for, according to his statement, it required but one day of rest to fill it, while now it takes two days and a half. Either of these hypothetical changes is possible, but none are very probable, nor are we obliged to resort to any of them. I suppose the Sabbatic River was always nearly what we find the stream below Mar Jirius now to be. The vagueness of general rumour, the love of the ancients for the marvellous, and a desire to conform this natural phenomenon to the Jewish division of time, will sufficiently account for the inaccuracies of these historians.

This account of the Sabbatic River furnishes the explanation of many similar fountains and streams in Syria. As stated above, the source of the Litany at 'Anjur is a remitting fountain of a very peculiar character. A constant stream issues from the pool, but there are frequent and vast augmentations in the volume of water, occurring at irregular periods, sometimes not more

Similar fountains

PART
II.

than twice in a day, while at others these augmentations take place every few hours. So, also, one of the largest fountains of the 'Aujah (the second river of Damascus) has singular intermissions, accompanied by loud noises, and other strange phenomena, on the return of the water. In Lebanon there are likewise fountains which either entirely intermit at stated periods, or are subject to partial remissions. Such, too, is the Fountain of the Virgin, in the valley of Jehoshaphat. All such instances can be explained by supposing either that the entire stream is subject to this siphonic action, as at the Sabbatic River and at Menbej, or that the constant regular stream is at times augmented by tributary intermitting fountains, as at Anjar and Siloam.

CHAPTER XIX.

KUDES—SAFED—KEFR BUR'IAM.

Kŭdes—Cydessa, or Kedesh-Naphtali.
Plain of Zaanaim.
The terebinth.
The dove—Scripture allusions.
Heber the Kenite.
Safed—the "city set on an hill?"
Meron—Meroz?

Beeriah—Beeroth?
Earthquakes.
The earthquake of 1837.
Marōn, burial-place of Rabbis.
Feast of burning.
Jish, or Giscala.
Kefr Bur'iam.

March 6th.

Kŭdes.

THE existing remains of this city of refuge show that it was once a place of importance, but I know very little of its history.

It has one, however, and sufficiently ancient too. Barak lived here, and to this spot he and Deborah gathered that brave band of Naphtalites who routed the army of Sisera in the plain of Esdraelon.[1] This is also the Cydessa or Kedasa of later days, and Josephus often mentions it under one or other of these names. To it Titus retired with his army from Giscala, which lies over yonder to the south-west a few miles. Josephus says it was a " strong Mediterranean village of the Tyrians, which always made war with the Jews,"—a statement which needs qualification, as do many others of that historian. There seems to be no propriety in calling it a Mediterranean village at all, unless because its inhabitants at that time were from the sea-coast of Tyre. We may perhaps infer from this notice that the population, even in those olden times, was as fluctuating as in our days, and possibly owing to the same cause—the extreme unhealthiness of the site. In another place the Jewish historian says that Cadesh lies between the land of the Tyrians and Galilee. It was, therefore, a border town, and subject to all the vicissitudes of such unfortunate localities. And it is remarkable that, so far as the circumstances

Formerly
Cydessa.

Un-
healthy
and inse-
cure.

[1] Judges iv. 10-17.

of the country admit of such a thing, it is still a border town, insecure, and often deserted.

The remains of its architecture bear witness to its varied fortunes. The hill on which the modern village stands was once fortified, and adorned with edifices very different from these wretched huts of mud and rubbish. Broken columns and handsome capitals indicate the presence of Greek artists; but the sarcophagi, and the ruins of large buildings on the plain down east of us, are certainly Jewish or Phœnician. They are, however, different from those at Maron, Yaron, Tell Hûm and other places in Galilee. The sarcophagi are very large, and some are double—a variety I have seen nowhere else in this country. The immense door-posts, twenty feet high, are doubtless of Jewish origin, and probably belonged to synagogues erected about the beginning of our era, possibly as late as the third century, at which period this region was crowded with Jews in peaceful and prosperous circumstances. In the mountain cliffs south-west of the village are many rock tombs, and altogether the marks of antiquity are numerous, and quite equal to the demands of her story.

Have you noticed the pretty plain sloping down to the north-east? Though on this elevated platform, so high above the Hûleh, it is wet and marshy in winter; and it is this, I suppose, that makes Kŭdes so unhealthy. It may be that "plain of Zaanaim which is by Kedesh,"[1] on which the Kenites pitched their tents; if, indeed, the *allon* in that verse should not be translated *terebinth* instead of "plain." This is one of the passages relied on to determine the signification of that word, but it does not do it. There is a fine plain here, "*by Keḍesh*," and therefore Heber may have pitched there; tent-dwellers, as he was, prefer the margin of such rich pastures. The Septuagint renders it *oak*, not *terebinth*, and Zaanaim it translates into *robbers:* So Heber pitched by the *oak* of the *robbers*. This very region, however, will favour those who wish to appropriate *allon* to the *terebinth*, for there are more of these trees on the hills between this and Mais el Jebel than in all the country besides. Ibrahim Pasha had them grafted with the pistachio from Aleppo, where that species abounds which bears the nut of the market. The peasants, however, destroyed the grafts, lest their crop of oil from the *berries* of these trees should be diminished, and thus this attempt at agricultural improvement was defeated.

It is very evident that Kŭdes and Zaanaim will never settle the controversy about the *allon;* so far as they are concerned, it may be a plain, or a terebinth, or an oak.

True enough; for there are magnificent *oaks* not far off, while the *plain* and the *terebinths* are in full view. And, finally, it is evident from Joshua xix. 33, that Allon Zaanaim was the *proper name* of one and the same place; and this is a matter of importance, as it gives us another point in the boundary of the

Marginal notes:
CHAPTER XIX.
Remains of architecture.
Plain of Zaanaim.
The terebinth.

---

tribe of Naphtali, for which any one who tries to run that line will be devoutly thankful.

THE TEREBINTH.

I have directed Salîm to take a guide and go across the country to Kefr Bur'iam, where we are to spend the coming night. We will make a detour to the south, and visit Safed. Our route lies along the base of these cliffs, and we shall soon descend into the Muaddŭmîyeh, one of the wildest wadies of Naphtali. It comes down from Jish, and, indeed, from far above and beyond it westward, and its terrible cliffs are full of caves and crevices, the favourite home of hawks and eagles. And there goes a flock of stout, compact, iron-grey pigeons, "flying as a cloud, and as doves to their windows."[1]

The dove.   Is this the dove, and these clefts in the rock the windows referred to by the prophet?

The Hebrew word is the general name for the Columba family, of which there are many varieties in this country. Ezekiel, speaking of the destruction of the Jews, says, "They that escape of them shall be on the mountains like doves of the *valleys;*"[2] or, as it should be, I think, the *heights* or lofty cliffs. *Flying "as a cloud."* The doves do not ordinarily fly in "clouds," but this variety does; and supposing pigeons, and not turtle-doves to be intended, we have before us both the windows and the clouds which suggested the figures of the text. When

---

[1] Isa. lx. 8.   [2] Ezek. vii. 16.

travelling in the north of Syria many years ago, I noticed in certain villages tall square buildings without roofs, whose walls were pierced inside by numberless pigeon-holes. In these nestled and bred thousands of these birds. They

PIGEON-HOUSE.

are very strong, swift of wing, and extremely wild. Their foraging excursions extend many miles in every direction, and it is curious to notice them returning to their "windows" like bees to their hives, or like clouds pouring over a sharp ridge into the deep wady below. I then supposed it was to such pigeonhouses full of windows that Isaiah referred, and it may have been so, but I have never seen them in Palestine. Perhaps the pigeons would not occupy them in this region, as there are in all directions natural windows in lofty cliffs where they can find a safer and more congenial home.

This would agree with their habits, as implied in Jeremiah's exhortation to Moab: "O ye that dwell in Moab, leave the cities and dwell in the rock, and be like the dove that maketh her nest in the sides of the hole's mouth."[1] Both Isaiah and Ezekiel speak of the mourning of the doves.[2]

Is there anything peculiar in their note in this country?

It is always mournful. The reference is to the turtle-dove, I suppose. Their low, sad plaint may be heard all day long at certain seasons in the olive-groves, and in the solitary and shady valleys among these mountains; I have,

Its "windows."

Nests "in the hole's mouth."

---

[1] Jer. xlviii. 28.   [2] Isa. lix. 11, and Ezek. vii. 16.

PART
II.

however, been more affected by it in the vast orchards round Damascus than anywhere else—so subdued, so very sorrowful among the trees, where the air

THE TURTLE-DOVE.

sighs softly, and little rills roll their melting murmurs down the flowery aisles. These birds can never be tamed. Confined in a cage, they droop, and, like Cowper, sigh for

" A lodge in some vast wilderness—some boundless contiguity of shade;"

Fleeing to the wilderness.

and no sooner are they set at liberty than they flee, as a bird, to their mountains.[1] David refers to their habits in this respect when his heart was sore pained within him : "O that I had wings like a dove! for then would I fly away, and be at rest. Lo, then would I wander far off, and remain in the wilderness."[2] And there you will meet these timid birds far away from the haunts of cruel hunters, of whose society they are peculiarly suspicious.

To what does Nahum allude when he says, " And Huzzab shall be led away captive ; she shall be brought up, and her maids shall lead her as with the voice of doves, tabering on their breasts ?"[3]

Tabering on the breast.

The prophet is probably not responsible for all this English ; but I suppose that Huzzab is another name for Nineveh, who was to go into captivity, led by her maidens tabering on their breasts as doves do,—for it was the mourners, and not the doves, who tabered. There is foundation, however, in the manners of our bird for the comparison. When about to utter their plaintive moan, they inflate the throat, and throw it forward until the neck rests upon the bosom. Thus they " taber" on their breasts. Now, if you have ever read the Thousand Nights, you will readily recall the favourite mode of introducing the

[1] Ps. xi. 1.   [2] Ps. lv. 6, 7.   [3] Nahum ii. 7.

great ladies who figure in those gorgeous and luxurious scenes. They are CHAPTER
preceded by troops of "high-bosomed beauties"—"a temptation to the ser- XIX.
vants of God"—bearing tabrets and other instruments, upon which they discourse soul-melting music. In the present case, these "high-bosomed"
damsels, with tabrets resting on their breasts, sang sorrowful strains before
their captive queen.

David speaks of a dove whose wings were "covered with silver, and her Wings of
feathers with yellow gold."[1] I have seen none that could have suggested silver and
these comparisons. feathers of
gold.

He refers to a kind found at Damascus, whose feathers, all except the wings,
are literally as yellow as gold; they
are very small, and kept in cages.
I have often had them in my house,
but their note was so very sad that
I could not endure it; besides, they
kept it up by night as well as by
day. Nothing can exceed the plain-
tiveness of their midnight lamentation.

Solomon repeatedly mentions the Doves
eyes of the dove: "Behold, thou eyes.
art fair, my love; thou hast doves'
eyes."[2] And again: "Thou hast
doves' eyes within thy locks, which"
(singularly enough) "are as a flock
of goats that appear from Mount
Gilead."[3] That is, her locks (not
the doves' eyes) were jet, glossy
black, like the Syrian goats; but
all Oriental poets are fond of doves'
eyes. The bride, also, repeats the

THE RING-DOVE.

compliment to her beloved, and even exaggerates it: "His eyes are as the eyes
of doves by the rivers of waters, washed with milk, and fitly set."[4] There is
a luxurious, delicious haze and indistinctness about such poetic extravagances
which captivate the Oriental imagination. Nor is the comparison wholly extravagant. Doves delight in clear water-brooks, and often bathe in them;
and then their liquid, loving eyes, "fitly set" within a border of softest skyey
blue, do look as though just washed in transparent milk.

To the millions who devoutly sing of the Emblem
of the
"Heavenly Dove, Holy
With all his quickening powers," Spirit.

no other symbol either in or out of the Bible suggests so much precious in-

---

[1] Ps. lxviii. 13.   [2] Song i. 15.   [3] Song iv. 1.   [4] Song v. 12.

PART II. struction and spiritual comfort as this sweet bird of ours. Pure and gentle, meek, loving, and faithful, the appropriate emblem of that Holy Spirit that descended from the opened heavens upon our blessed Lord at his baptism—O may that heavenly Dove

> " Kindle a flame of sacred love
> In these cold hearts of ours."

Our pleasant discourse has brought us up from the depths of Muaddŭmîyeh to this poor village of Alma.* Whether it be known to sacred history or not, its site is certainly that of a very ancient town. There is nothing of interest in the village itself; but those black tents which dot the hill side bring to mind the children of the Kenite, Moses' father-in-law, who left their original home in the desert, entered Palestine with Israel, and settled first at Jericho, and then in the wilderness of Judah. Some time after this, Heber severed himself from his brethren, came north, and pitched his tent at Zaanaim—plain, oak, or terebinth—near Kŭdes. There is a curious tradition of this thing lingering among the dwellers hereabouts, though confused, and mixed up with incredible fables. An old Metāwely sheikh once greatly amused me with his version of the story. It is not worth telling, but it is nevertheless worthy of note that such a tradition is still kept alive in this very neighbourhood, and it suggests the question whether these Arabs here may not sustain some remote relation to Heber and his heroic wife.

Heber the Kenite.

We are coming out upon a very naked and desolate country. It seems quite incapable of cultivation.

The path lies along the dividing ridge between the Hûleh and the great wady Leimûn, and such places are always barren. But if the peasants cannot grow corn, they find coin. When I last travelled this road, some children had just discovered a large deposit of silver coin of the Seleucidæ, kings of Antioch, on the mountain a short distance ahead of us, and the whole country was in an uproar about it. I purchased some of the coin for the worth of the silver, which was a fraction less than a dollar. But there is Safed directly before us, with its castle rising conspicuous in the centre. As our visit is not to the people, but to see the town and the magnificent prospect from the castle, we shall proceed at once to it. When I was here in 1833, the walls were entire, and the interior was a prison for political offenders against the recently established authority of Mohammed Ali. Not being of that class, I could not then gain admittance, but since that time I have often visited it, and the whole is perfectly familiar to me. Let us tie our horses in this interior fosse, and climb to the top. You observe that the shape of the hill is a well-described oval, and the wall corresponds to it. The bottom of the outer ditch is now a very flourishing vineyard, and the entire circuit is not far from half a mile. The wall is mostly modern, but built on one more ancient, portions of which can be seen on the east side. The interior summit rises about a hundred feet higher than

Ancient coin.

Safed.

---

* [Not the same village as the Alma mentioned afterwards, pp. 288, 295.—ED.]

this wall, and was a separate castle, strongly defended. By creeping under these broken vaults, you obtain a sight of the true antiquities of Safed. Here are *bevelled* stones, as heavy, and as aged in appearance as those of the most celebrated ruins in the country ; and they prove that this has been a place of importance from a remote age.

Is Safed mentioned in the Bible ?

It has been identified with the Bethulia of the Maccabees, but erroneously, of course. The fables of the rabbis do not deserve notice. Maundrell, Jowet, and others, throw out the hint that this was the city set on a hill, which could not be hid ;[1] and if that greatest of sermons was preached on the horns of Hüttîn, or near them, as tradition affirms, and if any *particular* city was referred to, there would be plausibility enough in the suggestion. These ancient parts of the castle render it all but certain that there was then a city or citadel on this most conspicuous "hill" top ; and our Lord might well point to it to illustrate and confirm his precept. The present Hebrew name is Zephath, and may either refer to its elevation like a watch-tower, or to the beauty and grandeur of the surrounding prospects. Certainly they are quite sufficient to suggest the name. There lies Gennesaret, like a mirror set in frame-work of dark mountains and many-faced hills. Beyond is the vast plateau of the Hauran, faintly shading with its rocky ranges the utmost horizon eastward. Thence the eye sweeps over Gilead and Bashan, Samaria and Carmel, the plains of Galilee, the coasts of Phœnicia, the hills of Naphtali, the long line of Lebanon, and the lofty head of Hermon—a vast panorama, embracing a thousand points of historic and sacred interest. Safed is truly a high tower on which to set the watchmen of Zion. My aneroid makes it 2650 feet above the Mediterranean. Tabor looks low, and Hüttîn seems to be in a valley.

"The city set on an hill."

For the history of this town you may consult Robinson, Wilson, or any of the tourists who enter into such matters. The important fact about it is, that, although now one of the four holy cities of the Jews, it has become such only within the last five hundred years.* The rabbis, therefore, know very little about its ancient story, and nothing is more unsatisfactory than their confused and contradictory fables about it. I am of opinion that the *castle* is that *Seph* which Josephus fortified in Upper Galilee. It is mentioned in immediate connection with the *rock Achabari* or *Akhbera*, that gigantic cliff down there to the south of us about five miles. (See Wars, b. ii. ch. xx. v. 6.)

Now a holy city of the Jews.

There are no antiquities in the present town of Safed, and therefore we will take a survey of its immediate surroundings, and then prosecute our ride. I

---

[1] Matt. v. 14.

* [" It was not till the sixteenth century that the schools of Safed became celebrated. Then a printing press was set up, many synagogues were built, and the rabbis of Safed were acknowledged to be among the chief ornaments of Hebrew literature. . . . . The sixteenth century was their golden age of literature. In the seventeenth, both learning and funds began to decline; and the terrible earthquake of 1837 gave a death-blow to the Jewish cause. . . . . The greater proportion of Jews are natives of Poland; but there are also representatives of most of the other countries of Europe." (*Hand-book for Syria and Palestine*, p. 439).—ED.]

PART
II.

Rock
Akhbera.

Meron—
Meroz?

once came directly here from Khan Minieh, at the north-west corner of the lake, and without a guide. From our present stand-point it seems so near that one is tempted to pitch pebbles into it; and this castle has the same deceptive appearance from below. I thought I could come directly up to it, but soon got entangled in rocky wadies, and after immense fatigue, found myself, at the end of two hours, looking off from the great rock Akhbera. This terrific precipice cannot be less than five hundred feet in perpendicular height, and it is traversed by interior passages, partly natural, partly artificial, quite to the top, with many windows in its face looking out upon the dizzy depth below. It was a famous den of robbers in the olden time, but is now surrendered to bats, owls, and eagles. At its base is a fountain called Ain Kehâly, and a single hut marks the site of an ancient town, with the Hebrew name of Hŭkŭb. The *village* of Kehâly lies in the wady above Akhbera, and beyond it the valley turns south-west, and unites with the Leimûny, which drains this broad and profound basin between us and that wooded mountain west of Safed, called Jebel Zebûd, and also Jermuk, from a village on its western slope. The great wady 'Amûd joins the Leimûny lower down, and the united stream issues, through a wild gorge, on to the plain of Gennesaret, and runs directly to the lake, without any connection with the Rubudîeh. The maps of this neighbourhood are generally very inaccurate.

The main source of the Leimûny is the fountain called 'Ain et Jin, which rises in a rocky glen high up the side of Jebel Zebûd. It is a good mill-stream, but at certain seasons it entirely intermits, and hence the name *Jin*, because its irregularities are supposed to be occasioned by these capricious spirits. It flows near Meron or Marōn—as it is differently pronounced—which you can just see on the slope of Zebûd, about two hours to the west of us. I identify it with the Meroz so bitterly cursed by Deborah, and I reach this conclusion thus: Barak resided in Kŭdes, from which we have just come. In his march to Tabor he would naturally pass under this Marōn, and would summon the inhabitants to join his expedition. They refused, probably with contempt and insult; hence the terrible imprecation in Deborah's triumphal ode: "Curse ye Meroz, said the angel of the Lord; curse ye bitterly the inhabitants thereof; because they came not to the help of the Lord, to the help of the Lord against the mighty."[1] It is rather a curious coincidence, if not an actual corroboration of this idea, that the Jews of this day have a tradition that Deborah actually passed by the place on her march with Barak to Tabor, and bathed in the fountain of Marōn; and hence they call it Deborah's fountain. The names Meroz and Marōn, or Meron, are almost identical, and the change of the final *nun* to zayn, in transcribing, might easily be made. The undoubted antiquity of Marōn, and its position on the direct road from Kŭdes to Tabor, lend additional probability to what I admit is, after all, only a fair guess.

---

[1] Judges v. 23.

I have a somewhat similar hypothetical identification of this Beerieh or CHAPTER Beria, on the north of Safed, with the site of those Beerites whom Joab sum- XIX. moned to aid him against Sheba, the son of Bichri, as we read in 2 Samuel Beeroth xx. 14. This would be on his route to Abel, and there is no other Beer in all and Beer- this region. Upon the same grounds, I suppose that the great host under ites? Jabin, king of Hazor, that came to fight against Joshua at the waters of Merom, may have assembled at this place. Josephus thus speaks about this matter : " So the kings that lived about Mount Libanus, who were Canaanites, and those Canaanites that dwelt in the plain country, with auxiliaries out of the land of the Philistines, pitched their camp at Beeroth, a *city of Upper Galilee*, not far from Cadesh." Now there is no other Beeroth in Upper Galilee. This is evidently an ancient site ; and Hazor, the capital of Jabin's kingdom, is at Hazere, some ten miles to the north-west, as I believe. If Jabin assembled his vast army there he would naturally march this way to Merom. The mountain immediately above Beerieh takes its name from the village, but the ridge south-east of it is called Jebel Canaan. May not this name have been given to it from the fact that the grand army of the Canaanites pitched their camp there on that most memorable occasion ? If those circum- stances render the identification satisfactory, we are now looking upon one of the most ancient sites known to history. The fact that it is at present a small village, in humble dependence upon its younger and more prosperous neighbour, forms no objection. The land abounds in such examples. Hazor itself is utterly extinct.

This town of Safed wears a fresher and more lively air than any other in this region. To what is that to be ascribed ?

It is, in fact, the newest. Not a house in it is twenty years old. The whole Earth- town was dashed to the ground in half a minute by the earthquake in 1837, quake of and these buildings have all been erected since that catastrophe. The pros- 1837. perity of Safed is entirely owing to the constant influx of foreign Jews, drawn hither by the sanctity of the place. The population may be about five thou- sand, more than half of them Jews—a strange assemblage from most of the nations of Europe. I have no heart to enter into their history, or dwell on Jews in their absurd superstitions, their intense fanaticism, or their social and domestic Safed. institutions and manners, comprising an incredible and grotesque *melange* of filth and finery, Pharisaic self-righteousness and Sadducean licentiousness. The following is a specimen of the puerilities enjoined and enforced by their learned rabbis : A Jew must not carry on the Sabbath even so much as a pocket handkerchief, except within the walls of the city. If there are no walls, it follows, according to their perverse logic, that he must not carry it at all. To avoid this difficulty here in Safed, they resort to what they call Erŭv. Poles are set up at the ends of the streets, and *strings* stretched from one to the other. This string *represents a wall*, and a conscientious Jew may carry his handkerchief anywhere within these strings. I was once amused by a devout Israelite who was walking with me, on his Sabbath, toward that grove of olive-trees on the north of the town where my tent was pitched. When we came to the end of the street the string *was gone*, and so, by another fiction, he supposed he was at liberty to go on without reference to what was in his pocket, because he *had not passed the wall*. The last time I was here they had abandoned this absurdity, probably to avoid the constant ridicule it brought upon them.

A profane and most quarrelsome fellow once handed me his watch to wind just after sunset on Friday evening. It was now his Sabbath, and he could not work. Thus they still tithe mint, and anise, and cummin, and teach for doctrines the commandments of men, making void the law of God by their traditions. It was such perverse traditions as these that our Lord rebuked when he declared that the Sabbath was made for man, not man for the Sabbath.

And now, free from this singular place, we must descend into this profound wady Leimûn, around whose upper expansions are seated half a score of villages, with hard names not necessary to repeat. Our path leads directly under Kŭditha, that wretched hamlet of black basalt immediately before us. It was utterly destroyed by the earthquake of 1837.

As we are in the centre of that awful catastrophe, I should like to hear some account of it.

These terrible calamities have often occurred in this country, and are frequently alluded to in the Bible. At the giving of the law, "Sinai was altogether on a smoke, because the Lord descended upon it in fire ; and the smoke thereof ascended as the smoke of a furnace, and the whole mount quaked greatly." [1] Then "the earth shook," sings Israel's great poet; "even Sinai itself was moved at the presence of God, the God of Israel." The mountains skipped like rams, the little hills like lambs.[2] On that memorable day when Jonathan overthrew the Philistines, "the earth quaked, so it was a very great trembling." [3] And when the Lord appeared to Elijah, "a strong wind rent the mountains, and brake in pieces the rocks; and after the wind an earthquake." [4] Isaiah also threatens Ariel, the city where David dwelt, with this awful judgment; and Amos says he was with the herdmen of Tekoa "two years before *the* earthquake;"[5] to which Zechariah refers when he says, "Yea, ye shall flee, like as ye fled from before the earthquake in the days of Uzziah king of Judah." [6] And so, too, our blessed Lord and his apostles familiarly allude to these dreadful visitations of God. Indeed, a large class of poetic imagery and prophetic commination is based upon them. They give point and emphasis to the most alarming threatenings of divine indignation, and, so far as my knowledge goes, they are, in this land of heavy stone houses, by far the most awful of all. Before them the very "knees of terror quake." When He arises to shake terribly the earth, all hearts fail, all faces gather blackness. Courage is of no avail; the boldest

---

[1] Exod. xix. 18.
[4] 1 Kings xix. 11.

[2] Ps. lxviii. 8 ; cxiv. 4, 6.
[5] Amos i. 1.

[3] 1 Sam. xiv. 15.
[6] Zech. xiv. 5.

fly, just as the feeble and timid do. *Why*, our narrative will abundantly show.

It was just before sunset on a quiet Sabbath evening—January 1, 1837— when the shock occurred. A pale, smoky haze obscured the sun, and threw an air of sadness over the closing day, and a lifeless and oppressive calm had settled down upon the face of nature. These phenomena are, however, not very uncommon in this country, and may have had no connection with the earthquake. Our native church at Beirût were gathered round the communion-table, when suddenly the house began to shake fearfully, and the stone floor to heave and roll like a ship in a storm. "Hezzy! Hezzy!"[1] burst from every trembling lip as all rushed out into the yard. The house was cracked from top to bottom, but no further injury was sustained. The shock was compara-tively slight in Beirût, but still many houses were seriously shattered, and some on the river entirely thrown down. During the week succeeding this Sabbath, there came flying reports from various quarters of towns and villages destroyed, and lives lost ; but so slow does information travel in this country, especially in winter, that it was not until eight days had elapsed that any reliable accounts were received. Then letters arrived from Safed with the startling intelligence that the whole town had been utterly overthrown, and that Tiberias, and many other places in this region, had shared the same fate. Some of the letters stated that not more than one in a hundred of the inhabit-ants had escaped.

As soon as these awful facts had been ascertained, collections were made at Beirût to relieve the survivors, and Mr. C—— and myself selected to visit this region, and distribute to the needy and the wounded. Passing by Sidon, we associated with ourselves Mr. A—— and two of his sons to act as physicians. In Sidon the work of destruction became very noticeable, and in Tyre still more so. We rode into the latter at midnight over her prostrate walls, and found some of the streets so choked up with fallen houses that we could not pass through them. I shall retain a vivid recollection of that dismal night while life lasts. The wind had risen to a cold, cross gale, which howled through shattered walls and broken windows its doleful wail over ruined Tyre. The people were sleeping in boats drawn up on shore, and in tents beside them, while half-suspended shutters and doors unhinged were creaking and banging in dreadful concert. On the 17th we reached Rumaish, where we met the first real confirmation of the letters from Safed. The village seemed quite destroyed. Thirty people had been crushed to death under their falling houses, and many more would have shared the same fate if they had not been at even-ing prayers in church. The building was low and compact, so that it was not seriously injured. After distributing medicine to the wounded and charity to the destitute, we went on to Jish. Of this village not one house remained ; all had been thrown down, and the church also, burying the entire congre-

---

[1] "Earthquake! earthquake!"

PART
II.

gation of one hundred and thirty-five persons under the ruins.   Not one
escaped except the priest, who was saved by a projection of the arch over the
altar.   The entire vaulted roof, with its enormous mass of superincumbent
stone and earth, fell *inward* in a moment, and of course escape was impossible.
Fourteen dead bodies lay there still unburied.

Effects of
earth-
quake at
Safed.

On the morning of the 18th we reached Safed, and I then understood, for
the first time, what desolations God can work when he ariseth to shake terribly
the earth.   Just before we began to ascend the hill, we met our consular agent
of Sidon returning with his widowed, childless sister.   Her husband, a merchant
of Safed, had been buried up to the neck by the ruins of his house, and in that
state remained several days, calling in vain for help, and at last perished
before he could be reached and set free.   As we ascended the hill, we saw
large rents and cracks in the earth and rocks, and, though not so large as a
chasm at Jish which I examined in the morning, still they gave fearful indications of what was to be expected.   But all anticipation, every imagination
was utterly confounded when the reality burst upon our sight.   I had all the
while refused to give full credit to the reports, but one frightful glance convinced me that it was not in the power of language to overdraw or exaggerate

Dreadful
scenes.

such a ruin.   We came first to the Jewish half of the town, which contained
about four thousand inhabitants two years before when I was there, and seemed
like a busy hive of Israelites ;—now not a house remained standing.   The town
was built, as its successor is, upon the side of the mountain, which is so steep
that the roofs of the houses below formed the street for those above ; when,
therefore, the shock dashed all to the ground, the highest fell on the next
below, that upon the third, and so on to the bottom, burying each successive
row of houses deeper and deeper under accumulated masses of rubbish.   From
this cause it happened that many who were not instantaneously killed perished
before they could be rescued, and others were rescued five, six, and even seven
days after the earthquake, still alive.   A friend of mine told me that he found
his wife dead, with one child under her arm, and the babe with the nipple in
its mouth : it had died of hunger, trying to draw life from its dead mother.
Parents heard their little ones crying, Papa ! Mamma ! fainter and fainter,
until hushed in death, while they were struggling to free themselves, or labouring with desperate energy to throw off the fallen rocks and timber from their
dying children.   O God of mercy ! my heart even now sickens at the thought
of that long black winter's night, which closed around the wretched remnants
of Safed in half an hour after the overthrow—without a light or possibility of
getting one, four-fifths of the population under the ruins, dead or dying, with
frightful groans, and shrieks of agony and despair, and the earth trembling
and shaking all the while, as if affrighted at the horrible desolation she had
wrought.

The chaos.

Most hideous spectacle, may I never see its like !   Nothing met the eye but
a vast chaos of stone and earth, timber and boards, tables, chairs, beds, cloth-
ing, and every kind of household furniture, mingled in horrible confusion ; men

everywhere at work, worn out and woe-begone, uncovering their houses in CHAPTER
search of the mangled bodies of lifeless friends, while here and there were XIX.
companies of two or three each, bearing away a dreadful load of corruption to
the tomb. I covered my face, and passed on through the wretched remnants
of Safed. Some were weeping in despair, others laughing in callousness still
more distressing; here an old man sat alone on the wreck of his once crowded
house; there a child at play, too young to realize that it had neither father
nor mother, nor relative of any name in the wide, wide world. They crowded
round us with loud lamentations, as if kindness unsealed the flood-gates of
their sorrow—husbands without wives, wives without husbands; parents childless, and children without parents, and not a few left the solitary remnants of
large families. The people were scattered abroad above and below the ruins,
in tents of old boards, old carpets, mats, brush, and earth, while some poor
creatures, wounded and bruised, were left among the tottering walls, exposed
to a horrible death from the loose and falling stones above them.

As soon as our tent was pitched and our medicines and stores opened, we set Sights of
out to visit the sufferers. But I have no heart to recall the sights and scenes suffering.
of that morning: bodies crushed and swollen out of all human shape, and in
every stage of mortification, dying hourly without hope of relief; they were
crowded into old vaults, where the air was tainted beyond endurance. Very
soon we returned, and commenced arrangements to erect a temporary hospital,
without which it was useless to attempt anything for the sufferers. On this
we all laboured incessantly, and by the 19th it was ready for their reception.
Having collected them in it, and distributed medicines and clean bandages in
abundance, we placed them under the care of a native doctor hired for the purpose, and then left for Tiberias. It was most refreshing to breathe once more
the pure air of the open country, free from the horrible sights and scents of
Safed. Nor shall I soon forget that pleasant ride to Tiberias, particularly in
the evening, and along the shore of the lake. Gennesaret lay like infancy
asleep. The sun settled quietly down behind the hills of Nazareth, and the
full moon shone kindly through the hazy atmosphere on lake and land, faintly
revealing the scenes where the Saviour of the world had wandered, and
preached, and healed all manner of disease.

The destruction of life in Tiberias had not been so great as at Safed, but the Tiberias.
houses and walls of the city were fearfully shattered. About six hundred
perished under the ruins, and there were scenes of individual suffering not
exceeded by any in Safed. Many of the wounded had been carried down to
the hot baths, where we visited them. They informed me that at the time
of the earthquake the quantity of water at these springs was immensely increased, and that it was so hot that people could not pass along the road across
which it flowed. This, I suppose, was fact; but the reports that smoke and
boiling water were seen to issue from many places, and flames of fire from
others, I believe were either fabrications or at least exaggerations. I could find
no one who had actually seen these phenomena, though all had heard of them.

PART
II.

Earth-
quake in
divers
places.

On the 22nd we left Tiberias, and reached Nazareth in the night, having distributed medicines and clothes at Lubieh, Sejera, Kefr Kenna, and Reîneh. In
all these villages, except Kefr Kenna, the earthquake had been very destructive, while in others on either side of us no injury had been sustained. This
erratic and apparently capricious course led one of my companions to remark
that it was the exact fulfilment of our Lord's words in Matthew xxiv. 7 :
"There shall be earthquakes in *divers* places." There may be something in the
geological formation of these plains and mountains which occasioned these extraordinary exceptions ; but whether we can or cannot explain the phenomenon, the fact is certain that some villages were entirely destroyed, and others
close to them suffered no injury. And though the present earthquake is in no
way referred to in that prophecy of our Lord, yet similar occurrences in ancient
times may have suggested, or rather may have rendered the reference appropriate. At Nazareth our mission terminated, and we returned by the ordinary route to Beirût, having been absent eighteen days in the middle of winter,
with bright, clear weather, so that even on the mountains we were able to
sleep in the tent without inconvenience.

I have somewhere seen it stated that these terrible judgments, instead of
softening the heart and working reformation in the life, produce effects the
very reverse.

Harden-
ing effects.

In this case it did so to an extraordinary degree. It was frightful to witness the intense selfishness and hideous rascality developed. The survivors in
the surrounding villages left their friends to die amid their own crumbling
houses, and hurried to Safed to strip the dead and plunder the living. Ibrahim Pasha sent a detachment of troops from Acre to protect the poor Jews
from robbery and murder, but they themselves were utterly callous in regard
to their fellow-sufferers. It is scarcely credible, and yet it is fact, that after
we had laboured night and day to build the hospital, we had to carry the
wounded to it ourselves, or *pay their surviving friends* exorbitant prices to
do it. So far as my experience goes (and wars, pestilence, cholera, and earthquakes have given me many opportunities to observe), the people will *not* learn
righteousness when *such* judgments are abroad in the land.

Marōn—
burial-
place of
Rabbi
Hillel.

But, to banish these painful pictures, let us turn to our present whereabouts. Over yonder, to our left, is Marōn, one of the sacred places of the
Jews. Dr. Wilson has given an extended account of the great rabbis whose
sepulchres are believed to be there. The most celebrated is Hillel, the grandfather of Gamaliel. His tomb is a chamber cut in solid rock, like multitudes
of others in this country, only larger, being twenty-five feet square, and having
thirty *loculi* or niches for the dead. There are several real sarcophagi in this
room, with enormous lids. It is curious that the whole room is often flooded
with water. The far-famed and truly infamous festival of "burning" is celebrated at these tombs. I never witnessed this extraordinary performance, and
never will. Professor Hacket gives a graphic account of it. The apartment
over the graves was lighted up by many lamps, and around the court were

stalls filled with people, their beds, and their travelling equipments. The pilgrims gave themselves up to intoxication, singing, dancing and clapping of hands; while some, more warlike, kept up an exhibition of sword-play. After dark the crowd filled the court, stalls, gallery, and corridor, almost to suffocation. A pillar supporting a stone trough stood at one corner of the gallery, and near it a vessel with oil, in which the articles to be burned were first dipped. At a given signal, a man with a blazing torch mounted the stairs to the gallery, and all were now intent with expectation. The first article burned was a costly shawl, the offering of a rich Jew from Joppa, who had paid about seventy-five dollars for the privilege of opening the ceremony. As the shawl began to blaze, the multitude raised a shout that made the welkin ring; men clapped their hands, and the women shrieked out the *zulghŭt*—a shrill tremulous cry, which one hears only in this country. Other offerings—shawls, scarfs, handkerchiefs, books, etc., etc.—were brought forward, dipped in oil, and consumed; while from time to time, as an article was seen to be of special value, or burned with uncommon brilliancy, the spectators broke forth into renewed expressions of delight. Thus this work of drunken madness went on until our informant was obliged to leave. It is, in fact, kept up all night, accompanied with scenes of such gross and indecent revelry, that all respectable Jews express the deepest regret and reprobation of the whole affair. I have never been able to ascertain the origin or real significance of this most absurd festival. It is, of course, intended to honour the great rabbis whose tombs are supposed to be there, and is also connected with some vague ideas of merit, by which the donors will derive benefit from the prayers or intercessions of these saints,—an error found among all Oriental sects in one form or another. But enough of such folly and extravagance. Here we have something more satisfactory, or at least more substantial. This deep pit on our right is probably an extinct crater. It is difficult to imagine what else it can be, and, as the entire region is volcanic, the thing is not in itself improbable. Yon village above and ahead of us is Jish, the modern representative of that Giscala where dwelt John, the arch-enemy of Josephus; and here stood that church whose roof fell in and buried the congregation alive while at their evening prayer. A road takes off north-west to Yarōn, which is about an hour and a quarter in that direction. It is too far out of the way, or I would take you thither, for there are many ancient remains about it well worth seeing. The most remarkable are the ruins of a church, and, as it differs from anything you will meet in the country, I will describe it. The length is eighty-six feet, the width fifty-three, with a double extension southward quite peculiar: the first twenty feet broad, and the length of the church; the other thirteen feet wide and fifty-five long. This is a sort of portico, supported by six columns. There were three doors in the west end, and a double row of columns extended from the wall in front of the doors to the altar; the architecture is Corinthian, and I noticed the Greek cross on some of the capitals; the entrances have posts eight feet high, and all of single blocks, standing on end like those of the old synagogues at Kŭdes,

PART
II.

Kefr Bu-
r'iam.

Ruins.

Marōn, and other places in this region. This may also have been originally a synagogue, or it may have been a church of the " Lower Empire," or both may have been built out of the ruins of a heathen temple more ancient than either. The remains lie about the hill, and are stuck into the embankment of their water-tank. I measured one stone fourteen feet long, curiously carved after the Jewish or Phœnician style. There are also many large sarcophagi in the neighbourhood, which certainly are neither Greek nor Roman. This is no doubt the Iron given to Naphtali,[1] and was in olden time a place of much importance. Beyond it is Bint Jebeîl, the capital of this district ; and farther north is 'Ain Atha, the Beth-Anath of the same tribe. This whole region is crowded with ancient sites, most of which, however, are unknown to history, either sacred or profane. And here is Kefr Bur'iam,* and it has taken us three hours and a quarter to come from Safed ; the distance, however, is not more than nine miles.

We have still to examine the antiquities of this village. This edifice among the houses is tolerably perfect, and the style of architecture is wholly peculiar. These sheaf-like carvings on the columns and cornices are neither Roman nor Greek. In its present form it probably was a synagogue of the second or third century. An old villager tells me that he remembers when there was a row of columns above those now seen, but the earthquake of 1837 threw them down, and all those along the north end of the edifice.

The other ruin, some thirty rods north of the village, is entirely prostrate, except the front entrance. This consists of two large upright posts supporting an entablature of a single stone more than ten feet long, richly ornamented with Jewish sculpture, and bearing a long inscription in Hebrew character, which, however, gives us no important information either as to the author, the age, or the character of the temple.

---

[1] Josh. xix. 38.

* ["Kefr Bur'iam was for many centuries a place of Jewish pilgrimage. It was said in the twelfth century to contain the tombs of Barak the conqueror of Sisera, and Obadiah the prophet; to these was added that of Queen Esther, in the sixteenth century. Round these shrines the Jews of Safed were wont to assemble each year on the feast of Purim, to 'eat, drink, and rejoice'— a few individuals of special sanctity still make a passing visit to the spot, to pray over tombs so traditionally holy " (Hand-Book for Syria and Palestine, p. 440).—ED.]

CHAPTER XX.

HAZOR—ALMA—ACRE.

Precious stones.
Hazere—Hazor.
Park-like scenery of Naphtali.
Wild beasts—Tigers.
Snow in Palestine.
Hosah—Râmy—Yârin.
Alma—Arab confederations.
Blood revenge—Sanctuaries.
Work for Christianity—One in Christ.
Mejawîse—Marrying relations.

A continual dropping.
The sirocco.
Ointment of the right hand.
Arabs—Tents and deserts.
The patriarchs not Bedawîns.
Wanderings in the wadies.
Conies and bees.
Tarshîha—An impostor.
Yanoah—Juth—Yerka—Kefr Yusif.
Acre.

March 7th.

THERE are manifest signs of a storm this morning, and we will do wisely to seek some safe retreat before it burst upon us. I have in charge to visit the Protestant community at Alma, and wish to spend the coming Sabbath there. You, however, would find but small entertainment in such a place, and therefore had better go direct to Acre. The muleteers know the road, and by riding hard you can reach the city before sunset. Travelling arrange-ments.

So be it; and when we meet in that far-famed fortress, I shall expect an account of your experiences among the peasants of Alma.

We part not yet. Our paths are the same for the first hour westward down this long wady toward Rûmeîsh. Very familiar to me is every foot of this valley, for in certain parts of it are beautiful geodes of chalcedony, which I have spent days, first and last, in gathering. In the spring of 1838 I sent four donkey-loads to Beirût, and from there they have been dispersed by friends to almost every part of the world. We have no time to meddle with them to-day, nor is it necessary. I have at home as much of this pretty mineral as you can possibly want. Some five years ago I discovered a new locality of it extending from Jisr Kuraone, below Mushgarah, quite up to the south end of the Buk'ah, at Jûb Jennîn. The whole country there for many miles is literally covered with these geodes, from the size of a walnut to that of a large melon —chalcedony enough to build the third foundation in the wall of the New Jerusalem.[1] Chalce-dony.

I have not yet seen any of the precious stones mentioned in the Bible, during our rambles through the country.

But few of them are to be found in Palestine. I have discoverd jasper and agate in great variety, and very beautiful, along the southern and eastern base of Mount Casius, and in a few other places; but the precious stones em- Precious stones of the Bible.

[1] Rev. xxi. 19.

PART
II.

ployed by Moses in making the priestly garments were doubtless procured in Egypt and Arabia, where they still abound. Of the twelve manner of stones in the breastplate of the high priest,[1] there are native to this country the jasper, the agate, the beryl, and the sardius. If the sapphire is the lapis lazuli, it is also met with in certain parts of Syria.

Biblical minera-logy ob-scure.

But Biblical mineralogy is yet involved in great obscurity, and a carefully prepared treatise on it is much needed. How many critics are there in the whole world, do you think, who have any definite knowledge of those gems only that are mentioned by Moses? I have yet to find one. Dr. Smith examined every available source of information while translating the Bible into Arabic, and, had he lived to complete that work, the student would have been able to cull from it the results of vast research. Some future scholar in these Oriental languages may yet be able to furnish to the world what is wanted, not merely in regard to gems, and the various ornaments made out of them, but also in reference to the resins, gums, spices, and ointments used by the ancient Hebrews, and likewise the medicinal and other plants, herbs, roots, flowers, and trees of the Bible.

Eastern love of gems.

It is worthy of remark that the Orientals always paid far more attention to gems and similar matters than we are accustomed to bestow in our day and country. And the same is true with these people around us. I venture to say that this donkey-boy coming to meet us could confound nine-tenths of Bible-readers in America by his familiar acquaintance with the names, appearance, and relative value of the precious stones mentioned in the Word of God. We need not be surprised, therefore, at the constant mention of them by plain and unlettered prophets and apostles. John was not a scholar nor a lapidary, and yet he is perfectly at home among precious stones, and without effort gives a list which has and does still puzzle our wisest scholars even to understand, nor are they yet agreed in regard to them. In our translation, and in every other with which I am acquainted, the same Hebrew word is made to stand for entirely different gems, and lexicographers, commentators, and critics are equally uncertain. But yonder is Rŭmeîsh, and the road to Acre here turns to the left. *Au revoir*, and a pleasant ride to you.

Acre, March 11th.

Safely back, and welcome; but where have you been all this while?

Not so fast; all in due time and order. Thanks first, rest and refreshment next, and then my story to your heart's content, and more plentifully, perhaps, than you desire.

Kûra.

Well, after we parted last Saturday, I passed Rŭmeîsh, and, turning to the north-west, came in half an hour to the ruins of an old city called Kûra, on the left of the entrance into the great wady el Aiyûn. The whole hill is perforated thickly with deep cisterns, most of them quite perfect in appearance, CHAPTER but all really "broken," so that they can hold no water. I know not the historic XX. name of this deserted city, if, indeed, it ever had one, but it must have been a place of importance in its day.

The only other site worth mentioning in this region is Hazere, midway be- Hazere. tween Dible, 'Ain Ible, and Cosa. This Hazere I identify with that Hazor which was the head of all those kingdoms whose armies, led by Jabin, were overthrown by Joshua at the waters of Merom. The remains of this very ancient city lie in a large natural basin, and spread far up the hill side toward the south. Heaps of hewn stone, old and rotten ; open pits, deep wells, and vast cisterns cut in the solid rock—these are the unequivocal indications of an important city. A large artificial cave, with an arch in front of a more modern date, is a celebrated mazar of the Metāwelies. I inquired of an old sheikh what saint was honoured there. In a voice loud and bold, as if to make a doubtful point certain, he replied, Neby Hazûr, who fought with Yeshua Ibn Nun. As this is a tradition purely native, handed down from remote antiquity, along with the name of the ruins, it adds probability to the identification. The situation meets sufficiently well the demands of all the Biblical notices we have of Hazor. It is true that Josephus, speaking in a loose and indefinite way, says that Hazor was over the Lake Samechonitis, and in like manner we may say that it is over the Hûleh. It is above it to the north-west, and in the centre of that mountainous district which overhangs the lake. And as Josephus never visited the site himself—wrote from memory in a distant land long after he had left his native country—his brief and incidental allusion to the position of Hazor is entitled to very little weight. Dr. Robinson, however, who was directed to this place by myself, does not accept the identification, nor will he admit that 'Ain Hazur, near el Mughar, is the En Hazor of Naph- The two tali ; but, until other sites with claims better established be discovered, I Hazors of shall continue to regard them as the two Hazors given to that tribe. Their Naphtali. names are identical, their positions satisfactory. In particular, I take this Hazere to be the site of that great city where Jabin resided and reigned—that Hazor which aforetime was head of all those kingdoms of Canaanites who pitched together at the waters of Merom to fight against Israel,[1] and which alone, of all the cities, did Joshua take and burn with fire.

It seems, however, to have recovered rapidly from its first overthrow, for a History of Jabin reigned in Hazor, and cruelly oppressed the Israelites in the days of Hazor. Deborah, until Barak routed his army on the plain of Esdraelon, and sent his chief captain fleeing on foot to the tent of Heber the Kenite, where, weary and fast asleep, he was slain by Heber's heroic wife; which deed of daring Deborah thus celebrates in her glowing song of victory : " Blessed above women shall Jael the wife of Heber the Kenite be ; blessed shall she be above women in the tent. With the hammer she smote Sisera ; she smote off his head, when

[1] Josh. xi. 5, 10, 12.

PART
II.

she had pierced and stricken through his temples. At her feet he bowed, he
fell, he lay down ; at her feet he bowed, he fell : where he bowed, there he fell
down dead.   So let all thine enemies perish, O Lord ; but let them that love
him be as the sun when he goeth forth in his strength." [1]   Josephus adds to
the Bible account that Barak killed Jabin in Hazor, and utterly overthrew
the city ; if so, it revived again, for it is often mentioned.   Solomon rebuilt it
once, and long after this it was of so much importance as to be named among
the chief cities of Galilee which Tiglath-Pileser conquered, about the year 740
before Christ.

But enough of Hazor and her story.   We must complete our journey to
Alma.   It is with a kind of pleasure altogether peculiar that one wanders over
Park-like
hills and
ravines of
Naphtali.
the park-like hills and through the solemn ravines of Naphtali.   With a sort
of breathless expectation, you dive into wild gorges deeper and deeper, ever on
the watch for a wolf, wild boar, or wild Arab, and held wide awake hour after
hour, communing with the grand, the beautiful, and the sublime.   It is only
by thus exploring the rocky mysteries of the country that we can discover
the wisdom of that divinely-established process of exterminating the original
inhabitants *little by little* before the Israelites.   "Thou mayest not consume
Wild
beasts.
them at once, lest the beasts of the field increase upon thee." [2]   I am not surprised to find this matter of wild beasts and their depredations often referred
to in the Bible, nor to read of lions, leopards, and bears in the very heart of
the land.   The lion, it is true, has been driven back into the desert; but, notwithstanding the multiplication of fire-arms, and other modes of destruction
far more effective than the ancients possessed, these wadies now abound in
large leopards, in bears, wolves, hyenas, and many other kinds of destructive
animals.   And although the farmer goes to his plough gun in hand, and every
shepherd is armed and followed by his dogs, yet it is all they can do to keep
the "beasts of the field from increasing upon them."   When Ibrahim Pasha
disarmed the country, they became so troublesome that he was obliged to
permit the farmers in such districts to procure guns, under certain restrictions.
Syrian
tigers.
Fierce Syrian tigers, as they are called, maintain their haunts directly beneath
large villages.

It is recorded in 1 Chronicles xi. 22, that Benaiah, who had done many acts
besides killing two lion-like men of Moab, "went down and slew a lion in a pit,
in a snowy day."   From this we learn several things : that lions abounded in
the land in the time of David ; that they retreated into pits ; and, lastly, that
Snow in
Palestine.
they had snowy days even in Palestine.   The battle of Benaiah reminds one
of the famous fight of Putnam with the wolf in his den.   This Jewish hero of
"many acts" doubtless tracked the lion to his lair by the fresh-fallen snow, as
Putnam did the wolf.

We have such snowy days occasionally, and they are attended with a species
of danger in certain parts of the country such as no man in America ever

---

[1] Judges v. 24–27, 31.   [2] Exod. xxiii. 29, 30.

thought of. Our doctor and quondam magician of Ibel was once passing over
the mountains in Belad Besharah, when he suddenly found himself at the
bottom of an ancient cistern, whose narrow mouth had been covered up with
snow. Not being hurt by the fall, he indulged in a hearty laugh at the exploit.
Soon, however, he saw with terror that the inside—shaped like a huge demi-
john—was as smooth as glass, so that it was utterly impossible to climb out.
After desperate but fruitless efforts, he had no resource but to call for help at
the top of his voice, in the hope that some chance passer-by might hear. Thus
he passed two dreadful days and nights before he was discovered and drawn
out more dead than alive. There are thousands of these ancient cisterns in
Upper Galilee, where Josephus says there were two hundred and forty cities
in his day, and the site of every one was pierced like a honey-comb with them.
One should always be on his guard while exploring these old sites, especially
if they are overgrown with grass and weeds. When peering into these dark
demijohn-cisterns I have often thought of poor Joseph, for it was doubtless a
forsaken cistern (beer is the word both in Hebrew and Arabic) into which he
was thrown by his barbarous brethren. The beer was empty; there was no
water in it.[1] And just such are now found about the site of old Dothan. It
is remarkable that, though dug in hard rock, and apparently sound, they are
nearly all dry even in winter.

They certainly furnish a very striking and significant commentary on the
expostulation of Jeremiah: "Be astonished, O ye heavens, at this, and be
horribly afraid, be ye very desolate, saith the Lord. For my people have committed two evils; they have forsaken me, the fountain of living waters, and
hewed them out cisterns, broken cisterns, that can hold no water."[2]

No comparison could more keenly rebuke the madness of a people who
changed their glory for that which doth not profit. The best cisterns, even
those in solid rock, are strangely liable to crack, and are a most unreliable
source of supply of that absolutely indispensable article, water; and if, by constant care, they are made to hold, yet the water, collected from clay roofs or
from marly soil, has the colour of weak soap-suds, the taste of the earth or the
stable, is full of worms, and in the hour of greatest need it utterly fails. Who
but a fool positive, or one gone mad in love of filth, would exchange the sweet,
wholesome stream of a living fountain for such an uncertain compound of
nastiness and vermin! I have never been able to tolerate this cistern-water
except in Jerusalem, where they are kept with scrupulous care, and filled from
roofs both clean and hard.

But to my story: where was I? Oh, stumbling over the ruins, and shouting down the throats of broken cisterns, to wake up the slumbering echoes of
old Hazor. From thence I climbed up to Cosa, some half an hour west of, and
eight hundred feet above Hazor. This may be the Hosah given to Asher by
Joshua.[3] Taking a hasty survey of her prostrate temples and ancient build-

---

[1] Gen. xxxvii. 24.   [2] Jer. ii. 12, 13.   [3] Josh. xix. 29.

PART
II.

Blât.

History
lost.

ings, I hastened on to Blât, which Mr. Van de Velde visited with so much tribulation of soul and travail of body. It is one hour and a half west of Cosa, and occupies the most conspicuous position in all this region. The architects of this temple were lovers of the sublime, and selected a spot on which to build and pray which commands prospects in all directions of great beauty. It was evidently a place of importance, but its history is utterly lost. The columns of the temple are visible to a vast distance, and all around are masses of ruins in wild confusion, and overgrown with thorns and briers. Far down the southern slope of the mountain are the remains of another place, almost concealed by a dense jungle of bushes, with the modern name of Khurbet el Bûsal (Ruin of the Onion), a name without a story, which is all that can be said of a hundred other sites in this region. With regret I descended to the regular road between Cosa and Alma, not far from Râmy,—the Ramah of Asher, I suppose, mentioned in Joshua xix. 29. There were yet three hours to Alma, but the road was good, down a very gradual descent westward. The country is well wooded and most lovely, but entirely deserted by all except tent-dwelling Arabs. In an hour and a half I came to Yarîn, having turned aside from the direct road to visit it.

Yarîn.

The broken houses of the ancient city cover a large natural tell, and lie there all ready for the future restorer of Israel's desolations. On the east side are the remains of a fine temple of Grecian architecture : possibly it may have been a church of early Christian days. The name Yarîn seems to be Hebrew, but I find no mention of it in the Bible, nor in Josephus. It was growing late, and the country thereabouts is full of Arabs, who bear a bad character; so I hastened on, and alighted at the door of our friend Zorab a little after sunset.

Alma.

During the night, the storm which had been gathering in the west burst upon us in winter's wildest fury. I was thankful for the shelter which even Alma's dark habitations afforded ; but I shall not trouble you with the history of those three days and nights of tribulation. The good people did what they could to make me comfortable, and were not to blame if my eyes could not bear to be smoked like bacon, nor my nerves endure the ceaseless titillation of fleas. The ladies were particularly distressed to find that my inner man rebelled against their savoury dishes. But the longest three days that ever rained or blew themselves into the past tense finally came to an end. The sun rose joyous and bright on the morning of the fourth, and happy was I to get abroad once more. In company with some of our friends, I spent the day in rambling about the country. We visited Kŭlaet Shem'ah, which appears to be on a level with Alma, and not more than three miles distant ; but at the end of an hour and a half we were farther from it than when we started. This great detour to the east had to be reached to get round the head of some of those gorges I have before mentioned. Several frightful ravines run down to the sea between Alma and Shem'ah, and so narrow that you have no idea of their existence until quite upon their brink. The continuity of the surface seems unbroken. I once undertook to go from Alma to this castle without a guide, but was brought up suddenly by one of these gorges, and obliged to CHAPTER return without accomplishing my object. XX.

The castle is quite modern, and does not answer to the magnificent appear- Castle of ance from a distance. The position on the top of a high natural tell over- Alma. looking the surrounding mountains, the beautiful plain and more beautiful sea of Tyre, gives to it this imposing aspect. But it is a modern ruin, built by the Wakady branch of the house of Ali es Sughîr about one hundred years ago. No doubt there were buildings there before this castle, just as there were on hundreds of other sites around it. Such remains of ancient towns and castles almost cover these mountains. The gigantic natural tell west of the castle, called Izmith, and Izmit, and also Izmid, has on it the ruins of an old castle, and the entire slope of the mountains down to the shore at Ras el Buiyâd is dotted over with ancient towers, to which the general name of Kusseîr is applied, apparently from their diminutive size. In a word, and once for all, let me say that no part of Palestine seems to have been more densely peopled than this Ladder of Tyre, and yet it has rarely been crossed Ladder of or even entered by the pilgrim or the explorer. Tyre.

How did you contrive to pass away those three dismal days of rain, and more dismal nights? It was bad enough even here in Acre.

The Arabs are great on such emergencies, and can fairly talk down the toughest storm that ever blew; and, indeed, we had plenty of important matters to discuss. I was particularly interested and even instructed by a long conversation one evening in regard to certain confederacies between Beit Zorab and some neighbouring families. One of these compacts did not at all please me, as it brings the Protestants there into close fellowship with the worst clans in the whole region. They are now involved in a case of murder by one of these fellows. It seems that long ago the Beit Zorab formed an Alliances alliance—to dignify small matters with large names—with these people for —offen- the sake of mutual protection, and to enable them to retaliate injuries. By defensive. these compacts, the parties are bound to stand by each other in case of need, to join in all quarrels, shelter each other when fleeing from the law or from the pursuit of enemies, and to bear their proportion of the fine incurred by any violation of property or injury to person. Especially must they aid in cases of manslaughter or murder; in the first instance, to conceal and further the escape of the slayer, and then to stand by his family to prevent a general massacre by the enraged relatives of the slain; and, finally, they must do all in their power to bring about a compromise, by inducing the other party to accept a ransom for the blood shed, and abandon their right of revenge. In the case in question, one of Zorab's allies had killed a Metâwely of 'Ain Ibel, and, as these Metâwelies are far the most numerous in this region, and delight to get an opportunity to assault the Christians, the whole village was immediately deserted, the terrified people seeking shelter and concealment among their confederates wherever they could find them. Our friend Zorab became involved in the matter by his relation as confederate with the family of the

PART
II.

slayer, and had to make frequent journeys to hush up the affair. He maintained that the present case was one of strict self-defence,—the man was obliged to kill or be killed ; and the character of the dead man renders this quite probable. But the whole affair, involving as it does the entire Protestant community of Alma, compelled me to look closely at the question as one of practical morals, which I had only thought of in theory before as a curious question of ancient history.

Blood-revenge.

One thing is obvious at first sight : these compacts, with all their consequences, are extra-judicial, are utterly ignored by the law of the land, and opposed to it. Their actual object seems to be to render the execution of the law impossible. But as in the Jewish community in the time of Moses, so here, the custom of blood-revenge is too deeply rooted to be under the control of these feudal lords of the land ; indeed, they themselves and their families are bound by it in its sternest demands. It is plain that Moses, clothed with all the influence and power of an inspired lawgiver, could not eradicate this dreadful custom, and was merely commissioned to mitigate its horrors by establishing cities of refuge, under certain humane regulations, which are fully detailed in Numbers xxxv. and in Deuteronomy xix. In process of time, many other places besides the six cities of refuge acquired the character of sanctuaries, to which persons could flee in the hour of danger. They were established, sanctioned, and sustained by necessity; and before we utterly condemn even such compacts as this of Beit Zorab, we must remember that both law and custom have abolished *all* sanctuaries. There is neither city nor shrine whose sanctity affords a refuge to one fleeing for dear life, and yet the law of retaliation remains in all its vigour, and is executed with energy by the non-Christian tribes around, who are the immense majority. And these compacts, these family treaties of alliance offensive and defensive, are intended to answer the same purpose that the ancient sanctuaries and cities of refuge did ; and they do it. When a man fleeing for life arrives among his allies, he is safe, so far as their utmost power to defend him can go ; and they are to pass him on to more distant retreats if necessary. For this purpose, these compacts are extended all over the land. For example, Zorab has allies in Beit Jallah, near Jerusalem, several days' ride to the south, and in Belad Baalbek, five days to the north of them, and in many other places. Thither the refugees are sent with the utmost despatch and secrecy. In the present instance the man-slayer is nowhere to be found.

Sanctuaries.

Objects of
the confederation.

Again : our friend says, in justification, that without these treaties of alliance they could not exist at all in this reign of lawless Moslems, Metáwelies, and Arabs. It is one of the cruel features of the *lex talionis,* that if the real murderer cannot be reached, the avengers of blood have a right to kill any other member of the family, then any relation, no matter how remote, and finally, any member of this blood confederation. The weak would hence be entirely at the mercy of the strong, were it not for these alliances ; and most of all would the few Christians in Belad Besharah fall victims to the fierce

non-Christian clans around them. This is their apology for such compacts, CHAPTER
and it is difficult to convince them that this, as they believe, their only means XX.
of safety, is immoral. If you tell them that they should make the government
their refuge, and appeal at once to the Pasha, they merely smile at your ignorance of the actual state of the country, and not without reason. Even in
Lebanon, which the Allied Powers have undertaken to look after, I have
known, not one, but many horrible tragedies. Several of my intimate acquaintances have literally been cut to pieces by the infuriated avengers of blood, and
in some instances, these poor victims had no possible implication with the
original murder, and only a remote connection with the clan involved in it.
Were it not for these confederations, there would be no safety in such emergencies, and they do actually furnish an important check to the murderous
designs of " avengers."

I once inquired of a friend if he were not afraid to go into a certain neigh- Compen-
bourhood where a murder had been committed by one of his confederation. sation for
" Oh no," he replied; " our aileh (confederation) can number twelve hundred
guns, and our enemies dare not touch me ; and, besides, the matter is to be
made up by our paying a ransom." This is the ordinary mode of settling such
questions. Zorab told me that last year a messenger came from their allies
in Beit Jallah to levy their proportion of the ransom for a murder committed
there, and they actually paid it. I read to him Numbers xxxv. 31; " Ye shall
take no satisfaction for the life of a murderer which is guilty of death, but he
shall surely be put to death." But he remarked, shrewdly enough, that this
was a Jewish law, and not at all applicable to them, for they were not in a
situation to investigate the cases, nor to execute any decision they might come
to. He further justified himself by saying that he and his immediate family
only *gave* to others according to the obligations of the compact, and did not
take from them. If their allies entered into an unrighteous compact to save
the life of a man who ought to be put to death, the sin was theirs, not his :
rather a nice distinction. He would never aid even one of his own family to
escape from the just demand of the law. I fear, however, that the pressure of
circumstances must always render his good resolutions useless. His own son
could put it out of his power to act with justice, by appealing from him to the
confederation of which he is a member.

One thing is certain : this system defeats nearly all the efforts of this weak Attempts
government to bring criminals to justice, and therefore it must be wicked in at sup-
its actual workings. It is equally certain that a good government would instantly crush the whole thing. The old Emir Beshir succeeded, after a few
terrible examples, in putting an end to it in Lebanon. But many a Druse
wove his smothered vengeance into his unshaven beard, and waited his opportunity during the long reign of that energetic prince. And this is the reason
why his downfall in 1840, by the action of the Allied Powers, was followed by
so many shocking tragedies. Long outstanding accounts were immediately
referred to a bloody arbitration, and settled in death.

PART
II.

Work for
Christi-
anity.

The introduction of a higher and more perfect development of Christianity among these Oriental sects has to encounter and overcome many other obstacles from customs adverse to its nature, which are at least as ancient as history. They have stiffened by old age into elements of unyielding resistance. I was reminded of this by a discussion at Alma concerning a matrimonial alliance which was being negotiated in behalf of one of the members of the community. We, as foreigners, interfere as little as possible, and must legislate very cautiously in such matters ; and yet the reception of the gospel, as we hold and teach it, must abolish or greatly modify certain of their customs, which have struck their roots down to the very heart of society.

Matrimo-
nial
clanism.

In addition to those alliances devised for external protection, there is another system of *matrimonial* clanism. There are certain families and circles called mejawîse, within which alone such alliances are permitted. They mutually give and take, and outside of these they must neither marry nor give in marriage. Treaty stipulations, such as Hamor and Shechem wished to establish between their people and the family of Jacob,[1] are still considered matters of the greatest importance, and long negotiations are often necessary before the high contracting powers can accomplish the difficult and delicate compact.

The men
of She-
chem.

The readiness with which the people of Shechem consented to the hard condition imposed by the treacherous sons of Israel proves beyond a doubt that they were highly respectable, and their alliance counted as an honour and a benefit. It would require very powerful arguments indeed to induce any village to accept such condition at this day. Then there is a sort of one-sided mejawîse, in which, from necessity, a family consents to *take* in order to get wives for their sons, but refuse to *give*, from an aristocratic feeling of superiority. It was a case of this kind about which the discussion arose in Alma. Now, a necessary result of becoming Protestants is to break up *all* these clans of mejawîse. Not only is our gospel largely eclectic, but it knows nothing of such distinctions. There are already Maronites, Greeks, Greek Catholics, Armenians, Catholic Armenians, Jacobites, Nestorians, Jews, and Druses in-

One in
Christ.

cluded in the one body of Syrian Protestants, and the gospel makes all one in Christ. There is neither Jew nor Greek.[2] Of course, all former matrimonial alliances and treaties are annulled by a sort of necessity. Not only do their ancient allies reject them, but the Protestants desire to abstain from all family alliances with those who cling to their old superstitions. You at once see that in such a country as Syria this single circumstance must revolutionize society just so far as evangelical religion prevails. Protestants pay no atten-

Mejawîse.

tion to these systems of mejawîse, and parents and parties concerned are often puzzled how to proceed or succeed.

Many of these matrimonial circles are extremely narrow, and seem to have for their main object the preservation of property within the immediate

---

family. The same purpose lay at the bottom of many Mosaic institutions, or original customs which he sanctioned. But it now acts badly, tends directly to deterioration of the race, and ends in insanity and extinction. I have known instances where there was not a single disposable bride within the entire circle of mejawise. This often leads to murder between contending candidates for a wife, oftener still to the marriage of mere children to very old men. One of my teachers, sixty years old, married a relative only thirteen. In non-Christian sects, the difficulty is sometimes got over by purchasing Georgian girls in the Constantinople market. The gospel must, of course, abolish this traffic, but at the same time it will throw down all these narrow enclosures, and open the way for marriages on better principles.

It will also abolish the very ancient system of marrying only relations. This custom prevailed in the family of Abraham even before he left Mesopotamia; and the reason assigned by Laban for giving his daughter to Jacob—because he was a relative—is still held to be binding. If there are two claimants for the same bride, and one is a relation, this is admitted to be a valid plea in his favour. But this is attended with all the objections mentioned under the preceding head, and causes many unnatural and compulsory marriages, with all their subsequent bad consequences. *Marrying relations.*

The gospel will likewise bring about an entire change in the mode of conducting matrimonial negotiations. This has always been managed in these countries by others than those most interested in the result. The parents, or the elder brother if there are no parents, make the bargain, and the poor bride has nothing to do but to submit. Her preferences and dislikes are treated with utter disregard, and I have known most horrible catastrophes from this cause. Now, true religion will educate and elevate the females, and introduce them into society, where they will have opportunity to become acquainted with those who seek them in marriage. Being free to accept or reject, they will not be married off while mere children to those they do not know, or knowing, abhor. The domestic institution will be placed on its true basis, and purified from a host of mischievous results, which flow necessarily from the present plan. Under the ameliorating agency of the gospel, the material veil of Oriental seclusion will give place to the veil of genuine modesty and self-respect, for which that has been in all ages but a miserable compensation. *Marriage negotiations.*

Again, the gospel will greatly narrow the list of prohibited degrees of relationship. That established by Moses is certainly wide enough, but ecclesiastical legislation in the East has added largely to it, and introduced the perfectly fictitious relationships of god-parents and foster-brothers, and I know not what. In practice, these rules are found to be so intolerable that the clergy have been obliged to invent and largely exercise the power of dispensation; but this opens a wide door to intrigue and bribery. More than half the quarrels between priest and people grow out of the manner in which this dispensing power is exercised. *Prohibited degrees.*

Certainly Christianity knows nothing about matters in themselves unlawful,

PART
II.
—

Priestly
dispensa-
tion.

but which may be made just and right by paying a few piastres to a priest This whole system, with all its appendages, will be abolished, and the priestly revenue derived therefrom be dried up. But such large changes in social habits and domestic institutions, to be brought about safely, must begin from within, and develop gradually, and not be rudely forced into society by foreign influence acting from without; and the Christian reformer should be contented to wait for this gradual development.

Betrothal.

Our discussion included the present system of betrothal, which, I suppose, is much the same as in ancient Bible days. It is a sort of half marriage, accompanied with religious ceremonies, and the settling of the nature and amount of dower which the bridegroom is to give,—a custom equally ancient. This, too, in its present form and essence, is destined to give way before the advancement of a higher Christianity, or at least to be so modified as to make marriage a less commercial transaction, in which the affections of the parties have no concern. As a part of that system by which relatives dispose of the hand and heart of a poor victim long before she is old enough to have any notions of her own, it needs to be greatly modified; I uniformly, however, refuse to take any active part in these negotiations, because the stand-point from which I regard the whole subject is altogether too far in advance of Syrian society to permit me to be a safe or practical guide in matters matrimonial.

A con-
tinual
dropping.

During the storm at Alma I suffered under the constant illustration of that proverb of Solomon, "A continual dropping in a very rainy day and a conten- tious woman are alike. Whosoever hideth her hideth the wind, and the oint- ment of his right hand, which bewrayeth itself."[1] The force of this proverb is well understood in all its details in this country. Such rains as we have had thoroughly soak through the flat earthen roofs of these mountain houses, and the water descends in numberless leaks all over the room. This continual dropping—tuk, tuk—all day and all night, is the most annoying thing in the world, unless it be the ceaseless clatter of a contentious woman. This, too, I had experienced in its most aggravated manifestation. A quarrel arose be- tween two neighbours about some trifling affair—a chicken, I believe—but it grew boisterous, and raged eleven hours by the watch. Through all these weary hours the "contentious woman" ceased not to scold, and scream, and curse her victim in a style quite original, and so loud that the whole neighbour- hood was disturbed. She would rush into the room, then bound out of it, and fly round the court like a fury, throw off her tarbouch, tear her hair, beat her breast, and wring her hands, screaming all the while at the top of her shrill voice. Sometimes she would snatch up her old shoe, fly at her enemy, and shake it under her very nose, trembling all the while in uncontrollable rage; nor could she be pacified until late in the evening, and then she continued mut- tering, like a thunder-storm working itself quiet behind a distant mountain.

And a con-
tentious
woman.

---

[1] Prov. xxvii. 15, 16.

Certainly he that hideth such a virago hideth the wind. It would puzzle even CHAPTER
XX.
Petruchio to tame such a shrew.

The reference to the wind has also a peculiar force in this country, especially The sion such promontories as the Ladder of Tyre, and during such gales as blew on rocco.
the 2nd of this month. But there is another wind still more pertinent to the
point in our proverb—the dry, hot sirocco. Who can either hide or abide it?
I have seen it in greatest power on the plain of Aleppo, and in the wadies
about Hasbeiya. The air becomes loaded with fine dust, which it whirls in
rainless clouds hither and thither at its own wild will; it rushes down every
gorge, bowing and breaking the trees, and tugging at each individual leaf; it
growls round the houses, romps and runs riot with your clothes, and flies away
with your hat; nor is there any escape from its impertinence. The eyes in-
flame, the lips blister, and the moisture of the body evaporates, under the
ceaseless application of this persecuting wind; you become languid, nervous,
irritable, and despairing. We shall meet this sirocco ere long, for it occurs
oftener in spring than in any other season of the year.

"The ointment of the right hand which bewrayeth itself." What does that
mean?

It refers to the custom of perfuming so common in ancient times, and not Ointment
unfrequent now. The odour of their cosmetics is so powerful that the very of the
street along which the person walks is highly scented. Such ointment cannot hand.
be concealed: it proclaims itself, as the Hebrew may be rendered, wherever it
comes. The right hand is mentioned because it is most honourable, most used
in anointing, and cannot be kept concealed in the bosom, as all salutations,
and the endless gestures in conversation, call it forth. The ointment of the
right hand will surely bewray itself, and so will a contentious woman: she
cannot be hid.

Where and what is this Alma? I never met the name in all my reading.

It is a small hamlet on the top of the Ladder of Tyre, about five miles from
the shore at Ras en Nakûra, and is the only inhabited village on that part of
the Ladder; but every hill top around it has a name and a ruin, some of which
were cities, not villages.

It is a singular fact that these old sites are now appropriated by fragments Arabs—
of Arab tribes, who pitch their black tents among the trees and bushes which tents and
have overgrown the ruins. Whenever you see a clump of large oaks, you may deserts.
be sure that *there* stood a city, and there, too, is the Bedawîn's tent. These
Arabs cultivate the soil, and pay taxes like other citizens, and are therefore
disowned and held in contempt by the regular sons of the desert; nor will
they intermarry with those degenerate clans who choose to gain their bread by
honest industry. But, then, these outcasts from the true Arab aristocracy
have their own scale of nobility, and would scorn to give their daughters to
those miserable wretches who dwell in houses, and follow the ways and avoca-
tions of civilization. What a bundle of absurdities and contradictions is man!
These Arabs live in squalid poverty and inexpressible filth, and yet are prouder

than Jupiter. One night, while keeping a bright look-out for my own integrity, having cows on two sides of me, goats and sheep all around, and fowls overhead, I was greatly amused by the complaints of my host against the filthy Arabs. "The beasts," said he, "ma byarifû jins en nudâfy—don't know anything about cleanliness!" Such testimony, person, place, and circumstances considered, was irresistible. I devoutly believed him.

But we may learn something from these tent-dwelling tillers of the soil, poor and despised though they be. My travelling companion over this region on a former occasion suggested that they offer an example of a custom among the agricultural population of the Jews, from which came the familiar proverb, "To your tents, O Israel;"[1] and perhaps the constant reference to dwelling in tents long after they had been settled permanently in Palestine may have been founded on fact. Daher Abûd, for many years a travelling doctor among the Arab tribes east of the Jordan, tells me that the population, even of such considerable towns as Salt and Kerak, pitch tents out in the country, and there spend their summers. He supposes that this was always customary to a considerable extent; nor is this improbable. The ancestors of the Jews all dwelt in tents, and during the forty years immediately preceding their entrance into Palestine, the whole nation lived in them; and it is extremely probable that many clung to their ancient manners, and spent most of their time in "tabernacles." In fact, the peasants in the south of Palestine do thus spend their summers to this day, and, were I an Arab farmer, I would do the same. Most gladly would I escape from the village, with its crowded houses, filthy within, and infested without by all the abominations which man and beast can congregate, to the bright sun, and joyous groves, and sweet air of the open country. Nor are houses necessary to the farmer in this delightful climate. Isaac dwelt in tents, and yet he "sowed in the land, and received in the same year an hundred-fold;"[2] and I know no reason why many of his descendants might not have been tent-dwelling tillers of the soil.

Dwelling
in tents.

The patriarchs
not Bedawîns.
May we not infer with certainty, from this and other passages in the history of the patriarchs, that they were not mere Bedawîn wanderers like those who now occupy the eastern deserts?

And curse the country by their annual incursions? Most certainly. Such representations are mere gratuitous slander. The Biblical patriarchs had large herds of cattle, which genuine Bedawîns have not; they tilled the ground, which those robbers never do; and they accommodated themselves, without difficulty or reluctance, to town and city when necessary, which wild Arabs cannot endure. From the first there was a sort of mixture of pastoral and city life in that age and in this climate altogether consistent with a fair degree of civilization and refinement.

But to my narrative. Yesterday I left Alma, and visited the great castle of Kŭreîn. Passing southward down a ravine called 'Ain Hor, we reached the

---

[1] 1 Kings xii.   [2] Gen. xxvi. 12.

great Wady Benna, at the end of an hour. The village of Benna lies under CHAPTER
mighty cliffs full of caverns, on the north side of the wady which trends XX.
round to the north-east toward Cosa. We ascended a branch wady to the Wander-
south-east, along a path which terminated at a large ruin called Summakh, and ings in the
left us in the woods, where we soon got lost. After wandering about for some wadies.
time, we discovered a Bedawy among the bushes, who threaded the tangled
wood like an American Indian, and brought us out on the northern brink of
Wady el Kurn, directly opposite the castle. The descent of six hundred and
ten feet to the bed of the river was more than difficult—really dangerous and
frightful. One held the horse by the head, and two by the tail, to keep him
from tumbling over the precipice, and by great care we all got safely down. I
was puzzled to make out the age and object of the building at the bottom of
the wady. It is about one hundred feet long and eighty high. The basement Singular
is a very strong vault, evidently ancient; above it is a group of groined arches, ruin.
mostly broken—they are apparently of Saracenic origin. One might suppose
that this was a church if he could find or fancy where the congregation was
to come from. A single granite column stops up the top of the stairway to the
tower, which may have been a campanila or a minaret, or neither, for there is
nothing about it to determine its character. A powerful *dam*, apparently
Roman, once turned the water of the river into the basement of this curious
edifice at the north-east corner. This favours the idea that the lower storey at
least was a mill; and in that case the upper part may have been a guard-house,
though it was finished off in a style more elaborate than is common for such
places. The dam would convert the river above it into an impassable fosse
for that side of the hill on which the castle stands. There is a tradition that
a covered way led down to the river from the castle, and, as the distance is not
great, the thing is possible ; and, indeed, the termination of what might have
been such a passage is seen in this basement-room.

   The ascent from this building to the top of the castle was extremely fatiguing. Castle.
It is only six hundred feet, but it is nearly perpendicular, and covered with
bushes and briers, through which one must burst his way upward. Where
the bold, sharp ridge of the castle joins the eastern mountain, it is only a few
feet across from north to south, with rugged cliffs descending on either side
to a great depth. Just here it is cut off by a broad and deep fosse, on the
west and lower edge of which stands the first part of the fortifications.

   The top of the ridge was widened by a wall built up from below, as was Its struc-
done by Solomon on Mount Moriah, to enlarge the platform of the Temple. ture.
This basement work is very solid, and exhibits very fine specimens of the old
Jewish or Phœnician bevel.   On this platform stood a noble tower, of extremely well-cut and very large stones, but not bevelled. They are all three
feet thick, and of various lengths up to ten feet. It must have been quite impregnable before the invention of cannon. The ridge falls down rapidly
toward the river in a direction nearly west, having the sides almost perpendicular. There are three other towers or departments, each lower than the

PART
II.

one above, and also wider, for the hill *bulges* out as it descends, and the lowest of all encloses a considerable area. These various departments were so connected as to form one castle, and yet so separated that each would have to be taken by itself. The second from the top has in it a beautiful octagonal pedestal of finely polished stone, about eight feet high, with a cornice; and over it stood eight demi-columns, united inwardly,—a column for each face of the pedestal. It probably supported an image or statue. Above all spread a lofty canopy of clustered arches like those in the building at the river. The entire castle and its hill are now clothed with a magnificent forest of oak, terebinth, bay, and other trees, whose ranks ascend, shade above shade,—

" A woody theatre of stateliest view; "

and underneath is a tangled net-work of briers and bushes, which makes it very difficult to explore the ruins. After groping about for two hours I was obliged to leave, though not half satiated with the scene, nor satisfied with my examinations of it. Indeed, Castle Hill is inexpressibly beautiful and imposing; a swelling pyramid of green, hung up in mid-heaven, with the grey old towers peering out here and there, as if to take a quiet look for themselves on the fair world around and below. And then the river gorge, who can describe it, with its lofty ramparts, where

"Woods over woods in gay theatric pride,"

climb clear up to the sky. The very eagles fly timidly through its dim and solemn avenues.

Object of the building.

It is not easy to comprehend the motive for erecting this castle in such a place. If the road from Zîb ever passed this way to the regions of Upper Galilee, then it would have served to command it; but there is no evidence that any such highway ever led up this wild gorge, and certainly no farther than to the castle itself. It may have been a frontier barrier, held by the Galileans to guard against incursions from the sea-board; or, if there was a time when Achzîb, on the sea-shore, was the sea-port of Naphtali and his neighbours, this castle might then have been of the utmost importance in maintaining safe communication with it. Achzîb was given to Asher, as we learn from Joshua xix. 29, but seems never to have been in their possession.

Conies.

When I first climbed into the castle, I was delighted to see, quietly sitting among the ruins, a beautiful little cony. It had shown that wisdom in selecting the rocks for its refuge which Solomon commends in Proverbs xxx. 26: " The conies are a feeble folk, yet make they their houses in the rocks." I have seen them on the wild cliffs of the Litany, below Blât, and also above the rocky pass of el Buiyad, on the Ladder of Tyre. In shape they resemble the rabbit, but are smaller, and of a dull russet colour. Our friends of Alma call them Tŭbsûn, and are well acquainted with them and their habits, as they are with the jerboa and many other animals rarely met with except in such rocky regions as this.

CONIES.

In a gigantic cliff of Wady Kŭrn immense swarms of bees have made their Bees. home. The people of M'alia, several years ago, let a man down the face of the rock by ropes. He was entirely protected from the assaults of the bees, and extracted a large amount of honey; but he was so terrified by the prodigious swarms of bees that he could not be induced to repeat the exploit. One is reminded by this of the promise to Jacob in that farewell ode of Moses, Deut. xxxii. 13 : " He made him to suck honey out of the rock." And Asaph, in the 81st Psalm, thus sings : " With honey out of the rock should I have satisfied thee." Such allusions prove that bees lived in the rocks long ago just as they do now, and perhaps they were more common than at present. I have seen no bees in the rocks except in a wady east of Tyre.

Parting from my guides, who returned to their homes, I took over the hills in a south-easterly direction, and passing M'alia, seated on a singular tell, once a walled town, and still showing specimens of ancient Jewish or Phœnician work, I stopped for the night at Tarshîha, half an hour farther on, and was hospitably entertained by the Greek priest of the village.

I spent the morning looking about this large village of Tarshîha, which gives Tarshîha name to a sub-governmental district of which it is the centre. There may be about three thousand inhabitants, of whom one-fifth are Christians, the rest Mohammedans, bearing a very bad character. Their brutal manners and fierce fanaticism have of late years been considerably ameliorated it is said, through the influence of Sheikh Aly el Mughraby, a sort of reforming prophet, who has his residence here. He is one of the religious impostors to which this country is ever giving birth. The number of his disciples is stated as high as twenty thousand.

Like the Mormons, he sends forth apostles to call men to his new Tarîkeh, A Mohammedan impostor. or new way, as it is named. They have produced a great sensation in Sidon, where he has many followers. His most zealous apostle there spent a whole forenoon in my study, labouring most earnestly at the work of my conversion,

PART
II.

Sheikh
Aly.

but finally gave up in despair. It was an amusing episode in our quiet life, and the style of argument was curious, and very characteristic of the Oriental mind. It is an interesting fact, however, that a man like Sheikh Aly can venture a reform which leaves Mohammed almost entirely out of the account, suffering only the name of Allah to be used in prayers and hymns—a sort of Moslem Protestantism from this point of view. He also inculcates charity, and respectful treatment of the Christians; which is an important improvement in the tone of Moslem manners, particularly in this region. As to the moral reformation, of which I had heard so much, the specimens at Tarshîha were far from satisfactory. The whole population seemed to me uncommonly profane, boorish, and insolent; still, their neighbours say it is a happy advance on the past, and ascribe the good work to Sheikh Aly. The sheikh himself I found dwelling very much at his ease, and caring little about the farther spread of his *Tarîkeh*. From the lowest level of pinching poverty he has risen to wealth, has a large harem, some of whom are from the highest families in the country, and in the enjoyment of his domestic paradise he has very much neglected the concerns of his followers.

M'alia.

Tarshîha sounds ancient and Jewish, but the name does not occur in the Bible, nor in Josephus, who performed his most warlike exploits in this neighbourhood, and could not well have avoided mentioning it, had it then been a place of importance. There are, indeed, few evidences of antiquity about it, and what are to be seen were brought, as I suppose, from the ruins of 'Alîa, on the edge of the pretty vale between Tarshîha and M'alia. Here was once a considerable city adorned with temples, the remains of which still cover that part of the plain. It is unknown in history, but the village of M'alia seems to derive its name from it. There was an Allon in Naphtali, and this 'Alîa may possibly be its representative. I was surrounded by many beautiful girls, but remarkably brazen-faced for Moslems. Perhaps they borrow brass from their head-dress called Semâdy, the most striking part of which consists of a thick roll of old coins, which is carried from the top of the head down the cheeks and under the chin. Their fine features are therefore set within this *metallic frame*, and it is no great wonder if they cannot *blush*. I never saw this peculiar head-dress in such perfection anywhere else. Those of the same kind about Nazareth are much smaller. Some of these weigh at least six pounds, others are said to weigh ten.

Sheikh el
Mujahîd.

Taking a guide, I went over the lofty hill south of Tarshîha, on which is a very conspicuous mazar, called Sheikh el Mujahîd. It commands a noble prospect in every direction, and especially over the south-western part of Galilee, drained by Wady el Kŭrn, with its wonderful ravines, wooded hills, and park-like glades. About a year ago, I came across this region from the north-east, and shall long remember that ride with great satisfaction.

Yanoah.

I reached Yanoah in about an hour from Tarshîha, and, as this name occurs among the cities which Tiglath-Pileser conquered, I was gratified to find in

and about it abundant evidences of extreme antiquity.[1] From Yanoah I
descended into the wady south-west of it, to examine the place called Juth or
Jeth. The ruins occupy the eastern end of an oblong saddle, lying between
Wady Maisely on the north, and the Medjnûny on the south—an isolated rock
about one thousand feet long and three hundred broad. The only approach to
it is from the plain, up Wady Maisely. The eastern end alone would require
much fortification, as everywhere else the rock terminates in frightful precipices. The whole of this eastern part is covered with vast quantities of rubbish, and the houses of the present village are built very high, and with thick
walls, as if to use up as much of the old stones as possible ; the rest is piled up
in heaps to clear the ground for cultivation. Perhaps this Juth is one of the
Gaths mentioned in the Bible. A Gath somewhere in this region was the
birth-place of the prophet Jonah; and though that site is thought to have
been east of Sephoris, yet that is by no means certain, and this, after all, may
be the real home of the prophet.

From Juth to Yerka is about an hour, and the road leads over wild rocky
ridges and through profound ravines, fatiguing to the horse, but charming to
the rider. Yerka, like Juth, occupies the site of an ancient town, as is evident
from the columns and other architectural remains, some of which have Greek
inscriptions on them. The inhabitants are all Druses, as are also those of
Yanoah and Juth. The prospect from Yerka is magnificent over the hills of
Samaria, along the dark ridge of Carmel, and round the Bay of Acre to the
great military fortress itself.

In the afternoon, I rode down the rocky declivity of the mountain to Kefr
Yusif, which lies at the edge of the plain. It bears the Moslem name of
Josephus, and has a large Jewish cemetery, held in great veneration by them.
They bring their dead from a distance to bury them there, though not a Jew
resides in the village. Two hours' easy riding across the plain brought me to
the gate of Acre, in good health, and cheerful courage to prosecute our pilgrimage.

---

2 Kings xv. 29.

CHAPTER XXI.*

LADDER OF TYRE—ACRE.

Ladder of Tyre.   Bŭssa—remarkable column.
Zîb—Achzîb—Ecdippa.   Acre—history, sieges, &c.
Castle of Jiddîn.   Boundaries of tribes—Asher—Zebulun.

March 12th.

WHILE we are quietly passing over this broad and fertile plain of Acre toward
Jiddîn, I call for your adventures after we parted at Rumeîsh last Saturday.

The account of that ride can soon be given; but let me remind you first,
that by taking the interior route by Banias, we have missed the entire road
from Tyre over the "Ladder" to Acre.

Road from   I can easily fill up that gap. The road follows the shore south of Tyre for
Tyre to   two hours to the Nahr Uzzîyeh, where are the remains of an old Roman bridge.
Acre.   This stream rises near Kefr Buri'am, passes by the site of Hazor under the
name of Wady el Aiyûn, and thence to the sea by a tortuous, wild, and wooded
gorge, like those we have looked into in other parts of Naphtali. Fifteen
minutes farther is a well called Medfeneh, south of which are ruins scattered
along the shore, with no other name than that of the well; but just at the
foot of the "Ladder" is el Hŭmra, a very ancient site, probably, of a castle
Ladder of   built to command the pass. The Ladder—the Promontorium Album of the
Tyre.   geographers—is a path cut in the cliff overhanging the sea for about a mile,
and rising two hundred feet above its surface. It makes even a bold man
nervous to look down where the waves dash against the perpendicular rocks,
and groan and bellow through the hollow caverns. The direction of the pass
is east and west, and the mountain rises boldly overhead several hundred feet,
in cliffs of white indurated marl, interlaced with seams of dark-coloured flint.
If you watch closely you will always see timid conies creeping about on these
cliffs. At the end of the pass the road turns south for a mile to the ruins of
Scanderûna, the Alexandroschene of the ancients; there is nothing about
them, however, indicative of an age older than the times of the Crusaders.
William of Tyre, in his History, lib. xi., sect. 29, 30, gives an account of the
repairing of this place in A.D. 1116 by Baldwin; but he derives its name from
Alexander the Great, and native tradition ascribes the road over the Ladder

---

* [The first part of this chapter glances at the sea-coast district between Tyre and Acre,
dwelling especially on the "Ladder of Tyre"—the name of a famous promontory, near Acre,
traversed by a road cut out of the cliff. Then an account is given of the road to Acre from
another point, Rumeîsh, noticed in last chapter, a considerable distance to the north-east; lastly
we are introduced to Acre itself.—ED.]

to the same hand ; but there was a road there long before Alexander's day, and CHAPTER
many others besides him have *repaired* it. XXI.

There are many specimens of Roman road in this vicinity, and a fountain of
delicious water flows out near the shore, most grateful to the weary traveller
along this desolate coast: no doubt the ancient city owed its existence to this
fountain. A mile farther south stands a solitary column on the hill side,
marking the site of a ruined temple and forsaken city. The place is now called
Em el 'Amed (mother of columns), and the remains are extensive, spreading Em el
up the valley—broken columns, prostrate houses, sarcophagi, and rock tombs. 'Amed.
The Wady Hamûl comes down from Alma to the sea at this point, but the
road up it is nearly impracticable, from the dense jungle of bushes, briers, and
ruins which choke this romantic valley. An aqueduct once led the water from
Neba Hamûl to Em el 'Amed, but it has long since been broken. One may
at least start the inquiry whether this may not be the Amad given to Asher
by Joshua.[1]

The coast from this place bends south-west for thirty minutes to Khan en Khan en
Nakûra, east of which is a village of the same name ; and on the shore stands Nakûra.
one of St. Helen's towers, in good preservation, tenanted by flocks below, and
hawks and owls above. From this khan the road lies along the shore westward for a mile, and then rising over Cape en Nakûra, descends deeply to the
sea, where the mountain terminates in bold and picturesque precipices. After
crossing a wady on an old Roman bridge half broken away, the path ascends
by a most villanous track for half an hour, to the ancient tower called Musheirifeh. The entire cape is about seven miles across, and has three distinct promontories : the first, the real Ladder, or Scala Tyrionum, which does not pro- Scala
ject into the sea more than a mile beyond the general line of the coast ; the Tyrionum.
second is Ras en Nakûra ; and the last is Ras el Musheîrifeh, which is the Mushei-
highest of all, and shows boldest toward the sea, and hence has been often con- rifeh.
founded with the true "Scala." This Musheîrifeh, with the noble fountains at
its base of the same name, I am disposed to indentify with the Misrephoth-
maim (waters of Misrephoth), to which that part of the Canaanitish host which Misre-
came from Dor, etc., fled from the battle of Merom ;[2] and I do this, notwith- photh.
standing the contradictory renderings of these words in the margin of our
Bibles, and all other philological criticisms whatsoever. The ancient and
modern names are nearly identical in form, and I believe in signification, and
both were suggested by the bright and glowing colour of those magnificent
cliffs which overhang the sea ; and any one who will study the route which the
division of Jabin's army that came from Dor must have taken to escape
Joshua's troops and reach home, will see that this is the spot where they
would most likely first find a safe and convenient halting-place on the shore.
The difficult pass, commanded by a castle, where the present Burj stands,
would be an effectual barrier against their enemies ; and the plain below, in pos-

[1] Josh. xix. 26.   [2] Josh. xi. 8.

session of Achzîb, which the Jews did not subdue, would afford a delightful place for them to rest and refresh themselves after the fatigues of that disastrous day. Let Musheîrifeh, therefore, stand for Misrephoth.

Below the old castle are picturesque caves, into which the waves tumble with tremendous uproar, and above one of them is a long inscription. I once descended the face of the cliff to the shore, and by creeping along a shelf of the rock several hundred feet long, and not more than six inches wide, I got within a few yards of this inscription. I had tried to reach it by boat several times, but the sea was always too rough. The result of this closer study left me in doubt whether, after all, it was not one of those unaccountable freaks of Nature, whose hand seems occasionally to sketch and scribble on the wild cliffs of the mountains, as if on purpose to puzzle antiquarian savants. If writing it be, there was a surface about fifteen feet square covered with some fifty lines, of the same length originally, but many of them now partially worn away. It is either Cufic of a very large pattern, and somewhat involved, or it is Egyptian hieroglyphics—possibly placed there when the kings of Egypt held Ptolemais, Ibrahim Pasha, the latest Egyptian potentate in possession of Acre, came to this place in a boat with a company of French savants, but neither could they get near enough to make anything out of it. If it is a freak of Nature, it is one of the strangest, and, at any rate, I hope some man of means and leisure will ere long solve the mystery. He should have two boats, with ladders, and means to suspend a scaffolding of some sort or other down the face of the cliff ; and, above all, the day must be absolutely calm.

I found thousands of petrified star-fish mingled in the white rock of the cliffs, like colossal plums in a mountain of pudding. They seemed to be about equally diffused through the entire thickness of the cape. The rock is intensely hard, and white as snow.

From the fountains at the foot of Musheîrifeh it is an hour to Zîb, the modern representative of ancient Achzib,[1] the Ecdippa of Roman geographers. The River Kûrn enters the sea near Zîb. The village stands on a mound, mainly of rubbish ; and it has evident traces of antiquity about it, though it could never have been a large city. The shore opens into small creeks, which afford a partial shelter for boats ; and this was probably the reason for building a city at this point. A grove of palm-trees, sheltering pyramids of bee-hives, will attract attention as the traveller hastens on to join the regular road to Acre at el Mŭzrah, where he will be sure to rest and regale himself with oranges, good water, and fine scenery. He will there have an excellent view of the great aqueduct which conveys water from Kabery to Acre. In half an hour more he will be at the Behajeh, the delightful but dilapidated palace of Abdallah Pasha, which our friend Jimmal has just purchased for sixty thousand piastres. This is two miles from Acre. The whole distance from Tyre is about twenty-eight miles. And now for your story.

Strange inscrip-tion.

Zîb—
Achzib.

---

[1] Josh. xix. 27.

Well, after parting from you at Rumeîsh, we ascended a wady southward, CHAPTER
called Kutamone, for half an hour, to a fountain, with an old castle on the hill ____XXI.____
east of it, all of the same name. The country thereabouts is densely wooded, Kuta-
and extremely beautiful, and, on that morning at least, alive with flocks and mone.
herds under the care of their shepherds. It also abounds, I was told, with
leopards, wolves, wild boars, gazelles, doves, partridges, and almost every
variety of birds found in this country. It was once densely peopled, too; for
Mohammed, who seemed to be perfectly at home there, gave me a long list of
ruins with outlandish names, which I did not venture to write. We climbed
out of Wady Kutamone by a steep path through most charming oak groves,
and immediately descended into another, called Bukra, which united below
with Wady el Kŭrn. From the top of the next ridge we saw a castle called Wady el
Deir, but as it lay out of our line to the west, we did not visit it.   Kŭrn.

I did on one of my trips through that region, and found two villages, in both
of which are remains of antiquity. The full name is Deir el Kasy, to distinguish it from another Deir farther south. The eastern part of the place is
mainly built within an ancient fort, some four hundred feet square, in its present form apparently Saracenic. From thence I descended into Wady el Kŭrn,
down a romantic path some fourteen hundred feet, and then toiled out of it
again to Tarshîha—a feat which took me two hours to accomplish.

We looked into it, and wisely kept round to the east, where it is less profound, and, passing Harfush, came to a considerable place, whose name I
spelled Sehemoita. We now had Tarshîha in a vale to the north-west of us;
and in an hour more we stopped to rest and lunch at Yanoah, which I took to be
very ancient. Descending from thence to the plain, we reached Acre just
before sunset, having been nine hours in the saddle. Thus ends my brief story.

And in good time, for we now commence to climb the mountain to Jiddîn,
whose castle sits proudly above us, as if in defiance of all enemies, and the
nature of the path forbids further conversation. But, before we begin the
ascent, let me call your attention to that village on the left. It is 'Amkah, 'Amkah or
supposed to mark the site of the Emek given to Asher.[1] The radicals are the Emek.
same in both Hebrew and Arabic.

Here we are at last, before the castle of Jiddîn; no great affair after all, and Castle of
far from equalling the promise that beckoned us on from the plain. This is Jiddîn.
owing to its position on the bold swell of the mountain facing the sea, and with
deep wadies on both sides. This modern castle was obviously built on the site
of one more ancient, and was, no doubt, an important place. Dr. Robinson
suggests that this wady may be the Jiphthah-el mentioned by Joshua as
belonging to Asher; but I think this can scarcely be so. Jiphthah-el was
farther south.

The castle need not detain us long. In its present form it was built by
Dahr el 'Amer, who preceded Jezzar Pasha in Acre—about a hundred years

[1] Josh. xix. 27.

PART II.

ago. It is like that of Shem'a, except that here there are more traces of antiquity. It is not easy to see any motive for building a castle at this spot. The position is not strong, and there is neither great road nor village, nor even a fountain of water near it. The view over the plain, however, is most beautiful, and it might have been designed as a sort of health-retreat for the pashas in those days when castles were necessary to safety. Like all other castles in Syria, this has been suffered to fall into decay, and the only inhabitants are these crabbed and sinister Arabs, their flocks, and their dogs. These invite us to be gone, and so does the declining sun, for if we return to Acre by Kabery, we have no time to spare. The path leads down the mountains diagonally toward the north-west, over a wild rocky region for fifty minutes. Such tracts

Waar, yaar, or forest.

are called *waar* by the Arabs, and the same word occurs very often in the Bible, and doubtless it indicates the same sort of country. Thus David, at the instance of the prophet Gad, departed from the hold of Mizpeh of Moab, and came into the "forest" (*yaar* or *waar*) of Hareth.[1] And again: the great battle against Absalom was in the "wood" (*yaar*) of Ephraim; and this yaar devoured more people that day than the sword devoured.[2] These waars are not pleasant, open forests, for the ground is too rocky for that—rocks piled in horrid confusion, and covered with prickly oak and other thorny coppice, which confound the unhappy traveller who gets entangled among them. The natives, when they wish to deter you from attempting a given road, shout in your ear *Waar, waar*, with a harsh, guttural emphasis, which bitter experience has taught me always to respect. Nothing is more impracticable than these stony, thorny waars, and I can readily believe that such a "wood" would devour more of a routed army than the sword of the victors. And now, escaped from our own waar, we descend into this beautiful vale of Kŭzrone which comes rambling down from Tarshîha and M'alia. In the cliffs higher up the country a little animal abounds, called senanûr, a kind of marten, not found anywhere else in Syria, I am told. What rich fields of wheat! and they spread down the widening wady to Kabery yonder on the edge of the

Fountains.

plain. There are two great fountains in the village, one of which is led directly into the aqueduct, and never pauses until it reaches the courts in Acre. The other is elevated in a *birkeh*, like those at Ras el 'Ain, and drives the mills that are built against it. The cluster of hamlets below bears the name of Nahr (river), and abounds in mills, orchards, and vegetable gardens. Near it

Aqueduct.

is seen the line of an ancient aqueduct, covered with immense masses of tufa, which not only proclaim the antiquity of the work, but also inform us that this water, like that at Ras el 'Ain, is far from pure. The people say that this aqueduct was built by Jezzar Pasha, and destroyed by Bonaparte—both incorrect. It was a ruin ages before Jezzar, and Bonaparte never destroyed such works. It can be traced along under Sheikh Daûd and Ghabsîyeh, and thence in a direct line toward Acre. The present aqueduct was made, it is said, by

---

[1] 1 Sam. xxii. 5.   [2] 2 Sam. xviii. 6–8.

Suleîman Pasha, and is therefore not fifty years old. This is doubtful; he perhaps only repaired it. It runs much lower down the plain than the ancient canal. This entire region, both in the plain and on the mountains, is full of ruins, which I once examined, but they are not historically important, so far as is known, and we have no time to devote to them to-day.

The distance from this to Acre is not far from ten miles, and my aneroid gives one hundred and seventy feet as the elevation above the sea—quite sufficient to carry the water over the walls, and to the tops of the highest houses in the city.

We shall return by Bŭssa, and thus take a look into the north-west corner Bussa. of this great plain. It abounds in antiquities beyond most parts even of this land of ruins. We shall find the explanation of these old quarries on the hill above us. This daughter of Jabal says those nearest remains are called Shwoizerîyeh—a very hard word, and apparently foreign.

Why call this curly-headed Bedawy by that name?

The Bible says that Jabal was the father of such as dwell in tents, and of "Father-hood." such as have cattle.[1] Now she dwells in one of those goat-hair tents on the mountain side, and she is tending this drove of poverty-smitten cattle. This Biblical form of expression is very common. Any one who should now invent tents, or the custom of living in tents, would be called the father not only of tents, but also of tent-dwelling; indeed the Arabs call a person distinguished for *any* peculiarity the father of it. Thus, a man with an uncommon beard is named *abu dŭkn*—father of a beard; and I have often heard myself called *abu tangera*—father of a saucepan—because the boys in the street fancied that my hat resembled that black article of kitchen furniture. And now we are among the ruins of Shwoizerîyeh: look closely to your path if you would not plunge headlong into an old cistern. These ancient sites are perfectly honey-combed with them. This entire region above us is covered with ruined sites, among which I have spent days of agreeable excitement, first and last; but there are no names of historic notoriety, and therefore we shall pass them by without notice. We will now cross this Wady el Kŭrn, and ride up to that Tall co-column, which stands like a solitary sentinel of by-gone generations. It has lumn. maintained its lonely watch over the plain for at least two thousand years. The shaft is composed of ten pieces, each three feet thick, and hence it is thirty feet long, standing on a base ten feet high and nine feet square. The entire elevation of this singular column is therefore forty feet, and it is sixteen feet in circumference. Of course it must have had a statue or something else on the top, to give it symmetry, but what that was, and how high, no one can tell; nor when, by whom, or for what it was erected. Those who sought to immortalize their names or deeds by it have utterly failed. This column is now called Hŭmsîn, and also Minawat, from this collection of ruins in its neighbourhood. Scattered over this hill side below the column are the remains

---

[1] Gen. iv. 20.

PART
II.

Extreme
antiquity.

of a large town, but without a name. From this to Bŭssa is a little more than half an hour, but we shall not go any farther than to this very ancient site, called 'Ammarîyeh, from which much of the stone used in building Bŭssa has been quarried. They are at it even now, and you see in this spot a striking proof of extreme antiquity. These men are digging out old foundations many feet deep in the soil, beneath an aged olive-tree which they are undermining. Now these houses were ancient ruins, buried thus deep under rubbish *before* this olive could have been planted, and the tree itself is many hundred years old. There is another very large ruin in the valley east of Bŭssa, called M'asûba, from which marble slabs and sarcophagi are also quarried, some of which have Greek inscriptions. And still farther up the country are other sites of ancient places, which I have examined on former occasions. The path to Alma leads over that rocky mountain to the north-east, and it takes about an hour and a quarter to reach it. But now for Acre; and we shall find ourselves shut out, unless we put our steeds to the gallop, for the gate closes at sun-set, and waits for no man.

How have you spent your time in Acre?

Acre—
few Bib-
lical
notices.

When not confined to the house by rain, I have been searching round the ruins of this famous fortress, and looking into its singular history. I find very few notices of it in the Bible. In Judges i. 31 it is said that Asher did not " drive out the inhabitants of Accho ;" which not only ascertains the fact of its existence at that early age, but also that it belonged to Asher, and was too strong to be subdued by that tribe. It is often mentioned in the apocryphal books under the name of Ptolemais, given to it by Ptolemy Soter; and in Acts xxi. 7, we read that Paul visited it on his way from Tyre to Cæsarea. These are all the Biblical notices I could find.

History.

And they include the whole; but a place so celebrated in general history is worthy of study for its own sake, as well as for the rank it so long held as the chief city on this coast. But it would take a volume to trace out its manifold vicissitudes and various fortunes,—a work we must leave to historians and antiquarians. That extraordinary young man, Hadrian Reland, has culled out of ancient authors nearly everything that has come down to our time about Acre, and you will find it in his "Palestina Illustrata." Perhaps the best modern compend of her history is that of Dr. Kitto, in his "Biblical Cyclopædia." The article on Acre seems to have been written by himself, and, notwithstanding the care and research bestowed upon it, he has fallen into some singular blun-

Errors of
Kitto.

ders. He says that the mountains of Anti-Lebanon are seen at the distance of about four leagues to the north ! North of Acre there is nothing but the sea, and no part of Anti-Lebanon can be seen from it, and if it could, it would be ten leagues instead of four. The bay of Acre *is* about three leagues wide, as he says; but " two leagues in depth" is a very equivocal expression. If he means to measure from the extreme north-western point of the base of Carmel to the mouth of the Kishon, it may be four miles, but at Acre the distance inward is not two. Dr. Kitto is also mistaken in supposing that the vaults mentioned

by Mr. Now were "designed to afford cool underground retreats to the inhabi- CHAPTER
tants during the heat of the day in summer." No such practice is known on XXI.
this coast. The heat does not require it, and the climate is so moist that even
upper rooms, if not constantly ventilated, become quickly covered with mould,
and are unfit to live in. It is true that at Bagdat, Mosul, and other places
along the valley of the Tigris, the houses are constructed with a sort of cellars
called surdab, to which the inhabitants retreat during the day; but then the
air is extremely dry there, and the thermometer ranges thirty degrees higher
than on this coast. In this country, however, castles, and nearly all sorts of
buildings, are erected on large vaults, and these lower apartments in dwelling-
houses are used for *winter*, not for summer. As soon as the heat begins, the
family reopen the upper storey, which has been partially deserted during the
cold months. Such speculations as the above mislead, and should be corrected;
they are in flat contradiction to facts.

Jeremiah speaks of a winter house in which Jehoiakim sat in the ninth The sum-
month, with a fire before him on the hearth;[1] and Amos mentions both winter mer and
and summer houses.[2] Such language is easily understood by an Oriental. In house.
common parlance, the lower apartments are simply *el beit*—the house; the
upper is the *ullîyeh*, which is the summer house. Every respectable dwelling
has both, and they are familiarly called beît *shetawy* and beît *seîfy*—winter
and summer house. If these are on the same storey, then the external and airy
apartment is the summer *house*, and that for winter is the interior and more
sheltered room. It is rare to meet a family that has an entirely separate
dwelling for summer. King Jehoiakim was therefore sitting in one of the
inner apartments of his palace, I suppose, when he cut up Jeremiah's prophetic roll with his penknife, and cast it into the fire.

A host of travellers have spoken of Acre, and such works on the Crusades
as Michaud's six volumes of rather confused annals enter largely into her
fortunes during the Middle Ages. It was the last point surrendered by the Sieges.
Knights of St. John, from whom it took the name of St. Jean d'Acre. They
gave it up to the Sultan of Egypt in A.D. 1291, and thus ended the anomalous
and wonderful kingdom of the Franks in Palestine. During my time it was
besieged for six months by Ibrahim Pasha, and when I visited it soon after he
had taken it, the whole place was a mass of ruins. But he immediately set
about repairing and fortifying it, and continued this work during the whole
time he held possession of Syria. It was blown to pieces by the British fleet
on November 3d, 1840, and again have the walls and castles been repaired
with great industry, and are now stronger, perhaps, than ever. But much of
the interior is in ruins, and will probably remain so, at least until a change of
dynasty brings in better times.

I have been round the fortifications, and estimate their circuit at about two Fortifica-
and a half miles. They seem to me to be skilfully planned, and very sub- tions.

---

[1] Jer. xxxvi. 22.   [2] Amos iii. 15.

PART
II.

stantial; but as any number of ships can bring their cannon to bear upon it, the guns on the walls can be silenced at once by overwhelming odds. This was done by Stopford and Napier in 1840. The number of pieces of all sorts is nearly 400, but most of them are of a very inferior character, and the carriages are old and rickety. They would be of very little service in actual combat. On a very large bronze cannon, commanding the harbour, is this somewhat satirical motto: "Ultima ratio regum." Alas! when they begin their "last argument," angels weep, Death on his pale horse goes forth to slay, and hell follows after to devour. The fortifications on the land side are almost concealed by admirably-constructed glacis without and beyond the deep ditch which runs round the wall. The piercings for cannon are so placed as to sweep every approach; and if Ibrahim Pasha had been permitted to complete the fosse, by which he intended to make Acre an island, by joining the sea from the north-west of the city to the bay at the south-east of it, the defences would have been nearly impregnable. The distance across is small, as the sea comes round the

Only a
military
place.

north-west corner for a considerable part of the way. In fact, Acre has the bay on the south-east and south, and the sea on the west and north-west; a position well adapted for a strong fort, which has always been its distinguishing characteristic, and is so now. It has no source of life or prosperity but what is dependent on its military occupation, and its manners and municipal regulations are governed by the rigid laws of war. There is but one gate on the land side, skilfully placed at the water's edge on the south-east angle and strongly defended. A sea gate leads to the shipping in the harbour; and both are shut at sunset. To one coming toward Acre across the plain, its surface seems considerably elevated above the general level, and the appearance is rather imposing. This elevation is owing to the accumulation of rubbish during its long life of wars, desolations, and reconstructions. The modern city, with all its works, stands on the ruins of many generations.

Environs.

At the summer palace of Abdallah Pasha, called el Behajeh, are some gardens and olive groves. A few palms and other trees are seen at Tell el Fakhar, a short distance south-east of the gate, and some fruit orchards and vegetable gardens are cultivated along the low banks of the Naamany. Otherwise the surroundings of Acre are very naked and uninteresting. It was not always so, even in modern times, if we are to believe the travellers who have spoken of it. Three things act together to keep down Acre: its military character, the unhealthiness of the climate, and the shallowness and insecurity

Khaifa a
rival.

of the harbour. Khaifa is, to a great degree, free from these drawbacks, and will probably lead away nearly all the trade from Acre. Indeed, it has done this already, and the merchants who reside in Acre are obliged to have their houses for business in Khaifa.

In the distribution of the land made by Joshua, Acre was given to Asher. Can you draw the boundary of this tribe with any degree of certainty?

Not at all. It had Carmel, which seems to have belonged, in part at least, to Zebulun, on the south, Naphtali on the east, and the sea-board on the west.

But we must leave a large uncertain margin between what we know belonged to Naphtali, and what was certainly the territory of Asher. And so also Asher and Zebulun met in the valley of Jiphthah-el, which may have been this wady of the Kishon ; but this is quite uncertain.

The reason why the boundaries of the different tribes were so eccentric originally, and are now so difficult to follow, was, that the "lots" were not meted out according to geographical lines, but lands of certain cities lying more or less contiguous were assigned to each tribe as its inheritance. These cities were the capitals of small principalities or districts, just as Tibnin, and Hŭnin, and Bint Jebail, etc., are now. The territory of one might extend far to the east of the city, that of the next to the west, etc. Suppose two such cities on the eastern border of Asher, for example : the line might lie along the edge of the plain of Acre, and thus include all the land belonging to the first, and then it must be drawn eastward far up the mountains in a most eccentric compass to embrace all the territory appertaining to the next, and so on throughout. Thus it is possible that Câbûl, and 'Umka, and Cosa, and Kanah, all lay along the eastern border of Asher. And thus it would happen that a village on the border of the plain would belong to Naphtali, and the next one, far east and on the mountains, to Asher. The coast was in the hands of Acre, Achzib, Tyre, and Sidon, which the Asherites could never conquer. There remains, therefore, generally the hills sloping toward the sea, with so much of the plains as they could subdue. Josephus is even more indefinite than Joshua. He says, " The tribe of Aser had that part which was called the *valley,* for *such it was,* and all that part which lay over against Sidon. The city Aser belonged to their share, which is also named Actipus." Now there *is* no valley to correspond to this description. The *plain* of Acre is full twenty miles long, and the upper part of this, with the eastern hills, we know formed a large part of Asher's "lot." But a plain is not a valley. Farther north they doubtless possessed the great promontory called the Ladder of Tyre, which is about a thousand feet high and eight miles across, and was crowded with towns and cities as it is now with ruins. Still farther on, in the same direction, they had what is called Sahil Kanah—the *plain* of Kanah—including the hills and the eastern margin of the plain of Tyre to the River Kasimîeh, in length about sixteen miles, and in breadth probably not more than eight. If they crossed the Kasimîeh so as to possess the parts over against Sidon, as Josephus says, then they had the hill country now called Shumar, and parts of the districts of Shukîf and Tiffah, above Sidon. This would give a length of not less than sixty miles, with a mean breadth of ten or twelve, but it is in no proper sense a valley.

Josephus was probably acquainted personally with only that part of Asher which extended along the east side of the plain of Acre, terminating at the sea near Burj el Musheîrifeh. This tract, seen from the neighbouring heights of Galilee, would look like a valley, for a line of low sand hills begins in front of Acre at Tell el Fakhar, and runs parallel to the coast northward to Nahr el

PART
II.

Kŭrn, in the vicinity of Zîb. The plain between this and the hills of Galilee formed a valuable part of Asher's "lot," and might have been called a valley. These remarks about boundaries may suffice once for all. It is now absolutely impossible to draw lines around the separate lots with any degree of certainty. Their general positions with relation to each other, however, can be ascertained with sufficient exactness for all important purposes in the study of Biblical geography.

Zebulun.

I have one more inquiry before you drop the subject. The sea-board from Acre to Sidon belonged to Asher, and the lot of Zebulun extended eastward toward Tabor. Now, how do you reconcile this with the prophecy of Jacob in Genesis xlix. 13: "Zebulun shall dwell at the haven of the sea, and he shall be for a haven of ships, *and his border shall be unto Zidon?*"

A Scripture difficulty.

There is, in fact, an apparent contradiction here between prophecy and history which I have not seen explained, or even noticed by ordinary commentators. That the territory of Zebulun did not reach to the *city* of Sidon is certain. Perhaps the following considerations may reconcile the prophecy of the dying patriarch with the subsequent history and home of Zebulun: *In the time of Jacob,* and at the distance of Egypt, Zidon was the representative of all Phœnicia. She was, in fact, the mother of that people, and was so spoken of by Homer several hundred years after the death of Jacob. Homer does not speak of Achzib, or Acre, or Dor, but only of Zidon, when he has occasion to mention this country. But Phœnicia, or *Sidonia* if you please, extended south of *Acre,* and Zebulun bordered on the sea for a considerable distance along that part of the coast; Jacob, therefore, spoke according to the received geography of his time, but with prophetic brevity mentioned only the parent city. When, however, Joshua, several hundred years later, came to divide the country between the tribes, it became necessary to specify the subordinate places, and no doubt some of the cities south of Sidon had by that time risen to importance, and might well give name to the coast in their vicinity; at all events, Joshua was obliged to mention them in defining the limits of the tribes. Hence, though Zebulun touched the sea far south of the city of Sidon, yet "his haven of ships" was actually a part of the general coast of Sidonia when Jacob gave forth his prophecy. Nor is it at all improbable that the *territory* of Sidon did originally extend southward to where Zebulun had his border at the sea, thus meeting the very letter of the promise.

CHAPTER XXII.

NEIGHBOURHOOD OF ACRE.

March 13th.

Our friends accompany us to Khaifa and Carmel this morning, and we may anticipate a pleasant ride round the head of this bay.

What dark and sluggish stream is this we are approaching?

It is the Nahr Naaman—the Belus, which Pliny says has its origin in a *River* lake called Cendevia. He speaks of its insalubrity, and no doubt the fevers *Belus.* which afflict Acre have their origin in the marshes of this stream. It rises below Shefa 'Amr in large fountains, now called Kurdany, which drive a number of mills. This Kurdany is doubtless Pliny's Cendevia. It is, in fact, a large marsh, called a lake by the same sort of courtesy that dignifies this brook with the name of river. The evil qualities of the water, and also its dark colour, are derived from the marshes at the head of it. I came near being swamped in its fathomless depths of mire. The *lake* is *made*, like that of Hums on the Orontes, by a strong and ancient dam across the lower end of the marshes. The whole area may be three miles in circuit, and the *river* at the mills is quite as large as here at the sea. The entire length is not more than six miles. It is pleasant to be able to confirm the statement of Pliny about this lake, for its existence has been denied by modern travellers.

Pliny repeats the story about the discovery of glass by sailors cooking their dinner on the sand at the mouth of this river. What have you to say to that?

When descending from Yerka to Acre several years ago, I noticed that the *Discover-* rock for many miles had a vitreous appearance, as if it had actually been *of glass.* *smelted* in some grand furnace of nature, and needed only to be melted over again and refined to make it genuine glass. The idea occurred to me at the time, that the disintegration of this vitreous rock might have furnished the glassy particles in the bed of the Belus and other brooks which fall into the sea along this part of the coast, and which first led to the discovery of glass; or, if these sailors supported their sauce-pans on pieces of rock placed round the fire, they might have melted so as to give the first hint which led to the discovery. The story may therefore have some foundation in fact.

PART
II.

Bay of
Acre.

Robbers.

Ship-
wrecks.

Their
cause.

This sandy beach, so smooth and solid, is one of the finest places in the world for a gallop, and there is always something exhilarating in a ride round the head of this bay. The city behind ; Carmel, with its holy traditions, in front ; the long reach of perfectly level shore, with men and animals diminishing in the distance either way down to the size of kittens ; the broad bay opening out upon the boundless sea, with its boats and ships ; these sandy downs, with feathery reeds running far inland, the chosen retreat of wild boars and wild Arabs,—all combine to excite the mind and enliven the spirits.

Then there is just enough of insecurity to keep the imagination in full play. The Arab robber lurks like a wolf among these sand-heaps, and often springs out suddenly upon the solitary traveller, robs him in a trice, and then plunges again into the wilderness of sand-hills and reedy downs, where pursuit is fruitless. Our friends are careful not to allow us to straggle about or lag behind ; and yet it seems absurd to fear a surprise here—Khaifa before, Acre in the rear, and travellers in sight on both sides. Robberies, however, do often occur, just where we now are. Strange country ! and it has always been so. There are a hundred allusions to just such things in the history, the Psalms, and the prophets of Israel. A whole class of imagery is based upon them. Thus, in Psalm x. 8–10 : " He sitteth in the lurking-places of the villages : in the secret places doth he murder the innocent. He lieth in wait secretly as a lion in his den : he lieth in wait to catch the poor : he doth catch the poor, when he draweth him into his net. He croucheth, and humbleth himself, that the poor may fall by his strong ones." And a thousand rascals, the living originals of this picture, are this day crouching and lying in wait all over the country to catch poor helpless travellers. You observe that all these people we meet or pass are armed ; nor would they venture to go from Acre to Khaifa without their musket, although the cannon of the castles seem to command every foot of the way. Strange, most strange land ! but it tallies wonderfully with its ancient story.

I see many wrecks of ships along this shore, and here are two not yet buried beneath the sand. They have been cast away by this last storm. To what do you attribute the insecurity of this anchorage ?

I have heard captains complain that there is something—either harsh seaweed or sharp rocks—which corrodes the cables. Others say that the bottom is not good and the anchor drags. My own opinion is, that the real cause of so many disasters is found in the nature of the shore and of the interior.

The high ridge of Carmel runs far down south-east, and between it and the mountains of Galilee on the north there is a narrow opening into the great plain of Esdraelon. Owing to this physical formation, the west sea wind is drawn inward with tremendous violence, and any accident happening to a ship's cable or anchor, she must inevitably come right on shore. There is no possibility of working out to sea. And although the headland from Carmel juts far into the bay to the north-west, yet the direction of the low flats of the Kishon along the base of the mountain draws the gales round this point into the bay, and they sweep down past the town of Khaifa toward the south-east with awful violence. The roadstead is wholly insecure in a gale from the west, and still more so during one from any intervening point between that and the north. You need not wonder, therefore, at the wrecks strewn along the shore, nor at the vast extent of these sandy downs, which stretch inland farther than we can see.

Here we have a confirmation of that proverb of our Lord, "Wheresoever the carcase is, there will the eagles be gathered together." [1]

Are those huge birds eagles?

Not all. Those smaller ones, of a dull white and yellow colour, are a species of vulture; they are a more gross and a much tamer bird. The eagles, you observe, have all retired to the tops of those sand-heaps, while the vultures only hop a little way up the beach as we approach.

Eagles and carcass.

EAGLES.

I did not know there were so many eagles in all this country. They must have gathered together from a great distance. And what "carcase" is this that has assembled such a congregation on the sea-beach?

[1] Matt. xxiv. 28.

Nothing but an immense turtle which the storm threw out on the shore.
You observe that his old back is covered with large and very strong barnacles,
of a species which I find only on these turtles. Do you notice that these eagles
have no feathers on the head and upper part of the neck ?

This reminds me of the advice of Micah to the houses of Achzîb back
yonder on this very shore : " Make thee bald, and poll thee for thy delicate
children ; enlarge thy baldness as the eagle." [1] They are a hideous-looking
bird.

But here we are at the Mukŭtta, as that " ancient river," the Kishon, is
now called. It is somewhat curious that both Kishon and Kŭtta are mentioned
by Joshua as *cities* in this neighbourhood; the one is the ancient Hebrew, and
the other the modern Arabic name of the *river*. You would scarcely suppose,
from the depth of the current, that one may pass along the beach three months
hence and find no river at all ; and yet so my experience proves. The first
time I came this way I crossed the Kishon in a boat, and swam the horses ;
the next time there was no river, not even a rill to be found. This is explained
by referring back to the *inward* winds I have spoken of. These ever drive the
waves, loaded with sand, up against the mouth of the river, and, as soon as
the dry season reduces its volume, the waves overcome it, and a large sand-
bank dams up the stream ; the river then spreads out into a large marsh, and
slowly percolates through the sand, and thus finds its way to the sea. It is
strong enough now, however, and if we watch not our opportunity and choose
our path wisely, following the sand-bank at its mouth, we shall fare badly
between it and the waves, which come rolling in to swell its dimensions.
Safely over, let me call your attention to this singular delta, with its apex at
the junction of the river with the sea, and its base resting against the foot of
Carmel. It is planted with picturesque and solemn palm-trees, the finest
grove of the kind in Syria.

Khaifa has much improved since my first visit twenty-three years ago ; and,
as the steamers between Beirût and Jaffa touch here, it must increase up to
a certain point ; but the natural advantages with reference to the interior are
not great, and it will never become a large city, unless a railroad from the east
should terminate at it ; then, indeed, it would speedily expand into a vast
emporium. This may be, the Sycamenon mentioned by Greek and Roman
geographers, though the distance from that place to Acre, according to the
Itineraries, was at least twice as great as from Acre to Khaifa. We have no
occasion to stop here, for there are no antiquities about it except rock tombs,
and our object is to visit the convent on the mountain. It will take us forty
minutes to climb it; but the view, widening as you ascend, and ever changing,
will richly repay any amount of toil ; and at the convent we shall rest and
refresh ourselves at the refectory of these Carmelite monks. The establishment
is, indeed, quite as much a hotel as a house of prayer.

---

[1] Micah i. 16.

Having now satisfied our curiosity and our appetites, we may pay our bill, and leave to others more in love with such matters the task of describing this great castle-convent, with its twenty monks chanting Latin to nobody, around holy places whose history is fabulous.

Our friend Scander has unconsciously exhibited an illustration of Isaiah xxii. 22, which struck me very forcibly : " And the key of the house of David *A key laid on a shoulder.* will I lay upon his shoulder : so he shall open, and none shall shut ; and he shall shut, and none shall open." The key with which Scander opened his magazine was large enough for a stout club, and it might well be laid on his shoulder.

True ; and I have seen keys more than twice as large. The material "house of David" was the stronghold of Zion, and such castles now have enormous wooden locks, with keys in proportion. I once spent a summer in an old castle whose great outer door had a lock and key which were almost a load to carry. This kind of lock is no doubt very ancient. Their construction is such that a false key can scarcely by any possible chance fit them, and the difficulty is increased in proportion to the number and eccentric position of the *wards* into which the movable metal drops are required to fall. The following cut will exhibit its nature more clearly than any amount of description can do.

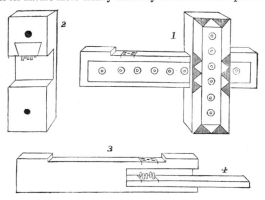

LOCK AND KEY.

These locks are placed on the *inside* of the doors of gardens and outer courts, *Door keys.* and even on those of inner rooms in some places. To enable the owner to unlock them, a *hole* is cut in the door, through which he thrusts his arm and inserts the key. All the garden doors about Sidon are thus arranged, and such must have been the custom at Jerusalem in the days of Solomon. In Song v. 4, he makes the bride say, " My beloved put in his hand by the hole of the door,"—that is, she saw him thrust in his hand to unlock the door, that he might enter. Solomon well knew the perturbations and delightful agitations of love; and a much more trivial thing than the hand of the beloved, and a much less significant action than the one here mentioned, will start the heart leaping and fluttering in irrepressible ecstasy. But it is time to return, lest Acre's inexorable gate be locked against us, and there is neither hole in it through which we can thrust our hand, nor wakeful heart on the other side to be "moved" by it if we could.

March 14*th*. Our ride to Shefa 'Amer to-day will complete the survey of this vast plain of Acre to the borders of Zebulun.

Almond-
tree.
As there is nothing special to claim attention in this part of the plain, let me ask an explanation of several passages of the Bible which I have marked in my Bible readings at Acre. But first tell me what tree is this on our right, dressed out in white blossoms so early in the season?

ALMOND-TREE.

That is the almond. It often blossoms in February, and this early activity is repeatedly alluded to in the Bible. Jeremiah opens his heavy
Early
blossom-
ing.
visions thus: "The word of the Lord came unto me, saying, Jeremiah, what seest thou? and I said, I see the rod of an almond-tree. Then said the Lord, Thou hast well seen, for I will *hasten* my word to perform it"—just as this tree hastens to bud and blossom long before any other has be-

gun to wake out of the repose of winter, and before it has put forth its own
leaves.

The same thing is implied, according to the general economy of miracles, in
the selection of rods from this tree by Moses to be laid up in the tabernacle, in
order to settle the controversy in regard to the family that should be clothed
with the priestly office: "And it came to pass, that on the morrow Moses went
into the tabernacle of witness; and, behold, the rod of Aaron, for the house of
Levi, was budded, and brought forth buds, and bloomed blossoms, and yielded
almonds."[1] This was miraculous rapidity certainly; but a rod was selected
for the purpose from that tree which, in its natural development, is the most
expeditious of all; and not only do the blossoms appear on it suddenly, but
the fruit *sets at once,* and *appears even while the flowers are yet on the tree,*
buds, blossoms, and almonds together on the same branch, as on this rod of
Moses.

In that affecting picture of the rapid and inevitable approach of old age
drawn by the royal preacher, it is said that "the almond-tree shall flourish" or
blossom.[2] The *point* of the figure is doubtless the fact that the *white* blossoms
completely cover the whole tree, without any mixture of green leaves, for these
do not appear until some time after. It is the expressive type of old age,
whose hair is white as wool, unrelieved with any other colour.

And now my texts: What do you understand by such expressions as, "He
drinketh up scorning like water ?"[3]

This idiom is very common in Arabic. It seems natural to the Oriental
mind to conceive of many operations under the idea of *eating* and *drinking,*
which we connect more directly with some other sense than that of taste, or
else mention abstractly. Thus they very commonly speak of *eating* a great
rain when they have been thoroughly drenched in a shower; so also they eat a
violent wind and a piercing cold. I frequently hear them say of one who has
been *bastinadoed* on the soles of his feet, that he has *eaten* fifty or five hundred
sticks, as the case may be. In like manner, they drink many strange potions.
In their self-conceit, they will offer to drink the whole course of scientific
education in three months. Persons not particularly encumbered with modesty
have assured me that they could drink the entire system of evangelical religion
with even greater expedition. There are many similar expressions in the Bible
which may claim our attention hereafter; at present let us turn up to that fine
Tell, from whose summit we shall enjoy a good view of this celebrated plain.
It is called Kezan, and was once a place of importance and strongly fortified.
These broken columns show that it was also adorned with superb temples and
other large edifices; but how utter the desolation that has laid these proud
towers in the dust! It cannot be less than half a mile in circuit and a hundred
feet high, after the degradation of many generations. There is one equally
large farther north, called Birweh, and others even larger to the south. From

---

[1] Num. xvii. 8.　　　　[2] Eccles. xii. 5.　　　　[3] Job xxxiv. 7.

PART
II.

the situation of these once fortified Tells, I suppose they were originally erected to command the passes into the interior. This is on the regular road to Nazareth. Tell Birweh is at the entrance into the district of Shaghûr, and Tells Daûk and Haruthîeh shut up the highway into the great plain of Esdraelon. They may have been held sometimes by the Gentiles of the sea-coast, and at others by the Jews of Galilee, or both may have held such castles at the same time, to watch each other.

Landscapes like this can never lose their charm, and the memory of this one will not be displaced by others, be they ever so grand or striking.

Plain of
Acre.

Flowers.

Birds.

We have made a long detour, not merely to see this tell, but also to escape the mud, for at this season a large part of the plain is wet and marshy. We must now hasten on to Shefa 'Amer. What an infinite array of flowers, fragrant and gay, adorn the plain! The anemones, and fiery poppies, and elegant orchises are specially conspicuous; and the humbler but sweeter hyacinths perfume the air with their spicy odours. The birds, too, are merry and musical as spring and love can make them. "Every prospect pleases, and only man is vile." There is something peculiarly sinister in the looks and ways of these peasants, and from this southward they bear a worse character than those of Lebanon. One reason no doubt is, that they are more oppressed by government, by wild Arabs, and by those who farm the country. These latter extort from them nearly all the produce of their lands in return for the doubtful advantage of having them stand between them and the officers of government. To secure this, they give these remorseless farmers of the revenue, thirty, forty, and even fifty per cent. on money thus advanced on their account. This kind of extortion has long cursed the country, for we find many allusions to it in the Bible. The *farmer* of a village has great powers accorded to him by contract, and enforced by government; he is, in fact, a petty tyrant, who takes *all* if he cannot otherwise get back what he has spent, and the iniquitous interest also. It is not strange, therefore, that these poor peasants, long subjected to such oppression, are a crabbed, ill-conditioned, and dishonest race. Treated without respect or mercy themselves, they are cruel to every body and thing under their power.

Tax-
gatherers.

This system of tax-gatherers greatly multiplies the petty lords and tyrants, who eat up the people as they eat bread. And something of the same sort has always been known in the East. Solomon says, "For the transgression of a land many are the princes thereof." [1]   And the Arabs have a current anecdote of a wise man who used this imprecation upon his enemies: "Allah kether mesheîkh kûm"—"May God multiply your sheikhs"—a fearful malediction! No more certain or expeditious plan to ruin one's enemies could be devised. The people familiarly ascribe such a calamity to the greatness of their sins. The multiplication of these lazy, licentious, and greedy rulers is, indeed, a sore visitation of God. One must have long and very closely observed the working

---

[1] Prov. xxviii. 2

of this mischief before he can even dream of the numberless ways in which CHAPTER
these bad men corrupt, oppress, and ruin the people. Though the proverbs of XXII.
the wise king and the wise Arab are identical in meaning, it is not probable
that the latter borrowed from the former. Experience and observation of the
same calamity originated the identity of thought. And the very next proverb
of Solomon repeats almost the same idea: "A poor man that oppresseth the "A sweep-
poor is like a sweeping rain, which leaveth no food."[1] The illustrative com- ing rain."
parison here is most impressive. It is founded upon a phenomenon which I
have frequently seen, and sometimes felt. A small black cloud traverses the
sky in the latter part of summer or the beginning of autumn, and pours down
a flood of rain that sweeps all before it. The Arabs call it *sale;* we, a water-
spout, or the bursting of a cloud. In the neighbourhood of Hermon I have
witnessed it repeatedly, and was caught in one last year which in five minutes
flooded the whole mountain side, washed away the fallen olives—the food of
the poor—overthrew stone walls, tore up by the roots large trees, and carried
off whatever the tumultuous torrents encountered, as they leaped madly down
from terrace to terrace in noisy cascades. Every summer threshing-floor along
the line of its march was swept bare of all precious food, cattle were drowned,
flocks disappeared, and the mills along the streams were ruined in half-an-hour
by this sudden deluge. Wherever it came it "left no food behind it." And
such is the oppression of a poor man that oppresseth the poor. These land-
lords, and sheikhs, and begs, and emirs, are generally poor, hungry, greedy,
remorseless, and they come in successive swarms, each more ravenous than
his predecessor. On a gigantic scale, every hungry pasha from the capital is
such a *sale*, sweeping over the distant provinces of the empire. Vast regions,
formerly covered with golden harvests in their season, and swarming with
people full of food and gladness, are now reduced to frightful deserts by their
rapacity.

The people of this country have an intense hatred of usury and the usurer, Hatred of
possibly connected with these farmers and their unrighteous exactions. But usury.
the mere *taking of interest*, and not the *rate*, is regarded as a sin by most
people. It is prohibited altogether by Mohammed, who seems to have understood the Mosaic precepts in this strict and literal sense, as, indeed, nearly
all Oriental Christians do. We read in Exodus xxii. 25, 26, 27, "If thou
lend money to any of my people that is poor by thee, thou shalt not be to him
as an usurer, neither shalt thou lay upon him usury. If thou at all take thy
neighbour's raiment to pledge, thou shalt deliver it unto him by that the sun
goeth down: for that is his covering only; it is his raiment for his skin:
wherein shall he sleep?" But, notwithstanding this abhorrence of both the
deed and the doer, nothing is more common. Everybody borrows who can, all
lend money who have it, and the *rate* is enormous. Twenty-five per cent. is
common. I have known fifty, sixty, and even a hundred per cent. asked and

---

[1] Prov. xxviii. 3.

21

PART
II.

given. The taking of pledges, even "from the poor," is equally common; but I never knew them to be restored "by that the sun goeth down," though for the *very* poor, who sleep in their *'aba* or outer garment, and have no other "raiment for their skin," it would be a very humane requisition. During the day, the poor, while at work, can and do dispense with this outside raiment, but at night it is greatly needed, even in the summer. The people in this country never sleep without being covered, even in the day-time; and in this, experience has made them wise, for it is dangerous to health. This furnishes a good reason why this sort of pledge should be restored before night; and I

Pledges
or pawns.

could wish that the law were still in force. In Deut. xxiv. 10-13 we have these precepts repeated, with some additions, as, "Thou shalt not sleep with his pledge;" also, "Thou shalt not go into his house to fetch his pledge. Thou shalt stand abroad, and the man to whom thou dost lend shall bring out the pledge abroad unto thee." A most kind and admirable precept, given to secure the poor man from having the privacy of his family rudely violated by these remorseless usurers. The strict laws regulating Oriental intercourse sufficiently guard the harems of all but the very poor. When the money-gatherer goes to any respectable house, he never rudely enters, but stands "abroad" and calls, and the owner comes forth to meet him, and, if convenient—if there are no women in the way—he is invited in. The divine law here throws its shield over the poor debtor's habitation, and protects his family from insolent intrusion, a thing intolerably humiliating in the East.

Ox-goad.

No wonder that people oppressed and robbed as these peasants are, become dishonest and cruel, and even vent their pent-up rage on everything under their control. Observe that ploughman armed with his long goad, with which he belabours and pricks his tiny oxen, as if it afforded peculiar pleasure to torment them.

Shamgar.

I have examined this implement of husbandry with much curiosity, and no longer wonder that Shamgar could convert it into a destructive weapon of war. His was, no doubt, very large,—made so purposely in those days when the Jews were not allowed to provide arms for defence. A strong pole ten feet long, with a sharp *chisel* at the butt end, would be a formidable spear, wielded by the strong arm of the son of Anath. But he must have been a giant, to kill six hundred Philistines with such a weapon, or, indeed, with any other.

Scripture
allusions.

This goad is an indispensable accompaniment of the plough. The upper end, with its pointed prick, serves instead of rein and lash to guide and urge on the lazy ox; and the other end with its chisel, as you call it, is used to clean off the share from earth and weeds, and to cut the roots and thorns that catch or choke the plough. It was to sharpen this part of the goads that the Philistines permitted the Jews to have a *file* in the early days of Saul.[1] The references to the goad in the Bible are numerous and interesting. Solomon says that "the words of the wise are as goads"[2] to guide and keep in the right path (or fur-

---

[1] 1 Sam. xiii. 21.   [2] Eccles. xii. 11.

row), and to stimulate the indolent to exertion. Our Lord, in his address to
Saul, says, " It is hard for thee to kick against the pricks "—a proverbial
expression, taken from the action of an unruly ox, which, when pricked by the
goads, kicks back in anger, and thus wounds himself more deeply. Commentators on this passage have collected many examples of the use of this exact
figure by classic authors. Thus Euripides says, " I, who am a frail mortal,
should rather sacrifice to him who is a god, than, by giving place to anger, *kick
against the goads.*" And so Terence : " These things have come to my recollection, for it is foolishness for thee to kick *against a goad.*" The proverb is
exceedingly expressive, and one which conveys to all the world where the goad
is known a most important lesson. The particular force of the expression is
unhappily lost by our translation. It is folly, certainly, to kick even a stone
against which one may have dashed his foot, and still more so to do this against
thorns that may have pierced us. But there is a deeper lesson in this proverb.
The ox kicks back against the goad with which he has been intentionally
pricked in order to bring him into the right path, or to prompt him to the
necessary activity, just as that ploughboy is constantly guiding and stimulating
his team. To kick back, therefore, is not merely impotent and injurious folly,
but it is *rebellion against him who guides.* This is the precise lesson which
our Lord intended to teach, and which heathen poets and moralists have drawn
from the proverb, or rather from the basis in agricultural life which suggested it.

But our journey lags, and we shall need the goad ourselves to remind us
that pleasant discourse will never bring us to Shefa 'Amer. It has an imposing appearance, with its large castle and houses of white stone.

Is there any mention of this place in the Bible ?

None that I know of ; nor has it yet been identified with any historic name.
In old Arabic authors it is written Shefr-am, and this looks like that Kefraim
which Eusebius says was six miles north of Legio. May it not also mark the
site of that Haphraim which was assigned to Issachar ?[1] If it was none of these,
then I know nothing about its history. The remains of an old church, and
those of some other buildings near it, indicate both antiquity and importance,
and so do the tombs in the rocks. The situation is conspicuous, and the surrounding country delightful. The inhabitants may number two thousand—a
mingled population of Druses, Moslems, Jews, and Christians, who not only
farm these hills and valleys, but trade with other towns, and with the Arab
tribes of the Desert. This oak wood extends northward beyond the district
of Shaghûr, and southward to the plain of Sharon, and is one of the largest
forests in the country. It also abounds in ancient sites,—Beit Lahm, Yafa,
Semmûnia, and many others, which we may visit hereafter. At present we
must return to Acre.

These days of bright warm weather have wakened up the instinct of the

---

[1] Josh. xix. 19.

Wild
geese.
wild geese, and prompted them to set out rather early on their annual migration to the north. Milton introduces this custom of certain birds in that
divine conversation on the creation, book seven :—

> ' The eagle and the stork
> On cliffs and cedar-tops their eyries build.
> Part loosely wing the region ; part more wise,
> In common, ranged in figure, *wedge* their way,
> Intelligent of seasons--
> 　　　　With mutual wing
> Easing their flight . . . . the air
> Floats as they pass, fanned with unnumber'd plumes."

Migration
of birds.
This is natural, beautiful, and even accurate. The eagles still on cliffs their
eyries build, and storks on cedar-tops ; and in their migrations, the storks
loosely wing the region, as you saw this morning in that immense disorderly
caravan that passed over Acre, going to tempt the frozen north quite too
early in the season ; and here these noisy geese, more wise, ranged in figure,
wedge their way. These migrations always interest me, particularly those of
Storks.
the storks. They come in countless flocks; the air floats as they pass, fanned
by unnumbered plumes. But that they or any other birds ease their flight
with *mutual* wing, is more than I am prepared to believe. As to the stork,
concerning which the tale is generally told, it is simply impossible. They are
a strange bird, however, as any one can learn by looking into their history.
A far-
travelled
stork.
They take a prodigious range in their migrations. In the year 1846, a stork,
becoming weary on its return from the distant south, alighted on that mountain near Safed, and was captured. Great was the astonishment of the captors
to find a silver locket suspended round its neck. They took it to the governor,
and he sent it to the Pasha of Acre, who forwarded the locket to our consul
in Beirût. It contained a letter from Octavia, a young countess of Gotzen, in
Germany, to the effect that this stork had for several years built its nest on an
old turret of her castle; that this year the turret fell and injured the bird. She
had it kindly cared for, and, when well enough to follow its companions, let it
go, with the locket on its neck. The enclosed letter contained a request that
whoever found the bird or the locket should send the writer word at any cost,
as she had a great curiosity to trace it in its wanderings. The consul wrote
to the young lady, giving all the particulars ; for which, in due time, he received a handsome acknowledgment. All this is simple fact, of which I
myself was cognizant. The poor stork died, and perhaps it had never recovered
entirely from its misfortune at Octavia's castle, and this compelled it to halt at
Safed, where it was captured. These singular birds do not breed in Syria, but
pass over it to Asia Minor, and into North-western Europe, where they not
only build in fir or pine trees upon the mountains, but also enter cities and
villages, and make their nests on houses, castles, and minarets. I saw multitudes of them in Brusa, which, indeed, seemed to be a favourite resort. Many
stories are told in regard to their intelligence, their partiality to Moslem
towns, where they are held sacred ; and also about their fidelity, kindness to

the old, the sick, etc. Take the following anecdote for a specimen: A stork built on a house in or near Brusa, and the owner put the egg of a duck in the nest. Great was the consternation and indignation of all storkhood in the place when the unknown duck was hatched. They assembled in noisy conclave round the nest, and, after a boisterous debate, not only the duckling was condemned to death, but the poor female stork also was torn to pieces by the other members of the community. I give the story as I heard it, without vouching for its truth. It is certain, however, that they are very strict, and even jealous in their domestic habits. It is also true

STORK.

that they are partial to the Moslem villages; indeed, they are themselves a sort of Moslems more ways than merely in their annual pilgrimages

PART II.

Habits of the stork.

towards Mecca. They are a solemn, austere bird ; stand for hours in one position, as if immersed in deep meditation, and do not hesitate to strike their sharp bill into any thing or person that disturbs them. They are of a dull white colour, with blackish feathers in various parts, have a slender body perched on tall legs, and a sharp bill at the end of a long neck, adapting them to wade in reedy marshes, and dive to the bottom to seize their prey. They live on frogs, mice, lizards, snakes, and all kinds of reptiles, which they seize with the rapidity of lightning. Owing to their diet, their flesh is coarse and unsavoury, and it was no great loss to the Jews to have it forbidden, as it is in Leviticus xi. 19, and Deuteronomy xiv. 18. The Druses, however, and some few others, do eat it, but by the great majority of the country it is rejected. The habits of this bird were known to David, who taught Milton

Nests on cedar-tops.

that it built its eyries in "cedar-tops."[1] And Jeremiah says, "The stork in the heaven knoweth her appointed times, and so do the turtle, and the crane, and the swallow;"[2] and this is still true. But these birds, "intelligent of seasons," have no settled calendar, and are very liable to be deceived by early warm weather. The poor little swallows were chattering about some days ago, and they will certainly find that they are quite too early.

Flight of the hawk.

While on the subject of birds and their migrations, let me inquire to what particular thing the author of Job refers when he asks, "Doth the hawk fly by thy wisdom, and *stretch her wings toward the south ?*"[3] I suppose this variety of hawk migrates like other birds ; but why particularize only their return *south*, and not their going to the north ?

There is a very singular reason for it. I have often seen them *returning* south during the latter part of September, but never saw them migrating northward. I can only account for this by supposing that in going they straggle along in single pairs, and at no particular time, or else by some distant interior route, but that when their young are grown they come back southward in flocks ; but even then they do not fly in groups, as do cranes, geese, and storks, but keep passing for days in straggling lines, like scattered ranks of a routed army. Here and there, as far as eye can reach, they come, flying every one apart, but *all going steadily to the south*. Job therefore states the fact just as he had seen it, and as you may also, on Lebanon, next September.

---

[1] Ps. civ. 17.   [2] Jer. viii. 7.   [3] Job xxxix. 26.

CHAPTER XXIII.*

ACRE—EL MUGHAR.

The Bible a country book.
Hero-worship—Sacred shrines—Relics.
Entrance to Galilee—Cabûl.
The land of sheep—Droves from Euphrates.
El Mughar.
Ramah of Naphtali.
Native dishonesty.

Government offices—Storehouses.
Ox-goring—Law of Moses.
Native laziness—Solomon's activity.
Olive-pressing—European machinery.
Typical relations of Palestine.
Burying-ground.
Fire-raising.

Monday, March 19th.

How delightful to be again in the open country! Acre is a positive prison to both soul and body. It seems to me that to read the Bible to best advantage one must be in the fields. When God would talk with Abraham, he brought him forth abroad;[1] and abroad we must go to meet and " hold converse" with the Lord our Maker.

There is more in your thought than would be likely to strike the careless ear. The Bible is not a city book; its scenes are mostly laid in the country—its themes suggested by, and its illustrations drawn from the same source; there most of it was thought, felt, spoken, acted, and even written. We are scarcely introduced to city life at all for the first three thousand years of Bible chronology. The Pentateuch was composed in tents during Israel's long sojourn in the wilderness, and ever after, the reader of the Holy Book is led forth to dwell in tabernacles with patriarchs, or in deserts with prophets and apostles. The poets also, and sweet singers of Israel, commune almost exclusively with Nature, her scenes and her scenery: from thence they draw their imagery, if not their inspirations. The same is eminently true of our blessed Saviour; and he who would bring his spirit most happily into communion with this divine Teacher, must follow him a-field,—must sit on the mountain side and hear him preach, must stand on the shore of Gennesaret and listen to the gracious words which proceed out of his mouth, must walk with him from village to village, and witness his miracles of healing mercy, and his tears of divine compassion. To reproduce and vitalize all this, we need the country, and best of all, *this* country; and if our Biblical studies "smell of the dew of herbs and

The Bible a country book.

Our Lord's love of the country.

---

* [Our travellers now commence what we have called their second tour through northern Palestine. Setting out from Acre, they again leave the Mediterranean Sea behind them, and proceed in an easterly direction towards the Lake of Galilee. The places noticed in this chapter are not of ancient fame, excepting, perhaps, "the land of Cabul," whose cities were presented by Solomon to Hiram. El Mughar, the resting-place for the night, is not mentioned by that name in Scripture, but it is in the immediate neighbourhood of En-hazor (Josh. xix. 37), now 'Ain Hazûr.—ED.]

[1] Gen. xv. 5.

PART
II.

of the breath of morning," rather than of the midnight lamp, I would have it so. They will be in closer correspondence thereby with the original masters, and more true also to the actual circumstances under which they have been prosecuted. We do, in fact, read, and study, and worship in Nature's holy temple, where God hath set a tabernacle for the sun, and made a way for the moon, with her starry train, to walk by night. In this many-aisled temple, eye, and ear, and heart, and every spirit avenue and sense of body share in the solemn worship. Oh! I do ever delight to linger there, and listen to hear the "piping wind" wake up the echoes that sleep in the wadies, and the softer melodies of brooks which run among the hills; and I do so love the flock-clad fields, and woods with singing birds, and vales full to the brim and running over with golden light from the setting sun, streaming down aslope through groves of steadfast oak and peaceful olive; and at early morn to breathe the air with odours loaded, and perfumes from countless flowers, sweet with the dewy baptism of the night. A thousand voices call to prayer, and praise ascends like clouds of incense to the throne eternal.

Voices of
nature.

Galilee.

Thus let it be to-day. We are going up to Galilee, where Immanuel the God-man, lived and toiled for thirty years. It were no idle superstition to take off the shoe of worldliness and sin as we enter this sacred temple where he so often sat, and taught those lessons of divine wisdom which we seek to study and explain.

Do you think it safe, or even Christian, to surrender one's mind to that reverential mood which men call *hero*-worship for want of a more appropriate name?

Hero-
worship

A very difficult and comprehensive question. The prompting principle of hero-worship is far too closely intertwined with the inner sanctities of man's moral nature ever to be eradicated. There are spiritual "high places" where men will ever continue to rear altars and burn incense. It is absurd to ignore their existence—might possibly be sacrilegious utterly to overthrow them. We may moralize, philosophize, and even theologize as we please, and still men will go on all the same to erect monuments, and build temples, and make pilgrimages to the birth-place, the home, and the tomb of prophet, poet, and hero. And if kings, nobles, and ministers of the gospel crowd to the place where Shakspeare was born, or died, or lies buried, and there weep and pray, and tremble and faint in seraphic ecstasy, should we wonder that the less cultivated and less sophisticated will do the same thing for the sacred prophet and the holy seer of antiquity? It is absurd to tolerate, admire, and even participate in the one, and yet condemn the other. Can we surround Plymouth Rock with reverential sanctities, because our forefathers landed there some two hundred years ago, and at the same time ridicule the Oriental who approaches Sinai with awe, or makes long pilgrimages to Mecca, or to Jerusalem, Hebron, Bethlehem, Nazareth, Tiberias, and a score of other places where holy men lived, wrought mighty miracles, and revealed to man the mysteries of God and eternity, and where they often sealed their testimony with their blood? I, at

Sacred
shrines.

least, cannot be so unjust and ridiculously partial. Still, the entire tendency should be closely watched. There is no end to the absurdities into which it will beguile the credulous or the imaginative. A candid and close comparison of ancient Bible customs with those things in our day which we call superstitions, will disclose the rather startling fact that the latter have their counterpart in the former. Thus Jacob had a remarkable vision ; the *place* was ever afterward holy, and was consecrated by religious rites. Moses put off his shoes before the burning bush, and so does the Oriental wherever the presence of God has been manifested, or is supposed still to be in any special manner. The chapel of the "burning bush" is never visited with sandaled foot. The Jews were forbidden to enter certain sacred places, to touch certain holy articles, or even to look upon certain things invested with peculiar sanctity. And thus, at this day, every sect and religion has the counterparts of all these things. The external instruments connected with working miracles had, in ancient times, transferred to them, in imagination, a portion of the sanctity and reverence due to him who used them, or to that divine power which was transmitted through them. This applied not only to the staves, robes, and mantles of prophets while living, but to the same things, to their bones also, and even to their very grave-stones, when dead. The same thing exists to this day, and even in an exaggerated form. Elisha took up Elijah's mantle and smote Jordan, saying, "Where is the Lord God of Elijah ?" He afterward sent Gehazi to lay his *staff* on the dead son of the Shunammite. It is now very common to bind on, or wrap round the sick, some part of the robes of reputed saints, in the belief that healing virtue will be communicated from it. The same faith, or rather feeling, led the people to bring out their sick into the streets, that even the shadow of Peter might overshadow some of them.[1] And so "from the body of Paul were brought unto the sick handkerchiefs or aprons, and the diseases departed from them, and evil spirits went out of them." [2] Even that wonderful superstition about relics, and the miraculous powers of dead saints' bones, is not without an antecedent reality in Bible history upon which to hang its stupendous absurdities. We read in 2 Kings xiii. 21, that people carrying a dead man to his grave, being frightened by a company of Moabites, threw the body hastily into the sepulchre of Elisha; and when the man was let down and touched the bones of Elisha, he revived and stood up on his feet. This train of comparison might be indefinitely extended, and the remark abundantly substantiated by facts, that there is scarcely a superstition among this people around us but what may have its origin traced far back to Bible times. And, moreover, when met with in those oldest records, it is frequently not at its birth or first institution that we see it, but as a custom whose origin is concealed in the twilight of remote antiquity. Now, up to a certain point, the feeling out of which this grows is natural, irresistible, and therefore innocent, if not even commendable. To one who really believes the evangelical narra-

---

[1] Acts v. 15.   [2] Acts xix. 12.

PART
II.

Reverence
for places.

tives, for example—to whom the records are *facts* and not *fables*,—the region we are about to enter will inevitably be invested with a sacredness which applies to no other on earth. It must be so. If any one visits these localities without being conscious of such reverence, it is *simply, only,* and *in every case,* because a latent unbelief has transferred the stupendous facts into the category of dreamy *myths.* No man *can* believe that here the Creator of the universe, his Lord and his Redeemer, really lived, and taught, and wrought miracles, and yet experience no other feelings than such as ordinary places awaken. Least of all can they do so, to whom that man of sorrows and acquainted with grief is the one altogether lovely, the chief among ten thousand. Love,—pure, warm, absorbing love, *will* invest these things with a sacredness, a preciousness beyond expression. It would argue a strange stupidity indeed, if we could walk over those acres once pressed by his sacred feet, and climb the mountains where he so often retired to meditate and pray, without emotion. We are in no danger of enacting such a piece of irreverence.

Entrance
to Galilee.

We study to-day no common lesson of earth's geography. Everything is interesting, and may be important. Let us, therefore, suffer nothing to pass unquestioned. You may begin with this large tell on our right. It stands at the very threshold of that country from which our Lord was called a Galilean. The modern name is Birweh, from this village above it. It is one hundred and twelve feet high, and eight hundred and eighty-eight paces round the base, and one hundred and eighty-six paces across at the top. It was once walled and entirely covered with buildings, and was probably designed to command the entrance into Galilee through this fine valley. The village shows signs of Phœnician or Jewish origin. It may have been a frontier castle, held by the latter to prevent the Canaanites of Acre from penetrating into the interior. That large village in the centre of Wady es Sh'ab is Damûn, and farther south,

Cabûl.

toward Abellîn, is er Ruaise; above it is Tŭmra, and higher still is Cabûl,—the same name as that which Hiram gave to the cities which Solomon presented to him.[1] The whole twenty cities, I suppose, were in this neighbourhood. If this is the Cabûl on the border of Asher, then this Wady es Sh'ab may be the Jiphthah-el mentioned in immediate connection with it.[2] It is impossible, however, now to draw any geographical lines from such uncertain points of departure. Josephus spent some time in Cabûl before he was shut up in Jotapata.[3] I have never passed through it, but am told that there is nothing about it remarkable. Over the hill beyond Cabûl is the rock Jefat, which Mr. Schulz identifies with Jotapata, and I think correctly. I have visited it from Cana of Galilee, from which it is distant about two miles, up Wady Jefat to the north-west.

This great Wady es Sh'ab, called also Halazûn, inclines somewhat to the south-east; and yonder is Maiar, high up on the southern side of it. Our path

[1] 1 Kings ix. 13.   [2] Josh. xix. 27.   [3] See *Life,* paragraphs 43, 45.

turns to the left through this gap, and ascends to the plain of Mejdel Kerûm. CHAPTER
Notice these lofty mountains on the north of this olive-planted plain. Can XXIII.
you tell which way the water is drained off?

Mejdel
It must be down the gap through which we have entered the plain, but it Kerûm.
is so level as to puzzle the eye.

Dr. Robinson says it has no proper outlet; which is scarcely correct, since it
is drained off south-west into Wady es Sh'ab, and south-east below Rameh by
the Wady Sulemiyeh. This Mejdel Kerûm is rather pretty, with its white
dome over some Moslem saint or other. The ruins of Gabera lie over that hill
to the south-east about three miles; it was celebrated in the wars of Josephus,
and was then an important town of Galilee. Here on our left are Deir el Asad
and el Ba'any close together: they have large remains of antiquity about them
—more, indeed, than are to be found in most of these Galilean villages. We
have now a rather blind path along the base of these northern mountains for a
mile due east to Nehf, below which is the regular road up the valley to Seijur.
Both these are ancient sites.

What a prodigious flock of sheep is wending this way down the valley! Sheep
Whence do they come, and what brings them along this unfrequented route? from Euphrates.
Several months ago they started from the plains around and south of the
head-waters of the Euphrates, and they are now on their way to Acre, and
other towns along the coast. The East is, and has ever been, the land of sheep,
as the Mississippi valley is of swine. Job had 14,000 sheep,[1] and Solomon sacrificed 120,000 at the dedication of the temple.[2] Nor will these numbers seem
incredible when examined and compared with what now exists in this country.
Every year sheep are brought down from the north in such multitudes as The land
to confound the imagination. In 1853 the interior route was unsafe, and all of sheep.
had to be passed along the sea-board. During the months of November and
December the whole line of coast was covered with them : they came from
Northern Syria and from Mesopotamia; and their shepherds, in dress, manners,
and language, closely resemble those of Abraham and Job, as I believe. At a
distance the flocks look exactly like droves of hogs going to Cincinnati ; their
progress is quite as slow, and their motions are very similar. The shepherds How
"put a space between drove and drove,"[3] and then lead on softly, as Jacob's driven.
shepherds did, and for the same reason. If they over-drive them the flock
dies; and even with the greatest care many give out, and, to prevent their dying
by the wayside, are slaughtered and sold to the poor, or are eaten by the
shepherds themselves. The flocks are also constantly thinning off as they go
south by selling on all occasions, and thus the whole country is supplied. How
vast must be the numbers when they first set out from the distant deserts of
the Euphrates ! Indeed, those northern plains literally swarm with sheep,
and hence the supply never fails. When these flocks have to be watered in a
region where wells are scarce, it is no wonder that there should be great strife,

---

[1] Job xlii. 12.   [2] 1 Kings viii. 63.   [3] Gen. xxxii. 16.

PART
II.as we often read of in patriarchal history.[1] Our road passes south of Rameh through these large olive orchards, planted among rocks, and left, in many places, to be choked with a dense jungle of oak and other bushes. And now we turn square round the base of this lofty mountain southward, into the pretty and well-watered Wady Sulemia (or Sulamy, as it is pronounced here). It has fine fountains, and we shall come upon some half-a-dozen mills at least, hid away in the romantic ravine below our path. These green hills are full of Arab tents at this season, and you can now hear the shouts of these wild men at their lagging flocks, and also their singular call to the camels scattered over the country. Here, too, game abounds, and on every side of us the red-legged partridge is calling responsive to its fellows; it is thus they welcome in the coming twilight. Our path now bends round to the east, having the broad wady Sulemia on our right, and el Mughar is just before us. Here comes our friend G—— J—— to meet us with his warm Arabic welcome.

El Mu-
ghar.

An Arabic
welcome.

Ahlan! Ahlan we Sahlan! Most happy to see you. Brother wrote that you were coming, but I had begun to despair of seeing you.

This interminable rain detained us prisoners in your house at Acre. But first of all, let us find a place for our tent. I have made a vow to avoid all fellaheen houses.

I cannot promise you very comfortable quarters, but, such as they are, you are most welcome to share them.

No, no; thank you. I am not to be caught that way. It is well enough for you, perhaps, but I should not sleep a minute; and, besides, our baggage would get full of fleas, to annoy us for a week to come.

Encamp-
ment on
house-top.

As you like; but there is not a level place in all the village large enough for the tent. You can pitch on the roof of the house.

That will do admirably; and it will also enable us to keep off the villagers, who have gathered round us like bees.

Well, this is something new. Are you sure we shall not break through and smother, or crush to death the family below?

No, I am not. It trembles rather suspiciously, but our friends assure us there is no danger.

Salim must find some sheltered place for our horses, or they will be unfit to ride to-morrow. Poor things, they are shivering in this cold mountain wind.

And now all our inquiries about friends, family, and politics are answered, my dear G——, I wish to get acquainted with your present whereabouts. It is all new territory to me, and somewhat savage. You ought to make large gains to remunerate you for this rough-and-tumble life among these fellaheen.

I do not find it disagreeable. I am busy all day long; the place is healthy, the people respectful and easily managed, and the proceeds of this farming operation quite satisfactory. We are nearly through with oil-pressing, and,

[1] Gen. xiii. 7, and xxvi. 20, 21.

although the crows have destroyed many thousand piastres worth of olives, we CHAPTER
XXIII. shall still make a handsome profit.

The orchards, I see, are very extensive.

Altogether too large for the population; and so, also, there is far more Olive cularable land than they can cultivate. There are thousands of olive-trees so ture. completely enveloped with thorny jungle that we cannot gather even what grows on them. If this jungle were cleared away, and the land properly dressed, we should at once double the crop. I am doing something at it, but Improvethese people are so lazy that but slow progress is made; in fact, they are ments. afraid to increase the number of bearing trees, lest their taxes should also be raised upon them. Thus a bad government paralyzes all desire to improve.

What are these people?

Druses and Greek Christians; and the same mixture of sects prevails in Rameh and other places.

This Rameh seems to be a large and important village.

About the same size as el Mughar. They are very anxious that I should farm their village also, but I have already quite as much on my hands as I can manage.

This is undoubtedly the Ramah of Naphtali, and this ruin above your Ramah of village, called 'Ain Hazûr, is the En-Hazor, I suppose, given by Joshua to the Naphtali. same tribe.[1]

Indeed! I did not know that our place was mentioned in the Bible.

El Mughar is not, but 'Ain Hazûr is. What do you call this broad wady south of you?

Sûlamy.

Are there any ruins of this name in the wady?

Yes; they lie between this and Deir Hanna, that castle to the south-west, Places in which you must have seen as you came toward our village,—but they are in- neighconsiderable.

bourhood

They are undoubtedly the remains of that Salamin which was fortified by Josephus.[2] Is this wady ever called Rŭbŭdîyeh?

There is a ruined village of that name in it, an hour and a half to the southeast of us, and between that and the lake it takes the name of the village.

What is that place on the opposite ridge of this wady?

It is 'Ailabûn; and over the hill beyond is another called Sabăna.

Where is 'Arraby? According to Josephus, it must be somewhere in this region.

It is west of Deir Hanna, on the southern side of the wady. You ought to ride over to this Deir. The castle built by the Dahar family of Acre is still inhabited, and is worth visiting. There was an ancient ruin there, from which it took its name *Deir*. Farther west is Sukhnîn.

That is Sogane, several times mentioned by Josephus. Is not Yâkûk in this neighbourhood?

---

[1] Josh. xix. 37.   [2] Josephus's Wars, book ii. 20, 6. Life, 37.

PART
II.

East of us, and directly above the plain of Gennesaret.

The similarity of name suggests that it is the site of the Hukkok given to Naphtali,[1] but I think this doubtful. I see not how any border line of that tribe could be drawn through Yâkûk, unless, indeed, the territory of that great tribe reached far down the Lake of Tiberias.

Do you find much trouble in conducting your agricultural speculations among this people?

Dishon-
esty of the
natives.

The greatest difficulties arise from dishonesty of the agents or *wakkeels.* Though I am on the ground, and watch everything closely, yet these men rob me right and left. I lose most by the peculations of those who oversee the gathering of olives; and in the time of threshing, unless I look strictly at the operations in person, I would be robbed of a large part of my harvest. The emirs and sheikhs, who commit this oversight to their servants, and the government, that deputes officers to gather its portion from the public lands, of course suffer still more severely.

Govern-
ment
officers.

No doubt; and yet the system followed by the present government for gathering up the produce of the country seems to be very ancient. Most of the kings of Judah and Israel engaged largely in agriculture. Besides arable lands for tillage, they had vine-yards, and olive-yards, and flocks, and camels, and asses; and they had agents like your *wakkeels,* and doubtless just as dishonest and oppressive. In 1 Chronicles xxvii. 25–31 we have a full list of these gentlemen appointed by David: Jehonathan was over the store-houses in the fields. In the Hûleh, and on the great plains of Askelon and Gaza, I saw large low huts built in the open country to store away the produce directly from the threshing-floors, thence to be carried home, as occasion required. Such, I suppose, were David's store-houses in the fields. Then follows a list of wakkeels over vineyards, over olive-trees, and even over the sycamores, whose fruit is now generally given to the poor.

Store-
houses in
the fields.

It seems to me to result, as a necessary deduction, that the reigning power in this country always pursued the ruinous policy of confiscating lands and property, and retaining them in their own hand, very much as the Turkish government does now; and this is the reason why we find so many places mentioned as deserts in the Bible history. The excuse for this agricultural policy on the part of the government in ancient times no doubt was, that the amount of money circulating among a people entirely agricultural or pastoral was small; the king must therefore necessarily take his taxes in *kind,* and depend for a large portion of his revenues upon the produce of the royal domains. But the Turkish government is pressed by no such necessity. The whole oppressive and ruinous system, by which large tracts of fertile territory are converted into deserts, ought to be abolished, and the government lands sold to those who cultivate the soil.

Govern-
ment
lands.

Your remark about stealing from the threshing-floors suggests the reason

---

[1] Josh. xix. 34.

why Boaz slept on his that night when he was visited by Ruth.[1] As he was CHAPTER
XXIII.
evidently a man of property, who employed many reapers, and did not work
himself, it must have been some urgent reason that could induce him to sleep Boaz,
in the open field among his workmen.

No doubt it was because he could not trust his servants; and what he did
must be done now. The owner, or some faithful agent, has to remain at the
floor day and night.

We encountered a drove of cattle to-day, some of which were fighting
furiously; and the herdsman, endeavouring to part them, was in danger of
being pushed over and gored to death by one of the belligerents. I had previously
imagined that the cattle of this country must have greatly degenerated since
the days when Moses thought it necessary to ordain that the ox which gored a
man should be stoned, and his carcass thrown away; and if he killed any one,
and was previously known to be vicious, the owner also should be put to death,
because he did not keep him in.[2]

Danger from this source has not ceased, especially among the half-wild Oxen gor-
ing.
droves that range over the luxuriant pastures in certain parts of the country.
And the law is still more in place which ordained that, "if one man's ox hurt
another's that he die, then they shall sell the live ox, and divide the money of
it; and the dead ox also they shall divide."[3] If this admirable statute were Law of
Moses.
faithfully administered, it would prevent many angry and sometimes fatal
feuds between herdsmen, and at the same time would be a very fair adjust-
ment of the questions of equity that grow out of such accidents.

Josephus very justly boasts of the wisdom and humanity of their great law- Humanity
of its
minute
regula-
tions.
giver, shown in minute regulations of this nature; and he gives as instances
not only these ordinances which we have noticed, but also another, of the
necessity for which I had a very practical intimation this afternoon. Founding his remark upon Exodus xxi. 33, 34, he says, "Let those that dig a well or
a pit be careful to lay planks over them, and so keep them shut up; not in
order to hinder any persons from drawing water, but that there may be no
danger of falling into them."[4] I came near falling into an uncovered well this Open
wells.
afternoon, when peering about an old ruin; and such accidents are not uncommon. A friend of mine lost a valuable horse in that way; and, according to the
Mosaic law, the owner of the pit should have paid the price of the horse.[5] I
have been astonished at the recklessness with which wells and pits are left uncovered and unprotected all over this country. It argues a disregard of life
which is highly criminal. I once saw a blind man walk right into one of these
unprotected wells. He fell to the bottom, but, as it was soft sand, he was not
so much injured as frightened.

March 20*th*. You are a late riser, my dear G——. I have had a long
ramble over your domains, enjoying the bright morning and the charming
scenery. The prospect over the hills, and down the broad wady Sulamy, and

---

[1] Ruth iii. 7.　　[2] Ex. xxi. 28-32.　　[3] Ex. xxi. 35.　　[4] Josephus, iv. 8, 37.　　[5] Exod. xxi. 34.

the ravine of Rŭbŭdîyeh to the lake, is exquisitely beautiful. But much land lies waste that might be tilled, and it is sad to see so many olive-trees entangled in jungles of thorns and bushes.

Much of this is owing to causes which we were discussing last night, but still more to the laziness of the people. A few are tolerably industrious, but the majority are far otherwise.

Laziness of natives. Laziness seems to have been a very prevalent vice in this country from days of old, giving rise to a multitude of popular proverbs, which the wise man has preserved in his collection. Indeed, there is scarcely any other subject so often mentioned, or so richly and scornfully illustrated by Solomon as this. His rebuke of the sluggard, drawn from the habits of the ant, is very appropriate and suggestive.[1] We need not now "consider her ways" in general, for all the world is or may be familiar with them. There are some circumstances, however, mentioned in this passage, which must have been suggested by actual life in this country. Thus the fact that the ant will faithfully and persever-ingly work *without guide*, or *overseer*, or *ruler*, is very striking. When I began to employ workmen in this country, nothing annoyed me more than the neces-sity to hire also an *overseer*, or to fulfil this office myself. But I soon found that this was universal and strictly necessary. Without an overseer very little work would be done, and nothing as it should be. The workmen, every way unlike the ant, will not work at all unless kept to it and directed in it by an overseer, who is himself a perfect specimen of laziness. He does absolutely nothing but smoke his pipe, order this, scold that one, and discuss the how and the why with the men themselves, or with idle passers-by, who are strangely prone to enter earnestly into everybody's business but their own. This over-seeing often costs more than the work overseen. Now the ants manage far better. Every one attends to his own business, and does it well.

The ant.

Overseers.

Improvi-dence. In another respect these provident creatures read a very necessary lesson to Oriental sluggards. In all warm climates there is a ruinous want of calcula-tion and forecast. Having enough for the current day, men are reckless as to the future. The idea of sickness, misfortune, or the necessities of old age exercise but little influence; they are not provident "to lay up for a rainy day" or dreary winter. Yet all these occasions come upon them, and they wake to want and pinching poverty. Now the ant provideth her meat in summer, and gathereth her food in the harvest. All summer long, and espe-cially in harvest, every denizen of their populous habitations is busy. As we walk or ride over the grassy plains, we notice paths leading in all directions from their subterranean granaries; at first broad, clean, and smooth, like roads near a city, but constantly branching off into smaller and less distinct, until they disappear in the herbage of the plain. Along these converging paths hurry thousands of ants, thickening inward until it becomes an unbroken column of busy beings going in search of, or returning with their food for future

[1] Prov. vi. 6–11.

need; there is no loitering or jostling; every one knows his business, and does not intermeddle with others. No thoroughfare of largest city is so crowded or better conducted than these highways to the ant-hills. They are great robbers, however, and plunder by night as well as by day; and the farmer must keep a sharp eye to his floor in harvest, or they will abstract a large quantity of grain in a single night.

Speaking of ants, what could have induced Herodotus to write that absurd story about the ants in India, "larger than a fox and less than a dog," which dug up gold, and tore to pieces those who came to gather it, and much more to the same purport?

As to Herodotus, he was a most courageous retailer of anecdotes, and used the privilege of great travellers without reserve. That Pliny should quote this fable is truly surprising.—See Herodotus, 170.

How long wilt thou sleep, O sluggard? Up, drowsy fool! no longer fold your hands in idleness, or the day of poverty will overtake you, as surely as a man who steadily travels on will come to the end of his journey. Though you see it not, yet the time of want draws near, direct and sure, and stern as an armed man who comes to bind and plunder.[1]

It is curious to notice how intensely Solomon hated this vice, and in how many ways he gave expression to his abhorrence and contempt of the sluggard. Thus, "The slothful man roasteth not that which he took in hunting."[2] The most good-for-nothing fellow may be roused by the excitement of the chase to endure the fatigue of hunting, but, when this violent stimulus is past, he is too indolent even to roast the game he has taken with so much toil. Again, "The soul of the sluggard desireth, and hath nothing."[3] Thus, too, "he is brother to him who is a great waster,"[4] and "he coveteth greedily all day long," and hath nothing, for "his hands refuse to labour."[5] "The way of the slothful is as an hedge of thorns:"[6] it pricks, lacerates, and entangles the miserable wretch. Slothfulness produces a sickly timidity, and is ever fruitful and expert in raising idle objections and imaginary dangers. "There is a lion without; I shall be slain in the streets."[7] "He will not plough by reason of the cold;"[8] and as ploughing and sowing cannot be carried on until the winter rains commence, he neglects altogether to sow his fields, "therefore shall he beg in harvest, and have nothing." I have often pitied the farmer when ploughing in the cold rains and pitiless winds, and it requires more decision of character than belongs to a sluggard to bear up against them; he therefore retreats into his hut, kindles a little fire, and dozes away his time by the side of it, enveloped in pungent smoke. Nor will he be roused: "A little more sleep, a little more folding of the hands." As the door on his hinges, so the sluggard on his bed rolls back and forth with many a creak and weary groan. He will put forth more arguments for his base conduct than seven men that can render a reason.

CHAPTER XXIII.

Herodotus on ants.

Solomon's dislike of sloth.

---

[1] Prov. vi. 11.   [2] Prov. xii. 27.   [3] Prov. xiii. 4.   [4] Prov. xviii. 9.
[5] Prov. xxi. 25, 26.   [6] Prov. xv. 19.   [7] Prov. xxii. 13.   [8] Prov. xx. 4.

There is a lion in the streets; it is too cold or too hot, too wet or too dry, too early or too late, time plenty or the time is past, the opportunity lost, and so on *ad infinitum*. "The slothful hideth his hand in his bosom; it grieveth him to bring it again to his mouth."[1]

Illustration of laziness.

Our Arab anecdotes go far beyond Solomon. A favourite illustration of extreme laziness is the case of a man that would not turn his head over on his pillow, though the muddy water leaking through the roof fell plump into his eye! But that description in the 24th chapter of Proverbs is the one which

The field of the sluggard.

strikes me as most appropriate to my poor fellaheen: "I went by the field of the slothful, and by the vineyard of the man void of understanding; and, lo, it was all grown over with thorns, and nettles had covered the face thereof, and the stone wall thereof was broken down."

Yes, that is true to nature, and to actual life in all its details. The stone terraces and garden walls soon tumble down when neglected; and this, beyond any country I have seen, is prolific in thorns and thistles. All your vineyards in this region are covered with them, and so thousands of your valuable olive-trees are completely choked up with briers and thorns, and their owners are too shiftless and indolent to clear them away.

As you are a large manufacturer of olive oil, I must embrace the opportunity to examine into this operation to-day.

Olive-pressing.

We are nearly through pressing for this year, but there is one mŭtrûf still in operation down by the brook Sulamy, to which we can walk after breakfast.

Does it not injure the quality of the oil to keep the olives so long?

Not materially, if proper care be taken to prevent heating and fermentation. Our olives are now quite black, and a person unacquainted with the matter might think them altogether spoiled; and yet, as you will see, the oil is clear and sweet, and the yield is equally good.

What is the difference between a mŭtrûf and a m'aserah?

The m'a-serah.

The m'aserah is worked by hand, and is only used for the olives which fall first in autumn, before the rains of winter raise the brooks which drive the mŭtrûf. The olives for the m'aserah are ground to a pulp in circular stone basins by rolling a large stone wheel over them. The mass is then put into small baskets of straw-work, which are placed one upon another, between two upright posts, and pressed by a screw which moves in the beam or entablature from above, like the screw in the standing-press of a bookbinder, or else by a beam-lever. After this first pressing, the pulp is taken out of the baskets, put into large copper pans, and, being sprinkled with water, is heated over a fire, and again pressed as before. This finishes the process, and the oil is put away in jars to use, or in cisterns, to be kept for future market.

The mŭ-trûf.

The mŭtrûf is driven like an ordinary mill, except that the apparatus for beating up the olives is an upright cylinder, with iron cross-bars at the lower end. This cylinder turns rapidly in a hollow tube of stone-work, into which

[1] Prov. xxvi. 13-16.

the olives are thrown from above, and beaten to a pulp by the revolving cross- CHAPTER
bars. The interior of the tube is kept hot, so that the mass is taken out below XXIII.
sufficiently heated to cause the oil to run freely. The same baskets are used
as in the m'aserah, but the press is a beam-lever, with heavy weights at the
end. This process is repeated a second time, as in the m'aserah, and then the
refuse is thrown away.

Well, these mŭtrûfs are about as filthy as any place I ever explored,
and the machinery is rude and clumsy in the extreme. Mr. B—— told me
recently that he had started a mŭtrûf at Nablûs, with European machinery, on European
quite a new plan, and that the work was done much cheaper and more expe- machin-
ditiously; the oil was clearer, and there was a gain of about thirty per cent. ery.
in the quantity. Certainly a little science applied to the matter would greatly
improve this important branch of Syrian agriculture. The m'aserah is,
however, the machinery used from the most remote times, as we know from
the basins, and wheels to crush the olives, still found in the ruins of old towns.
The huge stones upon the tops of the upright posts prove conclusively that
the ancients knew nothing of the screw, but employed beam-presses, as in
your mŭtrûfs.

Beam-presses are also employed in the m'aserah to this day, and I think the
use of screws is quite modern.

Have you any process for clarifying the oil?

None whatever, except to let it gradually settle on the lees in the cisterns
or large jars in which it is kept.

Certain villages are celebrated all over the country for producing oil particularly clear and sweet, and it commands a high price for table use.

Berjah, for example, above Neby Yunas, Deir Mîmâs in Merj Aiun, and et
Tîreh in Carmel. But the process there is very different. The olives are first
mashed as in the mŭtrûf, and then stirred rapidly in a large kettle of hot
water. The oil is thus separated, and rises to the top, when it is skimmed off
without pressing. The refuse is then thrown into vats of cold water, and an
inferior oil is gathered from the surface, which is only fit for making soap.

Micah speaks of *treading* out olives with the feet.[1] Is this ever done now? Treading
Not that I know of. And it could only be done when the olives have been out olives.
kept until they are very soft, as mine are at present.

I have heard it said that the blight, which has nearly destroyed the grapes
all over this country for the last few years, and which has ruined the vineyards
through the south of Europe, has also attacked the olives this year. Have you
noticed anything of the kind in your orchards?

There have been, perhaps, more withered olives than usual, but I do not
think it was from this blight. They do not show the same symptoms. The
olive dries up without developing, and falls off; but there is none of that
whitish mould, nor that offensive smell of corruption which the grape-blight

---

[1] Micah vi. 15.

occasions. The vineyards in this region are utterly ruined, and the people have cut them down and sowed the land with grain. This great calamity acts very mysteriously. The vines blossom and the young grapes *set* as usual, but, soon after, a silvery grey mould spreads over them, and as they enlarge they corrupt, with a very peculiar and offensive odour. Whole vineyards are thus ruined. There is this also strange about it: one year it attacks the vines raised on poles and running on trees, and those lying on the ground escape; the next year it is the reverse. Some vineyards, exposed to the winds, are wholly destroyed; others, sheltered from them, are uninjured. And again this is reversed. Hitherto no explanation has appeared to account for the calamity itself or for its eccentricities.

Moses and the prophets assign such visitations, without hesitation, to the displeasure of God. Moses says expressly that God would thus punish the inhabitants for their sins: "Thou shalt plant vineyards, and dress them, but shalt neither drink of the wine, nor gather the grapes: for the worms shall eat them. Thou shalt have olive-trees throughout all thy coasts, but thou shalt not anoint thyself with the oil: for thine olive shall cast his fruit."[1] And the sacred penmen often speak of blasting and mildew as chastisements sent directly from God. It seems very natural to refer like judgments in this same land, and upon a people whose moral and religious character so closely resemble those to whom the threatenings were first addressed, to the same source. The people themselves do, in fact, thus trace them back—"For the greatness of our sins," is the universal proverb.

Can it be mere imagination that there is somewhat peculiar in the providential dispensations experienced in this land? I think not. Certainly in
olden times there was much that was peculiar. God so made this land of Canaan that its physical conformation should furnish appropriate types and emblems, through which spiritual mysteries and invisible realities should be developed, and so pictured to the eye and the imagination as to affect the heart of man. These mountains point to heaven, this sunken Sea of Death to still lower depths. The valleys, the plains, the brooks and fountains, from the swellings of Jordan to the waters of Siloah, that go softly from under the altar of God, all were so made and disposed as to shadow forth dimly, but all the more impressively, divine revelations needful for universal man. There are no other groupings of natural objects so significant; no other names on earth can be substituted in our spiritual vocabulary for these, and what they formerly taught they teach now, and ever will, to all coming generations. It is this which invests even the physical features of Palestine with an interest and an importance which can belong to no other land. Jordan is much more than a mere river of water, Zion infinitely dearer than any ordinary mass of rock; in a word, the divine Architect constructed this country after a model, infolding in itself, and unfolding to the world, the dark mysteries of the life that is, and

---

[1] Deut. xxviii. 39, 40.

of that which is to be—of redemption and heaven, of perdition and hell. And these physical features are still preserved unchanged, to teach the same great truths to every successive generation. So God's more direct and daily providences toward this country and its inhabitants are made to repeat the same lessons that were addressed to ancient tribes, and their significance then expounded by divine teachers. Thus it is that blighting and mildew come, as they came of old, we know not how; God sends them. Thus come famine and dearth, when "the heaven that is over thy head is as brass, and the earth that is under thee as iron;"[1] and the Lord sends the burning sirocco with its rain of powder and dust, and summons his great army of locusts, and the caterpillar, and the palmer-worm, to devour. Thus, too, even in our day, he rises at times to shake terribly the earth, and overwhelm the cities of the guilty.

There is much more than a mere fortuitous conjunction of accidents in these and a hundred other items which might be mentioned. I can scarcely lift my eye without lighting upon something which repeats those lessons which God himself here taught to generations long since dead and gone. These poor women who are cutting up mallows by the bushes to mingle with their broth, are only doing that which want and famine, divinely sent, compelled the solitary to do in the days of Job.[2] And again: those men who have cleared away the earth, and are laying the axe at the very roots of that tree, in order to hew it down for firewood, are repeating the formula by which the Baptist teaches, that in the kingdom of heaven "every tree that bringeth not forth good fruit is hewn down and cast into the fire."[3] Your fellaheen value trees only as they bear good fruit: all others are cut down as cumberers of the ground; and they cut them from the very root, as John had seen them in his day. And yet once more: this man, with his load of dry weeds and grass, is going to remind us, at his tannûr, of "the day that shall burn as an oven, and all the proud, and all that do wickedly, shall be as stubble."[4] And we should further learn, from this operation, that "if God so clothe the grass of the field, which to-day is, and to-morrow is cast into the oven, shall he not much more clothe you, O ye of little faith?"[5] This lad who is setting fire to these briers and thorns is doing the very act which typified to Paul the awful state of those apostates whom it was impossible to renew again unto repentance. Oh, may we not be like that ground which "beareth thorns and briers—rejected, and nigh unto cursing, whose end is to be burned."[6]

Mallows.

Trees— value of.

Ovens.

Briers and thorns.

He finds it difficult to set the thorns on fire, for it is too late in the season. Before the rains came this whole mountain side was in a blaze. Thorns and briers grow so luxuriantly here, that they must be burned off always before the plough can operate. The peasants watch for a high wind, and then the fire catches easily, and spreads with great rapidity. It is really a beautiful sort of fire-works, especially seen at night.

Burning over ground

[1] Deut. xxviii. 23, 24. [2] Job xxx. 4. [3] Mark iii. 10.
[4] Mal. iv. 1. [5] Matt. vi. 30. [6] Heb. vi. 4, 8.

PART II.

Burning ground.

This practice of burning over the ground is very ancient in other lands besides this, and as there are neither fences nor habitations in the open country to be injured by the fire, there is no danger in it. Every schoolboy will remember what Virgil sings about it :—

> "Long practice has a sure improvement found,
> With kindled fires to burn the barren ground.
> When the light stubble, to the flames resigned,
> Is driven along, and crackles in the wind."

Yes, but these Arab peasants would think the poet but a stupid farmer, to puzzle himself with half a dozen speculations about the possible way in which this burning is beneficial; as, whether the "hollow womb of the earth is warmed by it," or some "latent vice is cured," or redundant humours "driven off, or that new breathings" are opened in the chapt earth, or the very reverse—

> "That the heat the gaping ground constrains,
> New knits the surface, and new strings the veins;
> Lest soaking showers should pierce her secret seat,
> Or freezing Boreas chill her genial heat,
> Or scorching suns too violently beat," &c., &c.

The Arab peasant would laugh at the whole of them, and tell you that two very good reasons not mentioned by the poet were all-sufficient: That it destroyed and removed out of the way of the plough weeds, grass, stubble, and thorn-bushes; and that the ashes of this consumed rubbish was a valuable manure to the land.

Scripture allusions.

David has a terrible imprecation against the enemies of God in the 83d Psalm, based upon this operation, perhaps : "As the fire burneth a wood, and as the flame setteth the mountain on fire, so persecute them with thy tempests, and make them afraid with thy storms." The woods of this country are almost exclusively on the mountains, and hence the allusion to them. I have known several such catastrophes since I came to Syria, and am always reminded by them of this passage.

In Nahum i. 10 the prophet has a striking comparison, or rather double allusion to thorns and fire. Speaking of the wicked, he says—"For while they be folden together as thorns, and while they are drunken as drunkards, they shall be devoured as stubble fully dry." Now these thorns, especially that kind called *bellan*, which covers the whole country, and is that which is thus burned, are so folden together as to be utterly inseparable, and being united by thousands of small intertwining branches, when the torch is applied they flash and flame instantly, like stubble fully dry ; indeed, the peasants always select this *bellan*, folden together, when they want to kindle a fire from their matches.

There is another allusion to the fire among thorns, which you, as a farmer in this neighbourhood, must have occasion to notice. Moses says—"If fire

---

[1] 1 Georgic.

break out and catch in thorns, so that the stacks of corn, or the standing corn, CHAPTER
or the field be consumed therewith, he that kindled the fire shall surely make XXIII.
restitution." [1]

Yes, we are obliged to charge our nâtûrs, or watchmen, as harvest-time Fire-
advances, to guard with the utmost care against fire. The reason why spreading.
Moses mentions its catching among thorns only, I suppose, is because thorns
grow all round our fields, and actually intermingle with the wheat. By harvest-time, they are not only dry themselves, but are choked up with tall
grass dry as powder. Fire, therefore, catches in them easily, and spreads
with great rapidity and uncontrollable fury; and as the grain is dead ripe, it
is impossible to extinguish it.

When I was crossing the plain of Gennesaret in 1848, during harvest, I Laws
stopped to lunch at 'Ain et Tîny, and my servant kindled a very small fire to against
make a cup of coffee. A man, detached from a company of reapers, came im- ing.
mediately and stood patiently by us until we had finished, without saying what
he wanted. As soon as we left, however, he carefully extinguished our little
fire; and upon inquiry I found he had been sent for that purpose. Burckhardt, while stopping at Tiberias, hired a guide to the caves in Wady el
Hamâm, and says that this man was constantly reproving him for the careless
manner in which he threw away the ashes from his pipe. He then adds, " The
Arabs who inhabit the valley of the Jordan invariably *put to death* any person who is known to have been even the innocent cause of firing the grass;
and they have made it a public law among themselves, that, even in the height
of intestine warfare, no one shall attempt to set his enemy's harvest on fire."
The ordinance of Moses on this subject was a wise regulation, designed to meet
a very urgent necessity. To understand the full value of the law, we must remember that the wheat is suffered to become dead ripe, and as dry as tinder,
before it is cut; and further, that the land is tilled in common, and the grain
sown in one vast field, without fence, ditch, or hedge, to separate the individual
portions. A fire catching in any part, and driven by the wind, would consume
the whole, and thus the entire population might be stripped of their year's
provisions in half an hour.

---

[1] Exod. xxii. 6.

CHAPTER XXIV.

EL MUGHAR TABIGA.*

March 21st.

Road to Genne-saret.

Our road for this day leads down to, and then along the shore of that beautiful Gennesaret, so interesting to every Christian mind, and to the ruins of those cities where our Lord wrought most of his mighty works. We are in the very centre of that region in which he passed the greater part of his life on earth, and on all sides are the deserted sites of villages and towns which he must have visited. They have the usual marks of antiquity, but nothing is known of their history. His eye, however, saw them crowded with inhabitants, and from them poured forth the thousands of Galilee to hear his sermons, eat his miraculous loaves, and be healed by his divine skill.

This half hour has brought us down in the world immensely.

Descent.

And there is still a heavy descent to the lake, which lies full six hundred feet below the Mediterranean, according to my aneroid. This small plain which we are now crossing is called Kaiserîyeh (Cæsarea) by some lost historical association; and below it we must pick our way over and through a very rocky waar for half an hour.

We are passing over limestone, with strata dipping at a sharp angle into the wady. I had expected to find trap rock as we approached the lake.

So we shall below Rŭbŭdîyeh, and the same volcanic formation continues to the south of us quite down to Beisan. And now we have reached the bottom of Wady Sulamy, and find it entirely dry. The stream that drove the mills west of el Mughar has vanished beneath the strata, only to reappear, however, lower down, where it takes the name of Rŭbŭdîyeh, and is carried by

* [In this chapter we reach the memorable plain of Gennesaret, and are surrounded by the scenes amid which our blessed Lord spent the chief part of his public ministry. The question of the true site of Capernaum is raised towards the end of the chapter. Dr. Robinson had fixed at a fountain in the plain of Gennesaret, called 'Ain et Tîny, and is followed in this by Mr. Porter in the "Hand-Book for Syria and Palestine." Dr. Thomson places Capernaum beyond the plain of Gennesaret, at Tell Hûm, near the mouth of the Jordan. Tabiga, which lies between 'Ain et Tîny and Tell Hûm, he regards as having been a manufacturing suburb of Capernaum. So that the difference between him and Dr. Robinson is in reality very small. All the three places are within three quarters of an hour of each other.—Ed.]

canals over a considerable part of the fertile plain of Gennesaret. This **CHAPTER**
Rŭbŭdîyeh was once a considerable town, as appears from the extent of ground   **XXIV.**
cumbered by these shapeless heaps of rubbish.

These farmers about us belong to el Mughar, and their land extends to the **Farmers.**
declivity immediately above Gennesaret, a distance of at least eight miles
from their village. Our farmers would think it hard to travel so far before
they began the day's work, and so would these if they had to do it every day;
but they drive their oxen before them, carry bed, bedding, and board, plough, **Their**
yoke, and seed on their donkeys, and expect to remain out in the open country **habits.**
until their task is accomplished. The mildness of the climate enables them to
do so without inconvenience or injury. How very different from the habits of
Western farmers! These men carry no cooking apparatus, and, we should think,
no provisions. They, however, have a quantity of their thin, tough bread, a
few olives, and perhaps a little cheese, in that leathern bag which hangs from
their shoulders—the "scrip" of the New Testament; and with this they are **"Scrip."**
contented. When hungry, they sit by the fountain, or the brook, and eat; if
weary or sleepy, they throw around them their loose 'aba, and lie down on the
ground as contentedly as the ox himself. At night they retire to a cave, sheltering rock, or shady tree, kindle a fire of thorn-bushes, heat over their stale
bread, and if they have shot a bird or caught a fish, they boil it on the coals;
and thus dinner and supper in one are achieved with the least possible trouble.
But their great luxury is smoking, and the whole evening is whiled away in
whiffing tobacco and bandying the rude jokes of the light-hearted peasant.
Such a life need not be disagreeable, nor is it necessarily a severe drudgery in
this delightful climate. The only thing they dread is an incursion of wild
Arabs from beyond the lake, and to meet them they are all armed as if going
forth to war.

Do you suppose that this wallet, in which
they carry their provisions, is the "scrip" which
the disciples were directed *not* to take in their
first missionary tours?[1]

No doubt; and the same, too, in which the
young David put the five smooth stones from the
brook.[2] All shepherds have them, and they are
the farmer's universal vade-mecum. They are
merely the skins of kids stripped off whole, and
tanned by a very simple process. By the way,

WALLET.

the entire "outfit" of these first missionaries shows that they were plain **Mission**
fishermen, farmers, or shepherds; and to such men there was no extraordinary **of the**
self-denial in the matter or the mode of their mission. We may expound the **twelve**
"instructions" given to these primitive evangelists somewhat after the fol- **apostles**
lowing manner:—Provide neither silver, nor gold, nor brass in your purses.[3]

---

[1] Matt. x. 10; Mark vi. 8; Luke ix. 3.   [2] 1 Sam. xvii. 40.   [3] Matt. x. 9, 10.

PART II.

Explanation of instructions. You are going to your brethren in the neighbouring villages, and the best way to get to their hearts and their confidence is to throw yourselves upon their hospitality. Nor was there any departure from the simple manners of the country in this. At this day the farmer sets out on excursions quite as extensive, without a para in his purse ; and the modern Moslem prophet of Tarshîha thus sends forth his apostles over this identical region. Neither do they encumber themselves with two coats. They are accustomed to sleep in the garments they have on during the day; and in this climate such plain people experience no inconvenience from it. They wear a coarse shoe, answering to the sandal of the ancients, but never take two pair of them ; and although the staff is an invariable companion of all wayfarers, they are content with *one*. Of course, such "instructions" can have only a general application to those who go forth, not to neighbours of the same faith and nation, but to distant climes, and to heathen tribes, and under conditions wholly diverse from those of the fishermen of Galilee; but there are general principles involved or implied, which should always be kept in mind by those who seek to carry the gospel to the masses of mankind either at home or abroad.

Why do you suppose our Lord commanded the disciples to "salute no man by the way?"[1] This seems to be a departure from the general rule, to become all things to all men. Would it not appear very churlish and offensive to refuse the salam even of a stranger ?

No time to be wasted. It would ; but I do not think that the prohibition extended so far. But the disciples were sent upon important and urgent business—they were ambassadors from their Lord and King—and were not to loiter by the way in idle conversation with friends whom they might chance to meet. The same is now required of special messengers. No doubt the customary salutations were formal and tedious, as they are now, particularly among Druses and other non-Christian sects, and consumed much valuable time. There is also such an amount of insincerity, flattery, and falsehood in the terms of salutation prescribed by etiquette, that our Lord, who is truth itself, desired his representatives to dispense with them as far as possible,—perhaps tacitly to rebuke them. These "instructions" were also intended to reprove another propensity which an Oriental can scarcely resist, no matter how urgent his business. If he meets an acquaintance, he must stop and make an endless number of inquiries, and answer as many. If they come upon men making a bargain or discussing any other matter, they must pause and intrude their own ideas, and enter Salutations. keenly into the business, though it in no wise concerns them ; and, more especially, an Oriental can never resist the temptation to assist *where accounts are being settled* or *money counted out*. The clink of coin has a positive fascination to them. Now, the command of our Saviour strictly forbade all such loiterings. They would waste time, distract attention, and in many ways hinder the prompt and faithful discharge of their important mission.

[1] Luke x. 4.

Upon the same principle he forbade them to go from house to house.[1] The reason is very obvious to one acquainted with Oriental customs. When a stranger arrives in a village or an encampment, the neighbours, one after another, must invite him to eat with them. There is a strict etiquette about it, involving much ostentation and hypocrisy; and a failure in the due observance of this system of hospitality is violently resented, and often leads to alienations and feuds among neighbours. It also consumes much time, causes unusual distraction of mind, leads to levity, and every way counteracts the success of a spiritual mission. On these accounts the evangelists were to avoid these feasts; they were sent, not to be honoured and feasted, but to call men to repentance, prepare the way of the Lord, and proclaim that the kingdom of heaven was at hand. They were, therefore, first to seek a becoming habitation to lodge in, and there abide until their work in that city was accomplished. " Go not from house to house" was a most important precept, and all evangelists in our own country must act upon the spirit of it whenever they go forth to call men to repentance.

CHAPTER XXIV.
Going from house to house.

Let us now turn southward a little, and examine 'Ain el Mudowerah, the famous Round Fountain, which for a long time was supposed to mark the site of Capernaum. This Gennesaret was and is extremely well watered. There are fountains far up Wady Hamam, which irrigate the south-western part of it. The streams from Rŭbŭdîyeh spread over the western side, and the Round Fountain waters the portion lying between it and the lake. Toward the northwest the Nahr 'Amûd, and the Leimûny from above Safed, cross the plain to the lake; and the north-eastern part was anciently fertilized by the powerful fountains of Tabiga. Here is the Round Fountain, covered up with bushes and briers. Dr. Robinson correctly describes it as " enclosed by a low circular wall of mason-work, forming a reservoir nearly a hundred feet in diameter. The water is perhaps two feet deep, beautifully limpid and sweet, bubbling up and flowing out rapidly in a large stream to water the plain below.

'Ain el Mu-dowerah, or Round Fountain.

Josephus thus boasts of the fertility of Gennesaret : "Its nature is wonderful as well as its beauty. Its soil is so fruitful that all sorts of trees can grow upon it, and the inhabitants, accordingly, plant all sorts of trees there; for the temperature of the air is so well mixed, that it agrees very well with those several sorts; particularly walnuts, which require the coldest air, flourish there in vast plenty. One may call this the ambition of Nature, where it forces those plants which are naturally enemies to one another to agree together. It is a happy conjunction of the seasons, as if every one laid claim to this country; for it not only nourishes different sorts of autumnal fruits beyond men's expectations, but preserves them a great while. It supplies men with the principal fruits; with grapes and figs continually during ten months of the year, and the rest of the fruits, as they become ripe, through the whole year; for, besides the good temperature of the air, it is also watered from a

Josephus' account of Gennesaret.

---

[1] Luke x. 7.

PART
II.
most fertile fountain. The people of the country call it Capernaum. Some have thought it a vein of the Nile, because it produces the *Coracin* fish, as well as that lake which is near Alexandria. The length of this country extends itself along the bank of this lake, that bears the same name, for thirty furlongs, and is in breadth twenty; and this is the nature of this place."

Changes now.
This extract shows, at least, the "ambition" of the historian to magnify his own country; but it is very interesting, as a vivid contrast between what this country was eighteen centuries ago and what it now is. The soil may be as good as ever, and the climate the same; but where are the walnuts, the figs, the olives, the grapes, and the other fruits coming on in their season the year round? Alas! all gone. The canal, too, from the fountain of Capernaum is broken, and there are no inhabitants to restore it, and to cultivate this " ambition of Nature."

Size of the plain.
The dimensions of the plain, as given by Josephus, are correct enough, though it is a little longer than thirty, and not quite twenty furlongs in breadth. In summer time all the streams which enter the plain disappear before they reach the lake. I once rode along the margin of the water from Mejdel to 'Ain et Tîny, and was often obliged to wade in the lake itself to get round sharp corners covered with bushes, and no brook of any sort or size at that season entered it from the plain. In winter and spring, however, both the Rŭbŭdîyeh and the Leimûny send strong brooks across to the lake. This Leimûny, where it issues forth from the mountains, has uncovered an immense formation of petrified cane and wood, such as I have seen in no other place.

Petrified wood.
I carried away a donkey-load on one of my visits to this region.

Gennesaret is now pre-eminently fruitful in thorns. They grow up among the grain, or the grain among them, and the reaper must pick the "harvest out of the thorns," as Job says the hungry robber shall do with that of the foolish, whose habitation he suddenly cursed.[1]

Thorns.
Do you suppose that Job refers to gleaning out that which grows thus among thorns? They would certainly take all the rest first; and so this threat would imply that the robbers would make thorough work of it, and leave nothing behind them, not even that which grew among the thorns.

There is another explanation possible. The farmers, after they have threshed out the grain, frequently lay it aside in the chaff in some private place near the floor, and cover it up with thorn-bushes, to keep it from being carried away or eaten by animals. Robbers who found and seized this would literally take it from among thorns; and the disappointment to the "silly one" would be aggravated by the reflection that he had gathered and threshed it, and needed only a day of wind to make it ready for storing in his granary. These farmers all need the exhortation of Jeremiah: "Break up your fallow ground, and sow not among thorns."[2] They are too apt to neglect this; and the thorns, springing up, choke the seed, so that it cannot come to maturity.

---

[1] Job v. 5.   [2] Jer. iv. 3.

And now here is the 'Ain et Tîny (Fountain of the Fig), concerning which Dr. Robinson has discoursed largely, and about which we shall have something to say by-and-by.

Does it take name from these wild fig-bushes growing in the cliff above it? Probably. There may have been, and I suppose were, such there in the days of Josephus ; they are always found at such places. The Jewish historian, however, does not mention this fountain, at least not under this name.

According to the parable of our Lord, we may know that summer is nigh from this fig-tree, for his branch is yet tender, and putteth forth leaves.[1]

True ; but in this sheltered spot, six hundred feet below the level of the ocean, summer comes on very early. The translator of my Josephus pauses to expound, in a note upon his assertion that fig-trees here yield fruit ten months in the year, that most difficult passage in Mark xi. 13, where our Saviour is said to have sought figs on a tree near Jerusalem at the time of the Passover, and found only leaves. The explanation is, that they were *old* leaves which he saw, and *old* figs that had remained on all winter which he expected to find ; for he supposes that in Gennesaret figs must have remained on the trees all winter through. But, whatever may be the true solution of the difficulty, this will not pass ; for fig leaves are among the very earliest to fall in autumn, and no old leaves could have been found on a tree on Olivet in the month of April, though *fresh* ones certainly might.

Have you met with any thing in this country which can clear away the apparent injustice of seeking figs *before the proper time for them ?*

There is a kind of tree which bears a large green-coloured fig that ripens very early. I have plucked them in May, from trees on Lebanon, a hundred and fifty miles north of Jerusalem, and where the trees are nearly a month later than in the south of Palestine ; it does not, therefore, seem impossible but that the same kind *might* have had ripe figs at Easter, in the warm, sheltered ravines of Olivet. The meaning of the phrase, "The time of figs had not yet come," may be that the ordinary season for them had not yet arrived, which would be true enough at any rate. The reason why he might legitimately (so to speak) seek fruit from this particular tree at that early day, was the ostentatious show of *leaves.* The fig often comes with, or even before the leaves, and especially on the early kind. If there was no fruit on this leafy tree, it might justly be condemned as barren ; and hence the propriety of the lesson it was made to teach,—That those who put forth in profusion only the leaves of empty profession are nigh unto cursing.

The objection that this tree did not belong to our Saviour, and therefore he had no right to take the fruit, is answered by a reference to the Mosaic law in such cases. Josephus thus expounds it : " You are not to prohibit those that pass by, when your fruits are ripe, to touch them, but to give them leave to fill themselves full of what you have." And the custom of plucking ripe figs, as

---

[1] Matt. xxiv. 32.

you pass by the orchards, is still universal in this country, especially from trees by the road side, and from all that are not enclosed. And after the "feast of the Cross," which occurs in September, the figs that remain on the trees are common property, and the poor have permission to enter the orchards and gather all they can find. This singular custom seems to have come down from remote antiquity, and is in beautiful correspondence with the spirit of more than one of the precepts of Moses.

Are *barren* fig-trees still found, and does their fruitfulness depend greatly upon careful culture, as may be inferred from the parable in Luke xiii. 6–9 ?

Need of culture.
There are many such trees now ; and if the ground is not properly cultivated, especially when the trees are young—as the one of the parable was, for only *three* years are mentioned—they do not bear at all ; and even when full grown they quickly fail and wither away if neglected. Those who expect to gather good crops of well-flavoured figs are particularly attentive to their culture—not only do they plough and dig about them frequently, and manure them plentifully, but they carefully gather out the stones from the orchards, contrary to their general slovenly habits. But here come our mules, and we will go on with them to Tabiga, where it will be more safe to spend the night than at this solitary 'Ain et Tîny. Take notice, in passing, that this Fountain of the Fig comes out close to the lake, and *on a level with the surface*, and therefore could not have irrigated the plain of Gennesaret. Our path is in the channel of the ancient canal which conveyed the water from Tabiga westward to this plain. The bold bluff above, with its artificial Tell, was once occupied by a castle, built, I suppose, to command this pass round the lake, and also the road to Jŭb Yûsŭf and Jisr Benat Yacobe. It is called Arreîmeh, and, when occupied as a fort, no one could pass this way without permission from its commander.

Tabiga.
It has taken us just fifteen minutes from 'Ain et Tîny to these great fountains of Tabiga ; and while the servants are pitching the tent and preparing dinner, we may ride on half an hour farther, to the site of Tell Hûm. These Arabs seem never to leave this shore, for I always find just such an exposé of semi-black, semi-naked urchins to stare and grin at me : Dr. Robinson also mentions them. Traces of old buildings extend nearly all the way along the *Tell Hûm.* shore from Tabiga to Tell Hûm, to which we must descend over these heaps of lava boulders which encumber the shore and the fields. Whatever we may conclude with regard to Tell Hûm, it is evident that there was once a large town at this place. The shapeless remains are piled up in utter confusion along the shore, extend up the hill northward for at least fifty rods, and are much more extensive and striking than those of any other ancient city on this part of the lake. With two exceptions, the houses were all built of basalt, quite black, *Remains.* and very compact. Like all such ruins, the stones were rudely cut ; but like them also, they are preserved entire, and will remain so for thousands of years. The stone of this temple, synagogue, church, or whatever it may have been, is a beautiful marble cut from the mountains yonder to the north-west, where it is seen in place, and very abundant. I think, with Dr. Robinson, that the

edifice was a synagogue, of the same age as those of Kŭdes, Kefr Bŭriam, CHAPTER XXIV.
Marone, and other places of Galilee ; the work, however, is more massive, and
in a higher style than at any of the above named places. The site of this
building was much more exposed when I was here many years ago than it is at
present, and I found more columns, entablatures, cornices, and other fragments
laid bare than can be seen now. Some of them were of a beautiful pale pink or
rose-coloured marble. These Arabs have piled up the ruins into a few rickety
huts for themselves and their cattle ; but when I was here in 1848 there was
not a human being in sight, and very probably he who comes here next spring
will find it equally solitary.

How luxuriantly everything grows about it ! These nettles and thistles are Luxuriant vegeta-tion.
the largest, sharpest, and most obstinate we have yet encountered.

They will be still more so two months hence ; and nowhere else will you see
such magnificent oleanders as at the head of this lake. I saw clumps of them
here twenty feet high, and a hundred in circumference,—one mass of rosy-red
flowers—a blushing pyramid of exquisite loveliness.

What can be more interesting ? A quiet ramble along the head of this
sacred sea ! The blessed feet of Immanuel have hallowed every acre, and the
eye of divine love has gazed a thousand times upon this fair expanse of lake
and land. Oh ! it is surpassingly beautiful at this evening hour. Those Evening.
western hills stretch their lengthening shadows over it, as loving mothers drop
the gauzy curtains round the cradle of their sleeping babes. Cold must be the
heart that throbs not with unwonted emotion. Son of God and Saviour of the
world ! with thee my thankful spirit seeks communion here on the threshold
of thine earthly home. All things remind me of thy presence and thy love.

> "There's nothing bright above, below,
> From flowers that bloom to stars that glow,
> But in its light my soul can see
> Some feature of thy Deity."

And I am thankful that God, manifest in the flesh, selected this lonely, lovely
shore for his dwelling-place, and sanctified it by his mighty miracles and deeds
of divine mercy. I would not have it otherwise ; and most sweet is it at this
calm and meditative hour,—

> "For twilight best
> Becomes even scenes the loveliest."

There is something spirituelle in the coming on of evening,—

> "Kindly calling
> Earth's many children to repose;
> While round the couch of nature falling,
> Gently the night's soft curtains close."

As you seem to run into the poetic, listen to another lay, such as your soft
muse in silk slippers never sang :—

" How pleasant to me thy deep blue wave,
    O Sea of Galilee!
For the glorious One who came to save
    Hath often stood by thee.

Fair are the lakes in the land I love,
    Where pine and heather grow,
But thou hast loveliness above
    What nature can bestow.

It is not that the wild gazelle
    Comes down to drink thy tide,
But He that was pierced to save from hell
    Oft wandered by thy side.

Graceful around thee the mountains meet,
    Thou calm reposing sea;
But ah! far more, the beautiful feet
    Of Jesus walked o'er thee.

Those days are past—Bethsaida, where?
    Chorazin, where art thou?
His tent the wild Arab pitches there,
    The wild reed shades thy brow.

Tell me, ye mouldering fragments, tell,
    Was the Saviour's city here?
Lifted to heaven, has it sunk to hell,
    With none to shed a tear?

O Saviour! gone to God's right hand,
    Yet the same Saviour still,
Graved on thy heart is this lovely strand,
    And every fragrant hill."

                                        M'CHEYNE.

Site of
Caper-
naum.

Is it certain that Tell Hûm marks the site of Capernaum ?
Far from it ; but of that we will converse in our tent, at leisure after dinner.

I feel more than usual interest in this inquiry about Capernaum. We know where the angel appeared unto Mary—where our Lord was born—where he spent nearly thirty years of his life before he commenced his public ministry —where he closed that ministry in death; and we know, also, from what place he ascended on high after his resurrection from the dead; and it seems as though I must find out the home where he resided most of the time while he manifested to men on earth the glory of the only begotten Son of God.

There is at this day no occasion to enter on those inquiries which fix the site of Capernaum to some spot at the head of this lake, for of this there is now no doubt; and there are here but two places whose claims are earnestly discussed, —Khan Minyeh, at 'Ain et Tîny, and this Tell Hûm. Dr. Robinson has very learnedly argued in favour of the former, and I am slow to dissent from the conclusions of such a man on a question of topography which he has so thoroughly studied. But the truth must be told: he has not convinced me. I believe the Doctor fails in his main argument. He endeavours to prove that 'Ain et

Tîny is the fountain of Capernaum. Now, what do we know of this fountain ? CHAPTER
Absolutely nothing but what is learned from Josephus. Will his account of it XXIV.

RUINS AT CAPERNAUM.

apply to 'Ain et Tîny ? I think not; and *if* not, then the whole argument 'Ain et
falls to the ground. In accounting *for the fertility* of the plain of Gennesaret, Tîny—ar-
the Jewish historian says, " It is *watered* by a most *fertilizing* fountain, called for and
Capernaum." The Doctor, aware that 'Ain et Tîny could not *water* the plain, against.
translates it "*most potable* fountain," and supposes that Josephus was not thinking of *irrigation*, but of water to *drink*. The Doctor, however, is alone in this
rendering. No translator of Josephus, in any language, has thus made him
speak of water to drink, when he is stating the reasons for the unparalleled
fertility of a *plain*. He *could not* have meant *potable*, because 'Ain et Tîny is
not good water, while the whole *lake itself lies within a few rods of it, and is
sweet and pleasant.* I can never abide this water of 'Ain et Tîny, but always
drink that of the lake. When, however, the fountain is full and strong, it can
be used. Still, Josephus could not have meant this fountain ; for, besides the
lake, everywhere accessible, and actually used by all the dwellers on Gennesaret, there are four streams of good water which cut across the plain from the

mountains to the lake, and half a dozen fountains in and around it, of far better water than this at Khan Minyeh. As, therefore, Josephus *could not* have meant to commend this for its potable qualities, so neither could he have mentioned it because of its fertilizing the plain by irrigation: for Dr. Robinson admits that it comes out on a *level* with the lake and *close to it*, so that it could not be made to irrigate an acre of the plain; and, moreover, if it could be elevated high enough, there is not sufficient water to make it worth while, especially in the season of the year when irrigation is needed. The conclusion is irresistible that 'Ain et Tîny is *not* the fountain of Capernaum, and Khan Minyeh, near it, does not mark the site of that city.

Again, the argument for 'Ain et Tîny drawn from the fable about the Nile and the fish Coracinus will be found equally untenable. We may admit that this fish was actually found in the fountain of Capernaum, and that this is a valid reason why the Round Fountain near the south end of Gennesaret could not be it, as Dr. Robinson observes; but this is no evidence that 'Ain et Tîny *is*. Certain kinds of fish delight to come out of the lakes and rivers in cold weather to those fountains that are *tepid* and slightly brackish, and they do so at more than one such fountain along the shores of this very lake, but *not* to 'Ain et

Springs of
Tabiga.

Tîny,—it has none of the qualities which attract them; but these great springs of Tabiga, where we are encamped, are one of their favourite places of resort, and I believe that here, in fact, is the *fountain* of Capernaum. It entirely meets every specification of Josephus, as to situation, quality, quantity, and office. They are at the head of the lake, and sufficiently copious to irrigate the plain. The cisterns by which the water was collected, and elevated to the proper height to flow along the canal, are still here; the canal itself can be traced quite round the cliff *to* the plain, rendering it certain that the water was thus employed; and, lastly, it is just such a fountain as would attract to it the fish from the lake, and there is no rival fountain to contest its claims in any of these essential attributes: there is, therefore, not another identification of an ancient site in this land more entirely to my mind than this. The fountain of Capernaum is at Tabiga.

Tell Hûm
the true
site.

All this, however, does not prove that Capernaum itself was at this precise spot, and I think it was not, but at Tell Hûm. In the first place, I attach great weight to the name. *Hûm* is the last syllable of *Kefr na hûm*, as it was anciently spelled, and it is a very common mode of curtailing old names to retain only the final syllable. Thus we have Zib for Ach*zib*, and Fîk for Aph*cah*, etc. In this instance *Kefr* has been changed to *Tell*—*why*, it is difficult to comprehend, for there is no proper Tell at that site. Still, a *deserted* site is generally named *Tell*, but not *Kefr* (which is applied to a village); and, when Capernaum became a heap of rubbish, it would be quite natural for the Arabs to drop the Kefr, and call it simply Tell Hûm; and this I believe they did. The ruins there are abundantly adequate to answer all the demands of her history, while those few foundations near Khan Minyeh are not. No one would think of them if he had not a theory to maintain which required them to represent

Capernaum. And, finally, in this connection, it seems to me that more import- ance should be attached to native tradition in this case than the Doctor is willing to accord. So far as I can discover, after spending many weeks in this neighbourhood off and on for a quarter of a century, the invariable tradition of the Arabs and the Jews fixes Capernaum at Tell Hûm, and I believe correctly.

It is very necessary to remark that Josephus does not locate either the foun- tain or the village of Capernaum *within* the plain of Gennesaret. It is Dr. Robinson that does this, by drawing his own inferences from certain passages in the Gospels. But it is an obvious remark that the Evangelists had no thought of giving topographical indications, while Josephus, on the contrary, was writing a laboured scenic description, and we should expect to find more light on this question in the latter than in the former; and this is the fact. And, moreover, the passages in the Gospels referred to admit, not to say require, an explanation in entire accordance with the supposition that Tell Hûm marks the site of Capernaum. The notices which bear upon this question are contained in the various accounts of the feeding of the five thousand, given in Matthew xiv., Mark vi., John vi., and Luke ix. This miracle was regarded by all the Evangelists as one of great importance; and as they, in their different narratives, have mentioned Capernaum and Bethsaida in such connections and relations as to have occasioned no small perplexity to sacred geographers, and finally led to the *invention* of a second Bethsaida at the head of this lake, we may be excused for developing our own ideas on the subject with some particularity of detail. But as we shall pass the very site where, I believe, the miracle was wrought, during our ride to-morrow morning, we had better postpone the discussion until we see the scene and the scenery; it will, however, necessarily throw light upon the questions we have been canvassing to-night, and, as I believe, add materially to the evidence that Tell Hûm is the true site of Capernaum.

Admitting this, what do you make of the ruins at 'Ain et Tîny.

They may, perhaps, mark the site of old Chinneroth. The greatest objection that occurs to me is the inconsiderable amount of them. Chinneroth was given to Naphtali; and from it both this plain and lake may have derived their names, for Genashur and Gennesaret are only different forms of Chinneroth, or Cinneroth—in Maccabees it is written Genasor, and also Nasor; and what more likely than that this city was on this plain, and gave name to it, and the lake also? I am aware that many entertain the idea that the predecessor of the city of Tiberias was Chinneroth; and it may have been so, but I think not. We may examine this point on the ground, and for the present rest on the suggestion that Chinneroth stood at the head of the pretty plain to which it gave name.

Tell Hûm being Capernaum, and Khan Minyeh Chinneroth, what do you make of this Tabiga?

It was the grand manufacturing suburb of Capernaum, and hence the foun- tains took name from the city. Here were the mills, not only for it, but for all the neighbourhood, as is now the case. So also the potteries, *tanneries,* and other operations of this sort, would be clustered around these great fountains; and the traces of the necessary buildings may be seen all around us. I even derive the name *Tabiga* from this business of *tanning*. Tabiga, or Tabaga, is nearly identical with *Dabbaga*, the Arabic name for tannery; and, no doubt, the tanneries of Capernaum were actually at these fountains, whatever may be true in regard to the name. And if a city should again arise in this vicinity, the tanneries belonging to it would certainly be located here, for the water is precisely the kind best adapted to that business.

As there is considerable marshy land about this Tabiga, may not this account for the prevalence of fevers at Capernaum? for here it was, of course, that Peter's wife's mother lay sick of a fever.[1]

Fevers of a very malignant type are still prevalent, particularly in summer and autumn; owing, no doubt, to the extreme heat acting upon these marshy plains, such as the Bŭtaiha, at the influx of the Jordan.

It must have been in this neighbourhood that our Lord was so pressed by the multitudes who flocked from all parts to hear him, that he was obliged to enter a ship, and have it thrust out a little from the shore, that from thence he might address them without interruption.

No doubt; and I was delighted to find small creeks or inlets between this and Tell Hûm, where the *ship* could ride in safety only a few feet from the shore, and where the multitudes, seated on both sides, and before the boat, could listen without distraction or fatigue. As if on purpose to furnish seats, the shore, on both sides of these narrow inlets, is piled up with smooth boulders of basalt. Somewhere hereabouts, also, Andrew and Peter were casting their nets into the sea, when our Lord, passing by, called them to follow him, and become fishers of men. And in one of these identical inlets, James, the son of Zebedee, and John his brother, were mending their nets, when they, being also called, immediately left the ship and their father Zebedee, and followed Jesus.[2] Here, yes, right here, began that organization which has spread over the earth and revolutionized the world. Viewed in this relation, is there a spot on earth that can rival this in interest?

---

[1] Matt. viii. 14.   [2] Matt. iv. 18–22.

CHAPTER XXV.

LAKE OF TIBERIAS—TABIGA—KERSEH.*

Thursday, March 23d.

I PROMISE you a most interesting ride to-day, and, while the loads go directly Route. along the shore to the entrance of the Jordan, we will ascend toward the north-east for half an hour, to visit the site of Chorazin. This triangular part of Naphtali, between the north-western corner of the lake and Jisr Benat Yacobe, has ever been a wild, semi-deserted region, destitute of water, of trees, and of human habitations ; and, of course, there are no *ruins* of importance upon it. It is, however, a fine pasture-field for the flocks of the Arabs, and Flocks in I found it covered, in mid-winter, with camels and cattle from the cold winter. Jaulan. Those parts adjacent to the shore have neither snow nor frost, and are clothed with grass and flowers in January ; but the ascent is very great,— not less than two thousand feet at the highest part of the road, and much higher west of it toward Safed, where the hills are often buried under deep snow. The flocks and their shepherds can, therefore, pass from winter to summer in an hour, and for several months can graduate their range so as to enjoy just the temperature which is most agreeable to their tastes. In May, however, the pasturage dries up, water fails, and the heat sends the flocks and herds to the higher and colder regions east of the Jordan. It is a ride of four hours from Khan Minyeh to the bridge, most of the distance over rough black basalt, interspersed in a few places with a white marble, intensely hard, and sufficiently compact to take a beautiful polish. Jub Yusuf—Well of Joseph Well of —where Moslem tradition locates the pit in which that unfortunate lad was Joseph. cast by his envious brethren, is midway between the lake and the bridge. The *khan* there is like this of Minyeh, but not so dilapidated, though equally

---

* [In this chapter our author visits the site of Chorazin ; states his reasons for believing in but one Bethsaida, built, however, partly on each side of the Jordan ; describes the little plain of Butaiha, on the north-east of the lake ; gives a full account of the upland district of Jaulan, formerly Golan and Gaulanitis, lying to the eastward ; and fixes on Gersa, or Kerza, as the scene of the miracle, in the country of the Gergashites, where the devils were sent into the herd of swine. In this chapter we have omitted, in this edition, a few paragraphs not essential to the object of the work.—ED.]

PART
II.

deserted. Indeed, there is not an inhabited house in the entire region. The land, however, is fertile, and in some coming day of peace and prosperity it will be a picturesque, fruitful, and most healthy province.

Arab
houses.

Before we pass entirely away from this vicinity, I wish to inquire whether there is anything in the construction of modern Arab houses to explain the manner in which the man sick of the palsy was placed at the feet of Jesus. I have never been able to understand it.

AN ARAB HOUSE.

The record in Mark ii. 1–12 and Luke v. 18–26 states that there was such a dense crowd around our Lord that the four men could not force their way through it, and therefore they went to the roof of the house, broke up part of it, and let down the sick man from above. The following considerations

Letting
down
through
roof.

may make this act intelligible. We must banish from our minds every form of European or American houses. Those of Capernaum, as is evident from the ruins, were, like those of modern villages in this same region, low, *very low*, with flat roofs, reached by a stairway from the yard or court. Jesus probably stood in the open *lewan*, and the crowd were around and in front of him. Those who carried the paralytic, not being able " to come at him for the press," ascended to the roof, removed so much of it as was necessary, and let down their patient through the aperture. Examine one of these houses, and you will see at once that the thing is natural, and easy to be accomplished. The roof is only a few feet high, and by stooping down, and holding the corners of the couch—merely a thickly-padded quilt, as at present in this region—they could let down the sick man without any apparatus of ropes or cords to assist them. And thus, I suppose, they did. The whole affair was the extemporaneous device of plain peasants, accustomed to open their roofs, and let down grain, straw, and other articles, as they still do in this country.

The only difficulty in this explanation is to understand how they could break up the roof without sending down such a shower of dust as to incommode our Lord and those around him. I have often seen it done, and have done it myself to houses in Lebanon ; but there is always more dust made than is agreeable. The materials now employed are beams about three feet apart, across which short sticks are arranged close together, and covered with the thickly-matted thorn-bush called *bellan*. Over this is spread a coat of stiff mortar, and then comes the marl or earth which makes the roof. Now it is easy to remove any part of this without injuring the rest. No objection, therefore, would be made on this score by the owners of the house. They had merely to scrape back the earth from a portion of the roof over the *lewan*, take up the thorns and the short sticks, and let down the couch between the beams at the very feet of Jesus. The end achieved, they could speedily restore the roof as it was before. I have the impression, however, that the covering, at least of the *lewan*, was not made of earth, but of materials more easily taken up. It may have been merely of coarse matting, like the walls and roofs of Turkman huts ; or it may have been made of boards, or even stone slabs (and such I have seen), that could be quickly removed. All that is necessary, however, for us to know is, that the roof was flat, low, easily reached, and easily opened, so as to let down the couch of the sick man; and all these points are rendered intelligible by an acquaintance with modern houses in the villages of Palestine.

But we must now make our way more to the east, across this Wady Nashif, as I hear it called by the Bedawîn. It runs directly down to the lake on the east side of Tell Hûm, and Khorazy lies over against us in that side valley which joins Wady Nashif directly below us. We may as well walk over these basaltic boulders, and each one take care of himself and horse as best he can. And here we are among the shapeless heaps of Chorazin, which attest most impressively the fulfilment of that prophetic curse of the Son of God. I have scarcely a doubt about the correctness of the identification, although Dr. Robinson rejects it, almost with contempt. But the name, Khorazy, is nearly the Arabic for Chorazin ; the situation—two miles north of Tell Hûm —is just where we might expect to find it ; the ruins are quite adequate to answer the demands of history ; *and there is no rival site.* I am utterly at a loss, therefore, to discover any other reason for rejecting it, but that its location at this point might seem to favour the claims of Tell Hûm to be Capernaum. To me, however, this is an additional evidence of the correctness of the identification in both cases. But we must leave the discussion of such questions to those who have leisure and learning, and turn down to

PART
II.

Bethsaida.

the south-east, over this vast field of black basalt, to visit the equally prostrate Bethsaida. Both fell beneath the same woe, and both have long been lost to the student and traveller. I am still in doubt as to the actual site of Bethsaida. The name is now generally affixed, in maps, to a *Tell* a short distance up the Jordan, on the east side ; but the only ruins of importance are below, along the foot of the hills bordering the vale of the Jordan, and at its debouchure on the west side. When I was here in 1855, the Bedawîn in the Butaiha applied the name Bethsaida to a bank on the shore of the lake, which is distinguished by a few palm-trees ; and in some modern maps this site is called Misadiyeh, a derivative from the same root as Bethsaida, both having reference to *fishing.* Mesady, however, is the name of a site on the rocky hill *west* of the Jordan, and higher up the gorge. Doubtless the city of Andrew and Peter derived its name from this act and occupation of fishing ; and, therefore, it is nearly certain that it was located on the shore, and not several miles from it, at the *Tell* to which the name is now affixed. Josephus also says that it was at the entrance of the Jordan into the lake.

Ruins on
west side
of Jordan.

I call your attention, in passing, to these remains of ancient buildings on the *west* side of the river, because we shall have occasion to refer to them hereafter. They mark that part of Bethsaida which was, as I suppose, on the *west* bank of the Jordan, and, of course, in Galilee ; while those on the east belong to that part which Philip repaired and called Julias. We shall come among them after crossing the river, which we might do on the sand-bar along the margin of the lake ; but I prefer the ford above, where the bottom is less marshy.

Buffaloes.

Again we meet the mire-loving buffaloes, and they seem as fond of the mud as the very swine.

They are ; and when they cannot find a marsh they bathe in pure water. I once ascended Olympus above Brusa, and near the very top buffaloes were lying in a pool of ice-water, collected from the surrounding snow-banks ; and they appeared to enjoy this cold bath as much as these do this black mud.

Josephus'
battle with
the
Romans.

By the way, it was just here that Josephus fought the Romans under Sylla ; concerning which battle he says, with his usual vanity, " I would have performed great things that day if a certain fate had not been my hindrance ; for the horse on which I rode, and upon whose back I fought, fell into a quagmire, and threw me on the ground, and I was bruised on my wrist, and was carried into a certain village called Caphernome or Capernaum." [1] This paragraph is not only curious in itself, but it confirms the idea that Capernaum was at Tell Hûm, and that it was then only a village. But turn up to the margin of this marsh along the foot of the hill, or you will encounter that certain fate which hindered Josephus from doing great exploits against Sylla. These black spongy places are treacherous to the last degree, as David appears to have found by sad experience ; for he speaks of sinking in deep mire to

---

[1] Life, 72nd paragraph.

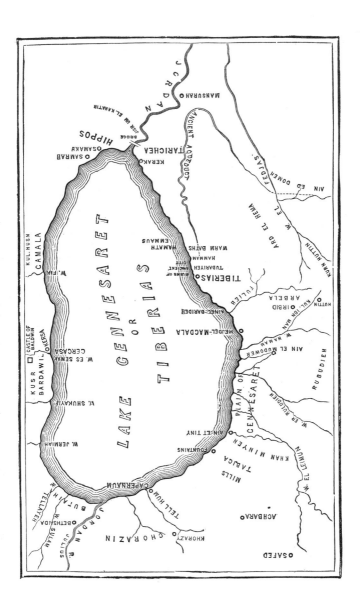

which there was no bottom. It is a curious fact that dry, rocky, and moun- CHAPTER
tainous as this country is, yet it abounds in bogs and quagmires to an extra- XXV.
ordinary extent. The rivers of Damascus all subside into vast swamps : the Swamps
Orontes creeps through them from Riblah to Antioch. The Jordan does the
same from Dan to Tiberias. The Kishon and the Naamany find their way to
the Bay of Acre through bottomless marshes, and so does the Zerka or Crocodile
River at Cæsarea, the Abu Zabûra, the Kanah, the Falej, and the Aujeh,
between that city and Jaffa. David was therefore perfectly familiar with these
deceitful and dangerous pits, and could speak of them from painful personal
experience.

Here we are at the ford, and though the water is not deep, the bottom is
rocky; and there down goes the mule, with all our bedding and wardrobe, into
the river. This " certain fate," however, is less painful than that of Josephus;
and, as the day is clear and warm, we shall be able to sun and dry everything
before night. And now we have the flowery but rather muddy Butaiha Plain of
through which to saunter for two hours. Dr. Robinson says correctly that it Butaiha.
resembles Gennesaret—the one on the north-west, and the other along the
north-east shore of the lake, both well watered and extremely fertile, and also
both very unhealthy. The Butaiha has the largest and most permanent
brooks. Gennesaret the most numerous and largest fountains. I can confirm
the statement of Burckhardt, that the Arabs of Butaiha have the earliest
cucumbers and melons in all this region. I once visited it in early spring
with a guide from Safed, who came, according to custom, to load his mules
with these vegetables for the market in that town. The vines are already
up and spreading rapidly; and there comes the gardener with a basket of
cucumbers to sell,—which, of course, we will purchase for our salad in the
evening.

LODGE AT BUTAIHA.

And that is the lodge, I suppose, which Isaiah speaks of ; just as the frail, Lodge in
temporary thing suggested that sad complaint of the prophet, " The daughter a garden
of Zion is left as a cottage in a vineyard, as a lodge in a garden of cucumbers." [1]

---

[1] Isaiah i. 8.

PART
II.

No doubt; but the true point of the comparison will not appear until the crop is over, and the lodge forsaken by the keeper. Then the poles fall down or lean every way, and those green boughs with which it is shaded will have been scattered by the wind, leaving only a ragged, sprawling wreck, —a most affecting type of utter desolation—"as Sodom, and like unto Gomorrah."

Julias
(Beth-
saida).

If this is the Julias which Philip built, and named in honour of the daughter of Cæsar, it was certainly no great compliment.

And yet Josephus says he advanced it to the dignity of a city, both by the number of inhabitants it contained and its other grandeur;[1] of which grandeur nothing now remains but these heaps of unmeaning rubbish. The fact is, that the Jewish historian is not to be trusted in such matters. I have visited all the cities which Philip is said to have built, and there neither is, nor could have been, much of royal magnificence about them. This is a fair specimen; and though Sogana and Seleucia were somewhat larger, they could never have been anything more than agricultural villages. I suppose Philip repaired and enlarged this part of Bethsaida in order to detach it from Galilee, and to secure to himself this rich plain of Butaiha, which appertained to it.

Jaulan, or
Golan.

As we have leisure enough while sauntering down this flowery plain, I should like to hear some account of this Jaulan above us. It is the Golan of the Hebrews, the Gaulanitis of the Greeks, and yet is almost an utter blank on our maps and in books of travel.

I have repeatedly explored parts of it, and once rode through it lengthwise from Hermon to the Jermuk. With a pleasant party of friends I started from Banias on the morning of February 28th, to visit first the ruins at Seid Yehuda. After examining these interesting remains of antiquity, we ascended the basaltic hills eastward for more than an hour, to Sujan, the Sogana of Philip. The surrounding country was once well cultivated, as appears evident from the broken terraces along the sides of the mountain; but at present it is absolutely deserted by all except lawless Bedawîn. The view from Sujan over the Hûleh and the surrounding regions is magnificent; and I imagine that one great attraction of the place was its cool and healthy atmosphere. From Sujan we wandered upward and eastward over vast fields of lava, without

Ruins of
Skaik.

road, or even path, for more than an hour, to Skaik, probably the Sacaca mentioned by Ptolemy. It is one of the largest ruins in Gaulanitis, and was better built than most cities of this region. My aneroid marked 2670 feet for the elevation of this site; and we found the air clear, cold, and bracing. Skaik was inhabited until modern times, and celebrated as the general rendezvous and point of departure for caravans to the east and south; and the existing remains of vast cisterns and caravanserais show that ample provision had been made for the accommodation of these large trading companies.

[1] Ant, xviii, 2, 1.

Half an hour south by west from Skaik is a large and very ancient ruin, called Summakah. This word seems to contain the elements of Samachonitis, the Greek name for the Hûleh. It is, however, pronounced as though written with a *koff* (*guttural k*) instead of *kaf;* and in that case it is the name for the bush sŭmmăk, the sumach of the tanner. Whatever be the origin and relations of the name, the position is beautiful, and it is supplied with a fine spring of water, flowing out from the base of the hill. Half an hour farther south are ruins called Joaiza; and there we encamped for the night, near the tent of the Emeer Hussein el Fŭdle—the supreme chief of all the Arabs in that part of the Jaulan. He is a young man of quiet manners and modest deport- ment, of few words, but sincere and truthful—all remarkable exceptions in his race and station. He traces his pedigree back directly to Mohammed, and the highest sheikhs and emeers of the Jaulan kiss his hand in acknowledgment of his superior rank. We were received with great respect; fresh coffee was roasted, and a sheep brought up, slaughtered, and quickly cooked before our tent, and the extemporaneous feast spread for us in presence of the emeer. Though he did not literally run to the herd and bring it himself, others did at his bidding, and the whole affair brought the patriarch Abraham most vividly to mind. Like our emeer, he dwelt in tents, and his dependants were encamped about him with their flocks and herds.

There were not more than thirty tents at this encampment; and, upon inquiry, I found, to my surprise, that the people were nearly all the slaves of the emeer. They and their ancestors have belonged to his family for so many generations that all trace of their real origin is lost. Their complexion also has softened into the bronze of the genuine Arab, and the Negro features are almost obliterated. The true Bedawîn, however, never intermarry with them, though the villagers and artisans who settle among them occasionally do. They are the property of the emeer in a restricted sense, and so are the flocks and herds which they are permitted to hold; and he does not hesitate to take what he wants, nor can they refuse his demands, whatever they may be. But then custom, or law, or both, utterly forbids him to sell them. I inquired into all these matters the next day as we rode through the country under the protection and guidance of his head servant, who reminded me constantly of "Eliezer of Damascus." In answer to my question, he exclaimed, in indignant surprise, "Sell us! *istugfar Allah*—God forbid!" They are, in fact, the home-born servants of the very ancient *house* of El Fŭdle; and, like the three hundred and eighteen in Abraham's family, they are his warriors in times of need,—which, in one way or another, happens almost daily. They seem to be attached to the emeer, or rather, perhaps, to his family name, rank, power, and honour. Their own honour, safety, and influence all depend upon him. I was almost startled to find that the emeer was entirely governed by one of his own slaves. He does nothing of himself; and this modern Eliezer not only disposes of his master's goods, but manages the affairs of government very much as he pleases. All the Arabs of the Hûleh and Jaulan greatly fear

PART
II.

and court this chief servant. He is shrewd, efficient, and sometimes cruel; nor is any man's life safe if its owner becomes obnoxious to Master Dauk. But a truce to him and his master. Other matters about this encampment of genuine Ishmaelites were equally interesting.

Gathering of flocks.

In the evening the flocks began to concentrate around this Joaiza from every part of the surrounding desert. It was a noisy, lively, and really beautiful scene. The young donkeys, calves, kids, and lambs, that had been kept up during the day, now let out from the folds, rushed bleating and braying every way, seeking their parents. They were finally shut in, and everything in the camp became quiet except the dogs. These kept up an incessant and angry barking all night long; and I understood that there were supposed to be robbers lurking about, who, but for these watchful sentinels, would carry off lambs, and even camels, from the outskirts of the encampment.

Bedawin dogs.

These dogs of the Bedawîn are extremely fierce, and it is not a little dangerous, as I have repeatedly experienced, to come upon an encampment in the night. They are an indispensable part of the shepherd's equipage, and

Country of Job.

appear to have been so even in the time of Job. And, by the way, this Jaulan was Job's country. His flocks and herds roamed over these same wild "walks," and were exposed to the very same dangers that now task the courage of these Arab shepherds. In these inaccessible ravines were the lion's den, the tiger's lair, and pits for bears and wolves; and across these vast plateaus the flying bands of Sabean robbers roved in search of plunder. The country, the people, the manners and customs, remain unchanged from remote antiquity. Job was a great emeer of the Hauran; and if he were there now, he might find the same kind of enemies to plunder and kill, and even natural phenomena very similar to the great fire that burnt up the sheep, and the mighty wind from the wilderness that overturned the houses of his children. Destructive fires often sweep over the desert, and angry hurricanes hurl to the ground the habitations of man. I would not, however, be understood to bring down the patient man of Uz to a level with the modern emeers of Arabia. He was an agriculturist as well as shepherd; an honest man, and not a robber; one that feared God and eschewed evil, and not a fanatical follower of the false prophet.

Frost and heat.

The night air at Joaiza was keen and cold; indeed, there was a sharp frost, and ice appeared on all the little pools about the camp. Jacob had experience of such alternations between blazing sun and biting frost. "In the day the drought consumed me, and the frost by night, and my sleep departed from me," was the indignant reply to his avaricious father-in-law.[1] In the present case the cold was owing mainly to the great elevation of the Jaulan—not less, on an average, than two thousand five hundred feet above the sea. It is a grand volcanic plateau, comparatively level, but with a line of singular *tells* running from Hermon southward to the Jermuk. The first is Tell Ahmar, south of

---

[1] Gen. xxxi. 40.

Lake Phiala. Three miles south of this is Tell Sheikha, then Tell Bŭrm, CHAPTER
next the great double Tell Aramein—the north peak called Aram, and the XXV.
south Abu Nidy. About four miles farther south is Tell Yusuf, and next it
Tell el Khanzîr. Tell el Farus is the last and the loftiest of the list. Few
persons, I presume, ever ride over the hills of Galilee without admiring these
tall, sugar-loaf land-marks on the eastern side of the Jordan, and wishing to Sugar-loaf
know their names and character. To such, at least, the above list will be hills.
satisfactory ; and the only additional statement I have to make in regard to
them is, that, though seen at such a great distance they appear small, they are,
in reality, rough volcanic *mounts*, and some of them very respectable *mountains*. Beyond them, eastward and southward, stretch the vast and fertile
plains of the Hauran, now and always the granary of Central Syria and
Northern Arabia. The Jaulan, however, is entirely given up to pasturage,
and, from the nature of the soil and climate, it will continue to be so,
although there are places which might be cultivated with any kind of grain,
and orchards would flourish everywhere. It is exceedingly well watered in
all parts, except the region between the Lakes Phiala and Tiberias. There
the fountains and streams dry up early in spring, and the weary traveller
must carry his water-bottle with him if he would not be " consumed with
drought."

We started early next morning with a letter and guide from the emeer to Fields of
Sheikh Fareij, whose camp was *somewhere*, about a day's journey in the lava.
desert southward of Joaiza. In that general direction our guide led us across
endless fields of lava, and most of the time without any road that I could see,
or my horse either. We crossed many tracks, however, which led down to the
Hûleh, to Jisr Benat Yacobe, and to this Butaiha, and encountered numerous
wadies, some shallow, others deep and ugly, which descend to the Jordan and
the lake. For the first hour we were surrounded by the droves and flocks of
the emeer, and I noticed a shepherd kindly carrying in his '*aba* a new-born
lamb, and a woman sedulously teaching a young calf what its mouth was made
for, and how to manage its spasmodic legs. Such acts not only remind one of
the patriarchs who dwelt in tents and tended cattle, but also of that Good
Shepherd from whose bosom no enemy shall ever be able to pluck even the
weakest lambkin of the flock.

Two miles from Joaiza I took " bearings " from an elevated site, called Sin-
diana; and a mile farther south is the pretty Tell Delwa, with a ruin upon, and Ruins
a wady descending from it toward the Jordan. Three miles farther we came
to Thûban and Kefr Neffakh, both very large ruins, but particularly the latter,
which exhibits an enormous mass of prostrate houses. After this we wandered about over broken ground for an hour in search of a Turkman sheikh,
and found his camp hid away in Wady Ghadarîyeh, which joins, lower down,
the far greater one of Ruzzanîyeh. This wady has many tributaries and much
water, and here, where it enters the Butaiha, is called Em el 'Ajaj, and also
Wady Sulam, incorrectly written Sunam on maps. Having procured a guide,

PART
II.

we reached Selukia—the Seleucia of Philip—in half an hour. The ruins of this place are extensive, but the position does not accord very well with the statements of Josephus. He, however, had never visited it, and spoke at random, as he often does in regard to matters with which he was not personally acquainted. Directly south is a place called 'Ain Selukia, from a collection of fountains whose water flows west, and unites with Wady Ruzzaniyeh. We had some difficulty in crossing another deep wady, about a mile farther south, named Tellaiya, from a number of low *tells*, a few miles east of our line of march. This Tellaiya may be the same that enters the Butaiha to the east of us, and is called Dalia by Dr. Robinson. It has cut a deep channel through the hard lava, and a fine stream of water rattles over its rocky bed.

Remains
of wood.

Down to this Wady Tellaiya the country had been more or less wooded. Though the oaks that cover the hills south of Banias and 'Ainfit gradually become more and more rare, smaller also, and more *scraggy*, still they are found, solitary or in groups, quite to the wady ; but south of it they disappear altogether, and the country is naked and cheerless. So, also, the flocks became more rare ; indeed, for many miles we saw none, although the pasturage is equally good, and water even more abundant than farther north. Lively little brooks crossed our track every five minutes ; but I suppose this deserted region is a sort of neutral territory between the northern and southern tribes, who are not always on such terms as render it safe to be caught too far away from their friends.

Ravine of
Jermaiah.

We were obliged to make a long detour to the east, in order to get round the impracticable gorge of the Jermaiah—that wady which comes down to the lake near the south-eastern corner of the Butaiha. It is the largest and most savage of all the ravines into which we looked during our ride of nine hours, and is said to be the chosen resort of leopards, wolves, hyenas, boars, and other

Game.

wild animals. In fact, the whole Gaulanitis abounds in game. We saw many gazelles, and another species of deer, called *waal*, considerably larger and more like our American deer ; partridges also, and grouse, ducks, geese, cranes, and pelicans delight in these solitudes, which their grand enemy, man, rarely invades, or if he does, has too many causes of solicitude to admit of delay, or to make it safe to have the crack of his musket heard.

After heading Wady Jermaiah we turned nearly west, down a gentle declivity for half an hour, and then came to a large ruin called Kunaitera ; not that of the same name on the road to Damascus from Jisr Benat Yacobe, but one

Sehm
Jaulan—
Golan ?

more ancient, and much larger than that ever was. *Sehm* Jaulan is the name of a well-known ruin to the east of this, and I suppose it marks the site of the Biblical Golan, from which this province takes its name. There is also a Khurbet Saida, some distance to the east of our track, but no Beit Saida. From Kunaitera to Khurbet Arba'in—*ruin of forty*—is half an hour. This city was originally well built for a place where no stone but basalt is found, and it must have been inhabited until a comparatively recent period. Crossing a smooth and fertile plain for some twǒ miles, we plunged abruptly into the CHAPTER gorge of Wady Shukaiyif by an almost perpendicular path, down which our XXV. animals slid rather than walked, greatly to their annoyance and our amusement; and here we found Sheikh Fareij, with his large camp, hid away so perfectly that it could not be seen until one is directly above it. Our nine hours' ride had made us all weary, and we gladly pitched our tent near that of the sheikh. He was not then at home, but a brother supplied his place, with a boisterous and rather ostentatious welcome. He berated our guide for bringing guests at an hour so late that it was impossible to give them such a reception and feast as were becoming. The sheep were all at a distance, and none could be got to sacrifice in honour of the occasion, and the parties, until morning, etc., etc. I assured him that we had all necessary provision for ourselves, and needed only provender for the horses. This was speedily brought, and everything arranged to our mutual satisfaction.

Just after our arrival a knot of Arabs gathered round the sheikh's tent, in A rescue. earnest and angry discussion, and I felt rather anxious to know whether or not we were the subject of controversy. Upon inquiry, it appeared that some of the sheikh's men had fallen in with a party of robbers that morning, who were driving off the cattle of these poor peasants who cultivate this Butaiha, and, after a skirmish with them, succeeded in rescuing the stolen cattle, and brought them into their camp. The owners had come to claim their property, and the rescuers demanded four hundred piastres before they would give them up. The case was brought before the sheikh, who ordered them to be restored without ransom; and, of course, there was grumbling on one side, and loud thanks on the other.

I noticed, at all the encampments which we passed, that the sheikh's tent Spear in was distinguished from the rest by a tall spear stuck upright in the ground in ground at front of it; and it is the custom, when a party is out on an excursion for tent. robbery or for war, that when they halt to rest, the spot where the chief reclines or sleeps is thus designated. So Saul, when he lay sleeping, had his spear stuck in the ground at his bolster, and Abner and the people lay round about him.[1] The whole of that scene is eminently Oriental and perfectly natural, even to the deep sleep into which all had fallen, so that David and Abishai could walk among them in safety. The Arabs sleep heavily, especially when fatigued. Often, when travelling, my muleteers and servants have resolved to watch by turns in places thought to be dangerous; but in every instance I soon found them fast asleep, and generally their slumbers were so profound that I could not only walk among them without their waking, but might have taken the very 'aba with which they were covered. Then the cruse of water Cruse of at Saul's head is in exact accordance with the customs of the people at this bolster. day. No one ventures to travel over these deserts without his cruse of water, and it is very common to place one at the "bolster," so that the owner can

---

[1] 1 Sam. xxvi. 7.

PART II. reach it during the night. The Arabs eat their dinner in the evening, and it is generally of such a nature as to create thirst ; and the quantity of water which they drink is enormous. The *cruse* is, therefore, in perpetual demand.

David and Saul

Saul and his party lay in a shady valley, steeped in heavy sleep, after the fatigue of a hot day. The camp-ground of Sheikh Fareij, in Wady Shukaiyif, is adapted in all respects to be the scene of the adventure. David, from above, marks the spot where the king slumbers, creeps cautiously down, and stands over his unconscious persecutor. Abishai asks permission to smite him once, only once, and promises not to smite a second time ; but David forbade him, and, taking the spear and cruse of water, ascended to the top of the hill afar off, and cried aloud to Abner : " Art not thou a valiant man ? and who is like to thee in Israel ? . . . . . As the Lord liveth, ye are worthy to die, because ye have not kept your master, the Lord's anointed. And now see where the king's spear is, and the cruse of water that was at his bolster." [1] What a strange sensation must have run through the camp as David's voice rang out these cutting taunts from the top of the hill ! But David was perfectly safe, and there are thousands of ravines where the whole scene could be enacted, every word be heard, and yet the speaker be quite beyond the reach of his enemies.

A young bride.

Among the incidents of that memorable ride was the following : A hardy little girl, about twelve years old, accompanied us on foot. She was the daughter of our guide, and he was bringing her to her husband, at this camp of Fareij, who had purchased her for a thousand piastres *(forty dollars)*. She had no companion or friend of any kind, except a young donkey, as little and as lively as herself. This she drove before her with infinite trouble. It was constantly running hither and thither, and she after it, over sharp rocks and through tangled thorns ; but still she never seemed to grow weary. I became quite interested in the brave girl, and from my heart hoped and prayed that she might find, in her hitherto unseen husband, a kind companion. When we arrived at the camp of Fareij, she was taken immediately into the harem of the sheikh, and I saw her no more. She carried nothing in the shape of outfit, except the little donkey. I noticed that when she left her mother's tent at Joaiza, she had on a pair of high red leather boots. These, however, she quickly drew off, and, tucking them under her sash or girdle, raced over the rocks after her pet in bare feet ; and this she did from early morning until after sunset. Our girls don't do such things on their wedding day.

An Arab sheikh.

Sheikh Fareij spent the evening in our tent, and greatly interested us by his dignified manner and intelligence, and by a certain air of sadness that pervaded his whole conversation and deportment. He complained bitterly of the course pursued by Government, whose tax-gatherers robbed and plundered the Arabs without mercy ; and he maintained that they were compelled to

plunder in turn. This was by way of apology for the admission which he CHAPTER
seemed somewhat ashamed to make, that robbing was their trade, and that he XXV.
and his men were engaged in it daily, either as aggressors or defenders. He
further lamented that the ancient, generous customs of the Bedawin were
being corrupted by Turkish oppression. They now robbed one another, and
even murder is often added to plunder. "I myself," said he, "live day by
day by the life of this good sword," striking his hand fiercely upon the formidable tool at his side. He admitted that, without my guide from the
emeer, I could not have reached his tent in safety ; and that, without similar
assistance from himself, I should not be able to proceed on the morrow round
the eastern shore of the lake. Of the truth of this I had certain and rather
startling evidence next morning ; for I found myself suddenly confronted by a
troop of the most savage Bedawin I ever encountered, and they made no
secret of the fact that they were restrained from plundering us solely by the
guard from Sheikh Fareij. What significance do' such incidents impart to a
thousand allusions to robbers in the Bible, particularly in the history of David,
and in his Psalms !

Your wanderings over the Jaulan must have led you near the track that Mizpah.
Jacob followed on his return from Mesopotamia. Could you hear anything
about that Mizpah where Laban overtook him ?

Mizpah must have been to the east of our track ; but I have never been
able to identify any of the places mentioned in that remarkable narrative.
The entire scene is eminently rich in allusions to Oriental manners and customs. The behaviour of Laban is true to life, and every expression is familiar Jacob and
to my ear "as household words." Laban says, "The God of your father Laban.
spake unto me yesternight, saying, Take thou heed that thou speak not to
Jacob either good or bad."[1] Now we should think that Laban was uttering
his own condemnation, and it appears strange that Jacob did not retort upon
him by asking, Why, then, have you followed me ? You have disobeyed the
command of God, according to your own admission. Jacob, however, knew
very well that such a plea would avail nothing. Laban believed that he fulfilled
the intent of the divine command merely by refraining to injure Jacob ; and
so the latter understood it. The terms of the order were most comprehensive
and stringent, but the real intention was to forbid violence ; and this sort of
construction must be applied to Oriental language in a thousand cases, or we
shall push simple narratives into absurdities, and make men, and even the God
of truth, utter contradictions.

The charge of stealing Laban's *teraphim* greatly provoked the idol-hating Teraphim.
Jacob, and he very likely thought it a mere device to conceal some evil purpose. But the thing is interesting to us as the earliest distinct notice we
have of the existence and worship of these images. They are frequently mentioned in after times, but here we first find them in this patriarchal family.

---

[1] Gen. xxxi. 29.

They must have been so small as to be easily concealed under the *saddle* of Rachel; and, by the way, it is still very common for Arabs to hide stolen property under the padding of their saddles. They probably resembled the small images of saints which are now carried about by Oriental Christians, and may have been honoured and consulted in much the same way. Some of those saints are celebrated for assistance given to women afflicted with Rachel's sorrow; and perhaps she herself had been driven to this sort of idolatry in her agony to become a mother. It would be Orientally feminine in an eminent degree if this was the cause of her *stealing* her father's gods. Nor does this act of stealing a god to worship strike these people about us as monstrous or absurd.

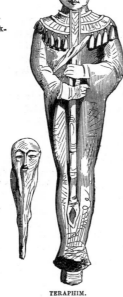

TERAPHIM.

Idolatry and wickedness.

I have known many such thefts of modern teraphim (pictures and images), and by women too. And why not? It is surely not absurd to *steal the god* whose aid you invoke to assist you to steal other things. It is well known that Greek pirates are most devout worshippers of the saints; and, what is even more monstrous, the Moslems, who claim to worship only the one true God, yet pray to this very Being for success even in their lowest intrigues and vilest lusts, and constantly mention his holy name in their lewd songs, blasphemously blessing him for success in their deeds of darkness. In this respect, as in most others, the "Thousand Nights" do but reflect the actual manners of the present generation of Arabs.

Oriental favouritism.

Another Oriental trait comes out very offensively in the conduct of Laban, and afterward in that of Jacob—a most undisguised and grievous *favouritism*. Laban searches all before he visits Rachel's tent, because she was the pet of his own and of Jacob's family. And so, when Jacob prepared for the worst, in the immediate prospect of a hostile visit from Esau, he placed the handmaids and his sons by them foremost, Leah and her children next, and Rachel and her son last; that, as he said about the cattle, "If Esau come to the one company and smite it, then the other company shall escape." Nor was there the least attempt to disguise this offensive and injurious favouritism, even in this hard extremity.

Jacob and Laban.

But to return to the meeting at Mizpah. The terms with which Laban and Jacob reproved each other are in admirable keeping with the parties and the story, and abound in allusions to Oriental customs, especially of a pastoral people. Twenty years long, cries Jacob, have I served thee. The ewes of thy flock have not cast their young. Evidence of most careful and successful CHAPTER treatment. The *rams* of thy flock have I not eaten. Implying that then, as XXV. now, the males of the flocks alone were used for food, or sold to the butcher. Then, as now, wild beasts tore some of the flock; but Jacob the shepherd, not Laban the landlord, bore the loss. Then, too, as at this day, thieves prowled about; but Jacob made good whatever was stolen. Of course, he had to watch by day and night, in winter's storms and summer's burning suns. It was, therefore, no mere figure of speech that the drought consumed him by day and the frost by night. Thus do the hardy shepherds suffer in the same regions at the present time.

We must not pass from these scenes in Jacob's history without noticing the admirable tact with which he appeased his justly-offended brother. He sends an embassy to him from a long distance. This itself was a compliment, and, no doubt, the ambassadors were the most respectable he could command. Then the *terms* of the message were the best possible to flatter and to conciliate an Oriental. He calls Esau his *lord*, himself his servant—or *slave*, as it might be rendered; and he thus tacitly, and without alluding to the old trick by which he cheated him of his birthright, acknowledges him to be the elder brother, and his superior. At the same time, by the large presents, and the exhibition of great wealth, Esau is led to infer that he is not returning a needy adventurer to claim a double portion of the paternal estate; and it would not be unoriental if there was intended to be conveyed by all this a sly intimation that Jacob was neither to be despised nor lightly meddled with. There was subtle flattery mingled with profound humility, but backed all the while by the quiet allusion to the substantial position and character of one whom *God had greatly blessed and prospered.* All this, however, failed, and the enraged brother set out to meet him with an army. Jacob was terribly alarmed; but, with his usual skill and presence of mind, he made another effort to appease Esau. The presents were well selected, admirably arranged, and sent forward one after another; and the drivers were directed to address Esau in the most respectful and humble terms: "They be thy *servant* Jacob's, a present unto my *lord* Esau; and be sure to say, Behold thy *servant* Jacob is behind us; for he said, I will appease him with the present that goeth before me, and afterward I will see his face." Jacob did not miscalculate the influence of his princely offerings, and I verily believe there is not an emeer or sheikh in all Gilead at this day who would not be appeased by such presents; and, from my personal knowledge of Orientals, I should say that Jacob need not have been in such great terror, following in their rear. Far less will now "make room," as Solomon says, for any offender, however atrocious, and bring him before great men with acceptance.[1]

Esau was mollified, and when near enough to see the lowly prostrations of his trembling brother, forgot everything but that he was Jacob, the son of his

[1] Prov. xviii. 16.

mother, the companion of his childhood. He *ran* to meet him, and embraced
him, and fell on his neck, and kissed him; *and they wept.* All this is beauti-

Meeting
of the
brothers.

ful, natural, Oriental; and so is their subsequent discourse, but we cannot
dwell upon it. It was obviously the purpose of God to bring his chosen servant
into these terrible trials, in order to work the deeper conviction of his former
sin, and the more thorough repentance and reformation. And *here it is* that
Jacob appears as a guide and model to all mankind. In his utmost distress
and alarm, he holds fast his hope and trust in God, wrestles with Him in
mighty supplication, and as a prince prevails: "I will not let thee go except
thou bless me. And he said, What is thy name? And he said, Jacob. And
he said, Thy name shall be called no more Jacob, but Israel; for as a prince
hast thou power with God and with men, and hast prevailed."[1]

Butaiha.

Our long ride through the Jaulan has whiled away the time and the road
quite to the end of this Butaiha, and this bold headland marks the spot,
according to my topography, where the five thousand were fed with five barley-
loaves and two small fishes.[2] From the four narratives of this stupendous
miracle we gather—1st, That the place belonged to Bethsaida; 2d, That it
was a desert place; 3d, That it was near the shore of the lake, for they came
to it by boat; 4th, That there was a mountain close at hand; 5th, That it was
a smooth, grassy spot, capable of seating many thousand people. Now all these
requisites are found in this exact locality, and nowhere else, so far as I can
discover. This Butaiha belonged to Bethsaida. At this extreme south-east
corner of it, the mountain shuts down upon the lake bleak and barren. It
was, doubtless, desert then as now, for it is not capable of cultivation. In this

Feeding
the five
thousand.

little cove the ships (boats) were anchored. On this beautiful sward at the
base of the rocky hill the people were seated to receive from the hands of the
Son of God the miraculous bread, emblematic of his body, which is the true
bread from heaven. When all had eaten, and the fragments were gathered
up, they departed in haste, for the day was far spent.

A vast amount of learning and critical research has been expended in efforts
to reconcile the different directions given (or supposed to be given) to the disciples by our Lord, and to make the entire narratives accord with the topo-

Scene of
the mi-
racle.

graphy of this region. According to John,[3] the disciples went over the sea
toward Capernaum, while Mark says that Jesus constrained them to get into
the ship and to go to the other side before unto Bethsaida. Looking back
from this point at the south-eastern extremity of the Butaiha, I see no difficulty in these statements. The case was this, I suppose: As the evening was
coming on, Jesus commanded the disciples to return home to Capernaum,
while he sent the people away. They were reluctant to go and leave him
alone in that desert place; probably remonstrated against his exposing himself
to the coming storm and the cold night air, and reminded him that he would
have many miles to walk round the head of the lake, and must cross the Jor-

---

[1] Gen. xxxii. 24, 27, 28.   [2] Matt. xiv. 15; John vi. 9.   [3] John vi. 17.

dan at Bethsaida before he could reach home. To quiet their minds, he may CHAPTER have then told them to go on before toward Bethsaida, while he dismissed the XXV. crowd, promising to join them in the night; which he intended to do, and actually did, though in a manner very different from what they expected. Still, they were reluctant to leave him, and had to be *constrained* to set sail. In this state of anxiety, they endeavoured to keep near the shore between this and Bethsaida, hoping, no doubt, to take in their beloved Master at some point along the coast. But a violent wind beat off the boat, so that they were not able to make Bethsaida, nor even Capernaum, but were driven past both; and when near the plain of Gennesaret, at the north-west corner of the lake, Landing- Jesus came unto them walking upon the sea. All this is topographically place. natural, and easy to be understood on the supposition that the miracle took place on this spot; that Bethsaida was at the mouth of the Jordan, and Capernaum at Tell Hûm. Nor is there need even of the marginal rendering in our Bible: " Over against Bethsaida." The disciples would naturally sail *toward* Bethsaida in order to reach Tell Hûm. Neither is there anything inconsistent with the statement of John,[1] that " the people took ship the next day, and came to Capernaum, seeking Jesus." They came from the south-east, where the miracle had been wrought, and would naturally seek him in Capernaum, for that was his home; but it seems that they did not find him there, for John immediately adds, " When they had found him *on the other side of the sea*,"—a very singular mode of expression if they found him in Capernaum itself, but perfectly natural on the supposition that they had *to go on* to the plain of Gennesaret, where he had landed. They would probably find him somewhere about 'Ain et Tîny, near which, I presume, the party reached the shore from their wonderful sail. But if it should appear to any one more probable that the people actually found Jesus in Capernaum, this might easily be, for Capernaum was not more than one hour's walk from the corner of Gennesaret, and he could easily have returned home, for they reached the shore very early in the morning. I, however, have very little doubt but that the people had to pass on from Tell Hûm to 'Ain et Tîny to find Him whom they sought.

It follows, of course, from this explanation, that Capernaum was *itself not in Gennesaret;* and I must add that neither Matthew, Mark, Luke, nor John locates it in that plain; nor does Josephus, nor any other ancient author. It is carried thither and anchored there by a modern theory, which, I think, is a mistake.

I am of opinion, also, that the *invention* of a second Bethsaida is wholly Bethsaida. unnecessary. Reland, who first started the idea, confesses that he has no authority for it, but merely resorts to it as an *ultimum refugium*, a last resort, to solve an otherwise invincible topographical difficulty. But I do not believe that another instance can be found of two cities of the *same* name close to-

---

[1] John vi. 24.

gether on the same part of a small lake ; and such hypothetical cities should not be created without absolute necessity, and no such necessity exists in this case. All admit that there was a Bethsaida at the entrance of the Jordan into the lake. The greater part of it, certainly that part which Philip repaired, lay on the east bank of the river, and, therefore, it is maintained, must have belonged to Gaulanitis, and not to Galilee; and as the Bethsaida of Andrew, Peter, and Philip, was a city of Galilee,[1] it is thought that we must have a second town of this name. But I think this unnecessary. Any city built at the mouth of the Jordan would almost necessarily have part of its houses on the west bank of the stream ; and this would be literally and geographically within the territory of Galilee. Peter, Andrew, and Philip were born there, and would be mentioned as Galileans. And further, I think it highly probable that the whole city, on both banks of the river, was ordinarily attached to Galilee, and that one object which Philip the tetrarch had in rebuilding the part on the east side, and changing its name, was to detach it entirely from its former relations, and establish his own right over it. I believe, therefore, that there was but *one* Bethsaida at the head of the lake, and that it was at the mouth of the Jordan ; and thus we settle the sites of all the places in this neighbourhood which are intimately related to the history of our blessed Lord and his disciples.

Storms on the lake.
My experience in this region enables me to sympathize with the disciples in their long night's contest with the wind. I spent a night in that Wady Shukaiyif, some three miles up it, to the left of us. The sun had scarcely set when the wind began to rush down toward the lake, and it continued all night long with constantly increasing violence, so that when we reached the shore next morning the face of the lake was like a huge boiling caldron. The wind howled down every wady from the north-east and east with such fury that no efforts of rowers could have brought a boat to shore at any point along that coast. In a wind like that, the disciples *must* have been driven quite across to Gennesaret, as we know they were. To understand the causes of these sudden and violent tempests, we must remember the lake lies low—six hundred feet lower than the ocean ; that the vast and naked plateaus of the Jaulan rise to a great height spreading backward to the wilds of the Hauran, and upward to snowy Hermon ; that the water-courses have cut out profound ravines and wild gorges, converging to the head of this lake, and that these act like gigantic *funnels* to draw down the cold winds from the mountains. On the occasion referred to, we subsequently pitched our tents at the shore, and remained for three days and nights exposed to this tremendous wind. We had to double pin all the tent-ropes, and frequently were obliged to hang with our whole weight upon them to keep the quivering tabernacle from being carried up bodily into the air. No wonder the disciples toiled and rowed hard all that night ; and how natural their amazement and terror at the sight of

---

[1] John xii. 21.

Jesus walking on the waves ! The faith of Peter, in desiring and *daring* to CHAPTER XXV.
set foot on such a sea, is most striking and impressive ; more so, indeed, than
its failure after he had made the attempt. The whole lake, as we had it, was Conduct
lashed into fury ; the waves repeatedly rolled up to our tent door, tumbling of Peter.
over the ropes with such violence as to carry away the tent-pins. And, moreover, those winds are not only violent, but they come down suddenly, and often
when the sky is perfectly clear. I once went in to swim near the hot baths,
and, before I was aware, a wind came rushing over the cliffs with such force
that it was with great difficulty I could regain the shore. Some such sudden
wind it was, I suppose, that filled the ship with waves, "so that it was now
full," while Jesus was asleep on a pillow in the hinder part of the ship ; nor is
it strange that the disciples aroused him with the cry of " Master ! Master !
carest thou not that we perish ? And he arose and rebuked the wind, and
said unto the sea, Peace, be still ; and the wind ceased, and there was a great
calm. And the disciples feared exceedingly, and said one to another, What
manner of man is this, that even the wind and the sea obey him ?" [1]

Salîm reminds me that we are to encamp early, in order to dry our bedding Wady
and clothes, and thinks that this Wady Semak is the best place for the pur- Semak.
pose that we are likely to find. While the men pitch the tents, we will stroll
up the valley, for exercise in part, and partly that I may show you the remains
of antiquity that are still to be found in it. Some four miles higher up are
the broken walls of Kusr Bardawîl, as the Castle of Baldwin, the famous
crusader, is called by the Arabs. We cannot go there, nor is there anything
worth the trouble at it. Here, however, is something of great interest to me,
and I think will be to you before we are done with it. The name of this Gersa, or
prostrate town is *Kerza* or *Gersa*, as my Bedawîn guide shouted it in my ear Gergesa.
the first time I visited it, on that windy day we have been describing. It
was a small place, but the walls can be traced all round, and there seem to
have been considerable suburbs. I identify these ruins with the long-lost
site of Gergesa, where our Lord healed the two men possessed with devils, and
suffered those malignant spirits to enter into the herd of swine. If this be
correct, it is a discovery of some importance. From Origen down to the last
critic who has tried his skill upon the Greek text of the New Testament, the
conflicting and contradictory readings of manuscripts in regard to the place
where the miracle was performed have furnished a fruitful source of discussion.
Matthew locates it at Gergesa,[2] Mark[3] and Luke[4] at Gadara. A few various
readings give Geresa. The Vulgate, Arabic, and others that follow the Vulgate, read Gergesa in all the evangelists ; nor are these all the discrepancies
in regard to the name of this place. Only one of these readings can be correct.
Which shall we select ? This is the question to be settled. Our inquiries
will, of course, be confined to the topographical indications which may have a
bearing upon the problem.

---

[1] Mark iv. 38–41.   [2] Matt. viii. 28.   [3] Mark v. 1.   [4] Luke viii. 26.

PART
II.

Not Ga-
dara.

Mountain
and
tombs.

Our first point is, that the miracle *could not have occurred at Gadara.* It is certain, from all the accounts we have of it, that the place was near the shore of the lake. Mark says that "when he came out of the ship, *immediately* there met him a man," etc. With this precise statement the tenor of all the narratives coincides, and therefore we *must* find a locality directly on the shore, and every place must be rejected that is not consistent with this ascertained fact. *Again*, the *city* itself, as well as the *country* of the Gergesenes, was at the shore of the lake. All the accounts imply this fact. *Lastly*, there was a steep mountain so near at hand, that the herd of swine, rushing down it, were precipitated into the lake. Now Gadara does not meet any one of these necessary conditions. I take for granted, what I believe to be true, that Um Keîs marks the site of Gadara ; and it was, therefore, about three hours to the south of the extreme shore of the lake in that direction. There is first a broad plain from Khurbet Samra to the Jermuk ; then the vast gorge of this river ; and after it an ascent for an hour and a half to Um Keîs. No one, I think, will maintain that this meets the requirements of the sacred narratives, but is in irreconcilable contradiction to them. It is true that a celebrated traveller, from his lofty stand-point at Um Keîs, overlooks all intervening obstacles, and makes the swine rush headlong into the lake from beneath his very feet. But to do this in fact (and the evangelists deal only in plain facts), they must have run down the mountain for an hour and a half, forded the deep Jermuk, quite as formidable as the Jordan itself, ascended its northern bank, and raced across a level plain several miles, before they could reach the nearest margin of the lake—a feat which no herd of swine would be likely to achieve, even though they were "possessed." The site of the miracle, therefore, *was not at Gadara.* This is an important result. Nor was it in the *country* of the Gadarenes, because that country lay south of the great river Jermuk ; and, besides, if the territory of that city did at any time reach to the south end of the lake, there is no mountain there above it adapted to the conditions of the miracle ; and further, the *city itself where it was wrought was evidently on the shore.* There we must find it, whatever be its name. And in this Gersa, or Chersa, we have a position which fulfils every requirement of the narratives, and with a name so near that in Matthew as to be in itself a strong corroboration of the truth of this identification. It is within a few rods of the shore, and an immense mountain rises directly above it, in which are ancient *t*ombs, out of some of which the two men possessed of the devils may have issued to meet Jesus. The lake is so near the base of the mountain, that the swine, rushing madly down it, could not stop, but would be hurried on into the water and drowned. The place is one which our Lord would be likely to visit—having Capernaum in full view to the north, and Galilee "over against it," as Luke says it was.[1] The *name*, however, pronounced by Bedawîn Arabs, is so similar to Gergesa, that, to all my inquiries for this place, they

---

[1] Luke viii. 26.

invariably said it was at Chersa; and they insisted that they were identical, CHAPTER
and I agree with them in this opinion.

XXV.

In studying the details of the miracle, I was obliged to modify one opinion
or impression which had grown up with me from childhood. *There is no bold* Not a per-
cliff overhanging the lake on the eastern side, nor, indeed, on any other, pendicular
cliff.
except just north of Tiberias. Everywhere along the north-eastern and eastern
shores, a smooth beach declines gently down to the water. There is no "*jump-
ing-off place*," nor, indeed, is any required. Take your stand a little south of
this Chersa. A great herd of swine, we will suppose, is feeding on this mountain that towers above it. They are seized with a sudden panic; rush madly
down the almost perpendicular declivity—those behind tumbling over and
thrusting forward those before; and, as there is neither time nor space to
recover on the narrow shelf between the base and the lake, they are crowded
headlong into the water, and perish. All is perfectly natural just at this
point; and here, I suppose, it did actually occur. Farther south the plain
becomes so broad that the herd might have recovered and recoiled from the
lake, whose domain they would not willingly invade.

How do you suppose these discrepancies in the name of this place crept
into the text?

We must leave that question to professed critics. I have an abiding con- Discrep-
viction, however, that Matthew wrote the name correctly. He was from this ancies in
evangel-
region, and personally knew the localities. His Gospel, also, was written first ists.
of all, and mainly circulated in the beginning, in these Oriental regions. John
does not mention the miracle, and Mark and Luke were strangers to this part
of the country, and may possibly have intended, by mentioning the *country* of
the *Gadarenes*, to point out to their distant Greek and Roman readers the
mere vicinity of the place where the miracle was wrought. Gergesa, or Gerasa,
or Chersa, however pronounced, was small and unknown; while Gadara was a
Greek city, celebrated for its temples and theatre, and for the warm baths on
the Hieromax just below it. They *may*, therefore, have written "*country* of
the Gadarenes." But I think it far more probable that intermeddling scho-
liasts made the change from Gergesa to Gadara, in order to indicate to the
unlearned the spot where the wonder took place. There is a certain resemblance between the names, and when once introduced into a leading manuscript, the basis for the controversy would be fairly laid down. Learned
annotators would be misled by the very extent of their geographical knowledge; which, however, would not be sufficiently exact to prove to them that
the miracle *could not* have taken place at Gadara. Origen, who, I believe,
first attempted to correct the text in those passages, seems to have been
acquainted with this very site we are upon; and this might well have been
the case, since he resided at Cæsarea. Still, his notice of it is confused, and
his criticisms had no valuable result. The mistake spread and became permanent. But, leaving to others more competent to decide how much weight
should be allowed to accurate topographical research in settling the reading of

PART
II.

a controverted *name* in manuscripts, we may certainly inquire, without presumption, whether it is safe to correct the text of Matthew by that of Luke (as some modern critics have done), and thus locate an important transaction in the life of our Saviour at a place where it could not possibly have occurred. One thing, I fear, is certain : if the light shed upon this question by careful topographical examinations cannot settle it, then must it remain for ever unsettled. Let any one examine the "various readings" of these passages as collected in Alford and Tregelles, and he will despair of ever arriving at even a safe probability from mere manuscript authority.

Wild
hogs.

And now, by way of relief, let me draw your attention to the fact that this Wady Semak is everywhere *ploughed* up by wild hogs in search of the esculent roots upon which they live at this season of the year. Whether there is any lineal connection between them and the herd that was feeding on this mountain, I leave you and every one else to decide according to his particular fancy. It is *fact*, however, that these creatures still abound at this place, and in a state as wild and fierce as though they were still " possessed."

CHAPTER XXVI.

KERSA—TIBERIAS.

March 24th.

A LONG ride and much to see promise a busy and a very pleasant day. We are to make the circuit of the entire southern half of the lake, and encamp among the ruins of that famous city from which it derives its present name. Here on the shore are warm, sulphureous springs, which emit steam with an odour intolerably offensive. The place is called Mizferah, and is probably what Burckhardt heard of as a ruined town at the mouth of Wady Semak, which he calls Medjeifera. There is no such *ruin*, and the names are very similar.

Sulphureous
springs.

Roman
road.

You observe that the plain (if so narrow a margin along the shore deserve such a name) is smooth, hard, and quite barren. A Roman road, or at least one well made, once ran along the shore quite to Kersa, whence it appears to have ascended to the Jaulan. We have now an excellent opportunity to study the grand geological characteristics of this region. The lower strata on our left are limestone, but all above is basaltic; and this CHAPTER formation is of vast thickness. The descent through Wady Shukaiyif from XXVI. the lofty plateau of the Jaulan is full two thousand feet before the trap gives place to calcareous rock. This immense volcanic field consists everywhere of Geological irregular heaps of amorphous lava and disintegrating scoriæ, with gigantic formation. mounds of globular basalt, which in a few localities shows a tendency to separate into rudely-shaped columns; but I have seen no genuine columnar basalt in the Jaulan. Were it not for the countless springs of water in the southern part, this whole province would be a black and barren wilderness, incapable of sustaining even the goats which now rejoice in its wild ravines.

Our Arab neighbours behaved very respectfully last night, and to-day I see no reason to apprehend any interruption to our researches.

A rare chance, and owing to political combinations in Tiberias, which render all parties particularly anxious to obtain or retain the good-will of the European consuls. This is especially true of 'Akil 'Aga, who now controls all these lawless tribes. We may well congratulate ourselves, for this is just the Dangers of most dangerous part of the country to traverse. When passing this way from the way. Banias, I took the precaution to get a letter from Sheikh Fareij to Sheikh Mahmood, then at the head of a large tribe encamped a little south of Kŭl'aet Hŭsn. With this, and three of his horsemen as guide and guard, we passed safely; but it was well we had them, for just at that little wady ahead of us we were suddenly confronted by a troop of Bedawîn robbers on their fleet horses, and armed with their tremendous spears. Our guard galloped up to them, and explained that we were under the protection of Sheikh Fareij, and must be allowed to pass. They grumbled a good deal, and looked viciously at our loaded mules, but did not dare to lay hands on anything belonging to our party. They acknowledged without a blush, however, that they Plunder- had come up from the Ghor (Valley of the Jordan) on an expedition for ing Be- plunder, and, when leaving us, said they intended to visit the Butaiha that dawin. very night. Alas for the poor peasants! Such visits, constantly repeated, desolate the country and drive the farmers farther and farther inland to find a place where these lawless villains dare not follow them. When such a *raid* breaks into a village, they compel the people to feed both themselves and their horses, and in the morning they march off with every valuable article they can find. Here is the true explanation of the wide-spread desolations of this beautiful country; and unless some stronger government than the Turkish shall come in to repress these intolerable robbers, the farmers will be driven toward the sea-board, until the whole interior is abandoned and changed to frightful deserts.

The marauding party that met us belonged to a tribe called Diab, which Tribe of interpreted means *Wolves*,—a most significant and appropriate name. I "Wolves." visited their camp, and after reading my letter and making some private inquiries of the guard, the sheikh was very gracious, though the reception

PART
II.

Resemblance of Arab tribes to Scottish clans.

at first was austere enough, and somewhat alarming. He was surrounded by a most villanous-looking troop. One aged warrior in particular might have sat for Rob Roy, or any other of Scott's wild Highland robbers. Indeed there are many points of resemblance between those Arab *tribes* and the Highland *clans* of former days. Perhaps the Arab is the more poetic, if not the more respectable character. The sheikh of these Diab urged me to spend the night with him; but finding me resolved to pass on, he rose and left the tent, saying that I must not go until he returned. After some time he came out of the *hareem*, or female department, with some fresh-baked bread and a plate of *dibs* (a kind of grape molasses), and, taking his seat by my side, he broke off a bit of bread, dipped it in the *dibs*, and gave it to me to eat; and in like manner he required all my companions to partake, and even had the muleteers called in to eat of it. After this, all those about the tent tasted of it. This was the ceremony, and he explained its significance

Covenant of bread and salt.

somewhat in this fashion: "We are now brethren. *There is bread and salt between us;* we are *brothers* and *allies*. You are at liberty to travel among us wherever you please; and, so far as my power extends, I am to aid, befriend, and succour you, *even to the loss of my own life*." The eating of this bread was the sign and seal of the covenant of *Brotherhood* (*Khûwy*, as they term it); and they tell us that this bread will *never* leave the heart of a true and loyal Bedawy; and, of course, the covenant of which it is the symbol can never be forgotten or renounced. They often upbraid the civilized Frank because he does not keep *bread and salt*—is not faithful to the covenant of brotherhood; and I have even heard them assert bluntly that *we have no bread and salt*.

Antiquity of the custom.

They tell us that this custom has come down to them from the remotest antiquity; and in reflecting upon this very striking incident, I have thought it not impossible that the apostles, who were plain fishermen, born and bred on this very shore, had been familiar with this custom, and fully appreciated

Possible appropriation of the custom by our Lord.

its significance; and that our blessed Lord, appropriated, expanded, and infinitely ennobled it in the bread of the Eucharistic Supper. The points of resemblance are many, extremely significant, and impressive. In both, the *element* and the *act* are almost identical; the bread in both is the symbol of a *covenant;* the act of eating is the seal of the covenant. In both it is a covenant of *brotherhood*, introducing the participants into that near and sacred relationship. The covenant is *perpetual;* the *bread* never leaves the loyal heart. In both it supposes the tenderest affection, and guarantees protection and succour *even unto death*. These are not all the points of resemblance, but they are sufficient, I think, to rescue the idea of connection between them from the charge of irreverence. If our Lord did actually base the Eucharistic Supper upon a custom well known to his disciples, and deeply significant, this would be in pleasing unison with other similar institutions. When he would enter into covenant with the earth that it should not be again destroyed by a deluge, he selected the beautiful and familiar bow that gilds the retiring storm-cloud to

be the sign and seal of the covenant. When, too, he made a covenant with CHAPTER
Abraham, it is more than doubted by the learned whether the remarkable XXVI.
seal of that covenant was an act then performed for the first time. And,
however this controversy may be settled, it is certain that *baptism*, which has
taken the place of *circumcision*, was known and extensively practised long
before our Lord appropriated and sanctified it to its present important office
in his Church. I see no objection, therefore, to the idea that we have in this
bread of the *Khâwy* an original and primitive custom, upon which our
Saviour ingrafted the precious institution of the supper; and the thought
throws around this Arab institution an inexpressible charm.

It certainly does; and may we not find traces of a custom somewhat similar Early
to this among those Bedawîn in early Bible history? Abraham, and Isaac, covenants.
and Jacob, to mention no others, appear to have *sealed* their covenants on
various occasions by *eating*. At first it may have been merely a friendly
repast; but having been associated for some time with the making and
the ratification of solemn contracts, it came to be regarded as a necessary
finale and seal of the transaction, and then to be the principal formula of the
covenant itself.

Such a transition would be natural, and is in itself highly probable; but we
must leave these speculations for the student and the commentator. They are
rather abstruse for a discussion on horseback.

Be it so; but, before we get on to some topic altogether foreign, I want to Salt and
make an inquiry which the Arab proverb about *bread and salt* suggested. Our its savour.
Lord, in the sermon on the mount, says, "Ye are the salt of the earth; but
if the salt have lost its savour, wherewith shall it be salted? It is thence-
forth good for nothing, but to be cast out and trodden under foot of men." [1] To
what fact in experience does he allude?

It is plainly implied that salt, under certain conditions so generally
known as to permit him to found his instruction upon them, did actually lose
its saltness; and our only business is to discover these conditions, not to
question their existence. Nor is this difficult. I have often seen just such
salt, and the identical disposition of it that our Lord has mentioned. A
merchant of Sidon having farmed of the Government the revenue from the
importation of salt, brought over an immense quantity from the marshes of
Cyprus—enough, in fact, to supply the whole province for at least twenty
years. This he had transferred to the mountains, to cheat the Government
out of some small percentage. Sixty-five houses in Jûne—Lady Stanhope's
village—were rented and filled with salt. These houses have merely earthen
floors, and the salt next the ground in a few years entirely spoiled. I saw
large quantities of it literally thrown into the street, to be trodden under foot
of men and beasts. It was "good for nothing." Similar magazines are common in this country, and have been from remote ages, as we learn from history

[1] Matt. v. 13.

PART
II.

both sacred and profane; and the sweeping out of the spoiled salt and casting it into the street are actions familiar to all men.

Manufac-
ture of salt.

It should be stated in this connection, that the salt used in this country is not manufactured by boiling clean salt water, nor quarried from mines, but is obtained from marshes along the sea-shore, as in Cyprus, or from salt lakes in the interior, which dry up in summer, as the one in the desert north of Palmyra, and the great Lake of Jebbûl, south-east of Aleppo. The salt of our Sidon merchant was from the vast marshes near Larnaca. I have seen these marshes covered with a thick crust of salt, and have also visited them when it had been gathered into heaps like hay-cocks in a meadow. The large winter lake south-east of Aleppo I found dried up by the last of August, and the entire basin, further than the eye could reach, was white as snow with an incrustation of coarse salt. Hundreds of people were out gathering and carrying it to Jebbûl, where the Government stores were kept.

Salt of Jeb-
bûl and
Usdum.

Maundrell, who visited the lake at Jebbûl, tells us that he found salt there which had entirely "lost its savour;" and the same abounds among the *debris* at Usdum, and in other localities of rock-salt at the south end of the Dead Sea. Indeed, it is a well-known fact that the salt of *this country*, when in contact with the ground, or exposed to rain and sun, does become insipid and useless. From the manner in which it is gathered, much earth and other impurities are necessarily collected with it. Not a little of it is so impure that it cannot be used at all; and such salt soon effloresces and turns to dust—not to fruitful soil, however. It is not only good for nothing itself, but it actually destroys all fertility wherever it is thrown; and this is the reason why it is cast into the street. There is a sort of verbal verisimilitude in the manner in which our Lord alludes to the act—"it is cast out" and "trodden under foot;" so troublesome is this corrupted salt, that it is carefully swept up, carried forth, and thrown into the street. There is no place about the house, yard, or garden where it can be tolerated. No man will allow it to be thrown on to his field, and the only place for it is the street; and there it is cast, to be trodden under foot of men.

An adieu.

But we must return to the tent of our new brother Mahmood. It would be an intolerable insult to depart without a courteous and somewhat cere-monious adieu. The sheikh accompanied us down to the road, and then sent two of his followers to guide us, as he said, to Semak, but, in reality, to guard us from some stray "brother," who might not be disposed to act in exact accordance with the claims of our extemporaneous relationship. One of these horsemen was very talkative, and among other matters stated, without the least reserve, that he wanted to have accompanied the marauding expedition which we encountered in the morning; but his sheikh would not permit him to go. "Well," said I, "if you had met me, would you have assisted to plunder me?" "Certainly, if you had not been protected by Sheikh Fareij." "What! rob your '*brother?*'" "Oh, you would not have

been my brother then." Strange customs, and most singular people ! It
was something novel to be riding gaily along this solitary shore with professed robbers, and these bushy ravines swarming with their comrades,
prowling about like beasts of prey. "He lieth in wait secretly as a lion in his
den ; he lieth in wait to catch the poor." [1]   My talkative " brother " gloried
in the title of robber ; and when I asked him why they did not cultivate the
rich valley of the Jordan, he curled his lip in disdain and exclaimed, " What !
a Bedawy drive the plough ? *istugfar Allah*—God forbid ! We are robbers.
This is our trade, and by this we will live, or, *wallah !* by this we will die,"
striking his terrible spear fiercely into the ground. This fellow (as usual)
was not satisfied with his present, and when I told him he might take or
leave it, just as he pleased, he went away, muttering to the servant that we
should meet him again in Wady Mandhour, " and then," said he, " *inshallah*
—if God please—I will *take* whatever I want." We remained encamped on
the shore of the lake at Semak three days, and I knew he watched us like a
lynx, and if we had attempted to enter Wady Mandhour he would have
made his threat good. Such insolence is intolerable, and I long for the day
when a strong government will take these wild Arabs in hand. They might
easily be tamed. Their ostentatious courage would utterly fail before even a
small force of European soldiers. They are great boasters, and, like all such,
great poltroons.

I am amazed to find sensible and highly cultivated gentlemen the
defenders and eulogists of the Bedawîn. Burckhardt was both a learned
man and an unsophisticated, straightforward writer, and yet he seems to
have been captivated with the character and customs of these wild Arabs.
But, according to his own account (which, so far as it goes, I can confirm),
they are a nation of universal liars, thieves, and robbers, with all the vices
which *must* ever attend such a course of life. They are also cowardly and
mean. Rarely, indeed, will they venture to attack even a very inferior party,
if armed and prepared to resist ; but wherever and whenever they overtake
a poor defenceless stranger, they pounce upon him like hungry wolves. Even
helpless women and children are robbed and stripped without mercy or
remorse. True, Burckhardt says that *some* of them turn their backs while
the *women are made to strip,* and are then so generous as to toss back a few
of the rags which they do not want. Wonderful generosity ! In accordance
with their whole character, they tyrannize over the women, who are, in fact,
their slaves, made to do all the degrading and severe drudgery incident to
their mode of life. The men lounge idly and lazily about the tent, smoke,
drink coffee, and play at games of hazard, of which they have a considerable
variety. They are execrably filthy and foul-mouthed, totally uneducated, and
supremely proud. Their very virtues are vices, or are contaminated by an
odious selfishness. Such is their one boasted virtue of hospitality. It is a

[1] Ps. x. 9.

25

PART
II.

Rascally
character.

mere social regulation; and without something of the kind, these troops of *land pirates* could not carry on their detestable vocation—could not even exist. Away, then, with all this mawkish complacency in the brutal character and habits of these insolent barbarians ! They would reduce Paradise itself to a howling wilderness in five years, and no civilized government could or would tolerate them for a day. This they well know, and hence they have an extreme dread and jealousy of the constant increase of European influence in this country. They do not hesitate to say that, whenever this influence becomes dominant, *they* must decamp for ever. So it certainly will be, and I should rejoice to witness the realization of their worst apprehensions. Not till then can this fair and fertile land be regenerated.

Gamala.

But yonder is the *hump* of the *camel* which constituted the citadel, and gave name to the famous fortress of *Gamala ;* for this is the Oriental word for camel, and it was appropriated to this isolated promontory from its resemblance to the back of that animal. By my aneroid it is eleven hundred and seventy feet above the lake, and we must leave our horses at its base, and climb on foot to its giddy summit as best we may. And now, within its mighty ramparts, let us sit down on one of these broken columns, and read Josephus until sufficiently rested to take a survey of this strongest of Jewish fortifications ; for Jewish it is, and no mistake, whatever may be said of other castles. It was the last that was sacked by Vespasian and Titus before the siege of Jerusalem, and it has remained to this day just as they left it. It has not been repaired, and the materials have never been wanted for any other place. He who would study the architecture and mode of fortification at the time of Christ, should visit this Kŭl'aet Hŭsn, as Gamala is now called. No other ruin in this country has remained so intact and perfect.

Now Kŭ-
l'aet Hŭsn.

Josephus informs us that, even after the taking of Jotapata and all other places in these regions, the people of Gamala refused to surrender to the Romans. "They relied upon the difficulty of the place, which was greater than that of Jotapata, for it was situated upon a rough ridge of a high mountain, with a kind of neck in the middle. Where it begins to ascend it lengthens itself, and declines as much downward before as behind, insomuch that it is like a camel in figure, from whence it is so named." He goes on to speak, in his accustomed style of exaggeration, of deep valleys all around it, and frightful precipices, which made every approach to it quite impossible. These were rendered still more impregnable by walls and towers above, and deep ditches below. This is sufficiently graphic, and *almost* accurate, for it is naturally one of the very strongest positions I have ever examined. But, notwithstanding this, it was doomed to utter destruction. On the last of September, in the year *sixty-nine* of our era, the invincible legions of Rome closed around it, never to leave while a living man remained in Gamala. The *Fifteenth* fortified their camp on that ridge over against us to the east ; the *Fifth* did the same further round toward the north, as I read Josephus ; and the *Tenth* filled up the ditches on the south-eastern part, along that narrow

Its siege.

neck which connects this citadel with the main mountain on the south. Strong CHAPTER detachments also watched and hemmed in the devoted city on all sides, so that XXVI. escape was impossible.

When the ditches were filled, and a way levelled up to a part of the wall that protected the lower city (there on the *neck*, I suppose), the battering-rams were made to play upon it in three places with such fury that it soon gave way and fell.   Through the gap rushed the iron-clad legions, with " mighty sound of trumpets, and noise of armour, and shout of soldiers."   But despair and frenzy nerved the hearts and arms of the Jews.   They threw The re- themselves madly upon their enemies, beat them back by main force, and pulse. overwhelmed them from above with darts, stones, and anything within reach. The Romans, hard pressed, rushed into the houses (that hung one over another along that steep declivity) in such numbers that the foundations gave way, and those above falling on those below, carried all away in their headlong descent, house upon house, in horrible confusion, burying up and crushing to death whole ranks in a moment.   Thus it happened that " a great number were ground to powder by those ruins, and a great many of those that got from under them lost some of their limbs, but a still greater number were suffocated by the dust that arose from those ruins."   Josephus was then a prisoner in the Roman camp, and witnessed the awful scene from a high point on this overhanging mountain.   His description is therefore very minute and graphic; true also, I suppose, for there was no particular temptation to exaggerate or falsify.   He says that the houses which fell with the Romans were low and not firm ; and an inspection of the place shows that none but very low houses could have stood there at all, for the face of the mountain is nearly perpendicular.   After immense confusion and wild disorder, in which Vespasian himself was in extreme danger of perishing, the Romans retreated to their camps, and the Gamalites celebrated their unexpected victory with the most extravagant rejoicings.

Brief was their triumph.   Vespasian comforted and encouraged his army in The cap- a set speech.   Titus came back from Syria with reinforcements ; a high tower ture. on the wall was undermined, and fell with prodigious noise; the soldiers rushed in again, led on by Titus himself; everything gave way, and went down before the ten-fold fury of the onset—the outer city first, and then this wonderful citadel itself was taken, and everything that breathed was put to Awful fate the sword, even to the women and helpless infants.   *Five thousand* of these of the
Jews. most miserable people, seeing escape impossible, destroyed themselves ; husbands threw their wives over the walls; parents seized their children and leaped madly from the ramparts, and were crushed into hideous masses in those yawning gulfs below.   Look over, if your head is steady enough, and see into what awful depths they must have plunged.   So fell Gamala on the 23d of October, A.D. 69, after a siege of twenty-nine days.   Of the entire population that thronged this city and citadel, only *two women* escaped.   The next act in the drama of Israel's destruction opens on the hills around Jerusalem, where the long bloody tragedy winds up with the total overthrow of the city and the holy temple, amid agonies and carnage never seen before and never to be repeated while the world stands.

Let us now take a walk around the fortifications of old Gamala. You observe that this " hump of the camel" extends from south-east to north-west. The diameter from the eastern gate to the one at the north-western extremity is *seven hundred and sixty-five paces*, and a straight and well-defined street ran from gate to gate. The average width was not quite half the length, and the entire shape of the summit approaches an oval. On all sides it is surrounded by deep ravines, except the narrow neck which joins it to the main mountain. This *neck* is much lower than the *hump*, and both are several hundred feet lower than the surrounding heights. Indeed, the *hump* looks as though it had broken away from those gigantic cliffs, pushed out lakewise to the north-west, and *sagged* down some five hundred feet below its original position, having only this narrow ridge to connect it with the parent mountain. Along this ridge, and particularly the eastern side of it, the exterior city was built; and in such fashion that Josephus says it looked as though it would fall down upon itself. The citadel, or *hump*, was entirely surrounded by a strong wall, which was carried along the very brink of the precipices; and in some parts arches had to be thrown from cliff to cliff, to secure a practicable foundation. Josephus intimates that he built this wall; which is simply absurd. But the man that could build the walls around the top of Tabor in *forty days*, might possibly construct those of Gamala in some idle moment! The fact is, that in neither case could Josephus have done more than slightly repair works which were already there.

This entire citadel, nearly a mile and a half in circuit, was covered with heavy buildings; and as the material was indestructible basalt, they remain very much as the Romans left them. This *tower* in the centre appears to have been the largest and highest of all. Near it once stood a temple or splendid

synagogue, and another to the north-east of it. Is it not marvellous to see the ground hereabout thickly strewn with granite columns from Egypt? How did they get them up to this giddy perch? There must have been great wealth in the city, and roads, and machinery, of which the Syrians of this day have no conception. The entire wealth and power of the present generation would be exhausted, and fail in the attempt, to carry any one of these columns from Tiberias to the top of this *hump* of the camel; and there are at least *thirty* of them in this immediate vicinity, and some of them more than fourteen feet long. On the east of this tower is an immense under-ground cistern, the vault of which is a fine specimen of the Roman arch. There were also numerous cisterns in every part of the citadel, and necessarily so, because there was no other supply of water. Here are some Corinthian capitals neatly cut in hard black basalt—a curiosity in their way. And these sarcophagi

and sepulchral stones are entirely peculiar to this city—at least I have seen nothing like them elsewhere. But what marks it as a genuine Hebrew city is, the total absence of inscriptions. There is not a solitary letter in any CHAPTER language. XXVI.

Josephus incidentally mentions a phenomenon which I happened to verify in my own experience. Speaking of the last assault upon the citadel, when Vespasian brought the whole army to support his son Titus, he says, "Now this upper part of the city was very rocky, and difficult of ascent, and elevated to a vast altitude, and very full of people on all sides, and encompassed with precipices, whereby the Jews cut off those that came up to them," etc. "How- A storm. ever, there arose such a *divine storm* against them as was instrumental in their destruction. This carried the Roman darts upon them, and made those which they threw return back, and drove them obliquely away from them. Nor could the Jews, indeed, *stand upon their precipices* by reason of the violence of the wind," etc., etc. Without supposing there was anything specially *divine* in the wind which blew down these ravines and over these ruins on my first visit, yet it was so vehement that I could not stand upon the ramparts for half a minute. Indeed, the depths below are so profound, in many parts, that no one can look into them without a shudder even in the calmest weather. It occurred to me at the time that this incidental notice by a contemporary of a furious wind rushing down toward and upon the lake, is a happy corroboration of the evangelical narratives, in which similar phenomena are repeatedly mentioned. To say the least, it is in beautiful correspondence with them.

With the single exception of Jerusalem, Gamala furnishes the most remarkable fulfilment on record of those terrible predictions of our Saviour concerning the destruction of the Jews; and in its haggard desolation and utter solitude it is at this day a much more impressive monument of divine judgment than even the Holy City itself.

We may now return, and thus relieve the real or pretended fears of our guide, who has been impatient of our long ramble. He says that this is a chosen resort of robbers; which, by the way, I do not believe. They rarely Searching frequent such a place as this, unless it be in search of hid treasure. When I for treasure. descended from here to the camp of Mahmood they were extremely suspicious of the purpose of my visit, and no explanations, reasonings, or protestations, had the slightest effect in removing their belief that I had gone there to search for gold. When I appealed to the fact that some of their own men were with me, they replied that all I did then was to take a copy of the localities where the treasure was, so that I might come back in the night and carry it away. When asked why they did not take it themselves, they gave two reasons: first, that they had no *daleel* or guide to the exact spot; and, secondly, that they had no *charm* of sufficient potency to subdue the spirits (jin) that keep guard over the treasure. The Bedawîn universally believe in the existence of such guards, and of charms or *names* which will subdue them. There is no tale on this subject in the "Thousand Nights," however extravagant, but what is to them credible and real. A large part of their conversation is made up of

PART
II.

Charms
and super-
stitions.
preposterous stories of this kind. They enter into the most minute details of the localities, the caves, rooms, closed doors, slabs with iron rings, etc., etc., ending always with some obstinate door which none of their *charms* could open; or, if they broke it open by main force, they were beaten back, thrown to the ground, blinded, suffocated with fumes of sulphur, or in some other miraculous way compelled by the guardian spirits to abandon the attempt. Of these creatures, also, they give the most outlandish descriptions, and appear firmly to believe their own stories. Several of the wildest of these romances have their locality in these very ruins of Gamala.

This amazing superstition is not only a source of constant annoyance to the traveller, but in these out-of-the-way parts of the country greatly increases the difficulties and the dangers of exploration. I am not sure but that my talkative guide from Sheikh Mahmood was induced to watch us so strictly under the idea that we either had or were intending to carry away their coveted treasure; and this absurd superstition might have cost us our lives if we had fallen into their hands in Wady Mandhour. Doubtless, too, it is this apprehension that induces Arabs often to conceal interesting localities from the traveller, or to refuse to accompany him to them; and, indeed, they have been known to mislead by false directions. This is one reason of the ridiculous blunders and topographical errors of certain tourists. Only this last year the British consul of Damascus (who had more influence over the Arabs of this country than any other man), in furnishing me with letters of protection to a large number of sheikhs in these mountains east of the Jordan, informed me that I must not take any instruments with me, nor be seen to take drawings, for it would certainly endanger my life, in spite of all the protection which the British Government could throw around me. These remarks, of course, apply chiefly to the remoter parts of the land—to routes and sites entirely under the control of the Bedawîn. Other places can be visited with but little annoyance from this cause; and yet, even in the most civilized districts, the people are provokingly pertinacious in ascribing our visits to old ruins to this, the only intelligible motive to their minds. The idea of coming far, toiling hard, and *spending money* merely to examine historic sites, is to them absurd and ridiculous.

Native
jealousy of
travellers.

Other
ruins.
Before we bid a final adieu to these mournful ruins, let us take a glance at their neighbours, some of which are 'not wanting in historic interest. That fortified rock on the north is called Nkeib, and the ruins upon it are evidently of the same age as these of Gamala. That sharp pinnacle further north, which resembles a church steeple, is Kureîn el Jerady. East of us about two miles is Fîk, a considerable village on the top of the mountain, occupying the site of the ancient Aphek, the city to which Benhadad fled after one hundred thousand of his soldiers had been slain in battle by Ahab. The city, however, proved almost as destructive as the army of Israel, for " a wall fell upon twenty and seven thousand of the men that were left."[1] This tremendous destruction

Fîk, or
Aphek.

---

[1] 1 Kings xx. 26–30.

was caused, as I suppose, by an earthquake; and after having seen the effects CHAPTER
of the earthquake in Safed and Tiberias, I can easily understand and readily ^{XXVI.}
credit this narrative. We are not required to limit the catastrophe to the
falling of a single wall; or, if this be insisted upon, we have only to suppose
that it was the wall of the city, and a little consideration will convince any one
familiar with Oriental fortifications that it might overwhelm a whole army.
Those ramparts were very lofty and massive. An open space was always left
along their base, and this would be packed full and tight, from end to end, by
the remnants of Benhadad's mighty host, and escape from the falling towers
would be impossible. The peculiar character of the site would render the
destruction only the more extensive and inevitable. I have not visited it, but
Burckhardt passed through it in 1812, and he informs us that the town is built
around the base of a hill in the shape of a crescent, not unlike the topography
of Safed, and it was this circumstance which rendered the overthrow of that
place so destructive. The Fîk of our day is a mere village, containing about
two hundred families, dwelling in huts built out of the rubbish of the ancient
city.

Burckhardt seems to have visited Kŭl'aet Hŭsn, or, at least, he heard of it, Argob.
and supposed that it marked the site of Argob, the capital of the kingdom of
Og. This is not very probable; indeed it is not certain, from the various
notices of Argob, that it was a city at all. In Deut. iii. 13, 14, we read of "the
region of Argob," and of "*all the country* of Argob;" and the same in 1 Kings
iv. 13; but nothing is said of a *city* of that name, nor can I hear of any such
ancient site. It is worthy of note, however, that the Bedawîn familiarly speak
of this whole district as Arkoob or Argoob. Thus they call the mountain on
which Um Keîs stands Argoob Um Keîs, and this mountain above us Argoob
Hŭsn; and although this word is applied to any rough, mountainous country,
I have nowhere else heard it thus used in common conversation; and since the
kingdom or district of Argob was in this immediate neighbourhood, I think it
nearly certain that we have the identical name still preserved among these
primitive inhabitants. And as this province is very wild and broken, may not
its own proper name have been transferred, as an adjective, to all similar
districts ?

Burckhardt speaks of a plain which extends from Fîk far into the interior of "A great
the Jaulan, and I myself passed over a portion of it, and thought it beautiful plain."
and very fertile. Josephus, in his account of the defeat of Benhadad, says he
pitched his camp *in the great plain*,[1]—a phrase often applied to Esdraelon, the
valley of the Jordan, and other places. In the present case he probably means
this very plain north of Fîk, since the remnants of his army fled into this city.

Directly south of el Hŭsn, on the mountain, is an inhabited village called
Kefr Hârib; and below it are the ruins of a castle, said to have belonged to it
in olden times. The plain between the shore and the mountain, you observe,

---

[1] Ant. vlii. 14, 4.

PART
II.

Geology.

widens as we advance, and becomes more fertile. The thickness of the super-incumbent trap also decreases, and yellow calcareous rock crops out nearer and nearer the surface, until, at the valley of the Jermuk, the former ceases altogether, and cretaceous limestone takes its place. The scenery becomes less savage and more picturesque, the soil richer, the pastures more luxuriant, and noble forests of oak, terebinth, and other trees adorn the hills and valleys. All tourists agree in representing this as one of the most charming regions of the East, and we draw the same conclusion from the incidental references to it in Bible history. I long to explore Gilead and Bashan, and hope to do it on some future occasion, but at present we must continue the even tenor of our way round the southern shore of this lake. Here are traces of an old village called Dueir Ban and a little further south is Khurbet Samra. A long low ridge divides the plain of the Ghor quite down to the Jermuk. It is called Tell et Tâlib, and also Kusr el Kelb, from an old castle of that name. Khan 'Agaba, mentioned by Burckhardt, is on the side of it. He says that this Khurbet Samra was inhabited when he passed this way in 1812; but, to judge from present appearances, he must have been mistaken, for it seems to have been an utter ruin for generations. It *may* have been occupied by a few Arab huts, and certainly there could have been nothing here forty years ago of a more substantial character. We should not be too positive, however, because the peasants in all this region build very ephemeral habitations with small stones and mud; which, if deserted, soon fall and melt away like summer snow on the mountains. It is surprising to see how quickly "houses which no man inhabiteth become heaps," as Job has it;[1] and Solomon noticed the same thing: "By much slothfulness the building decayeth; and through idleness of the hands the house droppeth through."[2] The roof of any of these huts, forsaken or neglected through idleness, will "drop through" in a single winter, and then the unprotected walls *wash down* by the rain, and speedily become mere shapeless "heaps." The cause is easily explained. The roof is made by heaping a thick stratum of earth over the brush, thorns, and cane which are laid on the beams to receive it. This earth, if not constantly *rolled*, or carefully plastered, so as to shed the rain, absorbs it, until the weight breaks the beams, and then the whole mass drops through, bursting out the feeble walls, which now have nothing to bind them together. The mortar used is without lime, and, when thoroughly saturated by the rain, becomes as slippery as soap; and thus the whole fabric tumbles into a dismal ruin. Indeed, such frail houses often fall suddenly during great storms, and crush the inhabitants to death. This is particularly the case where there is much snow, and the people cannot properly roll their terraces.

Slight
houses.

Untem-
pered
mortar.

It was such facts as these, perhaps, that suggested to Ezekiel the terms of that terrible rebuke to the prophets of Israel: "Because, even because they have seduced my people, saying, Peace; and there was no peace; and one built up a

[1] Job xv. 28.   [2] Eccles. x. 18.

wall, and, lo, others daubed it with untempered mortar : say unto them which CHAPTER daub it with untempered mortar, *that it shall fall.* There shall be an over- XXVI. flowing shower; and ye, O great hailstones, shall fall; and a stormy wind shall rend it." [1]

Yes, these are the very agencies by which the Lord now overthrows in a Villages night whole villages thus built with untempered mortar. " So will I break destroyed down the wall that ye have daubed with untempered mortar, and bring it down to the ground, so that the foundations thereof shall be discovered, and it shall fall, *and ye shall be consumed in the midst thereof*." A calamity this of very frequent occurrence. I have known many such during my residence in this land, and this whole passage is so graphic and true to experience, that the prophet, beyond a doubt, drew the picture from scenes with which he was personally familiar. This Samakh which we are approaching is a striking specimen of walls built and daubed with such mortar, and not a few of the houses threaten to crush their inhabitants beneath their ruins. It is at present the only inhabited village in this fertile delta formed by the lake, the Jordan, and the Jermuk, and it probably marks the site of the ancient Hippos. One or two of the houses, and the *menzâl* for strangers, are partly built of cut stones which belonged to the old city; but the remainder are made of small *cobblestones* from the shore and *untempered* mortar, loosely laid up, and daubed on the outside with the same.

The plain is some twenty feet above the lake, quite level, but declines Plain of rapidly to the junction of the Jordan and the Jermuk, some six miles to the Semak. south. It is a mere mud deposit, and indicates that the level of the lake has been, at some former period, much higher than it is now. The people of the village informed me that in very rainy years the water rises several feet above its present low mark, and should anything dam up the narrow exit of the Jordan, it would, of course, rise at once to the level of the plain.

I once spent several days encamped on the pebbly beach below Semak, and had ample time to explore the entire southern shore of the lake, as well as the Exit of outgoing of the Jordan. The shore is covered with pebbles of flint, jasper, Jordan chalcedony, and agate, mixed with several kinds of fresh-water shells. The largest is a variety of the *unio.* The exit of the Jordan is correctly laid down by Captain Lynch, but by no other author that I have seen. The ruins of an ancient bridge partly choke up the exit, and narrow it to about one hundred feet in width at low water; and even there it was not more than four feet deep; the current, however, is very swift. The shore and the river I found crowded with ducks, cranes, and other water-fowl, in the latter part of February; and, were it safe, it would be a delightful spot for the sportsman and the lover of fish and game. Semak has about two hundred wretched huts, packed together in the most uncomfortable manner possible. The inhabitants are all Moslems, and of course, or of necessity, confederates in robbery with their

[1] Ezek. xiii. 10–16.

PART II.

neighbours, those *Diabs—wolves*—whose tents we saw along the base of Tell Tâlib. No wonder the Bedawîn prefer the open country and the canvas cover to such an accumulation of dust, vermin, and every other abomination. Nothing could induce me to dwell in such a village. And yet it is situated on the shore of this sweet and beautiful lake, with the most interesting scenery in the world around it. Alas! it is a splendid "jewel in a swine's snout."[1]

Aspect of the lake.

The regular path leads directly to the ford below the broken bridge, Em el Kŭnâtur, but we will follow the shore to the exit of the Jordan. We have now a good view of the entire lake, and can see at a glance that it narrows rapidly on both sides, until it is not more than three miles wide at this extremity of it. The Jordan leaves it near the south-west corner, and its exit was commanded by those fortified tells on the north side, now called Tells of Kerak. The triangular plat north of them is the site of the ancient Taricea, or Tarichea, so famous in the wars of the Jews. A branch of the river once came down on the west side, and, of course, made the site of the city an island; nor would it be difficult to make that again the main outlet of the

Kerak.

river, as it probably was in former times. This Kerak was the great naval station of the Jews in the time of the Roman war. Josephus collected *two*

Two hundred and thirty ships.

hundred and thirty ships at this place to attack Tiberias, and here occurred the only sea-fight between the Jews and Romans. The ships probably lay at anchor within and around the exit of the Jordan, protected by towers upon these tells. The situation is admirable for the purpose, and there is no other safe harbour on the whole lake. It must, therefore, have been a place of great importance, so long as there were ships to need a refuge from the wild winds which often sweep over it. I have seen it lashed into fury for thirty consecutive hours by a tempest that would have wrecked a hundred fleets such as that of Josephus, had they been exposed to its violence.

How different the condition of these shores now from the time when Josephus could gather at this point more than two hundred ships in a single day! There is not at this hour a boat of any kind upon the lake, and I never but once saw a single sail unfurled upon its deserted bosom. Josephus, however, who lived, and sailed, and fought on it in the time of the apostles, abundantly corroborates their accounts of the ships that then sailed over it; and my own

Storms on the lake.

experience confirms all the other phenomena mentioned by them. Small as the lake is, and placid, in general, as a molten mirror, I have repeatedly seen it quiver, and leap, and boil like a caldron, when driven by fierce winds from the eastern mountains; and the waves ran high—high enough to fill or "cover" the ships, as Matthew has it.[2] In the midst of such a gale "calmly slept the Son of God," in the hinder part of the ship, until awakened by the terrified disciples.

Gadara

Gadara. with her prostrate temples and theatres, is seated on the top of

[1] Prov. xi. 22.   [2] Matt. viii. 24.

the mountain south of the great gorge of the Jermuk, and the celebrated hot baths of another Hammath are below on the bank of the river. The fountains are of immense size, and the entire locality extremely interesting and wild. Until quite recently, the Christians of Nazareth held a grand fair at those baths, and they still speak in raptures of the happy times they used to enjoy there, and curse these Arab wolves who now prowl about, and render it utterly impossible to hold their joyous festa.

The great highway from the west into Perea, Decapolis, and the distant Bridges. east, passed the Jordan at this bridge to which we are coming, now called Jisr el Kŭnâtur, in reference to the many high arches on which it rested. Jisr el Kŭnâtur. They appear to have been ten, but are all so broken and choked up with rubbish that one cannot be quite certain as to the number. The ford below it would be excellent were it not for the fragments of the bridge which strew the bottom. The river is about three hundred feet broad, and it is not more than three feet deep, except in early spring. The only bridge still in repair is Jisr el Mŭjamia, about seven miles below the lake. I spent a night and Jisr el Mŭjamia. day there last spring with 'Akil 'Aga, and then followed the west bank of the Jordan to this point. The junction of the Jermuk is in a rough, rocky channel, about a mile north of the Mŭjamia, and it is also spanned by a strong stone bridge. Further up the river is a ruined site called Dalhamia, or Dalhamia Dalmamia. One could make Dalmanutha out of this word, if the geography of the New Testament would admit the location here of that place, to which our Lord came on his return from Cæsarea Philippi (Banias) "through the midst of the coasts of Decapolis."[1] This journey of our Saviour appears to have been unusually extended and very circuitous. Departing from Tyre and Sidon, he came to this lake, not by the direct route, but, going first to Banias, he then made a circuit through the region of Decapolis, on the east of the lake and the Jordan. Now, if he visited Jerash, Pella, Gadara, and Hippos, he might return by this Dalhamia on his way home, or might come hither by boat, as Mark states. It must be remembered, however, that Matthew says Jesus "came into the coasts of *Magdala*"[2] after the very same miracle mentioned by Mark, just before he came to Dalmanutha; and this want of correspondence (for it is not a contradiction) between the two records my geographical knowledge does not enable me to clear up. It is generally supposed that the name in Mark is an error, and ought to be corrected into Magdala. This solution I do not accept. It is certain that but a *very few* points in this long journey are mentioned by any of the evangelists, and Jesus may well have gone to both Magdala and Dalmanutha ; and since he must have passed very near to this Dalhamia (as it is now called), it is not unlikely that he visited it. At any rate, there is abundant room in the country, and in the narratives, for *a* Dalmanutha, and I see no good reason for supposing that Mark has fallen into a geographical error. If this

---

[1] Mark vii. 31.　　　　　[2] Matt. xv. 39,

PART
II.

Dalhamia is not it, I confidently expect that some other more fortunate explorer will ere long reveal the true site. Let us wait patiently. Every extension of our knowledge in this department lessens the number of topographical obscurities, and in time all will be cleared away.

Windings
of Jordan.

How strangely the Jordan winds about, as if reluctant to leave its mother for the hard, downward race to the Sea of Death! On coming out of the lake it first runs northward, then west, south-west, and finally south, and all within a mile. Here at the bridge its course is south, but it soon departs from this western side of the plain, and makes a long detour to the east, and thus it continues meandering about in the most eccentric fashion, often darting along rocky rapids, or leaping down noisy cataracts, as if in sport, and then stealing silently away in some new direction, beneath overhanging willows and thick sycamores. On the whole, one is very much amused with its behaviour, and quite satisfied that the Jordan should be as peculiar in its character as it is unique in its history. Its manifold windings and doublings, with all the green islets enclosed, are accurately laid down in Captain Lynch's map, so far as I have followed the course of the river. There must have been far more water when he passed down it than there is now, or it would have been impossible to get the boats through the rocks in safety. To judge from the pictures we have of that expedition, the act of shooting these rapids must have been sufficiently perilous, even under the most favourable circumstances.

Abadîyeh.

About three miles lower down is a large village, on a singular tell near the river. It is called Abadîyeh, and the surrounding lands are well cultivated. South of that the entire valley of the Jordan is abandoned to the Bedawîn, and there is not an inhabited village until you reach Jericho. Beyond those nearest hills on our left is a deep wady called Fedjâs, which runs far up to the north-west. In it is a copious fountain, the water of which was anciently

Aqueduct.

carried along the declivity of the valley in an aqueduct which bent round the end of the ridge northward, and was taken to the old city of Tiberias. You can see the remains of that great work here above us on the side of the mountain. Those who built it seem not to have been acquainted with the *arch*, for the canal was frequently led into the heart of the hill, in order to get round some narrow ravine. I have not seen this curious old work noticed by any traveller, and I myself passed this way repeatedly without seeing it. The chief design of it, I suppose, was to *irrigate* the orchards and gardens of Tarichea, Emmaus, and Tiberias, because the water of Fedjâs is not particularly good to drink, and the inhabitants on this shore desire no better water than that of the lake itself. There are ruins of a building on the hill side, now called Tâhûn es Sŭkkar—that is, sugar-mill; and it seems to have been driven by water from the canal. It is not impossible that sugar-cane was once grown on this part of the Jordan valley (as it certainly was about Jericho), and that this canal was made to serve the double purpose of irrigating the sugar plantations and of driving the mills to crush the cane. This

double use of aqueducts is everywhere made, where the condition of the adjacent land will admit it. Of course this supposition implies that the canal has
been in use in comparatively modern times.

We have now an easy ride of an hour along the shore to the celebrated hot
baths of Tiberias. A castle once crowned this eminence on the left, and this
old wall ran from its base across the ancient bed of that branch of the Jordan
which ran on the west side of Tarichea. This wall and castle would entirely
command the road along the shore, so that it would be impossible to pass
without permission. The *wall* may also have served as a causeway to the city
when the delta on which it stood was surrounded by water.

This place on our left is now called Shŭgshab, but it must mark the site of
Sennabris according to Josephus; for the Roman army encamped at it was in
full view of Tiberias, and it is only at this spot (half an hour down the lake
from the baths) that this could have been true. There are traces of old buildings hereabout, and the name is sufficiently outlandish to have come down from
the dark ages.

There has been a smart shower here, while at Semak the ground was baked
hard, and the grain drooping sadly. The same was true on a former occasion
when I came up the Jordan valley. The ground in the Ghor was like a
parched desert. There had not been sufficient rain to bring up the grain, and
" the seed sown had rotted under the clod," while here at Tiberias the whole
country was a paradise of herbs and flowers. And thus it was in former
times. The Lord " caused it to rain upon one city," says Amos, and " caused
it not to rain upon another city: one piece was rained upon, and the piece
whereupon it rained not withered." [1] It was literally so about Semak and
'Abadîyeh, while their nearest neighbours were rejoicing in abundant showers.
There are other interesting allusions to matters in agricultural experience in
this passage of Amos. " I have withdrawn," says God, " the rain from you,
when there were yet three months to the harvest." This is utterly ruinous to
the hopes of the farmer. A little earlier or a little later would not be so fatal,
but drought *three months before harvest* is entirely destructive. In the eighth
verse we read, " So two or three cities wandered unto one city to drink water :
but they were not satisfied,"—a fact often repeated in this country. No longer
ago than last autumn it had its exemplification complete in Belad Besharah,
the ancient inheritance of Naphtali.

Here are the far-famed baths. They are often mentioned by Josephus,
who says they were a *little distance* from Tiberias, in a village called
Emmaus.[2] I am inclined to think that this was the Hammath given to
Naphtali; and if so, then Rakkath, mentioned in connection with it, may
have been the ancestor of Kerak at the outgoing of the Jordan. There is a
certain similarity in the names either in sound or in signification. Kerak
and Rakkath ring on the Arab ear alike; and Emmaus and Hammath are

---

[1] Amos iv. 7, 8.   [2] Ant. xviii. 2, 3.

PART
II.

but different modifications of the word from which Hammam, the name for warm baths, is derived. Tiberias itself *may* occupy the site of Chinneroth, from which the lake derived its primitive name, as it now gets that of Tiberias from its successor. We throw out these suppositions without vouching for their truth, or attempting to establish it. I cannot doubt, however, but that there was a city near Tiberias far older and more splendid than that built by Herod. The granite columns mingled among the now visible ruins must have an antiquity much higher than the first century of our era. I suppose the city of Herod occupied the same situation as the present town, for it is plainly implied in many notices by Josephus that it was at a considerable distance from the hot baths, while these ancient remains extend quite down to them. They cannot, therefore, be the ruins of Herod's city, but of one still older than it. Emmaus (*alias* Hammath) lay chiefly south of the baths, and its walls can be traced out without any doubt or difficulty. But this is quite enough of topography for once.

The water.

The water of these springs has a sulphureous and most disagreeable smell, and is so nauseous that it cannot be drunk, and is not used internally. The baths, however, have a great medicinal reputation, and their sanitary virtues are believed by the ignorant to be almost adequate to remove all the ills to which frail flesh is heir. The accommodations for bathing are everything but satisfactory, and the entire establishment is filthy and offensive in the extreme; and yet it is always crowded with the lame, the halt, the withered, and the leprous. There is but one common bathing cistern, where the water is hot enough to cook an egg, and it is always crowded with patients. What healthy person would dare to bathe in such a cistern, and with such company? How they can endure the water at from 130° to 140° of Fahrenheit is a mystery. I once had the bath cleared, and made the experiment, but should have fainted in a very short time if I had not made my escape from it. Little by little, however, they get used to it, and some delight to roll about in it by the hour, happy as a hippopotamus in the Nile.

Tempera-
ture.

The temperature of the fountains varies in different years, and at different seasons of the same year. According to my thermometers, it has ranged within the last twenty years from 136° to 144°. I was here in 1833, when Ibrahim Pasha was erecting these buildings, and they appeared quite pretty. The earthquake which destroyed Tiberias in 1837 did no injury to the baths, although the fountains were greatly disturbed, and threw out more water than usual, and of a much higher temperature. This disturbance, however, was only temporary, for when I came here about a month after the earthquake, they had settled down into their ordinary condition.

Are these hot springs ever mentioned in the Bible?

Bible allu-
sion.

The name of the place perhaps is, but the baths themselves are not alluded to either in the Old or the New Testament. There is a curious passage in Gen. xxxvi. 24, which I suspect refers to warm mineral springs and their

medicinal virtues. In our translation it reads thus : " This was that Anah
that found *the mules* in the wilderness, as he fed the asses of Zibeon his
father." The Hebrew word *yamim*, here translated *mules*, means *waters;*
and the Vulgate and Arabic translations render it *warm waters;* which rendering Jerome and others among the ancients favour, and not a few modern
critics agree with them. Of one thing I am well satisfied,—that Anah did not
find *mules*, whatever may be the true meaning of *yamim*. And since such hot
fountains exist, not only here, but in Wady Mandhour, below Gadara, and at
Callirrhoe, east of the Dead Sea, it is quite possible that Moses may have
become acquainted with them when in that region, and also with the fact
that Anah had first discovered them, or at least had found out their medicinal
virtues, and brought them into public notice. Perhaps some remarkable cures
upon Jews of distinction rendered it still further appropriate for Moses to
commemorate the discovery and the discoverer.

CHAPTER XXVII.

TIBERIAS.

March 25th.

You should have been out with me on the promontory which overhangs the Daybreak.
lake, to see the day break along the eastern mountains. At first it was intensely dark, but by-and-by it began to soften low down and far to the north.
Then suddenly the note of a lark rang out, silvery and joyous, as if from the
very midst of the stars. In rapid succession bird after bird rose up, hymning
their early matin, until the whole " marble vault of heaven " was vocal with
invisible choristers. One by one the stars faded out before the growing day,
and every moment the scene shifted and changed from bright to brighter—
from glory to glory, throwing down dark shadows from the eastern cliffs upon
the broad bosom of Gennesaret. At length the first rays of the sun gleamed
on the snowy head of Hermon, revealing deep wrinkles, which the storms of a
thousand generations have drawn across his stern, cold brow. It was the very
perfection of this style of beauty, nor do I understand how any one can call it
tame. Doubtless time and season, pleasant company, good health, and cheerful spirits, add immensely to the effect of such a scene. In the glare and burn-

PART
II.

Interest
of Genne-
saret.

ing heat of midsummer, a weary traveller, with eyes inflamed, might see nothing to admire; but I have never thus visited it. To me Gennesaret and its surroundings are ever fair, and always invested with unparalleled interest. Here our blessed Lord dwelt with men, and taught the way of life. Here he preached in a ship, slept in the storm, walked on the waves, rebuked the winds, and calmed the sea. Here is Magdala, Capernaum, Chorazin, and Bethsaida, with its desert place, where five thousand hungry souls were fed with miraculous bread; and Gergesa, where devils went from men to swine, and both together into the sea. Here he opened his mouth, and taught, with authority, that divine sermon on the mount; and on one of these solitary summits Moses and Elias, in shining robes, came down from heaven to converse with him in the glory of his transfiguration. And not least, from this shore he selected those wonderful men who were to erect his kingdom, and carry his gospel to the ends of the earth. Is there another spot on the globe that can compare with this?

Tiberias.

John is the only evangelist who mentions Tiberias; but he not only speaks of the city, but calls the lake by this name more than once.[1] May we not find in this an incidental corroboration of the opinion that his Gospel was written last of all, and toward the close of the first century, and for those who by that time had come to know the lake most familiarly by the name of Tiberias.

Its history.

This supposition becomes the most probable when we remember that it was quite a modern town when our Lord frequented this region, having been built and named by Herod about the time of his advent. Seventy years afterwards Josephus found it an important city, and no other in Galilee is so often mentioned by him. Almost every other city was destroyed by Vespasian and Titus, but this was spared, and rewarded for its adherence to the Romans by being made the capital of the province. John, writing many years after these events, would naturally mention both the city and the lake, and call the latter by its then most familiar name, Tiberias. But the other apostles wrote before these events had taken place, and therefore do not speak of Tiberias at all.

Not cer-
tain if
visited by
Jesus.

Is it not somewhat strange that our Saviour never entered Tiberias?

This is not quite certain, for he undoubtedly visited many places which are not mentioned by any of the evangelists; and if the tradition respecting the site of the present old church has any foundation in fact, he did actually enter it, and even after his resurrection. It is my opinion, however, that he never came to Tiberias, and for several reasons, which, by the aid of Josephus, we are able to discover. He tells us that Herod, in order to people his new city, brought many strangers, and people called Galileans, and many not even freemen, but slaves.[2] In short, Herod gathered up all classes, and compelled them to settle in Tiberias. This was not a population with which our Lord and his disciples would choose to associate. Josephus further states that to

---

[1] John vi. 1; xxi. 1; vi. 23.   [2] Ant. xviii. 2, 3.

Mount Hermon.

THE SEA OF GALILEE.

make this place habitable was to transgress the ancient laws of the Jews, be- CHAPTER XXVII.
cause "many sepulchres were here to be taken away in order to make room
for the city of Tiberias, whereas our law pronounces that such persons are
unclean for seven days." Jesus, therefore, *could not enter* this city without
becoming ceremonially unclean, and we know that both he and his disciples
scrupulously avoided any such violation of the law of Moses. He *never visited
Tiberias*, and thus the silence of the evangelists in regard to it is explained.

This piece of history suggests one or two other remarks. It is nearly certain Tiberias
that Tiberias was built, in part at least, upon the cemetery of a neighbouring built on a
city then in ruins; for without such a city whence came the many sepulchres cemetery.
spoken of? And that this city was ancient, and long since deserted, is evident from the fact that these sepulchres had no owners to be outraged by their
demolition. The people who once used that cemetery had totally disappeared
from the vicinity before Tiberias was erected. We may also determine with
certainty that this *former* city was *south* of the present one, for there is no
place for it on the north, or in any other direction but south. This confirms
the idea that the ruins between Tiberias and the baths are the remains of a
city more ancient than that built by Herod. The remark of Josephus about
the sepulchres also shows that the present town occupies the site of
Herod's city. The face of the hill on which the northern part of it stands
is covered with a very peculiar kind of tombs, and apparently as old as
the rock itself. Many of them were wholly destroyed when the wall was built,
for they extend under it, and into the city itself, while the whole hill side
north and north-west of it is crowded with them—the forsaken graves of
an extinct city and race. What was the name of this more ancient city must Ruins of
ever remain a matter of mere conjecture. It was many times larger than the an ancient city.
modern town, for it covered the plain and side of the mountain quite down
to the baths, and was a city of palaces, and temples, and splendid edifices,
as the remains abundantly show. Perhaps it was Hammath itself, named
from the hot baths, great and rich, from their celebrity in olden time.
Perhaps it was Chinneroth, from which the lake took its most ancient, as it
has derived its modern name from its successor. Perhaps—but it is idle to
multiply suppositions of this kind.

It would be tedious to enter minutely into the history of this city and its Tiberias a
varied fortunes; nor is this necessary. Reland, and Burckhardt, and Robin- rabbinical
son, and Wilson, and Kitto have done this at large. Ever since the destruc- city.
tion of Jerusalem, it has been chiefly celebrated in connection with the Jews,
and was for a long time the chief seat of rabbinical learning. It is still one of
their four holy cities. Among the Christians it also early rose to distinction,
and the old church, built upon the spot where our Lord gave his last charge
to Peter, is a choice bit of ecclesiastical antiquity. Though we need not
accept this age or origin, still I am not so sure as Dr. Robinson is, that,
because the arch of its vault is slightly *pointed*, its "antiquity must necessarily be limited to the time of the Crusaders at the earliest." If not greatly

PART
II.

mistaken, I have seen *such arches* far older than the twelfth century. But the entire subject of the *arch* is yet to be properly developed, and until this is done the unlearned must not be too positive. Let that pass. The present city is situated on the shore, at the north-east corner of this small plain. The walls enclose an irregular parallelogram, about one hundred rods from north to south, and in breadth not more than forty. They were strengthened by ten round towers on the west, five on the north, and eight on the south. There were also two or three towers along the shore to protect the city from attack by sea. Not much more than one-half of this small area is occupied by buildings of any kind, and the north end, which is a rocky hill, has nothing but the

Tiberias—
its filth.

ruins of the old palace. The earthquake of 1837 prostrated a large part of the walls, and they have not yet been repaired, and perhaps never will be. There is no town in Syria so utterly filthy as Tiberias, or so little to be desired as a residence. Being *six hundred* feet below the level of the ocean, and overhung on the west by a high mountain, which effectually shuts off the Mediterranean breezes, it is fearfully hot in summer. The last time I was encamped at the baths the thermometer stood at 100° *at midnight,* and a steam went up from the surface of the lake as from some huge smouldering volcano. Of course it swarms with all sorts of vermin. What can induce human beings to settle down in such a place ? And yet some two thousand of our race make it their chosen abode. They are chiefly Jews, attracted hither either to cleanse their leprous bodies in her baths, or to purify their unclean spirits by contact with her traditionary and ceremonial holiness.

The lake.

The lake itself is too well known to need much description. It is an irregular *oval,* with the large end to the north. I cannot make it more than four-

Size.

teen miles long, and nine wide from Mejdel to Wady Semak. It is about *six*

Depres-
sion.

hundred feet lower than the Mediterranean; and this great depression accounts for some of its remarkable phenomena. Seen from any point of the surrounding heights it is a fine sheet of water—a burnished mirror set in a framework of rounded hills and rugged mountains, which rise and roll backward and upward to where Hermon hangs the picture against the blue vault of heaven.

Cause of
depres-
sion.

This profound basin owes its origin, I suppose, to volcanic agency at some remote epoch in geological chronology. But it is not necessary to maintain that the whole of it was once an active crater. Perhaps no part of it was, though it is surrounded by vast regions of trap rock. It *may,* therefore, have been a gigantic crater, with waves of burning lava instead of water. The lake is fed mainly by the Jordan; but, besides this, there are the great fountains of Fûlîyeh, el Mudowera, 'Ain et Tîny, and Tabiga; and in winter the streams from wadies Haman, er Rŭbŭdîyeh, 'Amûd, and Leimŭn, from the west and north-west; and Sulam, Tellaiyeh, Jermaiah, Shŭkaiyif, and Semak on the east. During

Effect of
rain.

the rainy season these streams pour an immense amount of water into the lake, and raise its level several feet above its present mark. The effect is seen particularly along the southern end, and at the outlet of the Jordan.

The old story, told by Tacitus and others, that the Jordan flows directly CHAPTER through the centre without mingling with the lake, has no other foundation XXVII. than the fancy of those who repeat it. The water is sweet and wholesome, and the fish abundant and of an excellent quality. They are, however, but little troubled by either hook, net, or spear.

By the way, this reminds me that in all our rambles around this most Absence of Biblical of lakes, I have constantly missed two pictures with which it has boats and ever been associated in fancy's tablet—the little ships and the fishermen. The fishermen. absence of the former is easily explained. The few semi-savage Arabs who now frequent this shore have no occasion for ships. But why are there no fishers about Gennesaret? There are fish enough in these waters, as we have frequently seen.

The Arabs, particularly the Bedawîn and the peasant, have an invincible Arab dread and repugnance to the sea, nor can they be tempted to trust themselves dread of upon its treacherous bosom. Some of their favourite proverbs are intended the sea. to express this national aversion. If the lake were covered with boats, they would travel all round its shores on the slow-paced camel rather than sail directly across to our city. As there is no demand for boats, the very art of building them is lost. You could not find a carpenter on this whole coast who has either the materials, the tools, or the skill to construct one, or even to mend it if broken. They have no more use for boats than for well-made roads; both disappeared together when the Arabians conquered the country, and both will re-appear together as soon as a more civilized race rises to power.

The cause for the absence of fishermen is likewise found in the character Want of and habits of these Arabs. You could never persuade a genuine son of the patience. desert to sit or stand all day holding a rod over the water with a string and hook at the end of it. If you put it into his hands all ready baited, you would soon hear " Yŭkta 'amrû," as he flung the whole apparatus in the lake. Those who dwell in the cities and villages along the coast of the Mediterranean have partially departed from these primitive habits, and learned from Greeks and Franks the piscatory art; but even they have no enthusiasm for it. Out here it is held in utter contempt.

How do you account for the fact that so many of the apostles were chosen from this class of fishermen? It could not have been accidental.

Nothing in the kingdom of Christ is accidental or the result of caprice, least Apostles, of all the vital matter of its first teachers and founders. There was, no doubt, why an adaptation, a fitness in the occupation of these men to develop just those fishermen. attributes of character most needed in the apostolic office. There are various modes of fishing, and each calculated to cultivate and strengthen some particular moral quality of great importance in their mission. Thus angling requires *patience*, and great perseverance and caution. The line must be fine; the hook carefully concealed by the bait; and this, too, must be such as is suited to the capacity and taste of the fish you seek to catch. A mistake in any of these things defeats the object. If the hook is too big, or not well

PART
II.

covered,—the bait too large, or not adapted to the taste,—of course you take nothing, or bring up a useless crab. There may be deceptive nibbles, but nothing more. So, also, the line must not alarm them, nor will it do to dash the hook in impatiently. And the man must not put *himself* forward; *he should not be seen at all*.

Hand-net.

Then there is fishing with the hand-net. This is beautiful and picturesque. You see it to best advantage along the coast from Beirût to Sidon. The net is in shape like the top of a tent, with a long cord fastened to the apex. This is tied to his arm, and the net so folded that, when it is thrown, it expands to its utmost circumference, around which are strung beads of lead to make it drop suddenly to the bottom. Now, see the actor : half bent, and more than half naked, he keenly watches the playful surf, and there he spies his game tumbling in carelessly toward him. Forward he leaps to meet it. Away goes the net, expanding as it flies, and its leaded circumference strikes the bottom ere the silly fish is aware that its meshes have closed around him. By the aid of his cord the fisherman leisurely draws up the net, and the fish with it. This requires a keen eye, an active frame, and great skill in throwing the net. He, too, must be patient, watchful, wide awake, and prompt to seize the exact moment to throw.

Drag-net.

Then there is the great drag-net, the working of which teaches the value of united effort. Some must row the boat, some cast out the net, some on the shore pull the rope with all their strength, others throw stones and beat the water round the ends, to frighten the fish from escaping there; and as it approaches the shore, every one is active in holding up the edges, drawing it to land, and seizing the fish. This is that net which "gathered of every kind;" and, when drawn to the shore, the fishermen sit down and "gather the good into vessels, but cast the bad away."[1] I have watched this operation throughout a hundred times along the shore of the Mediterranean.

Bag-net.

Again there is the bag-net and basket-net, of various kinds, which are so constructed and worked as to enclose the fish out in deep water. I have seen them of almost every conceivable size and pattern. It was with some one of this sort, I suppose, that Simon had toiled all night without catching anything, but which, when let down at the command of Jesus, enclosed so great a multitude that the net broke, and they filled two ships with the fish until they

Night-fishing.

began to sink.[2] Peter here speaks of toiling all night; and there are certain kinds of fishing always carried on at night. It is a beautiful sight. With blazing torch, the boat glides over the flashing sea, and the men stand gazing keenly into it until their prey is sighted, when, quick as lightning, they fling their net or fly their spear; and often you see the tired fishermen come sullenly into harbour in the morning, having toiled all night in vain. Indeed, every kind of fishing is uncertain. A dozen times the angler jerks out a naked hook; the hand-net closes down on nothing; the drag-net brings in only weeds;

---

[1] Matt. xiii. 47, 48.　　　　[2] Luke v. 4–9.

the bag comes up empty. And then, again, every throw is successful, every net is full—and frequently without any other apparent reason than that of throwing it on the right side of the ship instead of the left, as it happened to the disciples here at Tiberias.[1]

It is wholly unnecessary to apply these things to the business of fishing for men in the great seas of sin. *That* we may leave to the commentator and the preacher. No one occupation of humble life—not even that of the shepherd—calls into exercise and develops so many of the elements necessary for the office of a religious teacher as this of fishing.

Are we to understand from John xxi. 7 that Peter was actually naked?

Not necessarily so. Here, in this hot climate, however, it is common to fish with nothing but a sort of shawl or napkin tied round the waist. The fisher's coat which he girt about him was the short *'abâyeh* which they now wear, and which they very often lay aside while fishing. They can doff and don it in a moment. When worn, it is girt tight about the loins with the zunnar; and Peter did this when hastening to meet the Lord.

The fisher's coat.

As to " ships," they have all disappeared; and there is but one small boat on the lake, and this is generally out of repair. The owner has been here, and told the servant that he will take us for a short sail this evening. We will go to Mejdel, and then you will have completed the entire circuit of this " sacred sea."

26*th*. What a charming sail on Gennesaret we had last night! I would not have missed it for any consideration.

Sail on Gennesaret.

It was indeed delightful, especially the row back after sunset, while twilight was fading into the solemn mysteries of night; and how prettily the stars came out, twinkling so sociably at us, like old friends! These very stars thus gazed with their loving eyes upon Him who made them, when he sailed over this same lake eighteen hundred years ago. Mystery of mysteries! The God-man, the Divine Logos, by whom all things were made which are in heaven and which are on earth, did actually sail over this identical sea in a boat, and by night, as we have done; and not stars only, but angels also beheld and wondered, and still do gaze, and ever will, " desiring earnestly to look into those things." This is not fancy, but fact; and shadowy indeed must be his faith in whose breast these sacred shores awaken no holier emotions than such as spring from common earth and ordinary lakes. He must be of those who have eyes but see not, ears but hear not, and hearts that cannot comprehend. Shame on us all, that we can frequent the haunts and the home of Him who came from heaven to die for our redemption with little reverence and less love. We would not plead for apocryphal relics or fabulous caverns. It is wise and well to refuse all homage to such cunning fabrications. But surely it is unnatural, if not impious, to withhold or restrain those emotions which the scenes we are contemplating are caculated to awaken, which they *will* inspire in every mind

The incarnation of Jesus.

---

[1] John xxi. 6.

PART II.
having faith enough to invest the Gospel narratives with reality and life. Depend upon it, the eye that looks unmoved on these shores is in the head of a practical infidel.

Localities of the gospel teaching.
I have always supposed that the Gospel narratives would be more interesting and better understood, and that the instructions of our divine Teacher would fall with more power upon the heart, in the places where they were first delivered, than when read or heard on the other side of the world; and to a limited extent I find this to be true. Still there is a sense of vagueness which I cannot dissipate. I regret this the more because it is so different from what I anticipated. It is a favourite theory of mine, that every true book has a birth-day and a home; so has every prophet and religious teacher; and we not only have a right to subject their recorded history and instructions to the test of time and place, to ascertain their authenticity and truthfulness, but, if they are genuine, such scrutiny will greatly illustrate and emphasize their meaning. Nor is it irreverent to apply these tests to the life and teachings of Him who spoke as man never spoke—as one having authority, and not as the scribes. Can we not do something toward gathering and concentrating the scattered rays of light which the wanderings about the home of our Lord have struck out?

Agreement of place and narrative.
Perhaps; at any rate we can *try*, and without the slightest apprehension that the record may prove a forgery. Everything will be found in most perfect agreement with all ascertained facts of chronology, topography, and history. The references to *time* are not very numerous or significant, but they agree most beautifully with the assumed age of our Lord's advent. When there is occasion to allude to matters in which this idea is involved, it is done with the utmost simplicity and naturalness. As an example—one of many equally pertinent—take the demand about the tribute-money, and the answer of Jesus, "Render unto Cæsar the things that are Cæsar's." We have examined the "image and superscription" of this Roman *penny* on the very spot where the tax-gatherer sat, and with the evidences scattered all around us that these lordly Romans were actually here. History, the treasured coin, and these prostrate ruins, unite in proving that the teacher Jesus, the cavilling Pharisees, and the tax-gathering Romans were all here, and the entire incident is admirably illustrated and confirmed.

Minute accuracy.
The references to topography are very numerous, and entirely satisfactory. We need only mention Nazareth, and Cana, and Capernaum, and Chorazin, and Bethsaida, and the regions around this lake. Everything is natural, and in accordance with ascertained facts, even to the omission of this city of Tiberias in the list of places visited by our Lord. There is also a sort of verbal accuracy at times, which it is always pleasant to meet. Thus Jesus is said to *go down* from Cana to Capernaum; and we now know that the latter place is not only the lowest, but actually six hundred feet lower than the Mediterranean Sea. And so, also, in the appeal to "a city set on an hill;" if he pointed to Safed, as he probably did, nothing could be more emphatic. This town is seen

from an immense distance, and cannot be hid. And if not Safed, there are many other towns all about the region where the remark was made, and a reference to any one of them was perfectly natural and emphatic.

The allusions to manners and customs are still more numerous than those to the topography of the land, and they agree most perfectly with the supposed age of the world and character of the people. It is implied in almost countless ways that those with whom our Lord associated on these shores were accustomed to out-door life. They meet on the mountain to hear him preach; they follow him into a desert place of Bethsaida to be fed; they spend whole days there without any apparent provision for either shelter, sleep, or food ; they are found in the open court of houses or on the shore of the lake at all times, etc., etc. Now all the specifications are here, just as they should be— the mountain, the desert place, the shore, the open court, the climate so warm as to lead the people into the open air, the present habits of the people— *everything* in exact accord with the Gospel narratives. The inhabitants not only go forth into the country as represented in the New Testament, but they remain there, and sleep in the open air, if occasion require, without the slightest inconvenience. Again the incidental mention of *women* and *children* in the great assemblies gathered around Jesus is true to Oriental life, strange as it may appear to those who read so much about *female seclusion in the East.* In the great gatherings of this day, at funerals, weddings, festas, and fairs, women and children often constitute the larger portion of the assemblies. I have seen hundreds of these gatherings in the open air ; and should a prophet now arise with a tithe of the celebrity of Jesus of Nazareth, there would quickly be immense assemblies about him "from Galilee, and from Decapolis, and from Jerusalem, and from Judea, and from beyond Jordan." Bad, and stupid, and ignorant, and worldly as the people are, their attention would be instantly arrested by the voice of a prophet, and they would flock from all parts to see, hear, and be healed. There is an irresistible bias in Orientals of all religions to run after the mere shadow of a prophet or a miracle-worker. A grand fraud was enacted in Lebanon a few years ago, in order to raise the wind to build a church. The water that burst out while the workmen were digging the foundation, it was published abroad, would restore the blind to sight ; and quickly multitudes of these unfortunate people, from all parts of Palestine and Syria, and even ship-loads from Egypt, hastened to the spot, to bathe their sore or sightless eye-balls in the wonder-working water. I myself saw long files of *blind leading the blind,* marching slowly and painfully on toward the blessed stream, and it was not until great suffering and loss that the insane multitude could be restrained from making the worse than useless pilgrimage. Such are Orientals of this day ; and to know what was the character, in these respects, of those to whom Christ preached, we need only study that of the people around us. In nothing does the East of this day throw more light upon New Testament history than just on this point, and it is certainly one of much importance.

LAB – AA

PART
II.

Out-door
Imagery.

Instructions addressed to such a people, assembled in the open country or on the sea side, would naturally, almost necessarily, abound in illustrations drawn from country life and from surrounding objects. No others would so seize upon their attention, be so readily comprehended, or so tenaciously remembered. Accordingly, we hear the divine Teacher exclaim at Shechem, "Lift up your eyes to the fields, already white to the harvest. Pray ye the Lord of the harvest to *send forth* labourers into the fields." Thus, too, He speaks of the vineyards; of the good branches *purged;* of the dry ones gathered *for the fire;* of the penny-a-day labourers *standing in the market waiting to be hired,* and of their receiving their wages at the close of each day. Such things as these we now see constantly, daily, and to the minutest shade of verbal accuracy. Again, the sparrows that chatter on every man's house teach lessons of filial trust in the providential care of our heavenly Father ; and lilies, more gloriously arrayed than Solomon, rebuke undue solicitude as to wherewithal we shall be clothed. Then we have the leaven and its lesson ; the mustardseed, with its prophetic promise to the Church ; the sower's four sorts of soil, and their diverse results ; the good seed, and the tares of the enemy ; the fig-tree, with its promise of spring, and its threatenings to the fruitless. Or, descending from the land to the lake, we have the fishermen, their ships, their nets, and their occupation, so suggestive to apostles and preachers, who must be fishers of men. We need not enlarge this list—every reader of the New Testament can add to it from his own recollection ; but it is important to remark, that all these allusions are perfectly natural and appropriate to the country, the people, the Teacher, the age, and every other circumstance mentioned or implied in the evangelical narratives. We have the *originals* still before us. The teachings and illustrations of our Lord would have been out of place in any other country except this. *They could not have been uttered anywhere else.*

Character
of the Jew.

There is one aspect of Christ's character, and one class of allusions in his public teaching, which deserves special consideration. Our Lord was most emphatically a religious teacher and reformer, and, of course, we expect to find constant reference to the manners and morals, the superstitions and religious ceremonies of the people ; and so there is, and with wonderful correspondence to the existing state of things in this same land. Contemplate, then, the man Jesus, the Teacher, the Reformer, as he stood on the shores of this lake eighteen hundred years ago. Who and what he was to the men of that age ? He was a Jew. But what was it to be an ordinary Jew of Nazareth in the year *thirty* of our era ? In very many respects just what it is to be one now in this Tiberias or in Safed—to be intensely and most offensively fanatical ; to regard one's self as pre-eminently holy, the special favourite of God, and to despise all others ; to be amazingly superstitious ; to hold obstinately and defend fiercely an infinite number of silly traditions and puerile fables ; to fritter away the whole life and power of religion in a rigid observance of trifling ceremonies. The common Jew of Tiberias is self-righteous, proud, ignorant, rude, quarrelsome, hypocritical, dishonest, selfish, avaricious, immoral ; and such, in the main, were his ancestors eighteen centuries ago. We *know* this, not so much from the New Testament as from Josephus, that special pleader and grand apologist for his nation. ^{CHAPTER XXVII.}

Now, here is a problem for the sceptic : How comes it that there is *nothing* of this Jew in Jesus ? How could "*the* model man"—ay, the *perfect pattern* for all ages and all lands—how, I say, could he grow, develop, and ripen in Nazareth ? Who taught him the maxims of the Sermon on the Mount ? Whose example of charity, kindness, and compassion did he copy ? How did he alone, of all Jews, nay, of all mankind, conceive, propound, and practise perfectly, a purely spiritual religion ? That he did all this, is undeniable, and it is for those who find in Jesus of Nazareth nothing but a common Jew to explain the wonderful phenomenon. ^{Jesus more than man.}

Again, Jesus grew up from his youth to manhood among a people intensely *mercenary.* This vice corrupted and debased every relation of life. Here, again, Josephus not only agrees with the writers of the New Testament, but goes far beyond them. We can fill up the outlines of his picture from the every-day life and manners of the people about us. Everybody trades, speculates, cheats. The shepherd-boy on the mountains talks of *piastres* from morning till night ; so does the muleteer on the road, the farmer in the field, the artisan in his shop, the merchant in his magazine, the pasha in his palace, the kady in the hall of judgment, the mullah in the mosque, the monk, the priest, the bishop—money, money, money ! the desire of every heart, the theme of every discourse, the end of every aim. Everything, too, is bought and sold. Each prayer has its price, every sin its tariff. Nothing for nothing, but everything for money—at the counter of the merchant, the divan of the judge, the gate of the palace, the altar of the priest. Now our Lord was an *Oriental,* and grew up among just such a people ; but who can or dare say that there is the faintest shadow of this mercenary spirit in his character ? With uncontrolled power to possess all, he owned nothing. He had no place to be born in but another man's stable, no closet to pray in but the wilderness, no place to die but on the cross of an enemy, and no grave but one lent by a friend. At his death he had absolutely nothing to bequeath to his mother. He was as free from the mercenary spirit as though he had belonged to a world where the very idea of property was unknown. And this total abstinence from all ownership was not of necessity, but of choice ; and I say there is nothing like it, nothing that approaches it, in the history of universal man. It stands out perfectly and divinely original. ^{Unlike other Jews.}

And, finally, Jesus was the founder of a new religion ; and the desire and effort of all merely human minds would be to secure its acceptance by connecting discipleship with personal pleasure or temporal advantage. Milton makes the devil say to Jesus,— ^{No temporal advantages for his followers.}

> " If at great things thou wouldst arrive,
> Get riches first, get wealth, and treasure heap."

PART
II.

And this temptation no man under such circumstances ever did or could resist. But Christ, from the first, took this position above the human race, and to the end retained it without an effort. He divorces his gospel from any alloy of earth. Money, property, and all they represent and control, have nothing to do with membership in his society, with citizenship in his kingdom. The very conception of the idea was divine. Not only is it not human, but it is every whit contrary to what is human. He could not have borrowed it, for he was surrounded by those who were not able to comprehend the idea—no, not even the apostles, until after the day of Pentecost. As to the multitude, they sought Jesus, not because they saw the miracles and were convinced, but because they ate and were filled. And so it always has been, and is now, in this same country. In this matter our missionary experience is most painful, and I hope *somewhat* peculiar. It would not be charitable—possibly not just—to say to every applicant, You seek us, not because you have examined our doctrines and believe them, but for the loaves and fishes of some worldly advantage which you hope to obtain ; and yet it is difficult for me at this moment to recall a single instance in which this was not the *first* moving

Mercenary spirit of the people.

motive. Nor does this apply to converts to Protestantism merely, but to all sects, and to all religious changes among the people. Religion is, in fact, a species of property, valued, not for its truth, but for its available price in the market. And thus it was in the time of our Saviour, and he knew it. He *knew* that the multitude followed him for the loaves and fishes ; that they sought to make him king that they might revel in ease, luxury, and power ; that they crowded about him to be healed as people now do around our physicians ; that one called him *master* to obtain a decision in his favour against his brother in regard to the estate, as many join the missionaries the better to press their claims in court. The determination to make religion, or the *profession* of it, a meritorious act, deserving temporal remuneration or personal favour, is almost universal. It was so in the time of Christ. According to the parable, some will even claim admittance into heaven because they had eaten and drunk in his presence ; and, still more absurd, because he had *taught in their streets.* Now, however ridiculous such pretensions may appear to men in the Western World, I have had applications for *money* in this country, urged earnestly, and even angrily, for precisely the same reasons. Our Lord founded the parable, *even to its external drapery and costume,* not on fancy, but on unexaggerated fact.

Worldli- ness of the apostles.

How utterly loathsome must have been such a spirit to the unworldly heart of Jesus ! and yet it was ever manifesting itself even in his chosen apostles. Here, again, Christ is our divine example. Hateful as was this earthly, grovelling spirit, yet how patiently he bears with it ! It is related of Dr. Chalmers that a certain man visited him several times as a religious inquirer, and when he imagined that he had awakened sufficient interest in his behalf, he cautiously let out the fact that he *was in want of money;* but no sooner was his object apparent than the wrath of the good doctor burst out in a furious tempest, and he almost kicked the mercenary wretch out of his house. If the doctor had been a missionary in this country, and had adopted the same summary mode with those who sought his presence from precisely the same motives, he might just as well have remained at home in his mother's nursery for all the good he would have effected here. But Christ did not thus dispose of the matter. He treated it as one, and only one, of the radical corruptions of religion which it was his mission to reform; and in attempting it he manifested the same divine wisdom and forbearance which characterize his whole course. He had to deal with it, even to the day of his death, in his chosen friends. They were constantly thinking of the temporal kingdom, and of seats of honour and power in his royal divan. Nor need we start and stare in amazement, as at some rare and monstrous development of selfishness. There are not half a dozen men in Syria who do not believe, or at least *feel*, that the assumption of the evangelical costume, for example, does, *ipso facto*, entitle the persons to share the temporalities of those by whom they have been discipled. This is neither slander nor exaggeration, and in numberless cases where this claim was denied even in the kindest possible manner, they have been offended, and forsook at once both the teacher and the gospel.

I have sought earnestly and painfully for the cause of this odious element in the religious character of Orientals. Customs so deeply rooted, and so general, and yet so manifestly base, must have their origin in powerful influences acting steadily and universally upon society. Close observation and long reflection lead me to the conclusion that there are, and have been from remote ages, several causes, all tending to connect religion indissolubly with man's selfish interests and his temporal affairs. They may all be traced, perhaps, to the *constitution of civil society.* There are two conditions in which men must seek and find some other security for property, liberty, and life, than what can be derived from government—*under absolute despotism* and in *lawless anarchy.* Where either of these prevails, man instinctively resorts to religion (or superstition) for an asylum ; and not in vain. Rarely is a tyrant so daring as to trample under foot the sanctions and safeguards of firmly-rooted religious rights ; and when any one has been mad enough to attempt such a violation, it has generally cost him his life. Even unbridled and ferocious anarchy is held in restraint, and ultimately subdued, by the sanctities and sanctions of religion. Now, the East has very generally been cursed with one or other, or with both of these tyrannies, and is at this hour. Hence the people have resorted, and do resort, to Religion for assistance and safety, and have designedly made her spread her protecting robes over the entire interests of society, temporal as well as spiritual. They have at length come to regard it mainly as a means to obtain and maintain the safety of person and property; and that religion which secures to its followers the greatest amount of relief and prosperity is the best. Hence, they are ready to embrace a new faith for a few piastres, for relief from a trifling tax, or for any other earthly advantage; and, naturally enough, they change back again with equal facility if disap-

Origin of the spirit.

Religion a check to despotism.

PART
II.

pointed, or if better prospects and promises solicit them. In this they are merely making that use of religion which they understand and think most valuable; nor do they feel ashamed of thus dealing with it. It is a legitimate use of the precious commodity. To us, who have always lived under a form of government where our temporal rights and privileges have been guarded by law, this is a monstrous perversion, and we cannot adequately appreciate the pressure which has crowded these people into such mercenary ways.

Religion the guardian of civil rights.

It is a fact, that to this hour Religion is made to throw her shelter around the separate existence and the temporal rights of the various classes and tribes that dwell in this country. They depend upon it, and employ it without scruple on all occasions. Even European influence in their behalf is mainly based upon it, and, to a certain extent, increases the evil. One nation protects the Maronites *because* they are Papists; another the Greeks *as such;* a third the Greek Catholics; a fourth the Druses, etc., through the whole list. True it is that in thus dealing with those tribes they do but avail themselves of customs inwrought into the very constitution of society and from remote antiquity. I know not when to date their beginning. The divinely established

Temporal element in Judaism.

economy of the Hebrews contained this element largely developed. The Hebrew commonwealth (or church) was a religious corporation which guaranteed to every faithful member of it extensive worldly advantages. The *letter* of its promises is almost wholly temporal; and if we glance back at the history of this land from Abraham to this day, we shall find that religion has been inseparably interwoven with the secular affairs of the people. This important fact accounts, in a great measure, for the present phenomena in regard to it. By a process short, natural, and certain to be adopted by corrupt human nature, religion has been made the servant of man's mercenary desires and evil passions.

Opposition of Jesus.

This miserable and fatal perversion Jesus of Nazareth alone, of all religious teachers, earnestly and honestly attempted to thoroughly correct. He laid the axe to the root of this old and corrupt tree. He revealed a pure spiritual religion, and established a kingdom not of this world; but, alas! his followers either could not or would not maintain it. They slid quickly down from his high position into bondage to the beggarly elements of this world, and nothing, apparently, but a second revelation of the same divine power can lift the gospel once more out of the mire of this pit into which it has fallen. He who is *Truth*—who came into the world to bear witness to the *truth,* divinely accomplished his mission. With the world and all its solicitations and comprehensive entanglements beneath his feet, he tolerated nothing in his kingdom but *truth.* This cut up by the roots the vast systems of *clannish* and *state religions,* founded on fables, and upheld by falsehood, force, and hypocrisy. He spurned with indignation the traditions of priests and the cunning adjustments of politicians. He would have nothing but truth for doctrine, nothing but honest faith in the disciple. To understand how vast the number of superstitions, lying vanities, idle fancies, vain ceremonies, abominable deceptions,

and foul corruptions which had overgrown religion in his day, it is only neces- CHAPTER
sary to examine that which claims to be religion in this same country at the XXVII.
present moment. And should this divine Truth again visit the land, with fan
in hand, he would scatter to the four winds, from the great threshing-floor of
his indignation, the mountains of chaff which have gathered there for ages, and
he would hurl the thunderbolts of his wrath against a thousand hypocritical
deceivers of mankind. Oh, how radical, profound, and far-reaching are the
simplest laws of Christ, and how prodigious the revolution they contemplate
and require! "Swear not at all." Why, the whole Arab race must quit Rules of
talking altogether. They *cannot* say simply Yea, yea—Nay, nay. "Lie not Christ.
one to another." Impossible! everything, within, without, and about you, is a
lie. "Do to others as ye would that they should do to you." This precept
seems to want a *not* somewhere or other. "Salute no man by the way."
Absurd! we *must* manufacture compliments as fast as possible, and utter
them with grace and gravity to friend and foe alike. But why multiply any
further comparisons and contrasts? The subject is inexhaustible, and enough
has been said or hinted to prove that Jesus did not borrow the lessons he
taught. They are not from man, of man, nor by man, *but they are of God.*

Shut the tent door, and put the candle outside, or we shall be overwhelmed Gnats.
by a deluge of gnats. This is one of the plagues of this filthy city. Once,
when encamped on this very spot, they came in such incredible swarms as
literally to cover up and extinguish the candle. In five minutes their dead
carcasses accumulated on the top so as to put it out. It seemed to me at the
time that Tiberias might be rendered absolutely uninhabitable by this insignificant, almost invisible enemy. Has it never occurred to you that the writers
of the Bible were very indifferent to those sources of annoyance which travellers now dwell upon with such vehement and pathetic lamentation? Gnats,
for example, are only mentioned once, and then not as an annoyance, but to
introduce and give point to a severe rebuke upon pharisaical scrupulosity : " Ye
blind guides, which strain at [or *out*] a gnat, and swallow a camel."[1] And certainly no comparison could better express the absurdity and hypocrisy of their
conduct.

As another instance of this indifference to small annoyances, I cannot but
think just now of the *flea.* These most troublesome creatures are only mentioned by David in his complaint to Saul: "After whom dost thou pursue?
after a dead dog, after a flea? For the king of Israel is come out to seek a
flea, as when one doth hunt a partridge in the mountains."[2]

True; but the reference is very emphatic. There are at this moment The flea.
myriads of men, women, and children, chasing these nimble creatures through
all the mysteries and hiding-places of their manifold garments. Still, it is remarkable that such an omnipresent source of vexation should not be more frequently mentioned, and the more so, as in this matter the Bible differs

---

[1] Matt. xxiii. 24.   [2] 1 Sam. xxiv. 14, and xxvi. 20.

PART II.

entirely from all Oriental writings. The Arabs, in their poetry, fables, stories, and general literature, not only mention the flea, but with every possible term of dislike and malediction. The Bedawîn, though filthy to a proverb, and patient *ad nauseam* of other vermin, have the greatest dread of the flea, and whenever they appear in their camp they break up and remove to another. Indeed, it is quite in the power of fleas to compel an evacuation. I have seen places where Arabs had been encamped literally swarming with them, as though the very dust had turned to fleas. One could not stand a moment on such a spot without having his legs quite black with them; and, beyond a doubt, if a person were bound and left there, he would soon be worried to death. An Arab proverb informs us that the king of the fleas holds his court in Tiberias. It is fortunate that etiquette does not oblige us to frequent it.

The centipede.

I was somewhat startled to find myself this morning in close proximity to a more formidable species of vermin than either gnats or fleas. While seated on a dilapidated sepulchre, an immense centipede crawled out cautiously, and made directly for my hand, which I quickly gave, and with it a smart stone, to add emphasis to the salutation. Are these ugly creatures really dangerous?

I am surprised to find them stirring so early in the spring, though Tiberias is hot enough for them or for anything else. The bite of the centipede is not fatal, but is said to be extremely painful, and very slow to heal. The Arabs say that it strikes its fore claws into the flesh, and there they break off and remain, thus rendering the wound more troublesome. I never saw a person bitten by them, but their mere appearance makes one's flesh creep. While the locusts were passing through Abeîh, they started up a very large centipede near my house, and I was greatly amused with its behaviour. As the living stream rolled over it without cessation for a moment, it became perfectly furious; bit on the right hand and the left; writhed, and squirmed, and floundered in impotent wrath; and was finally worried to death. During this extraordinary battle its look was almost satanic.

Donkeys.

How sweetly the day draws to a close around this warm and delightful lake! and there come the droves of cattle and donkeys down from the green hills where they pasture! I have seen no place where there are so many, or at least where they are brought home *together*, and in such crowds. Last night the thought struck me as they were entering the gate, and away I hurried after them, to see whether these Tiberian donkeys were as wise as those Isaiah mentions. True to life, no sooner had we got within the walls, than the drove began to disperse. Every ox knew perfectly well his owner, his house, and the way to it; nor did he get bewildered for a moment in the mazes of these

The master's crib.

narrow and crooked alleys. As for the asses, they walked straight to the door, and up to their master's "crib," without turning to bid good-night to their companions of the field. I followed one company clear into their habitation, and saw each take his appropriate manger, and begin his evening meal of dry *tibn*. Isaiah says in all this they were wiser than their owners, who neither knew nor considered, but forsook the Lord, and provoked the Holy One of Israel.[1]

These " cribs " of Isaiah are, I suppose, the " mangers " of the New Testament, in one of which the infant Redeemer was laid ?

It is so understood by the Arabs, so translated in their Bible, and I doubt not correctly. It is common to find two sides of the one room where the native farmer resides with his cattle fitted up with these mangers, and the remainder elevated about two feet higher for the accommodation of the family. The mangers are built of small stones and mortar, in the shape of a box, or rather of a kneading-trough; and, when cleaned up and whitewashed, as they often are in summer, they do very well to lay little babes in. Indeed, our own children have slept in them in our rude summer retreats on the mountains.

As to the donkey, he is a slandered and much abused animal. He is poorly fed, hard worked, overloaded, and beaten without reason or mercy. Their saddles are so ill-shaped, so hard, and so ragged, that they wound the back and shoulders; and the rough ropes which bind on the burdens lacerate the flesh wherever they come in contact with it. No wonder, therefore, that he has a gaunt frame, a tottering gait, ears which slouch heavily round his head, and a stupid and woe-begone stare out of hopeless eyes. But when young and unbroken, they are as lively and playful as kittens; and when well fed, the male is, without exception, the most pugnacious brute on earth. Dogs full of fire and fight as Dandy Dinmont's varieties of pepper will yet sometimes be at peace, but two fat male donkeys can never be brought together, night or day, in summer or in winter, without instant war.

CHAPTER XXVIII.

The manger.

Treatment of the ass.

CHAPTER XXVIII.

TIBERIAS TO NAZARETH.

Solitude of the lake.	Horns of Hŭttĭn.
Mustard.	Kefr Kenna and Cana of Galilee.
Locusts.	Plain of Zebulun.
Mejdel, or Magdala.	The Buttanf.
Tares and wheat.	Jotapata.
Wady Hamâm.	Nazareth.

March 28th.

It is six hours to Nazareth, but as there is nothing of special interest along the direct route by Lubieh, we will turn northward over this rocky shore to Mejdel. The path commands one of the finest views of the lake and surrounding scenery; and when the water was covered with boats and ships, and the land adorned with villas, orchards, and groves, the *tout ensemble* must have

Solitude of the lake.

---

[1] Isa. i. 3, 4.

PART
II.

been beautiful, and even magnificent. But now, how solitary and sad! There is something oppressive in this unbroken silence; the very ducks on the lake are "shockingly tame;" and the stupid fish gather in crowds, and stare up into one's face without the least alarm. Let us stop and look at them, congregated around these copious tepid and nauseous fountains of Fûlîyeh. Travellers call them 'Ain el Barideh—*Cold* Fountains; but I have not heard that name applied to them by the Arabs, and there is no propriety in it, for they are decidedly *warm*. Dr. Robinson says that the great road from the south comes down to the shore at this point, along this Wady 'Ammas; but, if this was formerly the case, it is nearly deserted now, and the main road descends Wady Hamâm. I myself have always ascended by that ravine, nor have I ever seen any one pass up this wady of Abu el Ammâs.

Ruins at
Fûlyeh.

These circular structures about Fûlîyeh have puzzled all travellers who have noticed them. They are ancient, and some think they are ruined baths; but there are no traces of any of the necessary accessories to such establishments, and without these they could not have been used for bathing. They do not appear to have been vaulted over; and the probability is, that they were erected, like those at Ras el 'Ain, near Tyre, and at Kabereh, to elevate the water of the fountains to irrigate this little vale of Fûlîyeh and to drive the mills of Mejdel. An inexhaustible mill stream must always have been of immense importance to the inhabitants of this neighbourhood.

Wild mus-
tard.

Is this wild mustard that is growing so luxuriantly and blossoming so fragrantly along our path?

Mustard-
tree.

It is; and I have always found it here in spring; and, a little later than this, the whole surface of the vale will be *gilded over* with its yellow flowers. I have seen this plant on the rich plain of Akkâr as tall as the horse and his rider. It has occurred to me on former visits that the mustard-tree of the parable probably grew at this spot, or possibly at Tabiga, near Capernaum, for the water in both is somewhat similar, and so are the vegetable productions. To furnish an adequate basis for the proverb, it is necessary to suppose that a variety of it was cultivated in the time of our Saviour, which grew to an enormous size, and shot forth large branches, so that the fowls of the air could lodge in the branches of it.[1] It may have been perennial, and have grown to a considerable tree, and there are traditions in the country of such so large that a man could climb into them; and after having seen *red pepper* bushes grow on, year after year, into tall shrubs, and the *castor bean* line the brooks about Damascus like the willows and the poplars, I can readily credit the existence of mustard-trees large enough to meet all the demands of our Lord's parable.

Irby and Mangles, going from the south end of the Dead Sea to Kerak, found a tree in great abundance, which had a berry growing in clusters like currants, and with the colour of a plum. The taste was pleasant, though

---

[1] Matt. xiii. 31, 32; Mark iv. 30–32; Luke xiii. 18.

strongly aromatic, and closely resembled that of mustard ; and, if taken in
considerable quantity, it had precisely the same effects as mustard. The

WILD MUSTARD.

leaves had the same pungent flavour as the seed, although not so strong.
They think this is the tree of the parable, and it may be so. They give no
name to this remarkable plant, but it well deserves a more careful and scientific examination. At any rate, I should not be surprised to find in some
such locality a *mustard plant* which, when grown, " is the greatest among
herbs, and becometh a tree, so that the birds of the air come and lodge in the
branches thereof." I once discovered a veritable *cabbage-tree* on the cliffs of
Dog River ; and many curious vegetable anomalies doubtless remain to be
detected and described.

We are not to suppose that the mustard-seed is the least of all seeds *in the* " Least of
world ; but it was the smallest which the husbandman was accustomed to seeds."
sow ; and the "tree," when full grown, was larger than the other herbs in his
garden. To press the *literal* meaning of the terms any further would be a

PART
II.

violation of one of the plainest canons of interpretation. This ample size, with branches shooting out in all directions, yet springing from the very smallest beginning, contains, as I suppose, the special meaning and intention of the parable. It is in this sense only that the kingdom of heaven is like a grain of mustard seed. Our Saviour did not select it because of any inherent qualities, medicinal or otherwise, which belonged to it. True, it is *pungent*, and *penetrating*, and *fiery*, and *searching*, and must be *bruised* or *crushed* before it will give out its special virtues; and one might go on enumerating such qualities, and multiplying analogies between these properties of mustard and certain attributes of true religion, or of the Church, or of the individual Christian; but they are foreign to any object that Jesus had in view, and must therefore be altogether fanciful. Such exposition dilutes the sense, and dissipates the force and point of his sayings, and should not be encouraged.

Locusts.

Here, on the side of this mountain above Fûlîyeh, I had my first introduction, some twenty years ago, to the far-famed locusts of the East. Noticing

SYRIAN LOCUST.

something peculiar on the hill side, I rode up to examine it, when, to my amazement, *the whole surface became agitated, and began to roll down the declivity.* My horse was so terrified that I was obliged to dismount. The locusts were very young—not yet able *even to jump;* they had the shape, however, of minute grasshoppers. Their numbers seemed infinite; and in their haste to get out of my way, they literally rolled over and over, like semi-fluid mortar an inch or two in thickness. Many years after this I became better acquainted with these extraordinary creatures in Abeîh on Lebanon.

Visitation
in 1845.

Early in the spring of 1845, these insects appeared in considerable numbers along the sea-coast and on the lower spurs of the mountains. They did no great injury at the time, and, having laid their eggs, immediately disappeared. The people, familiar with their habits, looked with anxiety to the time when these eggs would be hatched; nor were their fears groundless or exaggerated. For several days previous to the 1st of June we had heard that millions of young locusts were on their march up the valley toward our village, and at length I was told that they had reached the lower part of it. Summoning all the people I could collect, we went to meet and attack them, hoping to stop their progress altogether, or, at least, to turn aside the line of their march. Never shall I lose the impression produced by the first view of them. I had often passed through clouds of *flying* locusts, and they always struck my imagination with a sort of vague terror; but these we now confronted were without wings, and about the size of full-grown grasshoppers, which they closely resembled in appearance and behaviour. But their number was

Their
number.

astounding; the whole face of the mountain was black with them. On they CHAPTER
came like a living deluge. We dug trenches, and kindled fires, and beat, and XXVIII.
burned to death "heaps upon heaps;" but the effort was utterly useless.
Wave after wave *rolled up* the mountain side, and poured over rocks, walls,
ditches, and hedges—those behind covering up and bridging over the masses
already killed. After a long and fatiguing contest, I descended the mountain
to examine the *depth* of the column; but I could not see to the end of it.
Wearied with my hard walk over this living deluge, I returned, and gave over
the vain effort to stop its progress.

By the next morning the head of the column had reached my garden, and, Contest
hiring eight or ten people, I resolved to rescue at least my vegetables and with the
flowers. During this day we succeeded, by fire and by beating them off the locusts.
walls with brushes and branches, in keeping our little garden tolerably clear of
them; but it was perfectly appalling to watch this animated river as it flowed
up the road, and ascended the hill above my house. At length, worn out with
incessant skirmishing, I gave up the battle. Carrying the pots into the par-
lour, and covering up what else I could, I surrendered the remainder to the
conquerors. For four days they continued to pass on toward the east, and
finally only a few stragglers of the mighty host were left behind.

In every stage of their existence these locusts give a most impressive view
of the power of God to punish a wicked world. Look at the pioneers of the
host—those flying squadrons that appear in early spring. Watch the furious Produc-
impulse for the propagation of their devouring progeny. No power of man tion and
can interrupt it. Millions upon millions, with most fatal industry, deposit progress.
their innumerable eggs in the field, the plain, and the desert. This done, they
vanish like morning mist. But in six or eight weeks the very dust seems to
waken into life, and moulded into maggots, begins to creep. Soon this
animated earth becomes minute grasshoppers; and, creeping and jumping *all
in the same general direction*, they begin their destructive march. After a
few days their voracious appetite palls; they become sluggish, and *fast*, like
the silk-worms, for a short time. Like the silk-worms, too, they repeat this
fasting *four* times before they have completed their transmutations and are
accommodated with wings. I do not remember to have seen this fact in their
history noticed by any naturalist. In their march they devour every green
thing, and with wonderful expedition. A large vineyard and garden adjoining
mine was green as a meadow in the morning, but long before night it was
naked and bare as a newly-ploughed field or dusty road. The noise made in
marching and foraging was like that of a heavy shower on a distant forest.

The references to the habits and behaviour of locusts in the Bible are very Scripture
striking and accurate. Joel says, "He hath laid my vine waste, and barked allusions.
my fig-tree: he hath made it clean bare, and cast it away; the branches there- Joel.
of are made white."[1] These locusts at once strip the vines of every leaf and "Clean
bare."

---

[1] Joel i. 7.

cluster of grapes, and of every green twig. I also saw many large fig orchards "clean bare," not a leaf remaining; and as the bark of the fig-tree is of a silvery whiteness, the whole orchards, thus rifled of their green veils, spread abroad their branches "made white" in melancholy nakedness to the burning sun.

"Cut off before our eyes."

In view of the utter destruction which they effect, the prophet exclaims, "Alas for the day! for the day of the Lord is at hand, and as a destruction from the Almighty shall it come. Is not the meat cut off before our eyes?"[1] This is most emphatically true. I saw under my own eye not only a large vineyard loaded with young grapes, but whole fields of corn disappear as if by magic, and the hope of the husbandman vanish like smoke.

"The beasts groan."

Again, "How do the beasts groan! the herds of cattle are perplexed, because they have no pasture; yea, the flocks of sheep are made desolate."[2] This is poetic, but true. A field over which this flood of desolation has rolled shows not a blade for even a goat to nip. "The land is as the garden of Eden before them, and behind them a desolate wilderness; yea, and *nothing shall escape them.* Before their face the people shall be much pained;" (how emphatically true!) "all faces shall gather blackness. They shall run like mighty men; they shall climb the wall like men of war; and they shall march every one on his ways, and they shall not break their ranks."[3] When the head of the mighty column came in contact with the palace of the Emeer Asaad in Abeîh, they did not take the trouble to wheel round the corners, but climbed the wall like men of war, and marched over the top of it; so, when they reached the house of Dr. Van Dyck, in spite of all his efforts to prevent it, a living stream rolled right over the roof. "They shall run to and fro in the city; they shall run upon the wall; they shall climb up upon the houses; they shall enter in at the windows like a thief."[4] Every touch in the picture is to the life. If not carefully watched, they would have devoured the flowers which were carried into the inner rooms in pots.

Nahum.

Flight before the sun.

The prophet Nahum says that the locusts "camp in the hedges in the cold day; but when the sun ariseth they flee away, and the place is not known where they are."[5] Paxton and others have remarked that there is much difficulty in this passage; but to any one who has attentively watched the habits of the locust, it is not only plain, but very striking. In the evenings, as soon as the air became cool, at Abeîh they literally camped in the hedges and loose stone walls, covering them over like a swarm of bees settled on a bush. There they remained until the next day's sun waxed warm, when they again commenced their march. One of the days on which they were passing was quite cool, and the locusts scarcely moved at all from their *camps,* and multitudes remained actually stationary until the next morning. Those that did march crept along very heavily, as if cramped and stiff; but in a hot day they hurried forward in a very earnest, lively manner. It is an aggravation of the calamity

[1] Joel i. 15, 16.   [2] Joel i. 18.   [3] Joel ii. 3, 6, 7.   [4] Joel ii. 9.   [5] Nahum iii. 17.

if the weather continues cool ; for then they prolong their stay, and do far more CHAPTER damage. When the hot sun beats powerfully upon them, they literally "*flee* XXVIII. away, and the place is not known where they are." This is true even in regard to those which have not wings. One wonders where they have all gone to. Yesterday the whole earth seemed to be creeping and jumping,—to-day you see not a locust. And the disappearance of the clouds of flying locusts is still more sudden and complete.

David complains that he was "tossed up and down as the locust."[1] This David reference is to the flying locust. I have had frequent opportunities to notice "tossed up and how these squadrons are tossed up and down, and whirled round and round down." by the ever-varying currents of the mountain winds.

Solomon says, "The locusts have no king, yet go they forth all of them by Solomon bands."[2] Nothing in their habits is more striking than the pertinacity with which they all pursue the same line of march, like a disciplined army. As they have no king, they must be influenced by some common instinct.

I am not surprised that Pharaoh's servants remonstrated against his folly Plague of and madness when they heard the plague of locusts announced. "Let the locusts. men go," said they to their proud master, "that they may serve the Lord their God : knowest thou not yet *that Egypt is destroyed?* And when they came they were *very grievous*, for they covered the face of the whole earth, so that the land was darkened ; and they ate every herb of the land, and all the fruit of the trees, and there remained not any green thing in the trees, or in the herbs of the field." Moses declared that they should "cover the face of the earth so that one cannot be able to see the earth."[3] I have this dreadful picture indelibly fixed on my mind. For several nights after they came to Abeîh, as soon as I closed my eyes the whole earth seemed to be creeping and jumping, nor could I banish the ugly image from my brain.

The coming of locusts is a sore judgment from God. "If I command the locusts to devour the land," says the Lord to Solomon.[4] Yes, it is the command of God that brings these insects to scourge a land for the wickedness of the inhabitants thereof.

Do you suppose that the meat of John the Baptist was literally "locusts Food of and wild honey ?"[5] John the Baptist.

Why not ? by the Arabs they are eaten to this day. The perfectly trust-worthy Burckhardt thus speaks on this subject : "*All* the Bedawîn of Arabia, and the inhabitants of towns in Nejd and Hedjaz, are accustomed to eat lo-custs." "I have seen at Medina and Tayf *locust shops*, where these animals were sold by *measure*. In Egypt and Nubia they are only eaten by the poor-est beggars." "The Arabs, in preparing locusts as an article of food, throw them alive into boiling water with which a good deal of salt has been mixed. After a few minutes they are taken out and dried in the sun ; the head, feet, and wings are then torn off ; the bodies are cleansed from the salt and perfectly

---

[1] Ps. cix. 23.   [2] Prov. xxx. 27.   [3] Exod. x. 4–14.   [4] 2 Chron. vii. 13.   [5] Matt. iii. 4.

PART
II.

dried, after which process whole sacks are filled with them by the Bedawîn. They are sometimes eaten boiled in butter, and they often contribute materials for a breakfast when spread over unleavened bread mixed with butter." Thus far Burckhardt. Locusts are not eaten in Syria by any but the Bedawîn on the extreme frontiers, and it is always spoken of as a very inferior article of food, and regarded by most with disgust and loathing—tolerated only by the very poorest people. John the Baptist, however, was of this class, either from necessity or election. He also dwelt in the desert, where such food was and is still used; and therefore the text states the simple truth. His ordinary "meat" was dried locusts—probably fried in butter and mixed with honey, as is still frequently done. The honey, too, was the article made by *bees*, and not *dibs* from grapes, nor dates from the palm, nor anything else which ingenious commentators have invented. Wild honey is still gathered in large quantities from trees in the wilderness, and from rocks in the wadies, just where the Baptist sojourned, and where he came preaching the baptism of repentance.

The locust a "clean" animal.

Nor did John transgress the law of Moses by thus eating locusts. Disgusting and nauseous as this food appears to us, the Hebrews in the wilderness—probably in Egypt also—were accustomed to use it; and in Lev. xi. 22 it is declared to be clean in all its varieties, one of which is wrongly called *beetle* in our translation. No people ever eat any of the *beetle* tribe, so far as I can discover; and there can be no reasonable doubt but that *sal'am*, rendered *beetle*, and *khargal*, *grasshopper*, are both varieties of the locust.

Mejdel, or Magdala.

Here is Mejdel, seated on the southern margin of Gennesaret. It is a wretched hamlet of a dozen low huts huddled into one, and the whole ready to tumble into a dismal heap of black basaltic rubbish. This is the city of Mary Magdalene, out of whom went seven devils, and it seems to be in very significant keeping with the only incident that has given it a history. Evil spirits of some sort must possess the inhabitants, for they are about the worst specimen in the country; and yet they dwell on the shore of this silvery lake, and cultivate this plain of Gennesaret, which Josephus calls the "ambition of nature."

Plain of Gennesaret.

And so it well may be called, to judge from this large expanse of luxuriant barley and wheat. The whole plain is one waving field of grain, without hedge, ditch, or fence of any kind to break the even continuity.

Turn westward here, along the base of the mountain, and in half an hour we shall enter the great gorge of Wady Hamâm. Let me call your attention to these "tares" which are growing among the barley. The grain is just in the proper stage of development to illustrate the parable. In those parts where the grain has *headed out*, they have done the same, and *there* a child cannot mistake them for wheat or barley; but where both are less developed, the closest scrutiny will often fail to detect them. I cannot do it at all with any confidence. Even the farmers, who in this country generally *weed* their fields, do not attempt to separate the one from the other. They would not only mistake good grain for them, but very commonly the roots of the two are so intertwined that it is impossible to separate them without plucking up both.

Tares and wheat.

Both, therefore, must be left to *"grow together"* until the time of harvest."[1]

The common Arabic name for the
tare is *zowan*, and this, I presume, is
the root of the Greek name *zizanion.*
The tare abounds all over the East, and
is a great nuisance to the farmer.   It
resembles the American *cheat*, but the
head does not droop like cheat, nor
does it branch out like oats.   The grain,
also, is smaller, and is arranged along
the upper part of the stalk, which
stands perfectly erect.   The *taste* is
bitter, and when eaten separately, or
even when diffused in ordinary bread, it
causes dizziness, and often acts as a
violent emetic.   Barn-door fowls also
become dizzy from eating it.   In short,
it is a strong soporific poison, and must
be carefully winnowed, and picked out
of the wheat, grain by grain, before grinding, or the flour is not healthy. Of course
the farmers are very anxious to exter-
minate it, but this is nearly impossible.
Indeed, grain-growers in this country believe that in very wet seasons, and in
marshy ground, the *wheat itself turns
to tares.*   I have made diligent inquiries
on this point, and find this to be their
fixed opinion.   Nor is this a modern
notion, or one confined to the ignorant.
It is as old, at least, as the time of

TARES OF PALESTINE.

our Saviour, and is met with both in heathen writers and in the expositions of
the early fathers.   Still, I am not at all prepared to admit its truth.   If it
could be proved, as these old authors assert, that *zizanion* is merely a degenerated wheat or barley, it would be reasonable to allow that such degenera-
tion might occur in a soil and season adapted to cause it, but I do not believe
the fundamental fact in the question. *Zowan* differs so essentially from wheat,
that it will take the very strongest evidence to establish their original identity.
Besides, it does not accord with the general law of degeneracy that it is completed at *once*, and by a single process. Such changes are gradual, and require
successive production and reproduction, each adding to the gradual deteriora-

_____

[1] Matt. xiii 29, 30.

PART
II.

tion, before such a radical change can be effected. The farmers, however, stoutly maintain that they "sow good seed in their fields," and in clean ground, and yet that the whole is turned to *tares* in consequence of extraordinary rains during winter—that is, that perfect *wheat* is changed to perfect tares by one single process; and further, that this change is *permanent*. These extemporaneous tares ever after produce tares, and tares only, nor can you, by any legerdemain, *reverse* the process, and change *tares* back to wheat. *If* this be true, it is a species of original sin in the vegetable kingdom every way surprising.

Tares supplanting wheat.

But how are you to answer a farmer who takes you to a field nearly all tares, and declares that he there sowed clean seed, and that in previous years he always reaped good harvests of pure grain? Whence the present crop of tares? he asks, and so do you. I have repeatedly examined such fields with all the care in my power, and without finding an answer. It would be easy to say, as in the parable, "An enemy hath done this;" but, though I have read in authors *who never resided in Palestine* that bad men do thus injure their enemies, I have never found a person in the country itself who had either known or heard of such an act. It is certainly remarkable that Arab malice has never adopted this mode of injuring its victims; but the fact must be told—it is altogether unknown at the present day. It must have been done, however, in the time of our Saviour, or he would not have mentioned it in his parable. At all events, the farmers of this day will not admit that their fields have thus been filled with tares; and I believe them. We must, therefore, find some other solution of a phenomenon which occurs so often that I have myself had frequent opportunities to verify it. I suppose that several separate causes conspire to bring about the result. First, very wet weather in winter *drowns* and kills *wheat*, while it is the most favourable of all weather for *tares*. In a good season the wheat overgrows and chokes the tares, but in a wet one the reverse is true. The farmers all admit this, but still they ask, "Whence the *seed* of the tares? we sowed 'good seed.'" To this it may be answered, The tare is a very light grain, easily blown about by the wind; that a thousand little birds are ever carrying and dropping it over the fields; that myriads of ants are dragging it in all directions; that moles, and mice, and goats, and sheep, and nearly every other animal, are aiding in this work of dispersion; that much of the tares *shell out* in handling the grain in the field; that a large part of them is thrown out by the wind at the threshing-floor, which is always in the open country; that the heavy rains, which often deluge the country in autumn, carry down to the lower levels this outcast *zowan*, and sow them there; *and these are precisely the spots where the transmutation is said to occur.* It is my belief that in these and in similar ways the *tares* are *actually sown*, without the intervention of an enemy, and their presence is accounted for without having recourse to this incredible doctrine of *transmutation*.

Wady
Hamâm.

Enough about tares. We are just entering the throat of this tremendous gorge. It is called Hamâm, from the clouds of *pigeons* which "flock to their windows" in these rocks. Look up now to that cliff on the left. It is more than a thousand feet high, and a large part is absolutely perpendicular. It is perforated by a multitude of caverns, holes, and narrow passages, the chosen resort of robbers in former days. The walls and fortifications which united these caverns, and defended them against attack, are still visible. They are now called Kŭlaet Ibn M'an, but anciently they bore the name of Arbela, from a village on the top, a little back from the precipice, the ruins of which are now named Irbid.

Josephus has a graphic description of the capture of these caves by Herod the Great. After various expedients to expel them had failed, he let boxes filled with soldiers down the face of the precipice, and landed them at the entrance of the caverns. This was a most daring exploit, but it succeeded, and by fire and sword the robbers were entirely exterminated. Josephus himself afterward fortified this place, in preparation for the Roman war, but he does not appear to have made any use of it.

Caves— how taken by Herod the Great.

ASSAULT OF ROBBERS.

This is truly a most surprising gorge, and there is nothing in this region which leads the traveller to expect such precipices.

The country above is yet more deceitful, and one is on the very edge of the awful cliffs before he is aware of their existence. I have passed up this deep ravine many times, and yet can never get through without stopping again and again to gaze, admire, and almost shudder. But we have still a hard ascent to the top, and must no longer loiter here. See these prodigious blocks, each "large as a meeting-house." They have tumbled from those giddy heights, and nearly block up the wady. Some of them have fallen since I last came this road. Dr. Wilson is mistaken as to the size of this brook, but still here is a fountain of delicious water. My first ascent through this stupendous gorge had all the romance of a veritable discovery. I had never heard of it, and was almost wild with excitement.

The gorge and precipices

This is indeed a fatiguing ascent, but now we have gained the summit, what a beautiful plain spreads out to the south and west! and those cone-like hills must be the Horns of Hŭttîn.

They are, and that village at their base on the north has the same name. It is half an hour hence, and our path lies through it. Dr. Clarke and others have

PART
II.

Horns of
Hŭttîn.

A miracle-
working
mazar.

Battle of
the cru-
saders.

Ruinous
sites.

exaggerated the height of these "Horns," and the grandeur of the prospect from them; yet Dr. Robinson, who makes the criticism, scarcely does them justice. Neither the Horns themselves, nor the prospect of the plain, and gorge, and mountain, is to be despised.

Nor are these gigantic hedges of cactus which surround this village to be passed without remark.

They are very large, and you will find the same at Lûbieh, three miles south of us, and at Sejera, between that and Tabor. In fact, the cactus hedges form impenetrable ramparts around many of these villages in Galilee, which neither man nor beast will scale, and which fire cannot consume.

There are no antiquities of any significance in this Hŭttîn, and nothing else to detain us, except to get a drink of their good water. We shall find none equal to it between this and Nazareth. There is a Moslem *mazar* hid away in this ravine, which comes down from this nearest of the "Horns." It is called Neby Shaiyib, and is celebrated for the cure of insanity. Sheikh Yûsŭf of Abeîh was brought here several years ago, and two of our muleteers were of the party. They are now laughing at the foolish experiment. The poor sheikh derived no advantage from the long journey, hard usage, and silly ceremonies ; but that will not deter others from making a similar experiment. Ten thousand failures, a thousand times repeated, apparently have no tendency to cure the mania for miracles and miracle-working saints and shrines.

Was not the "Sermon on the Mount" preached upon one of these "Horns," according to ecclesiastical tradition ?

When I first passed from Nazareth to Tiberias, I was taken to the very stone upon which the Great Teacher was said to have stood. It lies round on the south-eastern slope of the second Horn, but it is needless to say that there is not the slightest evidence in favour of this locality. The same remark applies, with even more certainty, to the tradition that the feeding of the "five thousand" took place on this mountain; and this in spite of the half dozen "stones of the Christians"—Hajâr en Nusâra—which are still shown to substantiate the fact. These Horns of Hŭttîn, however, will always have a melancholy celebrity in memory of the miserable and utterly ruinous defeat of the crusaders in A.D. 1187, by the great Saladin. Michaud has given a minute account of this terrible battle in the second volume of his great work, and Dr. Robinson, in the third volume of his "Researches," a much better one, which you can consult at your leisure. Nothing so forcibly pictures to my mind the deplorable mismanagement of the crusaders, or the incapacity of their leaders, as the fact that they allowed themselves to be hemmed in upon these barren Horns of Hŭttîn to *die for want of water*, when there was this copious fountain at the base, within a bow-shot of their perishing ranks.

If you wish for an opportunity to cultivate your antiquarian ability, try it on this ancient ruin which we are approaching. It is now called Meskîna, and has evidently been a place of importance, to judge from the rock-tombs, cisterns, and old foundations scattered over the plain ; but I do not recall any such name either in the Bible or elsewhere. The same, however, is true of 'Ain Baida, 'Ain Mâhy, Em Jebeîl, and half a dozen other sites along the ridge upon our left, between Lûbieh and Kefr Kenna. That large village ahead of us, and almost concealed among the olive groves, is called Tûr'an, and from it this long narrow plain takes its name.

When riding up this road on a former occasion, I pestered everybody I could find on the right and the left, farmers, shepherds, Bedawîn, and travellers, with inquiries about the place where the *water was made wine*. With one consent they pointed to Kefr Kenna. Some of them knew of a ruin called Kânâ, on the north side of the great plain of Bŭttauf, but only one had ever heard of the word Jelîl as a part of the name; and, from the hesitancy with which this one admitted it, I was left in doubt whether he did not merely acquiesce in it at my suggestion. It is *certain* that very few even of the Moslems know the full name Kânâ el Jelîl; and yet I think Dr. Robinson has about settled the question in its favour as the true site of the miracle recorded in the second chapter of John. Kefr Kenna, however, is worth looking at for its own sake, and also because it has long borne the honours which are probably due to its neighbour, and *may* possibly have a right to them. It is prettily situated on the side of a shallow vale, has some ruins of ancient buildings, and some tolerably respectable modern ones, and, above all places in this vicinity, abounds in flourishing orchards of pomegranates. Pomegranates have a certain mystical office to perform in native marriages, and no doubt those from Kefr Kenna have special virtue and value. We shall not trouble ourselves to look up the fragments of the six water-pots which were shown to me long ago, nor any other fabulous antiquities of the place. Here, at this well, I always find a troop of bold but good-looking girls, like those of Nazareth. If this were the Cana of the New Testament, the servants doubtless drew water from this identical fountain, for the village has no other.

As we cannot now turn aside to visit the Kânâ on the other side of the Bŭttauf, I will give you an account of my ride thither on a former occasion. We obtained our guide from this village, and, as they are hunters, and familiar with every acre of this region, are the best that can be procured. Where the vale of Kefr Kenna unites with the plain of Tûr'an is a very ancient ruin, called Jiftah (or Geftah). This, I suspect, is the site of the Gath-hepher mentioned by Jerome as being two miles east of Sephoris, on the way to Tiberias. A respectable tradition makes this the birth-place of the prophet Jonah. His *tomb* is now shown by the Moslems of this neighbourhood at Meshhed, on a hill a little to the south of it. This Jiftah, with the curious addition of the article *el*, is the name of the important bounding valley, repeatedly mentioned by Joshua,[1] between Zebulun and Asher, and it is the only place that now bears that name. It is situated on the edge of the long

---

[1] Josh. xix. 14, 27.

PART
II.

Plain of
Zebulun.

valley of Tûr'an, which stretches from above Tiberias westward into the Bŭttauf, and thence south-west, under the name of Nehar el Mĕlĕk, down to the Kishon, at the base of Carmel, and there the boundaries of the two tribes might meet, for both extended to Carmel. I have the impression, therefore, that this is in reality the valley of Jiphthah; and as that part of it which spreads out into the Bŭttauf was doubtless the great plain of Zebulun, a new idea struck me while exploring it, as to the proper punctuation (if you choose) of that remarkable prophecy concerning the great light of the Sun of Righteousness that rose on Zebulun and Naphtali. Nazareth, Kefr Kenna, Kânâ, and all the regions adjacent, where our Lord lived, and where he commenced his ministry, and by his miracles "manifested forth his glory," were within the limits of Zebulun; but Capernaum, Chorazin, and Bethsaida were in Naphtali. It was this latter tribe that was "by the way of the sea, beyond Jordan, Galilee of the Gentiles."[1] Zebulun did not touch the Sea of Galilee at any point, but the territories of these two tribes met at the north-east corner of the Bŭttauf, not far from Kânâ, and within these two tribes thus united our Lord passed nearly the whole of his wonderful life. To others there may not appear to be much in these remarks, and yet the facts, as they came out clear and distinct during my ride round the "plain of Zebulun," seemed to me to add a beautiful corroboration of the ancient prophecy and promise.

The Bŭt-
tauf.

Rimmon
of Zebu-
lun.

But let this pass. Crossing the plain of Tûr'an toward the north-west, we followed the stream which drains off the water into the Bŭttauf. It is called Jerrûban, and was on that day a boisterous brook, in consequence of the heavy rain that, in spite of Mackintoshes and umbrellas, was soaking us to the skin, from head to foot. In an hour from Kefr Kenna we came to Rŭmmaneh, on the very edge of the Bŭttauf. This, no doubt, marks the site of the ancient Rimmon that belonged to Zebulun.[2] Between it and Seffûrieh is a ruin called Rûm—the Ruma, I suppose, mentioned by Josephus as the birth-place of two of his heroes of Jotapata.[3] The hills around the Bŭttauf, east, north, and west, are wild, picturesque, and crowded with ancient ruins, some of them with old columns, as at Em el 'Amûd and at Sûr, west and north-west of Hŭttîn. The day we crossed the Bŭttauf the eastern half of it was a lake, and the path from Rŭmmaneh to Kânâ led through the oozy, spongy end of it. It was the most *nervous* ride I ever made. For two miles the horses waded through mud and water to the knees, along a path less than two feet wide, which had been *tramped down* to a consistency sufficient to arrest the sinking foot for a moment; but if the careless or jaded nag stepped elsewhere, he sank instantly into a quivering quagmire. After several adventures of this sort, we "came to land" just at the foot of Kânâ.

Kânâ.

Leaving our tired animals to rest and crop the grass and shrubs, we ran eagerly up and down the hill on which the village was built. It faces the south-east, and rises boldly from the margin of the Bŭttauf. The hill itself

[1] Matt. iv. 15. [2] 1 Chron. vi. 77. [3] Wars, iii. 7, 21.

is nearly isolated. Wady Jefât comes down to, and then along the south- CHAPTER
western base of it, and another deep ravine cuts it off from the general range XXVIII.
on the north and north-east, and it is thus made to stand out like a huge
tell.

The houses were built of limestone, cut and laid up after the fashion still
common in this region, and some of them may have been inhabited within
the last fifty years. There are many ancient cisterns about it, and fragments
of water-jars in abundance, and both reminded us of the "beginning of
miracles."[1] Some of my companions gathered bits of these water-jars as
mementoes—witnesses they could hardly be, for those of the narrative were of
stone, while these were baked earth.

There is not now a habitable house in the humble village where our blessed Its deser-
Lord sanctioned, by his presence and miraculous assistance, the all-important tion.
and world-wide institution of marriage. This is a very curious fact, and might Its con-
suggest a whole chapter of most instructive reflections. It is a sort of divine nection
with mar-
law of development to hide away the beginnings of things the most momentous riage.
in some almost undiscoverable point. This is an example. Innumerable
millions in their happiest hours have had their thoughts and hearts directed
to Kânâ. Poor little lonely thing! the proudest cities on earth might envy
your lot. Nineveh and Babylon, and a thousand other names may be forgotten,
but not Cana of Galilee. It may even come to pass that Paris, London, and
New York will be dropped out of mind, and their very sites be lost; but to
the end of time, and to the end of the world, whenever and wherever there
shall be the voice of the bride and the bridegroom, then and there will Cana
of Galilee be remembered. Some names we pronounce with honour, some
with shame and sorrow, many with cold indifference, but *Cana* will ever
mingle in the song of the happy, to symbolize the peace and purity of domestic
happiness—the bliss of wedded love.

Kânâ is not only deserted itself, but so wild is the immediate neighbour- Wildness
hood, that it is the favourite hunting-ground of the Kefr Kennits. Ibrahim, of its
neigh-
our guide, had shot a large leopard among its broken houses only a week bourhood.
previous to our visit. He had been hunting wild boar in Wady Jefât; and up
this wady we next proceeded in search of Jotapata. It took just half an hour
to ride from Kânâ to the foot of the rock of Jefât, which Mr. Schultz first
identified with the site of that far-famed castle. It is therefore about two
miles west of Kânâ. The path is in the bed of Wady Jefât, and is easy
enough for a single horseman, but it would be quite impracticable for an army;
and this agrees well with the description of Josephus. The sides and lateral
ravines, of which there are many, are covered with a thick jungle of oak
coppice—the very best haunt for the wild boar, and wild Arabs too. We,
however, saw nothing more formidable than a jackal.

From the nature of the place and its surroundings, Jotapata could never Jotapata.

---

[1] John ii. 1-11.

PART II.

have been anything much more respectable than a retreat for robbers. Whatever appears greater than this in the account must be put down to the imagination or the *necessity* of the historian. The wadies about it are neither deeper nor more savage than scores of other wadies in Galilee, and Gamala was vastly more difficult to attack. The absence of fortifications on the top of Jefât can easily be explained. The original works were ephemeral, extemporized for the emergency, and built of the soft cretaceous rock of the place, and being demolished and deserted, they would crumble into just such rubbish as now covers the extreme edges of the rock. There are a few caves and old cisterns about it, quite sufficient for the story *reduced*, as this, above all others in Josephus, ought to be. He manifestly intended to rest his fame as a warrior upon the defence of Jotapata, and with this idea to stimulate his pen, there is scarcely any conceivable length of exaggeration to which he would not go.[1]

Nazareth.

But there lies Nazareth in its pretty vale, and I leave you to walk or ride down these slippery paths as you prefer, and to enjoy in silence your own reflections, which must be far more impressive than any words of mine.

CHAPTER XXIX.

NAZARETH.

March 29th.

View of Nazareth.

" CAN there any good thing come out of Nazareth ? Come and see," as Philip said to Nathanael.

Why not ? It appeared really charming last night as we came down the mountain from the north-east with the grateful shadows of evening falling softly around it. The vale is small, certainly, but then the different *swellings* of the surrounding hills give the idea of repose and protection ; and, for my part, I would infinitely prefer to have the home of Mary and her divine Son in such a quiet seclusion, than to be obliged to force my way to it through the dust, and confusion, and hard worldliness of any crowded city.

---

[1] See Wars, iii. 7, 8.

I most emphatically accord with that opinion, or rather *feeling;* and there is a sort of latent beauty and appropriateness in the arrangement by which He who made *all things out of nothing* should himself come forth to the world *out of a place that had no history.* The idea here tempts one to linger upon it and expatiate, but this would throw us quite off our present track, which is to go "round about" and describe this city of Nazareth and her neighbours.

It is certainly remarkable that this place, dearest to the Christian heart of all on earth except Jerusalem, is not mentioned in the Old Testament, nor even by Josephus, who was himself on every side of it, and names the villages all about it, but seems yet totally ignorant of its existence. It was probably a very small hamlet, hid away in this narrow vale, and of no political importance whatever. And so far as its subsequent history can be gathered from Eusebius, Jerome, and other ancient records, it never rose to distinction until the time of the Crusades. It was then made the seat of a bishopric; but long after this it was an insignificant village, and remained such through many a dark age of lawless violence. Within the last hundred years, however, it has gradually grown in size and risen into importance, until it has become the chief town of this district. It is now larger and more prosperous than in any former period in its history, and is still enlarging. The present population must exceed three thousand. But it can never become a great city. The position is not favourable, and there is a distressing want of water. Even at this early season there is an incessant contest for a jar of it around this Fountain of the "Annunciation," which is the only one in the village. The present growth of Nazareth is mainly owing to the unchecked inroads of the Arabs from beyond Jordan, which has rendered it unsafe to reside in Beisan and on the great plain of Esdraelon. Most of the villages have been recently deserted, and this work of destruction is still going on; and the villagers from the plains are here in Nazareth, at Jennin, and still further in toward the sea-board. Should a strong government again drive these Arabs over the Jordan, the population and importance of Nazareth would decline at once. It must, however, always be a spot sacred to the whole Christian world, for here our blessed Saviour passed the greater part of his life while on earth. But what a profound silence rests upon those thirty years of mysterious existence! We only know that here the child Jesus grew up from infancy to childhood and youth, increasing in stature as other children do, and in knowledge, and in favour both with God and man, as none ever have done. Here, too, he spent the years of his ripening manhood in humble labours and in sinless communion with God. How natural the desire to lift the veil that shrouds all this period in impenetrable darkness! Hence the spurious " Gospel of the Infancy of Christ," stuffed with puerile or profane fables.

Let any one, curious to see what weak, uninspired man makes of the history of Jesus, turn to the " First and Second Gospels of the Infancy," or the " Gospel according to Nicodemus," and he will be devoutly thankful to know that they

Its obscurity significant.

Its rise within last century.

Present populousness.

PART
II.

are miserable forgeries, so foolish that they are rejected by all; and so far from desiring to have the veil which covers the early life of the incomprehensible God-man lifted, he will adore the wisdom and the kindness that has thus concealed what we could not rightly appreciate nor even understand. Infinite wisdom decided that it was not well to encourage such inquiries, and has taken effectual care that they should never be answered. *There remains but one acknowledged anecdote of his life during all these years.* And further, I am most happy to believe that there is not a fragment of the ancient Nazareth itself which can be identified. It is nearly certain that every stone of the small hamlet where the Saviour of the world spent so many years has long ago dissolved back into the white marl of the hills from which it was quarried. This kind of rock disintegrates with great rapidity; and as the place was often almost or quite destroyed and forsaken, the soft stones thus exposed would not last fifty years.

No authentic remains of Nazareth.

Well, thus I would have it. I like to feel assured that the *church* of the annunciation, the *cave*, the *kitchen* of Mary, the *workshop* of Joseph, the *dining-table* of our Lord and his apostles, the *synagogue* where he read the prophet Isaiah, and the *precipice* down which his enraged fellow-villagers were determined to cast him headlong, *as now shown*, are all fabulous, apocryphal, and have no claims to my veneration or even respect. The eye rests on nothing with which our Lord was familiar except his own glorious works These remain the same. This narrow vale, on the side of which the village is built, climbing up the steep mountain back of it, is very much now what it was then. To this fountain the young Jesus came for water just as these fine healthy children now do with their "pitchers." Shut in on all sides by *fourteen* swelling eminences on the circling mountains, as Dr. Richardson counts them, Nazareth must have been always, as at present, very hot, particularly in the early part of the day. It was also wanting in prospects and distant views. Hence, no doubt, our Saviour would often climb to the top of this western hill, which rises at least five hundred feet above the bottom of the wady. There he could behold the distant sea, and breathe its fresh breeze. From thence, too, his eye would rove delighted over a vast expanse of sacred scenery. We can do the same, and in the doing of it hold converse with his spirit, and enjoy what he enjoyed, without one doubt to trouble or one fable of meddling monk to disturb. Let this suffice. God does not admit impertinent curiosity behind the veil of his own privacy.

Neighbouring places to Nazareth.

Of places which immediately surround Nazareth little need be said, because few of them are mentioned in the Bible, or have ever risen to any distinction. Tabor, and Debûrieh, and Ksalis, En-dor, and Nain, we shall visit hereafter. Yafa here, to the south-west two miles, is the Japhia of Zebulun. Semmûnia, mentioned along with it, is in the same great oak woods two or three miles still further west. Josephus also mentions Jibbata in the plain south of Semmûnia. Sefûrieh, the Sephoris which figures so largely in Josephus and during the Crusades—the Diocæsaria of the Romans and the Fathers—is about

five miles to the north-west. The fine fountains south of Sefûrieh, the more CHAPTER
valuable for their rarity in this region, have witnessed many a contest between XXIX.
Crusader and Saracen, as it was a favourite camp-ground for both. Though
it was an important city for several centuries after the advent of Christ, as
appears abundantly from Josephus and Roman authors, and had coins struck
with its name, yet it owes its celebrity mostly to the tradition that Joachim
and Anna, the supposed parents of the Virgin Mary, resided there. It is now
a considerable village, and flourishing for this region. The ruins of a castle,
probably built by the Crusaders, may still be seen on the hill above it; and
other remains, more ancient, are below on the west side. The latter may have
belonged to a church or convent of the middle ages. The place is favourably
situated, being nearly half way between Acre and Tiberias, with the fat and
fertile Bŭttauf on the north, the long vale of Tûr'an east, and the magnificent
oak glades for many miles to the south, west, and north-west. The inhabitants are not the most complacent to strangers, and I have never liked to
spend the night there.

30*th*. You have been making good use of this bright morning, I suppose, for
you left the tent at an early hour ?

I went at the call of the bell, and heard the monks say mass in their Chapel of
" Chapel of the Annunciation." The organ and the chant were quite affecting Annuncia-
tion.
in this strange land and sacred place at early dawn. But I have little satisfaction in looking at shrines in which I have no faith, or in examining the
cells of monks, for whose institutions and characters I entertain very little
respect. The convent appeared to me more like a castle than a house of
prayer; but I suppose it is none too strong to keep out Arab robbers. Issuing
through its iron gates, I strolled away in search of the Precipice of " Precipi- Mount of
tation;" and, were it not so far from the village, I should acquiesce in it at Precipita-
tion.
once, for it is well adapted to the murderous purpose which animated the
townsmen of our Lord. My guide pointed out a small ruin much nearer the
precipice, where, he said, the village was originally built; and this, if one
could place confidence in the tradition, would relieve the difficulty as to distance. I rather suspect, however, that the bold cliff which overhangs the
Esdraelon was selected because of its striking appearance, and the grand prospect which it commands.

On my way back through the upper part of the town, I found precipices
enough for all the requirements of the narrative in Luke.[1] Most of them, it
is true, appear to be partly *artificial*, but doubtless there were some of the
same sort in ancient days. I stopped also at the *Fountain* of the Annunciation, Fountain
according to the Greek tradition, and, among other things, attempted to pur- of Annun-
ciation.
chase one of those singular rolls of old coins which the girls of Nazareth bind
around their foreheads and cheeks; but I could not succeed in my negotiation, for they refused to sell at any price. Most travellers speak of the beauty

---

[1] Luke iv. 29.

PART II.

Girls of Nazareth.

of these girls, and not altogether without reason. To me, however, they appear unusually bold, and their obvious want of modesty greatly depreciates their good looks. I fear that a very intimate acquaintance with the Nazareth of this day might lead me to ask the very question of Nathanael, and therefore I am ready and quite willing to prosecute our pilgrimage.

Route.

The only preliminary is breakfast, and that has been waiting for half an hour. We send the tents to Sulam, and go thither ourselves by way of Tabor.

T A B O R.

March 30th.

It is about five miles nearly due east to the north-western base of Tabor, whence only it can be ascended on horseback. The road winds over the hills, and down a long wady to the plain, a short distance north of Debûrieh. We, however, shall not follow the valley, but keep round further north, and come upon the mount from the great oak woods which lie between it and Sejera. On one occasion I went directly up from Debûrieh with my aneroid, and found Height of the ascent from Esdraelon to be thirteen hundred and forty-five feet. I Tabor. had formerly made the base of the mountain about four hundred feet higher than the Bay of Acre, and the entire elevation, therefore, is not far from eighteen hundred feet. The southern face of Tabor is limestone rock, nearly naked; but the northern is clothed to the top with a forest of oak and tere-binth, mingled with the beautiful mock-orange (Syringa). The road (if road it may be called) winds up through them, and, notwithstanding the experi-ence of other travellers, I have always found it difficult, and in certain parts actually dangerous.

The mount is entirely composed of cretaceous limestone, as are the hills west and north of it; but all to the east is volcanic. I have never seen a picture of it that was perfectly satisfactory, although every artist who comes in sight of it is sure to take a sketch. Their views differ widely, owing mainly to the points whence they are taken. Seen from the south or north, Tabor describes nearly an arc of a great circle; from the east it is a broad truncated cone, rounded off at the top; from the west it is wedge-shaped, rising to a moderate height Its form. above the neighbouring hills. Its true figure is an elongated oval, the longi-tudinal diameter running nearly east and west. The most impressive view, perhaps, is from the plain between it and En-dor.

Esdraelon is seen to the greatest advantage, not from the summit, but from a projecting terrace some four hundred feet above Debûrieh. It appears like one vast carpet thrown back to the hills of Samaria and the foot of Carmel. In variety of patterns and richness of colours, it is not equalled by anything in View from this country. Both the Mediterranean and the Lake of Tiberias are visible Tabor. from a point near the summit, the former to the north-west, and the latter on the north-east. The Dead Sea, however, cannot be seen from any part of

Tabor, and those who have made the statement were probably deceived by the CHAPTER XXIX.
silvery haze which fills the ghor of the Jordan in that direction. There is
often an actual mirage, which would mislead any one who had not previously
examined the point on a day unperplexed by these phenomena. And now for
this exciting and romantic climb. I will lead the way, and leave you to your
own meditations, with the hint to look well to your horse, lest you change
romance to tragedy before we get up.

Here we are on the top of Tabor! Let us breathe our tired animals beneath Summit of Tabor
this fine old oak at the entrance into the fortress. You observe that a fossé
once protected the wall on all this part of the summit, because it is less
precipitous than elsewhere. This narrow plot on the north side, I suppose,
was levelled into its present shape by the inhabitants of the ancient city, for
gardens, or to make a hippodrome and parade-ground. South of this a rocky
ridge rises some fifty feet higher, and the entire summit was surrounded by a
heavy wall, strengthened with towers at suitable distances, and further
defended by a ditch when needed. These works are obviously of very different
ages, and history not only accounts for, but demands them. There was a
town here, and no doubt fortified, at or before the time of Joshua. Here Its his-
Barak and Deborah assembled the thousands of Naphtali to attack Sisera. tory.
And Tabor is never lost sight of either by Hebrew historian or poet. It
has, therefore, a story many times too long for us to repeat—Canaanitish,
Jewish, Græco-Macedonian, Roman, Christian, Saracenic, Frank, and Turk.
Parts of these fortifications are doubtless Jewish, but it is quite impossible to
distinguish the various ages of architecture with certainty. Nothing remains
now but a confused mass of broken walls, towers, vaults, cisterns, and houses,
some of which indicate the sites of the convents and churches erected by the
Crusaders. The Greek Church has recently fitted up, with the assistance of
Russian gold, two or three vaults here on the left, as a chapel and residence
of the solitary priest and keeper—a foreign monk, whose appearance is not
over-saintly, nor his cell particularly sweet. Both it and the chapel smelt of
arrack the last time I was here, and the red eyes and bloated countenance of
the priest did not indicate "total abstinence." The Latin monks from
Nazareth also celebrate mass here on certain festivals. I once saw a large
procession with drums and cymbals, singing and clapping hands, and the
indispensable roar of muskets, set out from that town to keep the Feast of the
Transfiguration here at these forsaken shrines.

Do you suppose that this is the scene of that stupendous event? I see it The Trans-
called in question by many modern tourists and critics. figuration

If I hesitate to admit the claims of Tabor to the honour of the Transfiguration, it is not from anything in the mount itself. No more noble or appropriate theatre for such a glorious manifestation could be found or desired.
Nor does the fact that there may have been a village on the top at that time
present any difficulty. There are many secluded and densely wooded terraces
on the north and north-east sides admirably adapted to the scenes of the Trans-

figuration. I have been delighted to wander through some of them, and certainly regretted that my early faith in this site had been disturbed by prying critics; and, after reading all that they have advanced against the current tradition, I am not fully convinced. You can examine this vexed question at your leisure, and have as good a right to form an independent opinion on it as anybody else, for all that is known about it is found in Matthew xvii., Mark ix., and Luke ix., which you can see at a glance contain nothing very decisive against the claims of Tabor. The topographical indications are very uncertain and obscure.

View from
Tabor.
But however we may dispose of this question, Tabor will always be a place of great interest. Its remarkable shape and striking position would attract admiration in any country, and the magnificent prospect from the top will always draw pilgrims and tourists thither. I have climbed to it many times, and shall certainly repeat my visits whenever I pass this way. It is from Tabor that one gets the best general view of central Palestine, and especially of the rise and direction of the different water courses by which the great plain of Esdraelon is drained. In common with others, I have carefully sought the summit-level of this part of the plain, and, until lately, without entire success. In my youthful days I was familiar with old maps which made the Kishon run in a broad, straight canal, from the Bay of Acre to the Jordan. Of course this is absurd in itself, and rendered still more so by the well-ascertained fact that the Jordan east of Tabor is seven or eight hundred feet lower than the Mediterranean. The old tradition, however, is not without a semblance of fact to rest upon. I once went directly across from Debûrieh to Nain, which you see to the south-west of us about four miles, on the slope of Jebel ed Dûhy. Between these two villages the plain is so perfectly level that I could not determine the exact line where the water would flow east, and where west, nor could the eye detect the slope either way except at a considerable

Course
of the
streams.
distance. An immense amount of water descends in winter from these oak-clad hills north and west of Tabor, and enters the plain between Ksalis and Debûrieh. It might well happen, therefore, that this flat space would be so flooded that a part would find its way westward to the Kishon, and another part descend along the base of Tabor into Wady Sherrar, and thence into the Jordan. And this it actually does, as I have clearly proved this winter. Being detained in Nazareth by a very heavy storm, our company set out, during a temporary lull, for a gallop to En-dor and Nain. Descending to the plain at Ksalis by the most frightful of all rideable paths, we struck out into Esdraelon direct for En-dor, and, of course, the path led diagonally across toward the south-east. It was all flooded with water, and *spongy* enough; but my search ended in palpable certainty. *All the water that came foaming off these hills east of Ksalis ran directly for this Wady Sherrar*, and no mistake; while all west of that village (and there was plenty of it) flowed without hesitation *westward* to the Kishon. So, also, the drainings of Jebel ed Dûhy from about En-dor, went to the *Sherrar* and the *Jordan*, while those to the west of it

MOUNT TABOR.

joined the Kishon. A line drawn from Ksalis to En-dor, therefore, passes CHAPTER
directly along the summit-level between the Kishon and the *Sherrar*. The   XXIX.
Wady Jalûd, however, on the other side of Jebel ed Dûhy, extends much The
further to the west than this, draining the central part of Esdraelon into the Kishon.
valley of Jezreel from about Fûlîeh. These two streams, the Jalûd and the The Jalûd.
Kishon, therefore, overlap one another for many miles, the arms of the latter,
north and south of Jezreel, carrying the waters from the mountains to the
Mediterranean, while the Jalûd takes those from the centre into the Jordan.
The winter torrents, which come down from the regions of Jelbûn east of
Jenîn, are the most distant branches of the Kishon ; but the most distant
perennial *source* of this famous river is the Fountain of Jenîn itself—the En- En-gan-
gannim (Fountain of Gardens) given to Issachar by Joshua.[1] This is reinforced nim.
on its way westward by the waters of Lejjûn, and many other rivulets from
the hills of Samaria and wadies of Carmel, and also from springs and marshes
in the lower part of the plain itself ; but they are not strong enough to keep
the river running during the summer and autumn. I have crossed the bed of
the Kishon (even after it enters the plain of Acre) in the early part of April,
when it was quite dry. The truth is, that the strictly permanent Kishon is
one of the shortest rivers in the world. You will find the source in the vast
fountains called Sa'adîyeh, not more than three miles east of Haifa. They
flow out from the very roots of Carmel, almost on a level with the sea, and the
water is brackish. They form a deep, broad stream at once, which creeps
sluggishly through an impracticable marsh to the sea; and it is *this* stream
which the traveller crosses on the shore. Of course, it is largely swollen during
the great rains of winter by the longer river from the interior. It is *then*
much easier to find than to get over. I once crossed diagonally through the
lower part of Esdraelon from Semmunia to Wady Kŭsab, and had no little
trouble with its bottomless mire and tangled grass.

I have described thus minutely this noble plain and "ancient river,"
partly because I have nowhere met with a good and correct account of them,
and partly to prepare the way for an intelligible conversation about some of
those Biblical scenes in which they figure most largely. I, of course, refer to
the battle of Barak, the sacrifice of Elijah, and the slaughter of Baal's priests
at the Kishon.

Is the battle-field of Barak visible from here?

Very distinctly. On the border of the plain to the south-west you can dis- Battle-
tinguish the bold artificial Tell el Mutsellim, near Lejjûn, the Megiddo of the field of
Bible. South-east of it is a village called Te'ennûkh, the Taanach of Judges. Barak.
Below these two, on the plain, the host of Sisera was encamped. Barak,
accompanied by the heroic Deborah, was where we now are, with their ten
thousand courageous Naphtalites from Kedesh. On the morning of that
eventful day, probably long before it was light, Deborah set the little army in

---

[1] Joshua xxi. 29.

PART II.

The attack.

motion with the energetic command and animating promise, " Up ; for this is the day in which the Lord hath delivered Sisera into thine hand. Is not the Lord gone out before thee ?" [1] Rapidly they descend the mountain, cross over by Nain into the valley of Jezreel, then incline to the left to avoid the low and marshy ground, and by the first faint light of the morning they are upon the sleeping host of the Canaanites. This assault, wholly unexpected, threw them into instant and irrecoverable confusion. But half awake, the whole army fled in dismay down the plain, hotly pursued by the victorious Barak. No time was allowed to recover from their panic. God also fought against them : " The earth trembled, the heavens dropped, the clouds also dropped water." Josephus adds that a storm from the east beat furiously in the *faces* of the Canaanites, but only on the *backs* of the Jews. The storm is required by both the narrative of the action and the song of victory. It was to this, I suppose, that Deborah alluded,—" Is not the Lord gone out before thee ?" and this it certainly was which swelled the Kishon, so that it swept away and drowned the flying host ; for it never could do that except during a great rain. The army of Sisera naturally sought to regain the strongly fortified Harosheth of the Gentiles, from which they had marched up to their camping-ground a short time before. This place is at the lower end of the narrow vale through which the Kishon passes out of Esdraelon into the plain of Acre, and this was

The rout. their only practicable line of retreat. The victorious enemy was behind them, on their left were the hills of Samaria, in the hand of their enemies ; on their right was the swollen river and the marshes of Thora; they had no alternative but to make for the narrow pass which led to Harosheth. The space, however, becomes more and more narrow, until within the *pass* it is only a few rods wide. There, horses, chariots, and men become mixed in horrible confusion, jostling and treading down one another ; and the river, here swifter and deeper than above, runs zigzag from side to side of the vale, until, just before it reaches the castle of Harosheth, it dashes sheer up against the perpendicular base of Carmel. There is no longer any possibility of avoiding it. Rank upon rank of the flying host plunge madly in, those behind crushing those before deeper and deeper in the tenacious mud. They stick fast, are overwhelmed, are swept away by thousands. Such are the conditions of this battle and battle-field that we can follow it out to the dire catastrophe. We

Harosheth. only need to know where Harosheth is, and that is now easily found and identified. The narrative of the battle leads us to seek it somewhere down the Kishon, for only in that direction would they fly from an attack coming from the north-east. Again, it cannot be very far from the camp, for the Hebrews pursued them to it. They had before the battle marched some ten or twelve miles, and we cannot suppose that they could pursue an enemy more than eight or ten miles further. Now, exactly in the line of their necessary retreat, and about eight miles from Megiddo, at the entrance of the pass

---

[1] Judges iv. 14,

to Esdraelon from the plain of Acre, is an enormous double mound, called
Harothîeh, which is the Arabic form of the Hebrew Harosheth, the signification of the word being the same in both languages. This *tell* is situated just
below the point where the Kishon in one of its turns beats against the rocky
base of Carmel, leaving no room even for a foot-path. A castle there effectually
commands the pass up the vale of the Kishon into Esdraelon, and such a
castle there was on this immense double tell of Harothîeh. It is still covered
with the remains of old walls and buildings. The village of the same name is
now on the other side of the river, a short distance higher up, and, of course,
nearer the battle-field. I have not the slightest doubt of this identification.
It was probably called Harosheth of the *Gentiles*, or *nations*, because it
belonged to those Gentiles of Acre and the neighbouring plains which we
know, from Judges i. 31, the Hebrews could not subdue; and, by the way, I
believe that Sisera pitched between Taanach and Megiddo, because, as is
stated in the passage from Judges, those towns were still in the hands of the
Canaanites.

It may be objected that our supposition makes the authority of Jabin ex- Kingdom
tend very far. It does; but, instead of weakening, this fact is rather confirm- of Jabin.
atory. Hazor, situated in the centre of the mountains of the present Belad
Beshara, we are distinctly informed by Joshua, was "the *head of all those
nations*" who assembled at the waters of Merom. Among them were the kings
of Dor, of Taanach, and Megiddo, and very likely of Acre itself. As Hazor
was rebuilt, and another king Jabin of the same dynasty now reigned in it,
the probabilities are great that he would still be the acknowledged "*head*" of all
these Canaanitish cities. Moreover, Jabin could only use his nine hundred
chariots of iron on the plains, such as those of Acre and Esdraelon, and no
better position for his horses and chariots could be found than just this site of
Harosheth, nor a more commanding position taken by his chief captain Sisera.

But if Harosheth is this Harothîeh, how comes it to pass that Jael, the
wife of Heber the Kenite, is found so near the battle-field that Sisera could
light down from his chariot and flee to her tent? We are told in this very
narrative that their home was near Kedesh, which is two days' travel to the
north-east of the battle-field.

Even this, when carefully examined, confirms our identification. It is men- Heber the
tioned in the 11th verse that "Heber the Kenite, which was of the children Kenite.
of Hobab, had severed himself from the Kenites, and pitched his tent unto
the plain of Zaanaim which is by Kedesh;" and I suppose the object of this
brief notice thus thrown into the narrative is, in reality, to account for the
appearance of Jael on this scene of action. The other Kenites were settled
in the hill country of Judah, not far from Hebron. If you ask, Why state How
that Heber had settled near Kedesh when you want to know how he came to Heber's
have his tent down at the bottom of Esdraelon? my answer is, that such was near the
the fact. Heber did settle there. And it is because he did, that there came battle-
to be "peace between Jabin and the Kenites," for Hazor was only a few miles field.

PART
II.

from Kedesh. An incident which happened to myself will explain why Heber was found at the bottom of this plain at the time of the battle. With a guide from Nazareth, I once crossed the lower part of Esdraelon in the winter. It was then full of Arab tents, and at first I felt a little nervous, but my guide assured me there was no danger, for he was well acquainted with these Arabs. Their home was in the mountains north of Nazareth, toward Safet, and they only came down here to pass the cold months of winter. This was the very thing that Heber did, and who knows but that these Arabs are lineal descendants of that heroic Jael? I peered curiously into the faces of the women, but they were all tawny brass or dirty bronze; and I could find none that looked at all heroic, though some of them seemed as if they could drive a nail into the temple of a sleeping enemy. To all this some one might object, that if Heber lived near Kedesh, why not descend to the Hûleh immediately below for the winter, rather than migrate to this distant place? For the simple reason, I answer, that this place was under the government of his ally Jabin, and the other was not. It is interesting to notice how all parts of this narrative, even to its remote and incidental implications, correspond and corroborate each other. In addition to the above, the habits of these tent-dwellers require that the battle should have occurred in the winter, or very early spring, for only then would Heber's tent be found here. Now this is nowhere stated in just so many words, but the song of victory says that "the clouds dropped down rain," and it only rains on Esdraelon in the winter. The same thing is necessarily implied by the fact that "the river of Kishon swept them away, that ancient river, the river Kishon;" and this it could not do except in winter.

Deed of
Jael.

What have you to say with regard to the deed of Jael, which is highly praised by Deborah? Dr. Kitto, after presenting the whole transaction and the supposed motives of the actor in the most unfavourable light, sums up the whole thus: "It was a most treacherous and cruel murder, wanting all those extenuations which were applicable to the assassination of King Eglon by Ehud." I feel unwilling to accept this explanation. It shocks my ideas altogether to suppose that an inspired prophetess should foretell the deed, and then celebrate it and its author in the highest strains of congratulation and eulogy, if it was a mere treacherous, cold-blooded murder.

Jael justified.

Certainly this is the very last conclusion we shall adopt. We need by no means take for granted that because the Kenites were not at war with the tyrannical Jabin, that therefore they were treated with justice by him. In the same neighbourhood at the present day, the tribes of settled Arabs (and the Kenites were of this class) are most cruelly oppressed by the sheikhs of the districts where they reside. They are at peace with them, however, through fear, and from inability to throw off the galling yoke, as Heber was with Jabin.

Relations
of Heber
and Jabin.

Now it is nearly certain that in those lawless times the defenceless Kenites would be oppressed by Jabin, and would sigh for and gladly embrace any opportunity to escape from this intolerable bondage. Their deliverer, therefore, would be esteemed a patriot and hero, not a murderer.

In the second place, if it must be supposed that Jabin was a kind friend CHAPTER
and just protector of the Kenites, it does not follow that *Jael* might not have XXIX.
had special reasons to fear and hate *Sisera*. He had the command of the
immediate neighbourhood where the Kenites were encamped, and, unless he
differed from modern commanders of Eastern tyrants, he would most certainly
abuse them, and allow them to be insulted without redress by his rude retainers. Jael might have thus been injured in the highest degree, if not by Sisera
himself, by some of his lewd captains. Or there may have been a recent
blood-feud between the tribe and this man or his family, which not only justified Jael, according to the law of retribution, but rendered it obligatory upon
her, and every one of the tribe, to take revenge upon their enemy.

In the third place, we are not to take for granted that certain fantastic
laws of the modern Bedawîn in regard to the asylum of the tent were in force
among these *settled* Kenites. These notions are carried to such an absurd
pitch in some tribes, that a man is obliged to protect the murderer of his
father if he succeeds in reaching the tent; but the *settled* Arabs know no such
laws, and I do not believe that the Kenites did.

Again, it may be assumed as nearly certain, that Jael would not have ventured upon this daring act unless she knew that her husband and her whole
tribe would not only justify, but rejoice in it as a righteous retribution upon
their oppressor, and as the means of escape from an intolerable bondage,
against which they were watching for an opportunity to revolt.

And yet once more. On the nearly incredible supposition that neither the
Kenites as a tribe, nor Jael as an individual, had any cause of complaint
against Sisera, we may fairly conclude that they were believers in Israel's God
and friends of *his* people. This their whole history confirms. They must
therefore have been deeply grieved at the cruel oppression which their
brethren in faith and worship suffered from Sisera. In their defenceless condition they had not dared to take sides openly against Jabin, but in heart
they were with the oppressed Israelites, and regarded it as a duty to help
them to the utmost of their power. The total overthrow of the Canaanites
offered the wished-for opportunity, and Jael boldly availed herself of it.

The reason why it is mentioned that the Kenites were neutral in this war Neutrality
was not to give the idea that they were under any obligation to take sides of the Kenites.
with Sisera or to protect him if defeated, nor even to account for the fact that
Sisera fled to Heber's tent. He *may*, and probably *had* little enough reason
to claim this protection. But it was necessary to make the statement about
the Kenites, as we have before said, in order to account for their being down
on Esdraelon at all when the army of Sisera was there. It deserves also to be
remembered that if the Kenites had attempted to shield and aid Sisera after
his defeat, they would have rendered themselves partisans in the war on the
losing side, and might have been treated as enemies by the now victorious
Israelites. On the whole, therefore, I conclude that if all the circumstances
and influences which impelled Jael to the daring act, and sustained her in it,

were known, we should find that she violated neither the customs of her people, nor the laws of war then in force, nor the abstract and greater laws of righteousness, by thus destroying the enemy of God's people and the oppressor of her own, who from necessity sought in her tent an asylum to which he had no right, and the granting of which might have involved her and her whole family in ruin.

Under these impressions, I can join with Deborah in celebrating the deed and the actor.

Song of
Deborah.

"Blessed above women shall Jael the wife of Heber the Kenite be, blessed shall she be above women in the tent. He asked water, and she gave him milk; she brought forth butter in a lordly dish. She put her hand to the nail, and her right hand to the workman's hammer; and with the hammer she smote Sisera, she smote off his head, when she had pierced and stricken through his temples. At her feet he bowed, he fell, he lay down: at her feet he bowed, he fell: where he bowed, there he fell down dead. The mother of Sisera looked out at a window, and cried through the lattice, Why is his chariot so long in coming? why tarry the wheels of his chariots? Her wise ladies answered her, yea, she returned answer to herself, Have they not sped? have they not divided the prey; to every man a damsel or two; to Sisera a prey of divers colours, of divers colours of needlework, a prey of divers colours of needlework on both sides, meet for the necks of them that take the spoil? So let *all thine enemies perish, O Lord; but let them that love him be as the sun when he goeth forth in his might.*"[1] There is nothing, ancient or modern, more beautiful, appropriate, or sublime, than this close of Deborah's triumphal ode. No gloss, paraphrase, or comment can add to its graces.

The nail.

There are a few allusions, however, in it which may be better understood by brief explanations. The "nail" which Jael used was a *tent-pin*, now, as then, called *wated;* and the "hammer" was the mallet with which it is driven into the ground. It is not necessary to suppose that either of them was of iron, as *nail* and *hammer* would imply. The *wated* was probably a sharp-pointed pin of hard wood, and the hammer was the ordinary mallet used by these tent-dwelling Arabs.

Allusion
to the
nail in
Isaiah.

There is a curious use of the word *nail* in Isaiah xxii. 23, 25, which must also refer to those wooden *wateds*, I suppose, for it is the same Hebrew word: "I will fasten him with a nail (yutad) in a sure place;" and again, in the 25th, this yutad, fastened in a sure place, shall be removed, and *cut down*, and fall. It is not every place that will hold the tent "nail" securely; it must be driven into suitable ground.

Doubtless a wooden pin or peg is here meant, not an iron nail. It is, however, not a tent-pin, but a peg driven into the *wall*, and used to hang clothes and household utensils upon. There is significance in the statement that it should be made fast in a *sure place*, because, in general, these pins are driven

---

[1] Judges v. 24–30.

into the wall through the plaster, and are everything but steady and secure. CHAPTER XXIX.
Not one in a score of them but what bend down, or get loose and fall out.
There is a reference to the same thing, and the same Hebrew word in Zech.
x. 4 : "Out of him came forth the corner, out of him the *nail—yutad*." And Zech. x. 4
this, by the way, gives an intelligible idea to this expression of Zechariah.
The tent-pin is absolutely essential to the stability and safety of the Arab's
habitation.

Again : it is absurd to suppose that Jael brought Sisera *butter* to drink. Butter or sour milk.
Neither the ancient nor the modern Orientals make *butter* at all, as we
understand the word, and what takes the place of it is never used as a bever-
age. Butter is the exponent of milk in the other member of the parallelism,
showing that sour milk, or *leben,* was meant ; and this, properly prepared,
makes a most cooling and refreshing drink.

Lastly : the entire soliloquy of Sisera's mother is worked out with admirable Mother of Sisera.
skill and truthfulness. When standing on the lofty tell of Harosheth, which
commands the view of the pass up the Kishon, and out into Esdraelon toward
Megiddo, I could fancy her ladyship sitting at a latticed window, and impatiently looking up the wady. She knew that a battle was to take place, was
certain of victory, and longed not so much to see her son as to grasp the spoils.
Knowing that those lewd warriors would chiefly value the fair damsels of the
Hebrews, she mentions them first, but does not appear to relish this sort of
" prey" for her house, and therefore does not give any to Sisera—most mothers
can understand and sympathize with her. But she feasted her imagination
with the goodly garment of divers colours which her son was to lay at her feet.
She looks at it again and again—turns it over first on this side, then on that,
to see and admire the " divers colours." This is eminently Oriental and
feminine ; and the childish repetition of " divers colours " is all the more
striking in an ode distinguished for rapid narrative, abrupt exclamation, and
the utmost conciseness of style and diction.

This Deborah was certainly a remarkable lady—prophetess, poet, judge, Deborah
and warrior. It is not a little singular that though her residence was near
Jerusalem, between Ramah and Bethel, yet we meet her far north, at Kedesh
in Naphtali, with Barak, who was of that city. We find her name also here,
at the foot of Tabor, perpetuated in this miserable village of Debûrieh.

As judge and inspired guide to Israel, she probably itinerated a good deal,
as did Samuel and other prophets ; and her patriotic zeal would lead her
wherever she could be of service to her oppressed people. I suppose she
dwelt in a tent, like her heroine Jael, under that palm-tree which bore her
name near Bethel, in Mount Ephraim. It was called *the palm-tree* of Deborah
(see the Hebrew).[1] It seems to me to be a fair inference from such expressions, that *trees* were as rare in Palestine, even at that early age, as they are
at the present day, or we should not so often read of *the* oak, *the* terebinth, *the*

---

[1] Judges iv. 5.

PART
II.

Remark-
able trees.

palm-tree, of this or that important place or event. If trees were abundant, such a designation would signify nothing, and would not have been employed.

And one other thought about these remarkable trees. This country abounds in them. We have sacred trees, and trees that are inhabited by *jin*, or evil spirits ; and we have single trees all over the land covered with bits of rags from the garments of passing villagers, hung up as acknowledgments or as deprecatory signals and charms ; and we find beautiful clumps of oak-trees sacred to a kind of beings called Jacob's daughters. These are doubtless relics of most ancient superstitions ; and in the fact that the old patriarchs and prophets lived, and prophesied, and were buried under such trees, we find, I imagine, the origin of this curious custom and belief.

Road to
Sulam.

But it is time to descend and pursue our ride to Sulam, whither our tents have preceded us. There is no path but the one we came up, for on the south and east the declivity is too precipitous for roads. I once attempted to find my way down toward Khan et Tejjar, but did not succeed, and was obliged to return to our present path. The road to the khan leads through this rough oak wood for more than an hour, when the forest and the limestone on which it grows terminate together. Below, and all east to the valley of the Jordan, the country is volcanic and destitute of trees. The wady in which the khans are situated is called Mîdy. It comes from the north-west, drains all that part of the forest, and passes down south-east to the Sherrar and the Jordan. There are two khans : one on a hill about one hundred feet square, and having octagonal towers on the corners. It served the double purpose of castle and caravanserai. The other is in the vale below, and was much larger. It had also a division through the centre, with vaults and magazines on either side of it, and the great advantage of a fountain of water within the walls. It was fitted up with rooms for the protection of merchandise and the accommodation of travellers. The place is now entirely deserted, nor is there an inhabited house in sight. Caravans do not spend the night there for fear of Arabs, who are always prowling about, watching for an opportunity to rob. I have never halted there for half an hour without having some of these rascals pass along and scrutinize my party closely, to see whether or not it would do to attack us.

Khan et
Tejjar.

Weekly
fair.

On Monday of each week a great fair is held at the khans, when, for a few hours, the scene is very lively and picturesque. These gatherings afford an excellent opportunity to observe Syrian manners, customs, and costumes, and to become acquainted with the character and quality of Syrian productions. Thousands of people assemble from all parts of the country, either to sell, trade, or purchase. Cotton is brought in bales from Nablûs ; barley, and wheat, and sesamum, and Indian corn from the Hûleh, the Hauran, and Esdraelon. From Gilead and Bashan, and the surrounding districts, come horses and donkeys, cattle and flocks, with cheese, *leben*, *semen*, honey, and similar articles. Then there are miscellaneous matters, such as chickens and eggs, figs, raisins, apples, melons, grapes, and all sorts of fruits and vegetables in their season. The pedlars open their packages of tempting fabrics ; the jeweller is there with

his trinkets ; the tailor with his ready-made garments ; the shoemaker with CHAPTER
his stock, from rough, hairy sandals to yellow and red morocco boots ; the   XXIX.
farrier is there with his tools, nails, and flat iron shoes, and drives a prosperous
business for a few hours ; and so does the saddler, with his coarse sacks and
gaily-trimmed cloths.   And thus it is with all the arts and occupations known
to this people.

The noise is incessant, and at a distance sounds like that " of many waters." The noise.
Every man is crying his wares at the top of his voice, chickens cackle and
squall, donkeys bray and fight, and the dogs bark.   Every living thing adds
somewhat to the many-toned and prodigious uproar.   It is now a miscellaneous
comedy in full operation, where every actor does his best, and is supremely
gratified with his own performance.

The people find many reasons for sustaining these antiquated and very Business
curious gatherings.   Every man, woman, and child has inherited a strong desire of the
for trading, and, of course, all classes meet at this grand *bourse* to talk over the fair.
state of the markets, from the price of a cucumber to that of cotton, or of a
five-thousand dollar horse from the Hauran.   Again, every Arab is a politician,
and groups gather around the outskirts of the crowd to discuss the doings of
the " allied powers," the last firman from the sultan, or the new tax demanded
by their own petty emeer.   Descending to more ordinary matters, these fairs
are great places for gossip and scandal.   Friends meet friends, and exchange
the news of weddings, births, and deaths, and all the multifarious incidents
and accidents between these grand extremes of human life.   In a word, these
fairs supply the places of many of the appliances of more civilized society.
They are the daily newspaper, for there is one for every day within a circuit
of forty miles.   They are the exchange, and the *forwarding office,* and the
political caucus, and the family gathering, and the grand festa and gala days;
and underlying the whole is the ever-present idea and aim of *making money.*

Thus it is at Khan et Tejjar (the Inn of the Merchants) on Monday morn- Descent to
ing, but long before sunset not a soul of this busy throng remains on the spot. the Jor-
All return home, or take refuge in some neighbouring village.   I attended dan.
once, and then took my way eastward to the valley of the Jordan, at Jisr el
Mujamia, in search of 'Akil 'Aga.   The country for the first three miles is a
rich volcanic plain.   The path then leads down to a brook, called Säära,
which descends from the north, past a village of the same name.   The water,
yellow-green and foul, flows.off in a deep gorge to the Sherrar.   Half an hour
further is M'ather, with hovels nearly concealed behind hills of manure.   The
only things at work about the village were the bees, of which there are more
hives than there are houses, and the air rings with the hum of these industrious purveyors of honey.   Two miles further east is Hadathy, large and
better built, with an enormous chasm, washed out of the surrounding bluffs by
fountains which run out from the crumbling banks.   This region was thickly
inhabited until quite recently ; and in little more than a mile from Hadathy
is 'Aolam, a large village in ruins.   It is probably the Ulama of the ancients.

PART
II.

It has excellent water, and very large fig-trees still flourishing, for it was sacked and destroyed by the Arabs only three years ago, as was also the next village, called Seerîn. Having thus ridden for three hours through this depopulated country, I *dived* suddenly into the valley of the Jordan, having the gorge of the Sherrar between me and Kaukab el Howa, the splendidly-situated castle of Belvoir. The descent to the Jisr was extremely steep, and greatly surprised me by its depth. It is difficult to remember, or practically realize, that the Jordan is there *eight hundred feet* lower than the ocean. Down,

The Ghor. down I walked, until, tired out, I resumed the saddle. The entire Ghor presented a most singular appearance. It is far from level,—tilted up, in fact, into fantastic hills and shelving bluffs by vast dikes of obtruding lava. Half way down I came upon ruins of a large place, called Yidma, evidently very ancient. The Ghor was alive with Arabs, dotted with tents, and clothed with flocks.

I pitched my tent at sunset near that of the aga, and tried in vain to sleep. An intensely hot sirocco had commenced to blow, and this made every man and beast in this large encampment almost as nervous and restless as myself. Early next morning, while sitting in my tent-door smoking an argely, I was startled to see a large panther (nimr) scouring the plain in full chase of a pack of dogs that had attacked him. Making a long circle, they swept around my tent, when the panther left the dogs, leaped over the corner of the tent, tossed my argely to the winds, and then bounded away after the dogs. In another minute he returned, sprang on the top of the tent, and laid himself down there. I was confounded, but sat still, and he soon jumped from the tent, and crouched down close to my feet ! He was out of breath, and panted fearfully. Though not at all pleased to have the fierce brute so near, I kept my eye steadily and sternly fixed on his. He remained quiet until his keeper

A panther. came from the aga's tent to recapture him. Then he growled fiercely, and was disposed to fight for his liberty ; nor was it until they brought some fresh meat that they were able to get hold of him. He was a tame one, so far as *nimrs* can be tamed, brought up by the aga to hunt gazelles. The aga told me that these *nimrs* require seven years to complete their growth, and a constant course of careful training all that time to make them good hunters. He is extremely cunning in his approaches towards his victim ; lies flat on his belly, and creeps almost insensibly toward the flock. His colour then is so like the surrounding grass and stubble that the aga said he could not keep track of him. He will thus manœuvre for hours, until finally within leaping distance, when he springs with one tremendous bound upon his terrified prey. If he misses it, he gives over for that time, nor will anything induce him to follow up the chase.

I was glad enough to get clear of my tiger, but, strange to say, I met him again under very different circumstances. Returning from Jaffa to Beirût some months after, when we came to Haifa, I saw a large cage coming in a boat toward the steamer, and there was my quondam acquaintance *en route* to Paris. The aga had sent him to the emperor through the French consul of Beirût. The poor fellow was miserably sea-sick, which made him perfectly furious. Leaping with all his might against the bars, he broke through, and seized a passenger who was standing near, and it was only by enveloping him in a heavy sail that he was subdued and forced back into his cage.

I think David must have been acquainted with the hunting habits of the panther. Speaking of the " wicked," he says, " He *croucheth* and *humbleth* himself that he may catch the poor."[1] It is true that the psalmist is speaking in this place of the lion, but the description applies so accurately to the wily manœuvres of this hunting *nimr*, that I imagine the royal poet must have also been acquainted with him and his ways.

This is certainly possible; and it is certain that, in his early pastoral life, David was familiar with the bear as well as the lion. Both these have dis- *The pan-* appeared from the hills where the son of Jesse tended his father's flocks, but *ther abun-* *dant in* these nimr still abound there. And now we have reached the foot of Tabor ; *Judea.* and this is Debûrieh, so called possibly from Deborah; but if so, this name has been *substituted* for some other one in the catalogue of places given to Zebulun by Joshua, for it is found in chapter xix. 12, though he wrote long *before* the time of the prophetess. These heavy stones may have belonged to the church said to have been erected here in the early ages of our era, or perhaps to some edifice still more ancient. The inhabitants have long borne a bad character, and my own reception among them has not inclined me to defend their reputation. The whole neighbourhood indeed is unsafe ; for the Arabs, from the Jordan and the lawless regions east of it, make frequent inroads up the plain, and plunder all whom they can conquer. We shall pass over to En-dor, and then around the eastern slope of " Little Hermon " to Sulam. This mount is now called Jebel ed Dûhy, and that small hamlet on the north-west corner of it is Nain, famous for the restoration of the widow's son to life. It was once a *Nain.* place of considerable extent, but is now little more than a cluster of ruins, among which dwell a few families of fanatical Moslems. It is in keeping with the one historic incident that renders it dear to the Christian, that its only antiquities are tombs. These are situated mainly on the east of the village, and it was in that direction, I presume, that the widow's son was being carried on that memorable occasion.[2] It took me just an hour to ride from the foot of Tabor to Nain, and the path lies near the water-shed between the Sherrar and the Kishon. The soil is deep and fertile, as it is along this road to 'Ain- *'Ain-dûr* dûr, as the home of Saul's far-famed witch is now called. *(En-dor)*

It is a most wretched-looking place, and yet the position, at the north-east corner of the mountain, facing Tabor, and overlooking the valley between them, is really beautiful. Jerome has said correctly that the distance from Tabor is four miles, for it has taken us an hour and ten minutes to ride it. There does not seem to be much to attract attention here, and, as it is growing late, I

---

[1] Ps. x. 10.   [2] Luke vii. 11–15.

PART
II.

think we had better move on, and find our tent before these straggling Bedawîn find us.

Caves of
En-dor.

It is only about an hour to Sulam, and there is just at present no particular danger of being robbed ; let us, therefore, before we leave this place of evil notoriety, look into some of its caves. You observe that the declivity of the mountain is everywhere perforated with them, and most of the habitations are merely walls built around the entrance to these caverns. Observe, too, that the cattle are stalled in them along with their owners; and so it was in the time of Saul. The " witch " doubtless occupied one of these caves, and in its dark recesses she secretly performed her " damnable sorceries." The whole place is in most striking accord with its ancient story ; and these old hags grinning at us from the yawning mouths of their blackened habitations, look more like witches than women. Hark, how they curse the *fathers* and *grandfathers* of us Christian dogs,—a kind of salutation you now never hear but from the very vilest people in the country. Whether witches or not, they are undoubtedly " possessed," and we may just as well pass on out of their sight.

Calves.

See, here are half a dozen little calves at the mouth of this cave, kept up from their mothers, who are at pasture under the care of the shepherd. I do not mean that there is anything unusual in this, but merely that just such a calf did the witch kill for Saul on that dismal night when he sought her dwelling.

She must have been extremely expeditious in her kitchen and cookery. A hungry man, as was Saul, would think it hard to wait for supper until a calf was slaughtered and cooked, and fresh bread baked, and all this after midnight.[1]

Rapid
cooking.

Such things are common even in our day. With the Bedawîn it is nearly universal to cook the meat immediately after it is butchered, and to bake fresh bread for every meal. Visit 'Akîl 'Aga, for example, whose tent is now in the valley below us, and you will experience the entire process. A sheep or calf will be brought and killed before you, thrust *instanter* into the great caldron which stands ready on the fire to receive it, and, ere you are aware, it will re-appear on the great copper-tray, with a bushel of *bûrgûl* (cracked wheat), or a *hill* of boiled rice and *leben*. In our native Cincinnati, a hog walks into a narrow passage on his own feet, and comes out at the other end bacon, ham, and half a dozen other commodities; at the aga's camp, it is a calf or sheep that walks past you into the caldron, and comes forth a smoking stew for dinner.

It seems that this killing, cooking, and eating in rapid succession is a very old custom. Abraham, and Manoah, and many others besides the witch of En-dor, were expert in getting up such *impromptu* feasts ; and our Saviour has given it a proverbial expression in the fatted calf of the " prodigal son."

Killing an
animal in
honour of
visitors.

Not only is this true, but among unsophisticated Arabs the killing of a sheep, calf, or kid, in honour of a visitor, is strictly required by their laws of

---

[1] 1 Sam. xxviii. 24.

hospitality, and the neglect of it keenly resented. They have a dozen caustic CHAPTER terms of contempt for the man who neglects to honour his guest with the usual XXX. *dŭbbthah* (sacrifice), as it is universally called—a name suggestive of the *ancient religious rites* of hospitality, and no less suggestive of the important fact that our own *dŭbbthah* is waiting for us. The very idea will quicken our pace over the shoulder of Mount Dûhy to our tent in Sulam.

CHAPTER XXX.

SULAM* TO JENIN.

March 31st.

THIS is the very luxury of travel : bright days and joyous,—air cool and fra- Luxury of grant,—hill side and vale robed in green and spangled with flowers,—bird, and travel. beast, and man himself gay and happy. Yes, give me the tent, the open country, and the clear blue sky, at least while spring lasts. And then these nights, so solemn, almost sad, and yet so very sweet—the bustling activities of the day laid aside, every harsh sound subdued, and the soul called home to rest or *reverize*. It is a sort of bliss merely to lie still and breathe. Thus, half waking and half asleep, hour after hour of last night stole away, while by-gone memories, historic associations, and recent experiences chased each other through all the labyrinths perplexed of fairy-land. Finally my dreamy Historic meditations arranged themselves into historic sequence, and the wonderful associa- deeds which immortalized this neighbourhood in olden times passed in review. tions.

First in order came those sad days when, " because of the Midianites, the The Mi- children of Israel made them the dens which are in the mountains, and caves, dianites. and strongholds. And when Israel had sown, the Midianites came up, and the Amalekites, and the children of the east, with their cattle and their tents, and they came as grasshoppers for multitude. Both they and their camels were without number, and they entered the land to destroy it." [1] In precisely the same manner do the Bedawîn Arabs, these modern Midianites, come up this Wady of Jezreel and Wady Sherrar, " after the people have sown," and

---

* [Sulam is the modern name of Shunem, memorable in Old Testament history as the place near which Gideon defeated the Midianites; also the place where the Philistines encamped before the battle of Gilboa; and the residence of the Shunammite woman, whose son Elisha restored to life. To these historical events allusion is made in this chapter. Jenîn represents the En-gannim of the Bible.—ED.]

[1] Judges vi. 2, 3, 5.

PART
II.

destroy the increase of the earth ; and not only destroy the increase of the field, but commit wholesale murder, as those did upon the brethren of Gideon at Tabor. In fact, the sacred historian expressly says that these Midianites were *Ishmaelites*, and we have under our very eyes the descendants of this ancient people committing similar depredations in the very same spot. Both these valleys are now swarming with these " children of the east," come over Jordan to consume the land.

Gideon.

But have you any Gideon to work out deliverance for this oppressed and impoverished country ?

Ophrah.

Alas ! no ; and I fear generations will pass away before any adequate liberator can arise ; and, by the way, this history of Gideon is very remarkable, and we are in the midst of scenes immortalized by his glorious achievements. Ophrah, the city of his inheritance, was on the general range of mountains south of Zer'in, and when he comes into notice the invaders lay along in this valley of Jezreel as *locusts* for multitude. It was harvest, and consequently a little later in the season than this. Gideon, instead of carrying his grain to the ordinary threshing-floor, took it into the midst of his vineyard, to hide both it and himself from the Ishmaelites. These summer threshing-floors are in the open country, and on an elevated position, to catch the wind when winnowing the grain, and of course they would be altogether unsafe at such a time, while the vineyards are hid away in the wadies and out on the wooded hills, and thus adapted for concealment. Indeed, I myself have seen grain thus concealed in this same country, during the lawless days of civil war. There, by the wine-press, the angel of the Lord appeared, and said to him, " The Lord is with thee, thou mighty man of valour."[1] After confirming his faith by wonderful miracles, he commissions him to destroy the enemies of Israel. The Lord looked upon him and said, " Go in this thy might ; have not I sent thee ?"

Thresh-
ing-floors
and vine-
yards.

This whole narrative reads most life-like and stirring here among the scenes described. The angel, who was no other than Immanuel—the Word in flesh assumed for the occasion—came and *sat under an oak*, as you and I would do, in one of those mountain vineyards, for the *harvest* sun renders the shade necessary, and the *oak* is the tree you will find near the wine-press. I have seen many such. The sacred narrative reveals the sad religious apostasy of even Gideon's family. His father had a grove and an altar to Baal, the abomination of the Zidonians. This, Gideon is commanded to destroy ; and from that act he received the name of Jerubbaal, " the *tryer* of Baal," to trans-late according to Arabic; and having performed this daring deed, he blows the trumpet, and assembles about him, out of Manasseh, Asher, Zebulun, and Naphtali, thirty-two thousand men. We are in the centre of these tribes, and can see at a glance from whence he gathered his army. It is worthy of re-mark that the men of Issachar are not mentioned, and we can from this point readily imagine the reason. The people of Issachar lived here on this great

The apos-
tasy of his
family.

His army.

---

[1] Judges vi. 12.

plain, and were, of course, altogether surrounded by and at the mercy of the Midianites, as these villages of Sulam, Shŭtta, Zer'in, etc., now are in the power of these Bedawîn. They therefore *could not* join the army of Gideon. Of those assembled, twenty-two thousand were afraid, and returned home at the first offer. Ten thousand more were dismissed by divine command at the " water," where " the three hundred" drank " by putting their hand to their mouth,"—a thing I have often seen done, and not always **by** heroes either. These three hundred alone were retained, and that very night this small band moved forward to the brow of that steep mountain which overhangs the vale and the fountain of Jezreel. Gideon, with Phurah his servant, let himself cautiously down from rock to rock until he stood among the tents of their enemies. There he overheard " a man tell his fellow" this strange story: " Behold, I dreamed a dream, and, lo ! a cake of barley bread tumbled into the host of Midian, and came unto a tent, and smote it that it fell, and overturned it that it lay along. And his fellow answered and said, This is nothing else save the sword of Gideon, the son of Joash, a man of Israel; for into his hand hath God delivered Midian, and all his host."[1] This dispelled every lingering doubt, and he returned to order the attack at once.

What possible analogy can there be between a sword and a cake of barley *The barley cake.* bread, that could have suggested this idea to the Midianite ?

Doubtless there was divine influence in the matter; but even this does not quite cover the whole case, I apprehend. Divine Wisdom ordinarily works with means adapted to produce the intended effect, and there is no conceivable reason why he should not suggest to this dreaming Midianite something calculated to bring Gideon into view; and so he doubtless did, and in a way best of all calculated to bring about the desired result. As to the line of connec- *Barley bread.* tion in the mind of the " interpreter," we may remember that *barley* bread is only eaten by the *poor* and the *unfortunate*. Nothing is more common than for these people, at this day, to complain that their oppressors have left them nothing but *barley bread* to eat. I remember that this was the identical lamentation of a wealthy farmer who rode with me last summer from Zer'in to Jenîn. This cake of barley bread was therefore naturally supposed to belong **to the** oppressed Israelites; it came down from the mountain where Gideon **was** known to be; it overthrew the tent so that it lay along, foreshadowing destruction from some quarter or other. It was a contemptible antagonist, and yet scarcely more so than Gideon in the eyes of the proud Midianites. That the interpreter should hit upon the explanation given is not, therefore, very wonderful; and if the Midianites were accustomed, in their extemporaneous songs, to call Gideon and his band " *eaters of barley bread*," as their successors, these haughty Bedawîn, often do to ridicule their enemies, the application would be all the more natural. At any rate, the interpreter read the riddle right, and reached the true intent of the prodigy.

---

[1] Judges vii. 13, 14.

PART
II.

The stra-
tagem.

Position.

What a strange stratagem was that of Gideon!

And yet it was well adapted to produce the effect intended; nor was the action, in the manner of it, at all remarkable. I have often seen the small oil lamp of the natives carried in a "pitcher" or earthen vessel at night. Armed with this curious weapon, the three companies took up their stations round the slumbering host. They would, no doubt, leave the road toward the Jordan open, for the enemy to take in his flight, and so one band of *lamp-bearers* must have planted themselves along the base of the hill there below Zer'in; another, between that and this Sulam, along the west side of the host; and the *third* band would stand along the brow of this hill, extending down eastward toward Shŭtta. The Midianites, we know, lay in the valley between this and Jezreel. Thus arranged around the slumbering host, at a given signal the *three hundred* pitchers are broken, *three hundred* trumpets bray harsh alarms on every side, and *three hundred lights,* as of so many different bands of assailants, flash upon their blinded eyes. It is not wonderful, therefore, that the Midianites rush in wild dismay and dire confusion one upon another. In the darkness they cannot distinguish friend from foe, and thus every man's sword was against his fellow. The very vastness of the army would render the rout more ruinous; and in that horrible slaughter "there fell an hundred and twenty thousand men that drew sword." [1]

How was it possible for the men of Manasseh, Asher, and Naphtali to hear the news and join in the pursuit of the Midianites in so short a time, and amid the urgencies of such a day?

The pur-
suit.

This is not difficult to explain. We are here on the very battle-ground, for the host lay in this valley, and, fleeing, they passed this Shŭtta to the east of us. Look around, and you find that we are in the centre of these tribes. The cities given to Manasseh, on the west of Jordan, were along the southern margin of Esdraelon and on the hills above. Asher came up to Carmel, at the bottom of this plain, and a swift runner could reach them in an hour. A portion of Naphtali occupied the western shore of the Lake of Tiberias, and could be reached in the same way, and in about the same time. It was possible, therefore, for them to receive the summons and respond to it. Of course, only those who lived adjacent to the scene of action are intended. The attack of Gideon was at night, and, in all probability, just before day. Gideon could not have made his visit, returned, and made all the necessary arrangements before the night was far spent; and, moreover, it is the invariable custom of these *modern* Midianites to select that hour for their assaults. It is proverbially the darkest, and both men and animals are then buried in deepest sleep. The very watch-dogs become drowsy. Besides, if successful, they want the opening light of day to complete the victory, and secure the plunder; and, if defeated, they need the light to gather up their scattered troops, and make good their retreat. Gideon, therefore, had the entire day, and that

[1] Judges viii. 10.

in harvest time, to collect the surrounding tribes, and pursue the flying chapter xxx. foes.

Is it still the custom for *men* among these Bedawîn "Ishmaelites" to wear Earrings. gold earrings ?

I have often seen them, and among certain of the tribes it is quite the fashion; but these golden earrings belonged, in part, no doubt, to the women. Bedawîn women not only have them in their ears, but also large rings are suspended from the nose. These are the *face* jewels, I suppose, which are mentioned very early in Biblical history.

But you interrupt the order of my midnight memories. "A change came over the spirit of my dream." I was back at En-dor, and the witch stood The scene at En-dor. within a dismal cavern, working out her wicked sorceries. Samuel arose " out of the earth, an old man covered with a mantle;" and God-forsaken Saul fell prostrate before the awful apparition.[1] I heard his voice sepulchral pronounce the dreadful decree, " To-morrow shalt thou and thy sons be with me; and the Lord also shall deliver the host of Israel into the hand of the Philistines." Poor Saul! doomed to death, and returning in despair to fight and fall with his sons and all Israel before the sword of Philistia! It was a fearful ride that dark night, for the Philistines were encamped in this very village of Shunem, directly between Gilboa and En-dor.[2] He probably kept to the east of Jezreel, crossed the valley below 'Ain Jalûd, and thence over the shoulder of this Jebel ed Dûhy to En-dor; but it must have been perilous in the extreme, and nothing could have induced Saul to venture thither but the agony of despair.

This Sulam affords an admirable camp-ground for a large army, Jebel ed Position of the armies. Dûhy rising abruptly behind, and the top of it commanding a perfect view of the great plain in every direction, so that there could be no surprise, nor could their march be impeded, or their retreat cut off. The fountain, it is true, is not very copious, but there are others toward Fûleh, and in the valley below. On the morning of that disastrous day, the lords of the Philistines passed on by hundreds and by thousands out of this valley of Jezreel, ascended by the city, and joined battle with Israel upon those rough mountains east of it. Israel was beaten and fled, closely pursued by their victorious enemies, and The defeat. Saul and his three sons were slain. "Tell it not in Gath, publish it not in the streets of Askelon. The beauty of Israel is slain upon thy high places : how are the mighty fallen ! Ye mountains of Gilboa, let there be no dew, neither let there be rain upon you, nor fields of offerings : for there the shields of the mighty were vilely cast away." We have the whole theatre of this bloody battle before us, memorable not only in itself and in its results, but as the occasion of that most touching lamentation of David over Saul and Jonathan.[3] The victorious Philistines descended to Beth-shan, and there fastened the body of Saul to the wall of the city. Sad, sad day to Israel, Song of the bow. and doubly sad to David. "O Jonathan! slain in thy high places. I am

---

1 1 Sam. xxviii. 13, 14.   2 1 Sam. xxviii. 4.   3 2 Sam. i. 17–27.

PART II.

distressed for thee, my brother Jonathan : very pleasant hast thou been unto me. Thy love to me was wonderful, passing the love of women. How are the mighty fallen, and the weapons of war perished !"

When I was young, it was the fashion to speak of Gilboa as still suffering the curse of David, and to this day I think of it as a withered wilderness, without dew, or rain, or any green thing to relieve its stern desolation. Of course, there is no foundation for such an idea?

The imprecation.

Certainly not. In my own personal experience I have had abundant evidence that both dew and rain descend there as copiously as elsewhere. David's poetic imprecation had no more influence upon the mountain, or on the clouds, than had Job's malediction upon the day of his birth; nor was either expected to produce any such malign effects. Similar expressions of profound sorrow or of deep displeasure are common in the East, and are found elsewhere in the Bible. Jeremiah says, " Cursed be the day when I was born; let not the day wherein my mother bare me be blessed,"[1] etc. The *thought* is natural, and who is there that hath not indulged it? The *child* vents its displeasure upon its rattle; the *boy* strikes the stone against which he stumbles ; the man curses adverse winds, and every senseless thing which annoys him, resists his will, or thwarts his plans.

Prophetic denunciations.

In regard to these imprecations, and others in the Bible like them, we should remember that they were never intended to act upon the physical and senseless elements of nature; and the same remark applies with equal truth to many of the " burdens " of prophecy. Though announced in figurative terms, which are drawn from natural objects, yet every child knows, or ought to know, that such things are not accountable agents. Even the denunciations against cities, such as Tyre, Damascus, Gaza, Askelon, Petra, Babylon, Jerusalem, and many others, must, in general, be restricted to the *inhabitants*, and not to their habitations. God has no controversy with earth, and rocks, and ruins; nor do I believe that this *land* of Palestine now lies under any physical curse, which renders it unfruitful or unhealthy. The rains, early, middle, and latter, are sufficiently abundant, and the dews as copious as ever ; the fields, also, yield as generous harvests to the careful cultivator as they ever did, or as do any others in the world.

This is perhaps true, and yet I have a " feeling " that it is not the *whole* truth.

The curse of the land.

We have not said that it was. It is not the sum-total of our own ideas on this subject, and at some other locality we may enlarge upon the matter. Such a place as the vale of Siddim, I suppose, was really burned and blasted by the direct agency of God ; and some other spots, once fertile, may now exhibit tokens of the displeasure of the Almighty " for the wickedness of the inhabitants thereof," and as a warning to the world. And there is a sense in which the whole earth has been smitten with a curse, and, in consequence, produces

---

[1] Jer. xx. 14.

thorns and thistles instead of wholesome fruits. But the desolation and barrenness of this glorious plain, for example, is in no sense the effect of any physical change in the soil or climate, but is owing entirely to the people who dwell here, and to the Bedawîn who destroy it; and the same is true of Gilboa.

This valley of Jezreel seems to expand, and to spread out an immense distance toward the south-east. To which of the tribes did it belong?

Esdraelon and its surrounding hills and vales constituted the portion of Issachar; and yet we learn from the 17th chapter of Joshua that many important cities in and about it were given to Manasseh. En-dor, and Beth-shan, and Taanach, and Megiddo, and this valley of Jezreel itself, belonged to that tribe; or, rather, were *assigned to* them, for they do not appear to have got possession of these cities. These "children of Joseph" complained that "all the Canaanites who dwell in the land of the valley have chariots of iron, both they of Beth-shean and her towns, and they who are of the valley of Jezreel;" and therefore they could not drive them out.[1] This is the earliest mention of Jezreel; and it is interesting to find that this famous valley still retains its original characteristics. Chariots of iron have indeed disappeared, but the inhabitants are eminently intractable and rebellious; and one can readily believe that when the "jumping chariot" raged through the vale of Jezreel, and down the Ghor of Beisan, the children of Joseph found it impossible to expel the inhabitants.

In my walk this morning I noticed an immense tell far down toward the Jordan: has it a name?

It is called Hŭsn, and is the centre of those ruins that mark the site of Beth-shan—the Scythopolis of the Greeks—the Beisan of the Arabs.

Indeed! it seems much nearer than that city should be, according to my geography; and it must be uncommonly high, and of gigantic proportions every way.

Though it is full three hours distant, and that much out of our line, still, if it were safe, we would spend the night there instead of Jenin, for it is well worth the ride and the time. But the ghor is said to be swarming with wild Bedawîn from beyond Jordan, and therefore we must abandon the idea of going into it.

Since our friends the Arabs will not allow us that pleasure, the next best thing is for you to describe it.

I once came to Beisan direct from Tiberias in a little more than six hours. The Itinerary, in brief, runs thus: Half an hour to the Baths; one and a half to Kerak, at the outgoing of the Jordan; two hours to El Mansûrah; two and a half to the entrance of the Jermuk into the Jordan; three hours to Jisr el Mujameah; and half an hour more to the camp of 'Akil 'Agâ, near the western hills, on the bank of the Sherrar, and just below Koukab el Howa.

---

[1] Joshua xvii. 16.

At four hours and forty minutes, passed a ruin with a few short columns, called Nusleh, near a large encampment of the Arabs of Rŭbâh.　At five

BEISAN.

hours is the great Wady Osheh (or Ushey), with a large tell of the same name; and in ten minutes further Wady Mukhŭrkŭsh crosses the plain on its way to the Jordan.　The ruined town, called es Soudah, half an hour south of this, has many columns and sarcophagi; and from that onward the remains of the great Beth-shan begin to appear, and constantly multiply for nearly an hour before you reach the castle.　We rode rapidly, and the distance from Tiberias cannot be far from twenty-four miles.　I have already led you over the route from Jisr el Mujameah to Tiberias, and need not repeat.　From the bridge, on this occasion, we ascended the western side of the ghor to 'Akil's tent under Koukabah, and then kept south along the base of the hills, with the plain of the Jordan on our left.　This plain constantly widened by the falling back of the hills, until at es Soudah the great valley of Jezreel, in which Beisan is situated, opens to the west its noble expanse.　From the city

Ghor
Beisan.

eastward it is called Ghor Beisan, and it spreads out to the south-east further than the eye can follow. For the last hour there is a steady ascent, and the aneriod indicates an elevation for the city above the Jordan of more than five hundred feet. Owing to this, the whole plain can be watered by the fountains that send their copious streams across the site of Beisan. In fact, few spots on earth, and none in this country, possess greater agricultural and manufacturing advantages than this ghor, and yet it is utterly desolate.

But to our description. Beisan is naturally one of the strongest places even in this country of strongholds. About half a mile south of the tell you saw is a square tower, constructed in part of large *bevelled* blocks of white limestone. Around this are grouped some forty or fifty wretched hovels of trap rock, loosely built, and ready to tumble down upon their inhabitants. These are as sinister a looking gang as can be found, and are, in fact, as great robbers as the Bedawîn themselves. The ancient city consisted of several distinct quarters, or wards, separated by deep ravines, with noisy cascades leaping over ledges of black basalt. I have seen no city except Damascus so abundantly supplied with water. Most of the streams take their rise in large marshes to the south-west of the city, and so high above it as to send their brooks over every part of the area; and it is evident, from the tufaceous deposits in all directions, that the inhabitants made good use of their privileges in this respect.

Streams.

The largest *wards* of the city appear to have been around the present castle, and on the west of Tell Hŭsn; but there are extensive ruins both to the east and north of it. The great Wady el Jalûd passes down on the north side of the tell, and Wady el L'ab on the south, meeting below, and thus almost surrounding it. The position of the tell is therefore very strong, and it rises about two hundred feet high, with the sides nearly perpendicular. A strong wall was carried round the summit, and the gateway was high up the steep declivity at the north-west angle. In the huge buttresses of this gateway are built fragments of columns, and handsome Corinthian capitals. It was on the wall of this tell, I suppose, that the bodies of Saul and his sons were fastened by the Philistines after the battle on Gilboa; and this supposition enables us to understand how the men of Jabesh-gilead could execute their daring exploit of carrying them away. Jabesh-gilead was on the mountain east of the Jordan, in full view of Beth-shan, and these brave men could creep up to the tell, along Wady Jalûd, without being seen, while the deafening roar of the brook would render it impossible for them to be heard. I have often been delighted with this achievement. The people of Jabesh had not a good character among their brethren. None of them came up to the great war against Benjamin[1] in the matter of the Levite and his concubine, and for this neglect they were condemned to utter destruction. In the days of Saul, however, it had again become a considerable city, and had acquired a fair

Exploit of the men of Jabesh.

[1] Judges xxi. 8–12.

PART
II.

reputation.[1] All Israel hastened, with almost incredible despatch, to rescue it from the cruel doom of Nahash the Ammonite. It was, no doubt, in gratitude for this deliverance, effected wholly through the energy of Saul, that the men of Jabesh hazarded their lives in order to secure his headless body from insult. History should always rejoice to record noble deeds, and most of all those instances of public gratitude which now and then throw a gleam of sunlight over its gloomy chronicles of selfishness and sin.

Remains
of Beth-
shan.

There is not much more to be said about Beisan. A bridge of extraordinary height spans the Jalûd east of Tell Hŭsn. It appears to have led from the south to the north quarter of the city. The *theatre* is in the wady south-west of the tell. It is built entirely of basalt, and much of it is thrown down. The chord of the circle is one hundred and ninety-three feet; and though the seats are nearly gone, the vomitories, with dens for wild beasts on either side, are almost perfect. Some of them are now used for stables. Beisan was a city of temples. They are now entirely destroyed, and most of the materials have long since been carried away for other buildings. Their number, however, can be ascertained, and their localities traced out, from partial foundations and prostrate columns. Some of these columns were four feet in diameter, mostly of white limestone from the neighbouring mountain, or of basalt from the place itself, and only a few are foreign granite. I do not think that the city could have been all embraced within one general wall, for it would have required one at least five miles long. It is more probable that the various wards, separated by deep ravines, had each its independent fortifications.

Important
site.

Whenever a good government shall restore order and security to this region, Beisan will rapidly rise to an important city. Its water privileges and other advantages will not only make it a delightful residence, but render it a great manufacturing centre. All kinds of machinery might be driven with the least possible expense by its abounding brooks; and then this lovely valley of Jezreel above it, irrigated by the Jalûd, and the Ghor Beisan below, watered in every part by many fertilizing streams, are capable of sustaining a little nation in and of themselves. Besides, Beisan is the natural highway from Bashan and the east to the sea-board at Haifa and Acre, and also to southern Palestine and Egypt. The ghor once teemed with inhabitants, as is evident from ruined sites, and from tells too old for ruins, which are scattered over the plain. I took down their names as now known to the Arabs, but none of them

Salim and
Ænon.
Succoth.
Tûbûkat
Fahel, or
Pella.

have any historic significance. Of Salim and Ænon, which must have been in the ghor at no great distance, I could hear nothing. Succoth is well known under the name of Sakût. Tûbûkat Fahel is in full view over the Jordan, and is, doubtless, the Pella of history. My guide assured me that *Felah* was the true name; and this is their way of pronouncing Pella, for, having no *p* in their language, they sometimes use *b*, and at others *f*, instead of it. Wady

Yabis, at the head of which was Jabesh-gilead, is a little to the south of
Tûbûkat Fahel.

Beth-shan has figured largely in the history of this country from a very early
age. It was given to Manasseh, but, like many other grants, seems never to
have been in their possession. At what time it took the name of Scythopolis,
and on what account, is uncertain. Some suppose it was so called from a
colony of Scythians who got possession of it. This is more probable than that
its name was derived from Succoth, a mere village many miles to the south-east
of it. Be this as it may, it is thus called in the apocryphal books of the Old
Testament, in Josephus, who often mentions it, and by nearly all profane
authors. It early became a Christian city, with a bishop of its own, and was
the ecclesiastical metropolis of the Third Palestine. *Beisan* is, of course,
merely the Arabic form of the original name, Beth-shan, given to it by these
barbarians, whose mission is destruction; and under their sway it soon fell into
decay and obscurity, and thus it must remain until they are driven over the
Jordan into their native desert.

But it is time for us to prosecute our journey. How sad to know that even
this pretty home of the Shunammite, with its orchards and gardens, will soon
be deserted and destroyed, unless these destructive Bedawîn be driven back by
the government! See! what a large encampment stretches down toward
Zer'in, and their black tabernacles dot the plain in all directions as far as the
eye can reach.

We are now on ground poetically, or rather prophetically illustrious. In
this immediate neighbourhood, the Tishbite, and his scarcely less wonderful
disciple Elisha, performed their amazing miracles. Here, in this very village,
dwelt that good Shunammite, who built "a little chamber" (an ullîyeh, upper
room) on the wall for the "holy man of God;" and put there a table, and a bed,
and a stool, and a candlestick.[1] In some parts of these fields which slope down
southward into Jezreel, her only son, given in reward for her hospitality to
Elisha, received a stroke of the sun while looking at the reapers; and I know
by experience that this valley glows like a furnace in harvest-time. The poor
lad cried out to his father, "My head! my head!"[2] and, being carried home,
he sat on his mother's knee till noon, and then died. Elisha was on Carmel
—probably near the altar of Elijah—at El Makhrakah, ten or twelve miles off.
The mother saddled an ass, and said to her servant, "Drive and go forward;
slack not thy riding for me, except I bid thee;" and away she flew past Fuliyeh,
and westward down the plain to the foot of Carmel. The man of God sees her
coming in such haste, fears some calamity, and sends Gehazi to meet her with
these three inquiries, "Is it well with thee? is it well with thy husband? is
it well with the lad?[3] She answered, "It is well;" but, at the same time,
she rushes up the "hill," and seizes the prophet by his feet. This scene is
natural, and very graphic. If you ask after a person whom you know to be

---

[1] 2 Kings iv. 8–10.   [2] 2 Kings iv. 19.   [3] 2 Kings iv. 26.

PART
II.

sick, the reply at first will invariably be, " *Well*, thank God," even when the very next sentence is to inform you that he is dying. Then the falling down, clasping the feet, etc., are actions witnessed every day. I have had this done to me often before I could prevent it. So, also, the officious zeal of the wicked Gehazi, who would thrust the broken-hearted mother away, probably thinking her touch pollution, agrees perfectly with what we know of the man, and of the customs of the East ; and so, likewise, are the injunctions to Gehazi : *Gird up thy loins* that you may run ; if *thou meet* any *man, salute him not ;* and if any salute thee, answer him not—this is no time for idle compliments. The mother followed with the man of God in company ; and when he had brought back her son to life, she *fell at his feet, bowed herself* to the *ground*, took up her son, and went out. Nothing can excel the touching simplicity of this narrative.

Loss of land.

How came it to pass that the good Shunammite lost her land by merely going to reside during the famine in the country of the Philistines, as we read in 2 Kings viii. 3 ?

It is still common for even petty sheikhs to confiscate the property of any person who is exiled for a time, or who moves away temporarily from his district. Especially is this true of widows and orphans, and the Shunammite was now a widow. And small is the chance to such of having their property restored, unless they can secure the mediation of some one more influential than themselves. The conversation between the king and Gehazi about his master is also in perfect keeping with the habits of eastern princes ; and the appearance of the widow and her son so opportunely would have precisely the same effect now that it had then. Not only the *land* but all the *fruits of it* would be restored. There is an air of genuine verisimilitude in such simple narratives which it is quite impossible for persons not intimately familiar with Oriental manners to appreciate, but which stamps the incidents with undoubted certainty. The thing happened just as recorded. It is too natural to be an invention or fabrication.

Elisha.

Elisha seems to have had no settled place of abode. We read of him in Carmel, in Shunem, in Jezreel, in Gilgal, on the banks of the Jordan, in Dothan, in Samaria, and even in Damascus.

Among his many miracles, I have long wanted to inquire what sort of wild gourd it was that poisoned the "pottage." [1] Is there anything satisfactory known about it ?

The poisonous gourd.

Not much more than the prophet's son that gathered them knew. The Septuagint does not *translate*, but gives the Hebrew word, showing that those learned men did not know *what* it was ; and if they could not determine the question, it is not likely that we can at this day. My Latin Bible calls it wild colocynth. I am not aware that there is any *tame* colocynth. The English renders it by the vague word *gourd*. I cannot believe it was colocynth, be-

---

[1] 2 Kings iv. 38–41.

cause this is so well known, so bitter, and so poisonous, that the most igno- CHAPTER
rant peasants never dream of eating it. Various other herbs have been XXX.

COLOCYNTH.

selected by "critics," as the *Cucumus prophetarum*, a small prickly gourd,
very rarely met with. The Hebrew root seems to point to some herb that
bursts or splits open, and I have thought it might be the Elaterium, which is
found all over the country, looks like a young squash, and is extremely poisonous. When green, it might be mistaken for an edible "gourd" or cucumber;
but when ripe it cannot be "gathered" at all, for it bursts on the slightest
pressure, with great violence, scattering the seeds in all directions. But all these
are mere conjectures, and we had better turn our thoughts to these sorry representatives of Jezreel,* to which our climb up this steep and rocky hill has
brought us.

There is certainly nothing royal about it now except its position. That, Jezreel
however, is very fine. East of it rises the high mountain called Jebel Jalûd,
and also Jebel Nûris, from a village of that name. Below it the valley of
Jezreel sweeps round southward to the Jordan. On the north, Jebel ed Dûhy
(Little Hermon) swells up like another Tabor; and to the west and south is
the magnificent Esdraelon, surrounded by the mountains of Galilee, the "ex-

* [The modern name of Jezreel is Zer'in.—ED.]

cellency of Carmel," and the fat hills of Samaria. There is little to claim attention in the village itself. A few stones, built here and there in the rude huts, seem to claim the honours of antiquity ; and these large sarcophagi are certainly relics of old Jezreel. The city could never have been large or splendid. The greater part was probably mere mud hovels; and yet there must have been some well-built palaces, when Ahab resided here with his bold but wicked queen. This apology for a castle may now stand upon the spot of that

Jehu. watch-tower from which the rebel Jehu was first seen driving furiously up the valley of Jezreel.[1] The south part of the plain at Beisan is marshy, and further this way the great fountain of Jalûd, with its spongy banks, renders the same side impassable. This fountain flows out from the base of the mountain below Nûris, and is immediately collected into a large pool by a dam of very ancient work, and from it the water is carried to a succession of mills stretching down the plain to the east. To avoid these mill-ponds, the road must have then passed along the valley, as it now does, not far from Kûmia. Jehu and his party could therefore be seen for at least six miles, and there was time enough to despatch messenger after messenger to meet him. He, of course, came past Beisan, because Jabesh-gilead was east of it, on the other side of Jordan, and he was commander of the garrison there when proclaimed king by his fellow-officers. Immediately he sets out in hot haste to slay Joram, and seize the government. The whole history of this revolution shows Jehu to have been a man of vehement energy and desperate daring. When he met his victim, he " drew a bow with his *full strength*, and smote Jehoram between his arms, and the arrow went out at his heart."[2] Nor did he hesitate a moment to kill Ahaziah king of Judah also. Then, entering the city, he ordered the

Jezebel. eunuchs to tumble the infamous Jezebel out of the window of her palace. " So they threw her down : and her blood was sprinkled on the wall, and *on the horses ;* and *he trode her under foot*."[3]

After this terrible day's work Jehu went in to eat and drink ; and, remembering Jezebel, he said, " Go, see now this cursed woman, and bury her, for she is a king's daughter."[4] "But they found no more of her than the skull, and the feet, and the palms of the hands." The word of the Lord by his servant Elijah was fulfilled, " In the portion of Jezreel shall dogs eat the flesh of Jezebel."[5]

The field of Naboth.   The field of Naboth which Ahab coveted was doubtless near the great fountain of Jalûd, at the bottom of the valley east of the city. Water was necessary for a garden of *herbs*, and there is no other perennial fountain in this neighbourhood. Joram, Ahab's son, went out against Jehu, who was coming up the valley of Jezreel, and they must have met somewhere near the fountain ; and Jehu, having killed Joram, ordered his body to be cast into the portion of the field of Naboth the Jezreelite ; "For," said he, "the Lord laid this burden

---

[1] 2 Kings ix. 17.   [2] 2 Kings ix. 24.   [3] 2 Kings ix. 33.
[4] 2 Kings ix. 34.   [5] 2 Kings ix. 35, 36.

upon him, Surely I have seen yesterday the blood of Naboth, and the blood of CHAPTER
his sons, saith the Lord." [1]   XXX.

The entire narrative in 2 Kings ix. is full of most emphatic lessons of instruction and warning to tyrants. The blood of Naboth was trebly avenged; first upon Ahab himself, then upon his son Joram, and finally on the wicked Jezebel, who had instigated the murder.

It must have been a strange state of things, when dogs were so abundant Dogs. and unscrupulous as to devour a human carcass in the streets of this city during the short time that elapsed before search was made for Jezebel's body; but the canine race always bear some resemblance in disposition to the character of the times and of their keepers. We may readily believe, therefore, that those under the palace of Jezebel were sufficiently savage. They may have been *taught to devour* the wretched victims of her cruelty; in which case the retribution would be remarkably appropriate and striking. What is meant by " making her eyes with paint," as the Hebrew has it?

Simply that which has been and is still the favourite mode of beautify- Painted ing the face among the ladies of this country. They eyes. " paint" or blacken the eyelids and brows with *kŏhl*, and prolong the application in a decreasing pencil, so as to lengthen and reduce the eye in appearance to what is called *almond shape.* The practice is extremely ancient,

PAINTED EYE.

for such painted eyes are found in the oldest Egyptian tombs. It imparts a peculiar brilliancy to the eye, and a languishing, amorous cast to the whole countenance. Brides are thus painted, and many heighten the effect by application to the cheeks of coloured cosmetics. The powder from which *kŏhl* is made is collected from burning almond shells, or frankincense, and is intensely black. Antimony, and various ores of lead, are also employed. The powder is kept in phials or pots, which are often disposed in a handsomely-worked cover or case; and it is applied to the eye by a small probe of wood, ivory, or silver, which is called *meel*, while the whole apparatus is named *mŭkhŭly.*

MEEL AND MUKHULY.

This neighbourhood is celebrated for its wheat, and a peculiar kind is called Grain of Nûrsy, from this village of that name on the mountain. The *grain* is long Jezreel. and slender, while that of the Hauran is short and *plump.* The latter bears the highest price in market. The name Jezreel—*God will sow*—seems to have reference to the adaptation of this place for growing grain.

---

[1] 2 King ix. 26.

PART
II.

Allusions
in Hosea.

Hosea[1] intimates that the final overthrow of Israel should be in this valley of Jezreel, where it is further said that God would punish the house of Jehu for the blood there shed by him. Treason and murder must be remembered and avenged, even though vengeance slumbers through many generations. What is the explanation of that singular passage in Hosea, chap. ii. 21-23: "It shall come to pass in that day, I will hear, saith the Lord, I will hear the heavens, and they shall hear the earth; and the earth shall hear the corn, and the wine, and the oil; *and they shall hear Jezreel?*"

You may read thus: The Lord will hear the heavens calling for the vapour and the clouds. These clouds shall hear the parched earth calling for rain. The earth, in turn, shall hear the languishing corn, and wine, and oil, and grant the nourishment required. Jezreel, also, the valley of vengeance and destruction, shall in that happy time be heard calling for the peaceful products of husbandry. Jezreel—God himself will sow her with the seed of peace and righteousness. The Orientals are delighted with this sort of hazy, indistinct figure. There is evidently a play upon the name Jezreel, and an unexpressed blending of the bloody tragedies enacted in this valley with promises of better things in reserve for the true people of Israel. The passage begins with another most obscure but pregnant figure: "I will give her [Israel] the *valley of Achor for a door of hope.*" That valley runs up from Gilgal toward Bethel. There Achan was stoned to death, and by that act the anger of the Lord was turned away from Israel, and the door of entrance to the promised inheritance thrown open. Achor means *trouble*, affliction,—from whence comes our word ache, perhaps. Thus the valley of affliction was the door through which Israel at first entered the land of Canaan. And thus again the Lord, by his prophet, promised to lead Israel to peace and rest through the valley of trouble. The very indistinctness makes this mode of speaking the more suggestive. The *valley of Achor—a door of hope—*not a bad motto for those who through much tribulation must enter the promised land, the Canaan of eternal peace and rest.

Valley of
Achor

Road to
Jenîn.

But it is time to pass away from Jezreel, with all its lessons of wisdom. There is nothing of interest in the plain itself from this to Jenîn. That village to which we are coming, called Jelâmy, is prettily situated, but nearly ruined; and Em Gabeleh (or Mukeibileh), south-west of it, is quite deserted. The one on the left among the hills is Arrâmy, celebrated for its wheat and tobacco. Between it and Jenîn the plain runs far up into the eastern hills, and at the head of it is Beit Kod. The mountain of Gilboa is that just in front of us to the south-east; that is, the name Jelbûn is now specifically attached only to this part,—but in ancient times, I think, the whole rocky region between Jelbûn and the valley of Jezreel was so called. Saul and Jonathan were probably slain somewhere further north, possibly on the lofty promontory of El Mazar. There may even be an allusion to this very conspicuous place

Mountain
of Gilboa.

in the opening stanza of David's lament: "The beauty of Israel is slain *upon* CHAPTER
thy high places." And this very name Mazar (a sacred tomb to which pilgrim- XXX.
ages are made) may have been given to it because the daughters of Israel
went thither to weep over Saul, who clothed them in scarlet, and put an ornament of gold upon their apparel.[1]

This dry channel proves that a large stream flows from Beit Kod and the
mountains above it during the winter rains. The soil appears to be eminently
fertile, and how beautifully the orchards of Jenîn stretch this way down the Jenîn.
plain! but I cannot yet see the town itself.

It is hid away in a ravine, and further concealed by the gardens and orchards.
Both they and the town owe their flourishing character to the fountain which
bursts out in the centre of the valley; and this, again, received its Hebrew
name (En-gannim—*Fountain of Gardens*) from the flourishing orchards
which anciently, as well as now, distinguished the place. This is the most
distant permanent source of the Kishon; but during summer and autumn the
water is all exhausted by irrigation, and none of it reaches beyond the margin
of these green fields.

Is Jenîn mentioned in the Bible?

It is, as I already remarked, the *En-gannim* which was given to Issachar.[2] The En-
Gannim is near enough to Jenîn, and the *En* is for the fountain. As the gannim
place grew in importance the prefix of *Ain* was dropped, and it became simply of Scrip-
Gannim. Josephus calls it Ginnea, and the Arabs Jenîn. It is now the
chief town between Nazareth and Nablûs; contains about two thousand inhabitants—nearly all Moslems; has a governor, secretaries, and a custom-house
posse. It deals largely in all the products of the country, and with the Bedawîn
on the east of Jordan; but the people are fanatical, rude, and rebellious.
They are almost always fighting among themselves or with their neighbours.
There are three leading families who keep up perpetual strife and bloodshed
throughout all this region—the 'Abd el Hâdy, and Beit Tokân of Nablûs and
'Arrâby, and the Beit Jerrar of this place. They are now actually fighting
with each other between this and Nablûs, and the travellers whom we met
this morning assert positively that we shall not be able to pass through the
country in that direction. We shall know more about this to-morrow.

---

[1] 2 Samuel i. 24.   [2] Joshua xix. 21.

30

CHAPTER XXXI.

JENIN TO SINDIANY.*

April 1st.

Native
uproar
and strife.

WHAT does all this uproar mean? We have had a most unquiet night.

I have been out to ascertain the cause, and it seems that the various parties that passed through in the evening with such barbarous uproar were Bedawîn from the Ghor, and from Jebel 'Ajlûn, east of the Jordan. They have been brought over by the *Beits* Jerrar and Tokân to aid them against 'Abd el Hâdy; and there has been a skirmish during the night, near Jeb'a, with the partisans of the latter from 'Arrâby. The people of Jenîn, who are of the Jerrar party, say that 'Abd el Hâdy was beaten; but the bloody work is still going on, and the smaller villages are being deserted. If you look out along the paths down the mountains, you will see women and children hastening hither with their miscellaneous furniture on donkeys, mules, and camels. This place is safe only because 'Akil Aga, who refuses to join in this war, lies encamped out on Esdraelon, and our guard is one of his relatives. I once before had to pass this plain when the Arabs were up in arms, when my own horse was seized by a robber; and I shall long remember the cool way in which my guard (also a cousin of the aga) told that party of marauders that if they touched any thing or person under *his* protection *there would be no more khûbs (bread) for them on this side the Jordan.* The same assurance will protect us to-day, but we shall have to make a long detour to get round the places where the people are actually fighting. They are divided among themselves. For example, one half of Seely—that village on the edge of the plain—is for 'Abd el Hâdy, and the other is for Beit Jerrar; and you can see the flash of their guns at this moment, as they fire at each other from their houses.

---

* [Besides describing the journey from Jenin to Sindiany (near Cæsarea), in the course of which the plain of Esdraelon is traversed from south to north, this chapter contains a short notice of Samaria and Shechem, the chief places in Central Palestine.— ED.]

The women about us are terribly enraged against 'Abd el Hâdy. Some of his party not long ago attacked the villages in the district of Er Rohah, killed some of the people, burned their houses, and drove off their cattle and flocks. But what most excites their wrath is, that these wretches maltreated, and even killed women and children. This is an enormity which they loudly declare has never been known among them before;.and, so far as my knowledge extends, they are correct. During the civil wars that desolated Lebanon in 1841 and in 1845, the women were not molested even in battle. I have repeatedly seen them on both sides running with water to their friends who were hard pressed with thirst, and I never knew any of them to be injured or insulted. The same deference to the women has always been shown in this region until the present outbreak, and hence the extreme exasperation of the different parties. If any of 'Abd el Hâdy's men fall into their hands, these women have vowed to roast them alive ! This universal exasperation renders it more than ordinarily dangerous to travel through this district, and our wisest policy is to get beyond the range of their bloody quarrel as soon as possible. Hassein is hurrying the muleteers, and now summons us to mount and be off.

He is leading us directly back over our route of yesterday. Would it not be much nearer and more interesting to pass down the southern side of the plain, past Taanach and Megiddo ?

Certainly it would; but the people are fighting with one another all along that line, and it would not be safe. We shall have a good view of these places and of many others by the longer route, and there are no antiquities at any of them to exaggerate our regret. Seely, where they are shooting each other, is surrounded by splendid groves of the " peaceful olive ;" but neither the whispers of the groves nor the innocent cultivation of the soil, nor the kindly offices of the shepherd can subdue the innate ferocity of these barbarians. Alas ! that such a country should be wasted by wild Arabs, and consumed by the fires of domestic war. But thus it has been for ages, and I fear it will continue thus for ages to come. In fact this plain has always been a great battle-field. The Canaanites and Philistines, Jews and Egyptians, Chaldeans and Persians, Greeks and Romans, Moslems and Christians, of almost every age and nation, have encamped around Megiddo, because of its commanding position, its abundant supply of water, and its rich pastures. There Ahaziah, who fled from Jehu, died of his wounds ; and there, also, the good king Josiah was defeated and slain by Pharaoh-necho. Under the name of Legio it is mentioned very often by the classic historians and geographers, and its modern name, Lejjûn, is merely the Arabic form of the same word. Of the many villages on the neighbouring mountains of old Samaria, the only ones of much importance are Kefr Kûd, the Capercotia of the Greeks; 'Arrâby, the original seat of the 'Abd el Hâdy family; and Em el Fahm, on this side of it. 'Arrâby is a large place, and capable of sending out a *thousand guns*, as they say in this country, and *there* is the centre of the present war.

PART
II.

I greatly regret that we have not been able to pass through these hills to Samaria and Nablûs.

We may yet visit these places from Jerusalem, if this feud quiets down as rapidly as they generally do. In the meanwhile, I will give you an account of them as we ride over this uninhabited plain. I have travelled the route from Jenîn to Samaria many times, but it is almost always disturbed by just such quarrels as the present. On leaving Jenîn, the road follows the Wady Bel'amy for the first half hour, passing on the right an ancient ruin of the same name. This wady is full of fountains in winter, and very muddy, but hot as a furnace in summer. Rising out of this, over a long hill, you come down again to a considerable town called Kŭbatîeh. The hills about this place are covered with groves of flourishing olive-trees, and the net-work of vales and plains west of it is extremely pretty and fertile. In one of them is the site of Dothan, called now Tell Dothaim. This *tell* was once inhabited, and at its base is a fountain where the brethren of Joseph may have watered their flocks. The neighbourhood affords the very best pasturage; and this was the reason, no doubt, why they came to it from Nablûs.[1] I am not aware that there still exist old cisterns about Dothaim, but there are very few ancient sites where they are not found; and, I presume, a careful search would reveal the very pit (*beer*) into which Joseph was cast. It is in pleasing agreement with the narrative in Genesis to find that the great highway from Gilead to Egypt still passes near this place. The caravans come up the Ghor Beisan, pass by Zer'in and Lejjûn, enter the hill country of Samaria by the wady of Dothaim, and thence go on to Ramleh, Gaza, and Egypt. The large caravansary north of Beisan, called Khan el Ahmar, marks one important station on this route. It was along this road that those "Ishmaelites came from Gilead with their camels bearing spices, and balm, and myrrh, going to carry them down to Egypt," to whom the poor lad Joseph was sold by his cruel and envious brethren. It is worthy of remark that these modern Ishmaelites would not now hesitate to make just such a purchase, and actually do in certain parts of the country; and it is also interesting to find *balm* connected with Gilead at that early day. Jeremiah, long after, exclaims, "Is there no balm in Gilead? is there no physician there?"[2]

What was this balm?

Not known with any certainty. Josephus frequently mentions it, and says that the tree which bore it grew about Jericho, and there only. In this he must have been mistaken, or the balm or balsam he speaks of was of a different kind from that mentioned in the Bible; for that was gathered at Engedi, in Gilead, and at other places. Josephus also says that the queen of Sheba first brought the balsam-bearing tree into the country as a present to Solomon; which must also be a mistake of our historian, if he means that the balm-tree was unknown in Palestine until her visit. However, it is probable that the

Road to Samaria.

Dothan.

Highway to Egypt.

Balm of Gilead.

[1] Gen. xxxvii. 14-17.　　[2] Jer. viii. 22.

balm he describes as so *very scarce* and *precious*, was a different kind from CHAPTER
that which the Midianites were taking to Egypt. I was shown in the jungle XXXI.
about the Fountain of Elisha, near Jericho, a rough thorn bush, like a *crab* or
haw tree, which the monks said yielded balm; and I actually purchased some
at the time, but without supposing it to be the Biblical article. The Hebrew
word has been translated very variously. According to the Septuagint, it may
mean any kind of *resinous gum;* the Latin has opobalsamum ; the Arabic has
snubar (pine), meaning apparently the pine-nuts, still an important article of
traffic. Some suppose it was the gum or juice of the *turpentine*-tree, which
still abounds in Gilead, and the resinous distillation from it is much celebrated
by the Arabs for its healing virtues. Josephus says that this balm of Jericho
was " an ointment, of all the most precious, which, upon any incision made in
the wood with a sharp stone, distils out thence like a juice." I suppose that
the balm which Jacob sent to Joseph,[1] and that which Jeremiah refers to for
its medicinal qualities,[2] were the same as that which our trading Ishmaelites
were transporting to Egypt, and that it was some resinous extract from the
forest-trees of Gilead.

Elisha was residing in this Dothan on that memorable occasion when the Elisha at
king of Syria sent horses, and chariots, and a great host to take him : " and Dothan.
when the servant of the man of God was risen early, and gone forth, behold, a
host compassed the city ;" and he cried out, " Alas, my master ! how shall we
do ?"[3] The position appeared desperate. The tell was completely surrounded
by the army, and escape seemed impossible. But " the mountain was full of
horses and chariots of fire round about Elisha." Well might he say to the terrified servant, " Fear not : for they that be with us are more than they that be
with them." And so it in reality is with the servants of God at all times; and
they alone of all men have no reason to fear. However many or threatening
their enemies, they that are with and for them are more numerous and more
powerful. This narrative seems to draw aside for a moment the veil which
conceals the spirit world, and affords us a hasty glimpse of those ministers of
flaming fire which are sent forth to minister for them who shall be heirs of salvation.[4] At the prayer of Elisha the Syrian host were smitten with blindness,
and then guided by the prophet himself into the midst of Samaria. I have
travelled along the path which this blinded army must have followed for several
hours, and such a march has no parallel in history. Indeed, this entire transaction is replete with instruction to all—of rebuke to proud enemies of God,
and of delightful encouragement to those who put their trust in him.

But we must not enter Samaria with this Syrian army, but go back and Road to
travel the road more leisurely. From Kŭbatîyeh we ascend a very rocky hill, Samaria
and then pass down through a low plain to Sanûr, which is two hours from
Jenîn. In winter this plain is a lake many miles in circumference, but it dries
up, and is sown with corn and vegetables in summer. The village of Sanûr is

[1] Gen. xliii. 11.   [2] Jer. viii. 22.   [3] 2 Kings vi. 13–23.   [4] Heb. i. 14.

PART
II.

within a castle, on an isolated hill, at the south-west corner of this plain; and it is, and long has been, occupied by a rude, fanatical population, ever ready to insult travellers and to stir up rebellion against the government. Jeba'is another large village, about an hour further on, strongly located on the brow of the mountain; and there the road to Samaria parts from that to Nablûs, inclining to the right along the base of the hill of Jeba. The whole route is beautifully and endlessly diversified with hill, and dale, and fertile plain, even now well cultivated and thickly settled. The villages stand out on every conspicuous position, and by the side of every gushing fountain. At the end of five hours from Jenîn you are at the base of the " hill of Samaria."

Hill of
Samaria.

The site of this celebrated capital is delightful, by universal consent. It is a very large, isolated hill, rising by successive terraces at least *six hundred* feet above the valleys which surround it. In shape it is oval, and the smaller and lower end unites it to the neighbouring mountain on the east. There is no fountain on the hill, and during a siege the inhabitants must have depended entirely upon cisterns. Water, however, is abundant in the neighbourhood. There is a good spring a short distance below to the south-east, and a brook from the mountains in the same direction, large enough to drive a mill; and in winter a fine mill-stream also flows past the north side of the hill. All these unite at the bottom of the plain north-west of the city, and, as I am told, form part of the river which, at the sea south of Cæsarea, is called Abu Zabûra.

The view from the topmost terrace of Samaria over the rich plains and hills around it, and far away to the blue Mediterranean, is truly magnificent. The remains of the ancient city consist mainly of colonnades, which certainly date back to the time of the Herods, and perhaps many of the columns are much older. There is a group of sixteen standing in a recess low down on the north-east side of the hill, and a similar group of sixteen on the top, though these last are larger; and there are many lying prostrate. The grand colonnade, however, runs along the south side of the hill, down a broad terrace, which descends rapidly toward the present village. The number of columns, whole or broken, along this line is nearly *one hundred*, and many others lie scattered about on lower terraces. They are of various sizes, and quite irregularly arranged, but when perfect it must have been a splendid colonnade. The entire hill is covered with rubbish, indicating the existence and repeated destruction of a large city. The modern village is on the south-eastern slope, adjacent to the ruined Church of St. John. You have seen so many views of what these ruins are *not*, that I despair of giving an accurate idea of what they *are*. The church, however, is an interesting specimen of mediæval architecture, which all look at with respect, and many with deep emotion. This is natural; though the tradition that associates the martyrdom of the Baptist with this spot is sufficiently doubtful, yet it augments the reverence with which one explores the vaults of this fine old ruin.

Remains
of Sama-
ria.

Nearly everything that is known about ancient Samaria is derived from the Bible and Josephus. This latter historian mentions it very often, and from him we learn that it derived its present name, Sebastia (or Sebustia, as the Arabs call it), from Herod, and in honour of Augustus. Herod rebuilt it after some one of its many overthrows, and most of the columns now visible are supposed to be remains of his edifices; but, as it was celebrated a thousand years before his time, and was for centuries the capital of a kingdom, I think it not unlikely that he built with the ruins of castles and temples much older than himself. It is remarkable that this place took its original name, Samaria, from the man who owned the hill, and not from Omri, the king who built the city.[1] It continued to be the capital of the " Ten Tribes," until they were carried captive into Assyria; and during the *twenty-five centuries* which have passed since that event its fortunes have been very various; often destroyed and again rebuilt, growing smaller by degrees, though *not beautifully* less, until it finally subsided into the insignificant village which now clings to the name and the site.

Like many other visitors, I have uniformly found the inhabitants of Sebustia rude, insolent, and sometimes even dangerous. They seem never to have had a good character, if we form our opinion from the language of the prophets. Many of the wonderful passages in the lives of Elijah and Elisha are connected with Samaria and her idolatrous and bloody rulers. I imagine that the level space on the topmost terrace of the hill, where are the sixteen large columns, marks the site of the great temple of Baal, which Jehu utterly " broke down," after that treacherous slaughter of Baal's priests and worshippers recorded in the 10th chapter of 2 Kings. It was to Samaria that Naaman the Damascene leper came to be healed—a very remarkable narrative, and very suggestive. This terrible disease still cleaves to Damascus, and is now, as it was then, incurable by man. It was this latter fact that alarmed the king of Israel in regard to the motive of Benhadad : " See how he seeketh a quarrel against me. Am I God, to kill and to make alive, that this man doth send unto me to recover a man of his leprosy ?"[2] exclaimed the perplexed king. One is tempted to inquire why this power of healing the leprosy, which so signally honoured the God of Israel in the eyes of all nations, should have been so rarely exercised. There were other lepers at that very time in Samaria under the eye of Elisha, as we learn from the next chapter. Indeed Christ says there were *many* of them, and of the children of Israel too, and yet " none of them was cleansed, saving Naaman the Syrian."[3] It is obvious, however, that this reserve in putting forth divine power is in strict accordance with the entire economy of miraculous manifestation. Gehazi, for his cupidity, had this terrible disease laid upon him, with the fearful doom added, " that it should cleave unto his seed *for ever ;*"[4] and who can tell but that the victims of this horrid plague now seen about this city and at Nablûs, the present home of all the Samaritans, may be the heirs of this heritage of Gehazi ?

The lepers mentioned in chapter vii. seem to have been shut out of Samaria

---

[1] 1 Kings xvi. 24. [2] 2 Kings v 15. [3] Luke iv. 27 [4] 2 Kings v. 27.

PART
II.

even when it was closely besieged by Benhadad. Is it common now to compel lepers to dwell outside of the city!

Not in all places, but they are everywhere regarded as unclean, shunned as dangerous, and obliged to live by themselves. Where there are considerable numbers of them, as at Jerusalem, there is a separate quarter to which they are confined, just *at* the gate, though *within* the walls of the city. At Samaria they were outside, and I have seen them thus cast out of the villages where they resided.

Doves'
dung.

What have you to say about that extraordinary article of food called "doves' dung," which was sold at a high price during that terrible siege of Benhadad?

I believe that the Hebrew chirîyonim, or khir yonim, was a name for a coarse and cheap sort of food, a kind of bean, as some think, to which this whimsical title was given on account of some fancied resemblance between the two. Nor am I at all surprised at it, for the Arabs give the most quaint, obscure, and ridiculous names to their extraordinary edible mixtures. I would, therefore, not translate at all, but let the passage read thus, " A fourth part of a cab of khir yonim for five pieces of silver;" and be content with that, until we know what khir yonim really is.

Nablûs
(She-
chem).

From Samaria to Nablûs is two hours' easy riding, first south, over the shoulder of the mountain, and then eastward, up the lovely vale of Nablûs. Nothing in Palestine surpasses it in fertility and natural beauty, and this is mainly due to the fine mill-stream which flows through it. The whole country is thickly studded with villages, the plains clothed with grass or grain, and the rounded hills with orchards of olive, fig, pomegranate, and other trees. Coming from Samaria, the ascent to the city from the valley is quite steep, and it climbs up the side of Gerizim to a very considerable elevation; indeed the perpendicular cliffs of the mountains overhang the upper part of the city. Travellers generally seek out the Samaritan quarter, which is near the southwestern corner, and sufficiently elevated to afford a good view of the whole town. Nablûs is a queer old place. The streets are narrow, and vaulted over; and in the winter time it is difficult to pass along many of them on account of brooks which rush over the pavement with deafening roar. In this respect I know no city with which to compare it except Brusa; and, like that city, it has mulberry, orange, pomegranate, and other trees, mingled in with the houses, whose odoriferous flowers load the air with delicious perfume during the months of April and May. Here the bilbûl delights to sit and sing, and thousands of other birds unite to swell the chorus. The inhabitants maintain that theirs is the most *musical* vale in Palestine, and my experience does not enable me to contradict them.

Ebal and
Gerizim.

Imagine that the lofty range of mountains running north and south was cleft open to its base by some tremendous convulsion of nature, at right angles to its own line of extension, and the broad fissure thus made is the vale of Nablûs, as it appears to one coming up the plain of Mukhna from Jerusalem.

Mount Ebal is on the north, Gerizim on the south, and the city between. Near the eastern end, the vale is not more than sixty rods wide ; and just there, I suppose, the tribes assembled to hear the " blessings and the cursings" read by the Levites. We have them *in extenso* in the 27th and 28th chapters of Deuteronomy ; and in Joshua[1] we are informed that it was actually done, and how. " Simeon, and Levi, and Judah, and Issachar, and Joseph, and Benjamin, stood on Gerizim; and Reuben, Gad, Asher, Zebulun, Dan, and Naphtali, on Ebal ;" while " all Israel, and their elders, and officers, and their judges, stood on this side of the ark, and on that side before the priests which bare the ark of the covenant of the Lord :" the whole nation of Israel, with the women and little ones, were there. And Joshua read all the words of the law—the blessings and the cursings; " there was not a word of all that Moses commanded which Joshua read not before all the congregation of Israel." This was, beyond question or comparison, the most august assembly the sun has ever shone upon; and I never stand in the narrow plain, with Ebal and Gerizim rising on either hand to the sky, without involuntarily recalling and reproducing the scene. I have shouted to hear the echo, and then fancied how it must have been when the loud-voiced Levites proclaimed from the naked cliffs of Ebal, " Cursed be the man that maketh any graven image, an abomination unto Jehovah." And then the tremendous Amen ! tenfold louder, from the mighty congregation, rising, and swelling, and re-echoing from Ebal to Gerizim, and from Gerizim to Ebal. Amen ! even so let him be accursed. No, there never was an assembly to compare with this.

It was part of the command of the Lord, and of Moses to Joshua, that, Joshua's having placed the " blessings and the cursings" on Gerizim and on Ebal, he pillars should write the whole law upon pillars of stone which he should rear up at this place. Do you suppose that the whole five books of Moses were thus engraven upon stone ?

I suppose not ; perhaps none of it was *engraved* on stone. A careful Writing examination of Deuteronomy xxvii. 4, 8, and Joshua viii. 30–32, will lead to on plaster. the opinion that the law was *written upon* or *in* the *plaster* with which these pillars were *coated.* This could easily be done ; and such writing was common in ancient times. I have seen numerous specimens of it certainly more than *two thousand years old,* and still as distinct as when they were first inscribed on the plaster. There seems to have been an unnecessary amount of learning bestowed upon this matter, and difficulties imagined where none exist. Michaëlis, in his " Commentary on the Laws of Moses,"[2] enters into a laboured examination of the passage. He gives and refutes various explanations, among others that of Kennicott, who supposes that the letters were cut out in black marble, the letters being raised, and the hollow intervals between them filled with white lime plaster. His own opinion, however, is, that Moses commanded Joshua to do as Sostratus, the architect of the Pharos, did, who

---

[1] Joshua vliii.   [2] Michaëlis, vol. i. book iii.

PART
II.

cut his own name on the solid marble, then plastered it over, and grooved the name of the king of Egypt on the cement. Moses, in like manner, ordered the law to be cut in the solid stone, and then to be plastered over with hard cement, so that when this plaster fell off, in after ages, the engraven law would be discovered entire and perfectly legible ! Now the main objection to these speculations is, that there is not the slightest foundation for them in the text. The direction there is perfectly plain, and needs none of these re-condite devices to render it intelligible and reasonable. That the Egyptians were accustomed to engrave on stone in various ways is well known, and Moses must have been familiar with it; but he was also familiar with the mode which he here commands to be followed, and he knew it to be sufficiently durable for all practical purposes. He therefore did not order such a Herculean labour as to grave the whole law in marble, but simply to write it *on* or *in* properly pre-pared cement. In this hot climate, where there is no frost to dissolve the cement, it will continue hard and unbroken for thousands of years—which is certainly long enough. The cement on Solomon's Pools remains in admirable preservation, though exposed to all the vicissitudes of the climate, and with no protection. The cement in the tombs about Sidon is still perfect, and the writing on them entire, though acted upon by the moist damp air always found in caverns, for perhaps two thousand years. What Joshua did, there-fore, when he erected those great stones at Mount Ebal, was merely to write *in* the still soft cement with a stile, or, more likely, *on* the polished surface, when dry, with red paint, as in ancient tombs. If properly sheltered, and not broken away by violence, they would have remained to this day. But every-thing that could be destroyed, has been long since, and again and again over-thrown, in the countless convulsions of this most rebellious neighbourhood; and the hope expressed by Michaëlis, that these (imaginary) marble slabs, with the law engraven upon them, were still in existence, buried beneath the rub-bish of Nablûs, and might one day be discovered, crumbles into dust along with the plaster upon which the commandments of the Lord were really written. Nor need we mourn over the loss. The printing-press preserves this same law to us far more securely than could any monument, though built of bronze or solid adamant.

Engraving on stone.

Antiquity of She-chem.

If Nablûs occupies the place of Shechem (and I suppose it does), it is one of the oldest cities in the world; nor is there anything improbable in this, for its natural advantages, great beauty, and abundant supply of water, mark out the site for a city. This latter fact, however, seems to prove that Shechem was not the Sychar mentioned in the 4th chapter of John. It is incredible that the " woman of Samaria " should have gone two miles away from these delicious fountains to draw water out of an immensely deep well. If we admit the identity of the present well of Jacob with that mentioned by John, there can be but little doubt that Sychar was a small Samaritan town not far from that spot; and there is a village north of it now called Aschâr. This is so like John's Sychar, that I feel inclined to adopt it. Of course, the " woman of

Samaria" belonged to the country or people of Samaria, not to the city of that name, which is some eight miles to the north-west of it.

I see no good reason to question the identity of this well with that of the patriarch; nor do I intend to disturb the bones of Joseph, concerning which he expressed so much solicitude when about to die in Egypt.[1] The Moslems point out his tomb at the base of Ebal in this vicinity; and this agrees well enough with Joshua xxiv. 32, where it is said that " the bones of Joseph, which the children of Israel brought up out of Egypt, buried they in Shechem, in a parcel of ground which Jacob bought of the sons of Hamor." Of course this " parcel of ground" must have been adjacent to the well; and tradition has located the sepulchre near enough to meet all the requirements of the history. Let his bones, therefore, rest in peace.

There is, after all, a mystery about this well which is not easily cleared up. Although we know that the patriarchs were given to well-digging, yet it is strange that Jacob should be at the expense of such a work when there is a fine fountain a little west of it, and the whole vale of Nablûs abounds in them beyond almost any other part of Palestine. The well, however, is a very *positive fact*, and it must have been dug by somebody, notwithstanding this abundance of fountains, and why not by Jacob? He was as likely to need it as any one, and as competent to execute the work. As to the reason for it, we may suppose that the fountains within the valley of Shechem were so appropriated as not to be available for Jacob's large family and larger flocks. Even now the inhabitants would not allow the flocks and herds of such an opulent tent-dwelling tribe to frequent their pretty vale; and as there are no fountains in that part of the eastern plain, and the streams from those within the valley run *westward*, Jacob probably found it necessary to dig this deep well for his own use. It is now deserted, and the surrounding terrace of rude masonry broken down, so that there is nothing distinctive or striking about it.

The ancient city of Shechem, I suppose, stood where Nablûs does now, and it is easy to comprehend how Jotham could stand above it, and deliver his cutting allegory in the hearing of the people, and then "run away" before they could take him.[2] Several lofty precipices of Gerizim literally overhang the city, any one of which would answer his purpose. Nor would it be difficult to be heard, as everybody knows who has listened to the *public crier* of villages on Lebanon. In the stillness of evening, after the people have returned home from their distant fields, he ascends the mountain side above the place, or to the roof of some prominent house, and there "lifts up his voice and cries," as Jotham did; and he gives forth his proclamation with such distinctness that all can hear and understand it. Indeed the people in these mountainous countries are able, from long practice, so to pitch their voices as to be heard distinctly at distances almost incredible. They talk with persons across enormous wadies, and give the most minute directions, which are perfectly

Marginal notes: Well of Jacob. / The well, why dug. / Jotham or Gerizim. / Distinct talking.

---

[1] Gen. l. 25.   [2] Judges ix. 7–21.

PART
II.

The trees.

understood; and in doing this they seem to speak very little louder than their usual tone of conversation. Jotham, therefore, might easily be heard by the greater part of the inhabitants of Shechem. The costume of his allegory is simple and natural, and the allusions are to the very trees which most abound at Nablûs,—the olive, the fig, the vine, and the bramble.

The Samaritans (and their patrons) claim for the site of their temple above Nablûs two very important Biblical events: that *here*, and not at Jerusalem, Melchizedek met Abraham; and that *on Gerizim*, and *not Moriah*, the patriarch offered his son Isaac;—and if I understand Mr. Stanley aright, he concurs in the justness of these pretensions.

Is Gerizim Moriah?

He does, and even devotes a long note of several pages to substantiate the claims; but this is not the most successful effort of that pleasant traveller and very clever writer. Mr. Stanley is a gentleman who yields cheerfully to the paramount authority of the Bible on all points where its indications are clear and decisive; and it seems to me that the positive assertion that Melchizedek was king of *Salem* makes it certain that Abraham did not meet him in *Gerizim*. *Shechem* was never called Salem, nor was there ever any place on Gerizim that bore this name. There was a Shalîm east of it, toward Jordan, and Jerome, after Theodotus, *supposed* that Melchizedek reigned there; but even this does not favour the cause of the Samaritans. The philological argument drawn from *Ar*-Gerizim has no appreciable weight in the case. And as to the probable route which Abraham would follow in returning from Dan to Hebron, I must

Abraham's route from Dan.

dissent entirely from the opinion of Mr. Stanley. Abraham would naturally return on the *western* side of the lakes Huleh and Tiberias. I have been round the eastern side of both, and affirm that he could not have selected that road, encumbered as he was with a large company of rescued prisoners and their baggage. Nor could he have followed the valley of the Jordan. No one who has ever traversed that impracticable *ghor* will believe that this great company took that path; and, after wandering over these regions in all directions, I am quite sure that the way by which Abraham led back the people of Sodom was along the ordinary road from Galilee to Jerusalem. This, it is true, would bring him near Nablûs; and if there were the remotest evidence that Melchizedek reigned there, the meeting might have taken place on Gerizim, as the Samaritans affirm; but there is *no* such evidence, and this route would bring Abraham to Jerusalem, where the king of Sodom would most naturally meet him. Mr. Stanley supposes that the king of Sodom went round the *eastern* shore of the Dead Sea; but that is quite impracticable, unless one makes a long detour through the interior. On the whole, I have not a doubt but that Abraham met Melchizedek at Jerusalem, and having restored the goods and the captives to the king of Sodom, he returned by way of Bethlehem to his

Salem.

home on the plain of Mamre. I cannot avoid the impression that the author of the "Hebrews" believed that *the* Salem of which the "priest of the most high God" was king was Jeru-*salem*; and in the 76th Psalm the Holy City is expressly called *Salem*. Add to this, that Josephus positively asserts that

Jerusalem was founded by Melchizedek, and we have a chain of evidence which cannot be broken by the weight of a hundred Samaritan traditions detailed with so much confidence by "our friend Jacob Shelaby" of Nablûs, sheikh of all the holy Samaritans, etc.

I cannot comprehend the motive for this partiality on behalf of Gerizim, nor by what authority Mr. Stanley asserts that the original sanctuary of the most high God was on that mountain, and not at Jerusalem. This is contrary to all the Biblical indications, so far as I can understand them. Salvation was of the *Jews*, not of the Samaritans; the spiritual worship of the Father was in Jerusalem, not on Gerizim; and from the days of Sanballat, and before, so far as we know, devout worshippers of Jehovah regarded the temple on Gerizim with abhorrence. Now, if this had been the original shrine, why was not this most important fact urged by Sanballat and his friends in their angry disputes with Nehemiah and Zerubbabel? and if Melchizedek reigned in Shechem, and Abraham offered up Isaac on Gerizim, why do we hear nothing of these things to strengthen their cause?

In regard to the question about the true site of that most wonderful act of Abraham, I believe it was on Mount Moriah, where the altar of burnt sacrifice was erected by Solomon, and near the spot where the greater sacrifice of an infinitely greater Son was finally offered; and it would take a vast amount of contrary evidence to force me to abandon this idea. Mr. Stanley's geographical argument is more than feeble. It is almost absurd to maintain that Abraham could come on his loaded ass from Beersheba to Nablûs in the time specified. On the third day he arrived early enough to leave the servants "afar off," and walk with Isaac bearing the sacrificial wood to the mountain which God had shown him—there build the altar, arrange the wood, bind his son, and stretch forth his hand to slay him; and there was time, too, to take and offer up the ram in Isaac's place. That all this could have been done *at Nablûs on the third day* of their journey is incredible. It has always appeared to me, since I first travelled over the country myself, that even Jerusalem was too far off from Beersheba for the tenor of the narrative, but Nablûs is two days' ride further north! Nor will the suggestion of Mr. Stanley, that Abraham came up through Philistia and then turned into the mountain, bear examination. The supposition is entirely gratuitous, and at variance with all the lines of patriarchal travel through the country, nor does it render the achievement of the journey in three days any more feasible. If Mr. Stanley had travelled over those interminable plains of Philistia and Sharon, as I have, he would not select this route for Abraham on his sad errand. Let us rejoice in being permitted to rest with entire confidence in the correctness of our received tradition, that the priest of the most high God reigned in Jerusalem, and that Abraham made the typical sacrifice of his son on Moriah, and not on Gerizim.

In regard to the famous temple of the Samaritans on Mount Gerizim, little need be said in addition to the information addressed to the eye by the plan of the *existing foundations*. The main edifice (I.) was nearly a square, being

Mount Moriah.

Mr. Stanley's vagaries.

Temple on Mount Gerizim.

two hundred and forty-one feet from east to west, and two hundred and fifty-five from north to south. In the centre of the court was an octagon (II.),

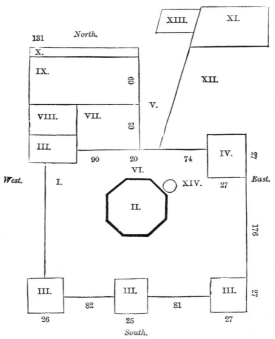

FOUNDATIONS OF SAMARITAN TEMPLE OF GERIZIM.

Plan of foundations. and near it a small but beautifully-rounded tank or cistern (XIV.) On the corners were square rooms (III.), and the one on the north-east (IV.) is covered with a white dome, and is used as an oratory. (V.) is a passage up from a lower platform on the north-east. (VI.) entrance to the grand court. (VII.) an open terrace, a few feet lower than the main court. (VIII.) used apparently as a cemetery. (IX.) a room about eighteen feet lower than No. (VII.)   (X.) portico or passage to the room (IX.)   (XI.) shapeless ruins. (XII.) now unoccupied, perhaps originally a yard or outer court. (XIII.) a room in ruins, object of it doubtful.

The walls are about six feet thick, and from seven to fifteen feet high. There are no ornamental carvings on any of the stones, but they are well cut, and *bevelled* after the Jewish or Phœnician manner. On the north there is a lower terrace of the mountain, covered with ruins, as of a village; and west of

the main edifice as a smooth plat, now used by the Samaritans for their tents, CHAPTER
when they go there to celebrate their feasts. For vastness and variety, the pro- XXXI.
spect from this temple is not surpassed by any in Palestine, unless it be the view View from
from Tabor, and many visitors think this from Gerizim the most interesting. Gerizim.

It was doubtless to this mountain, with its ruined temple, that our Saviour
pointed when he enunciated that cardinal truth in religion, "Woman, believe
me, the hour cometh when ye shall neither in *this mountain,* nor yet at
Jerusalem, worship the Father. God is a spirit; and they that worship him
must worship him in spirit and in truth."[1] Josephus tells us that this temple
was destroyed about a hundred and twenty-nine years before the birth of
Christ; but the site of it has been the place where the Samaritans have continued to "worship the Father" from that day to this, *not* in spirit nor in
truth, it is to be feared, but in form and fanaticism, according to the traditions
of their elders.

There are not now two hundred Samaritans, all told, in the world. They The Sama-
themselves mention one hundred and fifty as the correct census. They are a ritan rem-
strange people, clinging to their law, and to the sepulchres of their fathers, nant.
with invincible tenacity. Their chief priest will show you, with any amount
of sham reverence, their ancient copy of the Pentateuch; but though, like all The MS.
other travellers, I have given my *bŭksheesh* for the privilege of turning over Penta-
its time-stained pages, I have no faith in their legends in regard to it, estimate teuch.
its real value at a very low figure, and leave to others the minute description
of this curious relic of antiquity.

But it is time we should return from our long digression, and give some attention to this great plain through which we are led by our indefatigable guide
and protector. The central parts of Esdraelon seem to be entirely destitute Esdraelon.
of water, and this is the reason, I suppose, why it was never thickly inhabited.

That may have been one reason; another is, that it is hot in summer, and
unhealthy. As to water, I believe that it could be obtained in any quantity
by digging, as in all other great plains of this country. But it is by no means
certain that the central parts were always sparsely inhabited. There are
traces of many mud villages in it, and some of these have names, and a traditional history among the Arabs. There is a Lûd far down to the left,
which was probably settled by a colony from the Lûd which is near Jaffa; and
perhaps Jaffa, or Japhia, yonder on the hill-side below Nazareth, and Beit
Lahm, in the woods further west, were also colonized from the celebrated cities
of the same name in the south of Palestine.

Esdraelon is far from being a *dead* level, the western half having a decided
dip toward the sea, while its different parts roll up in long swells like gigantic
waves, terminating in Jebel ed Dûhy in the centre, and the rocky ridges of
Zer'in, and Em Gabileh toward the south. I have seen nothing to compare it

[1] John iv. 21, 24.

with except some of our rolling prairies in the West, and these lack Tabor, and
Little Hermon, and Gilboa, and Carmel, and a hundred other natural beauties
and historic memories with which this is everywhere surrounded and glorified.

French en-
gineering
project.
The French engineer who proposed to dig a ship canal from the Bay of
Acre, fill up the ghor, and thus open a channel to the Gulf of Akabah, must
have been profoundly ignorant of the topography with which he was dealing.
The " cutting " for this canal along the bed of the Kishon would gradually
deepen, until, at the water-shed of the valley of Jezreel, it would be several
hundred feet. This gigantic difficulty overcome, the sea must rush in with
volume sufficient to fill up the ghor from near Jisr Benat Yacobe to the Gulf
of Akabah, burying Tiberias six hundred feet deep, and all below it deeper
still, until, over the Dead Sea, it would be more than thirteen hundred feet;
and even then there would be required enormous excavation at the south end
before the connection with the gulf could be effected ! We may safely conclude
that, if there is no other way to unite the Red Sea and the Mediterranean
than this, the thing will never be done, and Tiberias, Gennesaret, and the
splendid valley of the Jordan are safe from this desolating inundation.

What is the name of this ruined castle which we are approaching ?

Castle of
Fûleh.
Fûleh, and west of it is 'Afûleh, both now deserted, though both were inhabited twenty-five years ago, when I first passed this way. Fûleh was occupied by the French in the time of Bonaparte, and about it were fought many
skirmishes with the Turks and Arabs. Many years ago, I spent a night at
Sejera, in the oak woods north of Tabor, and found several old men there who
remembered the battle of Kleber, and the wild rout of the Turks at the close
of it, when Bonaparte, with a troop of horse, came galloping up from Acre
to the scene of action. These people of Sejera spoke in the most exaggerated
terms of the desperate daring of these French cavaliers, a party of whom was
stationed at their village. This castle of Fûleh was circular, with a high wall
and a deep ditch. There was no water inside, but directly below it small
fountains *ooze* out of the ground in sufficient quantity for the demands of the
garrison, which could not have been large. The Bedawîn now resort to
them with their flocks and camels, and it was to secure this privilege that
they sacked and destroyed the castle; and by the same process the whole of
Esdraelon will soon be abandoned to them. Their system of desolation is
worked out after this fashion : They pitch their tents in the vicinity of a
village, and in such numbers as to bid defiance to the inhabitants. Of course,
their camels and flocks roam over the unfenced plain, and devour a large part
of the grain while growing; and when it is ripe, they either steal it or compel
the farmers to *present* them a heavy per centage as the price of their *protection*.

Plunder-
ing Arabs.
From the village itself, chickens, eggs, sheep, cows, and even horses disappear,
and can never be recovered. Many of the inhabitants soon move off to escape
from these annoyances, and the village being thereby weakened, the Arabs
provoke a quarrel; some one is wounded or killed, and then the place is sacked
and burned. The end aimed at is now reached, and the land belongs hence-

forth to the lawless Ishmaelite. In ten years more there will not be an in- CHAPTER
habited village in Esdraelon, unless this wretched work is checked; and even XXXI.
now it is unsafe to traverse this noble plain in any direction, and everybody
goes armed, and prepared to repel force by force.

But a small portion of the plain is under cultivation, and there are scarcely
any traces of antiquity upon it.

That is true, particularly in the centre and western part of it; and there
never were any very substantial buildings in those farming villages, I suppose.
The houses appear to have been made of unburnt brick, and, of course, it is
useless to look for them in our day. From the nature of the country and its
relative position, it was always subject to invasion, as the great highway for
armies, the battle-field of contending nations. The plain, therefore, was The towns
mainly cultivated by those who resided in towns upon its border; and there were on
the border
you will find ruins, as at Ksalis, Debûrieh, Nain, En-dor, Beisan, Solam, of the
Zer'in, Jenîn, Lejjun, Tell Caimon, and many other sites. At this place plain.
directly ahead of us, now called El Mezrah, there are many sarcophagi of a
most antique fashion, yet there is no other trace of an extinct city near it;
and the soil among the sarcophagi is ploughed and sowed like the rest of the
plain. There are also other sites where nothing but the tombs of those who
lived there remain to tell the story of their inhabitants.

Our guide, I see, is turning to the south, and intends to take us through
Wady Kŭsab, midway between Tell el Mutsellîm and Tell Caimon; and now,
before we enter this wady and bid adieu to Esdraelon, let us take a survey of Lower end
the lower end of it. It has become perfectly level, and I can tell you from of Esdraelon.
experience that in wet seasons it is extremely muddy; and then the Kishon
causes great danger to the muleteers. Rarely, indeed, do they get over it
without some of their animals sticking fast in its oozy bottom. You observe
that the hills of Samaria bend round to the base of Carmel, while those of
Galilee do the same on the opposite side, leaving a vale between them for
the Kishon only a few rods wide. The great tell, which, from our position,
seems to close up the entrance entirely, is called Kŭssîs (mound of the priest),
—a name probably commemorative of the slaughter of Baal's priests near its
base. The hills of Galilee are clothed, down to the bank of the river, with a Woods.
forest of oak, terebinth, mock-orange, and other trees and bushes. Hour after
hour you wander delighted through these lovely woods, over hills and through
wadies quite up to the Bŭttauf; and the same kind of grove re-appears on the
south of Carmel, and still forms the "ingens sylva" of the Roman geographers.

If you look down the Kishon, you can see a huge *double tell* at the further
end of the narrow vale. It is now called Harothîeh, and marks the site, I View
doubt not, of the old Harosheth of the Gentiles. The present village of that down the
Kishon.
name is in a recess of the hills, a short distance to the east of the tell. On
that bold promontory of Carmel directly facing us is the *Mŭkhrakah*, where Haro-
the great sacrifice was offered by Elijah. The shapeless ruins of El Mansûra thieh—
Haro-
are on a lower terrace to the south-east of it, and similar ruins are below on sheth.

31

PART
II.

the north side of the mountain. The great Wady Milhh passes southward round the end of Carmel; and through it, I believe, ran the ancient Roman road to Tantûra and Cæsarea. The large *tell* on this side of it is Caimôn, often mentioned by ancient geographers and itineraries. This lower end of Esdraelon is not more than six miles wide, and most of it is too flat and wet for cultivation; but the Arabs delight in it, particularly in winter, and it is even now dotted over with their black tabernacles. Overgrown as it is with tall thistles and long grass, it is the favourite haunt of the gazelle; and there goes a family of them bounding gaily toward Sheikh Bureîkh on the western margin of the plain. The solemn stork, too, frequents the more marshy parts of it, and adds much to the interest of this rather monotonous scene.

Ancient sites N.W. of the plain.

Around this north-western side of Esdraelon are clustered a number of interesting sites, which we may notice in passing. That large *tell* with a village upon it is Jibbata; and directly north of it, half an hour, is Semmûnia, on an immense *tell*, partly hid in a recess of the mountain. In the plain between the two, Josephus fought one of his battles with the Romans. Semmûnia is entirely deserted, but there is an excellent fountain of water at the south-west base of the tell; and the traveller along that road in summer will be thankful to know where he can slake his thirst and fill his "bottle." Two miles west of Semmûnia is Jeîda, on an old site full of rock tombs and surrounded with oak glades and rich vales of the most exquisite loveliness. West of this are Kŭskŭs and Tell'aum; and in the woods north of it are Zebda, Beît Lahm, and Em el 'Amed,—all ancient, and some of them historical.

Beauty of the region. Deserted.

Beautiful as paradise, yet that whole region is deserted; as "in the days of Shamgar, the son of Anath, in the days of Jael, the inhabitants of the villages cease, the highways are unoccupied, and the travellers walk through by-ways;"[1] and so we are doing at this moment, and for the same reason. The present state of the country is no novelty.

We are now passing through the scene of Barak's great battle with Sisera; and this same neighbourhood witnessed another contest more remarkable and vastly more important and impressive than the overthrow of that oppressor of Israel. It occurred during the reign of that wicked king Ahab, and his more wicked queen Jezebel; and the scene shifts from Esdraelon to Carmel, and from mountain to plain, in rapid succession. Elijah the Tishbite is the principal actor. Jezebel had successfully employed the power and patronage of the government to corrupt the faith of Israel, and the whole kingdom was overrun with the priests of Baal, that abomination of the Zidonians, while his idolatrous temples reared their insulting heads in every part of the land. To effect this apostasy, Jezebel had waged a bloody persecution against the prophets of the Lord. The Tishbite thus states the case, in reply to the question, "What doest thou here, Elijah? I have been very jealous for the Lord God of hosts," said he; "for the children of Israel have forsaken thy covenant,

Elijah and Jezebel.

---

[1] Judges v. 6, 7.

thrown down thine altars, and slain thy prophets with the sword; and I, even I only, am left, and they seek my life to take it away."[1]

To arrest this ruinous revolt, the Lord interposed by a series of awful judgments and stupendous miracles. At the prayer of the prophet he shut up the heavens for three years and six months, so that there was neither rain nor dew *The drought.* during all these years.[2] Near the close of this dreadful drought the king said to Obadiah, the governor of his house, " Go into the land, unto all fountains of water, and unto all brooks; peradventure we may find grass to save the horses and mules alive, that we lose not all the beasts. So Ahab went one way by himself, and Obadiah went another way by himself."[3] The latter went westward from Jezreel to the marshy grounds near Carmel, at the bottom of Esdraelon; and there Elijah met him, and said, " Go, tell thy lord, Behold, Elijah is here."[4] The good man was terrified at the thought of carrying such a message to the enraged king. " As the Lord thy God liveth," said he, " there is no nation or kingdom whither my Lord hath not sent to seek thee."[5] Elijah replied, " As the Lord of hosts liveth, before whom I stand, I will surely shew myself unto him to-day." Ahab seems to have been near at hand, for he quickly obeyed the summons; and when he saw Elijah he exclaimed, in anger, " Art thou he that troubleth Israel?"[6] " I have not troubled Israel," was the reply of the Tishbite; " but *thou* and thy father's house, in that ye have forsaken the commandments of the Lord, and thou hast followed Baalim. Now, therefore, send and gather me all Israel unto Mount Carmel, and the prophets of the groves, four hundred, which eat at Jezebel's table."[7] The wicked but weak-minded king sank before the daring servant of God, his more wicked and resolute wife not being by his side. He hastily gathered the people to a *The contest on Carmel.* remarkable and well-known spot on the eastern end of Carmel, where sacrifice had been offered to Jehovah in ancient times. But never before was there such a meeting as this, never such a momentous question to be discussed, such a mighty controversy to be settled. Elijah came unto all the people and said, " If the Lord be God, follow him; but if Baal, then follow him."[8] But the people, conscience-smitten, yet afraid of the king, answered him not a word. Then the prophet, to compel a choice, proposed the test of sacrifice, " and the God that answereth by fire, let him be God." The irresolute multitude ventured to approve; the king could not resist; the priests dared not refuse. Quickly the victims are upon the altars, and the priests call upon the name of Baal from morning until noon, saying, " O Baal, hear us! But there was no voice, nor any that answered." Then Elijah mocked them: " Cry aloud, for he is a god: either he is talking, or he is pursuing, or he is on a journey, or *peradventure he sleepeth, and must be awaked.*" The poor priests, goaded to madness by this scorching irony, leaped in frantic despair upon the altar, crying

[1] 1 Kings xix. 10. [2] 1 Kings xvii. 1. [3] 1 Kings xviii. 5, 6.
[4] 1 Kings xviii. 8. [5] 1 Kings xviii. 10. [6] 1 Kings xviii. 15–17.
[7] 1 Kings xviii. 18, 19. [8] 1 Kings xviii. 21.

PART
II.

aloud, "O Baal, hear us! and they cut themselves with knives and lancets after their manner, till the blood gushed out upon them." But in vain. "There was neither voice, nor any to answer, nor any that regarded." Thus they continued until the time of the evening sacrifice. Then Elijah repaired the *altar of Jehovah, which was broken down*, placing twelve stones, according to the number of the tribes of the sons of Jacob. A trench was dug round it, the wood arranged, the sacrifice upon it, and all was ready for the great decision; but, to make the trial doubly convincing, barrel after barrel of water was poured on, until it ran round about the altar and filled the trench. Then comes the solemn invocation: "Lord God of Abraham, Isaac, and of Israel, let it be known this day that thou art God in Israel, and that I thy servant have *done all these things at thy word*. Then the fire of the Lord fell, and consumed the burnt sacrifice, and the wood, and the stones, and the dust, and licked up the water that was in the trench." The whole multitude fell on their faces, crying out, "Jehovah, he is the God! Jehovah, he is the God!" And

Slaughter of Baal's prophets.

Elijah said to the people, "Take the prophets of Baal; let not one of them escape." They did so, and brought them down to the brook Kishon, and slew them there, near the base of that high Tell Kŭssîs which you see in the mouth of the valley. Then Elijah said to Ahab, "Get thee up, eat and drink, for there is a sound of abundance of rain." Elijah himself returned to the top of Carmel, cast himself upon the ground, put his face between his knees, and prayed—prayed earnestly for the rain; but it came not until his servant had gone up to the top and looked out on the Mediterranean seven times. Then the little cloud, as large as a man's hand, was seen to rise out of the sea, and Elijah sent word to the king, "Prepare thy chariot, and get thee down, that

The rain.

the rain stop thee not. In the meanwhile the heaven was black with clouds and wind, and there was a great rain." Thus the long drought of three years and a half was brought to a close. But the work of the prophet on this most eventful day was not yet ended. "Ahab rode and went home to Jezreel; and the hand of the Lord was on Elijah; and he girded up his loins and ran before Ahab to the entrance of Jezreel." This is the last, most strange, and most unexpected act of this great drama; and perhaps there is no one day's work in the whole history of man more wonderful than this.

El Man-sûrah.

Have you any confidence in the tradition which fixes the site of these scenes at the place called El Mŭkhrakah, near the ruined village of El Man-sûrah?

I have, and for many reasons. From the very nature of the case, it is nearly incredible that such a site should have been lost or forgotten. The narrative itself locates the scene on Carmel, and, by necessary implication, on the south-eastern end of it, looking off toward Jezreel. Within these narrow limits there is not much room for uncertainty or mistake. Again, it is clear from the 30th[1] verse that the place was sacred to the worship of Jehovah

---

[1] 1 Kings xviii. 30.

before the days of Elijah. There had been an altar there, which some one, most likely Jezebel, had caused to be thrown down; and after these stupendous miracles, it is not to be believed that the scene of them would be forgotten. They took place before all the people; and not in some far-off desert, difficult of access and rarely visited, but in the most conspicuous portion of a densely inhabited country, and one which has never ceased to be inhabited from that day to this. Accordingly, I believe it can be proved that the tradition of this site has never died out of the country. I have little doubt that this was the spot of the oracle on Carmel mentioned by Tacitus in his history of Vespasian, p. 410. His description is very remarkable: "Between Syria and Judæa stands a mountain known by the name of Mount Carmel, on the top of which *a god* is worshipped under no other title than that of the place, and, according to the *ancient* usage, *without a temple*, or *even a statue*. An altar is erected in the *open air*, and there adoration is made to the presiding deity. On *this spot* Vespasian offered a sacrifice," etc., etc. Let us carefully consider this bit of history.

Notice by Tacitus.

Vespasian at El Mûkhra-kah.

1. As to the precise place. The historian tells us that after their sacrifice Vespasian went to Cæsarea. Now I have already given my reasons for believing that the great Roman road down the coast from the north passes round the south-eastern end of Carmel. This conclusion I had reached long before I thought of its bearing on the point before us. But whether it did or not, the road from the interior did certainly follow this route to Cæsarea, and Vespasian marched along it. *This would bring him directly beneath this Mûkhrakah.*

Identified with scene of Elijah's contest.

2. The place is simply designated as "*the spot.*" There was no temple, no image—only an altar in the open air; and this was according to the *ancient custom* of the place. All this is precisely what we should expect at the seat of Elijah's wonderful miracle, and in striking agreement with what we now actually find there. There is no temple, and no evidence that there ever was one. There is only a "spot" on a natural platform of naked rock, surrounded by a low wall, which, from appearance, may have been there in the days of Elijah, or even before. Within this uncovered enclosure is the *sacred spot*, without a mark,—without a title, as Tacitus has it.

3. It is mentioned by pilgrims in subsequent ages, briefly, according to their custom, yet in such a way as to leave no doubt that the site was still kept in remembrance. One of the "*stations*" of ancient pilgrimage derived its name from it.

4. It is still well known and reverenced by all the inhabitants of this neighbourhood, Jews, Christians, Moslems, Druses, and Bedawîn, and *as the site of these miracles of Elijah*. My guide to it, a Druse, approached it with great reverence, and even awe; and this present veneration of all sects tallies admirably with the history of Tacitus. It was then in the hands of heathen priests or of corrupt Samaritans, but was so celebrated that pilgrims and worshippers of all nations resorted to it. This is natural, and in agreement with even the

present customs of this country. Very many shrines of the Moslems, and other races, owe all their sanctity to events recorded only in Biblical history. In this particular case it is highly probable that those mingled people who were transported hither from Assyria, "who feared the Lord and served Baal," would immediately appropriate to the uses of their superstitions this most celebrated "spot." Their descendants may have held possession of it when Vespasian passed this way, and the fame of its oracle induced even him, the master of the Roman world, to consult it.

5. The name Mŭkhrakah, signifying the place that was *burned*, or the place of *burning*, is so far confirmatory of the tradition. Such native and significant names do not fasten upon any spot without an adequate reason, and there is, in almost every case, some foundation in truth for them. In this instance it is the very name we should expect, and is applied to the spot most likely of all to be the true one.

6. Lastly, there is no other place with opposing claims. It has no rival. This is remarkable in a country where there are so many conflicting traditions in regard to almost every celebrated site. But not only is there nothing to contradict its claims or disturb its title, but the closest scrutiny into the history, even to the most minute incidents and implications, will corroborate and confirm them. Why, therefore, should there be a doubt about the matter? I confess, with hearty good-will, that I am troubled with none.

Mr. Van de Velde, who visited this place in company with Dr. Kalley, was the first in our day, so far as I know, who has published a description of the Mŭkhrakah, and his account is sufficiently accurate. I cannot agree with him, however, that the water poured upon the sacrifice was procured from the fountain he mentions. That fountain was nearly dry when I saw it, nor do I think it could hold out through the dry season even of one ordinary summer. How, then, could it last through three years and a half of total absence of rain? Nor are there any marks of antiquity about it. The water was obtained, as I suppose, from those permanent sources of the Kishon at the base of Carmel which I have before mentioned. It is even doubtful whether any of these, except the great one of Saadîeh, could stand such a protracted drought; and the distance even to that is not so great as to create any difficulty. Perhaps there might have been water in the marshes about Tell Thora, east of Tell Kŭssîs. The path from the place of sacrifice brought me to the Kishon at this great tell; and, from the nature of the mountain, the priests must have been brought down the same track. They were, therefore, in all probability, actually put to death near it; and, naturally enough, the act would fasten its name to the tell as the most conspicuous permanent object in the neighbourhood. If Elijah returned to the place of sacrifice after the slaughter of the priests, his servants would have to go but a short distance to obtain an extensive view of the sea, both towards Cæsarea and also over the plain of Acre to the north-west. I suppose that both Elijah and Ahab did return to the Mŭkhrakah—Ahab to partake of the feast prepared and spread some-

where near at hand, which always formed part of these sacrifices, and Elijah CHAPTER
to pray for rain. This is implied by the words of the prophet to the king— XXXI.
" Get *thee up*, eat and drink ;" and again, "Get *thee down*, that the rain stop
thee not."

The best way to reach the Mŭkhrakah is to go from Haifa, along the base Way to
of Carmel, past Tell Harothîeh, to Tell Kŭssîs, and then ascend the moun- Mŭkh-
tain by some ruins on a bold swell of Carmel, which my guide said bore the rakah.
name also of El Mansûrah, the same as on the south-eastern end of the mountain. But without a guide it is next to impossible to find the spot, so dense
is the jungle of thorn-bushes on that part of Carmel. I once undertook to
reach it from the south-west, got lost, and finally had to procure a guide from
Idjzîm, and then scramble across frightful gorges and up steep precipices, to
the no small danger and fatigue of both horse and rider.

How large a portion of these wonderful actions are we to suppose took place
on the day of the sacrifice ?

The whole of them after the people assembled to the return of the king to
Jezreel.

This reminds me of the feat performed by the prophet at the winding up of
this wonderful drama : "The hand of the Lord was upon Elijah, and he girded
up his loins, and ran before Ahab to the entrance of Jezreel." This has always
appeared to me most extraordinary conduct for a man of his age, character,
and office.

And yet, when rightly understood, it was beautiful, and full of important Elijah
instruction. Elijah, as God's minister, had overwhelmed the king with shame running
and confusion in the presence of his subjects. The natural tendency of this Ahab.
would be to lower him in their eyes, and lessen their respect for his authority.
It was not the intention, however, to weaken the government nor to encourage
rebellion. The prophet was therefore divinely directed to give a testimony of
respect and honour to the king as public and striking as from necessity had
been the opposition and rebuke to his idolatry. The mode of doing honour to
Ahab by running before his chariot was in accordance with the customs of the
East, even to this day. I was reminded of this incident more than twenty
years ago at Jaffa, when Mohammed Aly came to that city with a large army to
quell the rebellion of Palestine. The camp was on the sand hills south of the
city, while Mohammed Aly stopped inside the walls. The officers were constantly going and coming, preceded by runners, who always kept just ahead of
the horses, no matter how furiously they were ridden ; and, in order to run
with the greater ease, they not only "girded their loins" very tightly, but also
tucked up their loose garments under the girdle, lest they should be incom-
moded by them. Thus, no doubt, did Elijah. The distance from the base of
Carmel across the plain to Jezreel is not less than twelve miles ; and the race
was probably accomplished in two hours, in the face of a tremendous storm of
rain and wind. It was necessary that the "hand of the Lord should be upon"
the prophet, or he would not have been able to achieve it.

PART
II.

Meeting
of Elijah
and Ahab.

It is easy to fancy the place of meeting between Elijah and the angry king of Israel. The prophet was returning from Sarepta along the common highway which led up this wady of Kishon to Megiddo, and had reached that immediate neighbourhood where the permanent fountains of the river begin. There he found Obadiah, with part of the " beasts," seeking grass to keep them alive. It is evident that Ahab himself was not far off. Probably he had gone out on that marshy part of the plain near Tell Thora, hoping also to meet with grass. The only other part of this region where grass could be sought at the end of such a drought would be down the Wady Jezreel, east of the city, around the great fountain now called 'Ain Jalûd. But the narrative does not countenance the idea that Ahab was at such a distance from Carmel. The place of meeting was therefore at the south-east end of this mountain, not far from Tell Kŭssîs.

Extent
of the
drought.

Are we to suppose that the *drought* extended over all this country ?

I think not. Probably only over the kingdom of Israel, on whose account it was sent. It, however, involved the plain of Sarepta, but that lies within the proper territorial limits of Israel. In order to understand how it was possible to keep any part of this kingdom from being absolutely depopulated, we may remember, that although all the crops fail even when there is a drought of only a few months in spring, and that in a single dry summer all the ordinary fountains cease, yet there are others, such as 'Ain Jalûd, in the valley of Jezreel, and some of the sources of the Kishon at the base of Carmel, which have never been known to dry up entirely. Moreover, there is no reason to suppose that the drought extended to Hermon and Lebanon, and hence the great fountains of the Jordan would keep the lakes and the river full and strong, and water could be brought from these sources of supply on camels and mules, and by other means of transportation. It is certain, too, that a portion of the people would remove to the vicinity of these supplies, and to more distant neighbourhoods. As to provisions, the Mediterranean was on their western border, and corn from Egypt could be brought in any quantity, as is still done in seasons of scarcity. By these and other means a remnant would be preserved. But we are not to lessen the calamity too much in our account of these resources. The wandering of the king in search of grass ; his angry salutation to the prophet ; the dying destitution of the widow at Sarepta,—all show the fearful extent and severity of the famine. And now we are about to leave this interesting region for one almost a desert.

It may be desert, but it is very green and inviting ; and what a beautiful brook comes babbling down the wady !

Wady
Kusab.

If it derived its name, *Kŭsab*, from the abundance of *cane* on its banks, they seem all to have disappeared ; but here are splendid oleanders in their place, and I see that the guide has halted for our noonday rest and lunch under a pyramid of these flowery bushes. We shall not be detained long, I daresay, in this solitary place. Hasseîn is evidently uneasy, and looks suspiciously at those horsemen coming down the wady. They are acquaintances,

MOUNT CARMEL.

however, I perceive ; and, while they discuss Arab politics, we will discuss CHAPTER bread and cheese, chicken and ham. XXXI.

As I expected. These men advise us to be moving, and to keep close together until we reach the next village, after which there is no danger ; and so we are off. It is well we improved the time, or we might have had a long ride on an empty stomach.

These hills are entirely naked, and mostly barren, or, rather, uncultivated, for I see nothing to prevent their being planted with orchards and vineyards.

Nothing but insecurity, and the ferocity of the people in this region. As we advance, you perceive that the wady splits into many branches. We take this one on the west, and our track opens on to beautiful views of Carmel in the north. That village about three miles to the west of us is called Um Ezzêinat, and the one south of it Rehanîeh. The name of the district is Belad er Rohah, and it includes the south-eastern border of Carmel down to Cæsarea. As we are taking leave of Carmel, let us while away the time spent in climbing these tedious hills with a few facts and remarks in regard to that celébrated mountain. It is steep and lofty only at the north-west corner, and Mount on that face which overlooks the plains of Acre and Esdraelon. The ascent Carmel. is comparatively easy from the sea, and it sinks down gradually to the south into the wooded hills of Samaria and the rich plain of Cæsarea. There are, however, deep ravines, in some of which I became entangled on my way from Tantûra to the Mŭkhrakah, and had no small trouble to extricate myself from their perplexing sinuosities and abrupt precipices. There is no special " excellency " in Carmel at present, whatever may be said of Sharon.[1] Its name, *Kerm el*, signifies " vineyard of God ;" and we read that Uzziah, who loved husbandry, had vine-dressers in Carmel.[2] These vineyards have all disappeared, and, in fact, so have the *forests,* which were celebrated in ancient song. It is Scripture a glorious mountain, however—one to swear by, according to Jeremiah : " As I allusions. live, saith the King, whose name is the Lord of hosts, Surely as Tabor is Jeremiah among the mountains, and *as Carmel by the sea,* so shall he come."[3] Amos Amos. lets us know that in his day the top of it was a famous place to hide in ; nor has it changed its character in this respect : " Though they dig into hell, thence shall my hand take them ; though they climb up to heaven, thence will I bring them down ; and though they hide themselves in the top of Carmel, I will search and take them out thence."[4] My experience would not have prompted me to place the " top of Carmel" third in such a series of hiding-places, but yet I can fully appreciate the comparison. Ascending it from the south, we followed a wild gorge, through which my guide thought we could get up, and therefore led us on into the most frightful chasms, overhung by trees, bushes, and dark creepers, until it became absolutely impracticable, and we were obliged to find our way back again. And even after we reached the summit, it was so rough and broken, and the thorn-bushes so thick-set and

[1] Isa. xxxv. 2.   [2] 2 Chron. xxvi. 10.   [3] Jer. xlvi. 18.   [4] Amos ix. 2, 3.

PART
II.

Micah.

sharp, that our clothes were torn and our hands and faces severely lacerated; nor could I see my guide ten steps ahead of me. It was a noble pasture-field, however, and in reference to this characteristic Micah utters this sweet prayer: "Feed thy people with thy rod, the flock of thy heritage, which dwell solitarily in the wood in the midst of Carmel."[1] From these and other hints we may believe that Carmel was not very thickly inhabited. There are now some ten or eleven small villages on and around it, occupied by Moslems and Druses; and, besides these, I have the names of eight ruins, none of which, however, are large or historical. Carmel was a habitation of shepherds,[2] and it is implied that its pastures were not liable to wither. This may in part be occasioned by the heavy dews which its great elevation, so near the sea, causes to distil nightly upon its thirsty head. I found it quite green and flowery in midsummer. Our road now begins to descend toward the south-west, and the village to which we are coming is called Dalia er Rohah, to distinguish it from another of the same name on the top of Carmel, settled by Druses from Lebanon.

Deceitful
brooks.

This is a singular brook which we are following down the wady. Back yonder I thought of watering my horse, but, supposing the stream would become larger, I omitted it, and here it has vanished altogether, like one of Job's[3] deceitful friends—I mean brooks.

The phenomena of streams in this country aptly illustrate the character of his false friends. In winter, when there is no need of them, they are full, and strong, and loud in their bustling professions and promises; but in the heat of summer, when they are wanted, they disappoint your hope. You think your fields will be irrigated, and yourself and your flocks refreshed by them, when, lo! they deal deceitfully and pass away. Nearly all the streams of this country, "what time they wax warm," thus vanish, go to nothing, and perish.

Like Job's
friends.

Such were Job's friends. There is another illustration equally pertinent. You meet a clear, sparkling brook, and, so long as you follow it among the cool mountains, it holds cheerful converse with you by its merry gambols over the rocks; but as soon as you reach the plain, "where it is hot," it begins to dwindle, grow sad and discouraged, and finally fails altogether. Those which suggested the comparison of Job probably flowed down from the high lands of Gilead and Bashan, and came to nothing in the neighbouring desert; for it is added that the "troops of Teman looked, the companies of Sheba waited for them, and were confounded because they had hoped." It was on those high mountains only that Job could become familiar with the winter phenomena, where the streams are "blackish by reason of the ice;" for not only are Lebanon and Hermon covered with snow in winter, and the brooks there frozen, but the same is true also of the higher parts of the Hauran, and of the mountains to the south of it, where Job is supposed to have resided. We shall follow this Wady Dalia, called also Shukkah, for an hour at least; and,

---

[1] Micah vii. 14.   [2] Amos i. 2.   [3] Job vi. 15-19.

owing to some peculiarity in the strata, the water repeatedly sinks away and CHAPTER
then re-appears lower down. The pastures on either side are extremely rich ; XXXI.
and, when I passed along it in February, it was all glowing and blushing with
an infinite number and variety of flowers, sending up incense to the skies, and
offering their honeyed cups to millions of bees. I saw here a flower altogether
new to me. The stem resembles a strong rank pea; but the flowers hang in
pendent clusters like hops. The upper part is a light bronze colour, dashed
with purple; the rest, pure white. I could get no name for it.

We now leave this Wady Dalia, and go over the hill southward for half an Sindiany.
hour to Sŭbbarîn, near the head of another valley, which bears the name of
Sindiany, from a village of that name further down toward Cæsarea. Perhaps
both wady and village are so called from the *oak* woods with which the whole
country is clothed. I shall not soon forget the ride on that lovely evening of
February when I first passed this way. The setting sun glowed and trembled
among the tree-tops, and, streaming down aslope, filled the valley with transparent gold and living emerald full up to the brim and running over. It
seemed like fairy-land, and I no longer questioned the unequalled charms of
Cæsarea and her surroundings. From our present position we can gaze
through this glorious vista of oak glades, and along many a solemn aisle, leading every way far into the deep forests. I was taken by surprise, having
anticipated nothing but a barren desert, when I met with rural beauty un-
surpassed by anything in this country. The scene now is changed : the fields
are white for the harvest, the flowers have faded and fallen, and the grass is
sear and dead. But the same round hills are here, and the grand old oaks,
with their robes of fadeless green. It never can be less than lovely while
they remain. But our guide beckons us onward, and with reason, for there
is yet another hour to Sindiany ; and this neighbourhood has a villanous
reputation.

> "Every prospect pleases,
> And only man is vile."

However, my experience enables me to trust the people of Sindiany ; and
there is a charming camp-ground just north of the village. Take notice of
this fountain of Sŭbbarîn. We shall meet it to-morrow where one would
least expect it.

CHAPTER XXXII.

SINDIANY—CÆSAREA.

Oaks —Wood of Ephraim.
Road to Cæsarea.
Remarkable kŭsr.
Aqueduct.
Cæsarea—History.
Remains.

The Zerka, or Crocodile River.
Crocodiles.
Coast from Haifa to Cæsarea.
Athleet.
Tantûra.
The Mufjûr.

April 2d.

Oaks.

I HAVE had a delightful ramble this morning in these grand old forests, and now understand perfectly how Absalom could be caught by the thick branches of an oak. The strong arms of these trees spread out so near the ground that one cannot walk erect beneath them ; and on a frightened mule, such a head of hair as that vain and wicked son "polled every year" would certainly become inextricably entangled.

Wood of
Ephraim.

No doubt ; and it is interesting to know that the region where that battle was fought is still covered with such forests—that "wood of Ephraim," with thick oaks, and tangled bushes, and thorny creepers growing over rugged rocks, and ruinous precipices, down which the rebel army plunged in wild dismay, horses and men crushing each other to death in remediless ruin. Thus 20,000 men perished in that fatal wood, which "devoured more people that day than the sword devoured." [1]

Heaps of
stones.

The great heap of stones over the pit into which Absalom was thrown was not raised in honour of the king's son, but in detestation of the traitor's enormous crime ; and you will find miniature heaps of the same kind and significance all over the country. It is a wide-spread custom for each one as he passes the spot where any notorious murderer has been buried, to cast a stone upon it. I have often seen this done, and, yielding to the popular indignation, have thrown my stone with the rest. I am reminded of all this by the conduct of my guide, who has actually dismounted to *spit* upon this heap, and add his pebble to the growing pile. He says the wretch who lies buried there was a notorious robber who infested this road, and committed many cruel murders ; and he is using the incident to enforce his admonitions upon us to keep together in this part of our ride ; which we will of course conform to as long as it suits our purpose.

Morning
in mist.

Yesterday I thought your description of this valley extravagant, but withdraw the criticism this morning. When the early light began to reveal the character of the scene around me, the country from north to south was buried under a dense, low-lying fog, which left the many-shaped hill-tops peering

[1] 2 Sam. xviii. 7, 8.

above it like green islets in the bosom of a placid lake. I was breathless with CHAPTER
surprise and admiration. When the sun arose, this grey, silvery sea, as if XXXII.
startled by some invisible spirit, became agitated in an extraordinary manner,
and vast pyramids of shining vapour burst up from beneath, swelling higher
and higher among the oaks, until it escaped through their thick boughs, and
vanished away in the clear vault of heaven. All this commotion and gorgeous
display, I found, was owing to a brisk breeze which came up the valley from
the sea at Cæsarea. Acting from below, and itself turned about by every bend
and swell of the hills, it swayed and twisted the yielding waves of vapour
according to its own eccentric will.

There was something of the kind in February last, and it is indeed singu- Fogs com-
larly beautiful. Such fogs, however, are quite common on the great plains mon in
along the coast, as we shall see in the land of the Philistines. But let us the plains.
follow our company down the valley, for we have a busy day, with just enough
of danger to make it exciting. That village on our left is called Khŭbbaizy, the
Arabic name for the *malva*, the Hebrew nearly for the *rose;* and both malvas
and wild roses adorn this sweet vale. Many other hamlets repose in the bosom
of these glorious woods, but we cannot load our memories with their obscure
and ignoble names. Did you observe that the dew rolled off our tent this
morning like rain? And now the early sunbeams " sow the earth with pearls
and diamonds," as Milton's muse describes these pendent drops that glitter
and sparkle from every leaf in the forest and blade in the field.

If I remember correctly, this place on our right bears the ominous name of Road to
'Ain Maiety (Dead Fountain); and the tell east of it is *sit Leîla*,—a name more Cæsarea.
frequently heard in Arab song than any other. We now turn westward toward
Cæsarea, leaving the main road, which keeps on southward through the plain
of Sharon to Lydd and Ramleh. The whole of this region is as fertile as
beautiful ; but most of it is uncultivated, and all infested with robbers. When Robbers.
at Sindiany last year, I wanted to send my baggage directly across to Tantûra,
while I came round this way to Cæsarea, and I had to hire a guard sufficiently
large not merely to protect my muleteers in going, but also the men themselves in returning. The people could not then venture from village to village
but in companies and well armed. It is not so bad now, and we shall send
our tents on to the mills of Zerka, three miles north of Cæsarea, where alone we
can pass the night in safety. Left to ourselves for the day, with our faithful
guard to watch for us, we will ramble about *ad libitum* among these remains
of antiquity.

That large building some two miles to the north-west of us is the kŭsr we
heard so much about from our friends at Sindiany; and to reach it we must
pick our way through these bushes and tall reeds, over a country not a little
infested with bottomless mud. Ignorant of these treacherous bogs, on my first Bogs.
visit I struck directly across the plain for the kŭsr, and was soon floundering
in unsubstantial mire up to the belly of my horse, and was glad to get safely
out again on the same side by which I entered. Here we are at one of these

PART
II.

brooks, sluggish and black as ink, but the bottom is not very *distant,* and we can easily pass over.

Where does this stream come from? There was no water in the wady down which we have travelled this morning.

It is the joint contribution of many springs which rise out of this spongy plain in all directions, and we shall soon see more of them. Between this and the kŭsr are immense fountains, now called Miamās, the water of which was collected in a large pool, and then carried by an aqueduct to Cæsarea. These works are of course broken, and we must pass round them on the north in order to find a practicable path to the kŭsr.

Remark-
able kŭsr.

There seem to have been many substantial buildings hereabout; and, indeed, we are floundering over the grass-covered ruins of a considerable city. The kŭsr itself must have been an immense affair, and in a style of architecture quite peculiar.

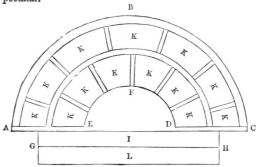

A B C D E F A, Cavea.
F D, Pulpitum.
G H, Scene.
I, Proscenium.

K, K, K, Cunei separated scalæ.
F E D F, Orchestra.
L, Postscenium.

The vomitories are beneath the cavea.

PLAN OF THEATRE.

A theatre.

It was doubtless one of Cæsarea's theatres, and the plan of a *Roman* theatre, which I brought along for the purpose, will enable you to comprehend at once the details of the edifice. It is semicircular, and the *chord* is a hundred and sixty-six feet. The seats are all gone, and the *cavea* much changed, but the vomitories and vaults beneath are in good preservation, and are now used for stables and granaries by the peasants. This tower on the south-eastern corner, and these huts inside, are comparatively modern, and were erected probably when the building was turned into a Moslem castle. The prospect over the wooded hills of Samaria and the far-spreading plain of Sharon is very beautiful, and hither flocked the laughter-loving Greeks of Cæsarea to enjoy the excitement of theatrical games and the pleasures of the open country at the

same time. The topography of the place is decidedly interesting. Directly CHAPTER
XXXII.
north of the kŭsr terminate the last spurs of Carmel in a bold promontory
called Khŭshm en Nazûr. South of it is the great marsh Ez Zoar, fading
out into the sandy downs and brushy slopes of the Upper Sharon. The ruined
villages of Em el 'Alŭk and Muallŭkah (both names suggestive of the "horse-
leech," which greatly abounds in this marsh of Zoar) appear on the northern
ridge; and Bureikîeh, three miles distant in the same direction, is inhabited
by the peasants who cultivate the land around these fountains of Miamās.
The fountain near Sŭbbarîn, which I pointed out to you yesterday, was in
former times led down by Bureikîeh to the kŭsr, where it was associated with
the stream from Miamās, and the two united were carried along the perpendicular base of Mount Khŭshm, across the swamp of Zoar, to the shore, and
thence southward to the city. This was a remarkable work, and most of it is
still quite perfect. Our road is now upon, or rather, *within* this aqueduct
until we get over the various brooks which, passing beneath it, are lost in the
general marsh.

This is, indeed, a narrow and somewhat *nervous* pathway, especially as one
sees on either side of him bogs of bottomless mud.

There is some danger, no doubt, but with nerves sufficiently steady we An aque-
might follow on the top of this *double* aqueduct quite to the western side of duct.
the marsh; for, if I remember aright, there is not a broken arch in the entire
line. I, however, have no fancy for such *high* ways, and the ground south of
it is here sufficiently solid to justify the attempt to reach the sandy plain beyond. Safely through! Look back now at the long file of arches on columns
which span the entire width of the Zoar. But the difficulties of our position
are not yet ended. Here is a very suspicious-looking stream *soaking* its way
through tall reeds and flags, and beyond it is a second and a third, all pouring
their blackish water into the marsh. The largest of these brooks, called
Shukeîŭk and Shŭkkauk, is said to rise in Wady Sŭfsâfy, about two hours to
the south-east. All these streams run northward into the swamp, and not
to the sea, in consequence of that low rocky ridge which extends parallel to
the coast and about half a mile from it. This formation is the same fossili-
ferous *sandy* limestone as that out of which nearly all the cities on the sea-
board are built; and it has been hewn and cut up by quarriers in the most
extraordinary manner; indeed the cuttings and quarrying are more extensive
than those of any other city on this coast. I once spent several hours searching among them for inscriptions, but found none; and the only important
discovery was, that such enormous quarryings were never made by the short-
lived city of Cæsarea, and that this was merely the Roman name for a more
ancient city. I had read this before, but I was convinced that the original
name could not have been *Strato's Tower*, for that was Latin, and these quar- An an-
ries were opened long before they ever appeared in Syria. This primitive cient city.
city, I suppose, was the frontier town in this direction of the Phœnicians, and I
leave to the lovers of antiquarian research the discovery of its name and history.

And there lie the ruins of all your three cities together, directly in front of us. What could have induced Herod to select this place for a harbour, as it is an open coast, without projecting headland or protection of any kind ?

The rich country back of it to Samaria and Nablûs probably furnishes the explanation. It is also in the centre of a long *reach* of coast entirely destitute of harbours, and this offers another reason ; and, moreover, it is not quite true that there is no natural protection to serve as the basis for an artificial harbour. Several ledges of rock run out into the sea from the shore, and the king took advantage of two, between which the water was deepest, and there constructed great moles, *enclosing a space larger than the Piræus.* Josephus says so, not I. It never could have been sufficiently long to protect a single first-class Boston clipper.

Cæsarea has always been invested with a peculiar interest to my mind, not so much for its own eventful history, nor because it was the capital of Palestine, but chiefly on account of its honourable and most important connection with the Apostolic Church. It was here that the good Cornelius fasted, prayed, and gave alms, which came up before God as a memorial, until an angel of the Lord appeared, and directed him to "send unto Joppa for Simon, whose surname is Peter." There another vision revealed to that apostle the great fact "that God is no respecter of persons; but that in every nation he that feareth him, and worketh righteousness, is accepted with him ;"[1] and thereby prepared this bearer of the "keys of the kingdom of heaven" to unlock the door to the Gentile world. Here the "apostle of the circumcision" first learned that he must "not call *any man* common or unclean ;"[2] *here* the Holy Ghost was first granted to the heathen ; and *here* took place the first Gentile baptism. Certainly we Gentiles have abundant reason to cherish the memory of Cæsarea. Paul, the apostle of the Gentiles and greatest of foreign missionaries, often visited it, and was here held prisoner for two whole years. Standing in chains where some of these ruins now lie, he made his noble speeches before Felix, and Festus and Drusilla, Agrippa, and Bernice, characters somewhat famous, and most of them not a little infamous in their day. Eusebius the historian was born and lived in Cæsarea, and here Origen studied and wrote commentaries. But we need not prolong the list of her honours. They do but exaggerate her present utter desolation.

These ruins remain precisely as they were twenty-five years ago, upon my first visit. The area enclosed by the wall extends along the shore about the fourth of a mile, and is some forty rods wide from east to west. The wall was built of small but well-cut stones, was strengthened by sixteen square towers, and protected by a broad ditch; but still it could not have been a place of much strength, nor is it celebrated for any great military events. We are not to suppose that its vast population, stated as high as 200,000, was confined

[1] Acts x. 34, 35.   [2] Acts x. 28.

within these narrow limits. On the contrary, there are abundant traces of chapter suburbs scattered all over the plain, and the enclosed area was little more than XXXII. the acropolis of the city. The harbour was at the south-west corner of this citadel, and we can trace its whole extent by the existing remains. Look at Exagge- them, and then turn to Josephus,[1] and see if you can discover any resemblance. ration of Josephus. Beyond all doubt, much of that description is magniloquent Josephian hyperbole. Who can read of the *mole*, two hundred feet broad, built of stones more than fifty feet long, eighteen wide, and nine deep, without a smile? Why, the whole harbour enclosed by it is not much broader. But it is useless to

MOLE OF THE HARBOUR OF CÆSAREA.

criticise this extraordinary piece of exaggeration; I cannot refrain, however, from remarking that the historian must have forgotten that there is no appreciable *tide* at the head of the Mediterranean, when he says, "The sea itself,

Ant. xv. 9, 6.

32

PART
II.

upon the flux of the tide from without, came into the city and washed it all clean!" There is enough here, however, besides the name, to convince us that the historian is actually speaking of this place, though the exaggeration is so egregious that one seems to be walking in his sleep. It was doubtless this south-western mole which Herod named Procymatia—" wave-breaker." Where exactly the Tower of Drusus stood, I am at a loss to decide.

Remains
of Cæ-
sarea.

In one respect, these remains of the first century of our era are extremely interesting and important. They present the best criterion by which to judge *architecturally* of other ruins, and show conclusively that many of them are far more ancient. A moment's examination will also prove that Herod built with materials furnished to his hands by ruins of a city older, and, I believe, much more magnificent than his own. This immense number of granite columns built into his moles speaks of an antecedent and wealthy metropolis, with splendid temples, which had been overthrown long before Herod began his work. Nor do I believe that Strato's Tower (as the place was then called, and which he changed to Cæsarea) was the original name. That is of foreign derivation, given by the Romans, while these columns and other relics speak of Greek or Phœnician times and architects. Josephus says that Herod built a temple on this southern mole, and a splendid theatre near the harbour; and without the city, on the south side, an amphitheatre capable of holding a vast multitude of people. All have disappeared. These tall buttresses, which make the most show of any part of the present ruins, evidently belonged to a Christian church, possibly of Crusader times. Cæsarea has the misfortune to be inseparably associated with the incipient causes and first outbreaks of that dreadful war in which Jerusalem, the Temple, and the Jewish nation were destroyed. Herod, by erecting heathen temples and theatres, and placing idol statues in the city, greatly displeased the Jews, and the disputes between them and their idolatrous fellow-citizens finally became so bitter and exasperated that they rushed blindly into open revolt. One of the first acts of the bloody tragedy was the massacre of 20,000 Jews in this city by the Greeks. The whole Jewish nation then flew to arms, and ceased to fight only when they ceased to be a people.

Its for-
saken
state.

How comes it that Cæsarea has for many ages been utterly deserted? It is the only considerable city on the coast that has been thus absolutely forsaken.

Several things have conspired to work out this result. The mole being overthrown, the harbour became utterly unsafe. Not a single ship could ride securely in it. This destroyed her commerce. The aqueducts broken, there was no longer an adequate supply of water; and this gone, the surrounding country relapsed into its natural state of a barren desert, and the sand, constantly accumulating from the sea, buried up every green thing. Thus solitary in itself, it early became infested with robbers, so that no one could live here in safety; and thus it continues to this hour; nor is there much reason to hope that it will again become an important city, for it has not a single natural advantage.

But it is time to seek our tent at Towahîn ez Zerka, an hour to the north-east of us. Let us follow the line of these lofty canals—two in one—by which we shall obtain a better idea of the ancient suburbs, and likewise observe the great size of the aqueducts, which were carried along parallel to the shore for about two miles. They served as a defence against the sands of the sea, and the whole space on the east of them seems to have been occupied with buildings. We can see into the covered canals in many places; and the stories of the natives, that a man could pass inside of them on horseback from the city to the mills of Zerka, do not seem to be incredible fables. They are in such preservation that it would not cost a large sum to clear them of the sand, and again bring the water to the harbour. It is not true, however, as some travellers assert, that ships frequently put in here to obtain water from these aqueducts, for they have been broken for many centuries. Boats often call in summer to load with stones from the ruins, and much of the recent building in Jaffa and Acre is constructed out of them. I once spent a day here while my boat was thus being freighted for Jaffa; and this is the only *trade* carried on with this ancient capital of Palestine. Shepherds, who water their flocks from the well near the southern gate, visit it by day, and robbers by night lie in wait to plunder any unprotected traveller who may chance to pass,—which, however, is of rare occurrence. Comparatively few now follow this desolate coast, and none venture alone if they can in any way avoid it.

Canals.

Here are the mills; and, by the advice of the miller, I daresay our tent is pitched in a very good position for defence. There is no disguising the fact that we must pass the night surrounded by robbers, and for once it will be necessary to keep a strict guard. We have time enough before sunset to examine this extraordinary locality. It appears that the river Zerka, whose various branches we crossed in the morning, had here broken through the low, rocky ridge which runs parallel to the shore, and in some remote age this opening was shut up by this powerful wall, thus raising the water twenty-five feet high. This wall is two hundred and thirty paces long and twenty feet thick, and the road still passes along its top—the grandest mill-dam I have ever seen. The water falls directly from the top on the wheels below. There are some eight or ten mills now in motion, and many are in ruins, and at least twenty might be ranged side by side below the wall. It is this dam that causes the marsh of Zoar, the whole of which would be effectually drained by simply breaking it down, and many thousand acres of the richest land would thus be regained to cultivation.

Mills.

This Zerka is undoubtedly the Crocodile River of the ancients, and you will be surprised to hear that there are now living crocodiles in the marsh at our side: but such is the fact. These millers say they have seen them often; and the government agent, a respectable Christian, assures me that they recently killed one eighteen spans long, and as thick as his body. I suspect that, long ages ago, some Egyptians, accustomed to worship this ugly creature,

The Zerka, or Croco-dile River. Croco-diles.

PART II.

settled here, and brought their gods with them. Once here, they would not easily be exterminated; for no better place could be desired by them than this vast jungle and impracticable swamp. I was delighted, on my first visit, many years since, to find these creatures still on hand to confirm the assertions of Greek and Roman geographers. The historians of the Crusades speak of this marsh, which they call a lake, and also say that there were crocodiles in it in their day. If the locality would admit, I should identify this Zerka with the Shihor-libnath of Joshua xix. 26, for Shihor is one of the names of the Nile, the very home of the crocodile; but the river in question was given to Ashur, and is probably the Naaman (the Belus of ancient geographers), and the marshes at its source are as suitable for this ugly beast as these of Zoar.

Coast from Haifa to Cæsarea.

By taking the interior route on the east and south of Carmel, we have missed a long stretch of the coast. Is there anything of interest on the shore from Haifa to Cæsarea?

The best answer is to pass it in review; and it is about as profitable, and far more pleasant to traverse this nine hours in imagination than to ride them on horseback. By way of introduction, listen to some remarks on the general character of the Syrian sea-board. From Carmel and northward there are numerous headlands, with bays on the north of them more or less deep, by which the line of the coast falls back to the east, as it were, by successive steps. Carmel itself, with the Bay of Acre, is not only the first, but one of the most striking. North of Acre is the Ladder of Tyre, which consists of three such capes,—el Musheîrifeh, en Nakûrah, and el Bŭyăd. Between Tyre and Sidon is the low headland of Sarafend, and from Sidon to Beirût are three rocky *Nakûrahs*, with the retreating coves of Rumeîleh, Neby Yûnus, and Damûr. Then comes the projecting cape Ras Beirût, with its Bay of St. George falling back to the deeper cove of Jûn. The next salient point is the Theoprosopon of the ancients, north of Bŭtrûn; beyond which, by successive steps, at Cape Enfeh and the *mina* of Tripoli, the coast enters far eastward into the plain of Akkar. With lesser indentations at Ruad and Balinas, we come to the long, low promontory of Ladakîyeh. Finally, stretching across the open sea at the so-called Bay of Antioch, we pass Ras el Khanzîr, and enter the Bay of Scandaroon. Such is the configuration of the northern half of this coast; but from Carmel southward it runs in a direct line a little west of south, in long unvaried *reaches*, far as the eye can see, and further too, past Athleet, past Tantûra, Cæsarea, Jaffa, Askelon, Gaza, and quite on round to Egypt.

Head-lands.

After this rapid survey, we will begin again at the point of Carmel. It is three hours thence to Athleet, with no important villages or ruins intervening. Athleet, however, presents the greatest historic and architectural puzzle found at the head of this sea. I cannot identify it with any ancient site whatever. Neither the Bible, nor Josephus, nor any profane historian or geographer mentions it, nor does its name appear in the old itineraries; and yet the

Athleet.

remains of antiquity at it are more numerous, more striking, and in better preservation than at any other city of Phœnicia. The exterior wall, built of great stones, and protected by a ditch, cut through the solid rock where necessary, enclosed a large quadrangular space reaching quite across the headland on which the city stood. Most of *this* wall has been carried away to build those of Acre during the long centuries of the past. The acropolis was at the extremity of the cape, cut off from the outer city by a wall prodigiously strong, whose heavy stones are bevelled after the purest Phœnician style. Large sections of it remain entire, and just as they were first put up. There is no *patch-work*, no broken columns or other fragments, as in the oldest Greek and Roman structures in Syria. It is pure, unmixed Phœnician. Just within this wall stands a portion of a gigantic building, whose character it is difficult to comprehend. It was erected on *vaults* of very great strength, and the fragment of the east wall towers up at least *eighty* feet high. There it stands in its loneliness, unbroken by a hundred earthquakes, the first object that strikes the eye of the traveller either up or down the coast. Near the top, on the interior, so high that it strains the neck to look at them, are the flying buttresses (finished off below with the heads of men and beasts) from which sprung the arches of the *great dome*. It must have been superb—sublime. Now, who erected this magnificent temple, and when? The only history we have of Athleet begins with the Crusaders, who call it Castellum Peregrinorum (Pilgrims' Castle), because they used to land there when Acre was in the hands of the Saracens. But they built none of these edifices. There are also other remarkable indications of extreme antiquity about Athleet. This low, rocky ridge on which we are encamped, and which occasions this marsh of Zoar, begins a little to the north of Athleet, and in front of the city it rises to a considerable elevation, and is there cut up in a singular manner by old quarries. Directly east of the city, a broad road was hewn through the ridge, which is still the common highway for the surrounding country, and well-worn tracks of chariot-wheels are still to be seen along this remarkable passage. Mr. Van de Velde supposes that these were for *railroad* cars, and makes some further *guesses* on the subject, which must have required a good deal of nerve to pen and publish.

Interior remains.

Now the question returns, What is Athleet, either by this or any other name? I have no answer. The Hebrew writers may have had no occasion to mention it, because that part of the coast was not in their possession. The Roman and Greek writers and travellers generally passed round on the east of Cæsarea, as I believe, and did not visit it. Strabo says, "After Acre is the Tower of Strato, having a station for ships. Between them is Mount Carmel, and *names* of cities, but nothing besides; the City of Sycamenon, Bucolon, and the City of Crocodiles." The ruins of this last town are here at the mouth of this River Zerka. This silence of Strabo with regard to both Athleet and Dor favours the idea that the Roman road passed on the east of Carmel. Sycamenon is probably Caimon. The Bible repeatedly mentions Tantûra

Mystery of Athleet

and her towns by the name of Dor; and Athleet may have been one of her "towns," though it was immensely superior to Dor. But enough about Athleet, except that her people are great villains; and so are those of Et.Tirêh, at the foot of Carmel, north-east of it. En Haud, on the brow of the mountain, may possibly mark the site of En Haddah, given to Issachar. It is nearly three hours from Athleet to Tantûra, and the two villages, Kefr Lam and Sarafend, both apparently ancient, are between them. Further inland are Yebla and 'Ain Gazzal. The name Yebla resembles Ibleam, which was assigned to Manasseh, though belonging to the lot of Issachar.

Tantûra. Tantûra merits very little attention. It is a sad and sickly hamlet of wretched huts, on a naked sea-beach, with a marshy flat between it and the base of the eastern hills. The sheikh's *palace* and the public *menzûl* for travellers are the only respectable houses. Dor never could have been a large city, for there are no remains. The artificial tell, with a fragment of the *kŭsr* standing like a column upon it, was probably the most ancient site. In front of the present village are five small islets, by the aid of which an artificial harbour could easily be constructed, the entrance to which would be by the inlet at the foot of the kŭsr; and should "Dor and her towns" ever rise again into wealth and importance, such a harbour will assuredly be made.

The Muf-jûr. Twenty minutes south of Tantûra, a considerable stream, called Mufjûr, enters the sea. It descends from Belad er Roha, and is probably the same as Wady Dalia. The beach is thickly strewn with pretty shells, and the sand is solid enough to make the ride along the rippling surf delightful. It is two hours to the mouth of the River Zerka, where are the remains of the old City of Crocodiles; and thus we have reached our camp-ground, and the hour when wearied travellers seek repose.

PART III.—THE SEA-COAST PLAINS—SHARON AND PHILISTIA.

[The third section of the tour may now be said to commence: The district which we are now to travel is the largest plain of Palestine, embracing the celebrated Sharon on the north, and Philistia on the south. Sharon was more celebrated in poetry than in history; and the number of remarkable places in it is but small. The ancient and celebrated sea-port of Joppa may be said to separate Sharon from Philistia. After visiting the ruins of several of the well-known cities of the Philistines, we climb the mountains of Judah, and pass into the southern district of the land.—ED.]

CHAPTER XXXIII.

CÆSAREA TO JAFFA.

Reminiscences of Cæsarea.	Sand downs—Brooks—Pine forests.
Water-spout—Flying fish.	Nahr Falej—Palsy River.
Abû Zabûra—River Kanah?	Plain of Sharon—Roses—Sea-shells.
Sparrows—Melons—Granaries—Ants.	Jaffa.

April 3d.

THE hurry and bustle of our early start have crowded out our usual morning *Morning.* worship. Let us therefore turn aside and take a lesson from the works and ways of nature, while the grey dawn grows into the full broad day. This is the season and this the hour when poets love to sing,—

> " Sweet is the breath of morn, her rising sweet,
> With charm of earliest birds."

The lark is already on high, saluting the first ray that gilds the dappled east with his cheerful matin. All nature hears the call, shakes off dull sleep, and hastens to join the general welcome to the coming king of day; and yonder he comes, over the head of Carmel, " rejoicing as a strong man to run a race." See ! even the vegetable kingdom shares the universal joy. Notice these flowers all around us, how they turn smiling to his ardent gaze, *bend forward* in seeming reverence, *throw open their pretty cups*, and cast abroad *their sweetest perfume*. This silent adoration of ten thousand thousand flowers is most beautiful and impressive, and nowhere else beheld in higher perfection than among the lilies and roses of this sacred plain of Sharon.

Now this " powerful king of day " is but the faint shadow of his Maker—the Sun of Righteousness ; and when He rises " with healing in his wings," [1]

---

[1] Mal. iv. 2.

PART
III.

may we be ever ready to meet him with analogous welcome and superior joy. Let us even now listen to the many voices around us calling to prayer. " O come, let us worship and bow down ; let us kneel before the Lord our maker ; for he is our God, and we are the people of his pasture, and the sheep of his hand."[1]

We have done well to commence our ride with the dawn, for it is the longest, and will be the most fatiguing which we have yet accomplished. " He who goes not to bed will be early up," says an Oriental proverb; and so it has been with me. I can never sleep in such a place as this, and therefore merely wrapped my cloak about me and sat down patiently to watch our boastful guard; for I never yet found them faithful through a whole night. Talking, smoking, and joking, they managed to stave off sleep until one o'clock, and then all except Hammûd gave up the effort. He held on for nearly another hour, humming to himself more and more drowsily, till finally his head subsided on his chest, and his song into a gurgling snore. Poor fellow ! let him sleep and dream of home.

Midnight.

Lifting his gun quietly from his knee, I walked out on this ancient causeway, and set myself to count the stars, and listen to the sounds that startle the dull ear of night. I deemed myself familiar with every noise and note that mark the transit of those leaden hours : the surf's low murmur dying out on the shore—the sobbing of the winds among the trees and rocks—the monotonous response of the night-hawk to his mate—the muffled flutter of the circling bat—the howl of the wolf—the jackal's wail—the bark of the fox—and the ban-dog's cross bay from the distant fold. To these and such as these I have listened with the listening stars a thousand times, and again last night. But there was something additional to render my solitary watch upon this old dam strange, and doubtful, and expectant. Above the clattering of mill-stones and the rush of water-wheels there came, every now and then, a loud splash and hollow roar never heard by me before. Did they come from the slimy crocodiles which crawl through this hideous swamp in search of prey ? The idea made me nervous. Ere long, however, my musings wandered off to more interesting themes. I recalled the day and night I spent among Cæsarea's broken walls and prostrate columns more than twenty years ago. Fresh from scenes of war, and earthquake, and sickness, and death in Jerusalem, I then felt a mysterious sympathy with these sad and forsaken ruins. Cæsarea is, in some respects, the most interesting site on the earth to the missionary. Here the Holy Ghost was first poured out upon Gentiles as upon the Jews, and thus the middle wall of partition broken down. From this spot the glad tidings set forth to run among the nations north, and south, and east, and west— west, far west—and, after eighteen centuries, from that New World, westward, far beyond the dream of prophet or apostle, returns the herald of that gospel to mingle his tears with the dust and ashes of this cradle of the Gentile Church.

Interest of
Cæsarea
to the mis-
sionary.

---

[1] Ps. xcv. 6, 7.

How wonderful the ways of God! In this place the greatest missionary that ever lived was shut up in prison two whole years, and at a most critical time in the history of the Church, when his presence and preaching seemed indispensable. One cannot help feeling that Paul made a mistake when he came here from Acre *en route* to Jerusalem. He should have listened to Philip's four prophetic daughters, and to Agabus, who took Paul's girdle and bound his own hands and feet, and said, "Thus saith the Holy Ghost, So shall the Jews at Jerusalem bind the man that owneth this girdle."[1] But the lion-hearted apostle could not be persuaded. "What mean ye," saith he, "to weep and to break my heart? for I am ready not only to be bound, but to *die* at Jerusalem for the name of the Lord Jesus." And speedily and right nobly did he redeem his pledge.

Having escaped terrific mobs and horrible conspiracies at Jerusalem, he was brought back to this place in chains, and here held prisoner by Felix, that corrupt and tyrannical governor. How often he must have dragged his chain to the top of the castle during those two long years, and gazed on the green hills of Palestine, and out upon the blue sea over which he had sailed many times on messages of mercy to heathen nations along its distant shores. One longs to know something of the musings and occupations of that wonderful man during the tedium of those many months. But inspiration is silent, and even tradition fails us. The supposition that he superintended the writing of Luke's Gospel is a mere guess, with no historic basis.

Here we are again within Cæsarea's prostrate walls. Doubtless some of these mounds of rubbish mark the exact site of Paul's prison, and from this sandy margin of the harbour he stepped on board that ship of Adramyttium in which he sailed for Italy to prosecute his appeal before Cæsar.[2] Repeatedly have I passed over these same seas, and followed the apostle step by step in that tedious and unfortunate voyage. They evidently had a pleasant run to Sidon, where they touched the next day, and Paul was allowed to go on shore and refresh himself among his friends. The wind must have then hauled round to the west, for the ship could not pursue the direct course to Italy south of Cyprus, but ran north between the island and the Syrian coast, and then west over the Sea of Cilicia and Pamphylia; working westward in the teeth of the wind, it was a tedious and dangerous passage. But we may not follow that celebrated voyage any further at present, nor longer linger here at Cæsarea; so take your last look at these remains of the city, and harbour, and sandy suburbs, and let us hasten after our luggage, now far ahead of us.

In passing through from Cæsarea to Jaffa, we do but follow the example of ancient geographers and itineraries. They stretch their lines from the one to the other, as though there were nothing worth attention in the twelve intervening hours. Nor were they much mistaken, for there is, perhaps, no ride of so many miles in any other part of Palestine more solitary and barren

Margin notes:
CHAPTER XXXIII.

Paul.

His captivity.

Road to Jaffa.

---

[1] Acts xxi. 8–11.   [2] Acts xxvii. 2.

PART
III.

of historic interest. Strabo says, " After Strato's Tower there is a great wood, and then Joppa." The Roman road was evidently carried east of these sandy downs which lie along the shore, both to avoid them and also to find suitable places to throw their bridges over the rivers which enter the sea. Following that route, we should first pass through a dreary wood of dwarfish pines and entangled bushes, and then down the long plain of Sharon direct to Lydd, the Diospolis of the ancients. But, as this would be much longer, we shall keep to the coast, although the sand is deep and heavy.

Before taking leave of this interesting site, let us examine these traces of a city on the south of it, whose remains appear to be much older than those of Cæsarea. Those inlets along the rocky shore, I suppose, were the harbour of that primitive city which was called Strato's Tower before and at the time of Herod; but this could scarcely have been its original name. It was somewhere in this vicinity, south of the city and near the sea, that Herod built his great amphitheatre, and these half-buried foundations may have belonged to that vast edifice.

Land of the Philistines.

We have now taken leave of Phœnicia and entered the territory of the Philistines. These people came from Egypt, and we shall see, as we go south, that even the present inhabitants approach more and more closely to the Egyptian type, in physiognomy, in costume, language, manners, and customs.

A people from Egypt.

Dr. Kitto has a long and laboured article to prove that they were the "shepherd kings" expelled from Egypt. Others more competent must decide whether or not he makes good his hypothesis, but the mere supposition adds fresh interest to this people and to the country which they occupied.

What are these high *tells* ahead of us, overhanging the sea?

Cliffs of Abu Zabûr.

They are one hour from Cæsarea, and are called Abu Zabûr. The encroachment of the sea has worn them half away, but on the top of this first one are some half dozen very large columns of bluish marble, which must have formed part of a temple, or possibly of a mausoleum. The spot is still used as a burying-ground by some of the Arab tribes in this region. It commands a noble view of the sea westward, and of Strabo's " ingens sylva " in the interior. This wilderness is covered by shifting sand, which has overflowed the country, and whose presence is easily explained. The rock of the shore is a loose friable sandstone, constantly washed to pieces by the waves, and driven inward by the west winds. This holds good along the entire coast wherever loose sand encumbers the plain, but here it is unusually abundant and troublesome; and we shall have high hills of it on our left, and this soft beach to wade through for two full hours yet, therefore let us be patient, and plod steadily onward.

Water-spouts.

There is always something to amuse and instruct in this country. Look at those clouds, which hang like a heavy pall of sackcloth over the sea along the western horizon. From them, on such windy days as these, are formed *waterspouts*, and I have already noticed several incipient " spouts " lengthening downward from their lower edge. These remarkable phenomena occur most

frequently in spring, but I have also seen them in autumn. They are not CHAPTER
accompanied with much rain, and between the dark stratum above and the XXXIII.

WATER-SPOUT.

sea, the sky is clear and bright. Here and there fragments of black vapour, Water-
shaped like long funnels, are drawn down from the clouds toward the sea, and spout
are seen to be in violent agitation, whirling round on themselves as they are described.
driven along by the wind. Directly beneath them the surface of the sea is
also in commotion by a whirlwind, which travels onward in concert with the
spout above. I have often seen the two actually unite in mid air and rush
toward the mountains, writhing, and twisting, and bending like a huge serpent with its head in the clouds and its tail on the deep.

They make a loud noise, of course, and appear very frightful. " Deep Noise of
calleth unto deep at the noise of thy water-spouts; all thy waves and thy water-
billows are gone over me," said David, when his soul was cast down within meeting.
him.[1] But, though formidable in appearance, they do very little injury. I
have never heard of more than one instance in which they proved destructive
even to boats, though the sailors are extremely afraid of them. As soon as
they approach the shore they dissolve and disappear.

[1] Ps. xlii. 7.

PART
III.

That kind of water-spout which bursts on the mountains, generally in the dry months of summer, does immense mischief. In a few minutes the wadies along its track are swollen into furious rivers, which sweep away grain, olives, raisins, and every other produce of the farmer. I have frequently known them to carry off and drown flocks of sheep and goats, and even cows, horses, and their owners also.

Flying-
fish.

This is one of those days when the sea is just sufficiently disturbed to set the flying-fish in motion; and I have already seen several flocks of them frightened out of their proper element to try their glossy wings in the air. They are generally supposed to do this to escape some ravenous fish that is pursuing them; but there are no voracious dolphins in this sea, and they often start up in shoals before Arab boats. Their flight is always short, spasmodic, and painful; and when their *web-wings* become dry, they instantly collapse, and the poor little aeronaut drops into the water like a stone. I have had them repeatedly fall into my boat when attempting to sail over it.

Desolation
of the
coast.

How melancholy is this utter desolation! Not a house, not a trace of inhabitants, not even shepherds, seen everywhere else, appear to relieve the dull monotony. I wonder if it was thus when Peter came along from Joppa to Cæsarea?

The coast itself was doubtless what it is now, but the road could not have been so utterly deserted. Cæsarea was then a great capital and a grand commercial emporium, and this now solitary track was crowded with multitudes hastening to the grand centre of business, pleasure, and ambition.

Did Paul travel this route to and from Jerusalem?

I suppose not. As I said before, the Roman road, even to Joppa, went inland from Cæsarea, and no doubt it united with the great highway which came down by Sindiany, and continued along the plain southward to Lydd, Ramleh, Eleutheropolis, and onward into the desert toward the Red Sea at Akabah. A few miles further down, a branch went off to the south-east through the mountains to Jerusalem; and we know that Paul was brought down that way by the Roman soldiers, and this was the direct route which he always pursued unless turned aside by some special call. Antipatris lies between Cæsarea and Lydd; and its site, restored to its original name, Kefr Saba, is now well known.

Zabûra.

Here we come to what is called Minet Zabûr, or Harbour of Zabûra; and around this small inlet was once a village of some size, as is indicated by the quantity of broken pottery scattered over the surface. This is an infallible sign of an ancient site. If there ever were any but mud hovels here, however, every stone has been carried away, or has dissolved to sand and dust. The Riber Abû Zabûra enters the sea a short distance ahead of us, but, as this has been a remarkably dry season, we can doubtless cross on the beach, though, when I passed this way in 1833, I had to make a long detour into the interior over these sand hills, and finally got across with great difficulty. It is celebrated for quicksands and bottomless mud ; and it was partly to avoid such impracticable rivers that the Romans carried their highways down the interior; for it was their system never to make a road where they could not construct bridges. I have an idea that this Abû Zabûra is the River Kânâh, which formed the south-western border between Ephraim and Manasseh. The country on the north of it belonged to Manasseh, that on the south to Ephraim.[1] Dr. Robinson, however, thinks he has identified this river with a wady now called Kanah, west of Nablûs, which, he says, " turns south-west, joins the Aujeh, and so enters the sea near Jaffa." But I can scarcely believe that the lot of Manasseh reached so far south. The text in Joshua intimates that the border followed the River Kanah to the sea; which it may have done if this Abû Zabûra is it, but not if the River Kanah became swallowed up in the 'Aujeh. The Doctor may possibly have been misled in regard to the final direction of his Wady Kanah, for nothing is more eccentric than the course of the streams after they enter these plains. Kitto makes the river of Arsûf, which enters the sea between Em Khâlid and El Haram, to be the Kanah of the Bible; and this is certainly far more probable than that the Aujeh is, but even this seems to carry the border of Manasseh too far south.

We must allow our horses to drink at the ford, for it is a long stretch to the next brook. Here is a shepherd with some cattle, to relieve this utter solitude. Hammûd exclaimed, when he saw this wild Arab shepherd, " *El hamdu-lillah shûfna ensân*—Thank God, we have seen a man !" He may be thankful, also, that the Bedawy is *one* and that we are many, for every denizen of these wild downs is a robber by profession.

These cliffs, below which we have been trailing our slow and weary march since crossing the Zabûra, are very singular geological specimens—absolutely perpendicular—composed of very thin strata, piled up like *dog-eared paste-board* in a bookbindery—not horizontal, but crumpled, twisted, and *bulging* out in all possible angles and shapes.

Yes, and the same extraordinary formation continues almost to Jaffa. This long line of cliffs is called Durb el Kheît—*road of a chord*—probably because they stretch in a straight line for so many miles. But our horses are becoming quite exhausted with this deep sand ; let us, therefore, strike out into the country, and pass over these sand hills to a village called Em Khâlid, forty-five minutes to the south-east of us. There has been a fight there this week between the villagers and the Arabs, as I was told at the mills last night; but we are a strong party, and they will not venture to molest us. There we shall find water, take our lunch, and refresh our weary horses.

What sort of birds are these which make such a noise among the trees and bushes ?

They are field sparrows, and this is the largest congregation of them I have ever seen. The trees and even the shrubs are stuffed full of their nests ; and

---

[1] Joshua xvii. 9.

these hawks, which are soaring about seeking for prey, cause all this alarm and hubbub among the sparrows. You remember we saw something like this on the Hûleh, only the birds are ten times more numerous here; in fact, they seem to be without number. They live upon the wild oats which Splendid cover these sand hills as if they had been sown by man. Now we have gained view. the summit, see what a splendid prospect opens upon the eye. The great plain of Sharon stretches southward quite beyond the range of vision, while the mountains of Manasseh and Ephraim, crowded with villages, picturesquely perched upon their many-shaped declivities, bound the horizon in that direction. Below us, to the south-east, is Em Khâlid, and most welcome to man and beast, for we have been riding five hours, and at a rapid pace.

Twenty-three years ago I arrived at this village from Tantûra, and slept under this identical old sycamore, which the west wind has forced to spread its branches down the hill to the east. How little of the romance of that first journey through Palestine can I now get up, with all the appliances and luxuries of modern travel! Without tent, canteen, or even cook, sleeping under trees, hedges, or rocks, as it happened, I passed from Beirût to the Dead Sea, and back through the interior by Nablûs, Nazareth, and Tiberias. But there was more romance than common sense in the matter, and before that first summer was over I lay on my bed for many weeks, consumed by that low, nervous, Dead Sea fever, which has proved fatal to so many Syrian travellers.

Water-
melons.

This Em Khâlid is famous for water-melons beyond almost any village in Palestine, and vast quantities are taken by boat to Beirût, and other towns along the coast.

Are these melons the *abattachim* of Egypt, the remembrance of which augmented the murmurs of the Israelites in the wilderness ?[1]

In all probability the same. The Arabic name *bŭtteekh* is only a variation of the Hebrew, and nothing could be more regretted in the burning desert than these delicious melons, whose exuberant juice is so refreshing to the thirsty pilgrim. It is among the most extraordinary eccentricities of the vegetable kingdom, that these melons, so large and so full of water, should flourish best on such soil as this around Em Khâlid. Into this dry sand the vine thrusts its short root, and that in the hottest season of the year. Yet a thousand boat-loads of this most juicy melon are gathered from these sand heaps for market every summer. The leaves themselves must have the power of absorbing moisture from the heavy dews of the night. The villagers are telling our people that, for fear of the Arabs, they have not dared to plant their more distant fields this spring, and therefore there will be few of their melons in the city markets; which bit of information has stirred the wrath of the muleteers, and they are pouring maledictions upon them—upon their heads, their eyes, their beards, and everything else pertaining to them. And really

---

[1] Numbers xi. 5.

one feels a sort of sympathy with these feelings. I am conscious of a degree CHAPTER
of dislike toward these Bedawîn robbers more intense than I allow toward any XXXIII.
other of God's creatures, nor have I any patience with them ; but let us leave
them before I am startled out of all due decorum. Our lunch over, we must
ride steadily and fast, for it is yet more than six hours to Jaffa.

Look well before your horse's head, or you may fall into some of these open-
mouthed cisterns. The whole face of the hill is pierced with them.

I see ; but what are they for? Not to hold water certainly, for there is no
way in which they could be filled.

They are wells or cisterns for grain. In them the farmers store their crops Grain cis-
of all kinds after the grain is threshed and winnowed. These cisterns are cool, terns.
perfectly dry, and tight. The top is hermetically sealed with plaster, and
covered with a deep bed of earth; and thus they keep out rats, mice, and even
ants,—the latter by no means a contemptible enemy.

By the way, I read lately, in a work of some pretension, that ants do not
carry away wheat or barley. This was by way of comment on the words of the
wise man, that the ant " gathereth her food in the harvest." [1] What have you
to say of the criticism ?

That it is nonsense. Tell it to these farmers, and they will laugh in your Ants.
face. Ants not pilfer from the floor and the granary !—they are the greatest
robbers in the land. Leave a bushel of wheat in the vicinity of one of their
subterranean cities, and in a surprisingly short time the whole commonwealth
will be summoned to plunder. A broad, black column stretches from the wheat
to their hole, and you are startled by the result. As if by magic, every grain
seems to be accommodated with legs, and walks off in a hurry along the moving
column. The farmers remorselessly set fire to every ant city they find in the
neighbourhood of their threshing-floors.

Are these Eastern granaries mentioned or alluded to in the Bible ?

The custom is doubtless an ancient one, and it extended from this country Scripture
through the Carthaginians of North Africa into Spain. They seem to be allusions
alluded to by those ten men who said to Ishmael, " Slay us not ; for we have ries.
treasures in the field, of wheat, and of barley, and of oil, and of honey," [2] and
thus they saved their lives from the treacherous Ishmael. These cisterns not
only preserve the grain and other stores deposited in them from insects and
mice, but they are admirably adapted to conceal them from robbers. These
ten men had doubtless thus hid their treasures to avoid being plundered in
that time of utter lawlessness ; and in a similar time I found people storing
away grain in cisterns far out in the open country between Aleppo and Hamath;
and they told me it was to hide it from the government tax-gatherers. It is
quite dangerous to come upon a deserted site full of these open cisterns and
wells, especially at night, as I have often found. Frequently they are entirely
concealed by the grass, and the path leads right among them. They must

---

PART
III.

always be dug in dry places; generally, as here, on the side of a sloping hill, They would not answer in a wet country, but in these dry climates stores have been found quite fresh and sound many years after they were thus buried. The farmers also resort to various expedients to keep the grain from injury. One of the most common is to mingle quicksilver with oil, or with the white of an egg, and rub it in well with the wheat. This will preserve it free from insects of all kinds. Joseph in Egypt must have understood how to preserve grain, at least for seven years; and I suppose that in ancient times, when cities and fortresses *were liable to very long sieges*, it was of the utmost importance to know the best methods of preserving their stores. Askelon is said to have been besieged *twenty-eight years*, and of course the people must have had immense provisions laid up and well preserved. That this was common is implied in the parable of the rich fool, who built greater store-houses and laid up provisions for *many years.*[1]   If there had been no such store-houses in the land, and the custom of laying up grain for many years was unknown, the terms of the parable would have lacked verisimilitude,—a defect in construction which attaches to none of our Lord's sayings.

Sand
downs.

Are we to suppose that these vast downs have really been formed by sand blown in from the sea-shore? All the way from Cæsarea we have had them, and here they are three miles broad and several hundred feet high.

Yes; and they continue, with only partial interruptions, far down the coast beyond Gaza toward Egypt. But, extensive as they are, they are all the work of the winds and waves, acting in the same manner through countless ages. The gradual encroachment of the sea is slowly wearing away this underlying rock, as we have seen in the strange cliffs along the shore, and the new-made sand is being driven further and further inland. If this process goes on long enough, the entire plain will be buried under this slow-creeping desolation. There are many parts of the coast where this has actually been accomplished, and the sea now lashes the perpendicular cliffs of the mountains; and along this valley of Sharon are places where the sandy deluge has reached nearly to the foot of the hills, leaving only a narrow strip of fertile soil between them.

Brooks.

These shifting banks greatly perplex the brooks which cross the plain. They are not sufficiently powerful to keep their channels open during summer, and hence they are often dammed up at the mouth, and form large marshes along the very margin of the sand. We shall encounter one of these a short distance ahead of us. Strong, permanent streams, like the 'Aujeh, maintain their right of passage at all times, and have done so in all ages. The 'Aujeh, in fact, effects an entire break in this line of sand hills; but, south of Joppa, the weaker and less permanent brooks are constantly shut up during summer, and when swollen by winter rains, flood the country, until they can force open a channel to the sea.

The plain here has evidently been buried deep under this sand long ages

ago, precisely as at Beirût; and here are the usual pine forests growing upon CHAPTER
it.   These are the finest specimens we have seen in Palestine, though every XXXIII.
sandy ridge of Lebanon and Hermon is clothed with them, and often of a much Pine for-
larger growth.   They are not seen on the *mountains* of Palestine, because ests.
that peculiar sandy formation is not found there.   This tree the Arabs call
snubar, and in my opinion it is the Hebrew *berosh*, concerning which there is
so much confusion in the various translations of the Bible.   In the English
it is generally rendered *fir*, but many modern critics think that it should be
cypress.   I, however, suppose that *berosh* is the generic name for the pine, of
which there are several varieties on Lebanon.   Cypress is rarely found there,
but pine everywhere, and it is *the* tree used for beams and rafters.   *Ers* is
the distinctive name for the cedar, *berosh* for the pine.

This tree bears a very large and compact cone, from which is obtained the Pine cone.
nut of the market.   This cone,
when ripe, is gathered by the
owners of the forests, and when
thoroughly dried on the roof, or
thrown for a few minutes into
the fire, it separates into many
compartments, from each of
which drops a smooth white nut,
in shape like the *seed* of the
date.   The *shell* is very hard,
and within it is the fruit, which
is much used in making pillau
and other preparations of rice,
and also in various kinds of
sweetmeats.   In the Arabic
Bible, the *myrrh*, which the
Ishmaelites who bought Joseph
were carrying into Egypt, is
called *snubar;* and if this is in
truth the *berosh* of the Bible,
scarcely any other tree is more
frequently mentioned ; and this
would be in exact correspondence
with its actual value.

CONE OF THE PINE.

The variety of pine which we
saw on the north of Em Khâlid, and in which the field sparrows have made
their nests, is found all over Lebanon, but it never grows tall, and is but
little used in building or in the arts ; and the same is true of all other kinds
in this country, except the stone pine of this grove.

There is your sand-perplexed brook, with its accompanying marsh, I sup- Nahr
pose ?   33   Fulej.

Yes; it is called Nahr Falej—the Palsy River. On the shore near its mouth is Arsûf; and from it the river takes that name on many maps. Arsûf is generally supposed to mark the site of the ancient Apollonia. You observe that the banks of the Falej are shaded with a dense jungle of those mop-headed canes called *babeer*, which cover the great marshes of the Hûleh. By keeping up the bank for some distance we shall find an easy ford near some old mills, where the river breaks through a ledge of rocks and enters this verdant vale. It has taken an hour and a half from Em Khâlid, and another hour and a half will bring us to El Haram, on a bold cliff overhanging the sea.

Do you know, I was very suspicious of those Arab horsemen who joined us out of the jungle upon our left. But you seemed to enjoy their society amazingly.

PINUS ORIENTALIS.

They had no intention of molesting us. The main speaker was the sheikh of a tribe whose tents are concealed by the bushes to the south-east of us. He was very anxious to hear the news from the Crimea; and, to judge from his talk, you would think him a most zealous partisan of the Sultan and the Ingleese (English); but he soon turned from war to discuss the merits of the splendid mare upon which he sat so proudly. He had heard that the English were buying horses, and was anxious to sell. He only asked the modest sum of 18,000 piastres (720 dollars) for his mare! She is, in reality, a splendid creature, and walks over this sandy soil as if she were built on springs; nevertheless I should be sorry to give 18,000 piastres for her.

Let us quicken our pace to this Haram, for there is something to examine on the north of it. The walls of an ancient city, or immense quadrangular fort, can be traced all round ; and on the north-west corner was a citadel overhanging the sea, and cut off from the rest by a deep ditch. It must have been a very strong place. There are also other traces of antiquity in various directions.

What an extensive view this elevation commands ! The precipice breaks sheer down to the sea, while to the east the country declines gently over many a mile of this sandy desert. Isaiah says that Sharon shall be a wilderness,[1] and the prediction has become a sad and impressive reality. And so these flocks of the Arabs fulfil that other prophecy, " Sharon shall be a fold of flocks."[2] Why is Sharon always joined with Carmel ?

Because, as we remarked when turning round the extreme end of it to Cæsarea, the broad vale which stretches southward to this distance and a great deal further does actually commence at the base of that mountain. This long plain seems always to have been celebrated for its flocks and herds. David appointed one of his great officers—Shitrai, the Sharonite[3]—over the herds that fed in Sharon.

By the way, we have skirted this plain for so many miles without meeting any of those roses about which Solomon sings so sweetly.[4]

There are wild roses enough in some parts, with their ever-accompanying Roses thorny thickets ; and, if the Hebrew word khŭbbaizly may be interpreted by the Arabic khŭbbaizy (malva), I have seen thousands of Solomon's roses on Sharon ; and, before you explode at the thought of degrading the poetic *rose* into *marsh-mallows*, let me tell you that certain kinds of mallows grow into a stout bush, and bear thousands of beautiful flowers. However, I will not contend for the identity of *khŭbbaizly* and *khŭbbaizy*, for that would exclude our favourite rose from the Bible altogether,—a calamity which the critics seem determined to bring about at any rate, for some of them maintain that the khŭbbaizly is the *narcissus*, others that it is the *asphodel*, and some translators call it *lily*.

But come, bid adieu to El Haram, and, for the present, to Sharon also, and slide down this steep declivity to the shore, along which our track lies all the way to Jaffa, a distance of three hours. You may go to sleep for the first two, for there is nothing to attract attention except the infinite quantity of shells, Sea shells of which there are banks many miles long and several feet thick. A whole fleet might be loaded with them.

And now we shall have to wait at this 'Aujeh, and take off the loads from our mules ; for I see, by that horseman who is fording it, that the water will come up to the sides of the mules, and wet our clothes and books. I never before attempted to cross at this place ; but the people of El Haram said that, owing to the scarcity of rain, it could easily be done ; and so it can, by all except the loaded animals. However, we shall quickly pass the things over

---

[1] Isa. xxxiii. 9.   [2] Isa. lxv. 10.   [3] 1 Chron. xxvii. 29.   [4] Song. ii. 1.

PART
III.

Jaffa.

on the shoulders of the men, then another hour will bring us safely to the *biarah* of our worthy and hospitable friend Mr. Murad.

Jaffa appears well, bathed in the soft light of sunset. We see almost every house, for they are built on the steep northern declivity of the cape, and the roof of the range below is on a level with the street of those above. The city therefore shows to best advantage from the sea as one comes from the north. The cape itself is merely a sand conglomerate, like the cliffs of Durb el Kheît; it is, in fact, the continuation of that ridge, broken up for a short distance by the joint influence of the 'Aujeh and the sea.

CHAPTER XXXIV.

JAFFA, OR JOPPA.

April 10th.

Antiquity
of Jaffa.

JAFFA is one of the oldest cities in the world. It was given to Dan, in the distribution of the land by Joshua, and it has been known to history ever since. It owes its existence to the low ledge of rocks which extends into the sea from the extremity of the little cape on which the city stands, and forms a small harbour. Insignificant as it is, and insecure, yet there being no other on all this coast, it was sufficient to cause a city to spring up around it even in the earliest times, and to sustain its life through numberless changes of dynasties, races, and religions, down to the present hour. It was, in fact, the only harbour of any notoriety possessed by the Jews throughout the greater part of their national existence. To it the timber for both the temples of Jerusalem was brought from Lebanon; and no doubt a lucrative trade in cedar and pine was always carried on through it with the nations who had possession of the forests of Lebanon. Through it also nearly all the foreign commerce of the Jews was conducted until the artificial port of Cæsarea was built by Herod. Hither Jonah came to find a ship in which to flee from the presence of the Lord, and from it he sailed for Tarshish.

Story of
Andro-
meda and
Perseus.

By-the-by, do you think there is any foundation for the idea of Reland and others, that the story about Andromeda and Perseus originated from some confused account of Jonah and the whale which had reached the Greeks through sailors of Tarshish?

Possibly; and it is certainly curious that Pliny, after alluding to the story of Andromeda, says that M. Scaurus, among other wonderful relics, showed the bones of a wild beast brought, during his ædileship, to Rome from Joppa,

a walled town of Judea.   The length was forty feet, the elevation of the ribs CHAPTER
greater than the height of an Indian elephant, and the thickness of the skin XXXIV.
was a foot and a half!   This may well have been *a* whale, if not the identical Skeleton
one in whose belly Jonah passed three days.   The fact, also, that in the of a whale
mythical fable of Perseus and Andromeda the name Iapolis frequently occurs
as that of a city connected with the same, strongly favours the original identity
of the stories.   But we leave all such questions to the learned.   Joppa has a History of
history not made up of fables, but, alas! for the most part written in blood. Joppa.
Scarcely any other town has been so often overthrown, sacked, pillaged, burned,
and rebuilt.   It would be tedious to enter into minute detail of these disasters,
and they may be gathered from the Bible—the books of the Maccabees,
Josephus, the Greek and Roman historians, Eusebius, Jerome, and others of
the fathers, and from the chronicles of the Crusades in the " Gesta Dei per
Francos."   In our day it has acquired an unhappy notoriety in connection with
Bonaparte, the plague, and the poisoning of sick soldiers.   I myself was held
prisoner in it for forty days in 1834, while it was besieged by the mountaineers
in revolt against Ibrahim Pasha.   Mr. Arutîn Murad, our consul at the time,
told me that the present city was then not a hundred years old.   In consequence of the pirates which infested this coast during the early life of his
father, Jaffa was entirely deserted, and the inhabitants retired to Ramleh and
Lydd.   He himself remembered when there was only a single guard-house,
occupied by a few soldiers, who gave notice to the merchants in Ramleh when
a ship arrived.   With this agrees the account of the desolation of Tyre at the
same period, and from the same cause.   Such facts lay open the wretched state
of the country during those times of utter anarchy.   When Bonaparte came
along, however, Jaffa had again risen to some importance, and it has been
growing ever since.   Twenty-five years ago the inhabitants of city and gardens Recent
were about 6000 ; now there must be 15,000 at least, and commerce has growth.
increased at even a greater ratio.   Several sources of prosperity account for the
existence and rapid increase of Jaffa.   It is the natural landing-place of
pilgrims to Jerusalem, both Christians and Jews, and they have created a
considerable trade.   The Holy City itself has also been constantly rising in
importance during the present generation.   Then there are extensive soap
factories, not only here, but in Ramleh, Lydd, Nablûs, and Jerusalem, much Its trade.
of which is exported from this port to all the cities along the coast, to Egypt,
and even to Asia Minor through Tarsus.   The fruit trade from Jaffa is likewise
quite considerable, and lately there have been large shipments of corn to
Europe.   Add to this that silk is now being cultivated extensively along the
River 'Aujeh, and in the gardens about the city, and the present prosperity
of Jaffa is fully explained.   And unless European enterprise shall hereafter
construct a railway which will carry off those sources of wealth to some more
secure harbour, Jaffa must continue to rise in importance for ages to come.
The harbour, however, is very inconvenient and insecure.   Vessels of any Harbour.
considerable burden must lie out in the open roadstead,—a very uneasy berth

at all times; and even a moderate wind will oblige them to slip cable and run out to sea, or seek anchorage at Haifa, sixty miles distant. The landing also is most inconvenient, and often extremely dangerous. More boats upset, and more lives are lost in the breakers at the north end of the ledge of rocks that defend the inner harbour, than anywhere else on this coast. I have been in imminent danger myself, with all my family in the boat, and never look without a shudder at this treacherous port, with its noisy surf tumbling over the rocks, as if on purpose to swallow up unfortunate boats. This is the *true monster* which has devoured many an Andromeda, for whose deliverance no gallant Perseus was at hand.

Gardens and orchards. Jaffa is celebrated in modern times for her gardens and orchards of delicious fruit more than for anything else. They are very extensive, flourishing, and profitable; but their very existence depends upon the fact that water to any amount can be procured in every garden, and at a moderate depth. The entire plain seems to cover a river of vast breadth, percolating through the sand *en route* to the sea. A thousand Persian wheels working night and day

NA'URA—PERSIAN WATER-WHEEL.

produce no sensible diminution; and this inexhaustible source of wealth

underlies the whole territory of the Philistines down to Gaza at least, and
probably much further south.

Have we any reason to believe that these Persian wheels were here in
ancient days of Jewish history? I have been greatly interested in them, and
they seem admirably adapted for the purpose intended—simple in construction,
cheap, quickly made, soon repaired, easily worked, and they raise an immense
quantity of water.

Many efforts have been made to introduce pumps, but they aways fail and
get out of repair; and as there is no one able to mend them, they are thrown
aside, and the gardener returns to his *na'ura*. The whole of this machinery
is quickly enumerated and described. A wide cog-wheel is carried round
horizontally by a mule with a *sweep*. This turns a larger one perpendicularly,
which is directly above the mouth of the well. Over this revolve two rough
hawsers, or thick ropes, made of twigs and branches twisted together, and
upon them are fastened small jars or wooden buckets. One side descends
while the other rises, carrying the small buckets with them, those descending
empty, those ascending full, and as they pass over the top they discharge into
a trough which conveys the water to the cistern. The length of these hawsers
and the number of the buckets depend, of course, upon the depth of the well, for
the buckets are fastened on the hawser about two feet apart. The depth of
wells in Jaffa varies from ten to forty feet. If the mule turns the wheel
rapidly, which he rarely does, a bucket with about two gallons of water will be
carried over the top of it and be discharged into the trough every second; and
it must be a good pump that will steadily do as much. The hawser is made
of twigs, generally of myrtle branches, not merely because it is cheap and
easily plaited by the gardener himself, but because its extreme roughness
prevents it from *slipping* on the wheel, as an ordinary rope would do, and thus
fail to carry up the loaded buckets.

There are other kinds of water-wheels in this country. The shadûf, so conspicuous on the Nile, is nowhere to be seen in Palestine, but the well-sweep
and bucket are used in many places; and I once saw an Egyptian working an
apparatus much like the shadûf on the shore of the lake a little north of the
city of Tiberias.

Another apparatus is common in this land of Philistia, which I have also
seen on the plains of Central Syria. A large buffalo skin is so attached to
cords that, when let down into the well, it opens and is instantly filled, and,
being drawn up, it closes so as to retain the water. The rope by which it is
hoisted to the top works over a wheel, and is drawn by oxen, mules, or camels,
that walk directly from the well to the length of the rope, and then return,
only to repeat the operation until a sufficient quantity of water is raised. This
also is a very successful mode of drawing water.

The wheel and bucket (of different sorts and sizes) is an apparatus much
used where the water is near the surface, and also along rapid rivers. For
shallow wells it is merely a wheel, whose diameter equals the desired elevation

PART
III.

of the water. The *rim* of this wheel is large, hollow, and divided into compartments answering the place of *buckets*. A hole near the top of each *bucket*

SHADUF.

allows it to fill, as that part of the rim, in revolving, dips under the water. This, of course, will be discharged when the *bucket* begins to descend, and thus a constant succession of streams falls into the cistern. The wheel itself is turned by oxen or mules.

Large
wheels.

This system of wheels is seen on a grand scale at Hums Hamath, and all along the Orontes. The wheels there are of enormous size. The diameter of some of those at Hamath is eighty or ninety feet. The great advantage of this apparatus is that it is driven by the river itself. Small *paddles* are attached to the rim, and the stream is turned upon them by a low dam with sufficient force to carry the huge wheel around with all its load of ascending buckets. There is, perhaps, no hydraulic machinery in the world by which so much water is raised to so great an elevation at so small an expense. Certainly I have seen none half so picturesque or so musical. These wheels, with their enormous loads, slowly revolve on their groaning axles, and all day and all night each one sings a different tune, with every imaginable variation of tone—sobs, sighs, shrieks, and groans—loud, louder, loudest, down to the bottom of the gamut—a concert wholly unique, and half infernal in the night, which, heard once, will never be forgotten.

Watering
with the
foot.

To what does Moses refer in Deuteronomy xi. 10? "For the land, whither thou goest in to possess it, is not as the land of Egypt, from whence ye came out, where thou sowedst thy seed. and wateredst it with thy foot, as a garden of herbs."

The reference, perhaps, is to the manner of conducting the water about from plant to plant, and from furrow to furrow, in irrigating a garden of herbs. I have often watched the gardener at this fatiguing and unhealthy work. When one place is sufficiently saturated, he pushes aside the sandy soil between it and the next furrow with his foot, and thus continues to do until all are watered. He is thus knee-deep in mud, and many are the diseases generated by this slavish work.

Or the reference may be to certain kinds of hydraulic machines which were turned by the feet. I have seen small water-wheels, on the plain of Acre and elsewhere, which were thus worked; and it appeared to me to be very tedious and toilsome, and, if the whole country had to be irrigated by such a process, it would require a nation of slaves like the Hebrews, and taskmasters like the Egyptians, to make it succeed. Whatever may have been the meaning of Moses, the Hebrews, no doubt, had learned by bitter experience what it was to *water with the foot;* and this would add great force to the allusion, and render doubly precious the goodly land which drank of the rain of heaven, and required no such drudgery to make it fruitful.

The fruits of Jaffa are the same as those of Sidon, but with certain varia- Fruits of tions in their character. Sidon has the best bananas, Jaffa furnishes the best Jaffa. pomegranates. The oranges of Sidon are more juicy and of a richer flavour than those of Jaffa; but the latter hang on the trees much later, and will bear to be shipped to distant regions. They are therefore more valuable to the producer. It is here only that you see in perfection fragrant blossoms encircling golden fruit. In March and April these Jaffa gardens are indeed enchanting. The air is overloaded with the mingled spicery of orange, lemon, apple, apricot, quince, plum, and china trees in blossom. The people then frequent the groves, sit on mats beneath their grateful shade, sip coffee, smoke the argela, sing, converse, or sleep, as best suits their individual idiosyncrasies, till evening, when they slowly return to their homes in the city. To us of the restless West, this way of making *kaif* soon wearies by its slumberous monotony, but it is Elysium to the Arabs.

Are these orchards remunerative in a pecuniary point of view?

I am informed that they yield ten per cent. on the capital invested, clear of Profit of all expense. Our friend Murad tells me that a *biarah* (the technical name of orchards. a watered garden) which costs 100,000 piastres will produce annually 15,000; but 5000 of this must be expended in irrigation, ploughing, planting, and manuring. This allows the proprietor 10,000 piastres, which is a very fair per-centage on capital invested in agricultural pursuits.

I have been strolling along the streets, or rather *street* of Jaffa, for there Thorough seems to be but one, and a more crowded thoroughfare I never saw. I had to fare of force my way through the motley crowd of busy citizens, wild Arabs, foreign Jaffa. pilgrims, camels, mules, horses, and donkeys. Then what a strange rabble outside the gate, noisy, quarrelsome, ragged, and filthy! Many are blind, or at least have some painful defect about their eyes, and some are leprous. The

PART
III.

Dorcas.

peasants hereabout must be very poor, to judge by their rags and squalid appearance. I was reminded of Dorcas and the widows around Peter exhibiting the *coats* and garments which that benevolent lady had made, and I devoutly wished she might be raised again, at least in spirit, for there is need of a dozen Dorcas societies in Jaffa at the present time.

Grave of
Dorcas.

Did you find her house ? No ! Well, our consul discovered *her grave* in one of his gardens, and gave it to the Armenian convent of Jerusalem. I examined the sarcophagus in its original bed, and there was this *negative* evidence in favour of Tabitha that there was no counter claim whatever. If not Tabitha's, whose tomb was it, pray ?

Though not so fortunate as you, I was taken to the house were *Simon the tanner* resided. It is certainly by the sea-side, and that is something, but then so is all Jaffa. A stout earthquake might shake half of it into the sea.

Tanneries.

If Simon lived near his business, his house was probably on the shore *south of the city*, where the *tanneries* now are located, and most likely were in Peter's day. These manufacturing establishments are generally removed to a distance beyond the walls; and with good reason, for they are extremely offensive, as well as prejudicial to health. But there is no reason to suppose that Simon's *dwelling-house* was near his tannery, and it *may* have occupied the identical site now assigned to it.

Pottery.

I have been out on the shore again, examining a native manufactory of pottery, and was delighted to find the whole Biblical apparatus complete, and in full operation. There was the potter sitting at his "frame," and turning the

Potter's
wheel.

"wheel" with his foot. He had a heap of the prepared clay near him, and a pan of water by his side. Taking a lump in his hand, he placed it on the top of the wheel (which revolves horizontally), and smoothed it into a low cone, like the upper end of a sugar-loaf ; then thrusting his thumb into the top of it, he opened a hole down through the centre, and this he constantly widened by pressing the edges of the revolving cone between his hands. As it enlarged and became thinner, he gave it whatever shape he pleased with the utmost ease and expedition. This, I suppose, is the exact

Scripture
allusions.

point of those Biblical comparisons between the human and the Divine Potter : " O house of Israel, cannot I do with you as this potter ? saith the Lord. Behold, as the clay is in the potter's hand, so are ye in my hand, saith the Lord." [1] And the same idea is found in many other passages. When Jeremiah was watching the potter, the vessel was marred in his hand, and " so he made it again another vessel, as seemed good to the potter to make it." [2] I had to wait a long time for that, but it happened at last. From some defect in the clay, or because he had taken too little, the potter suddenly changed his mind, crushed his growing jar instantly into a shapeless mass of mud, and beginning anew, fashioned it into a totally different vessel. This idea Paul has ex-

---

[1] Jer. xviii 6.   [2] Jer. xviii. 4.

pounded and employed, in the ninth chapter of the Romans, to soften some of CHAPTER
those things which Peter says are hard to be understood: "Shall the thing XXXIV.

THE POTTER AND WHEEL.

formed say to him that formed it, Why hast thou made me thus? Hath not
the potter power over the clay, of the same lump to make one vessel unto honour,
and another unto dishonour?" Certainly he has, and I saw him do it, but
I did not see thereby much further into the great mystery which the apostle
was illustrating. That, I fear, will ever remain among the "hard things" which
the unlearned and unstable will wrest unto their own destruction.

It is evident, from numerous expressions in the Bible, that the potter's Scripture
vessel was the synonym of utter fragility; and to say that the wicked should allusions.
be broken to pieces as a potter's vessel, was to threaten the most ruinous
destruction. In this day of glass and other fragile fabrics, and of strong stone
pottery, we should hardly have adopted this language.

Perhaps not; but for this country it is still as appropriate and forcible as
ever. Arab jars are so thin and frail that they are literally "dashed to Arab jars.
shivers" by the slightest stroke. Water-jars are often broken by merely
putting them down upon the floor, and nothing is more common than for the
servant to return from the fountain empty handed, having had all his jars
smashed to atoms by some irregular behaviour of his donkey.

To what does Isaiah refer in the 14th verse of the 30th chapter, where he
says, "He shall break it as the breaking of the potter's vessel that is broken in

pieces; he shall not spare : so that there shall not be found in the bursting of it a sherd to take fire from the hearth, or to take water withal out of the pit ?"

Potsherd.

Your inquiry refers, I suppose, to the *sherd to take fire from the hearth,* or to *take water out of the pit.* This last you must have seen many times during our rambles. It is very common to find at the spring or " pit " pieces of broken jars, to be used as ladles either to drink from or fill with ; and bits of fractured jars are preserved for this purpose. But the destruction mentioned by Isaiah was to be so complete that there would not be a piece left large enough for that. The other allusion in this passage you may not have noticed, but I have a hundred times and more. Take your stand near any of the public ovens in Sidon (or here in Jaffa, I presume,) in the evening, and you will see the children of the poor coming with " sherds " of pottery in their hands, into which the baker pours a small quantity of hot embers and a few coals with which to warm up their evening meal. Isaiah's vessels, however, were to be broken into such small bits that there would not be a sherd of sufficient size to carry away a few embers from the hearth. These comparisons are exceedingly expressive where the actions referred to are of constant occurrence, as they are in all our cities to this present day.

Fountain.

The only building about Jaffa that has the slightest claim to even Saracenic beauty, is the fountain near the gate. This is really striking; and its surrounding courts furnish admirable specimens of Arab countenances and costumes for the pencil of the artist and the study of the phrenologist. I rarely pass out of the city without turning aside there to taste its cool water, and amuse myself with the ever-shifting scene.

"Void space" in the gate.

Did you not also notice the " void space " about Jaffa's only gate, and the crowds of people that always gather there in the afternoon ? I have seen both the governor and the kady, with their suites, sitting there, decreeing and executing judgment precisely as such things are spoken of in the Bible. As the city is surrounded by a wall and ditch, and has but this one gate, all must go in and out through it, and hence the great crowd that chokes up the passage; and hence, too, it happens that there is scarcely an allusion in the Bible to matters transacted in " the gate," but what you may see enacted every day about this one of Jaffa.

April 13th. I am quite satisfied with Jaffa, and it is a relief to get beyond this sea of green trees into open plain. How many hours' ride have we before us to-day ?

That depends upon the rate of travel. It is about three hours to the main source of the 'Aujeh at Er Ras, nearly the same distance back to Lydd, and three quarters of an hour further to Ramleh, where we are to find our tent.

Plain of Sharon and Philistia.

This is truly a magnificent plain, much larger than those of Tyre, Acre, or even Esdraelon.

In its whole extent it certainly is the largest on the west side of the Jordan,

for it includes the entire territory of the Philistines. Far from being a flat, CHAPTER
dead level, it is, like Esdraelon, agreeably varied by long swells, growing into XXXIV.
sandy ridges, and even rocky tells and hills, which afford sightly positions for
villages. Of these there are more than in other plains, more populous also,
and surrounded often by olive and fruit orchards, which impart an air of
cheerfulness not seen elsewhere in Palestine. Yonder, on the plain to the
south-east of us, is a beautiful mirage. This optical illusion is often so per- Mirage.
fect, that even the experienced traveller finds it difficult to believe that he is
not approaching an actual lake of transparent water. Dr. Wilson tells us that
the name for mirage in Sanscrit means " the thirst of the antelope;" and nothing could be more poetical. I once gave chase to a flock of gazelles on the
plain of Tireh, south-east of Aleppo. The day was intensely hot, and the
antelopes made direct towards a vast mirage, which covered the whole eastern
horizon. To me they seemed to be literally leaping through the water, and I
could see their figures *below* the surface, and *reversed*, with the utmost distinctness. No wonder *they* were deceived, for even their pursuers were utterly
confounded. But the pursuit of the mirage is like chasing the rainbow, which
retreats as you advance, and can never be overtaken. The Arab name is *serab*,
and it is doubtless to this deceitful phenomenon that Isaiah refers,[1] where the
promise is that this *serab* shall become a real lake. Our translators have
missed the exact meaning of this most emphatic figure. *Serab* is not " parched
ground," but a simmering, tantalizing phantom of a lake. Sale, in his Koran,
chapter xxiv., translates serab by *vapour:* " The works of unbelievers are like
the *vapour serab* in a plain, which the thirsty thinketh to be water, until,
when he cometh thereto, he findeth it nothing." Mohammed meant the
mirage, and he gave the proper name for it.

The peasants of Sharon differ strikingly from those in the north. All these Peasants
around us appear to me to be of Egyptian origin. Do you suppose that there of Sharon.
is sufficient of the old Philistine blood in their veins to account for their
peculiar physiognomy?

There is enough of the Egypto-African about them to explain all peculiari- Supposed
ties of colour, contour, and character. I hold that the Philistines came from origin of
the neighbouring coast of Africa, perhaps from Lower Egypt, though Josephus tines.
seems to place Caphtor, their ancient home, higher up the valley of the Nile.
There is much plausibility in the theory which identifies the shepherd
kings, who conquered Lower Egypt about the time of Abraham, with the
Philistines. They may have been a great roving race of Bedawîn until the
time of that conquest. By remaining masters of that highly enlightened
people for so many generations, they acquired much of their civilization ; and,
when finally expelled, they came north into Palestine, drove the original inhabitants from the coast and the great plain of Sharon, and there built their
cities, carried on agriculture and commerce, and became a powerful confeder-

---

[1] Isa. xxxv. 7.

acy, quite able to protect themselves from their neighbours. This seems to me best to agree with the various notices of them found in the Bible, in the fragments of Manetho, the history of Josephus, and with all other hints which can be gathered up from ancient authors, the traditions of nations, and the architectural indications derived from the monuments which still exist. I cannot think that the Philistines emigrated originally from Crete, or from Cappadocia, nor even from Cyprus. Such theories show the skill and learning of their inventors more than they illustrate the true origin of nations. Who can believe that these islands were so overstocked with inhabitants at that *very early* age after the Deluge as to require, or even to admit such an emigration? And if they had been forcibly expelled from either of those countries, would there not have been some tradition of such a great fact in their national history?

To which of the tribes did this part of the plain belong?

Tribes of
Dan and
Ephraim.
The border over against Jaffa was assigned to Dan, and Ephraim was north of it. The 'Aujeh *may* have been the boundary betwixt them. The Jews do not seem to have obtained possession of this neighbourhood, at least not until the time of David. There, to the south of us, on the road from Jaffa to Lydd,

Beit Du-
jan.
is Beit Dujan, "the house of Dagon," which was probably held by the Philistines, and named from their famous god.

Silk gar-
dens.
Within the last fifteen years certain persons from Beirût planted along this fertile valley of the 'Aujeh large mulberry orchards which are succeeding well, and the cultivation of silk is extending rapidly to many other parts of this plain. The attempt was made to introduce this valuable crop many years ago, but for some reason or other failed. The fountains here at the *Ras* rise low in the earth, and the engineers of Ibrahim Pasha decided that the water could not be carried to Jaffa at a sufficient elevation to irrigate the gardens; and the project was therefore abandoned. If it could be achieved, such a canal would relieve the farmers from a very large part of the expense of cultivating their orchards, and would irrigate them much more thoroughly. I think it by no means fully ascertained that the water could not be elevated at this great source, as it is at Ras el 'Ain, near Tyre, and at other places, by building strong cisterns. They would, of course, be very large and expensive; but then the supply of water, greater than even that near Tyre, would be invaluable, and convert the whole of Sharon into a paradise. Let us ride up to that mosque, and take a bird's-eye view of the country. About an hour to the north is Jiljulieh, pro-

Jiljulieh—
Gilgal?
bably the site of that Gilgal whose king is called "king of the nations" in Joshua (xii. 23). If this is the Gilgal of the "Onomasticon," there seems to be a mistake of *south* for *north* in that invaluable work, because Gilgal is placed six Roman miles north of Antipatris, whereas it is that much south of it. The latter place, now called Kefr Saba, is seen beyond it on the edge of the plain.

It is useless to endeavour to remember these non-historic names which our guide is rattling off at such a rate, so we will turn our horses southward, and pursue the regular old Roman road toward Lydd. It was along this route, doubtless, that Paul was brought by the soldiers who guarded him to Cæsarea.

Here we have the village Renthieh before us, and, as Dr. Robinson remarks, CHAPTER
it is sufficiently like Arimathea to be assumed as the site of that place; and, XXXIV.
from what Jerome says, it seems to me quite probable that this was really the Renthieh
city of that "honourable counsellor, which also waited for the kingdom of —Arima-
God," who "went in boldly unto Pilate, and craved the body of Jesus."[1] thea?

The map of Dr. Robinson has some mistakes in this region which deserve
to be corrected.* The situation of Lydd is correctly laid down with respect
to Jaffa and Ramleh, but Kubab is where Beit Dujan should be, and Safuriyeh is too near Lydd. Kubab is between Ramleh and Latron; Amwas (Emmaus, Nicopolis) is half an hour *north*, not south of Latron. On the north of
Beit Dujan is a village called Yafa; and south of Safuriyeh, a little off the
road to Ramleh, is Sarafend, the third of the name between this and Sidon.
We are now approaching the orchards of Lydd, that village where Peter was Orchards
when summoned to Jaffa on account of the death of Dorcas. Its greatest of Lydd.
celebrity, however, is derived from St. George, who is said to have been both Church of
born and buried there. Dr. Robinson has given an excellent description of St. George
the church as its ruins now are, and a rapid sketch of the long and somewhat
eventful history of the city. No one will examine the remains of the church
without being impressed with a certain air of grandeur which it wears. The
arch of the south aisle is particularly fine and striking. The edifice is at the
south-west corner of the village, and it seems always to have been outside the
ancient city, or on its wall. It was a little more than seventy feet wide, and
one hundred long, though it is impossible to get the exact length on account
of a mosque which is built on the corner of it. The material is a pale yellow
rock, cut from quarries on the road to Jerusalem. It takes a good polish,
and is very hard and durable.

Lydd is a flourishing village of some two thousand inhabitants, embosomed
in noble orchards of olive, fig, pomegranate, mulberry, sycamore, and other
trees, and surrounded every way by a very fertile neighbourhood. The inhabitants are evidently industrious and thriving, and the whole country between
this and Ramleh is fast being filled up with their flourishing orchards. Rarely Pro-
have I beheld a rural scene more delightful than this presented in early har- sperity.
vest, when I rode from Ramleh hither through the fields on the east of the
common path. A thousand reapers, gleaners, and carriers were abroad and
busy when the morning sun shot his first rays down through the olive-trees
upon the animated groups. The wheat and barley grew among the olive-trees,
which half hid, half revealed the merry harvesters—men, women, and children
—the first reaping, the second gleaning and guiding the loaded camels, and
the children at play, or watching the flocks and herds, which were allowed to
follow the *gleaners.* But no description can reproduce such a tableau. It
must be seen, heard, and enjoyed to be appreciated.

---

[1] Mark xv. 43.
* [Some of these have been corrected in the second edition of Robinson.—ED.]

PART III.

Ancient trade.

Lydd, like most other towns in this country, has seen better days, and that, too, in times not very remote. There are remains of large and well-constructed buildings mingled with the modern huts, and several extensive soap factories are now also deserted and falling to decay. These times of recent prosperity were probably when Jaffa was abandoned on account of the pirates; for in those days the trade of Syria and Palestine was carried on over land. Large caravans came from Aleppo through the Bŭk'âh, and down Wady et Teim to Khan Minieh; from Bagdad and Damascus across the Jaulan, by Jisr Benat Yacobe, to the same place; and from the Hauran by Beisan and Zer'in. All these lines, meeting near Lejjun, passed down by Antipatris to this place, and thence, by Ramleh and Gaza, to Egypt. That was the time when the long lines of khans, *caravanserais*, and castles were needed and maintained. But no sooner did the sea, freed from pirates, offer a cheaper conveyance, than this entire system was abandoned. Commerce sought the nearest ports along the coast, and was thence shipped to its destination. Hence all these khans have gone to ruin, and those great highways are deserted. Many other towns besides Lydd and Ramleh have lost by this change of route, and the cities on the coast have gained in equal if not greater proportion.

Historical interest.

Let us ride through the village, to get a better idea of a place which has figured so largely in Jewish, Macedonian, Roman, Saracenic, Frank, Arab, and Turkish dynasties. From the earliest ages of the Church to the present hour it has been frequented by pilgrims, and during the Crusades it was specially honoured on account of St. George.

Women grinding at the mill.

This little circuit has afforded me a beautiful illustration of Scripture. Two women are sitting before the door of their house, upon a large piece of sackcloth, grinding on a hand-mill. I heard the ring of this apparatus some time before I saw it, and I now understand what is meant by the preacher when he says, "The sound of the grinding is low, because the grinders are few."[1] Jeremiah also saddens his picture of Israel's desolation by Nebuchadnezzar, by adding that the sound of the mill-stones should cease.[2] And upon Babylon, whose king thus stilled the voice of the grinding in Jerusalem, John, with apocalyptic thunders, denounces the like desolation: "The sound of a millstone shall be heard no more at all in thee."[3]

From this on southward through Philistia there are no mill-streams, and we shall not cease to hear the hum of the hand-mill at every village and Arab camp morning and evening, and often deep into the night. I like it, and go to sleep on it as a child to its mother's lullaby. It is suggestive of hot bread and a warm welcome when hungry and weary. You observe that *two women* sit at the mill facing each other; both have hold of the handle by which the upper is turned round on the "nether" mill-stone. The one whose right hand is disengaged throws in the grain as occasion requires through the hole in the upper stone, which is called the rekkab (rider) in Arabic, as it was long ago in

Mode of working

---

[1] Eccles. xii. 4.　　　　[2] Jer. xxv. 10.　　　　[3] Rev. xviii. 22.

Hebrew.   It is not correct to say that one pushes it half round, and then the CHAPTER
other seizes the handle.   This would be slow work, and would give a spasmodic XXXIV.

WOMEN GRINDING AT A MILL.

motion to the stone.   Both retain their hold, and pull *to*, or push *from*, as
men do with the whip or cross-cut saw.   The proverb of our Saviour[1] is true
to life, for *women* only grind.   I cannot recall an instance in which men were
at the mill.   It is tedious, fatiguing work, and slaves, or lowest servants, are Slaving
set at it.[2]   From the king to the maid-servant behind the mill, therefore, work.
embraced all, from the very highest to the very lowest inhabitants of Egypt.[3]
This grinding at the mill was often imposed upon captives taken in war.
Thus Samson was abused by the Philistines,[4] and, with Milton for his poet,
bitterly laments his cruel lot :—

> "To grind in brazen fetters, under task,
> Eyeless, in Gaza, at the mill with slaves."

[1] Matt. xxiv. 41.   [2] Isa. xlvii. 2.   [3] Exod. xi. 5.   [4] Judges xvi. 21.

PART
III.

"Nether"
millstone.

Damascus
mulberry.

Ramleh.

What is the foundation for the comparison, "Hard as the *nether* mill-stone ?"[1] Is the lower harder than the upper ?

Not always. They are often both of the same porous lava, brought from the Hauran; but I have seen the *nether* made of a compact sandstone, and quite thick, while the upper was of this lava,—probably because, from its lightness, it is the more easily driven round with the hand.

What tree is this mingled with the olive and the almond, and loaded with a pale green berry ?

That is the *tût shamy*—the Damascus mulberry. It is grown for its fruit, not for the silk-worm. Pass this way in the middle of May, and you will find these trees bending under a load of berries so exactly resembling our largest blackberries in America that you cannot distinguish them from each other. There are more of these Damascus mulberry-trees here than all I have seen elsewhere in my life, and they yield their glossy black fruit more abundantly than in other places. It has a sharper acid than that of the ripe blackberry, and when eaten in large quantities is unhealthy. It is one of those fruits, now found all over Palestine, which are not mentioned in the Bible; and the same remark applies to the prickly pear, which flourishes in such impenetrable thickets around these villages.

Let us incline a little to the right, pass round to the west of Ramleh, and examine that tower which overlooks the whole country. Here we cross the road from Jaffa, and you observe this large open cistern in ruins to the south of it. There are many vaulted cisterns between this and the tower, and other indications that this vicinity was once either the seat of Ramleh itself, or of some more ancient town. These cisterns may be almost of any age, and a city at this place would have them, of course. In Mohammedan times we can find an adequate cause for them in the fact that there were here large *khans* for the accommodation of the trading caravans which passed this way into Egypt.

This noble tower is generally believed to be a minaret, but the style of architecture differs from that of any minaret known to have been erected by the Moslems, at least so far as I have seen. There are a few minarets in some of the cities of Syria which resemble this, but they are in every case attached to mosques which were originally Christian churches. In my opinion this tower is one of them, and was the campanile of a magnificent church. Of its age I know nothing. That there is an Arabic inscription over the entrance to the interior stairway, bearing date A.H. 710, A.D. 1310, establishes only the fact that this record was placed there at that date, for Mohammedan rulers often insert slabs with pompous inscriptions over entrances to buildings which they did not erect. There are scores of such vaunting records on castles, temples, and churches which are much older than the era of Mohammed. The nature of those ancient buildings renders this matter quite easy, and the architects

---

[1] Job xli. 24.

of this country are so skilled in these insertions that the forgery cannot readily CHAPTER
be detected. I am inclined, therefore, to ascribe an early date to the cisterns XXXIV.
found all through the olive orchards hereabout, and the same to the tower Remains
itself. That the Moslems did destroy Christian churches at Ramleh is certain, of
and in doing this it would be quite natural to leave the tower standing, to churches.
serve as a minaret to mosques, which, after their usual custom, they erected
at or near the same site. These mosques, being less substantial, subsequently
fell into decay, or were thrown down by earthquakes or by the Crusaders.
The confused tradition of such events, mingled up with fables of various ages,
have, therefore, as I suppose, a foundation in fact. Dr. Robinson has a long
and learned epitome of these historical and traditionary notices, and, though
we may not always fully sympathize with him in his depreciation of ecclesiastical tradition, nor feel anxious to strip all these cherished sites of their sacred
associations, yet we can never fail to be instructed by his learned researches.

These vaults beneath the area enclosed by the ancient buildings are in them- Ancient
selves, and apart from all historical questions, very remarkable. The one vaults.
under the south side is about one hundred and fifty feet long, forty wide, and
twenty-five deep. The roof is sustained in the centre by a row of nine square
columns. The cistern on the west end is nearly seventy-five feet *square* and
twenty deep, and the roof is supported by a *double row* of columns. The *third*
is parallel to the *first*, which it also resembles in its details. Besides these,
there are smaller vaults and cisterns, so perfect, even yet, as to hold water.
The great vaults, well plastered with hard stucco, are dry, lighted from above,
and may have been used as store-houses for the caravans ; but if so, the case
is unique, for there is no other example of the kind in Syria, and no reason
can be assigned why resort should have been had to such expensive subterraneous magazines in Ramleh alone. In all other khans the magazines were
built round the hollow square enclosed by the exterior walls, nor can I believe
that the Moslems constructed these vast vaults for that purpose. Probably
they were connected with the more ancient cathedral or convent, or both
united, of which they and the tower are the only remaining monuments. But
enough of this antiquarian discussion. Here lies a heavy marble slab, or,
rather, square column, written over from end to end with an Arabic inscription
which refers to the erection of mosques on this spot subsequent to the times
of the Crusades.

Let us now enter and ascend this *campanile* by its winding stairs of one Campan-
hundred and twenty-six steps. The entire height cannot be much less than ile.
one hundred feet. Twenty-three years ago, after this tower had been rudely
shaken by an earthquake, which cracked nearly all the houses in Ramleh, and
threw down many, I ascended to see if it had been injured ; but it stood precisely as before, not a rent or crack from bottom to top, and thus it has stood
a hundred earthquakes uninjured. It is twenty-five feet square at the base,
and diminishes by graceful offsets, dividing it into different storeys, with various-
shaped windows and architectural embellishments. The summit has been

accommodated with a round tower and balcony, to fit it for the muezzin of the mosque; but this is obviously an anomalous addition to the original structure, and most of it has been shaken down by those earthquakes which have had no effect on the body of the tower.

At the time I speak of, the whole of this country was in revolt against Ibrahim Pasha and Mohammed Aly of Egypt. I was shut up in Ramleh for many anxious days, and often came to this lofty look-out to watch the movements of the opposing forces with a heavy heart, for my family was in Jerusalem —the only Franks there, with one exception—and the city was in the hands of the rebels. After returning from one of these sad and solitary watchings, I wrote in my journal as follows: "The view from the top of the tower is inexpressibly grand. The whole plain of Sharon, from the mountains of Judea and Samaria to the sea, and from the foot of Carmel to the sandy deserts of Philistia, lies spread out like an illuminated map. Beautiful as vast, and diversified as beautiful, the eye is fascinated, the imagination enchanted, especially when the last rays of the setting sun light up the white villages which sit or hang upon the many-shaped declivities of the mountains. Then the lengthening shadows retreat over the plain and ascend the hill sides, while all below fades out of view under the misty and mellow haze of summer's twilight. The weary reapers return from their toil, the flocks come frisking to their folds, and the solemn hush of Nature shutting up her manifold works and retiring to rest, all conspire to soothe the troubled heart into sympathetic repose. At such an hour I saw it once and again, and often lingered until the stars looked out from the deep sky, and the breezes of evening shed soft dews on the feverish land. What a paradise was here when Solomon reigned in Jerusalem, and sang of the 'rose of Sharon!' Better still will it be when He that is greater than Solomon shall sit on the throne of David his father; for 'in his days shall the righteous flourish, and abundance of peace so long as the moon endureth. The mountains shall bring peace to the people, and the little hills by righteousness.'[1]

> "'Fly swifter round, ye wheels of time,
> And bring the promised day.'"

Lovely Sharon, good-night! our tent awaits us at the Birkeh on the eastern side of the village.

Is there reason to believe that Ramleh is the Arimathea of Joseph?

Some understand Jerome to mean this place when he speaks of Arimathea as being near to Diospolis—that is Lydd; but he may have had in mind Renthieh, on the north of Lydd. The tradition which connects Joseph with this place, however, is quite ancient, confused, and doubtful, though it may be. Dr. Robinson discusses the question with his usual learning; and with his usual distrust of tradition he settles it against Ramleh. There is too little

Marginal notes: View from top.   Is Ramleh Arimathea?

---

[1] Ps. lxxii. 3, 7.

resemblance between the names of Ramleh—*sand*—and Arimathea, derived from a root which means *high*, and is applied to towns on elevated sites, to build anything upon the mere name ; but those who have faith in ecclesiastical tradition will scarcely give up Ramleh on this account. The assertion of Abu el Fida, that *Ramleh* as it now is was built after Mohammed, scarcely touches the question, for the Mohammedans rarely built entirely *de novo*, and I am quite sure they did not here. The old city *might* have been called Ramathaim; and the form of the word, not being according to Arab taste and idiom, was changed to Ramleh for their new town. I am unable to decide the question, because I cannot be certain that both Eusebius and Jerome do not speak of this as the Arimathea of Joseph. They must have had better opportunities for correct information than we can procure, and if they locate it here I shall not dispute their decision.

Ramleh is a larger town than Lydd, and has now about three thousand five Its size. hundred inhabitants, a greater proportion of whom are Christians than in any other place on this plain. There are many good houses, several churches and convents for pilgrims, and some large well-built soap factories. An immense old church, once dedicated to St. John, is now the chief mosque of the place. It always fills me with indignation to see these ancient edifices thus perverted, and I believe it would be an act of real justice if the Christian nations would compel the restitution of this, and all others like it, to the native Christians. Most of the European nations have consular agents here, and there is more wealth and a greater approximation to the style and manners of a city than in other towns of the same size in Palestine. This is doubtless owing to constant intercourse with pilgrims and European travellers.

CHAPTER XXXV.

RAMLEH TO ASHDOD.

Soap manufacture.	Wady Sûrar.
Neby Danyâl.	Gaza—Ethiopian eunuch.
Beit Ur (Beth-horon).	The sirocco.
Biblical sites.	Yebna—Threshing
Kuryet el 'Ainub.	Usdûd—Ashdod.
Modin—Latron.	Fog—"cloudy dew."

April 14th.

A RAMBLE through the streets this morning has not increased my respect for Ramleh. I got bewildered among narrow crooked lanes which lead nowhere in particular ; and with dogs, hairless and scabby, had a regular battle, until a one-eyed man kindly drove them away, and guided me out of the perplexing labyrinth. Are these large mounds of grey rubbish the ashes of soap factories ? Soap manufactories. They are, and they speak of an extensive business continued through many centuries. You will see similar heaps at Gaza, Jerusalem, and many other places, but by far the largest are at Edlip; and there, too, are the most extensive olive orchards in the country. I cannot account for these immense hills of ashes, except on the supposition that the *kŭly* (alkali) used in the manufacture of soap has been very impure, leaving a large residuum to be cast out upon these heaps.

Soap.

From whence is this *kŭly*, and by what process is it manufactured?

In Syria it is obtained mostly from the Arabs of the frontier deserts, where it is made by burning the *glasswort* and other saliferous plants that grow on those arid plains. The *kŭly* resembles in appearance cakes of coarse salt, and it is generally adulterated with sand, earth, and ashes, which make the residuum very large, and from it these vast *tells* of rubbish gradually accumulate around the places where soap is manufactured. The growth of these mounds, however, is so slow, that it must have taken hundreds, if not thousands of years for those at Edlip to reach their present enormous size. The mineral alkali called *natron*, found in Egypt, and employed from remotest antiquity for various purposes besides making soap, as we learn from Herodotus and other old authors, is not used in this country.

Scriptural allusions.

Both kinds of alkali are mentioned, I suppose, in the Bible. Jeremiah says of the degenerate Jews of his day, "Though thou wash thee with *nitre*, and take thee much soap, yet thine iniquity is marked before me, saith the Lord God." [1] This *borith*, here translated soap, was doubtless some cleansing preparation of vegetable alkali, and the *nitre* was the mineral *natron* of Egypt. Malachi also speaks of "fullers' soap," [2] where the same word *borith* is used. Solomon was acquainted with the natron of Egypt, and also with the fact that it effervesced violently when brought into contact with vinegar; and he says that this is like singing songs to a heavy heart; [3]—that is, it throws the heavy heart into a sour, angry fermentation, as when *natron* is cast into a pot of vinegar.

Soap ashes.

In one respect, at least, these ashes are very mischievous. They not only add to the heat of summer, which renders Ramleh almost uninhabitable, but on the occurrence of the slightest wind the air is filled with a fine pungent dust, which is very injurious to the eyes. I once walked the streets counting all that were either blind or had defective eyes, and they amounted to about one-half of the *male* population. The women I could not count, for they are more rigidly veiled in Ramleh than in any other town in the country. I never saw the faces of those in whose house I resided for a month. Whenever I had occasion to go out or come in, a servant, or one of the sons, always preceded me, calling out, "*Et tarîûk! et tarîûk!—the way! the way!*" when the women fled and concealed themselves, in their own apartments. But we must leave Ramleh, and I fear we shall encounter a sirocco to-day, for there are premonitory puffs of hot air which rarely deceive.

[1] Jer. ii. 22.   [2] Mal. iii. 2.   [3] Prov. xxv. 20.

The muleteers will go directly to Ashdod, while we make a detour, to gain CHAPTER a better knowledge of the plain, and also to visit Jamnia, which lies to the XXXV. west of the regular road from Ramleh. We will ride through these olive Road to orchards to an elevated point in the ridge, which commands a prospect of great Ashdod. rural beauty and rich historic interest. On the east you can trace the road from Lydd to Jerusalem, far up the mountain toward Beth-horon ; and to the south-east the path that goes by Emmaus quite to Latron, at the entrance into Wady 'Aly. As we do not take either of these roads to the Holy City, this is the spot from which to point out to you what there is to be seen along them. I have been over them so often that every salient rock and stunted bush is perfectly familiar to me. From Lydd the path leads down into a wady, which it partly follows for three miles, to a place called Jimzû,—no doubt Jimzû the Gimzo reconquered by the Philistines, with other cities in the low country, in the days of Ahaz.[1] Neby Danyâl—Prophet Daniel—is some two miles in Neby this direction ; and on the north of Jimzû is a large tell covered with rubbish, Danyâl. and now named Daheriyeh or Duheîry. The road keeps up a valley north of Jimzû, which I heard called Wady Zicheriyeh—Zechariah ; and in it are some remarkable caverns and old foundations, marking an ancient site, which also bears the name of this prophet. The extensive quarries along this wady were probably made by the builders of Lydd and Ramleh. Bufilîya lies over the ridge to the south, in a wady called Suleiman, along which there is a road leading to Jîb. Above Zicheriyeh is Shilta, a ruin on the left ; and east of it another called Kŭrakûr. Half an hour further is an extensive site called Keferrût,—possibly the Chephirah of the Gideonites who deceived Joshua.[2] There is a willy there called Khŭrîyeh. Sŭffah is a village one mile south-east of Keferrût, and in about an hour more Beit Ur et Tahta, a site manifestly Beit Ur ancient, and admitted on all hands to be the lower Beth-horon, so often (Beth-horon). mentioned in the Bible. I have always found the Moslems there particularly austere and uncivil. It is just an hour from this to the upper Beit Ur—heavy climbing over an extremely rough road. This place we shall visit from Jerusalem, and may now return by a track leading south-west into a broad wady called Merj Ibn Omeir, on the south side of which is situated Yalo, the modern representative of that Ajalon over which Joshua commanded the moon to stand still on that memorable day when his victorious army pursued the routed host of the five kings. They evidently fled from Gibeon down by the upper Beth-horon to the lower, and then southward into this Merj Ibn Omeir. All these places are still found, and in exact agreement with the account of that great victory recorded in the 10th chapter of Joshua. The water from this Merj, *when it flows at all*, runs down a narrow channel, passes off to the *north*-west along Wady Atallah, east of Lydd, and thence across the great plain to the 'Aujeh. Wady 'Aly bends round Latron, and then *northward* below Kebab to the same valley east of Lydd, and not *south-west* toward

---

[1] 2 Chron. xxviii. 18.　　　　　　[2] Joshua ix. 17

PART
III.

Ekron, as in most maps of this region, in which, also, Amwas is placed *south* of Latron, whereas its true position is north.

Biblical sites. Amwas— Emmaus? What a nest of Biblical sites are in view! but that which interests me most is Amwas. Do you suppose it is the site of the Emmaus toward which the two disciples were pursuing their sad walk when the risen Saviour joined them, and in which he was made known to them by the breaking of bread?

So thought Eusebius and Jerome, but there are almost insurmountable objections against it. Luke says it was *threescore* furlongs from Jerusalem,[1] and this site is twice that distance as the crow flies. Besides, if we were at liberty to correct the text, as has been suggested, and make it read one hundred and sixty furlongs instead of sixty, that might bring you to Amwas; but how were the disciples to get back to Jerusalem that same night, before the people had retired to sleep, as we are told expressly that they did?[2] "The day was far spent" when the three reached Emmaus. They had their meal to get ready, and it was certainly evening when they sat down to meat. They could not, therefore, have started back before dark, and it is six hours' hard walking over rough mountains from this Emmaus to Jerusalem. If this had been the place, they could not have reached home until after midnight. This is certainly possible, but not probable, and therefore I cannot believe that we have before us the scene of that interesting conversation and miracle recorded in the 24th chapter of Luke. This is yet to be found somewhere much nearer the Holy City; and Josephus states[3] that Cæsar, after the destruction of Jerusalem, gave Emmaus, a village *sixty* furlongs from the city, to eight hundred of his soldiers, whom he had dismissed from his army. This I believe to be identical with the Emmaus of Luke.

Kuryet el 'Ainub. I regard with respect the tradition that the Emmaus of Luke is Kuryet el 'Ainub, which Dr. Robinson identifies with Kirjath-jearim. It is the right distance from Jerusalem, and it would be a very appropriate situation to plant a colony of disbanded troops, for they would command the road from the seaboard to Jerusalem. The two things do not clash, for Kuryet el 'Ainub *may* be both Kirjath-jearim and Emmaus; and it renders the place more interesting to find it not only the resting-place of the *ark*, but, long after, of *Him* who was infinitely greater than the ark.

Nicopolis. But, though this is not the Emmaus of Luke, it early became celebrated, and there are still the remains of a church there, and other indications of antiquity. It was called Nicopolis by Julius Africanus, who caused it to be rebuilt early in the third century; and under this name it is often mentioned by Eusebius, Jerome, and other early writers. It also figures largely in the Crusades, as does also Beit Nuba, that village a short distance north of it, which marks the end of Richard the Lion-hearted's wild career in this country. He loitered weeks there, and then returned crest-fallen to Ramleh. There are fine fountains below Emmaus, which Pliny mentions;[4] and good water in

[1] Luke xxiv. 13.　　[2] Luke xxiv. 33.　　[3] Wars, vii. 6, 6.　　[4] Book vi. 14.

this neighbourhood is most acceptable even in spring, as the pilgrims have CHAPTER abundant reason to remember, for the road is lined with boys and girls with XXXV. jars of it, which they sell at exorbitant prices.

Where is Modin, so celebrated in the Maccabees and in Josephus? Modin.

The site has not yet been discovered, but I suspect that it is identical with Latron, seated about two miles south of Amwas, upon a high hill directly in Latron. front of the entrance into Wady 'Aly. This site seems best to agree with all the notices of Modin which we have; and the *pyramids*, built there by the Maccabean family, could well be seen from the sea, as they are said to have been; and the large ruins now covering the hill at Latron require something of the kind to account for them. It was a strong castle, and an important station during the Crusades, for which its position is admirably adapted, for it completely commands the entrance into Wady 'Aly, up which is the ordinary road to Jerusalem. The monks say that this Latron was the city of the penitent thief, whom they call Disma, and who, according to their legends, used to rob pilgrims and travellers in Wady 'Aly. Hence the name of the place, Latron or Ladrone,—robber.

Wady 'Aly is the easiest route to Jerusalem, but there is neither water nor Wady any monument of antiquity in it except the tomb of the Imam 'Aly, below 'Aly. Saris, from which the valley takes its name. After gaining the top of the mountain—three good hours from Latron—you descend to Kuryet el 'Ainub, which, for the last half century, has had a bad notoriety as the seat of the mountain robber Abu Gush. We shall visit that neighbourhood from the Holy City, and now let us turn westward to Yebna. This little village to the south, Yebna. with its pretty gardens, is 'Akir, no doubt the modern heir of the celebrated Ekron. Josephus says the god of Ekron was a fly, and I certainly found plenty Ekron. of them there when I visited it two years ago. From this place the ark of God was sent back, and the unbroken and unguided kine took the direct road across the plain to Beth-shemesh; which city was near the mouth of Wady Wady Sûrar, behind that long rocky spur which strikes down from the mountains Sûrar. south of Latron.[1] There is *'Ain* es Shems at the present day, and somewhere near it was the city to which came the cart with its mysterious burden. We can now easily understand how the lords of the Philistines could follow until they saw it taken possession of by the Bethshemites, and then return the same day to Ekron. It might be said by those ignorant of the country, that, the whole distance being a level plain, there was no great miracle needed to secure the safe transmission of the ark over this comparatively short distance; but let them make a similar experiment, and stake their scepticism upon its success, if they have the courage to do so, or let them even try to reach 'Ain es Shems themselves without a guide, and see how they will succeed.

My thoughts have often followed Philip and the eunuch in their ride across Ethiopian eunuch.

---

[1] 1 Sam. vi. 10–12.

this plain, and I have wished to know what sort of country they passed through.

If the eunuch came down Wady 'Aly from Jerusalem, he would follow nearly the same track from Latron that I once took, and this is now regarded as the easiest and safest route ; if he came by Wady Sûrar, entering the plain near Beth-shemesh, he would cross it further south ; and if he descended by Eleutheropolis, his route would be still nearer the southern desert. Then another question is, whether Philip set out from Samaria or from Jerusalem ; most probably from Samaria, as I think, for he appears to have been in that city when he received the command to go.[1] He would then have met the Ethiopian chariot somewhere south-west of Latron. There is a fine stream of water, called Murŭbbah, deep enough even in June to satisfy the utmost wishes of our Baptist friends. This Murŭbbah is merely a local name for the great Wady Sûrar, given to it on account of copious fountains which supply it with water during summer. Above them the wady was entirely dry in the month of April, at which time the transaction took place, I suppose. I know of no brook on the route from Beth-shemesh to Gaza, but there may be one. Dr. Robinson found water in the wady below Tell el Hâsy, which is midway between Beit Jibrîn and Gaza, and on the direct line between them. This route would lead them near, if not quite into the desert. The same, however, might have been true of either of the routes, out in the centre of the plain, as it is at this day. Some, perhaps most people, suppose that it was Gaza which was desert, and not the country through which the road passed ; and the Greek is as indefinite as the English ; but Philip did not go to the city, neither was it desert or deserted at the time when the angel commanded him to take this excursion ; nor do I believe it has ever been an *eremos*—desert— since the earliest days of history. It has often been sacked, plundered, and sometimes burned, and it suffered one of these reverses about thirty years after the journey of Philip; but these Oriental cities spring up from their ashes, like the phœnix, with wonderful rapidity ; and I cannot suppose that Gaza itself could, with any propriety, be called desert either then or at any other time from that day to this.

Ethiopian eunuch's road.

Gaza.

That Philip was found at Azotus, which is Ashdod, after the baptism of the eunuch, seems to imply that it took place not far from that city, which is rather against the idea that they followed the road from Beit Jibrîn to Gaza, since that would carry them many miles south of Ashdod.

These filmy apologies for clouds which lounge about the sky seem to act rather as condensers to concentrate the heat than as a cooling shadow. There is something extremely oppressive in this air.

Sirocco.
We have two kinds of sirocco, one accompanied with vehement wind, which fills the air with dust and fine sand. I have often seen the whole heavens veiled in gloom with this sort of sand-cloud, through which the sun, shorn of

---

[1] Acts viii. 5, and 25–27,

his beams, looked like a globe of dull smouldering fire. It may have been CHAPTER
XXXV.
this phenomenon which suggested that strong prophetic figure of Joel, quoted
by Peter on the day of Pentecost :[1] " Wonders in the heaven above, and
signs in the earth beneath ; blood, and fire, and pillars of smoke ; the sun
shall be turned into darkness, and the moon into blood."[2] The pillars of
smoke are probably those columns of sand and dust raised high in the air
by local whirlwinds, which often accompany the sirocco. On the great desert
of the Hauran I have seen a score of them marching with great rapidity over
the plain, and they closely resembled "pillars of smoke."

The sirocco to-day is of the quiet kind, and they are often more overpower-
ing than the others. I encountered one a year ago on my way from Lydd to
Jerusalem. Just such clouds covered the sky, collecting, as these are doing,
into darker groups about the tops of the mountains, and a stranger to the
country would have expected rain. Pale lightnings played through the air
like forked tongues of burnished steel, but there was no thunder and no wind.
The heat, however, became intolerable, and I escaped from the burning highway into a dark vaulted room at the lower Beth-horon. I then fully understood
what Isaiah meant when he said, " Thou shalt bring down the noise of the *Heat with*
strangers as the heat in a dry place, as the heat with the shadow of a cloud ;"[3] *shadow of*
that is, as such heat brings down the noise and makes the earth quiet—a *a cloud.*
figure used by Job when he says, " Thy garments are warm when he quieteth
the earth by the south wind."[4] We can testify that the garments are not
only warm, but *hot.* This sensation of dry hot clothes is only experienced
during the siroccos ; and on such a day, too, one understands the other effects
mentioned by the prophet,—bringing down the noise, and *quieting* the earth.
There is no living thing abroad to make a noise. The birds hide in thickest
shades ; the fowls pant under the walls with open mouth and drooping wings ;
the flocks and herds take shelter in caves and under great rocks ; the labourers
retire from the fields, and close the windows and doors of their houses ; and
travellers hasten, as I did, to take shelter in the first cool place they can find.
No one has energy enough to make a noise, and the very air is too weak and
languid to stir the pendent leaves even of the tall poplars. Such a south
wind with the heat of a cloud does indeed bring down the noise and quiet the
earth.

Here we are at Yebna, as the Jamnia of the classic geographers is now *Yebna—*
pronounced. Yebna, however, was the ancient Hebrew name, as appears *Jamnia.*
from 2 Chron. xxvi. 6, and the Arabs have restored it to its proper place. It
has always been a flourishing town, and is so still. There are traces of old
buildings about it, but no remains of any remarkable edifice ; yet the ancient
inhabitants must have had temples and idols in abundance, for when Judas
Maccabeus had overthrown Gorgias here at Jamnia, he " found under the coats
of every one that was slain things consecrated to the idols of the Jamnites.

---

[1] Joel ii. 30, 31.   [2] Acts ii. 19, 20.   [3] Isa. xxv. 5.   [4] Job xxxvii. 17.

PART
III.

Then every man saw that this was the cause for which they were slain."[1]
Strabo says that Jamnia and its vicinity were so densely inhabited that it sent
forth forty thousand armed men.   Pliny mentions two Jamnias—this before
us, and another on the sea-board.   This last is mentioned in 2 Macc. xii. 9 ;
and there Judas is said to have " set fire to the haven and the navy, so that the
light of the fire was seen at Jerusalem !"   The sea is behind these sandy downs,
about three miles distant, but the harbour has entirely disappeared.

Jaffa to
Yebna.

From Yebna to Jaffa is three hours and a half.   Coming this way, the road
leads through gardens for more than half an hour, and then keeps along the
border of these downs of white sand for nearly two hours to Wady Haneîn, in
which are traces of ancient buildings at different places.   The remains of old
Sarafend are up this wady to the north-east, and the wady runs down to the
sea on the north side of a remarkable tell called Rubîn, where is also a willy
of the same name.   A considerable ridge extends back eastward, and spreads
out in different directions, on the southern slope of which is Kebab, and El
Mughar twenty minutes east of it.   Between these and Yebna is a deep valley,
through the centre of which descends the brook of Wady Sûrar, which turns
round to the north-west, and then unites with Wady Haneîn near the tell
Rubîn.   The ancient harbour of Yebna was at the mouth of this wady.

Yebna is pleasantly situated on this hill, which declines westward toward
the sea ; and there may be three thousand inhabitants, all Moslems, and all
given to agriculture.   Their territory is large and of surpassing fertility.   Our
steam ploughs would work wonders in the plain of Philistia, and the time
must come when they, or something better, will take the place of these ridiculous Arab machines.   And yet, with even this imperfect mode of cultivation,
the harvests of Yebna are very abundant.   When I passed this way two years
ago there were hundreds of men, women, and children reaping, gleaning, and
carrying away the grain to their great threshing-floors.   Long lines of camels,
bearing on their backs burdens many times larger than themselves, were slowly
converging to a point here at Yebna from every part of the plain, and the grain
lay in heaps almost mountain-high.

Rich har-
vests.

The threshing-floors were arranged all round the town, and the scene was
picturesque and novel even to me.   The most common mode of threshing is
with the ordinary slab, called *mowrej*, which is drawn over the floor by a horse
or yoke of oxen, until not only the grain is shelled out, but the straw itself
is ground into chaff.   To facilitate this operation, bits of rough lava are
fastened into the bottom of the *mowrej*, and the driver sits or stands upon it.
It is rare sport for the children to sit on these slabs, and even our own
delight to get out to the *baidar*, as the floor is called, and ride round on the
mowrej.

Thresh-
ing-floors.

The Egyptian mowrej is a little different from this, having rollers which
revolve on the grain ; and the driver has a seat upon it,—which is certainly

The mow-
rej.

more comfortable. In the plains of Hamath I saw this machine improved by CHAPTER
having *circular saws* attached to these rollers. It is to this instrument, I XXXV.

SUMMER THRESHING-FLOOR.

MOWREJ.

suppose, that Isaiah refers in the 41st chapter of his prophecies : " Behold, I Threshing
will make thee a new sharp threshing instrument *having teeth*. Thou shalt instru-
thresh the mountains, and beat them small, and shalt make the hills as chaff. ment hav-
Thou shalt fan them, and the wind shall carry them away, and the whirlwind
shall scatter them." [1] This passage has several allusions which we can readily
understand and explain in this country.   The intention of the farmer is to beat

---

[1] Isa. xli. 15, 16.

and grind down his hills of grain to chaff, and much of it is reduced to fine dust, which the wind carries away. Very little use is now made of the *fan*,

but I have seen it employed to *purge the floor* of the refuse dust, which the owner throws away as useless. The references to the wind which drives off the chaff are numerous in the Bible, and very forcible. The grain, as it is threshed, is heaped up in the centre of the "floor," until it frequently becomes a little mound much higher than the workmen. This is particularly the case when there is no wind for several days; for the only way adopted to separate the chaff from the wheat is to toss it up into the air, when the grain falls in one place, and the chaff is carried on to another. Isaiah here speaks of the whirlwinds, and it is a curious fact that whirling currents are extremely common on the plains. They start up as if by magic or spirit influence, and rush furiously onward, swooping dust and chaff up to the clouds in their wild career.

Treading out corn.
The sacred writers speak of *treading out* the corn. Is this mode still practised by these farmers of Philistia?

On some floors here at Yebna there was no machine of any kind, and boys rode and drove horses round on the grain, somewhat as we did in our barns when I was a boy. It was this, in part, which made the scene so peculiar. Some ran round from left to right, and others the reverse, and no one continued long in the same direction, but changed every few minutes, to keep the animals from getting dizzy.

Muzzling the ox.
The command of Moses not to muzzle the ox that treadeth out the corn is literally obeyed to this day by most farmers, and you often see the oxen that draw the mowrej eating from the floor as they revolve. There are niggardly peasants, however, who *do muzzle* the ox,—enough to show the need of the com-

mand; and Paul intimates that there were just such in the Church in his day: CHAPTER XXXV.
"Doth God take care for oxen? or saith he it altogether for our sakes? For
our sakes, no doubt, this is written; that he that plougheth shall plough in
hope; and that he that thresheth in hope should be partaker of his hope."[1]

The Peutingerian Tables make the distance between Yebna and Ashdod to
be ten miles, and we shall find it two hours and a half fair riding over the level
plain. The only village that divides with Yebna the produce of this region is
El Hamamy, just visible to the east of us. Here is a deep channel coming
down toward the sea, with a bridge over it, for which I have no name but that
of Usdûd. In the plain above, it has various branches, one of which passes Usdûd.
down by a ruin called Mukhazin, and another comes from Mesmia, two hours
east of Usdûd. I hope our tent will be under the shady trees near the large
ruined khan of Usdûd, on the west of the village, for there alone we shall find
refuge from this persecuting wind.

There seem to be extensive orchards and large groves of sycamore about it,
but the sand from the shore comes quite up to the town.

Yes; and at no distant day it will entirely overwhelm it, and Ashdod will Sand.
then be nothing but a heap of barren moving sand. The site, however, is
protected by these groves, which break the course of the wind, and is further
sheltered by this artificial tell, on the eastern side of which most of the houses
are built. The tell was most likely the acropolis of the old city.

Hot as it is, I must take a stroll round this ancient capital of the Philistines.

As you like; but I have seen enough of it on former occasions to dispense
with a further survey in such air as this.

Well, you are soon satisfied. Did you find the marble columns of the Remains
temple of Dagon, or the grassy hill of Volney? of Ashdod.

You may as well stop. I saw nothing ancient, and think there is nothing
to be seen except a few old stone buildings stowed away among the wretched
mud hovels, so as not to be easily examined. The people, too, are so rude,
that I was glad to escape from their impertinent curiosity. The village is
buried beneath forests of cactus, and overshadowed by sycamores, which impart
a singular aspect to the place. I saw camels drawing up water from deep
wells with the Persian water-wheel. The plain eastward seems boundless,
very fertile, and well cultivated. This is the extent of my discoveries; and
there is more evidence of antiquity at this old khan and *mazar* than anywhere
else about Ashdod.

You have enumerated nearly everything that is to be seen, and we cannot
do better just now than discuss our dinner, which has been waiting this last
half hour. And yet I would not imply that Ashdod, even in ruins, is destitute
of interest. This high and ample mound, I suspect, constituted that impregnable acropolis which it took Psammetichus of Egypt *twenty-nine years* to sub- Acropolis.

[1] 1 Cor. ix. 9, 10.

PART
III.

due. Herodotus says this was the longest siege that any city ever sustained
Ashdod, like Jamnia, had a port, which, like that, also, has entirely disappeared. The sea is some two miles distant, and the intervening space is a
desert of moving sand, which has reached the outskirts of the town. If you
are anxious to see what vicissitudes this city of Dagon has passed through,
and on what occasions it has played a part in the great drama of history, you

Bible re-
ferences to
Ashdod.

can consult Joshua, and First Samuel, and Second Chronicles, and Nehemiah,
and the Maccabees, and Josephus, and Luke, who calls it Azotus in the eighth
chapter of Acts.[1] The Greek and Roman historians and geographers often
speak of it, as also Eusebius, Jerome, and other Christian fathers, under the
same name. It figures likewise largely in the Crusades, and, indeed, in nearly
all other wars that have ever desolated the country of the Philistines. This
long and eventful story proclaims its inherent importance and the tenacity of
its life; but it has finally fallen under the heavy " burden" of prophecy, and
sunk to the miserable village from which you have just escaped.

The Phi-
listian
plain.

You are quite correct about the eastern plain, for it is exceedingly fertile,
and crowded with flourishing villages, more so than any part of Philistia. I
once came from Latron diagonally across the country to this place in a little
more than six hours. The whole distance must be about twenty-five miles,
for I rode fast. For the first hour and a half the country was diversified by
alternate fat valleys and low rocky spurs from the mountains west of 'Ain es
Shems. Leaving Khŭlda on a high hill a little to the right, I crossed the
brook Murŭbbah—a name for this part of Wady Sûrar—and, after following
down its reedy bank for a mile, I left it where it inclines to the north-west,
and, riding nearly two hours further, through an ocean of ripe wheat, came to
Mesmia just as the sun set. There I pitched for the night. It is a large
agricultural village, mud hovels packed together like stacks in a barn-yard,
and nearly concealed by vast mounds of manure on all sides of it. During the

Fog.

night a dense fog settled down flat upon the face of the plain, through which
you could not see ten steps, and the scene in the morning was extraordinary
and highly exciting. Before it was light the village was all *a buz* like a bee-
hive. Forth issued party after party, driving camels, horses, mules, donkeys,
cows, sheep, goats, and even poultry before them. To every body and thing
there was a separate call, and the roar and uproar were prodigious. The
parties separated in all directions out into the plain, shouting for the same
reason that steamers whistle, blow horns, and ring bells in foggy weather.
Ere long all were lost in the dense mist, and by degrees the thousand-tongued
hubbub died away in the distance. Taking a guide from Mesmia, we also set
out for this Usdûd, directing our course a little north of west. It was a
strange ride, for, during the grey and foggy dawn, we saw camels in the air,
and " men as trees walking," and often heard all sorts of noises about us without seeing anything. At length, a sea breeze coming to the assistance of the

[1] Josh. xv. 46, 47; 1 Sam. v. vi.; 2 Chron. xxvi. 6; Acts viii. 40; Neh. xiii. 23, 24.

sun, the fog began to rise and wheel about, now hither, now thither, in fantas- tic evolutions, until, at the end of an hour, we came out into the clear light of day near Yazûr. This village is seated at the south end of a high ridge, is better built, and has more trees about it than Mesmia, but is not so populous. Turning somewhat to the south of west, we came in half an hour to Bûtany es Sharkîyeh, and thence to Bûtany el Gharbîyeh, and from this last to Usdûd —two hours and a half in all from Mesmia, through as fertile a country as the sun ever shone upon.

Isaiah makes the Lord say, " I will take my rest, I will consider in my dwell- ing like a clear heat upon herbs, and like a cloud of dew in the heat of har- vest." [1] This latter comparison, I have no doubt, was suggested by some such cloud as this which I have described. In the morning it absolutely *reposed* upon the vast harvest-field of Philistia, lying on the corn serene and quiet as infancy asleep. I have never seen such a cloud in this country except "in the heat of harvest." To what natural phenomenon exactly the poetic prophet refers in the preceding clause is doubtful; "like a clear heat upon herbs" is scarcely intelligible in this connection. I at least have noticed nothing of this kind which could suggest the thought of repose and meditation. Nor does it improve the matter to read, "like a clear heat *after rain*," as it is in the margin. The Hebrew itself is obscure, but in the Arabic it is "like the shining light of *noonday*." This is very suggestive of retirement to some cool, quiet place of rest, and there are many references to it in other passages of the Bible. I have often been struck with the quietude of sultry noon. Neither man, nor beast, nor bird is astir. The flocks gather under shady trees, or be- hind walls and great rocks, and drowsily ruminate; the feeble breeze slumbers among the tree-tops, and the very shadows appear stationary and dreamy. If the allusion is to these phenomena, it is very expressive indeed.

It is during such rides that one sees life as it is in Philistia. When the fog dispersed the whole plain appeared to be dotted over with harvesting- parties, men reaping, women and children gleaning and gathering the grain into bundles, or taking care of the flocks which followed closely upon the foot- steps of the gleaners. All seemed to be in good humour, enjoying the cool air of the morning. There was singing alone and in chorus, incessant talking, home-made jokes, and laughing long and loud.

The grain is not bound in sheaves as in America, but gathered into large bundles. Two of these, secured in a large net-work of rope, are placed a few feet apart. The camel is made to kneel down between them, the large bundles are fastened to his pack-saddle, and, at a signal from the driver, up rises the peaceful beast and marches off toward the threshing-floor near the village. Arrived there, the patient beast kneels down again, and is relieved of his awk- ward load only to repeat the same operation all day long, and for many weeks together, for the Syrian harvest extends through several months. On the

[1] Isa. xviii. 4.

plain of Philistia it commences in April and ends in June; and this not only gives ample time, but it has this great advantage, that the villagers from the mountains can assist the farmers on the plain, since their own crops are not yet ripe. I was struck with this fact when at Mesmia. Several Christians from Bethlehem, who had thus come to reap, spent the evening at my tent, and one of them explained to me the advantages derived from thus labouring on the plain. He not only received wages for his own and his wife's labour, but his children were permitted to follow after them and glean on their own account, as Boaz allowed Ruth to do in their native village.

Unburnt brick.

In that ride through Philistia I saw many villages built entirely of unburned brick, made by tramping up the soil into thick mud mixed with *tibn* from the threshing-floor. It was this kind of brick which the Israelites were required to make in Egypt, and the manufacture of them is certainly the most dirty and slavish work in which the peasant engages.

Digging through houses.

It would be easy to dig through houses built of these soft bricks, as did Ezekiel when enacting the signs of captivity before the people.[1]

Or as robbers and other bad men, bent on evil errands, did in Job's day.[2] The fact is that these mud houses and mud villages are ephemeral, insecure, and every way uncomfortable; low, filthy, and earthy, without light or ventilation, all packed together; no privacy of any kind possible; no relief from incessant noise from man, and beast, and creeping things; no shelter from a burning sun; no escape from clouds of dust;—in a word, they are dens of wretchedness and endless discomfort. The natives, however, seem insensible to these annoyances, and are measurably happy. They have also some wise and good *institutions* among them. One is the public wells, where the water is raised by *wheel and bucket-work*, called sâkîeh, at the common cost and for common use. The one near my tent at Mesmia had four stout mules allotted to it, and was kept in motion night and day. The well was one hundred and twenty feet deep, and the water was cool, sweet, and inexhaustible.

Public wells.

CHAPTER XXXVI.

ASHDOD TO GAZA.

April 15th.

FORTUNATELY our sirocco has subsided into a soft south-west wind, and without rain, giving us a bright morning and the prospect of an agreeable day.

---

[1] Ezek. xii. 5.   [2] Job xxiv. 16.

This plain over which we have ridden from Usdûd is constantly being encroached upon by this desolating sand, along the border of which the path has led, rising occasionally over the advanced swells of the coming flood. The first village on our left was Beit Daras, the next further out is Jûlis, eastward of which a little more than an hour is Gustiny, all of them rich agricultural towns, which sit very prettily on the rolling plain. We shall now turn off from the regular road to Gaza, which keeps more inland, and make for Askelon, by that village called Hamamy. It is about six miles from Usdûd, and, like it, seems just about to be overwhelmed by the sand. It is a thriving village, however, and has traces of a more prosperous antiquity. By the direct line over the sand hills it is three miles to Askelon, but much further by the regular road from Hamamy. We shall take the former, not because it is the nearest, but because there is something sadly appropriate in this approach to Philistia's capital, over such swells and ridges of barren sand. The modern village is a little north of the old site, and the houses which are not made of sun-dried bricks are built out of the fragments of old Askelon. It will take us two hours to run even hastily over the ruins, and the baggage had better pass on to some sycamore-trees near a large Moslem willy on the south-east side of the city. There we will lunch and rest, for I give you warning that the ramble will be very fatiguing. We will pass down here on the north side to the shore, and there hand our horses to these boys to be taken to our lunching-ground, for it is impossible to explore the interior on horseback.

Askelon differs from the other celebrated cities of the Philistines, being seated on the sea, while Ekron, Gath, Jamnia, Ashdod, and Gaza are in the interior. It never could have been a harbour of any considerable size, however, and what once existed appears to have been filled up by Sultan Bibars of Egypt, that great scourge of mankind, and destroyer of cities in this country. The topography of this place is very peculiar. A lofty and abrupt ridge begins near the shore, runs up eastward, bends round to the south, then to the west, and finally north-west to the sea again, forming an irregular amphitheatre. On the top of this ridge ran the wall, which was defended at its salient angles by strong towers. The specimens which still exist along the south-east and west sides show that it was very high and thick,—built, however, of small stones, and bound together by broken columns of granite and marble. This clearly proves that it is patch-work, and not Askelon's original rampart. These extraordinary fragments, tilted up in strange confusion along the sandy ridge, are what generally appear in the pictures of Askelon, and impart such an air of desolation to the view. The position, however, is one of the fairest along this part of the Mediterranean coast; and when the interior of this amphitheatre was crowded with splendid temples and palaces, ascending, rank above rank, from north-west to south-east, the appearance from the sea must have been very imposing. Now the whole area is planted over with orchards of the various kinds of fruit which flourish on this coast. It is especially celebrated for its apples, which are the largest and best I have ever seen in this country.

Road to Askelon

Hamamy.

Askelon.

Desolation.

Fruits.

When I was here in June quite a caravan started for Jerusalem loaded with them, and they would not have disgraced even an American orchard. Dr. Kitto has laboured in several of his works to prove that the Hebrew word taffûah, translated "apples," means citron; but I think this is one of his least happy criticisms. The Arabic word for apple is almost the same as the Hebrew, and it is as perfectly definite, to say the least, as our English word,—as much as the word for grape, and just as well understood; and so is that for citron,—but this is a comparatively rare fruit. Citrons are also very large, weighing several pounds each, and are so hard and indigestible that they cannot be used except when made into preserves. The tree is small, slender, and must be propped up, or the fruit will bend it down to the ground. Nobody ever thinks of sitting under its shadow, for it is too small and straggling to make a shade. I cannot believe, therefore, that it is spoken of in the Canticles. It can scarcely be called a *tree* at all, much less would it be singled out as among the choice trees of the wood. As to the smell and colour, all the demands of the Biblical allusions are fully met by these apples of Askelon; and no doubt, in ancient times and in royal gardens, their cultivation was far superior to what it is now, and the fruit larger and more fragrant. Let taffûah, therefore, stand for apple, as our noble translation has it.

The sycamore fig grows larger here, and of a darker blue colour than in any other place I have visited. They are gathered, and carried in baskets to Gaza. None of these fruits are ripe yet, but the orchards promise a generous crop. There are no buildings of the ancient city now standing, but broken columns are mixed up with the soil, and the number of old wells and cisterns still kept in repair enables the peasants to water their orchards and gardens abundantly, without which all would quickly perish.

Let us climb to the top of these tall fragments at the south-east angle of the wall, and we shall have the whole scene of desolation before us, stretching, terrace after terrace, quite down to the sea on the north-west. The walls must have been blown to pieces by powder, for not even earthquakes could toss these gigantic masses of masonry into such extraordinary attitudes. No site in this country has so deeply impressed my mind with sadness. O man, savage, ferocious, brutal, what desolations thou hast wrought in the earth! They have stretched out upon Askelon the line of confusion and the stones of emptiness. Thorns have come up in her palaces, and *brambles in the fortresses thereof*, and it is a habitation of dragons and a court for owls.[1]

This is the impression "before dinner." Let us descend to our cheerful lunch, spread on the clean sand under those giant sycamores, and the view after dinner will be much less gloomy. Askelon will surely be rebuilt at some future day of prosperity for this unhappy land. The position is altogether too advantageous to allow it to sink into total neglect. The inhabitants call the place El Jore, but they are also acquainted with the name Askelon, and in

---

[1] Isa. xxxiv. 11, 13.

some degree with her ancient story, which closely resembles that of her CHAPTER XXXVI. neighbours, Ashdod and Gaza, and is to be found in the same books, sacred and profane. In the Crusades it played a more illustrious part than either of them, but we shall not enter into details, which may be found in the same authors referred to for the history of Usdûd. If this place was ever celebrated for aromatic plants, as Strabo, Pliny, and Dioscorides assert, they probably grew on these sand hills north and south of the city.

Askelon was famous for the worship of Venus under the name of Derceto, Worship of Venus. as Herodotus informs us; but if there ever was a deep lake near it, abounding in fish, into which she, ashamed of some of her misdeeds, plunged, and was transformed into a fish, it has totally disappeared. It is a curious fact, however, that there are still sacred fish kept in consecrated fountains in several parts of this country. Is this a remnant of the old fish-worship of Syria, Origin of fish-worship. springing originally from, or connected with these fables about Venus? I think so; for it is difficult to account for these sacred fish on any other supposition. I have visited several of these fountains, but the largest and most remarkable is situated a short distance north of Tripoli.

We must now pursue our journey, and for the first half hour over this naked ridge to N'alia, a village nearly surrounded by sand hills. Mejdel, buried up Mejdel. in a forest of tall olive-trees, lies nearly due east of Askelon, but it has exchanged places with Hamamy on modern maps. Mejdel is a large town, with mosque and minaret, and some good houses. It has also a governor and cadi, and is regarded as a sort of capital for the region about Askelon. The direct road from Usdûd to Gaza keeps further inland, having Beit Timah, El Villages. Jîyeh, and Beit Jirjia on the east of it, in the order named. Beit Timah is a considerable distance out on the plain, the others are near the road, and all of them are surrounded by large olive-groves. The next village southward is Deir Senad, and near it is a bridge, broad and substantial, over a deep channel, always dry when I have been here, but which has a vast volume of water during the winter rains. It is called Senad from this village, but higher up it takes the name of Wady Simsim. This river does not run north-west, as put down on maps, but breaks through the sand ridge to the sea, west of Deir Senad. Here is Beit Hanûn on our left, and between us and the sea is Beit Lahia, and further on is Jebala. These villages are famous for their fruit and vegetables, with which the markets of Gaza are supplied. Jebala is a sort of suburb to Gaza, and at it a great part of the oil gathered from these immense groves is made into soap. And now the tall palm-trees and taller minarets of this last city of Palestine toward Egypt come into view. We shall seek quarters in a khan, in order to escape annoyance from this rude population. They bear a bad character, and have lately shown symptoms of Moslem fanaticism and insubordination, which render it safest and wisest to avoid all occasion of trouble.

In wandering over the ruins of this curious city I came upon an immense serpent, which had just caught one of these pretty crown-larks. The screams Serpent. and fluttering of the poor captive drew me to the spot, and I succeeded in killing the snake, but the bird was dead. This adventure reminded me of an inquiry I have often wished to make in regard to the curse pronounced upon the serpent in Eden : " Dust shalt thou eat," etc., etc.[1] Are there any snakes in the East that eat dust or earth ? In our country they are carnivorous or insectivorous—gather their food from the grass, the rocks, the trees, the water —insects, worms, frogs, birds, and mice, while the larger devour squirrels and hares. We know that in Africa and the East the gigantic anaconda and boa crush to death and swallow whole gazelles and other animals, but I never heard or read of any that eat dust.

Eating
dust.
Perhaps the phrase " eat dust" has a metaphorical meaning, equivalent to " bite the dust," which from time immemorial has been the favourite boast of the Eastern warrior over his enemy. To make him eat dust, or, as the Persians have it, *dirt*, is the most insulting threat that can be uttered. In pronouncing sentence upon the serpent, we need not suppose that God used the identical *Hebrew* words which Moses wrote some thousands of years afterward, but the Jewish lawgiver was guided to a proverb which fully expressed the purport of that divine commination. We may paraphrase it after this fashion : Boast not of thy triumph over a feeble woman, proud, deceitful spirit ; you shall be overthrown, and reduced to the most abject degradation. The seed of this feeble victim of thy treachery shall yet plant his heel upon thy accursed head, and make thee bite the dust. This explanation agrees well with the manner in which Isaiah uses the proverb. Speaking of the triumph of the Redeemer's kingdom, he adds, " And dust shall be the serpent's meat," what time the wolf and the lamb shall feed together, and the lion shall eat straw like the bullock. Then shall this most ancient and most glorious prophecy and promise receive its full accomplishment, and the old serpent, with all his evil brood, be made to bite the dust. May we not find here an allusion to the manner in which the serpent has always been killed—by crushing his head into the earth ?

Flying
serpents.
Moses speaks repeatedly of fiery serpents,[2] and Isaiah mentions fiery flying serpents :[3] are there any kind of snakes which can properly be said to fly ?

In all these cases the Hebrew word is suraph, and Arab scholars identify it with a kind of serpent that *darts* with prodigious velocity upon its victims, and, when enraged, against its enemies. A thousand incredible stories are related in reference to it. I have been assured by those who professed to speak from personal knowledge, that it will spring, leap, or, as they call it, *fly* to an immense distance, and with such force as literally to penetrate and pass quite through any soft substance with which it comes in contact. The children of Israel encountered these flying serpents in the *wilderness ;* and, in strict agreement with this, the scene of all these marvellous stories is laid in the great deserts. Though I by no means credit all these anecdotes, at least in

[1] Gen. iii. 14.   [2] Num. xxi. 6.   [3] Isa. xxx. 6.

their exaggerations, yet they are too numerous and consistent to be mere fic- CHAPTER
tions. Niebuhr, and many other respectable travellers into Arabia and Chaldea, XXXVJ.
also speak of them, not as fables, but as well-known realities. The name,
flying serpents, does not necessarily imply that they had wings, as Orientals
familiarly apply this to multitudes of things to which such appendages do not,
and are never supposed to belong. The epithet *fiery* would be given to them
either from their fiery temper, colour, and motions when enraged, or from the
burning pain of their bite. They are regarded as very dangerous, and even
mysteriously dreadful.

16*th*. We have had a pleasant excursion through the different parts of this
celebrated city. How many inhabitants is it supposed to contain?

There are one hundred and fifty taxable Greeks, which may give seven Popula-
hundred for the entire Christian population. The kady told me last night tion of
that there were *fourteen thousand males* among the Moslems. This, if ap- Gaza.
plied to the *whole province*, may be correct; if restricted to the *city*, it is
simply absurd, as it would give a population of about fifty thousand Mohammedans. Both Christians and Moslems maintain that Gaza is larger than
Jerusalem, and the entire population may be sixteen or eighteen thousand.
The city is built partly on an oblong hill, partly in the valleys south and
north of it. There are now neither walls nor forts, but the places of certain
gates belonging to ancient walls are pointed out. The only one that interests
me is that which bears the name of Samson, from the tradition that it was
from that place that he carried off the gate, bar and all. It is on the east
side of the hill-part of the city, looking toward Hebron, and near it is a mazar,
or willy, to his honour. Gaza is municipally divided into five *haras*, or *wards*.
Two are in the broad vale on the south-east, and both called *Sejarîyeh*—
woody. They are the *new* town, and indicate growth and advancement. The
other three are *et Tuffah*—the *apples; Daraj*—*steps;* and *Zeitûn*—*olive.*

The original city stood on the hill where the palace, mosques, khans, and Original
nearly all the stone houses now are. This was its position when Alexander site.
besieged and took it, according to Arrian; and many granite and marble
columns, and heavy old stones, mingled with more recent work, on this hill, go
to confirm the fact. This, too, is the tradition of the place; and the people
know of no other site for ancient Gaza. I suppose, therefore, that Dr. Keith
is mistaken in his theory on that subject. There is, however, an old tradition
given by Reland, that the original city was deserted, and a new Gaza erected
on another spot. Jerome also seems to intimate something of this kind; but
perhaps nothing more is meant than some new suburb around the old site on
the main hill, just as the two *haras* or wards, called *Sejarîyeh*, have arisen
in the vale to the south-east of the present town. An air of decay hangs over Appear-
Gaza, partly because many buildings are really falling to ruins, and partly ance of
because the stone out of which it is built is old and saturated with saltpetre, decay.
which effloresces, and disintegrates with great rapidity. A house soon comes
to look old that is built of these rotten ruins. On the south-west of the city

PART
III.

are the quarantine buildings, erected by the present government out of this same description of stone, and they already show signs of decay. The mosque, most conspicuous for its massive minaret, is believed to have been a Christian church, and is still known by the name of Dier Hannah. Dr. Robinson gives a particular description of this church, and thinks it may possibly date back as far as the *beginning* of the fifth century. Bonaparte is said to have destroyed this castle east of our *khan*, and, at any rate, its overthrow is comparatively recent. Those travellers are mistaken who say that the sea is not visible from Gaza. We have seen it from various points, over and beyond the great olive-groves ; but, of course, it cannot be seen from lower parts of the city. The harbour is a little north of west, near two willys, now called 'Adjlûn and Sheikh Hasan. The ancient name seems to have been Majumas. It is a mere open roadstead, and there is no village, nor even a magazine cn the shore.

Wells.

The wells at Gaza are very deep, some of them one hundred and fifty feet ; but the natives greatly praise the quality of the water. I found the air cool in June, and all agree that the city is healthy. The houses are full of sparrows, and the gardens alive with doves and other birds, which keep up a constant *roar* of music, aided by rooks in abundance from the tops of the feathery palm. The commerce of Gaza with the Arabs is considerable, but the great trade of the city is in soap, which is carried over the desert to Cairo. They send none by ship, as the sea air damages the soap. A *cantar*—about five hundred and fifty pounds—is transferred on camels to Cairo for four dollars and a half, though the journey takes fifteen days. Latterly, a large trade in wheat, barley, and sesamum has sprung up with Europe, shipped mostly from Jaffa. With a harbour at hand and a government to protect from the Bedawîn, Gaza would rapidly rise in importance. It is admirably situated for trade with all the eastern tribes of Arabs, and with Egypt. At no very distant day a railroad will pass down from the plains of Northern Syria, and the valleys of the Euphrates and Tigris, to Egypt, and then again Gaza, as the frontier city, will become populous and flourishing.

Commerce.

Antiquity.

Gaza is among the very oldest cities in the world. The name occurs in the 10th chapter of Genesis;[1] and in Joshua[2] it is mentioned as one of the three cities in which alone Anakim still existed. In the distribution of the land it was assigned to Judah, and after the death of Joshua it was actually conquered by that tribe ; but they did not long keep possession of it, for when it again appears in sacred history it is as a city of the Philistines, in connection with the romantic adventures and exploits of Samson.

That reminds me that he was here imprisoned and made to grind at the mill. I saw this operation going on in several places during our ramble about the city, and we heard its ringing " sound" until a late hour last night. To what an abject condition that renowned champion of Israel was reduced,—

Samson in
fetters at
Gaza.

"To grind in brazen fetters under task,
Eyeless, in Gaza, at the mill with slaves!

[1] Gen. x. 19.   [2] Josh. xi. 22.

> Oh, change beyond report, thought, or belief!
> See how he lies at random, carelessly diffused!
>   Can this be he
> Who tore the lion as the lion tears the kid;
> Ran on embattled armies clad in iron,
> In scorn of their proud arms and warlike tools;
> Spurned them to death by troops? The bold Ascalonite
> Fled from his lion ramp; old warriors turned
> Their plated backs under his heel,
> Or, grovelling, soiled their crested helmets in the dust.
> Then, with what trivial weapon come to hand,
> The jaw of a dead ass his sword of bone,
> A thousand foreskins fell, the flower of Palestine,
> In Ramath-lechi, famous to this day
> Then by main force pulled up and on his shoulders bore
> The gates of Gaza, post, and massy bar,
> Up to the hill of Hebron, seat of giants old."

Thus Milton sings his glorious deeds.

Yes, and with what shame, remorse, and horror he is made to bewail his unequalled folly in having divulged the secret gift of God—

> "To a deceitful woman. . . . Delilah,
> That specious monster, my accomplished snare,
>   Who shore me,
> Like a tame wether, of my precious fleece,
> Then turned me out ridiculous, despoiled,
> Shaven and disarmed among mine enemies.
>   Tell me, friends,
> Am I not sung and proverbed for a fool
> In every street?"

By far the most wonderful exhibition of his giant strength he ever made was in this city, not only in walking off with the gates to the top of yonder hill toward Hebron, though any one who knows what the doors of a city gate are, will not think this a small achievement, but chiefly in pulling down the vast temple of Dagon, by which he himself perished, with three thousand of his enemies. I looked at some of the old columns near the brow of Castle Hill with great interest, and I fancied that they once formed part of Dagon's temple. I suppose that the three thousand were partly on the flat roof and partly below, and all were crushed together in an unparalleled calamity. Have you never felt it difficult to believe that such strength could reside in or be put forth by any combination of human bone and sinews? *(margin: Carrying off the gates.)*

It was divine power acting through these limbs of Samson. This renders it easy and simple. Samson himself, according to Milton, was rather disposed to understate the gift:— *(margin: Dagon's temple.)*

> "What is strength without a double share
> Of wisdom? Vast, unwieldy, burdensome.
> God, when he gave me strength, to show withal
> How slight the gift was, *hung it in my hair*."

It is one of those pleasant coincidences, that here at Gaza, where we read so incidentally of the "grinding at the mill" in that ancient story, we still have *(margin: Grinding at the mill)* the same operation ringing in our ears. The reason is, that this city has no mill-stream near it ; there is neither wind nor steam mill, and hence the primitive apparatus is found in every house, and heard in every street. Nor can it be mere fancy that these modern Philistines bear a close resemblance to their proud, vindictive, and licentious ancestors.

The three hundred foxes.
How do you understand the matter about the three hundred foxes ? I have often heard it quoted as proof of the incredibility of some of the Bible narratives, by sceptics, who deny the possibility of one man catching so many foxes.

It is probable that by foxes jackals are intended, and these are even now extremely numerous. I have had more than one race after them, and over the very theatre of Samson's exploit. When encamped out in the plain, with a part of Ibrahim Pasha's army, in 1834, we were serenaded all night long by troops of these hideous howlers. But if we must limit Samson to the ordinary meaning of fox, even these are to be found here. I started up and chased one when I passed over that part of the plain where Timnath is believed to have been situated. It must be admitted, however, that the number seems not only large in view of the difficulty of capturing them, but also far too great for the purpose intended. The object was to set fire to the dry corn which covered the plains of the Philistines. Now a spark would seem sufficient to accomplish this. During the summer months the whole country is one sea of dead-ripe grain, dry as tinder. There is neither break, nor hedge, nor fence, nor any cause of interruption. Once in a blaze, it would create a wind for itself, even if it were calm to begin with. And it would seem that a less number could have answered all the purposes of Samson ; but to this it is obvious to remark that he meditated no limited revenge. He therefore planned to set the fields of a great many towns and villages on fire at the same moment, so that the people would be confounded and bewildered by beholding the conflagration on all sides of them ; and each being intent on saving his own crop, no one could help his neighbour. Besides, the text implies that certain parts were already reaped, and this would produce interruptions in the continuity of the fields ; and, also, we know not the modes of cultivation at that early period. Part of the land may have been permitted to lie fallow, or might have been planted with " summer fruits," which, being green, would stop the conflagration, and render necessary a greater number of firebrands.

Difficulty of capturing.
As to the difficulty of capturing so many foxes, we must remember that Samson was judge or governor of Israel at that time. He no more caught these creatures himself than Solomon built the temple with his own hands : and if we take two or three other facts into account, it will not appear incredible that the governor of a nation could gather such a number of foxes when he had occasion for them. The first is, that in those days this country was infested with all sorts of wild animals to an extent which seems to us almost incredible. This is evident from almost numberless incidental allusions in the Bible ; but the use of fire-arms for so many centuries has either totally exterminated

whole classes, or obliged them to retire into the remote and unfrequented deserts. No doubt, therefore, foxes and jackals were far more numerous in the days of Samson than at present. The second fact is, that, not having fire-arms, the ancients were much more skilful than the moderns in the use of snares, nets, and pits for capturing wild animals. A large class of Biblical figures and allusions necessarily presuppose this state of things. Job, and David, and all the poets and prophets, continually refer in their complaints to snares, nets, pits, etc. We are justified, therefore, in believing that, at the time in question, the commander of Israel could, with no great difficulty, collect even three hundred foxes. He was not limited to a day or a week; and though it may be true that in the whole country there are not now so many killed in an entire year, yet this does not prove that this number could not have been then gathered by Samson from the territories of Judah, Dan, and Simeon, over which his authority more particularly extended. We therefore want no correction of the text to render the whole account credible, nor need we call in the aid of miracles. It was merely a cunning device of Israel's champion to inflict a terrible chastisement upon his enemies.

That it was felt to be a most serious calamity is shown by the cruel punishment inflicted upon the indirect cause of it. Not being able to reach Samson, they wreaked their vengeance upon his wife and all her house, and they destroyed them with the same element which had consumed their harvest. And when we remember that so great is the dread of fire in harvest-time, that the Arabs punish with death any one who sets fire to a wheat-field, even though done by accident, we will not greatly wonder that the Philistines should have thus dealt with the family whose injurious conduct had excited their dreaded enemy to this ruinous exploit.

Philistian revenge.

Have you been able to discover any remnants of that famous temple which Samson overthrew with such terrible slaughter of the laughter-loving Philistines?

I have never seen them except in pictures, with the mighty man "bowing himself with all his might" between two of the toppling columns.

The edifice must have been of enormous size, for "there were *upon the roof* about three thousand men and women, that beheld while Samson made sport."[1] It is not easy for me to understand how the tearing of a column or two from so vast a temple could have brought the whole to the ground.

The temple of Dagon.

The roofs in Gaza were then flat as they are now, and it does not require a *very* large space for three thousand people, who stand as close as they can be packed. So much for the size of the building. A further explanation may be found in the peculiar topography of Gaza. Most of it is built on hills, which, though comparatively low, have declivities exceedingly steep. The temple was erected over one of these, beyond a doubt, for such was and is the custom in the East; and in such a position, if the central columns were taken out,

Its probable position.

---

[1] Judges xvi. 27.

PART
III.

Temple of
Dagon.

the whole edifice would be precipitated down the hill in ruinous confusion. There is such a steep declivity on the north-east corner of the present city, near the old dilapidated castle and palace, and the houses in that vicinity have fragments of columns wrought into the walls and laid down as *sills* for their gates. Somewhere in that neighbourhood, I suppose, the temple stood; and it coincides with this conjecture that the *willy* of Samson is in a garden a little east of it.

How over-
thrown.

Is it not a fair deduction from the story of the overthrow of this temple, that *columns* large enough to sustain immense roofs were common at that very early day? And may not those which are found in many of the ruined cities of Palestine date back to the same age? Such has long been my opinion; and I am further inclined to believe that the immense roof which rested upon these columns was sustained by *arches*. If this were so, and the centre columns stood on the brow of the declivity, near the old castle, the whole edifice would be precipitated down the hill merely by tearing away those centre supports.

There seems to be an unusual amount of noise and confusion in the street. To what is this owing?

Wedding.

Salim says it is a procession in honour of the marriage of the governor's oldest son. Let us take our stand on the roof of the *khan*, from which we can have a full view of this Oriental cavalcade. Playing the jereed is the most animating spectacle of the whole; but this, I perceive, has already taken place out on the plain, for their panting steeds are still covered with froth and foam. There are a thousand pictures of this sport, but none that does justice to it, and, indeed, it must be seen to be understood and appreciated. The sheikhs and emeers of Lebanon and Hermon are the best jereed-players. Gaily dressed, and superbly mounted, they take their stations at opposite ends of the hippodrome. At length one plunges his sharp *shovel* stirrups into the quivering side of his horse, and away he bounds like a thunderbolt until within a short distance of his opponent, when he wheels sharp round as if on a pivot, flings his "reed" with all his might, and then darts back again, hotly pursued by his antagonist. Others now join in, until the whole hippodrome resounds with the general *mêlée*. Many are the accidents which occur in this rough play, and what begins in sport often ends in downright earnest; but, notwithstanding this, the young emeers are extravagantly fond of it, for nowhere else can they exhibit either their horses or themselves to so great advantage; and from every latticed window that looks out upon the hippodrome they well know they are keenly watched by the invisible houris of their midnight dreams. Some of the players perform almost incredible feats of daring and agility. Not only will they catch the "reed" of their antagonist in their hand while on the run, but I have seen them hang to the saddle by the upper part of the leg, throw themselves down so low as to catch up from the ground their own reed, and regain their seat again, and all this while their horse was at the top of his speed. There is always more or less of this jereed-playing at the weddings of the great, and upon all important state occasions.

Jereed-
playing.

CHAPTER
XXXVI.

Harlequin
musicians

Caval-
cade.

Here comes a new farce: musicians in harlequin attire, with fox-tails
dangling from conical caps, blowing, beating, and braying any amount of dis-
cordant music.   Following them is a company of dancers at sword-play. They
are fierce-looking fellows, and their crooked Damascus blades flash around
their heads in most perilous vehemence and vicinity.   This, I suppose, is the
first time you have seen a real shield, or heard its ring beneath the thick-falling
blows of the sword.   The next in this procession are genuine Bedawîn Arabs,
with their tremendous spears.   This is because Gaza is on the borders of the
desert, and the governor finds it to his interest to court the sheikhs of these
powerful robbers.   And now comes the governor and suite, with the bridegroom
and his friends—a gay cavalcade, in long silk robes ; some of them are olive-
green, and heavily loaded with silver and gold lace.   Such is high life in Gaza.

DANCING-GIRLS.

The whole night will be spent in feasting, singing, dancing, and rude buffoonery, in the open court by the men, and in the *harem*, in equally boisterous
games and dances, by the women.   These are great occasions for the dancing-

girls ; and many, not of the "profession," take part in the sport. We see little to admire in their performances. They move forward, and backward, and sideways, now slowly, then rapidly, throwing their arms and heads about at random, and rolling the eye, and *wriggling* the body into various preposterous attitudes, languishing, lascivious, and sometimes indecent ; and this is repeated over and over, singly, or in pairs or groups. One thing is to be said in their favour : the different sexes do not intermingle in those indecorous sports. In my opinion, the dances spoken of in ancient Biblical times were in most points just such as we have been describing.*

CHAPTER XXXVII.

GAZA TO BEIT JIBRIN.

Beauty and fertility of Philistia.
Gerar—Wells—Lahai-roi.
Character of Isaac.
Um Lakis—Lachish.
"Gulgal."

Beit Jibrîn or Eleutheropolis—Bethogabra?
Country of Samson—Timnath.
Lion—Bees—Treachery of wives.
David and Goliath.
David with Achish.

April 17th.

I AM now more than ready to leave this rude and fanatical city. What sort of country have we before us to-day ?

Road to
Beit Jib-
rîn.
Beautiful in itself, but monotonous—wheat, wheat, a very ocean of wheat. Our road to Beit Jibrîn leads diagonally across the whole territory of Philistia, and offers an opportunity to become familiar with its physical features and its present productions ; but there is not a single sight of much importance along the entire distance.

This I shall not regret, for I am almost disgusted with ruins, and fatigued by the effort to trace out the history of extinct races and magnificent cities among mud hovels and semi-savage Arabs. Give me for one day the open country, and soil unpolluted by these vulgar people, and unencumbered with shapeless heaps of unmeaning rubbish.

I cannot promise freedom from Arabs, not even from Bedawîn robbers, for we ride along the very borders of their desert homes, and they frequently make inroads quite beyond our track. Neither is the country anything like what we mean by virgin soil in America. It has been ploughed for thousands of years, and probably very much as it is at present ; but in one very remarkable respect it is not what it once was. There was doubtless a time, long, long ago, when it was covered with dense primeval forests, and there have been ages of prosperity and peace since then, when it was crowded with towns and

---

* [The author must allude here to such dancing as that of the daughter of Herodias before Herod. The dancing which sometimes accompanied worship must have been very different.— ED.]

villages, enclosed in and surrounded by beautiful gardens and orchards. But, ever since Moslem rule began, the land has become the property, not of the cultivator, but of the government; and while this ruinous régime lasts, this splendid country will remain as it is. No man will plant orchards and make improvements on land not his own; but give him a secure title, and, under the crude husbandry of even these ignorant peasants, Philistia will quickly be studded with villages, and beautified with vineyards, olive-yards, and orange-groves. This, however, will never be realized until a strong government subdue or drive back the Bedawîn to their deep deserts. Neither vineyards, nor fig orchards, nor vegetable gardens can exist, while these people are allowed to roam at will with their all-devouring herds and droves of camels.

The first time I came into this region I was agreeably surprised to find it not a flat, barren country, approaching to a sandy desert; one must go much further south to encounter anything resembling that. From the distant mountains it indeed has the appearance of a level plain, but the view is so vast that even very considerable hills are lost to the eye. In reality, Philistia closely resembles some of the most beautiful regions of our own glorious West. True, it lacks our fine forests, and one misses our charming country-houses, with their orchards; but that is owing to the inhabitants. The country is equally lovely and no less fertile than the very best of the Mississippi Valley. Nay, owing to something in the nature of the soil, or of the climate, or both, the sources of its fertility are even more inexhaustible than in any part of our own land. Without manure, and with a style of ploughing and general culture which would secure nothing but failure in America, this vast plain continues to produce splendid crops every year; and this, too, be it remembered, after forty centuries of such tillage.

In what part of this plain was Gerar, where Isaac resided so many years? It seems to have been extremely fertile, for he reaped a hundred-fold in that valley: "And the man waxed great, and went forward, and grew until he became very great,"[1]—as any other farmer would who reaped such harvests.

The site has not yet been discovered; but I doubt not it can and will be, just so soon as it is safe to travel in that region. It must be somewhere to the south-east of us, and not above fifteen miles distant. According to the "Onomasticon," it was twenty miles to the south of Eleutheropolis. Beginning, therefore, at Beit Jibrîn, and going southward about seven hours, the traveller encounters the great Wady Sheriah, called by some Wady Gaza; and in it, or in one of its fertile branches, there is little doubt but that the lost site will be found. Arabs who frequent Gaza from that neighbourhood speak of a ruined city somewhere there, which careful examination may yet decide to be the ancient Gerar. Isaac went there from Beersheba, the site of which is now known to be a few hours to the east of this region. There was a Wady Gerar in ancient times, which no doubt took its name from the

---

[1] Gen. xxvi. 12, 13.

PART
III.

city ; and, with such data to guide the future explorer, the place will surely be found.

Gerar—
Mr. Row-
lands' nar-
rative.

It is, perhaps, scarcely proper to speak of this site as even now absolutely unknown. The Rev. J. Rowlands believes that he not only found Gerar, but also the lost Kadesh-barnea. He thus writes to his friend Mr. Williams: "From Gaza our course was to Khalasa. On our way we discovered ancient Gerar. We had heard of it at Gaza under the name of Joorf el Gerar—the Rush or Rapid of Gerar, which we found to lie three hours south-south-east of Gaza. Within Wady Gaza, a deep and broad channel coming down from the south-east, and running a little higher up than this spot, is Wady es Sheriah, from the east-north-east. Near Joorf el Gerar are the traces of an ancient city called Khirbet el Gerar—the Ruins of Gerar. Our road beyond Khalasa lay along a plain slightly undulating. This plain must be the land of Gerar. Here we sojourned for two days (one of which was Sunday) with Abraham in Gerar." This is rather a meagre account of such a celebrated and unknown region and city, but it is the best we have at present. Mr. Rowlands then went southward to Suez, passing by Khalasa, or Khulasah as Dr. Robinson spells it, and identifies it with the Greek Elusa ; but Mr. Rowlands thinks it marks the site of the Chesil of Joshua xv. 30, one of the cities in the south of Judah. Both may be correct. Mr. Rowlands does not seem to have been aware that Dr. Robinson not only visited the place, but gave an extensive description and history of it. Our fortunate traveller, passing in a direct line across the desert from Khalasa to Suez, came, in two hours and a half, to an

Sebâta—
Zephath.

old site called Sebâta, which he identifies with Zephath, called Hormah— "destruction"—in Numbers xxi. 3, where the Israelites vowed a vow to utterly destroy the place, on account of the attack of king Arad ; and subsequently, in Judges i. 17, after Judah and Simeon had utterly overthrown it, this name "Destruction" was attached to it a second time. Near this place is also a well, called Bir Rohebeh, and the ruins of a city with the same name, which

Rehoboth.

he has no doubt was the Rehoboth of Genesis xxvi. 22. The ruins are extensive, and in remarkably good preservation. Ten camel hours (twenty-five miles) further toward Suez, Mr. Rowlands found Moilâhi, which he believes,

Beer-
lahai-roi.

for half a dozen reasons, to be Beer-lahai-roi, where Hagar found water, and called it after the name of the Lord that spake unto her, Lahai-roi—"Thou God, seest me."[1]   Our traveller is now in the vast wilderness, plain, or desert of Paran, called also the wilderness of Kadesh, so famous in early Bible story, and

Kadesh-
barnea.

he discovers more than one interesting locality. We shall only refer to Kadesh-barnea. He finds it twelve miles east-south-east of Moilâhi ; and as he stood at the base of the rock that was smitten by Moses, and gazed upon the beautiful brook of delicious water still gushing forth from it, and leaping down into the desert over many a lovely cascade, he was quite wild with enthusiastic excitement,—and well he might be, with his firm faith in the identification.

[1] Gen. xvi. 13, 14.

The history of Isaac's sojourn in Gerar is very curious and instructive. Com- CHAPTER
XXXVII. bining both pastoral and agricultural industry, it is not strange that he grew very great. The vast grazing plains around and south of his position enabled Isaac in him to multiply his flocks indefinitely, while the "hundred-fold" harvests Gerar. furnished bread for his numerous servants; and, in addition to these advantages, the blessing of the Lord was on the labour of his hands in a manner altogether extraordinary. These things made the Philistines envy and fear him; and therefore Abimelech, king of Gerar, demanded and obtained a covenant of peace with him. Just so at this day the towns, and even cities, such as Hamath and Hums in the north, and Gaza and Hebron in this region, cultivate with great care friendly relations with the sheikhs of prosperous tribes on their borders. It appears that the country was deficient in water, Scarcity of and that wells, dug at great expense, were regarded as very valuable posses- water. sions. Isaac was a great well-digger, prompted thereto by the necessities of Wells. his vast flocks; and in those days this was an operation of such expense and difficulty as to be mentioned among the acts which rendered illustrious even kings.[1] The strife for possession of them was a fruitful source of annoyance to the peaceful patriarch, as it had been the cause of separation between Abraham and Lot before him; and such contests are now very common all over the country, but more especially in these southern deserts. It was the custom in former times to erect towers or castles to command and secure the possession of valuable watering-places; thus Uzziah built towers in connection with "his many wells."[2] And to stop up wells was the most pernicious and destructive species of vengeance—the surest way to convert a flourishing country into a frightful wilderness. Israel was commanded thus to destroy the land of the Moabites, by stopping all the wells of water.[3] It would be a curious inquiry for the explorer to seek out these wells, nor would it be surprising if they should be found still bearing the significant names which Isaac gave them. All travellers agree that water is so scarce and valuable in that region, that the places where it is to be found are as well known by the Arabs as are the most flourishing towns in other parts of the country. Isaac's place of residence was the well Lahai-roi, as we read in Genesis xxv. 11, and xxiv. Lahai-roi. 62—the same that was so named by Hagar.[4] It may have been first discovered by her, or miraculously produced by "the God that saw her," for the salvation of the maternal ancestor of the Arab race and her unborn son, as the fountain of Kadesh afterward was for all Israel,[5] and perhaps that of Lehi for Samson.[6] It seems to have been the usual mode to designate the dwelling-place in patriarchal times, and indeed long after, by some circumstance or fact which made it memorable. Abraham dwelt under *the* oak at Mamre; Isaac at this well; Jacob hid the idols of his family under *the* oak at Shechem;[7] and long after, Joshua took a great stone and set it up under the same oak, as I

---

[1] 2 Chron. xxvi. 10. [2] 2 Chron. xxvi. 9. [3] 2 Kings iii. 19, 25. [4] Gen. xvi. 14.
[5] Num. xx. 11. [6] Judges xv. 19. [7] Gen. xxxv. 4.

PART III.

suppose.[1] Thus, also, Deborah dwelt under *the palm*-tree of Deborah;[2] the angel of the Lord that was sent to Gideon came down and sat under an oak which was in Ophrah;[3] king Saul is said to have tarried under a pomegranate-tree in Migron;[4] and it is yet quite common to find a village better known by some remarkable tree or fountain near it than by its proper name. The knowledge of these places and things is perpetuated from generation to generation; and I doubt not many of these wells in the south could be discovered, if one had time and liberty to explore.

Coincidences in patriarchal life.

There are some curious coincidences in the patriarchal connections with Gerar. Both Abraham and Isaac came from Beersheba to that city; both adopted the same prevarication in regard to their wives, for the same reason and with the same result. It would appear that these ladies must have been beautiful in comparison with the darker daughters of Philistia, and this even when they were far advanced in life. Both were taken into the *harem* of the king, and both rescued by similar divine interpositions. The king, in either case, was called Abimelech, and each had a chief commander called Phicol. Both Abraham and Isaac made covenants with these Abimelechs; the place of meeting in both cases was a well; and from the seven ewe lambs the well was called Beersheba—" the well of seven," or " well of the oath."

How do you account for these strange coincidences?

It is fair to conclude that Abimelech was the royal title, just as Pharaoh was in Egypt, and Cæsar in Rome. *Phicol* may also have been a name of office, as mudîr or mushîr now is in this country. If one of these officers is spoken of, his *name* is rarely mentioned. I, indeed, never know any but the official title of these Turkish officers. I suppose it was the custom of these Abimelechs to augment their state and glory by introducing into their *harems* illustrious ladies, and that often without respect to their age. To enable them to do this, they sometimes killed their husbands; and such things are not unknown even in our day. I could point to more than one such transaction among the emeers and sheikhs of this country. This was the temptation which led both Abraham and Isaac to that culpable deception which is recorded of them. As to the other repetitions of similar acts, there is no difficulty in understanding them. After the lapse of many years it would be quite in accordance with Oriental usages for the successors of the first Abimelech to renew the covenant of peace with Isaac, who had grown so great as to be both envied and feared. The *mode* of contracting alliance was the same, because in both cases an established custom was followed; and that the well should have been twice named Beersheba, from this double transaction made at it, is not surprising. It may have been intended also, by that divine providence which guided all such proceedings of the patriots, to settle, by these remarkable acts, a well-known point to determine in future ages the extreme southern border of the Promised Land.

Coveting wives.

---

[1] Josh. xxiv. 25–27.   [2] Judges iv. 5.   [3] Judges vi. 11.   [4] 1 Sam. xiv. 2.

The character of Isaac is very marked and peculiar. He never travelled far
from this spot during his long life of one hundred and eighty years—probably
never removed from Wady Gerar and its neighbouring city. There are but
few acts of his life on record, and several of these are not much to his credit.
He seems to have been an industrious, quiet man, disposed to wander alone
and meditate,—at least when he had such an interesting theme to think about
as the coming of the camels with his expected bride. He preferred peace to
strife, even when the right was on his side, and he was "much mightier" than
those who annoyed and injured him. This silent submission to injury was
objected to by Abimelech in the question of the wells, and with much apparent
justice. The king, when reproved about those which his servants had violently
taken away, replied, in substance, Why did you lay up this grudge in your
heart all this while? You should have had more confidence in my justice,
and instead of tacitly implying that I was a party to this violence, you ought
to have reported the case to me. I do not feel flattered by this concealment,
nor very well pleased that it should be cast in my teeth on this particular
occasion. The same injurious suspicion is more prominent in Isaac's conversation about his wife. He there distinctly states his apprehension that Abimelech was a lawless tyrant, who would not stick at murder in order to get
Rebekah into his harem. Neither Isaac nor Rebekah appears to advantage
in this discussion with Abimelech. I say *appears*, because it is by no means
certain that the king was not capable of doing just what Isaac feared; while
Isaac would sooner have lost his right hand, or even his life, than be guilty of
such enormous wickedness. And it is often the case that a very bad man may
be able to set his conduct in such a light as to seem more honourable and
generous than those much better than himself. This should be remembered
when we study the exhibitions of character made by Jacob and Esau at their
meeting in Gilead. Esau carries off the whole credit of the interview, and
his brother seems cold, suspicious, cunning, unbrotherly. And while I do
not pretend to admire certain traits in Jacob's character, yet he was far more
upright and religious than Esau. Jacob knew him and his four hundred men
too well to venture into his society and power. Hence all the shuffling and
backing out, and even deception, which he gave in return for his injured
brother's forgiveness, warm-hearted welcome, and generous offers of assistance. Jacob *dared* not accept them, and yet to reject them under such circumstances could not but place him in great embarrassment.

How could Isaac have been so grossly deceived by Jacob and his mother?

He was not only blind, but old, so that he could not distinguish with accuracy, either by the touch of his shrivelled hand or by the ear, now dull of
hearing. It must be further remembered that Esau was from his birth a hairy
person. He was now a man, full grown, and no doubt as rough and shaggy as
any he-goat. Jacob was of the same age, and his whole history shows that he
was eminently shrewd and cunning. He got that from his mother, who on this
occasion plied all her arts to make the deception perfect. She fitted out Jacob

PART
III.

History of
Isaac.

with Esau's well-known clothes, strongly scented with such odours as he was accustomed to use. The ladies and dandies in ancient times delighted to make their " raiment smell like the smell of a field which the Lord had blessed ;" and at this day they scent their gala garments with such rich and powerful spicery that the very street along which they walk is perfumed. It is highly probable that Jacob, a plain man, given to cattle and husbandry, utterly eschewed these odoriferous vanities, and this would greatly aid in the deception. Poor old Isaac felt the garments, and smelled the still more distinguishing perfumes of Esau, and though the voice was Jacob's, yet he could not doubt that the person before him was—what he solemnly protested that he was —his first-born. The extreme improbability of deception would make him less suspicious, and, so far as the hair and the perfume are concerned, I have seen many Arabs who might now play such a game with entire success.

All this is easy and plain in comparison with the great fact that this treachery and perjury, under most aggravating accompaniments, should be in a sense ratified and prospered by the all-seeing God of justice. It is well to remember, however, that though the blessing, once solemnly bestowed, according to established custom in such cases, could not be recalled, yet, in the overruling providence of God, the guilty parties were made to eat the bitter fruit of their sin during their whole lives. In this matter they sowed to the wind and reaped the whirlwind.

Retribution.

We set out on this line of remark by saying that in several of the known incidents of Isaac's history, few though they be, he does not appear to advantage. Even in this transaction, where he, now old, blind, and helpless, was so cruelly betrayed by his wife and deceived by his son, he is unfortunately at fault in the main question. He was wrong and Rebekah was right on the real point of issue ; and, what is more, Isaac's judgment in regard to the person most proper to be invested with the great office of transmitting the true faith and the true line of descent for the promised Messiah was determined by a pitiful relish and longing for " savoury meat." Alas, for poor human nature ! There is none of it without dross ; and mountains of mud must be washed to get one diamond as large as a pea.

We have taken no note of time during this long digression, nor have I even noticed the face of the country.

Not much lost thereby, for our track has been the ordinary road to Beit Jibrîn. After emerging from the great olive-grove north of Gaza, we had Beit Hanûn on our left ; then Demreh, on the same side, upon the bank of Wady Simsim, and Nejid on the south of our path. The village we have just passed is Simsim, and this one to which we are coming is Burîer. Time from Gaza three hours ; direction, north-east ; country, a rich, rolling, agricultural plain. Our next village is Um Lakis, which, I have little doubt, *derives its name* from the Lachish so celebrated in Bible story and prophecy. The city itself seems to have been more to the south, and nearer Beit Jibrîn, according to the " Onomasticon " and other notices. Even that is not certain, however, and

Um Lakis.

the great similarity of name, for a site so close to the locality of the ancient city, is not to be forgotten.   My company at Mesmia gave me names of villages, ruins, old sites, tells, and wells sufficient to fill two pages.   None in this direction, however, seemed to be of any historic interest except 'Aglan and this Lakis.   We shall come to 'Aglan in half an hour.   There are no ruins at either of these places to remind one of ancient glory; but the same remark applies to all the sites on this plain, and that for two reasons: the cities were built chiefly of unburned brick; and such parts as were of stone were either taken from that soft arenaceous formation which is found all along the coast, or from that cretaceous rock which is so characteristic of all these southern hills of Judea, and which is often nothing more than indurated marl.   We are not, therefore, to expect ruins; and the name, with a tell of greater or less height, composed of such debris, pottery scattered over the neighbourhood, and a well or two, with a sarcophagus or a stone trough—these are the things by which we identify old sites in Philistia.

Brick buildings.

The plain from this to Beit Jibrîn is destitute of villages and barren of historic interest ; and, after taking our lunch at this 'Aglan, we must quicken our pace, or we shall be out on this desert later than is exactly safe.   The whole distance, at our rate of riding, is nine hours, and this may be taken as the utmost breadth of the proper territory of the Philistines.   The great Wady Simsim branches out to the north-east and south, but it is everywhere destitute of water except in winter.   The largest of these branches, called Wady el Hasy, wanders about in a general direction toward the south-east, and drains the western slopes of the mountains of Hebron.

What sort of vegetable is this whose stems our muleteers are cutting up and chewing with so much relish ?

It is the wild artichoke.   We can amuse ourselves with it and its behaviour for a while, and may possibly extract something more valuable than the insipid juice of which our men are so fond.   You observe that in growing it throws out numerous branches of equal size and length in all directions, forming a sort of sphere or globe a foot or more in diameter.   When ripe and dry in autumn, these branches become rigid and light as a feather, the parent stem breaks off at the ground, and the wind carries these vegetable globes whither-soever it pleaseth.   At the proper season thousands of them come scudding over the plain, rolling, leaping, bounding with vast racket, to the dismay both of the horse and his rider.   Once, on the plain north of Hamath, my horse became quite unmanageable among them.   They charged down upon us on the wings of the wind, which broke them from their moorings, and sent them careering over the desert in countless numbers.   Our excellent native itinerant, A—— F——, had a similar encounter with them on the eastern desert, beyond the Hauran, and his horse was so terrified that he was obliged to alight and lead him.   I have long suspected that this wild artichoke is the *gulgal*, which, in Psalm lxxxiii. 13, is rendered *wheel*, and in Isaiah xvii. 13, a *rolling* thing.   Evidently our translators knew not what to call it.   The

Wild artichoke.

Vegetable globes.

Gulgal.

first passage reads thus: " O my God, make them like a wheel (*gulgal*), as the stubble before the wind;" and the second, " Rebuke them, and they shall flee far off, and shall be chased as the chaff of the mountains before the wind, and like a rolling thing (*gulgal*) before the whirlwind." Now, from the nature of the parallelism, the *gulgal* cannot be a " wheel," but something corresponding to chaff. It must also be something that does not fly like the chaff, but, in a striking manner *rolls* before the wind. The signification of *gulgal* in Hebrew, and its equivalent in other Shemitic dialects, require this, and this rolling artichoke meets the case most emphatically, and especially when it rolls before the whirlwind. In the encounter referred to north of Hamath, my eyes were half blinded with the stubble and chaff which filled the air; but it was the extraordinary behaviour of this "rolling thing" that rivetted my attention. Hundreds of these globes, all bounding like gazelles in one direction over the desert, would suddenly wheel short round, at the bidding of a counter-blast, and dash away with equal speed on their new course. An Arab proverb addresses this rolling thing thus: " Ho! 'akkûb, where do you put up to-night?" to which it answers as it flies, "Where the wind puts up." They also derive one of their many forms of cursing from this plant: " May you be whirled, like the 'akkûb, before the wind, until you are caught in the thorns, or plunged into the sea." If this is not the "wheel" of David and the "rolling thing" of Isaiah, I have seen nothing in the country to suggest the comparison.

April 18th. How is it ascertained that this Beit Jibrîn is the site of the ancient Eleutheropolis?

The identification is due to the skill of Robinson and Smith, and the process of discovery and verification is detailed with great care in their " Researches." Owing to the fact that Eusebius and Jerome take this as the central station from which to mark the direction and distance of many other places, there are few geographical points in the country of greater value, and Dr. Robinson very justly magnifies its importance. Having myself derived the highest gratification in following out his results in my own excursions in this region, I gladly embrace every opportunity to express my obligations. There is a

whole nest of sacred sites scattered around this important centre. On the east we have Beit Nusib—Nezib; and further over the hills to the north-east Jeb'a—the Gibeah of Judah; and north, a little east, we find Shochoh in Shuwiekeh; and beyond it Jarmuth in Yarmuk. 'Ain Shemsh is Beth-shemesh; and north-west of this, Tibneh is the Timnath of Samson's wife. North-east of this is Zorah, the city of his father; and south-east of that is Zanuah. The wady in which Zorah lies is called Wady es Sumpt, and this is probably the battle-field of David and Goliath of Gath. Dr. Robinson thinks that Gath may have been at or near

Deir Dubban, where are very remarkable excavations and other indications of an ancient city. It appears to me that Bethogabra—Eleutheropolis—Beit Jibrîn, and *Gath* are all one and the same city. Khurbet Get—ruins of Gath

—is the name now applied to one of the heaps of rubbish a short distance westward from the castle of Beit Jibrin. The Hebrew word Bethogabra and the Arabic Beit Jibrîn may be rendered *house of giants*,—which reminds us of Goliath of Gath and his family. And further, I think that the Mareshah of Joshua xv. 44, which was rebuilt by Rehoboam, and is repeatedly mentioned in connection with Gath,[1] was a suburb of this great capital of the Philistines. Benjamin of Tudela makes Mareshah and Beit Jibrîn identical, and Jerome places them so near each other that they may be regarded as one and the same place. Micah probably wrote "Moresheth-gath" in order to fix the location of the suburb by the name of the main city.[2] All these identifications lend additional interest to this vicinity. Not only did Goliath and his family of giants reside here, but in this beautiful valley king Asa achieved that grand victory over Zerah the Ethiopian, with his host of "a thousand thousand, and three hundred chariots;" for the battle was at Mareshah, in the valley of Zephathah. These facts and suggestions will be sure to quicken your zeal for this day's explorations, notwithstanding your growing disgust with old ruins. There are, in fact, many things about Beit Jibrîn which merit a careful examination. The most striking is this immense quadrangular enclosure which marks out the boundaries of an old castle. It is about six hundred feet square, and was built of large heavy stone. Then, too, the castle within this inclosure has points of interest. Some parts of it appear very ancient, while this confused mass of arches, vaults, and broken walls speaks of Saracenic and crusading times. Besides this building there are immense artificial caverns hewn out of these cretaceous hills, and some of them carefully ornamented. They are found chiefly in the wady which runs up south by east, and in which is situated the ruined church called Mar Hannah. Dr. Robinson has given a detailed account of these remarkable excavations, the object of which he is at a loss to comprehend. Some of them were undoubtedly cisterns, and it is not impossible that all were originally such, but subsequently some of them may have been enlarged into temples and under-ground chapels, and others made into granaries.

In travelling through this sacred territory, few things please me more than to light upon those circumstances which prove the accuracy of ancient Bible narratives even in the most incidental remarks and the minutest allusions. We are now not far from Zorah, the birth-place of Samson,[3] and it is pleasant to find his home still in existence, in that secluded mountain village above 'Ain Shemsh. On one of the hard rocks of that village Manoah placed his sacrifice, and the angel of the Lord did wondrously while Manoah and his wife looked on; "for it came to pass, when the flame went up toward heaven from off the altar, that the angel of the Lord ascended in the flame."[4]

Josephus has a curious addition to the Bible narrative of these transactions, in which, after extolling the beauty of Manoah's wife, he says that her husband was exceedingly jealous; and when he heard her expatiate upon the

Marginal notes: Mareshah—Gath. Castle of Beit Jibrîn. Country of Samson.

---

[1] 2 Chron. xi. 8.   [2] Micah i. 14.   [3] Judges xiii. 2.   [4] Judges xiii. 20.

PART
III.

Timnath.

Lion.

Bees.

Wedding
feast in
Timnath.

beauty of the man who had appeared to her and announced the birth of a son, he was so consumed with this terrible passion that he besought God to send the messenger again, that he might see him—and much more to the same purport. But to return to the history. It is said that Samson went *down* to Timnath, and there saw the woman whom he desired to marry. Now Timnath still exists on the plain, and to reach it from Zorah you must *descend* through wild, rocky gorges,—just where one would expect to find a lion in those days, when wild beasts were far more common than at present. Nor is it more remarkable that lions should be met with in such places than that fierce leopards should now maintain their position in the thickly settled parts of Lebanon, and even in these very mountains, within a few hundred rods of large villages. Yet such I know is the fact.

There were then vineyards belonging to Timnath, as there now are in all these hamlets along the base of the hills and upon the mountain sides. These vineyards are very often far out from the villages, climbing up rough wadies and wild cliffs, in one of which Samson encountered the young lion. He threw the dead body aside, and the next time he went down to Timnath he found a swarm of bees in the carcass. This, it must be confessed, is an extraordinary occurrence. The word for bees is the *Arabic* for *hornets*, and these, we know, are very fond of flesh, and devour it with the greatest avidity. I have myself seen a swarm of hornets build their comb in the skull of a dead camel; and this would incline me to believe that it was really our *debabir—hornets—*that had settled in the carcass of Samson's lion, if it were known that they manufactured honey enough to meet the demands of the story. However, we find that not long after this, bees were so abundant in a wood at no great distance from this spot, that the honey dropped down from the trees on the ground; and I have explored densely wooded gorges in Hermon and in southern Lebanon where wild bees are still found, both in trees and in the clefts of the rocks. It keeps up the verisimilitude of the narrative that these are just the places where wild beasts still abound; and though *bees* ordinarily avoid dead carcasses, it is possible that they on this occasion selected that of the lion for their hive.

The circumstances of the wedding-feast in Timnath are also in keeping with such occasions at the present day. Even the weddings of ordinary people are celebrated with great rejoicings, which are kept up several days. Samson, however, was not an ordinary peasant, but the son of an emeer or nobleman, and the marriages of such are attended with quite as much display as that of Samson. The games and sports also, by which the companions of the bridegroom pass away the time, are not unlike those mentioned in the 14th chapter of Judges; and such occasions frequently end in quarrels, and even bloodshed. I have known many fatal feuds grow out of the sports of these boisterous festivals. And yet one thing more: Samson's wife was a weak and wicked woman, who had no real love for her husband; and this is certainly common enough at the present day. Wives are procured now as then by the intervention of parents, and without any of that personal attachment between the parties which we deem essential. They are also very often ready to enter into any treacherous conspiracy against their husbands by which they can gain some desired advantage either for themselves or their friends. Indeed, there are very many husbands in this country who neither will nor dare trust their wives. On the contrary, they watch them with the utmost distrust, and keep everything locked up for fear of their treachery. And yet these distrusted but cunning wives have wonderful power over their husbands. Though uneducated in all that is good, they are perfect masters of craft and deceit. By their arts and their *importunity* they carry their point, often to the utter and obvious ruin of their husbands, and this, too, when there is really no love between them. It is not at all contrary to present experience, therefore, that Samson's wife should conspire against him in the matter of the riddle, nor that she should succeed in teasing him out of the secret.

We are now in the neighbourhood where David began his illustrious career by slaying Goliath of Gath. The Philistines went up against Judah and pitched near Shochoh,—which site is ascertained to be at Shuwiekeh, about six miles to the north-east of us. Beit Netif is on a hill some three miles nearly north of it, and between them is the deep Wady es Sumpt, which passes down the plain, by Timnath, to the great Wady Surar. Dr. Robinson identifies this Wady Sumpt with the Elah of 1 Samuel xvii. 2, by which Saul encamped, probably on the north side, opposite the Philistines; and it was into this wady that the champion of the "uncircumcised" descended every day to defy the armies of the living God: his height nearly ten feet, his proportions enormous, his visage terrible; covered with a shining coat of mail weighing five thousand shekels, a helmet of brass on his head, a target of brass between his shoulders, and greaves of brass on his legs, he appeared like a brazen statue of colossal size, holding a spear whose staff was like a weaver's beam. No wonder the stoutest heart quailed, and that " all the men of Israel, when they saw the man, fled from him and were sore afraid." Forty days did this terrible giant come into the valley, morning and evening, to defy the hosts of Israel, exclaiming, with impious insolence, " Give me a man, that we may fight together." Thus he stood and cried in the morning when the youthful David drew nigh with the parched corn and the ten loaves which his father had sent to his elder brothers. He hears the tumult, and the defiance, and his heroic soul takes fire. Eagerly he inquires into the case, and, undeterred by the rebukes of his envious brothers, he offers to meet the dreadful champion. He is brought before Saul, who said unto him, "Thou are not able to go against this Philistine to fight with him; thou art but a youth." David modestly replies that, though young, he had already performed, by God's aid, deeds as daring and desperate as this could be. He had killed both a lion and a bear with his empty hands: " And the Lord that delivered me out of the paw of the lion, and out of the paw of the bear, will deliver me out of the hand of this Philistine."[1] Declining armour

CHAPTER XXXVII.

Treachery of wives.

David and Goliath.

---

[1] 1 Sam. xvii. 37

PART
III.

and helmet, coat of mail and sword, he took merely his shepherd's staff, and the sling with which he had often practised while tending his father's sheep on the mountains. He came down into the wady, put five smooth stones into his scrip, and went on boldly to meet the giant. One of these, hurled with his whole force and with unerring aim, sank deep into the giant's insolent forehead. He staggers convulsively, and with a mighty clang falls prostrate upon his face. David is upon him in a moment, and with his own great sword strikes off his head, which he bears back to Saul in triumph. Thus were verified David's confidence and piety. He fought "that all the earth might know that there is a God in Israel."

David not recognised.

How do you account for the fact that neither Saul nor Abner, either before or after the battle, recognised David ? In the verses immediately preceding the account of Goliath, we are informed that David had been summoned from Bethlehem to play on his harp before Saul, when the evil spirit from the Lord came upon him; and Jesse had sent him upon an ass, laden with bread, and a bottle of wine, and a kid. It is added that "Saul loved David greatly, and he became his armour-bearer." He also requested his father to leave David with him, for he had found favour in his sight. But the very next notice is that David is quietly tending sheep at Bethlehem, and his three older brothers are with the army. David re-appears before the king, and is not recognised either by him or by his servants. To me this has always appeared very strange.

Order of incidents.

It is, indeed, so strange as to suggest the query whether the incidents in this part of David's life are arranged in the exact order of time in which they occurred. The account in the 17th chapter has throughout the air of a first acquaintance. Abner said, in reply to the inquiry of the king, "As thy soul liveth, O king, I cannot tell who he is." David himself gives not the slightest hint, either before or after the fight, that he had ever seen the king before. This is a reserve, a stretch of modesty unparalleled, upon the supposition that he had not only been with him before, but had been greatly beloved by him, and selected to be his armour-bearer—implying the closest intimacy and largest confidence. It is no part of Oriental character to refrain, through modesty, from claiming previous acquaintanceship with superiors, and the present instance is so far beyond the bounds of probability that I hesitate to believe it while there is any other possible explanation. How could the king, and Abner, and all the other attendants of the royal household, have so utterly forgotten the wonderful harper, who had charmed away the evil spirit, and had been so beloved ? It seems to me much more probable that this incident of playing on the harp before the king belongs to some period subsequent to the battle with Goliath. This is rendered more credible from the fact that there are some circumstances introduced into the account of that day's adventures which could not have taken place until long after; as, for example, in the 54th verse, where it is said that "David took the head of the Philistine and brought it to Jerusalem, but he put his armour in his tent." Now David *had no tent at the time*, and did not *go to Jerusalem* until after the lapse of many eventful years.

If, however, we were shut up to the necessity of accepting the narrative as to time just in the order in which it is recorded, I have only to remark that we do not know how long a period intervened between the return of David to his father's house and his appearance before the king on the morning of the *duel* with Goliath. If it were two or three years, it is possible that David had, in the meanwhile, suddenly shot up from boyhood to youth, tall and robust, and his personal appearance might have so changed as to bear little resemblance to the ruddy lad who played skilfully on the harp. It is a fact that lads of this country, particularly of the higher classes, are often very fair, full-faced, and handsome, until about fourteen years of age, but during the next two or three years a surprising change takes place. They not only spring into full-grown manhood as if by magic, but all their former beauty disappears ; their complexion becomes dark, their features harsh and angular, and the whole expression of countenance stern, and even disagreeable. I have often been accosted by such persons, formerly intimate acquaintances, but who had suddenly grown entirely out of my knowledge, nor could I, without difficulty, recognise them. David had become a shepherd after leaving the king's palace, —an occupation which of all others would most rapidly change his fair complexion into a dirty bronze. He appeared before Saul in his shepherd's attire, not in the gay dress of a courtier in the king's palace, and he *may*, therefore, not have been recognised. But, as before remarked, if this were so, it is not only remarkable in itself, but it follows that David was at an early age possessed of a wisdom, modesty, and self-control, without a parallel in the history of mankind.

Change of appearance.

In after life, David had much to do with this part of the country. Twice he fled to Gath for fear of Saul. Is it not strange that he should select the city of Goliath for his asylum ?

David in Gath.

He was hard pressed, and had only a choice of dangers. Gath was near his native mountains, and, probably, had more friendly relations with the Israelites than the more distant cities of the Philistines. King Achish, also, appears to have been an open-hearted, unsuspecting, and generous character, probably of that chivalrous temperament which led him to admire such a hero as David. At any rate, he treated him very kindly, and presented him with Ziklag, a village which seems to have been long retained and highly prized by the royal family.

How do you dispose of the deception practised by David toward his protector in the matter of the excursions against the Amalekites and others down south of us ?

Deceiving of Achish.

That David acted under the pressure of very powerful motives, and was by them urged aside from the plain, open path of rectitude. We are under no obligation to justify all his conduct. It is but common justice, however, to give him the benefit of all palliating circumstances ; and when these are duly weighed we shall not find occasion to pass a severe judgment upon him. He was an exile, hunted out of his home like a partridge on the mountains, and

PART
III.

obliged to reside among enemies—was surrounded on all sides by difficulties and dangers, and with a large troop of friends and followers, for whom he must find the means of support; he had also been set apart by God himself to be the deliverer of his people from these very Amalekites, who had been condemned to total destruction for their enormous wickedness by the Sovereign Ruler of all nations. David, therefore, felt that he had a divine warrant for attacking and exterminating them; and they were actually within the borders of his own tribe of Judah as settled by Joshua. The wrong, therefore, if wrong there were, was in the deception practised upon Achish, and not in the invading and destroying of the Amalekites. This God had sternly enjoined upon the Israelites to do. Let it be remembered, however, that Achish had no real right to know where David went, nor was David under any obligation to tell him the whole truth. What he did say was true in the letter of it, for David did really make an inroad into those places which he mentioned, though not against the Jews.

Ziklag.

Ziklag, you suppose, was somewhere in this neighbourhood ?

We infer this from the notices of it in the Bible, but the site has been long lost. Connected with it is one of the most remarkable incidents in the life of David. While he was with Achish and the Philistine army in the plain of Esdraelon, these bordering Amalekites invaded the south, and Ziklag, which they burned with fire, and carried all the inhabitants away captive. This terrible calamity threw David and his whole company into the most violent transports of grief. " They lifted up their voice and wept, until they had no more power to weep;" and the people, in their madness and despair, even talked of stoning David.[1] He, however, succeeded in inspiring them with courage to pursue their enemies. They overtook them in the night some distance south of the brook Besor, and falling suddenly upon them while they were eating, and drinking, and dancing, because of the great spoil they had taken, the victory was complete, and all that had been taken from Ziklag were recovered, together with a vast amount of booty which these Amalekites had gathered up from the land of the Philistines. There is a remarkable resemblance between this victory of David and that of Abraham over the kings who had carried Lot away captive.

I was reminded of the poor Egyptian whom David found half dead, and brought to life again by giving him " a piece of a cake of figs and two clusters of raisins" to eat, and water to drink, by an incident which occurred to me

Sick
Egyptian.

when crossing the plain to Askelon. Far from any village, a sick Egyptian was lying by the road side in the burning sun, and apparently almost dead with a terrible fever. He wanted nothing but "*water! water!*" which we were fortunately able to give him from our travelling-bottle; but we were obliged to pass on and leave him to his fate, whatever that might be.

This victory over the Amalekites was probably achieved on the very day that Saul was defeated and slain on Gilboa; and David, when he had heard of that

[1] 1 Sam. xxx. 3-6.

event—by which the way to the throne of Israel was open to himself—took of CHAPTER the spoils, and sent presents to all the towns and villages where he used for- XXXVII. merly to resort. He acted in this matter upon a principle which his wise son Gifts. has expressed after this fashion: "A man's gift maketh room for him, and bringeth him before great men."[1] His gifts speedily made room for him in Hebron, and prepared the hearts of all Judah to welcome him as their king.

It seems to have tasked all David's firmness and tact in government to control his heterogeneous troop of followers.

There were certainly some churlish sons of Belial among them, but this was David's not their general character. The servants of Nabal, in Carmel, gave a very troop. different testimony concerning them: "The men were very good unto us, and we were not hurt, nor missed we anything as long as we were conversant with them when we were in the fields."[2] They were, therefore, in no sense a lawless set of robbers. Nabal's taunt to the messengers, "Who is David, and who is the son of Jesse? there be many servants now-a-days that break away every man from his master,"[3] was as unjust as it was insolent; but he was, in fact, "such a son of Belial that a man could not speak to him;" or, as his not very polite wife has it, "As his name is, so is he. Nabal is his name, and folly is with him."[4] It does not follow that because "every one that was in distress, and every one that was in debt, and every one that was discontented," or, rather, *bitter of soul*, "gathered themselves unto David,"[5] that therefore they were the refuse and offscouring of the land, like a troop of irregular Turkish cavalry, or the followers of an outlawed Druse sheikh. The government of Saul had degenerated into a cruel despotism. David himself, and all his relations, had been obliged to flee from his outrageous and murderous jealousy, and there is abundant evidence that they were honourable and respectable people. Nor is it any wonder that many were in distress, and bitter of soul, under a king who could employ a savage Edomite to kill the whole family of the chief priest of the nation, merely because David had been innocently entertained for a day by them. The madness and ferocity of such a king would compel the noblest spirits in the land to flee unto David, and a large proportion of his retinue was actually composed of such men.

Even the debtors, in such a time of misrule, were, in most cases, better men Debtors. than their creditors. Nearly everybody is in debt in these Oriental countries, and, owing to the tenure of land, the modes of raising taxes, and the claims of feudal chiefs, it is impossible for the villagers to keep free from it, either personally or as part of a community loaded with heavy liabilities; and, even in the cities, the number who are more or less involved is far greater than those who stand square with the world. I hardly ever knew an estate in this country which was not found thus encumbered when the death of the owner brought out the truth; and very generally those who are the creditors are cold,

---

[1] Prov. xviii. 16.   [2] 1 Sam. xxv. 15.   [3] 1 Sam. xxv. 10.
[4] 1 Sam. xxv. 25.   [5] 1 Sam. xxii. 2.

cunning usurers, hated and hateful. The fact, therefore, that a man is in debt is no reflection on his character ; and in times of misrule and apprehension like that of Saul, the best families are suddenly reduced by extortion to utter poverty. To raise the enormous sums demanded of the head of the house, and enforced by the bastinado, the wife and children sell and pledge everything they possess to those lenders, and raise money at ruinous rates of interest. The tyrant, also, from motives easily understood, enforces the collection of such debts with a rigour that knows neither delay nor mercy. That some of David's company fled from just such extortion is highly probable, and they may have been the most estimable people of the land. It is pleasant to believe that the noble and generous David was surrounded by a fair proportion of kindred spirits, and that in the midst of his sore trials and perplexities his heart was sustained and comforted by the reflection that he was able to furnish an asylum to many innocent victims of regal oppression. This is distinctly stated in the case of Abiathar, who escaped from the slaughter of the priests at Nob, and must have been equally so in regard to his own father and all his family.

These modern dwellers about old Gath appear to be actually taller and more warlike than the average inhabitants of this region.

The sheikh and his family might well be the descendants of the ancient giants, for they are rough, fierce-looking fellows ; and, indeed, the whole population now make a very savage display of guns, pistols, crooked swords, double-edged *khan-jars*, long knives, and whatever else can aid them to cut, stab, and hack the human body to pieces. The sheikh says that they are thus armed in order to keep at a distance the Bedawîn Arabs, who would otherwise eat up their ripening harvests. This may be so, though I have never seen them without arms ; and those who can get nothing better carry tremendous clubs, like the weaver's beam of the giant, and in handling them they are as expert as any Irishman with his shillalah, and far more dangerous.

Do these people now make any use of the sling, which, in the hand of David, was so fatal to their famous townsman ?

The only place where I have seen the sling used is at Hasbeîya, on Mount Hermon, and there merely in mimic warfare, waged by the boys of the town. The deep gorge of the Busîs divides Hasbeîya into two parts, and when the war-spirit is up in the community, the lads collect on opposite sides of this gorge, and fight desperate battles with their slings. They chase one another from cliff to cliff, as in real warfare, until one of the parties gives way, and retreats up the mountain. I have seen the air almost darkened by their ringing, whizzing pebbles, and so many serious accidents occur that the " authorities " have often interfered to abolish the rude sport ; but, whenever there occurs a fresh feud, or a revolt against the government among the old folks, the young ones return again to the fight with slings across the Busîs.

It must have required careful drilling and long practice before the seven hundred left-handed Benjamites "could sling stones at a hair-breadth, and not

Marginal notes:

Modern weapons.

The sling.

The seven hundred Benjamites.

miss;"[1] but this is a region where such a mode of warfare would be culti- CHAPTER
vated in ancient times, and be very effective. The stones for the sling are XXXVII.
everywhere at hand, and the country is cut up by deep gorges, with impracticable banks; and, before the invention of guns, there was no other weapon that
could carry across these profound depths and reach the ranks of the enemy.
David, while following his flocks over these rough mountains, practised other
arts besides that of playing on the shepherd's pipe, for he became as expert
in the use of the sling as any of the chosen men of Benjamin. He was manifestly one of nature's noblemen, born to excel in everything he undertook.
Not only was he the most skilful musician, but the greatest poet; not only David's
the most daring shepherd, but the bravest soldier and the most success- strength.
ful general. It is nowhere stated in so many words that he possessed
great physical strength, but this is implied in several anecdotes of his life.
Without this he could not have wielded the sword of Goliath, and yet he chose
that of all others for himself; and again, none but the very strongest could
kill a lion and a bear in fair fight. What the lion is we all know, or at least The lion
imagine, and yet David says, "I caught him by his beard, and smote him, and and the
slew him."[2] The Syrian bear—still found on the higher mountains of this bear.
country—is perhaps equally to be dreaded in a close personal encounter. The
inhabitants of Hermon say that when he is chased up the mountain he will
cast back large stones upon his pursuers with terrible force and unerring aim.
The stoutest hunter will not venture to attack him alone, nor without being
thoroughly armed for the deadly strife. David, however, caught him as he
was running away with a kid from his flock, and slew him; and this when he
was but a youth, ruddy, and of a fair countenance, so that Goliath disdained
him as an antagonist. It is interesting to remember that these personal adventures of David, both with giants and with wild beasts, took place in these
mountains immediately above us.

---

[1] Judges xx. 16.   [2] 1 Sam. xvii. 35.

PART IV.—SOUTHERN PALESTINE.

[In this, the concluding section of the journey, our travellers advance by Hebron, through the hill-country of Judea, to the northern angle of the Dead Sea, visiting the localities of Gilgal and Jericho; then proceed westward to Jerusalem, and devote the closing portion of their tour to the Holy City and places around.—ED.]

CHAPTER XXXVIII.

HEBRON.

April 19th.

Road from Beit Jibrîn to Hebron. OWING to the wretched headache which tormented me all day, our ride from Beit Jibrîn to this city has left no distinct trace on my memory, except that of a very fatiguing ascent from Idna toward Taffuah.

I can readily refresh your memory this morning by passing in review yesterday's journey, which was one of great interest to me. While the muleteers were packing up and loading, I rode out and again examined the excavations on the south-east of Beit Jibrîn. My guide led me on horseback through a **Caverns.** long succession of caverns, all dug out of the white cretaceous rock of the hill above the city. They closely resemble ancient cisterns, having a hole at the top as if to draw water from ; but their number and vast size fill the mind with astonishment, and suggest doubts with regard to the original purpose for which they were made. They, however, were hewn out of the rock precisely as cisterns were, and the mark of the pickaxe is distinctly seen on the sides of those that are tolerably perfect. Multitudes of them, however, have fallen in from above, and the partition-walls of others have dissolved by time, thus throwing many into one. Indeed, they appear to have been originally connected by doors and galleries cut through the rock. But it would require a separate memoir adequately to describe these remarkable caverns, and this I certainly have no disposition to write, nor would you have patience to hear. They are all circular, and I measured one which was sixty-five feet in diame-

ter, and ninety-one to the top of the dome from the rubbish which covered the CHAPTER
floor, ten feet deep at least. The entire height of this cistern must therefore XXXVIII.
have been more than a hundred feet. On the north side, and about midway
to the top, are several figures of idols cut in the rock—rude images of Dagon Idols.
himself perhaps. In several of the caverns further south are inscriptions very
high up, in a large and mixed Cufic and Phœnician character. I have copies
of them, and also of the images, kept rather as curiosities than for any light
which they shed upon the mysteries of their location. The only theory I can Immense
entertain in regard to these gigantic excavations is, that they were cisterns of cisterns.
old Gath, made thus numerous, and on such an immense scale, to secure a supply
of water against all emergencies of drought or of war; and this idea is corroborated by the existence, at the present day, of similar cisterns in more than
one of the neighbouring villages. At Zikrîn, some six miles north-west of

WATER-JARS AND " BOTTLES."

Beit Jibrîn, are vast excavations beneath a broad platform of hard rock which
covers several acres, and it is pierced by forty openings or doors—*bâbs* in Ara-

bic—through which water is drawn up by the villagers.   The excavations underneath this flooring closely resemble these of Beit Jibrîn both in shape and size, and the separate cisterns are so connected by galleries and doors that the water passes from one to the other, and stands in all at the same elevation.   The overlying rock at Zikrîn is so hard that the roof has nowhere caved in, and the cisterns are therefore in good preservation, and afford an inexhaustible supply of water.   This is all I have to suggest on the subject, and now for the ride to Hebron.

**Valley of
Senaber.**

I overtook you at Deir en Nukhaz, slowly sauntering up the pretty valley of Senaber, which village we reached in an hour from our camp-ground.   The valley, you remember, was broad and fertile, and the ascent for the first three hours very gradual.   As we advanced, side valleys came in from the right and left, opening long vistas into the bosom of the surrounding country.   In the mouth of the wady which descends from the vicinity of Turkumieh (Tricomia) we saw a large and picturesque encampment of Arabs, with whose goats, and dogs, and naked children we were highly entertained.

Escaping from the half-begging, half-plundering importunity of these Ishmaelites, we rode another hour, and stopped to lunch at 'Ain el Kuf, which is

**'Ain el
Kuf.**

the only fountain in this entire valley. Here we saw many people coming and going with pitchers and jars, and not a few with large " bottles " of skin,— an unmistakable evidence that good water is very scarce in that region; and had we not filled our own " bottles," we should have suffered no slight inconvenience in the long ascent, for we found no water from that on to this vale of Hebron.

**Leather
bottles.**

I remember that ascent with sufficient distinctness, and also that we stopped to rest about half way up Wady 'Ain el Kuf, at a sheep-fold under the southern cliff of the ravine; and there, for the first time, I saw the mandrake, with

**Man-
drakes.**

MANDRAKE—LEAF, FLOWER, AND ROOT.

its broad leaves and green " apples," and my curiosity was excited by the discussion which followed about the singular contract between Rachel and Leah for Reuben's mandrakes.[1] CHAPTER XXXVIII.

Into that we shall not now enter, nor will we pry with curious eye into the motives which urged Rachel to make the purchase. I, for one, don't know. As to the mandrakes themselves something may be said. Reuben gathered them in wheat-harvest, and it is then that they are still found ripe and eatable on the lower ranges of Lebanon and Hermon, where I have most frequently seen them. The apple becomes of a very pale yellow colour, partially soft, and of an insipid, *sickish* taste. They are said to produce dizziness; but I have seen people eat them without experiencing any such effect. The Arabs, however, believe them to be exhilarating and stimulating even to insanity, and hence the name *tuffah el jan*—" apples of the jan;" but we may safely leave the disputed questions concerning mandrakes to those who have time and inclination for such inquiries, and hasten on to our camp-ground in the pretty valley of Mamre, here on the hill side, near the quarantine of Hebron. Vale of Mamre.

Whatever may be true in regard to the road hither, the appearance of Hebron itself, lying in deep repose along the vale of Mamre, was quite beautiful. The time of our visit is doubtless most favourable, for nature upon these mountains is now in her holiday dress; and when we began to descend toward the city, the lengthening shadows of the western hills had just dropped their sober curtains over the scene, softening its somewhat rugged features, thereby greatly enhancing its charms. Seen under circumstances not so favourable, the impression might be much less agreeable; but, apart from natural scenery, no intelligent traveller can approach Hebron with indifference. No city in Palestine so carries one back to earliest patriarchal times. Manners and customs, and modes of action, and even idioms of speech, have changed but little since the Bible was written, or from what they were when Abraham dwelt here among "the sons of Heth." Take the account of the death and burial of Sarah, as it is found in the 23d chapter of Genesis, as an example : " Sarah died in Kirjath-arba; the same is Hebron : and Abraham came to mourn for Sarah, and to weep for her." There is something formal in this remark, but it is in perfect accordance with present customs. Should such a person die here tomorrow, there would be a solemn public mourning and weeping,—not as indicating the grief of the family so much as in honour of the dead. The customs of the people demand that there should be loud, boisterous, uncontrollable weeping, mourning, beating of the breast, and every other external manifestation of great sorrow. Such was this funeral mourning of the great emeer Abraham; but, besides this public tribute to the memory of Sarah, he, no doubt, sincerely lamented her death in the privacy of his own tent. Appearance of Hebron. Mourning for the dead.

Abraham's negotiation for a sepulchre is also very Oriental and striking. Such a purchase was quite necessary. There has always been in this country Purchase of tombs.

[1] Gen. xxx. 14—16.

the utmost exclusiveness in regard to tombs; and although these polite Hittites said, "Hear us, my lord: thou art a mighty prince among us; in the choice of our sepulchres bury thy dead; none of us shall withhold from thee his sepulchre, but that thou mayest bury thy dead," Abraham was too experienced an Oriental not to know that this was merely compliment. The thing was quite out of the question; nor would Abraham himself have consented thus to mingle his dead with the dust and bones of strangers, even if they had been willing. He knew well how to understand the offer, and therefore pressed his request to be allowed to purchase. Nor is such a negotiation easily arranged. If you or I had occasion to make a similar contract to-day from these modern Hittites, we should find it even more delicate and tedious than did Abraham. I do not believe we could succeed, even with the aid of all the mediators we could employ. In concluding the purchase with Ephron, we see the process of a modern bargain admirably carried out. The polite son of Zohar says, "Nay, my lord, hear me: the field *give* I thee, and the cave that is therein, I *give* it thee. In the presence of the sons of my people *give* I it thee; bury thy dead." Of course! and just so I have had a hundred houses, and fields, and horses given to me, and the by-standers called upon to witness the deed, and a score of protestations and oaths taken to seal the truth of the donation; all which, of course, meant nothing whatever, just as Abraham understood the true intent and value of Ephron's *buksheesh.* He therefore urged forward the purchase, and finally brought the owner to state definitely his price, which he did at four hundred shekels of silver. Now, without knowing the relation between silver and a bit of barren rock at that time and in this place, my experience of such transactions leads me to suppose that this price was treble the actual value of the field. "But," says the courteous Hittite, "four hundred shekels! what is *that* betwixt me and thee!" Oh, how often you hear these identical words on similar occasions, and yet, acting upon their apparent import, you would soon find out what and how much they meant. Abraham knew that too; and as he was then in no humour to chaffer with the owner, whatever might be his price, he proceeded forthwith to *weigh* out the money. Even this is still common; for, although coins have now a definite name, size, and value, yet every merchant carries a small apparatus by which he weighs each coin, to see that it has not been tampered with by Jewish clippers. In like manner, the *specifications* in the contract are just such as are found in modern deeds. It is not enough that you purchase a well-known lot; the contract must mention everything that belongs to it, and certify that fountains or wells in it, trees upon it, etc., are sold with the field. If you rent a house, not only the building itself, but every room in it, above and below, down to the kitchen, pantry, stable, and hen-coop, must be specified. Thus Abraham bought the field, "*and* the cave which was therein, *and* all the trees that were in the field, *and* that were in all the borders round about, were made sure." I see this negotiation in all its details enacted before me, and hear the identical words that passed between the parties. The venerable patriarch,

bowed down with sorrow, rises from beside the couch on which lay the lifeless CHAPTER
body of his beloved Sarah. He *stands* before the people—the attitude of re- XXXVIII.
spect which etiquette still demands. He addresses them as *beni Heth*—sons
of Heth ; and in the same words he would address these Arabs about us as
beni Keis, beni Yemen, etc., etc., according as each tribe is now designated.
Again, Abraham begins his plea with a reference to his condition among them
as a stranger—the very idiom now in use—I, a stranger, *ana ghurîb;* and
this plea appeals strongly to the sympathies of the hearers. It is by such an Manner of
appeal that the beggar now seeks to enlist your compassion, and succeeds, be- conduct-
cause all over the East the stranger is greatly to be pitied. He is liable to be tracts.
plundered and treated as an enemy; and among these denizens of the desert
strangers *are* generally enemies, and dealt with as such. The plea, therefore,
was natural and effective. Abraham stood and *bowed* himself to the children
of Heth;—another act of respect in accordance with modern manners; and the
next step is equally so. He does not apply directly to the owner of the field,
but requests the neighbours to act as mediators on his behalf ; and were we
anxious to succeed in a similar bargain with these people, we must resort to
the same round-about mode. There is scarcely anything in the habits of
Orientals more annoying to us Occidentals than this universal custom of
employing mediators to pass between you and those with whom you wish to do
business. Nothing can be done without them. A merchant cannot sell a piece
of print, nor a farmer a yoke of oxen, nor any one rent a house, buy a horse,
or get a wife, without a succession of go-betweens. Of course Abraham knew
that this matter of the field could not be brought about without the intervention of the neighbours of Ephron, and therefore he applies to them first. How
much manœuvring, taking aside, whispering, nodding of heads, and clasping
of hands there was before the real owner was brought within reasonable terms,
we are not told, but at length all the preliminary obstacles and conventional
impediments are surmounted according to the most approved style of
etiquette, and the contract is closed in the *audience of all the people that* Witnesses.
went in at the gate of the city. This also is true to life. When any sale is now
to be effected in a town or village, the whole population gather about the
parties at the usual place of concourse, around or near the gate, where there
is one. There all take part and enter into the pros and cons with as much
earnestness as if it were their own individual affair. By these means, the
operation, in all its circumstances and details, is known to many witnesses,
and the thing is made *sure,* without any written contract. In fact, up to this
day, in this very city, a purchase thus witnessed is legal, while the best drawn
deeds of a London lawyer, though signed and sealed, would be of no avail
without such living witnesses.

Well, Abraham thus obtained the cave of Machpelah for the possession of Cave of
a burying-place for himself and his descendants, and thus became legal pro- Machpe-
prietor of a portion of the promised inheritance. "There," as Jacob, when lah.
dying, said, " they buried Abraham and Sarah his wife ; there they buried

PART
IV.

Isaac and Rebekah his wife; and there I buried Leah."[1] And thither, too, his sons carried Jacob out of Egypt when he died, and buried him by the side of his wife.

Funeral
of Jacob—
Atad, or
Abel-miz-
raim.

Dr. Kitto maintains that Joseph carried his father through the Great Desert, round the south end of the Dead Sea, then through the land of Moab, and crossing the Jordan near Jericho, there held the great mourning of the Egyptians in the floor of Atad, which he locates between Jericho and the Jordan ; and the Doctor rather complains that no one has taken the trouble to notice this extraordinary fact. The reason, I suppose, is, that no one believes the story. There is not a particle of evidence for such a wonderful journey in the Bible account of the funeral, nor does Josephus give a hint that he had ever heard of it. Moses, who wrote on the *east* of the Jordan, simply says that the floor of Atad, called Abel-mizraim, was on the other, or *west* side of it, without stating where. Jerome, indeed, indentifies it with Bethagla, and locates that village near Jericho; but this identification has no authority in itself ; and besides, there was another Bethagla in the land of the Philistines, much more likely to be the Abel-mizraim of Genesis, if the two places had in reality any relation to each other. In a word, nothing less than the positive assertion of the Bible would enable me to believe this theory of Dr. Kitto, for it would be the most extraordinary journey on record.

Do you suppose that this *El Haram* encloses the identical cave, and the graves of the six ancestors of the Hebrew nation ?

I have no doubt of it, and therefore I regard it as the most interesting of all spots on the face of the earth. Others might be equally sacred and precious could we be sure of their identity—the manger at Bethlehem, Calvary in Jerusalem, or the last resting-place of Adam or Noah, for example ; but doubt and obscurity, absolute and impenetrable, rest on all such sites. Here, however, there is no room for scepticism. We have before us the identical cave in which these patriarchs, with their wives, were reverently " gathered unto their people," one after another, by their children. Such a cave may last as long as the " everlasting hills" of which it is a part ; and from that to this day it has so come to pass, in the providence of God, that no nation or people has had possession of Machpelah who would have been disposed to disturb the ashes of the illustrious dead within it.

I have been out examining this venerable edifice as closely as the insolent keepers would allow, and it seems to bear marks of a higher antiquity than anything I have yet seen in the country.

Machpe-
lah.

It is doubtless very ancient—is probably of Jewish workmanship, though I cannot think that it dates back to Solomon, or to any time anterior, to the captivity. The stones are large, but with a shallow bevel, and the face is worked off smooth, like some parts of the wall about the area of the Temple at Jerusalem. The square pilasters, without capitals or any well-defined cor-

[1] Gen. xlix. 31.

nice, are a feature wholly unique, and marks it off from any other edifice I have examined. There are sixteen of these on each side, and eight on the ends. The height, including the more recent additions of the Saracens, is at least fifty feet, perhaps more. Dr. Robinson gives two hundred feet for the length, one hundred and fifty for the breadth, and sixty for the height, and this is as near the truth as any guess of our own could be. It is located on the declivity of the hill, with the town mostly below in the wady south and west of it. The rock above it is intensely hard, and portions of it are of a pale red colour, like that from which books, crosses, and other curiosities are made for the pilgrims. I succeeded, in 1838, in breaking off specimens of it, though not without danger of a mob. The *cave* is beneath this foundation of hard rock. Up to this day we have no good description of the interior of the edifice. I have studied Aly Bey's drawings, and his very unsatisfactory account explanatory of them, but am unable to say whether or not they confirm the following particulars gleaned from other sources. The most interesting items we have are from Benjamin of Tudela, a traveller of the twelfth century, upon whom I have wished on many occasions to be able to rely, and never more than in this instance. He says the real sepulchres are not shown to ordinary visitors, but if a rich Jew arrives, the keepers open an iron door which has been there *ever since the days of our forefathers,*—that is, of the patriarchs themselves! Through this they enter; descend into a first cave, which is empty, traverse a second, which is also empty; and reach a third, which contains six sepulchres—those of Abraham, Isaac, and Jacob, and of Sarah, Rebekah, and Leah, one opposite the other! He says, also, that all these sepulchres have inscriptions, the letters being engraved, that of Abraham thus:—"This is the sepulchre of our father Abraham, upon whom be peace;" and so of all the rest. O Benjamin! why did you allow yourself to write so carelessly in other instances, where we can follow you, as to shake our faith when we *cannot?* Well, the day is not far off when this and every other sacred locality will be thrown open to the inspection of all who wish to know the truth; and until then we must rest contented with what information floats about, without any very satisfactory authority. All agree, and my own Moslem servants testify to it, that within this exterior edifice is a large building which may have been an ancient church, but is now used as a mosque. The *cave* is beneath its dome. Monro the traveller thus speaks of it, but most certainly from hearsay; " The mosque is a square building, with little external decoration. Behind it is a small cupola, with eight or ten windows, beneath which is the tomb of Esau. Ascending from the street at the corner of the mosque, you pass through an arched way, by a flight of steps, to a wide platform, at the end of which is another short ascent. To the left is the court, out of which, to the left again, you enter the mosque." Not very intelligible; but let that pass. " The dimensions within are about forty paces by twenty-five. Immediately on the right of the door is the tomb of Sarah, and beyond it that of Abraham, having a passage between them into the court. Corresponding to these, on the opposite side of the mosque, are the tombs of Isaac and Rebekah; and behind them is a recess for prayer, and a pulpit. These tombs resemble small huts, with a window on each side, and folding doors in front, the lower parts of which are of wood and the upper of iron, or of bronze plated. Within each of these is an *imitation* of the sarcophagus which lies in the cave below the mosque, and which no one is allowed to enter. Those seen above resemble coffins, with pyramidal tops, and are covered with green silk, lettered with verses from the Koran. The doors of these tombs are left constantly open, but no one enters those of the women—at least men do not. In the mosque is a baldachin, supported by four columns, over an octagonal figure of black and white marble inlaid, around a small hole in the foremost, through which passes a cord from the top of the canopy to a lamp which is kept continually burning in the cave of Machpelah, where the actual sarcophagi rest. At the upper end of the court is the chief place of prayer, and on the opposite of the mosque are two large tombs, where are deposited the two larger sarcophagi of Jacob and Leah."[1] This whole description has the air of something composed from the account of an intelligent Moslem, who had been employed by Mr. Monro to bring back the best account of it he could. If it will not bear a very rigid criticism, it is probably a tolerably close approximation to the reality, and with it we must be content.

Houses in Hebron. Hebron appears to be well built. The houses are generally two storeys high, and have flattened domes, such as we saw at Jaffa, Ramleh, Gaza, and other places in the south part of this country.

The same as at Jerusalem; and the reason is, that beams are too scarce and dear to admit of flat roofs. I presume it was the same in the days of Solomon, for he had to bring the beams and boards for the Temple from Lebanon ; and what is now used in these cities is brought from thence by sea to Jaffa, and afterward carried on camels. Hence the rooms are all vaults, even where there is a second and a third storey. The roofs, however, may be made flat by raising the exterior walls, and filling in until level with the top of the arch. This is done on the convents and other heavy buildings, by which a fine promenade is secured.

Population. What may be the population of Hebron ?

I estimated it at between seven and eight thousand in 1838, and it remains about what it was then. Some think this estimate too low, while others speak of only five thousand ; but this is certainly below the truth. There are some seven hundred Jews ; all the rest are Moslems, and of a most bigoted and insolent character. There are no Christians either in the town or district. Hebron furnishes another refutation of the ancient fable about the cities of refuge, that they were situated in conspicuous positions. Here it lies in this long valley, with no prospect in any direction except toward the south-east, and even that is not very extensive.

[1] Summer's Ramble, i. 245.

If it were of any importance, we might refer to a tradition as old, at least, CHAPTER XXXVIII. as Benjamin of Tudela, that the original city did actually occupy the north-western hill. I do not, however, believe it; there is nothing there to support Tradition of former site. it; and many things in and about the present town seem to settle its claims to be one of the oldest cities in the world on an immovable basis. These immense *birkehs* or pools are certainly very ancient. The one furthest down the Pools. valley is one hundred and thirty-three feet square, and about twenty-two feet deep. The upper one is eighty-five by fifty-five, and nineteen feet deep. They are rarely full of water, though I have seen them overflowing in a very rainy season. Stone steps lead down to the water from the corner, and people are constantly descending and ascending with large skin "bottles" on their backs. Indeed, the town seems now to depend entirely upon them, though the water is none of the purest, and there are two or three fountains at no great distance up the valley. It was not always thus, for there are two or three broken aqueducts in the valley to the west and north-west of the city, which must have been in use down to a comparatively recent period.

All the visitors speak of the vineyards of Hebron; and it is a very ancient Vine-yards. tradition that the clusters which the spies carried back from Eshcol were from this valley. Certainly in no other part of Palestine are the vineyards so extensive, so well kept, or so productive. They cover the sloping hill sides for a long distance to the west and north-west of the town. As the Moslems do not make wine, the grapes not disposed of in the market are dried into raisins, or the juice is boiled down into *dibs*, a kind of thick grape molasses, frequently mentioned in the Bible under the kindred name of *debash*, in some places translated "honey," and in others "manna!" Besides grapes, the olive and the fig are the most important fruits of Hebron; but apricots, pomegranates, quinces, apples, pears, and plums also flourish, with proper care.

There are some pomegranate bushes in this neighbourhood which may even Pome-granates be called trees by way of courtesy, but in reality these large and delicious "apples" grow on a stout thorny bush. There are several kinds of them in this country. In Jebaah, on Lebanon, there is a variety perfectly black on the outside. The general colour, however, is a dull green, inclining to yellow, and some even have a blush of red spread over a part of their surface. The outside rind is thin but tough, and the bitter juice of it stains everything it touches with an undefined but indelible blue. The average size is about that of the orange, but some of those from Jaffa are as large as the egg of an ostrich. Within, the "grains" are arranged in longitudinal compartments as compactly as corn on the cob, and they closely resemble those of pale red corn, except that they are nearly transparent and very beautiful. A dish filled with these "grains" *shelled out* is a very handsome ornament on any table, and the fruit is as sweet to the taste as it is pleasant to the eye. They are ripe about the middle of October, and remain in good condition all winter. Suspended in the pantry, they are kept partially dried through the whole year.

The flower of the pomegranate is bell or tulip shaped, and is of a beautiful

PART
IV.

orange-red, deepening into crimson on some bushes. There is a kind very
large and double, but this bears no fruit, and is cultivated merely for its
brilliant blossoms, which are put forth profusely during the whole summer.

Orna-
ments.

This fruit was greatly esteemed in ancient times, and is mentioned by Moses
as one of the excellences of the promised land ;[1] and, by divine command, he
was to make pomegranates on the hem of the ephod,—a golden bell (the

POMEGRANATES.

blossom) and a pomegranate alternately round about the hem of the robe ;[2]
and they were reproduced in the Temple, upon the net-work that covered the
chapiters on the top of "Jachin and Boaz,"—those noble pillars of brass,—
two hundred pomegranates, in rows, round about. Solomon, of course, adorns
his Song of Songs with allusions to this beautiful and pleasant fruit; and, while
admiring it, we may enter more readily into the gorgeous chamber of imagery
where that poetic monarch delighted to dwell and to revel.

Glass
manufac-
tory.

The only manufacture peculiar to Hebron is that of glass. I was not a little
amused, on my first visit, with this business. Having not long before examined the great glass factories at Pittsburg, I entered these with no little
curiosity ; but what a contrast ! In an old rickety room were three or four
small furnaces of earth, all in a glow with the melted matter. The men were
then making rings for bracelets, or rather armlets, to supply the Jerusalem market. The process was extremely simple: an iron rod was thrust
into the melted mass, to the end of which a small portion adhered. This was
rapidly twisted and pressed into a circular shape, merely by the dexterous use
of a long blade like that of a knife. It was a second time thrust into the furnace, and, when sufficiently softened, was stretched to the proper size by the
aid of another iron rod. This was the entire process. The various colours

---

[1] Deut. viii. 8.   [2] Exod. xxviii. 33.

seen in these rings and seals are mingled into the general mass while in the CHAPTER furnace, not laid on afterward. Some are nearly black, others quite white, XXXVIII. and others variegated with all the intermediate shades. I did not see them make lamps, although they manufacture large quantities for this country and for Egypt.

Hebron, having been "built seven years before Zoan in Egypt," has, of History. course, a very long history from that day to this; and from the fact that Abraham, Isaac, and Jacob spent much of their lives in and near it, and, with their wives, were buried here, it has always been held in high veneration by their descendants. Not only Jews, but all who claim to be related to them, Arabs and Edomites, and other Oriental tribes, have shared in this veneration ; and since the Gentile world has adopted the religion of Abraham—that father of the faithful—its name and fame have extended to the ends of the earth, and must continue till time shall be no more. When the spies came this way, the giants of the Anakim family resided in it; but they were expelled by Caleb, to whom the place was given by Joshua. After this we hear but little of Hebron till the time of David, who made it his residence during the seven years in which he reigned over the tribe of Judah. When he became king of all Israel he removed to Jerusalem, made that city the permanent capital of the Jewish commonwealth, and Hebron is rarely mentioned after this in sacred history. Neither the prophets nor the evangelists name it, nor does the Saviour appear to have visited it ; yet we know from the Maccabees and Josephus that it continued to be an important city even subsequent to the time of the captivity; and Eusebius, Jerome, and a host of later writers speak of it, generally in connection with the tombs of the patriarchs. The Moslems got possession in the seventh century, and have continued to inhabit it ever since, with short interruptions during the time of the Crusades. Thus its existence and identity have been perpetuated and guaranteed without a break to our day.

Is it not strange that the historians of the Crusades, who must have had Unsatis- free access to the cave of Machpelah, have given us no intelligible description factory histories of it ? of the Cru-

Not to those who have waded through their confused and rambling annals, sades. where one finds everything he does not want, and very little of what he does. Every valuable geographical and topographical fact contained in the large folios of the " Gesta Dei per Francos" might be condensed into a few pages ; and yet this collection embodies the most important remaining records of those eventful times. If there had then been a single intelligent student of Biblical geography in the world, we might now have had important light from the Middle Ages to guide us in many a doubtful ramble after a lost locality.

The Anakims of ancient Arba seem to have been the proverbial type of those Anakims. giants so often mentioned in the Bible. We hear of them in Moab under the name of Emims, " a people great and many, and tall as the Anakims, which also were accounted giants." The same were found among the Ammonites, and

---

PART IV.

Giants.

called Zamzummims; and Og, king of Bashan, remained of the giants at the time of Moses. What are we to understand, and how much, from these and other notices of this peculiar race?

Nothing less, certainly, than that there existed men of gigantic stature from the remotest antiquity, even before the Deluge; for these " men of renown" are mentioned in the sixth of Genesis. That there were in times past men of extraordinary size is a tradition wonderfully prevalent to this day all over the East. It not only runs through their legendary lore, but is embodied in numerous monuments of a more substantial character, as the tomb of Noah at Kerak, in the Buk'ah, and that of Seth at Neby Sheet, on the eastern side of the same plain. To what extent such fables corroborate the historic facts of the Bible every one must decide for himself; but the traditions themselves, and these commemorative monuments, are extremely ancient, reaching back to the times of myth and fable. The truth appears to be, that there were among the governing races of primitive times certain families of gigantic stature. This peculiarity was carefully perpetuated and increased by such marriage restrictions as tended to that result; and something similar has been found among the inhabitants of the Pacific islands. For anything beyond this, tradition, that delights in the marvellous and monstrous, is probably accountable. Every distant object seen through her telescope is distorted and vastly exaggerated.

Exaggerations.

If we pass from fact to fable, we may pause a moment on the first step in the scale of exaggeration, and hear the returned spies terrifying their brethren at Kadesh by their false report: " All the people that we saw in the land are men of great stature. There we saw the giants, the sons of Anak, which come of the giants: and we were in our own sight as grasshoppers, and so we were in their sight." [1] You may now enter any coffee-shop on a mild summer evening, and, as twilight shadows settle on the silent auditors, listen to the professional *hakwatieh* amplifying the dimensions of these ancient men of renown, until —the coffee sipped and the argela out—the hearers separate, stroking their beards, and muttering *Masha Allah!*—"God is great!" But the flights of these story-tellers are tame and timid in comparison with the unfettered excursions of rabbinical imagination. Hear what they say about Og, king of Bashan: The soles of his feet were forty miles long, and the waters of the Deluge only reached to his ankles. He, being one of the antediluvian giants, escaped the general destruction, and re-appears in subsequent history as Eliezer of Damascus, Abraham's servant. Abraham, who was only of the size of seventy-four ordinary men, could yet scold most terribly. Under his rebuke Og trembled so violently that one of his double teeth dropped out; and this the patriarch made into an ivory bedstead for himself, and ever after slept upon it. When Moses, who was ten ells high, attacked this same Og—by this time king of Bashan—he seized an axe ten ells in length, jumped ten ells high, and then

Story-tellers.

Og.

[1] Num. xiii. 32, 33.

struck with all his might—*where?* why, on *his ankle*. That blow finally killed CHAPTER him, for Rabbi Jochanan says, " I have been a grave-digger, and once, when I was XXXVIII. chasing a roe, it fled into a shin-bone. I ran after it and followed it for three miles, but could neither overtake it nor see any end to the bone; so I returned and was told that this was the shin-bone of Og, king of Bashan." But enough of this nonsense. Go to Kanah, and the old Metāwely sheikh there will entertain you till midnight with an account of the process by which Abraham tamed this unruly servant into obedience somewhere in the marshes of the Hûleh, below Tell el Kady. Coming back from such grotesque and monstrous fables, we may be thankful for the sober and credible statements of the Bible, which only require us to believe that there were in primitive times certain persons of very large stature, who were called giants.

April 20*th.* In my rambles about the outskirts of the town last evening I lit upon a company of Ishmaelites sitting round a large saucepan, regaling themselves with their dinner. As they said " *Tufuddal*" very earnestly, I sat down among them, and doubling some of their bread spoon-fashion, plunged into the saucepan as they did, and I found their food very savoury indeed. The composition was made of that red kind of lentiles which we examined in Pottage of the market, and I can readily believe that to a hungry hunter it must have lentiles. been very tempting.

It is a singular fact that our Frank children born in this country are extravagantly fond of this same *adis* pottage. Generally, however, it is made out of the brown or bronze-coloured, and not of this red kind. I can testify, also, that when cooking it diffuses far and wide an odour extremely grateful to a hungry man. It was, therefore, no slight temptation to Esau, returning weary and famished from an unsuccessful hunt in this burning climate. I have known modern hunters so utterly spent as to feel, like him, that they were about to die.

It has always seemed to me an act peculiarly unlovely and unbrotherly in Jacob to seize such an opportunity to cheat Esau out of his birthright.

Doubtless it was so; nor do I suppose that it was the first time he had Jacob and overreached his careless brother. This, however, deserved to be recorded, Esau. because it was the grand pivot upon which turned all Jacob's life,—the antecedent act which led directly on to that odious deception practised upon poor old blind Isaac, then to Jacob's flight into Mesopotamia, his marriages, etc., etc. It is instructive to notice how one sin prepares the way for and seduces to the commission of greater. This private purchase would do Jacob no good unless the father confirmed the sale. When, therefore, Isaac was about to transmit, by an act of solemn blessing, the birthright, with all its rich covenants and promises, to Esau, Jacob and his mother saw that their whole previous manœuvres to secure these would utterly fail unless they could now succeed in deluding the helpless father also.

It is not difficult to imagine by what process of sophistry Jacob might Conduct reconcile his conduct with his conscience. I believe the unsophisticated of Jacob

PART
IV.

Jacob and
Esau.

reason of man always refuses to ratify the rights of mere primogeniture as established by custom or law among many nations. In the case of Jacob and Esau it is also to be remembered that they were twins, born at the same time, and Jacob no doubt felt that his brother had really no valid claims of precedence which should entitle him to the inestimable blessings involved in this instance in the question of birthright; so also thought his mother—and to that extent I agree with them. Then it is highly probable that Jacob knew that Esau disbelieved, or at least despised, the religious covenants and promises connected with the line of family descent, and that he was utterly unfit to be trusted with matters of such high import. And in this also he judged correctly. And further, it is nearly certain that Jacob had largely augmented the common estate, while Esau, by his wild and idle life, had rather squandered than added to it. He therefore felt that he had the best right to it,—and so he had. Add to this a spice of chagrin at the obvious partiality of the father for the idle Esau, for no better reason, as appears, than because he ate of his savoury venison; and we have materials enough from which Jacob could work out a tissue of specious reasons for self-justification.

Chastise-
ment of
Jacob.

Success in fraud, as usual, entails a long train of retributive sorrows. Jacob was immediately obliged to fly from his beloved home; and his fond mother, largely implicated in the crime, never again saw her darling son. After a long and perilous journey to Mesopotamia, he was subjected to a series of cruel deceptions and frauds practised upon him by his selfish father-in-law; and when compelled to flee from this intolerable annoyance, he had to humble himself to the dust and plead for his life before the brother he had so often and so grossly injured; and, long after this, he was again deceived by his own sons, in the matter of his lost beloved son Joseph. Few histories are more instructive than this of Jacob, or better illustrate the, to us, involved and complicated machinery of divine providence.

Emeers
cooking.

There are some curious incidents in this long story which let us into the habits and manners of those primitive times. For example, it appears that Jacob, though the son of a wealthy emeer, was actually cooking his own mess of pottage.

There is nothing in this contrary even to present usage in this country. I have often seen rich and luxurious citizens occupied in the same way, and this is still more common among the Arabs of the desert. So also Esau, one would have thought, might easily have sent some of the numerous servants to hunt for venison on the important occasion of receiving the parental blessing; but this too is quite natural in the East. I have had an opportunity to see the great sheikhs of the Anizy, Bini Sukhr, and other tribes of Arabs, and they were in no way distinguished either by dress or manners from their humblest followers. Their garments were even more worn and greasy than those of the servants, and I could not see that they refused to bear their full share of any business that was going on. Indeed, there is a rude etiquette which requires these chiefs to be foremost in all hardships which they and their followers

encounter. So also the fact that Laban's daughters were keeping the flocks, CHAPTER
and Jacob's mother carrying water from the well, and other similar examples, XXXVIII.
do not contradict the customs of wealthy Eastern shepherds. And who that
has travelled much in this country has not often arrived at a well in the heat
of the day which was surrounded with numerous flocks of sheep waiting to be
watered. I once saw such a scene in the burning plains of northern Syria.
Half-naked, fierce-looking men were drawing up water in leather buckets; Drawing
flock after flock was brought up, watered, and sent away; and after all the water.
men had ended their work, then several women and girls brought up their
flocks and drew water for them. Thus it was with Jethro's daughters when
Moses stood up and aided them; and thus, no doubt, it would have been with
Rachel, if Jacob had not rolled away the stone and watered her sheep. I
have frequently seen wells closed up with large stones, though in this part of
the country it is not commonly done, because water is not so scarce and precious. It is otherwise, however, in the dreary deserts.

Cisterns are very generally covered over with a large slab, having a round Closed
hole in it large enough to let down the leather bucket or earthen jar. Into wells.
this hole a heavy stone is thrust, often such as to require the united strength
of two or three shepherds to remove. The same is seen occasionally over *wells*
of "living water;" but where they are large and the supply abundant no such
precaution is needed. It was either at one of these cisterns, or less abundant
and more precious wells, that Jacob met Rachel; and being a stout man,
nearly seventy years of age, he was able to remove the stone and water the
flock.

I have repeatedly found wells closed up tight and the mouth plastered over Fountain
with mortar. Such wells are reserved until times of greatest need, when all opened.
other sources of supply have failed. This may illustrate that passage in
Zechariah xiii. 1 : "In that day there shall be a fountain opened to the house
of David, and to the inhabitants of Jerusalem, for sin and for uncleanness."
This is indeed a beautiful and significant promise, which many actions and
customs in this country may shed light upon and render emphatic. Not only
are fountains often sealed up until times of utmost need, and then opened for
public use, but when this is not the case they are commonly far off from the
villages, in secluded valleys, and on account of the difficulty of carrying water
to their homes, the women take their soiled clothes, a kettle, and some wood
down to them, and there do their washing. Again, the inhabitants of most
villages select one or more sheep in autumn, which they feed with the greatest
care for their winter's supply of cooking-fat. They not only stuff them with
vine and mulberry leaves, as is done in our country with poultry, but every
evening they take them to the open fountain and thoroughly wash them from
all defilements. This greatly adds to the richness and sweetness of the mutton.
The figure may have been suggested to Zechariah by this custom. Now Fountain
Christ is not only the good shepherd, and his people the sheep of his pasture, for un-
but he is also the fountain in which their sins and pollutions are washed away. cleanness.

This fountain, long sealed up, was opened by the nails and the spear on Calvary, and not merely for the house of David and the inhabitants of Jerusalem, but for all whom they represent and include. Millions have been washed in the gospel fountain, and yet its waters are as abundant and efficacious to cleanse from sin as ever. It is the very heart and core of the glad tidings to all nations that this fountain has indeed been opened, and whosoever will may wash and be clean.

What does this curious and irregular procession signify?

Circumcision.

Our friend here says it is a circumcision, and it is generally attended with just such music and buffoonery.

Well, that is interesting, certainly, to find this rite still practised in the very place where it was first instituted by command of God to Abraham, nearly four thousand years ago. Ishmael, too, the great ancestor of these Arabs, was among the very first to receive the rite.[1]

If you have any curiosity to study this subject in detail, you will find the process, and the accompanying feasts and ceremonies, minutely explained by Lane in his " Modern Egyptians." This before us is evidently a small affair, for the rabble accompanying the victim are rude in the extreme, and poorly clad. The whole thing resembles a drunken frolic more than a religious ceremony; but even in the processions of the rich on such occasions, there are commonly two or three buffoons along with the musicians, to make sport by their outlandish costume and ridiculous behaviour.

What do you say to the arguments of those who maintain that Abraham was not the first that practised circumcision—that, in fact, the Father of the Faithful borrowed it from the Egyptians, the Ethiopians, or Colchians?

Origin of circumcision.

I have very little interest in such speculations. The Bible is false—let us say so at once—if Abraham did not receive this rite by revelation, and adopt it in obedience to a direct command of God. He received it also as the seal of a most important covenant. I care not whether anybody ever used a somewhat similar custom or not before the time of Abraham. It may be so, though there is no satisfactory evidence of the fact. To me it seems far more probable that the rite was communicated to the priests in Egypt through Joseph, who married into their family or tribe, than that the Israelites borrowed it from them. As to the testimony of Herodotus, who came into Egypt *fifteen centuries* after, and, with great learning and research, often writes a good deal of nonsense, I refuse utterly to put it in the same category with that of Moses. The great founder of the Jewish commonwealth—the greatest lawgiver on record—born and bred in Egypt, states the facts in relation to the introduction of circumcision among his people. A mere traveller and historian—a foreigner and a *Greek*—comes along very much later, and makes statements which are partly true, partly erroneous, as Josephus shows in his answer to Apion; and then sceptical authors, more than twenty centuries

---

[1] Gen. xvii. 28.

later than Herodotus, bring up his imperfect statements, and, twisting and *CHAPTER* expanding them, attempt to prove that Abraham did not receive circumcision *XXXVIII.* from God (as Moses plainly says he did), but from the Egyptians! Not with such weapons can the veracity of Moses be successfully assailed.

It is, however, very remarkable that this singular rite did actually spread Its exteninto many countries,—that it has been retained not only by Jews and Moslems sion. all over the world, but that even some Christian sects have adopted it, as the Copts and Abyssinians. We need not pursue this subject any further at present, but it is certainly a fine corroboration of the Book of Genesis, to stand in the plain of Mamre and witness the ceremonies of that solemn religious rite which Abraham here received "as a seal of the righteousness of faith which he had yet being uncircumcised."[1]

We are reminded by the firing of guns, the beating of the everlasting *tubble,* Eliezer, the singing and clapping of hands, and the general hubbub always attendant Abraupon native weddings, that it was from this place Abraham sent his faithful ham's servant into Mesopotamia to find and to bring a wife for Isaac.

Yes; and the account of this embassy in the 24th chapter of Genesis furnishes many allusions to Oriental customs which modern manners beautifully illustrate. We have already had occasion to notice the great influence and authority which chief servants in the families of emeers and sheikhs still exercise. Such was the confidence and respect accorded to Eliezer, that Abraham at one time seriously contemplated making him his heir,—a result not uncommon in these Oriental countries in all ages down to the present time.

Another thing very noticeable, and to which also we have before alluded, is the great solicitude of Abraham to have his son marry *one of his own kindred.* This is in exact correspondence with the customs of the Eastern nobility; nor need we limit the remark to the higher classes. Certain degrees of affinity excepted, a relative always has the preference in matrimonial negotiations. The strict injunction of Abraham, therefore, to bring none but a *relative* from his own family, though enforced by religious considerations, was in no sense a departure from established usages and social laws in regard to marriage.

The mode of swearing fidelity required of Eliezer, by placing his hand under Swearing the thigh of Abraham, seems to have been peculiar to the patriarchs, and *may* fidelity. have had reference to that promised seed who was to proceed from Abraham's loins, according to the then figurative style of speaking on this subject. In the present case there would be more than ordinary propriety in this significant action, inasmuch as the oath taken had direct and exclusive reference to the preservation of that line of descent through which this promised seed was to come.

The preparation and outfit for this journey agree in all respects with the Eliezer's persons concerned, the nature of the country, and the habits of the people. Journey. Eliezer took ten camels loaded with provisions and presents; and such an

---

[1] Rom. iv. 11.

expedition would not now be undertaken from Hebron with any other animals, nor with a less number. The diligent servant, no doubt, selected the most direct route, which would be through Palestine, along the west side of the Jordan and the lakes, into the Buk'ah, and out through the land of Hamath to the Euphrates, and thence to the city of Nahor in Mesopotamia. Such a journey is both long and dangerous,—far beyond what is indicated to a Western reader by the brief statement that Eliezer "arose and went to Mesopotamia;" but what befell him by the way we know not. The narrative leaps the whole distance, and so must we, with the simple assurance that the Lord God of Israel led him by the right way.

Customs.

Every phrase of the eleventh verse contains an allusion to matters Oriental. Arrived at the town of Nahor, "he made his camels *kneel down without the city by a well of water at the time of evening—the time that women go out to draw water.*" He made the camels kneel—a mode of expression taken from actual life. The action is literally *kneeling;* not stooping, sitting, or lying down on the side like a horse, but *kneeling* on his *knees;* and this the camel is taught to do from his youth. The *place* is said to have been by a well of water, and this well was outside the city. In the East, where wells are scarce, and water indispensable, the existence of a well or fountain determines the site of the village. The people build near it, but prefer to have it outside the "city," to avoid the noise, dust, and confusion always occurring at it, and especially if the place is on the public highway. It is around the fountain that the thirsty traveller and the wearied caravan assemble; and if you have become separated from your own company before arriving at a town, you need only inquire for the fountain, and there you will find them. It was perfectly natural, therefore, for Eliezer to *halt at the well.* The *time* was evening; but it is further stated that it was when the *women* go forth to draw water. True to life again. At that hour the peasant returns home from his labour, and the women are busy preparing the evening meal, which is to be ready at sunset. Cool fresh water is then demanded, and of course there is a great concourse around the well. But why limit it to the *women?* Simply because such is the fact. About great cities men often carry water, both on donkeys and on their own backs; but in the country, among the unsophisticated natives, *women only* go to the well or the fountain; and often, when travelling, have I seen long files of them going and returning with their pitchers "at the time when women go out to draw water."

Camels
kneeling.

A well
outside
the city.

Rebekah.

Again: the description of Rebekah, the account she gives of herself, and the whole dialogue with Eliezer, agree admirably with Oriental customs. Even the statement as to the manner of carrying her pitcher, or rather jar, is exact—*on her shoulder.* The Egyptian and the negro carry on the head, the Syrian on the shoulder or the hip. She went *down* to the well; and nearly all wells in the East are in wadies, and many of them have steps down to the water—fountains of course have. Eliezer asks water to drink; she hastens and *lets down the pitcher on her hand.* How often have I had this identical

act performed for myself, when travelling in this thirsty land! Rebekah's CHAPTER
address to the *servant*, "Drink, my lord"—*Ishrub ya seedy*—will be given to XXXVIII.
you in the exact idiom by the first gentle Rebekah you ask water from. But
I have never found any young lady so generous as this fair daughter of Bethuel.
She drew for all his camels, and for nothing, while I have often found it
difficult to get my horse watered even for money. Rebekah emptied her
pitcher into the *trough*—an article always found about wells, and frequently
made of stone. The jewels, also, for the *face*, forehead, and arms, are still
as popular among the same class of people as they were in the days of
Abraham. Not only are the head, neck, and arms adorned with a profusion
of gold and silver rings, chains, and other ornaments, but rings are suspended
on the face, from the side of the nose, etc, etc.

Laban's address, " Come in, thou blessed of the Lord," is still in good taste. Laban's
I have often been welcomed in set phrases even more complimentary and welcome.
sacred. The camels, as appears from the 32d verse, were included in the
invitation, and were brought *into the house ;* and I have often slept in the
same room with these peaceful animals, in company with their owner and all
his family. *Straw* and provender were given to them ; that is, *tibn* and
some kind of pulse or grain. There is no *hay* in the East. Water to wash
the feet of the wearied travellers was of course given ; and the same kind act
will be done to you under similar circumstances. So, also, the mode of
negotiating the marriage contract, the presenting of gifts, etc., are all in perfect accordance with modern usages. The parents manage the whole affair,
often, however, with the advice of the eldest son and heir, as Laban was in
this case. And if the father be dead, the eldest son takes his place, and
assumes his authority in the disposal of his sisters. Presents are absolutely
essential in betrothals. They are given with much ceremony before witnesses,
and the articles presented are described in a written document, so that, if the
match be broken off, the bridegroom can obtain them back again, or their value,
and something more as a compensation for the injury.

Finally, the behaviour of Rebekah, when about to meet Isaac, was such as Behaviour
modern etiquette requires. It is customary for both men and women, when of Rebe-
an emeer or great personage is approaching, to alight some time before he kah.
comes up with them. Women frequently refuse to ride in the presence of
men ; and when a company of them are to pass through a town, they often
dismount and walk. It was, no doubt, a point of Syrian etiquette for Rebekah
to stop, descend from her camel, and cover herself with a veil in the presence
of her future husband. In a word, this Biblical narrative is so natural to one
familiar with the East, so beautiful also, and life-like, that the entire scene
seems to be an affair in which he has himself been but recently an actor.

CHAPTER XXXIX.

HEBRON TO SANTA SABA.

April 21st.

Donkeys,
saddles,
and sacks.

RETURNING from my ramble down the vale of Hebron this morning, I met a company of men and donkeys going out apparently for grain, and I was struck with the resemblance of the animals themselves to those in pictures now found on the monuments of Egypt. The saddles and sacks of some appeared to be

EGYPTIAN DONKEYS.

precisely like those used in the days when the sons of Jacob descended along the same valley to get corn from Egypt.

Doubtless there has been but little change in all these matters from that CHAPTER XXXIX. time to this, and the resemblance is often still more exact from the fact that, when the crops of this country fail through drought or other causes, the people still go down to Egypt to buy corn, as they did in the time of the patriarchs. Going to Egypt. It has also frequently occurred to me, when passing a large company of donkeys on their way to buy food, that we are not to suppose that only the eleven donkeys on which the brethren of Joseph rode composed the whole caravan. One man often leads or drives half a dozen ; and, besides, I apprehend that Jacob's sons had many servants along with them. Eleven sacks of Servants grain, such as donkeys would carry, would not sustain a household like his for a week. It is no objection to this supposition that these servants are not mentioned. There was no occasion to allude to them, and such a reference would have disturbed the perfect *unity* and touching simplicity of that most beautiful narrative ; and it is in accordance with the general practice of Moses, in sketching the lives of the patriarchs, not to confuse the story by introducing non-historic characters. Thus, had it not been for the capture of Lot by Chedorlaomer, we should not have known that Abraham had three hundred and eighteen full-grown men in his household ; and so, also, had it not been necessary for Jacob to send company after company to guide his large presents to meet Esau, we might have been left to suppose that he and his sons alone conducted his flocks in his flight from Mesopotamia. But it is certain that he had a large retinue of servants ; and so, doubtless, each of his sons had servants, and it is incredible that they should have gone down to Egypt without them ; on the contrary, there is every reason to believe that there was a large caravan. The fact, also, that the sons themselves took part in the work, and that each had his sack under him, is in exact correspondence with the customs of tent-dwelling shepherds at this day. The highest sheikhs dress and fare precisely as their followers do, and bear their full share in the operations of the company, whatever they may be.

This leads me to suggest another idea, which I have long entertained in Number of the Israelites in Egypt. regard to the actual number of persons that went down to Egypt with Jacob. It was strictly true that "all the souls that *came out of Jacob's loins*, besides his sons' wives, were threescore and six ;"[1] and these being, so to speak, historic characters, are, according to the usual practice, specifically mentioned : but there must have been a very large company belonging to them, of both men-servants, maid-servants, and children ; and, beyond a doubt, these remained, were incorporated with, and multiplied as rapidly as their masters. May we not in this fact find an explanation of the vast multitude to which this company had grown in so short a time ? I have myself no doubt on the Servants included. subject. Israel did not sell his home-born servants, but took them into Egypt. There they were absorbed into the Hebrew nation during those generations when all were reduced by their tyrannical masters to one common lot of hard

----

[1] Gen. xlvi. 26.

bondage.　And thus it came to pass that there were six hundred thousand men that went up harnessed and fit for war.　Nor is this custom of absorbing into the different tribes those servants that belonged to them at variance with either ancient or modern practice.　That the freedmen were incorporated with and adopted the family name of their masters, is a well-known fact in the history of the great Roman commonwealth.

That company of donkeys you met were doubtless going to the distant fields to bring in to the threshing-floors the *'adis* or lentiles from which Esau's pottage was made.　Just below us is a field in which it is not yet ripe, and another yonder, on the southern slope of the mountain, where they are gathering it.　You notice that it does not grow more than six or eight inches high, and is *pulled* like flax, not cut with the sickle.　When green, it resembles an incipient pea-vine, only the leaves are differently arranged, smaller, and more delicate,—somewhat like those of the mimosa or sensitive plant.

LENTILES ('ADIS).

Road to St. Saba.　Our muleteers anticipate a hard day's march to St. Saba, and therefore are more than usually expeditious in starting.　Allowing them to pursue the regular road toward the Pools of Solomon, we will pass up to the north-west, and visit the great oak of Abraham.

Pools of Hebron.　Do you suppose that this large pool we are now passing is ancient ?

I see no reason to doubt that both this and also the smaller one, higher up the valley, date back to the days of the Jews.　Whether either of them is mentioned in 2 Sam. iv. 12, as the place where David hung up the murderers of Ishbosheth, is, of course, doubtful ; but both of them may have then been in existence, for works of this kind, and in such localities, last as long as the cities for whose accommodation they were made.

Vineyards.　We are now riding through the most extensive and best-kept vineyards that I have seen in this country.

All travellers are struck with them, and no one fails, or can fail, of being CHAPTER XXXIX. reminded by them of that extraordinary cluster of grapes which the spies car-

LOWER POOL OF HEBRON.

ried " between two upon a staff;" for the valley of Hebron is the place from Vines. whence they bore this proof of the fertility of the promised land.[1]   I have been here in the season of grapes, and, though they are larger than in most other localities, and the clusters very long, yet I have never seen any so heavy as to require to be borne between two upon a staff.

These houses and rude towers in the vineyards are for the vine-dressers, I suppose ?

The houses are for the families of the owners of these vineyards ; and should you come this way in September or October, you will find the city deserted, and these gardens crowded with grape-gatherers of every age and sex. The Vintage. whole population then live abroad, each under his own vine and fig-tree. Most of them sleep beneath these vine-arbours, and the houses are for the safe keeping of their utensils and their raisins, while they are out gathering grapes. A large part of the crop is eaten or sold at the time ; the remainder is dried into raisins, or pressed, and the juice boiled down to a thick molasses, called *dibs ;* for the Moslems, as you are aware, make no wine.

These towers stationed around on commanding points are for the *natûrs,* or Towers. watchmen ; and they are already there, keeping a keen eye upon the entire range of vineyards.   One of them is coming toward us from his tower, and his object is to see who we are, and what may be our business out here among the

[1] Num. xiiL 28.

vineyards. We will take him as our guide to the oak; for, although it is in full view, there are innumerable turns yet to be made in our tortuous path before we can reach it. These watchmen are very celebrated characters in the Bible, and figure largely both in prose and poetry. Isaiah has a beautiful reference to them in the 52d chapter of his prophecies: "Thy watchmen shall lift up the voice; with the voice together shall they sing: for they shall see eye to eye, when the Lord shall bring again Zion."[1]

Do you believe that the watchmen here mentioned were these *natûrs* over the fields and vineyards? I had supposed that the prophet refers in that passage to the military sentinels in time of danger.

Doubtless the reference is in many places to such sentinels stationed upon lofty mountains, or upon the fortifications of the city. Thus, in the 62d chapter, "I have set watchmen upon thy walls, O Jerusalem, which shall never hold their peace day nor night;" and again in the 52d chapter, "How beautiful upon the mountains are the feet of him that bringeth good tidings, that publisheth peace; that bringeth good tidings of good, that publisheth salvation; that saith unto Zion, Thy God reigneth!" If you conceive of Zion as a city defended by walls and towers, and guarded by soldiers, the illustration is natural and striking, particularly in time of war. Then, as I myself have seen at Jerusalem, these watchmen are multiplied, and so stationed that every yard of the wall falls under their surveillance, and thus they literally see eye to eye. They never remit their watchfulness, nor do they keep silence, especially at night. When danger is apprehended they are obliged to call to one another and to respond every few minutes. The guard on the look-out at the Tower of David, for instance, lifts up his voice in a long call, the one next south of him takes up the note and repeats it, and thus it runs quite round the circuit of the walls. At Sidon the custom-house guards stationed around the city are required to keep one another awake and alert in the same way, particularly when there is danger of smuggling.

There is, however, another set of scenes which seems to me to correspond better to the drapery of the passage from Isaiah. Zion, or the Church of God, is frequently described under the similitude of a garden or vineyard; and such is the case here. Her watchmen are not on walls, but stand upon the mountains, and the costume of the entire scene is rural, not mural. It breathes of the country, not of the city. To understand and enjoy this noble passage, one needs to go forth to the fields at the time of the vintage. The vineyards are generally planted on the sides of mountains, often climbing, by successive terraces, quite to the summit. As they are far from the village, and without fence or hedge, they must be carefully guarded, and the stoutest and boldest young men are selected for *natûrs*. They take their stations on the highest part of the mountain which they have to watch, and are so arranged that the *eye of one surveys the entire series of vineyards up to the point where the eye of the other reaches* Thus eye meets eye, and every part is brought under CHAPTER XXXIX. constant surveillance. "They shall lift up the voice," etc. This is very natural and beautiful. When an animal or thief appears, or any other cause of alarm occurs, the watchman who observes it lifts up a long-toned cry at the very top of his voice, and is immediately responded to by his fellows at the other stations; and the attention of all being aroused, it is his duty whose part is threatened with injury to attend to the case at once. Thus it will be with *Zion* in the happy days foreshadowed by this prophecy. The watchmen being sufficient in number, rightly located, all intent upon their work of watching, and ready to afford each other information of danger and assistance in repelling it, then will Zion dwell safely. Wild beasts may threaten to break in and devour, and robbers may prowl about, but the system of defence will be perfect, and the watchmen " scorn surprise."

This explanation coincides best with the 7th verse: "How beautiful upon Feet upon the mountains are the feet of him that bringeth good tidings, that *publisheth* tains. *peace!*" These *natûrs*, standing upon the very pinnacle of the mountain, have a very striking appearance, particularly when seen below, far off, at a great elevation, in picturesque costumes, their outline drawn sharply upon the clear blue sky beyond;—they seem in fancy's eye like aerial beings, guardian angels, hovering in mid heaven over their peaceful charge. The *feet* are mentioned, perhaps, because they are seen *standing*, as if alert and prompt to fulfil the duties of their office. They do, in fact, *stand, not sit or lounge;* and the same idea is implied in the 5th verse of the 61st chapter of Isaiah: "Strangers shall *stand* and feed your flocks." Good shepherds do not sit down in careless neglect of their charge, and I have often been reminded of this promise to Israel when looking at the shepherd *standing out* in bold relief upon some towering cliff, from which he could see every member of his flock.

It is only on rare occasions that one now finds all the circumstances here alluded to combined in the same scene, and never but in elevated and retired parts of Lebanon, during the months of September and October. When pass- Singing ing through vineyards thus situated and thus guarded on that goodly mountain, together. I have been suddenly startled by a long, loud note of warning, swelling up the steep cliffs of the mountains, and responded to by others before and behind, "singing together" in concert, and waking the echoes that sleep in the wadies and among the ragged rocks; then one of the watchmen, leaving his lofty station, would descend to meet me with hands laden with the best clusters for my acceptance, and this, too, "without money and without price." Courteously accompanying me to the end of the vineyards, he would then dismiss me with a graceful bow, and the prayer of peace on his lips. If, however, one attempts to take without permission, these watchmen are required to resist even unto death,—and in the execution of their office they are extremely bold and resolute. I have known many serious and some fatal rencounters of this kind.

Here we are at the famous oak, and a moment's inspection will show to one Abra- acquainted with such matters that it can have no connection with Abraham, ham's oak nor, indeed, with any one else who lived more than a thousand years ago. We have oaks in Lebanon twice the size of this, and every way more striking and majestic. It is a fine old *baluta* (evergreen oak), however, twenty-six feet in girth at the ground, and its thick branches extend over an area ninety-three feet in diameter. Some six feet from the ground the tree *forks* into three great arms, which again divide as they ascend into innumerable limbs. The location is beautiful, near the head of this wady Sebta, and about two miles north-west of the city, and many a pic-nic is achieved by the Jews of Hebron upon the soft sward that is allowed to grow beneath this noble oak of their father Abraham.

We must now pursue our ride to the north-east, and join our company below Beled en Nussarah (town of the Christians), where they are to wait for us. In the valley south of this ruined *Beled* is a fountain of the same name,

Abra-
ham's
house.

from which an aqueduct once carried the water to Hebron. Beyond is the *house* of Abraham, which lies some distance to the east of the regular road from Hebron to Bethlehem, on a path that leads to Tekoa, and which we would follow if our men knew the way, as it would take us nearer the cave of Adullam, which we wish to visit. This house of Abraham appears never to have been finished, and at present there remain but two courses of great stones, some of them fifteen feet in length, and more than three thick. The builder, whoever he was, appears to have projected a strong castle or palace, two hundred feet long and a hundred and sixty feet broad; but, like many who begin, he was not able to finish, and has left these courses of hewn stones out on this lone mountain to puzzle the brains of antiquarians and tourists to the end of time.

Places on
the way.

We now begin to descend northward to Dirweh, where is a fountain of water with large stone troughs, and many old quarries in the neighbourhood. The place is doubtless ancient, though its name does not occur in the Bible. Directly east of it, however, is Hŭlhŭl, the ancient Halhûl, which was given to Judah, and which was near Hebron, according to the "Onomasticon." From this to the Pools of Solomon one may go to sleep, so far as pretty scenery or interesting historic sites are concerned. We are now coming to a deserted village, called Kûfîn and west of it a short distance is Beit Ummar, while on the east of our path is a considerable ruin, called Bazata, or Beth Zeita.

Though our present road is destitute of historic sites, this region of country abounds in them; and if the season were not so far advanced, and the country had been less disturbed, it would have been pleasant to spend a few days in making excursions around Hebron. Scarcely any part of Palestine has pre-served so many ancient names as the district of which this city is the centre.

Ancient
sites.

On the south are Adoraim, and Anab, and Shochoh, Juttah, Ziph, Eshtemoa, Anim, Maon, and Carmel, from whence David got his wife, after Nabal, "that son of Belial," had died in his drunken debauch, as recorded in the twenty-fifth chapter of First Samuel; on the west and north are Beth-tappuah, Ramah, Beth-zur, and Halhûl, and many more, according as we extend the circle.

These names, however, are nearly all destitute of Biblical interest, and what there is of ruins about the sites worthy of notice we must commit to the care of tourists and explorers, who make it their business to search out, measure, and describe them. The people of Ziph obtained an odious reputation in the time of David by betraying his hiding-place in the hill of Hachilah to king Saul. One of these rough hills below Ziph must doubtless be the scene of that venturesome visit of David into the camp of his enemy while he and all his troop were asleep.[1] That entire region is now almost deserted except by Bedawîn robbers, who render it at least as dangerous to honest shepherds as it seems to have been before David and his company frequented it. The men of Carmel mention it as something remarkable that they were not *hurt*, neither missed anything as long as they were conversant with them in the fields. "They were a wall unto us night and day, all the while we were with them keeping the sheep."[2] It is refreshing to read such a testimony to David's admirable government over the band that followed him; and if there were now such an emeer in that same region, we might have safely extended our rambles down to the Dead Sea, at the famous castle of Masada, and then passed on northward by 'Ain Jidy to Jericho. As it is, we are only able to get some such view of these districts as Moses had from the top of Pisgah. The result of such a survey on my mind, however, has always been far less satisfactory and refreshing than it appears to have been to Moses; for no other part of Palestine is so dreary and uninteresting as this,—and it grows more and more so as you approach the Sea of Sodom, until the barren, bronze-coloured rocks terminate in the tremendous cliff of Masada. It has never been my privilege to visit that celebrated castle, and the best account I have seen of it is from the pen of Mr. Wolcott, who was also the first in modern times to visit and identify it. The most striking *views* were drawn by his travelling companion, Mr. Tipping, and appear in Mr. Traill's new translation of Josephus. Their visit was made in the winter of 1842, and since then many travellers have been there, including several of the exploring expedition of Captain Lynch. All who have visited this terrific crag and strange castle seem to have been smitten with the spirit of exaggeration, but no one, except perhaps M. De Saulcey, has equalled Josephus. You can read his account in the 8th chapter of the 7th book of his Wars. He thus speaks of the approach to it along the path called "the *serpent*," "as resembling that animal in its narrowness and its perpetual windings, for it is broken off at the prominent precipices of the rock, and returns frequently into itself; and lengthening again by little and little, hath much ado to proceed forward, and he that would walk along it must first go on one leg and then on the other; and there is also nothing but destruction in case your foot slip; for on each side there is a vastly deep chasm and precipice, sufficient to quell the courage of anybody by the terror it infuses into the mind," etc., etc.

CHAPTER
XXXIX.

Ziph.

Masada.

Exaggerated accounts.

1 1 Sam. xxvi. 1–12.　　　2 1 Sam. xxv. 15, 16.

PART
IV.

The historian informs us that Jonathan the high priest first of all built a fortress on this cliff, and called it Masada; but the great wall around the entire
summit, seven furlongs in length, was the work of Herod, who erected a palace
there, and spent vast sums in preparing it to be a last retreat for himself in
case of need. He, however, died elsewhere, and had no occasion for such a
stronghold; but after the destruction of Jerusalem, a band of robbers, whom
Josephus calls Siccarii, seized upon it, and dared to set at defiance the conquerors of the world; and upon its hard and blackened summit was enacted
the very last scene in the tragedy of Israel's destruction.

Tragedy
of Masada.

The wall built by Silva to hem in the besieged can still be traced quite
round the rock, and also the remains of the Roman camp; and when the
place was subdued by famine, and the defences were stormed, the people,
unable to escape, and maddened by the speech of Eleazar their chief, "embraced their wives, took their children in their arms, and gave the longest
parting kisses," and with bitter tears then plunged their dripping daggers to
their hearts, and laid them all dead in one ghastly funeral pile. They then
chose ten men by lot to slay all the rest, and every one laid himself down by his
wife and children, and, with his arms around their lifeless bodies, offered his
neck to the sword of the executioner. This bloody butchery accomplished,
one of the ten killed all the rest, and finally himself. Thus perished nine
hundred and sixty men, women, and children, the last great sacrifice on
the altar of divine retribution, and only two women and five children survived to tell the tale. Such tragedies are far more than mere incidents in
man's general history. They are the voice of the Almighty One, setting
the seal of truth divine to a thousand admonitions and prophetic warnings
scattered everywhere through his holy Word; and, thus regarded, there is
no stronger evidence for the divine origin of the Bible than the seven books
of Jewish Wars by Josephus.

En-gedi.

There is no other point of much interest along the western shore of the
Dead Sea, except 'Ain Jidy—Fountain of the Goat—the En-gedi of the Bible,
which was given to Judah, and mentioned by Joshua along with the city of
Salt.[1] It is in a wild ravine, and the cliffs on either side are full of natural and
artificial caves and sepulchres. It was in the strongholds of En-gedi that the
persecuted David at one time dwelt; and into one of the caves there Saul
went "to cover his feet," when David, who lay hid deep within, arose and
cut off the skirt of his robe, and might have slain the wearer also, had he not
feared to stretch forth his hand against the Lord's anointed.[2] Owing to
copious fountains in this warm ravine, there were, in ancient times, fragrant
orchards and spicy gardens at En-gedi, to which Solomon, in his Song of
Songs, compares his beloved: "My beloved is unto me as a cluster of camphire in the vintage of En-gedi."[3] What camphire was precisely, cannot now
be determined, but it must have been very pleasant. In the margin it is

---

[1] Josh. xv. 62.   [2] 1 Sam. xxiii. 29, and xxiv. 1–6.   Song i. 14.

translated " cypress,"—something equally unknown to me. Dr. Kitto argues CHAPTER
that this *kopher* was the *henneh;* and certainly the long " clusters" of henneh XXXIX.
flowers are extremely fragrant. The Orientals, also, are extravagantly fond of
their odour, and they have an intimate association with love and marriage, so
that Solomon might very appropriately compare his beloved to such a cluster.
It is my opinion, however, that *kopher* is merely a poetic name for a very
fragrant species of grape that flourished most luxuriously in these vineyards
of En-gedi. The Arabs of the present day distinguish their choice varieties
of grapes by names every way analogous to this.

In the account of Saul's pursuit of David to En-gedi, two circumstances are
mentioned which are worthy of a passing remark. The first is, that there
were *sheep-cotes* there in connection with the cave into which Saul retired. I Sheep-
have seen hundreds of them around the mouth of caverns, and, indeed, there cotes.
is scarcely a cave in the land whose location will admit of being thus occupied,
but has such a " cote" in front of it, generally made by piling up loose stones
into a circular wall, which is covered with thorns as a further protection against
robbers and wild beasts. During cold storms, and in the night, the flocks
retreat into the cave, but at other times they remain in this enclosed cote.
The cavern may have been full of them when the king entered ; nor would
his presence have disturbed them—as I have found on many occasions—while
their constant tramping about the sleeping Saul would have rendered the
approach of David wholly unnoticed. I have had them step over me when
resting in such caves, and have seen them actually tramp on their sleeping
shepherd without disturbing his slumbers. Moreover, these caverns are as
dark as midnight, and the keenest eye cannot see five paces *inward;* but one
who has been long within, and is looking *outward* toward the entrance, can
observe with perfect distinctness all that takes place in that direction. David,
therefore, could watch Saul as he came in, and notice the exact place where
he " covered his feet," while he could see nothing but impenetrable darkness.

The other fact is, that the cliffs about En-gedi were then called "the rocks Wild
of the wild goats ;" and from them, doubtless, the place received its name, goats.
En-gedi ('Ain Jidy)—the Fountain of the Goats. Now it is a remarkable and
a pleasing circumstance that these bold and hardy dwellers upon the rocks are
still found in the wild ravines about 'Ain Jidy. I have seen the skin and
powerful horns of one that was shot there by an Arab hunter.

But here we are at El Burak, as the Pools of Solomon are now called, and Pools of
there we will take our noon-day lunch, and drink of that " sealed foun- Solomon.
tain" which furnished the king another pretty figure with which to compare his " beloved ;" at least such is monastic identification and exposition of
Song iv. 12.

While I arrange for our repast under the wall of this dilapidated old castle,
you may satisfy your curiosity by a survey of these great cisterns. Well, do
they equal their name and fame ?

They are worthy of Solomon, and that is the highest note I can think of at present.

WILD GOATS.

Size of
pools.

They are certainly gigantic cisterns, and all the more impressive is this utter solitude, where there are no other structures with which to compare them, or to divide the interest which they inspire. The proportions of the one furthest to the east are truly royal: nearly six hundred feet long, two hundred wide, and fifty deep. When full, it would float the largest man-of-war that ever ploughed the ocean.[1]

The first time I saw these Burak there was very little water in any of them, but I have since been here when the two upper ones were full and overflowing into the third. The stream from the only fountain in this

---

[1] Dr. Robinson, with his usual accuracy, gives the measurement of the three as follows:— The first is 582 by 207, and 50 feet deep; the second is 423 by 250, and 39 deep; the third is 380 by 236, and 25 deep. All of them, however, are considerably *narrower* at the upper end, the first being 148, the second 160, and the third 229 feet.

vicinity was then led along an open canal on the north side, directly into the aqueduct east of the pools, and thus carried round the shoulder of the hill, apparently to irrigate gardens in that direction. I examined the under-ground rooms in the southwest corner of this old castle, where the water first appears, brought there by an artificial channel, many feet below the surface, from the fountainhead, which is some forty rods to the north-west. Tradition makes this "the spring shut up, the fountain sealed," to which the "sister spouse" is compared in Song iv. 12; and if so, the "garden enclosed" was near at hand, perhaps in this little plain which spreads up to the fountain from the pools. If Solomon really constructed these vast reservoirs—and even Dr. Robinson is disposed to admit the fact—it is probable that it was on the neighbouring hills, and in the valleys to the north-east of them, that he planted the vineyards, made the gardens and orchards of all kinds of fruits, and made pools of water, to water therewith the wood that bringeth forth trees;[1] by which and other like data he worked out the great problem of human affairs to the final product of "vanity of vanities." Josephus, however, says that these gardens were at Etam,—which our friends in Jerusalem have identified with Urtas, its fountains and fine gardens.

Well, at Urtas let it be, or wherever you please: I am tired of doubting everything. Besides, I think there is good reason to rest in the *general* correctness of this identification; and the thought that the wise king of Israel

Possibly the work of Solomon.

GROUND PLAN OF SOLOMON'S POOLS.

Length 380 feet.

Length 423 feet.

Length 582 feet.

---

[1] Eccles. ii. 4–6.

PART
IV.

had often retired to those then well-wooded and well-watered hills and valleys, adds immensely to the charm of this day's most delightful and instructive ramble.

Urtas.

Aqueduct.

We must now pursue our ride, and the path lies down the valley below Urtas, and we shall follow for some time the line of the canal by which the water was conveyed to Jerusalem. This aqueduct is probably less ancient than the pools; but that is not certain, for I have often noticed that such canals, where the line followed along the surface of the country, were constructed of small stones, laid up in a careless manner, and this, too, where we know that the work dates back at least to the beginning of our era. The ephemeral character of the present aqueduct, therefore, does not *prove* that it is modern. It followed the sinuosities of the hills, passed east and below Bethlehem and the Convent of Elijah, and near Jerusalem was carried along the west side of Gihon to the north end of the lower pool, where it crossed to the east side, and descended around the southern declivity of Zion, below Neby Daûd, and finally entered the south-western corner of the Temple area, where the water was employed in the various services of the sanctuary.

Tekoa.

I once struck across the wild region east of us, to visit Tekoa and the so-called cave of Adullam. Of Tekoa little need be said. The name is applied to a ruined site lying on the north-eastern slope of a high ridge, an hour and a half to the south-east of the pools. The whole country is now deserted, except by the Arabs, who pasture their flocks on those barren hills. They are a rude and sinister-looking generation. I hope the herdsmen of Tekoa, with whom Amos says he associated, were better men and more civilized than their present successors. Joab, I am sure, would search Tekoa in vain for a wise woman to fetch about that cunning form of speech by which David was induced to recall Absalom from banishment.[1]

Cave of
Adullam.

Having passed eastward of Tekoa, we descended a shallow wady for about a mile, to some curious old buildings which overhang the tremendous gorge of Wady Urtas, there called Khureitûn, which is also the name of the ruins. Leaving our horses in charge of wild Arabs, and taking one for a guide, we started for the cave, having a fearful gorge below, gigantic cliffs above, and the path winding along a shelf of the rock, narrow enough to make the nervous among us shudder. At length, from a great rock hanging on the edge of this shelf, we sprang by a long leap into a low window which opened into the perpendicular face of the cliff. We were then within the hold of David,[2] and, creeping half doubled through a narrow crevice for a few rods, we stood beneath the dark vault of the first grand chamber of this mysterious and oppressive cavern. Our whole collection of lights did little more than make the damp darkness visible. After groping about as long as we had time to spare, we returned to the light of day, fully convinced that, with David and his lion-hearted fol-

---

[1] 2 Sam. xiv.   [2] 1 Sam. xxii. 4, 5.

lowers inside, all the strength of Israel under Saul could not have forced an entrance—would not have even attempted it.

I see no reason to disturb the tradition which makes this the *hold* into which David retired with his father's house and his faithful followers when he fled from Gath. David, as a shepherd leading his flocks over these hills, was doubtless acquainted from his boyhood with all the intricacies of this fearful cavern, just as these Arab shepherds, his successors, now are ; and what more natural, therefore, than that he should flee thither in the day of his extremity ? It was out in the wild desert, far from the haunts of Saul, and not likely to be visited by him. It was also in the direction of Moab, whither he sent his parents and the women of his train, while he abode still in the hold. Again, we know that many of his subsequent exploits and escapes from Saul were in this region and south of it. And, finally, there is a sort of verbal accuracy in speaking of the topography—David's family are said to have gone *down* to him from Bethlehem. Now this cavern is nearly two hours to the south-east of that village, and the path *descends* rapidly nearly the entire distance. Let us therefore acquiesce in the tradition that this is the Adullam into which David fled from Gath, and in which he first collected and organized his band of trusty followers.

Of course, this is not the *city* Adullam, so often mentioned in the oldest books of the Bible, and which appears to have been in the neighbourhood of Gath. But enough about this cave. After escaping from it, we returned up the same shallow wady for a mile or more, and then descended by one of the vilest roads in the world into Wady Urtas, and passed up northward round the western base of Jebel Fureîdîs. We had not time to ascend it, but it seemed very high—I should say eight hundred feet from the bottom of the wady—an enormous natural mound, as trimly turned and as steep as a haystack. It is doubtless the Herodium of Josephus, which he somewhat fancifully compares to the breast of a woman. It has every appearance of an extinct crater, and yet I noticed no indication of volcanic agency in that immediate vicinity.

This Fureîdîs was called Frank Mountain by the Crusaders, and must have been a strong fortification during all the ages in which isolated tells afforded the natural platform for castles. There is none of equal height and size in Palestine. Leaving it on the right, we had Bethlehem in full view about three miles westward, and the setting sun threw a mild and subdued light over the plains where the shepherds were keeping watch. Somehow or other we made but slow progress, and night came upon us bewildered in a labyrinth of wadies, while there were yet two long hours to Mar Saba, whither the mule-teers had preceded us, and which we had to reach, or otherwise sleep out in the wilderness supperless, and at the mercy of our villanous guides. On we marched, up and down, and down and up, on sharp ridges, in deep wadies, and over slippery rocks, or through stiff mud, but finally, without accident or injury of any kind, we dismounted at the entrance of the convent. I shall never forget that evening ride. Our imaginations had been held wide awake

PART
IV.

Convent
of Mar
Saba.

hour after hour by bad roads, doubtful guides, and the dismal notes of owls and jackals. The moon, rising over the brown hills of Moab, flashed and trembled on the Dead Sea, giving just light enough to make the crags appear more stern, and the chasms more horrible. At the convent, two towers, one on either brow of the gorge, loomed up through the misty moonbeams, like grim old giants, to guard the access. We entered through a low iron door, went down, turned round through a second door, then down again by winding stairs, across queer courts, and along dark passages, until we reached at length our rooms, hanging between cliffs that towered to the stars, or seemed to, and yawning gulfs which darkness made bottomless and dreadful. I was struck dumb with astonishment. It was a transition sudden and unexpected, from the wild mountain to the yet wilder, more vague, and mysterious scenes of Oriental enchantment. Lights gleamed out fitfully from hanging rocks and doubtful caverns. Winding stairs, with balustrade and iron rail, ran right up the perpendicular cliffs into rock chambers, where the solitary monk was drowsily muttering his midnight prayers. It was long after that hour before sleep visited my eyes, and then my dreams were of Arabs, and frightful chasms, and enchanted castles.

Sights of
Mar Saba.

Daylight next morning stripped off much of the wild and fearful from the midnight view through the pale beams of the waning moon; but even then Mar Saba is the strangest convent that I have ever seen. We, of course, visited the curiosities of the place: St. Saba's sepulchre, beneath an octagonal mausoleum; the numerous chapels, covered with pictures and Greek inscriptions; the really splendid church, blazing with silver and gold; the vault, filled with fourteen thousand skulls of martyred monks! and I know not what besides, with which this convent-castle is crowded. No description had in the least prepared me for what I saw, and no pen-picture could do justice to the original. It must be seen, and every visitor will be well rewarded for his three hours' ride. The stupendous cliffs of the Kidron, full of caverns, now the home of bats and owls instead of monks and hermits, are not the least impressive of the many wonders that cluster around this strange retirement of Santa Saba.

Urtas—
Etam.

Our *present* approach will be by the sober light of day, and must lack every element of romance, so we may as well interest ourselves with this fine valley of Urtas. This is believed to be the Etam of the ancient Hebrew kings,—a name which rarely occurs in the Bible, and nowhere in such relation to other places as to indicate this locality, unless it be in 2 Chronicles xi. 6, where it is named along with Bethlehem and Tekoa. The truth is that its celebrity depends upon the fables of the rabbis more than the pages of sober history. The fountain near the village, however, must have always filled the valley below it with orchards and flourishing gardens; and it is not an unreasonable supposition that David, who so intensely longed for even a drink of water from his native Bethlehem, would have shown a similar partiality for this pretty valley below it, where he must have often played while a child. Not unlikely he had

purchased it before he died, and when Solomon came into possession, he
further adorned it with his pools and orchards ; and in traversing this vale, I
always love to reproduce in imagination the gorgeous scene when it was filled
with fruits and flowers, and these many-shaped hills on either side, and on all
sides, were terraced to their tops, and dotted everywhere with country villas,
amid olive-groves, fig-orchards, and clustering vines. Thus it certainly was
through many long ages of peace and prosperity ; and it is my belief that
thus it will be once more, in that happy day "when the Lord shall bring
again Zion."

CHAPTER XL.

'AIN ES SULTAN—JERICHO.

April 24th.

THE tent never was so welcome to me as at the close of this long day's ride.
I am glad we have taken it, but shall never wish to repeat it.

The reasons of this unusual weariness are, that we have actually been in the
saddle more than twelve hours, and then the greater part of the day and of
the ride has been in this depressed and hot region of the Dead Sea. The fact
is, our visit is nearly a month too late both for pleasure and health. But the
fatigue is over, and we may now sit down and review at our leisure this most
interesting excursion.

Among the multiplicity of sights and scenes which drew my attention View near
hither and thither in rapid succession, only a few points have impressed their Santa
features upon my memory. In the morning, as soon as the gate of the convent was opened, I climbed to the top of the tower on the south of the
ravine. From there my eye roamed over a wilderness of rusty brown hills, the
most dreary and blasted that I ever beheld. Beyond and below it is the Dead
Sea, bordered on the east by the abrupt cliffs of Moab. Turning to what was
beneath me, the wonderful chasm of the Kidron struck me with amazement.
We have seen nothing so profound or so wild in all our travels.

I am glad you have had an opportunity to spend one night in an Oriental Attrac-
convent, and become acquainted with these remarkable institutions. Santa tions of
Saba is among the very best specimens, and, in addition to its distinctive religious character, it seems always to have been a sort of frontier castle in the

PART
IV.

heart of this stern desert of Judea. Saint Saba was probably attracted to the spot by those very savage aspects of the scene which strike our minds with such horror. The howling wilderness, the stern desolation, the terrific chasms, the oppressive solitude, the countless caverns, the ever-prevalent dangers from wild beasts and wild robbers,—these and such as these were the charms that fascinated his morbid imagination. We would not judge the dead, however, nor ought we to forget the shelter and good dinner which his institution afforded us last night. It is really, in our day, a very respectable hotel, and gentlemen—not ladies—can scarcely do better than to spend one of the two nights there which an excursion from Jerusalem to the Dead Sea and the Jordan necessarily requires. The régime, it is true, partakes of both military sternness and conventual austerity, so far as the fortress itself and the monks within it are concerned; but both are necessary, the one to meet the requirements of the Church, the other to repel the attacks of the Bedawîn, who prowl about at all seasons, watching for an opportunity to force an entrance and to plunder the rich treasures of the establishment.

Valley of
Fire.

As to the ride from St. Saba to the Dead Sea, you surely cannot have forgotten the path along the perpendicular cliffs of Wady en Nar— *Valley of Fire*—as the wonderful gorge of the Kidron is there called; nor the long descent to and ascent from it; nor the naked hills over which we toiled in the broiling sun for seven hours, frequently losing the path amid tangled ravines and shelving gullies washed out of sand-hills; nor will you cease to remember the delight with which we galloped over the level plain after we had escaped from this perplexing net-work of wadies.

Of all these things I have but a faint recollection, but I remember attempting to shelter my aching head from the burning sun under a stunted juniper-tree.

Juniper-
tree.

Yes; and, in your disappointment, said that, if Elijah's juniper afforded no better shade than yours, it was not at all surprising that he requested for himself that he might die.[1] And certainly these straggling bushes cast but a doubtful shade at all times, and lend no effectual protection against such a sun and wind as beat upon us in *our* "wilderness." Still, the prophet slept under one, and the Bedawîn do the same, when wandering in the desert, where they often furnish the only shelter that can be found. Job, as translated, has a curious reference to this tree in the 30th chapter of his remarkable dialogues. He says that those contemptible children whose *fathers he would have disdained to set with the dogs of his flock*, flee into the wilderness, and for want and famine cut up mallows by the bushes, and juniper roots for their meat.[2] These mallows are a coarse kind of *greens*, which the poor boil as a relish for their dry bread. I have often seen the children of the poor cutting them up under the hedges and by the bushes in early spring; so that this rendering seems natural and appropriate to us who reside in the country, and

Mallows.

---

[1] 1 Kings xix. 4.   [2] Job xxx. 1-4.

therefore I accept the rendering, without noticing the arguments of learned
critics against it. What sort of juniper roots can be used for food is more than

JUNIPER.

I can discover or comprehend. They are excessively bitter, and nothing but Coals of the fire will devour them. Burckhardt found the Bedawîn of Sinai burning Juniper. them into coal, and says that they make the best charcoal, and throw out the most intense heat. The same thing seems to be implied in Psalm cxx. 4, where David threatens the false tongue "with sharp arrows of the mighty, with *coals of juniper*." Perhaps the meaning of Job is, that the poor cut up mallows to *eat*, and juniper roots with which to cook them. This would give a sense in accordance with the known use of these roots, and still preserve the connection with the food of the poor. The Arabic word is *retem*,—the same as the Hebrew; and Forskal calls it *genista raetam*. It is, therefore, a species of broom, and not that kind of juniper which bears the famous berries, and whose oil assists in the composition of certain varnishes. This tree is also found in the country, and, if you had met with it, you would have had less occasion to complain of the want of shade.

Some of these things will certainly be remembered, nor shall I ever forget the unexpected appearance of Mount Hermon towering to the sky far, far up the ghor to the north (which convinced me that Moses also saw it from the mountains of Moab); nor the sombre and shadowy surface and shores of the Dead Sea, nor the indescribable feeling of disappointment at the Jordan.

First sight of Jordan. While approaching it over that melancholy desert of soft deep sand, I eagerly watched the line of willow-trees which you said marked out the tortuous line of the river, expecting it to burst on my delighted eyes; but not until we were actually on the very brink did I see water enough to fill a thimble, and when there it was hard to believe that what I saw was the whole Jordan. Finding, however, that it was, I endeavoured to reconcile my previous anticipations with the vastly ensmalled reality by noticing the rapidity of the current and the depth of the stream.

"Jordan's stormy banks." This, however, was not your first acquaintance with the river; but I cannot smile at your forgetfulness of this fact, for, though I have looked at the Upper Jordan a thousand times, yet down here at Jericho I too am always disappointed. When boys, we used to sing with vast enthusiasm, "On Jordan's *stormy* banks I stand," and supposed that it was big as the Ohio at least, and as stormy as the North-West Passage; and something like this must have been in the mind of Watts when he applied the word *stormy* to this little river rambling over this low plain where everlasting *summer* abides. It is not an epithet which personal acquaintance would have suggested.

Prejudices. I begin to feel that there is more fancy than fact in the costume and drapery of many of our hymns; but that is allowable, perhaps. I found, however, that my traditionary notions in regard to matters of fact were about equally fanciful. What, for example, becomes of one's hereditary ideas of the prodigious fertility of the plain of Jericho? From the river to 'Ain Hajla there was nothing but a most unprofitable extension of simmering sand, bare and barren of everything except stunted thorn bushes and ugly black lizards.

You must not forget that the day has been excessively hot, you very tired, and, more than all, that the cultivated part of the plain has just been shorn of its luxuriant harvests, and also that the vegetation elsewhere has entirely dried up, except the "summer crops" which are irrigated from 'Ain Hajla, the brook Krith, and this fountain of Elisha. If your temper had not been somewhat like the day, and your anticipations had been moderated by reflection, you would have brought away impressions more just as well as more agreeable.

'Ain Hajla— Beth-hoglah. I see that 'Ain Hajla stands on modern maps for Beth-hoglah.

And correctly, I think; but that the Gilgal where Joshua made his first encampment within the promised land, and where the ark and tabernacle remained for so many years after the conquest, was immediately above it, as located on some modern maps, remains yet to be proved. Josephus says that Joshua pitched his camp fifty furlongs from the river, and ten from Jericho.[1] Now, *if* he crossed due east of the city, and *if* Josephus is correct in his **Gilgal.** numbers, then Gilgal must have been very near the present Riha; and this,

[1] Ant. vi. 4.

again, may have been true, on the supposition that ancient Jericho was in the CHAPTER
immediate neighbourhood of this 'Ain es Sultan, as I suspect it really was; XL.
for Riha is about six miles from the Jordan, and a city below this Fountain of
the Sultan would not be much more than ten furlongs from it. All these
things are mere suppositions, I admit, and, indeed, there probably never was
any permanent *city* called Gilgal in this plain; and if there was, it had passed
away, and the name and site were lost even before Josephus wrote his history.

I have never seen this plain so entirely deserted as it is at present. Even Riha.
the few inhabitants of Riha have gone to other parts to labour, since their own
harvests are already gathered. On my first visit the whole valley was lively
enough, for I was one of several thousand pilgrims drawn hither from all parts
of the world to bathe in this holy river.

This is a ceremony which we have missed, somewhat to my regret, as it was
one of the scenes I had always associated with my intended visit to the Jordan.

Well, since you cannot *see*, the next best thing is to *hear;* and if you will
put yourself into the most comfortable position to listen, I will read from notes,
taken a quarter of a century ago, the adventures of my first visit to Jericho.
Early in the morning of April 16th, 1833, we left the Convent of Archangel, Procession
and passed down the Via Dolorosa to the Palace, where the guard was already of pilgrims
in motion, and from thence, with the white flag of the pilgrim in front, and Jordan.
the green of the prophet in the rear, we set forward. It was a merry hour,
apparently, to everybody. The whole population of the city, of either sex and
of every age, in their best, lined the zigzag path along which the pilgrim host
was to pass. With noise and pomp such as Arabs only can affect, we passed Road from
out at St. Stephen's Gate, wound our way down into the narrow vale of Jeho- Jerusalem
to Jericho.
shaphat, over the south point of Olivet, by the miserable remains of the city
of Mary, Martha, and Lazarus, and then prepared ourselves to descend, for
you remember that we must go "*down* to Jericho." And, sure enough, *down,*
down we did go, over slippery rocks, for more than a mile, when the path became less precipitous. Still, however, the road follows the dry channel of a
brook for several miles further, as if descending into the very bowels of the
earth. How admirably calculated for "robbers!"

After leaving the brook, which turns aside too far to the south, we ascended
and descended naked hills for several miles, the prospect gradually becoming
more and more gloomy. Not a house, nor even a tree, is to be seen; and the
only remains are those of a large khan, *said* to have been the inn to which the
good Samaritan brought the wounded Jew. Not far from here, in a narrow
defile, an English traveller was attacked, shot, and robbed in 1820. As you
approach the plain, the mountains wear a more doleful appearance, the ravines
become more frightful, and the narrow passages less and less passable. At
length the weary pilgrim reaches the plain by a long, steep declivity, and
doubtless expects to step immediately into Jericho. But alas! no city appears,
and after a full hour's ride he pitches his tent (if he have one) in a dry, sultry
plain of sand, sparsely sprinkled over with burnt-up grass. If he have no

tent, a shrivelled thorn bush is better than nothing; and if he cannot get that, let him do as we did—sit down under the burning sun, and bear it as well as he can.

Finding it intolerably hot, we passed through the camp, and went on to the village, about a mile distant, and took shelter under some fig-trees which grew around the sheikh's palace, a square, castle-like house,—the only one of any size in the place, and where, tradition says, the little Zaccheus once dwelt. In the immediate vicinity are some forty or fifty of the most forlorn habitations that I have ever seen. And this is Jericho! These houses, or rather huts, are surrounded by a peculiar kind of fortification, made of nubk, a species of bush very abundant in the plain. Its thorns are so sharp and the branches are so plaited together that neither horse nor man will attack it.

The Arabs of Jericho and the plain are many shades darker than the same class on the mountains only a few miles distant. This is easily accounted for by the great difference in climate. We shivered in our cloaks upon the hills, and broiled in the shade on the plain.

After looking about the village, and riding a mile or two to the north-west to see the great fountain 'Ain es Sultan, we returned to the camp about sunset for protection. Having sung "The voice of free grace," and "There is a land of pure delight," we wrapped our cloaks about us and prepared to sleep; but the scenes of the day and the circumstances with which we were surrounded were too novel and exciting to allow of sleep. East and west of us, in parallel lines, stretched the mountains of Moab and Palestine like perpendicular walls reared to heaven by the Creator to guard this favoured spot. At our feet flowed the Jordan, the most interesting river on earth; a little to the south slept in mysterious silence the bitter waters of the Dead Sea; while underneath were the mouldering ruins of old Jericho, whose walls fell prostrate at the blast of Israel's priests. What an assemblage of interesting objects! How well calculated to awaken deep and solemn reflection! Here the swellings of the Jordan rolled back, that Israel's chosen race might take possession of the promised land; and thus, "when on Jordan's stormy banks we stand," if the Ark of God be there, the angry billows shall flee away at the presence of Him who hath said, "When thou passest through the waters, I will be with thee; and through the rivers, they shall not overflow thee."[1] Here, too, the smitten Jordan parted hither and thither when the prophet of the Lord went over to be carried to the skies in a chariot of fire. We drink of the fountain which was sweetened by Elisha's cruse of salt. Here, also, our blessed Saviour was baptized, the heavens were opened, the Spirit descended upon him in the form of a dove, and the voice from the Father said, "This is my beloved Son, in whom I am well pleased." O ye guilty cities of the plain! even here do ye lie sealed up unto the judgment day, "suffering the vengeance of eternal fire." Tremble, O my soul, lest thou be overthrown and consumed with that fire

---

[1] Isa. xliii. 2.

FORDS OF THE JORDAN.

which shall never be quenched, and be cast into that other lake of which this CHAPTER
XL.
is such a solemn type.

About three o'clock in the morning there was a buzz in the camp, which in Morning
march of
a short time became like the "noise of many waters," and at four precisely we pilgrims.
set forward toward the Jordan, going to the south-east. A large company of
guards went before, bearing on long poles flaming torches made of turpentine
and old rags, which threw over the plain a brilliant light, revealing double
ranks of armed horsemen on either side of the host, careering in genuine Arab
style, and plunging with fearless impetuosity through the grass and bushes to
drive out any Bedawîn that might be lurking there. The governor, with his
body-guard, brought up the rear, and thus we were defended on all sides. Nor
was this caution misplaced. One poor fellow from Poland, having fallen behind,
was attacked, robbed, and stripped naked.

After a two hours' ride over an uneven plain, we reached the Jordan as the Pilgrims
bathing.
sun rose above the mountains of Moab. Immediately the pilgrims rushed
headlong into the stream—men, women, and children—in one undistinguished
mass. The haughty Turk sat upon his beautiful horse, and looked in scorn upon
this exposure of the "Christian dogs." The pilgrims, however, were highly
delighted with their bath. The men *ducked* the women somewhat as the
farmers do their sheep, while the little children were carried and plunged
under water, trembling like so many lambs. Some had water poured on
their heads, in imitation of the baptism of the Saviour; for it is part of the
tradition that our blessed Lord was here baptized, and the ruins of an old
convent near at hand ascertain the exact locality to the perfect satisfaction of
the devout pilgrim. The Latins, however, maintain that the event took place
higher up the stream, and hence they bathe there. I hope they have a more
convenient place than the Greeks. It could scarcely be more unsuitable. The
banks are nearly perpendicular, and very muddy, while the current is astonish-
ingly rapid, and at least ten feet deep. It required the most expert swimmers
to cross it, and one less skilled must inevitably be carried away, as we had
melancholy proof. Two Christians and a Turk, who ventured too far, were Drowning.
drowned without the possibility of rescue; and the wonder is that many more
did not share the same fate where thousands were bathing at once. This sad
accident, which would have cast a shade over the whole assembly in America,
produced very little sensation among the pilgrims. In fact, this pilgrimaging
seems to obliterate every benevolent feeling from the heart. When we left
Jerusalem, the guard immediately in front of me, in careering and curveting
with his horse, fired a pistol, and shot a woman dead, and yet I never heard
the affair mentioned afterward but with levity. As we came along, if any poor
woman fell from her horse, and rolled down among the rocks, it called forth
only loud laughter from the passing crowd.
Insignifi-
The Jordan would scarcely be dignified with the name of River in America, cant appearance
and its appearance is, in reality, quite insignificant. It is, however, deep, of the Jor-
narrow, and very muddy, and hurries away to the sea with great velocity. In dan.

approaching the river, you descend several benches or terraces; and, though much swollen with the rains and the melting snows of Lebanon at that time, it was still fifteen or twenty feet below its proper banks. It has also a very winding course, and resembles the streams of the Mississippi Valley, having on one side a perpendicular bluff, and on the opposite a low beach covered with weeds, bushes, and drift, and these alternate constantly. These low flats vary in width. At the bathing-place it was about twenty rods wide, and the whole of it had recently been inundated. These are the banks that were flooded when the Israelites passed over. Nor was the miracle unnecessary. It would be impossible for such a host to cross the Jordan at the same season of the year without either a bridge or a miracle, for boats could do nothing in such a current, and it is too deep to ford. Travellers have differed widely in their description of the Jordan, principally from two causes—visiting it at different *seasons* of the year, and at different *places*. When and where I saw it, the width might have been twenty yards, and its depth ten feet.

Dead Sea.   After the pilgrims had bathed, we left them, and turned down to the south, with three or four English travellers and a guard from the governor, to visit the Dead Sea; and having ridden across plains of barren sand for an hour and a half, we stood upon the shore of this memorable lake. Without any reference to what others have said, I can testify to the following facts:—The water is perfectly clear and transparent. The taste is bitter and salt, far beyond that of the ocean. It acts upon the tongue and mouth like alum; smarts in the eye like camphor; produces a burning, pricking sensation; and it stiffens the hair of the head much like pomatum. The water has a much greater specific gravity than the human body, and hence I did not sink lower than to the arms when standing perpendicularly in it. Although there is evidence in the sand and brushwood thrown upon the beach that in great storms there are waves, still there is some foundation for the reports about its immobility. There was a considerable breeze, yet the water lay perfectly calm and motionless. We saw no fish nor living animals in the water, though birds were flying *over* it unharmed. All of us noticed an unnatural gloom, not upon the sea only, but also over the whole plain below Jericho. This, too, is mentioned by ancient historians. It had the appearance of Indian summer in America, and, like a vast funeral pall let down from heaven, it hung heavily over the lifeless bosom of this mysterious lake. Having gathered some curious pebbles from the shore, and filled our cans with the water, we returned to the camp about noon, highly pleased with our excursion.

**'Ain es
Sultan.**   In the afternoon we visited again 'Ain es Sultan. This fountain rises at the base of a hill which has the appearance of an Indian mound, though rather too large for a work of art. But there are many similar tells in the plain, and they were probably thrown up for the same purpose as those which are so numerous in America. The water is sufficiently abundant to turn a large mill, is beautifully transparent, sweet, and cool, and swarms with small fish. There seems to be no reason to doubt the tradition that this is the identical

fountain whose bitter waters Elisha healed. On the margin of this delightful CHAPTER XL.
brook grow great numbers of bushes, bearing a yellow apple, about the size
and having very much the appearance, of a small apricot,—beautiful to the eye, Apple of
but nauseous to the taste, and said to be poisonous. I can do as others have Sodom.
done before me—inquire. Is this the apple of Sodom ?

Directly west, at the distance of a mile and a half, is the high and precipi- Mount
tous mountain called Quarantania, from a tradition that our Saviour here fasted Quarantania.
forty days and nights, and also that this is the "high mountain" from whose
top the tempter exhibited "all the kingdoms of the world, and the glory of
them." The side facing the plain is as perpendicular, and apparently as high
as the rock of Gibraltar, and upon the very summit are still visible the ruins
of an ancient convent. Midway below are caverns hewn in the perpendicular
rock, where hermits formerly retired to fast and pray in imitation of the "forty
days;" and it is said that even at the present time there is to be found an
occasional Copt or Abyssinian languishing out his *quarantania* in this doleful
place. We found it, however, inhabited only by Bedawîn, several of whom
made their appearance, well armed, many hundred feet above us. Leaving
the company here, I struck southward across the plain, in order to look for the
site of ancient Jericho. It appeared to me highly probable that the original
city took in the great fountain 'Ain es Sultan, as there was nothing to prevent
it, and, if left without the walls, an enemy could compel them to surrender by
cutting off their supply of water. Accordingly, the plain to the south and
south-west of the fountain is covered in many parts with very ancient remains.
There are evidences of walls stretching in different directions, and many indications of decayed buildings. The rocks are black and honey-combed, and the
walls can only be traced by continuous elevations of the turf, with an occasional
bit of foundation appearing through the grass. Whether these mark the site
of old Jericho, of course, cannot at present be decided, but they are evidently
more ancient than the ruins of Tyre or of Cæsarea, and there are no others
visible in this vicinity.

18*th*. Spent the first part of the night in walking about the camp. The Camp of
scene was very picturesque. Spread abroad over the plain lay men, women, the pilgrims.
and children, of almost every nation under heaven, of all languages, every
variety of costume, and of all colours, from the black of Africa to the white of
Poland. All denominations of this sectarian world were there—Mohammedans,
Druses, Maronites, Catholics, Greeks, Armenians, Copts, Syrians, Jews, Epis-
copalians, Lutherans, Presbyterians, Methodists, and infidels, in one vast congregation—faint image of that great congregation when the trumpet shall
sound and wake the dead. The camp did not become quiet at all, and about
midnight everything was again set in motion. We hastily mounted our animals to keep from being trampled under foot, and, falling into a line with a
long train of lights, set forward toward the narrow pass down which we came
at first. A similar line of torches, about a mile to the south, marked out the
course of another division of the host. The night was exceedingly dark, and,

PART
IV.

as we approached the defile leading up the mountain, the confusion became horrible,—women screaming in terror, when about to be trampled down by a long line of camels coupled together; parents calling for their children; friends hallooing for friends ; muleteers beating and cursing their animals, to force them up the steep rocks; those above calling to those below; while the guards, stationed upon projecting rocks, kept up a constant discharge of musketry, whose lurid glare and hollow reverberations down the deep ravines startled the "leaden ear of night," and rendered sublime what would otherwise have been

Move-
ments by
night.

ridiculous. After we were fairly up the mountain we came in view of the southern division, and the prospect was grand beyond description. For miles the long train of torches rose and sunk in graceful curves, corresponding to the hills and vales over which they marched, while the same discharge of fire-arms continued with even magnified effect. In about an hour we united our lines, and hurried on to the Holy City, which we reached a little after sunrise, shivering with the cold wind of the mountains, but thankful that we had been permitted to perform this interesting tour with so much ease and safety.

Your account of the separation of parents and children in this returning host of pilgrims reminds me of the one single incident in the youthful life of our blessed Lord which is recorded in the New Testament.[1]

It is not, in fact, surprising that, in the midst of such a crowd, Joseph and his mother should suppose that Jesus was in the company with his "kinsfolk and acquaintance;" nor is the time that elapsed before they became so alarmed at his absence as to turn back and search for him at all remarkable. I question whether there is ever a pilgrimage made from Jerusalem to the Jordan at this day without the separation of parents and children equally prolonged ; and, in the case we are considering, it was the absence of a youth who, his parents well knew, had never done in his whole life one unwise or improper act. They would not, therefore, be easily alarmed on his account.

OVERFLOW OF THE JORDAN.

Passage of
the Israel-
ites.

Among the stupendous miracles that have rendered this neighbourhood illustrious, the most wonderful and the most suggestive was the passage of the Hebrew nation through the Jordan to their promised inheritance. The twelve stones that bore witness to the fact have long since disappeared, and even the precise spot where the passage was made is a matter of dispute ; and in view of the superstitious abuses to which such sites are perverted, I am quite contented to have them all thus hidden, as was the sepulchre of Moses. We have the hills of Moab on the other side; the river itself that was divided; the sea into which the water, cut off from above, subsided ; and Jericho, over against which the grand miracle was performed: and these are enough for the

---

[1] Luke ii. 41–50.

confirmation of our faith; nor would I walk a mile or turn a stone to make the identification any closer or more perfect. There is an incidental allusion, however, in the account of the miracle, which infidels have employed to throw discredit on the entire narrative, and even upon the Bible itself, and which it is highly proper that we should explain if we can. It is said in Joshua iii. 15 that " Jordan overfloweth all his banks all the time of harvest." This is the statement, and the objections against its accuracy and truthfulness are, that the Jordan is a short and rapid river which soon runs down, and that, therefore, it could not have overflowed all its banks in harvest, for the rains have entirely ceased, and the tributaries of the river have dried up;—and this plausible reasoning is strengthened and confirmed by the unqualified assertion that the Jordan does not overflow its banks at all, not even in the rainy season.

To meet and refute these injurious assertions, various suppositions and suggestions have been put forward by the friends of revelation. It has been maintained that the channel of the river has been deepened since the time of Joshua,—and this is indeed very probable; and again, that from various causes, less water now falls upon the country of the Jordan than did anciently, and that the rains cease earlier in the spring,—and this may possibly be true, and, if there were any need of such hypothetical assistance to establish the veracity of the sacred historian, we should not hesitate to employ it for what it is worth, but I am persuaded that the matter in question needs no such aid. It is a plain, honest statement of a simple fact, as literally true now as it was when Joshua led the ransomed tribes into Canaan. All we need in order to clear the passage from obscurity or doubt is an adequate acquaintance with the phenomena of the country and the river. Let us subject the passage and the scenery to a careful scrutiny and analysis, and we shall find that here, as in a thousand other places, the Land illustrates and confirms the Book.

The river overflows during harvest; but *where* was the harvest spoken of, and what is the time of it? These inquiries are strictly essential. I visited the scene of this miracle on the 1st of April, and found barley harvest about Jericho already ended. I also found the river full to the brim, and saw evidence in abundance that it had overflowed its banks very recently. Harvest in the vale of the Lower Jordan comes on about the middle of March. This seems early, and it is long before the crops are ready for the sickle on the neighbouring mountains, or even around the fountains of the Upper Jordan. But the reason is obvious. The valley at Jericho is thirteen hundred feet below the level of the ocean, is sheltered from cold winds on all sides by mountains of great height, and is open to the warm southern breezes from the deeper basin of the Dead Sea. It has therefore the climate of the tropics, though in the latitude of Jerusalem.

Still, the rains are over, and most of the tributary streams have dwindled down to inconsiderable rills, even at this early season of the year, and how comes it, therefore, that the Jordan alone is full to overflowing? This is easily explained. The Jordan does not depend upon tributaries for its steady

PART
IV.

Fountains
of the Jordan.

supply of water, but is almost wholly formed and fed by certain great fountains, which arise far north, around the base of snowy Hermon. The largest of these is called El Leddan, at Tell el Kady; the next in size is at Banias. These are the two great sources mentioned by Josephus under the names Greater and Lesser Jordan. The one from Tell el Kady is about three times as large as that from Banias, and its course is south, a little west, through the plain of the Hûleh, for about five miles, where it is joined by the Baniasy, and, in less than a mile further south, by the Hasbâny. The Jordan is thus formed by the union of these three rivers, and, winding southward through extensive marshes, flows into Lake Hûleh—the Merom of Joshua. The Hasbâny is a beautiful river, whose furthest permanent source is near Hasbeîya, some eighteen miles north of Tell El Kady. The torrents from Wady et Teim greatly augment its size in the rainy season, but it depends for its permanent volume of water upon three fountains: the Fuarr, at Hasbeîya; the Sareid, below Kafr Shubah; and the Luisany, at El Ghujar. To complete the account of the sources of the Jordan, the fountains of Derdara, in Merj Aiun, and the Ruahiny, must be mentioned, and also those of Blata and El Mellahah. We need not pause to notice the River Jermuk, nor the fountains which flow directly into the different lakes. Those we have named are sufficient for the purpose of our illustration. The Jordan is thus made up from the joint contributions of great permanent springs, and in this fact we find the explanation of the overflow of the river so late in the season as March. These immense fountains do not feel the effects of the early winter rains at all. It requires

Lateness
of the
overflow.

the heavy and long-continued storms of mid-winter before they are moved in the least; and it is not until toward the close of winter, when the melting snows of Hermon and Lebanon, with the heavy rains of the season, have penetrated through the mighty masses of these mountains, and filled to overflowing their hidden chambers and vast reservoirs, that the streams gush forth in their full volume. The Hûleh—*marsh* and *lake*—is filled, and then Gennesaret rises, and pours its accumulated waters into the swelling Jordan about the 1st of March. Thus it comes to pass that it does actually "overflow all its banks during all the time of harvest;" nor does it soon subside, as other short rivers do, when the rains cease. These fountains continue to pour forth their contributions for months with undiminished volume, and the river keeps full and strong all through March into April, and the proper banks of the river are still full to overflowing in the time of harvest.

Two series
of banks.

To understand the passage correctly, we must also remember that Jordan has two series of banks, and in some places three, but it is the lower only which are overflowed, either now or at any former period within the history of man; and to these the reference in Joshua is unquestionably made. The low *flat*, or river *bottom*, thus inundated is nowhere wide, and is generally covered with a thick jungle of willow, sycamore, and other trees. It was from these

Swellings
of Jordan.

thickets that "the swellings of Jordan," in ancient days, expelled the lion from his lair: a poetic allusion, which bears incidental testimony to the historic statement. At present there are no lions to be roused; but the wild boar, the jackal, and the wolf occupy his place, and, like him, flee before the swellings of this river.

I think it not improbable that the rise and fall of the Jordan are, in reality, somewhat earlier now and more rapid than in the days of Joshua. The cutting off of the forests of Lebanon and Hermon may cause the snows to dissolve sooner ; and the clearing away much of the marshes at the head of the Hûleh allows the floods a quicker passage, and thus the river *may* be at its height, in ordinary seasons, a few days sooner than was the case three thousand years ago. It is nearly certain, also, that the channel of the Jordan has deepened, and especially near the Dead Sea, so that the *extent* of the overflow may now be less than then, and of shorter duration. But, without referring to these circumstances, the preceding facts and explanations are sufficient to establish the accuracy of the statement in Joshua, that the " Jordan overfloweth all his banks all the time of harvest."

It will be easy for us to overtake the company while they are climbing the long ascent out of the valley of the Jordan, and therefore we may linger an hour on this hill, to study the features of this melancholy but eminently interesting scene. Jericho was called " the city of palm-trees," but the one only palm that a quarter of a century ago stood, like a solitary sentinel, near the old tower is gone, and thus has passed away the last vestige of that great forest which gave name to the city. The forest, however, might be restored, and then the best dates would again come from Jericho. The soil and climate are admirably adapted to this tree, and, indeed, there is nothing required but cultivation and irrigation to make the whole plain of the Lower Jordan fruitful as the garden of the Lord. Such it will certainly become at no very distant day. Every acre of it might be watered from the strong brook in Wady Kelt, from this great fountain Es Sultan, from those of Wady Dûk, and from the Jordan itself. This river winds incessantly, falls everywhere rapidly, and has about thirty distinct cascades. Here is unappropriated water-power to drive any amount of machinery, and elevation sufficient to allow every part of this valley to be irrigated at all times of the year. Thus treated, and subjected to the science and the modern mechanical appliances in agriculture, the valley of the Jordan could sustain half a million of inhabitants. Cotton, rice, sugarcane, indigo, and nearly every other valuable product for the use of man, would flourish most luxuriantly. There were, in fact, sugar plantations here long before America was discovered ; and it is quite possible that this plant was taken from this very spot to Tripoli, and thence to Spain by the Crusaders, from whence it was carried to the West Indies. Those edifices to the west of 'Ain es Sultan are the remains of ancient sugar-mills, and are still called Towahîn es Sukkar. They seem to have been driven by a canal brought along the base of Quarantania from Wady Dûk.

Now how desolate and barren ! Just around 'Ain es Sultan, and between it and Riha, the plain is covered with a forest of thorn-trees ; but look elsewhere, and the eye aches from the glare of naked sand fields glowing beneath a burning sun.

Many of these thorn bushes through which we have been carefully picking our way are the zŭkŭm. This bush looks like a crab apple-tree, and bears a small nut, from which a kind of liquid balsam is made, and sold by the monks as the balm of Gilead, so famous in ancient times. I purchased a phial of it when on my first visit to the Jordan with the pilgrims, but could not discover that it possessed any particular medicinal virtues. And now we must cross this Wady Kelt, and begin to climb the mountain. In the winter this is a powerful stream, and the remnants of aqueducts in several places show that the inhabitants once knew how to employ its fertilizing powers upon the desert of the Jordan and Dead Sea.

Balm of Gilead.

I notice traces of ancient structures on each side of the wady, and some of them were made with small stones, cut and fitted into the wall like tesselated pavement. We have nowhere else seen any such buildings.

It is, in fact, the only specimen of the kind. This must always have been a pass of great importance, and hence these mounds and old castles in front of it. The one nearest the pass is called 'Akabet ed Deir. Turn now and take your last view of the Jordan, as it loses itself in the bitter waters of the Dead Sea. Captain Lynch says, that a short distance above the sea it was forty yards wide and twelve feet deep; then fifty yards wide and eleven feet deep; then eighty yards by seven feet; and, finally, one hundred yards and only three feet deep upon the bar. Thus this sweet type of life subsides into the Sea of Death, and is lost for ever.

I have still some inquiries to make about the Dead Sea, and we may as well while away this fatiguing climb and this desolate road by discussing them.

Gorge of Wady Kelt.

Allow me first to call your attention to this gorge of Wady Kelt, on the right of the path. It is grand, wild, and stern, almost beyond a parallel.

Do you suppose that this is the Cherith to which Elijah was sent to be fed by ravens?

Cherith?

The name favours the opinion, but not so the situation. It is far from the prophet's usual abode, and in returning back again to Sarepta he would be obliged to pass through the kingdom of his enemy,—which would certainly be a long and critical journey. The brook itself, however, is admirably adapted to the purpose for which Elijah retired to it; and there come sailing down the tremendous gorge a family of ravens, to remind us that God can feed his people by means the most unlikely. And now for your inquiries about the Dead Sea.

They refer rather to the south end of it, and concern particularly the location of the cities of the plain which were destroyed. All agree that Sodom and her associated towns were around the south end of this sea, and since the exploration of Lynch and others it has appeared very probable that the shallow part, which is some fifteen miles long, was originally a plain on which the

cities stood, and that this plain was submerged at the time they were overthrown. Admitting this to be true, or at least probable, how are we to understand what is said of the fertility of that region in the time when Lot chose it
for his residence? " It was well watered everywhere, before the Lord destroyed
Sodom and Gomorrah, even as the garden of the Lord, like the land of
Egypt, as thou comest unto Zoar." [1] Lot resided at the south end of the Dead
Sea, and it seems to be implied that the land there belonged to the valley of
the Jordan, was watered by that river, and that therefore it was immensely
fertile.

Chapter XL.

Dead Sea —former state.

And such, I think, was the fact. The River Jordan begins in the valleys
of Hermon, and terminates in this sea; and it is my opinion that, until the
destruction of Sodom, this was a fresh-water lake, and that its character was
changed at that time by the obtrusion from below of rock salt and other volcanic products, which have rendered it so extremely bitter and nauseous. The
evidences of such action and obtrusion are to be seen in the ridge of rock salt
called Usdum, at the south end of the sea, and in the presence of naphtha
and bitumen in its waters. The lake being originally shorter by the length of
these plains of Sodom and Gomorrah, would necessarily rise much higher
during the rainy season than it does now; and the water being fresh, it would
subside by evaporation, and perhaps by irrigation, much more rapidly than at
present, though there is a much greater rise and fall in this sea than was
formerly supposed. This great southern extension is thirteen feet deep in
winter, but late in autumn it is only *three*, and is then forded, not only by
camels, but even by donkeys. Now for my specific answer to your inquiry.
I suppose that this southern plain on which the cities stood was actually
flooded by fresh water during the rise of the lake, just as the Nile floods the
land of Egypt " as thou comest unto Zoar;" and that when the water subsided
the whole plain was sown, just as Egypt was and is. There are many examples
of this operation about smaller lakes and ponds; and places thus overflowed
are the most productive in the country. We have only to suppose that the
inhabitants knew how to control the rising of the lake by embankments, as
the Egyptians did the Nile, and the whole mystery about the fertility of this
plain is explained. It seems to me nearly certain that, if this had been then
a salt sea, the whole territories of those cities must have been about as blasted
and barren as are the desolate shores at present; which would be in flat contradiction to the statement in Genesis. The obtrusion of rock salt at Usdum
must, therefore, have been subsequent to, or, rather, it accompanied the
catastrophe. I have not examined this matter at the place itself, but I have
seen no statement which would render such an obtrusion a geological impossi-
bility, while instances of the submergence of tracts much larger than this plain
are well ascertained historical facts.

Southern plain flooded.

Fertility of the plain ex-plained.

Of course, the old and rather taking theory, that the Jordan, before the

PART
IV.

destruction of Sodom, ran through Wady 'Arabah to the Gulf of 'Akabah, must be abandoned. This would demand geological changes, reaching from the Lake of Tiberias to the Red Sea, too stupendous to have occurred within the period of man's residence upon the earth. Still, this grand chasm, valley, or *crevasse*, running, as it does, between the two Lebanons, through the whole length of the Jordan, and along the 'Arabah to the Elanitic Gulf, and even down that gulf itself into the Red Sea, is among the most remarkable phenomena of our globe; and it is not certain to my mind but that there was at one time a water communication throughout this long and unbroken depression.

How do you account for the nauseous and malignant character of the water of the Dead Sea ?

This is owing to the extraordinary amount of mineral salts held in solution. The analyses of chemists, however, show very different results. Some give only seventy parts of water to the hundred, while others give eighty, or even more. I account for these differences by supposing that the specimens analyzed are taken at different seasons of the year, and at different distances from the Jordan. Water brought from near the mouth of that river might be comparatively fresh, and that taken in winter from *any part* would be less salt and bitter than what was brought away in autumn.

Analysis
of Dead
Sea water.

One analysis shows, chloride of sodium, 8; potassium, 1; calcium, 3. The very last I have seen gives calcium, $2\frac{4}{5}$; chloride of magnesium, $10\frac{1}{2}$; of potassium, $1\frac{1}{3}$; of sodium, $6\frac{1}{2}$. The specific gravity may average about 1200, that of distilled water being 1000. This, however, will vary according to the time and the place from whence the specimens are taken.

CHAPTER XLI.

JERUSALEM.

April 26th.

Quarters
on Mount
Olivet.

A FRIEND has placed at our disposal a small cottage near the top of Olivet, which commands a charming view of the city in all its extent; and, as we are to remain some time at this true capital of the Christian world, we will accept the kind offer. By this arrangement our time will be as much at command as though we kept to the tent; we shall also escape the annoyance of Jerusa-

JERUSALEM FROM THE MOUNT OF OLIVES.

lem's inexorable gates, and be able to prolong our walks and rides in the evening at pleasure. To reach the cottage, we must take this rather blind path from Bethany over the summit of the mount, and we at once experience the advantage of this arrangement, for it is already too late in the evening to enter the city; nor can we now stop to examine these misshapen ruins that mark the home of that happy family whom Jesus loved. Our cottage, however, will be within a short walk of it, and we shall have opportunities to visit it at our leisure.

CHAPTER XLI.

27th. From the top of this Mount of Olives the view eastward and southward, over the regions through which we have wandered for the last few days, is most peculiar and impressive. It is the Creator's own conception realized of desolation absolute—hills behind hills, sinking far down to the Dead Sea, with Edom and Moab beyond. As the rising sun revealed them, I have been watching their worn and haggard features with a strange sort of fascination, for I doubt not it was into this " wilderness" that Jesus was led after his baptism in the Jordan—what particular part of it I care not to know. Enough for me that on these doleful hills the great temptation was borne by the suffering Son of God for forty days and forty nights—that here the prince of darkness was baffled at every point, and his accursed dominion overthrown and that for ever.

"The wilderness."

Our position on this mount is indeed delightful, and whichever way one turns, he sees objects of the highest and most sacred interest. From a dozen points I have been gazing down into the Holy City, and my utmost anticipations are more than realized. Jerusalem, as I see it this morning, is all I could desire; and if a nearer acquaintance is going to disappoint and disgust, let me not enter, but depart from this " Mount of Ascension," carrying away the picture already imprinted on my heart.

Views of Jerusalem.

Such a result is not inevitable, though this your first is by far the best view you will ever have. Your introduction to the Holy City differs widely from mine. Wearied with a long ride from Jaffa, I approached from the west when the shadows of evening were falling heavily over the blank walls and unpicturesque ramparts of Zion. I could see nothing of the city, and entered the gate dissatisfied and sadly disappointed. Subsequently, while residing here, this first impression wore off, and was succeeded by feelings of deep reverence and earnest affection. Be not discouraged, therefore, if you return from the first walk about Zion hungry, weary, half-roasted, and with a sensation of disgust tugging desperately at your heart. As you repeat your rambles with less excitement and hurry, and become familiar with the localities and their sacred associations, an intelligent and abiding interest in the very dust and stones of Jerusalem will grow up vigorous and refreshing, you scarcely know how.

View from the west.

At any rate, I am resolved to make myself thoroughly acquainted with the Holy City and its environs, cost what it may.

A very sensible resolution; but I give your fair warning that I am not to be your guide and *cicerone.* It is no child's play, at this season of the year, to

Guides

PART
IV.

walk down and up Mount Olivet, and explore sites and scenes from the bottom of Jehoshaphat to the top of Zion. I have gone the rounds a hundred times, and intend now to rest. Guides in abundance can be procured, and the city is before you. As to "helps and helpers," you are in danger of being bewildered with an *embarras du richesse*. Not to name the Bible and Josephus, here are Eusebius and Jerome, Reland, Maundrell, Chateaubriand, Williams, Wilson, Schultz, Robinson, and any number of minor works. In charts, plans, and views we are equally rich—Catherwood's, Robinson's, Wilson's, Schultz's, Williams's, and many others; and, most satisfactory of all, you have the living original spread out beneath your eye, and ready to be questioned at all hours of day and night. Do not set out, however, like Mr. Solesby, resolved to make

"Discoveries."

discoveries. There is not a foot of ground that has not been already scrutinized by a thousand eyes as keen as yours; and the old adage, "If *true*, not *new;* if *new*, not *true*," may be applied to Jerusalem and her monuments with more propriety than to any other place on earth.

I am in no mood to allow my enthusiasm to be extinguished by such a damper as that. To me everything is invested with the charm of novelty, and I shall taste all the pleasure of discovery without claiming any of its honours. Jerusalem is the common property of the whole Christian world—belongs neither to Greek nor Latin—is neither Papist nor Protestant. *I* claim a share in Zion and Moriah, Olivet and Siloah, Gethsemane and Calvary; and I mean to pursue my studies and researches with as much freedom and zest as though no eye but mine had ever scanned these sacred sites.

So be it; but do not dream of reaching results in all cases clear and satisfactory even to yourself, much less to others.

Conflicting theories of places.

It would be entertaining, at least, if not instructive, to submit the topography of Jerusalem and her environs to a conclave composed of devout padres, learned authors, and intelligent gentlemen from Europe and America, now residing in the Holy City. They would scarcely agree on a single point. Poor Josephus would be so tortured, and twisted, and perplexed, as not to know what he meant himself; and, by the same process, every text in the Bible that had any bearing upon this topography would be mystified and confounded; and thus, too, would be treated the "fathers," and every pilgrim and visitor who unfortunately published a sentence about Jerusalem. They would be completely bewildered, and then dismissed from the witness-box as incompetent, or otherwise unworthy of credit. Now, I would learn from this imaginary congress of conflicting theorizers to walk softly over such doubtful territory, and not to dogmatize where opinions of the learned clash.

Difficulty of reconstruction.

It is my own decided impression that no ingenuity can reconstruct this city as our Saviour saw it, or as Josephus describes it. No man on earth *knows* the line of the *eastern* and *south-eastern* portions of the *first* wall; nor where the *second* began, nor how it ran after it began; nor where the *third* wall commenced, nor one foot of its circuit afterward; and of necessity the locations of castles, towers, corners, gates, pools, sepulchres, etc., etc., depending upon *supposed* starting-points and directions, are merely hypothetical. One hypo- thesis may have more probability than another, but all must share the uncertainty which hangs over the data assumed by the theorizers.

Well, leaving speculations and their results to take care of themselves, may we not find some important points and boundaries about which there can be no reasonable doubts?

Certainly there are such outlines, strongly drawn and ineffaceable, which make it absolutely certain that we have the Holy City, with all its interesting localities, before us. For example, this mount on which our cottage stands is Olivet without a doubt; the deep valley at its base is the channel of Kidron; that broad ravine that joins it from the west, at the Well of Joab, is the Valley of Hinnom, which is prolonged northward and then westward under the ordinary name of Gihon. The rocky region lying in between these valleys is the platform of ancient Jerusalem—*the whole of it.* Within these limits there was nothing else, and beyond them the city never extended. Thus I understand the language of Josephus when he is speaking of Jerusalem, *one* and *entire.*

I go a step further in generalizing, and with considerable confidence. This platform of Jerusalem is divided into two nearly equal parts by a valley which commences to the north-west of the Damascus Gate, shallow and broad at first, but deepening rapidly in its course down along the west side of the Temple area, until it unites with the Kidron at the Pool of Siloam. The city, therefore, was built upon two parallel ridges, with a valley between them, and these grand land-marks are perfectly distinct to this day. The eastern ridge is Moriah, on which stood the Temple; the western is Mount Zion; and the valley between them is that of the Cheesemongers. These ridges are parallel to each other, and that of Zion is everywhere the higher of the two; that is, the part of it without the present south wall towers above Ophel, which is over against it; the Temple area is much lower than that part of Zion which is west of it, and the north-west corner of the city overlooks the whole of the ridge on which the Temple stood. This accords with the express and repeated assertion of Josephus, that Zion, which sustained the Upper Market-place, or the Upper City, was much the highest of all. The houses built down the *eastern* slopes of Zion everywhere face those on the *western* slopes of the opposite ridge, and the corresponding rows of houses meet in this intervening valley just as Josephus represents them to have done in his day. The historian wrote his description with an eye to Titus and the Roman army, and I cannot doubt but that, up to our present point of generalization, we have laid down the outlines of Jerusalem *as they saw and conquered it.* If we now proceed from generalities to particulars, we shall encounter obscurity and perplexing difficulties at every turn, and these will thicken around us just in proportion as we descend to details more and more minute. For example, perhaps all *planographists* of the Holy City agree that the lower part of the interior valley is that of the Cheesemongers, but higher up, where, under the name of Tyropean, it must define the supposed position of a certain tower, the course of this

PART
IV.

valley is very earnestly contested. And thus, too, all agree that the ridge *south* of Jaffa Gate is Zion, but some maintain that it terminates there at the Tower of David, while others believe that Zion continued up northward to the Castle of Goliath, and even beyond it. Some authors assume that the Tyropean commences at the Tower of David, and descends first eastward and then to the south-east, under the Temple area and down to Siloam, and that traces of such a valley can still be seen. Other eyes absolutely fail to discover it, and their owners say that the rain from heaven and the theodolite of the engineer

Acra.

obstinately refuse to acknowledge any such valley. Some place Acra north of Jaffa Gate, and others north-east of the Temple area. But we need not extend the list of conflicting theories any further, for it includes nearly every rod of the entire city—the line of every wall, the position of every castle, the name of every pool, the place of every gate, the site of every scene, etc., etc. On most of these questions I have my own opinions, but to state and defend them would be a most wearisome business, and as useless as it would be endless.

The walls.

It is probable that a considerable part of the present western wall, and possibly some of the northern, occupy nearly the line of the *ancient first wall*. That part east of Damascus Gate may be on the line of the *second wall*, as far as that wall extended in that direction, and from the corner of the Temple area northward it must follow very closely that of the *third wall*. That part which crosses Zion from the lower Pool of Gihon to the Mosque of El Aksa is modern. These walls, as is well known, were built, or, more correctly, I suspect, largely repaired by Sultan Suleiman in 1542, A.H. 948. They are from ten to fifteen feet thick, and from twenty-five to forty feet high, according to the nature of the ground. They have salient angles and square towers, with battlements and loop-holes. A path, protected by a breastwork, runs all round on the top of these walls, and from many parts of this promenade the tourist obtains his most satisfactory views of the city. The stone employed is evidently the fragments and remains of ancient structures. They vary greatly in size and appearance. Along the eastern line of the Temple area are portions of very ancient walls—huge stones, well cut, and laid down with the utmost regularity; probably the work of Herod. Where the south wall crosses the Tyropean it is built of large irregular blocks, evidently the fragments of the Temple and its substructions. Near the Damascus Gate, also, were some fine specimens of ancient work. The entire length of these walls, according to Dr. Robinson's measurements, is four thousand three hundred and twenty-six yards —a little less than two miles and a half. This makes nearly twenty of the thirty-three stadii which Josephus says was the entire circuit of the exterior walls, and leaves but thirteen stadii for the south end of Zion, the hill Ophel, and the quarter of Bezetha, on the north of the Temple. The ancient third wall, therefore, could not have extended very far to the north of the present city.

Gates.

Where the gates of ancient Jerusalem were located I do not know, and, therefore, I will leave it to others to station them according to their different theories. The present city has five gates : that at the Tower of David takes the name of Jaffa, Bethlehem, or Hebron Gate, because from it the roads to CHAPTER those places depart ; Damascus Gate on the north, St. Stephen's on the east ;   XLI. Bab el Mugharabeh, leading down to Siloam ; and the Gate of Zion.   Some of these have other names, but it is not necessary to charge the memory with many titles for the same things.   There are also two or three old gates, now walled up, as that of Herod on the north-east, and the Golden Gate in the east wall of the Temple area.   The architecture of all these entrances to the Holy City is Saracenic, except the last, which is ancient, and the interior of it ornamented with rich and elaborate carving in good Grecian style.

It will facilitate your study of Jerusalem to fix in your memory the names and direction of a few of the leading thoroughfares of the city.   The streets Streets. are, with rare exceptions, short, narrow, and crooked.   A few, however, are sufficiently long and important as thoroughfares to be put down on a chart. I prefer the plan of Mr. Williams, and we will use his division of streets, and, to avoid confusion, his nomenclature also.   There are only some half a dozen streets which are much frequented by travellers.

1. The Street of David, entering into Temple Street, which descends from Jaffa Gate, and crosses the Tyropean to the Temple area.

2. The Street of the Patriarch, leading north from David Street to the Church of the Holy Sepulchre.

3. Via Dolorosa, which is a sort of eastern continuation of the Street of the Holy Sepulchre, and leads finally to the Gate of St. Stephen.

4. The Street of St. Stephen, which passes through the markets to the Gate of Damascus.   Zion Street is a southern continuation of it.

5. The street leading from the Armenian Convent to Zion Gate.   There are many more, and a multitude of blind alleys, traversed only by those who are in search of some particular locality.   These streets are paved with smooth stone, not a little dangerous to timid riders, especially where the descent is steep.

The only castle of any particular importance is that at the Jaffa Gate, com- Tower of monly called the Tower of David.   The lower part of it is built of huge stones, David. roughly cut, and with a deep *bevel* round the edges.   They are undoubtedly ancient, but the interspersed patch-work proves that they are not in their ori- ginal positions.   I have been within it, and carefully explored all parts of it that are now accessible, but found nothing which could cast any light upon its history.   It is believed by many to be the Hippicus of Josephus, and to this Hippicus? idea it owes its chief importance, for the historian makes that the point of de- parture in laying down the line of the ancient walls of Jerusalem.   Volumes have been written in our day for and against the correctness of this identifica- tion, and the contest is still undecided ; but, interesting as may be the result, we may safely leave it with those who are now conducting the controversy, and turn to matters more in unison with our particular inquiries.   Everything that can be said about this grand old tower will be found in the voluminous works of Williams, Robinson, Schultz, Wilson, Fergusson, and other able writers on the topography of the Holy City.

TOWER OF DAVID.

Mount
Zion.

After riding through the city, I spent this morning in walking about Mount Zion, particularly that part of it which is without the walls, and have been struck with the wonderful fulfilment of the prophecies of Jeremiah and Micah that Zion should be ploughed as a field.[1]

It has so happened that my visits to Jerusalem have been at the season when luxuriant crops of grain were growing on all the south-eastern face of the mount. The full force of the prophecy is not reached unless we remember what Zion was—the stronghold, by nature and by art almost impregnable. Even the Jebusites scornfully said to David, "Except thou take away the lame and the blind, thou canst not come up hither,"[2] so confident were they that it could not be captured. David, having made it the capital of his kingdom, greatly strengthened the fortifications, and other kings, in after ages, added to them, and it was, no doubt, densely crowded with the best and the strongest edifices in Jerusalem at the time these prophecies were uttered. That such a place should become a common wheat-field, where, generation after

Zion a
ploughed
field.

---

[1] Jer. xxvi. 18; Micah iii. 12.   [2] 2 Sam. v. 6.

generation, the husbandman should quietly gather rich harvests, was, indeed, CHAPTER
a most daring prediction, and yet it has long since been most literally fulfilled. XLI.

What is there, or was there, about Zion to justify the high eulogium of David:
"Beautiful for situation, the joy of the whole earth, is Mount Zion, on the
sides of the north, the city of the great King?"[1]

The situation is indeed eminently adapted to be the platform of a magnifi- Situation
cent citadel. Rising high above the deep Valley of Gihon and Hinnom on the
west and south, and the scarcely less deep one of the Cheesemongers on the
east, it could only be assailed from the north-west; and then "on the sides of
the north" it was magnificently beautiful, and fortified by walls, towers, and
bulwarks, the wonder and terror of the nations: "For the kings were assembled; they passed by together. They saw it, and so they marvelled;
they were troubled, and hasted away." At the thought of it the royal psalmist
again bursts forth in triumph: "Walk about Zion, and go round about her;
tell the towers thereof; mark ye well her bulwarks; consider her palaces, that
ye may tell it to the generation following."[2] Alas! her towers have long since
fallen to the ground, her bulwarks have been overthrown, her palaces have
crumbled to dust, and we who now walk about Zion can tell no other story
than this to the generation following.

There is another Zion, however, whose towers are still more glorious, and The true
shall never be overthrown. "God is known in her palaces for a refuge."[3] And Zion.
"this God is our God for ever and ever." How often is this name synonymous
with the Church of the living God, and no other spot but one can divide with
it the affection of his people—no other name but one can awaken such joyful
hopes in the Christian's heart. The temporal Zion is now in the dust, but
the true Zion is rising and shaking herself from it, and putting on her beautiful
garments to welcome her King when he comes to reign over the whole earth.

There are very few stations to be visited on Zion. Inside the walls is the Stations
Armenian Convent, with its fine church and large gardens; and on the outside on Zion.
is the house of Caiaphas, near the gate,—an ill-shaped building, in itself meriting
no attention, but it is enriched with some choice relics. The Armenians here
show the identical stone slab which closed the door of the sepulchre, and the
precise spot where the cock stood when he crowed three times before Peter
completed his miserable denial of the Lord. You may lay this up along with
the olive-tree in which the ram was caught by the horns, and substituted on
the altar for Isaac. It is growing near Abraham's Chapel, on the north side of
Calvary.

The only other building of any note on Zion is the Tomb of David—now a Tomb of
mosque, which has been so often drawn by artists that its appearance is fa- David.
miliar to all. Belonging to it is the Cœnaculum—a large, dreary "upper room" The Cœ-
of stone, fifty or sixty feet long, by some thirty in width. An ancient tradition naculum.
says that our blessed Lord here celebrated his last Passover, and at the close

---

[1] Ps. xlviii. 2.   [2] Ps. xlviii. 12, 13.   [3] Ps. xlviii. 3.

PART
IV.

of it instituted the "Supper." Here, too, he gave that most affecting lesson on humility, when he rose from supper, laid aside his garments, girded himself with a napkin, and washed the feet of his disciples.[1] Whether there is any foundation for this, or for the equally old tradition that this was the place where the apostles had assembled on the day of Pentecost, when the miracle of cloven tongues was shown, I care not to inquire. There was an *old* chapel there in the *fourth* century, to commemorate these events, and I please myself with the idea that there may be truth in the traditions. What a pity that both it and the reputed Tomb of David below should be in the hands of Moslems! No Christian is permitted to enter the latter on any account, and it is guarded with more jealousy than even the Mosque of Omar.

Ceme-
teries.

On this south part of Zion are the cemeteries of the different Christian denominations, and, among others, that of our own nation, north-west of the Tomb of David ; and that of the English, to the south-west, on the very declivity of the mount, above the Valley of Hinnom. The high school of Bishop Gobat is located at the same place, and the whole establishment forms an interesting group in a most remarkable position.

The south-eastern face of Zion declines, by many a winding terrace, down to the level of the Kidron at the Pool of Siloam, and the line of the aqueduct from the Pools of Solomon can be traced quite round the shoulder of the mount to the place where it passed under the city wall, some distance east of, and far below Zion Gate.

VALLEY OF JEHOSHAPHAT.

Valley
of the
Kidron.

Why the valley of the Kidron has this name, or when it first received it, I believe to be wholly unknown. It commences far round to the north-west, toward the Tombs of the Judges, and is there broad and shallow. Passing eastward, it has Scopus and the general platform of the city south of it. Meeting the north-eastern corner of Olivet, it turns due south, and pursues this direction to Beer 'Ayub, where it bends again to the south-east. From the Church of the Virgin southward it becomes a narrow ravine, and sinks down between Olivet and Ophel very rapidly, so that at the Well of Job it is more than five

Tombs.

hundred feet below the top of Zion. I had visited this lower part, to the Fountain of the Virgin, previously, and to-day I examined the sepulchral monuments above it. They are in the steep, rocky termination of that part of Olivet directly north of Kefr Silwan, and the entire base of the mountain has been cut and hewn into perpendicular faces by Jerusalem's ancient quarriers. In these faces are many sepulchres of the ordinary kind, but the tombs which

Tomb of
Zechariah.

merit special attention are—first, the monolith of Zechariah. It is a cubical block about twenty feet every way, and surmounted by a flattened pyramid of

---

[1] John xiii. 4, 17.

at least ten feet elevation, so that the entire height is thirty feet.   It has no CHAPTER
XLI.
mason-work about it, but is one solid mass hewn out of the mountain, the adjacent rock being cut away, so that it stands entirely detached.   Each of the
sides has two columns and two demi-columns, and the corners are finished off
with square pilasters.   The capitals are plain Ionic, and a broad cornice, worked
with acanthus leaves, runs round the top below the pyramid.   There is no
known entrance.

Second, the Tomb of St. James, which is near to the north side of this mono- Tomb of
lith.   It shows a fine front to the west, ornamented with four short Doric St. James.
columns.   The entrance is not by these columns, but from a passage cut
through the rock, in the north-east corner of the space around the Tomb of
Zechariah.   The *Cave* of St. James extends forty or fifty feet back into the
mountain.

Some two hundred feet north of this is the Tomb of Absalom.   The lower Tomb of
part of this monument resembles that of Zechariah.   Mr. Willis gives the fol- Absalom.
lowing description of its architectural composition   The square has a pilaster
at each angle, and a quarter column attached to it; and also, two half columns
between these have Ionic capitals, and sustain an entablature of a singularly
mixed character   Its frieze and architrave are Doric, and have triglyphs and
guttæ.   The metope is occupied by a circular disk or shield, but in lieu of the
regular cornice there is
one which resembles the
Egyptian cornice, con-
sisting of a deep and
high corvetto, and a
bold torus below it.
Above this is a square
attic rather more than
seven feet in height.
Upon this is a circu-
lar attic.   The whole is
finished off with what
Dr. Robinson calls a
small dome, running up
into a low spire, which
spreads a little at the
top like an opening
flower.   The   entire
height of this very
striking "pillar" can-
not be less than forty
feet, but the lower part
is not a little encum-
bered with stones and rubbish.   Believing it to be Absalom's Tomb, the

ABSALOM'S TOMB (RESTORED).

PART
IV.

natives throw stones against and spit at it as they pass by. This tomb has been much broken on the north side, and an opening made into a small sepulchral chamber within the solid part of it.

Tomb of Jehoshaphat.

Close to this monument, on the north-east, is the reputed Tomb of Jehoshaphat,—and from it the valley may have taken this name. It has an ornamental portal in the perpendicular face of the rock, but the sepulchre is wholly subterranean, and in no way remarkable. I examined these monuments with special pleasure and interest, not because they really had any connection with the individuals whose names they bear, but because they remain very much as they were at the time of our Saviour. I know not whether there is a single edifice, or part of one, in Jerusalem, upon which his eye of compassion rested, when from this Olivet he beheld the city and wept over it; but these sepulchral monuments appear now just as they did then to Him, and he must have often seen, admired, and spoken of them.

From these tombs I went north to look at the subterranean Church and Sepulchre of St. Mary. It was closed, and so was the so-called Garden of Gethsemane, a short distance to the south-east of it, and I could only examine the outside wall.

Gethsemane.

The authenticity of this sacred garden Mr. Williams says he chooses rather to believe than to defend. I do not even choose to believe. When I first came to Jerusalem, and for many years afterward, this plot of ground was open to all, whenever they chose to come and meditate beneath its very old olive-trees. The Latins, however, have, within the last few years, succeeded in gaining sole possession; have built a high wall around it, plastered and white-washed; and, by planting it with trees, seem disposed to make it like what they suppose it was when our Lord retired thither with his disciples on that mournful night of his "agony." Whatever may be thought of this idea, all travellers regret the exclusiveness which makes access difficult, and renders it impossible for most of them to visit the spot at all. The Greeks have invented another site a little north of it, and, of course, contend that they have the true Gethsemane. My own impression is that both are wrong. The position is too near the city, and so close to what must have always been the great thoroughfare eastward, that our Lord would scarcely have selected it for *retirement* on that dangerous and dismal night. In the broad recess north-east of the Church of Mary there must have been gardens far larger and more secluded; and, as we have before suggested, it is nearly certain that all the gardens around the city were thrown open, during the great feasts, for the accommodation of the pilgrims, so that he could select the one best adapted to the purpose for which he retired from the crowded city. I am inclined, therefore, to place the garden in the secluded vale several hundred yards to the north-east of the present Gethsemane, and hidden, as I hope for ever, from the idolatrous intrusion of all sects and denominations. The traditions in favour of the present location, however old, have but little weight, and fail to convince the mind; and there is no reason to think that a single tree, bush, or stone on either of these had any connection with the mysterious agony of the Son of God, when "his sweat was, as it were, great drops of blood falling down to the ground."

As to the Church and Sepulchre of the Virgin Mary, I have had more than one opportunity to examine it. There is a descent of sixty steps to the church, which, consequently, lies almost entirely under the bed of the Valley of Jehoshaphat. The steps, however, are partly outside and partly within the door which leads down to the body of the church. Seen from above, when this is lighted up, the church presents a most striking appearance. On the right of the descent are shown the chapel and tombs of Joachim and Anna; that of St. Joseph on the left; and toward the east of the church is the supposed tomb of Mary, bearing a general resemblance to the Holy Sepulchre, and probably modelled after its pattern. The various altars bear witness to the divisions of Christendom, and its joint occupation by the various countries contributes to perpetuate their miserable feuds; nor does the influence of Gethsemane, which is hard by, seem to allay their animosity, or to inculcate Christian charity.

There are other sepulchres in and around Jerusalem which are well worth examining. They are found in astonishing numbers along the south side of Hinnom; and, indeed, almost everywhere within and without the city, where the accumulated rubbish is removed, these tombs are met with, generally hewn into the perpendicular faces of the rocks, made in quarrying for building stone. They are of all sizes and shapes. Some are merely single rock-graves; other are small rooms, entered by a door in front, and having two, three, or more niches for the bodies; others, again, are much more extensive—a sort of catacomb, room within and beyond room, each having several niches. The best examples of these are the Tombs of the Kings and those of the Judges. Those of the kings are in the olive grove about half a mile north of the Damascus Gate, and a few rods east of the great road to Nablûs. A court is sunk in the solid rock about ninety feet square and twenty deep. On the west side of this court is a sort of portico, thirty-nine feet long, seventeen deep, and fifteen high. It was originally ornamented with grapes, garlands, and festoons, beautifully wrought on the cornice; and the columns in the centre, and the pilasters at the corners, appear to have resembled the Corinthian order. A *very low* door in the south end of the portico opens into the antechamber—nineteen feet square, and seven or eight high. From this three passages conduct into other rooms, two of them, to the south, having five or six crypts. A passage also leads from the west room down several steps into a large vault running north, where are crypts parallel to the sides. These rooms are all cut in rock intensely hard, and the entrances were originally closed with stone doors, wrought with panels and hung on stone hinges, which are now all broken. The whole series of tombs indicates the hand of royalty and the leisure of years, but by whom and for whom they were made is a mere matter of conjecture. I know no good reason for ascribing them to Helena of Adiabene. Most travellers and writers are inclined to make them the sepulchres of the Asmonean kings.

TOMBS OF THE KINGS.

Tombs
of the
Judges.

The Tombs of the Judges are about a mile north-west of those of the kings. The vestibule in front of them is highly ornamented, but after an entirely different pattern from those of the kings. It faces the west, and from it a door leads into a room about twenty feet square and eight feet high. On the north side are seven *loculi*, seven feet deep, prependicular to the side of the room. Above these are three arched recesses, two feet and a half deep, probably for the reception of sarcophagi. Perpendicular to these recesses, two long loculi penetrate the rock from the back part. Doors on the south and east conduct to small rooms, which have three long niches perpendicular to their three sides, the doors occupying the fourth. There is also an arched recess over the loculi in these rooms. From the north-east corner of the ante-room a flight of steps goes down into a small vestibule, neatly cut, and ornamented by recesses and a slightly-arched roof like a dome. A passage leads into another chamber further east, nine feet square and six high, each of whose three sides has an arched recess parallel to it, from the back of which perpendicular loculi enter into the rock. In some respects this is a more remarkable catacomb than that of the kings, and the arrangement is more

varied and complicated. Why the name, Tombs of the Judges, is given, no
one can assign any plausible explanation. In all directions from this locality,

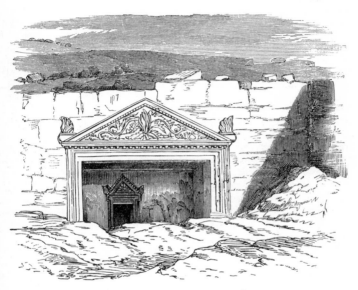

TOMBS OF THE JUDGES—FRONT VIEW.[1]

but especially toward the city, the strata of the mountain have been cut and
carved into perpendicular faces by ancient quarriers, and in them are innumerable tombs, of every variety of pattern. Indeed, the prodigious extent of
these quarries and tombs is one of the most striking indications of a great city,
and of a long succession of prosperous ages, which the environs of Jerusalem
furnish.

The Tombs of the Prophets are here, near the southern summit of Olivet. I
have never examined them with much care, but they are regarded as very
mysterious excavations by antiquarians. Mr. Williams thus describes them :
Through a long gallery, first serpentine and then direct, but winding as you
advance, one passes into a circular hall, rising into a conical dome about
twenty-four feet in diameter. From this hall run three passages, communicat-
ing with two semicircular galleries connective with the hall, the outer one of
which contains in its back wall numerous recesses for the corpses, radiating

*Tombs
of the
Prophets*

---

[1] For Interior View, see p. 107.

PART
IV.

Grotto of
Jeremiah.

Excava-
tions
under
ridge.

toward the centre hall. No inscriptions or remains of any kind have been discovered to elucidate the mysteries of these mansions for the dead.

The so-called Grotto of Jeremiah is beneath the high tell of Ez Zahera,
about forty rods to the north-east of the Damascus Gate. This tell, no doubt,
once formed the termination of the ridge [of Acra ?], and the rock between it
and the wall of the city has been quarried away. Nor will the magnitude of
this work stumble any one who examines the vast subterranean quarries
within and beneath the city, the opening to which is nearly south of Jeremiah's
Cave. The high perpendicular cuttings which sustain the wall are directly
opposite to similar cuttings over the cave, and each is about fifty feet high.
The yawning Cavern of Jeremiah extends under the cliff about one hundred
feet, and there are various buildings, graves, and sacred spots arranged
irregularly about it, walled off, plastered, and whitewashed. Under the floor
of the cavern are vast cisterns. Lighting our tapers, we descended about forty
feet, into the deepest one. The roof is supported by huge square columns, and
the whole, neatly plastered, is now used as a cistern. The water was pure, cold,
and sweet. This place is in Moslem hands, but the keepers allowed us to explore every part of it at our leisure. In any other part of the world it would
be considered a remarkable work, but here, in the vicinity of such excavations
as undermine the whole ridge within the city, it dwindles into insignificance.
There is no evidence to connect it in any way with Jeremiah, and no modern
theory has sufficient probability to claim attention.

The excavations under the ridge which extends from the north-west corner
of the Temple area to the north wall of the city are most extraordinary. I
spent a large part of this forenoon examining them with a company of friends
from the city. Passing out at the Damascus Gate, we ascended the hill of
rubbish east of it, and just under the high precipice over which the wall is
carried, we crept, or rather *backed* through a narrow opening, and, letting ourselves down some five feet on the inside, we stood within the cavern. Lighting
our candles, we began to explore. For some distance the descent southward
was rapid, down a vast bed of soft earth. Pausing to take breath and look
about, I was surprised at the immense dimensions of the room. The roof of
rock is about thirty feet high, even above the huge heaps of rubbish, and is
sustained by large, shapeless columns of the original rock, left for that purpose by the quarriers, I suppose. On we went, down, down, from one depth
to a lower, wandering now this, now that way, and ever in danger of getting
lost, or of falling over some of the many precipices into the yawning darkness
beneath. In some places we climbed with difficulty over large masses of rock,
which appear to have been shaken down from the roof, and suggest to the
nervous the possibility of being ground to powder by similar masses which hang
overhead. In other parts our progress was arrested by pyramids of rubbish
which had fallen from above, through apertures in the vault, either natural or
artificial. We found water trickling down in several places, and in one there
was a small natural pool full to the brim. This trickling water has covered

many parts with crystalline incrustations, pure and white; in others, stalac- CHAPTER
tites hang from the roof, and stalagmites have grown up from the floor.   The   XLI.
entire rock is remarkably white, and, though not very hard, will take a polish
quite sufficient for architectural beauty.

The general direction of these excavations is south-east, and about parallel Direction
with the valley which descends from the Damascus Gate. I suspect that they and ex-
extend down to the Temple area, and also that it was into these caverns that tent.
many of the Jews retired when Titus took the Temple, as we read in Josephus.
The whole city might be stowed away in them; and it is my opinion that a
great part of the very white stone of the Temple must have been taken from
these subterranean quarries.

TOMBS OF SIMON THE JUST AND OF THE SANHEDRIM.

These curious sepulchres are rarely visited. They are in the valley of the
Kidron, a short distance north-east of the Tombs of the Kings, and under the
cliffs on the north side of the wady. They are frequented exclusively by the
Jews, and mostly on their festival days. I once entered them on the thirty-
third day after the Passover—a day consecrated to the honour of Simon. Many Tomb of
Jews were there with their children. Like all other sects in the East, they Simon.
make vows in reference to shaving off the hair from their own and their children's heads in honour of some saint or shrine. A number had that day been
clipped, the hair weighed, and a sum distributed to the poor in proportion to
the weight. The surrounding fields and olive orchards were crowded with
gaily-dressed and merry Hebrews. I never saw so many pretty Jewesses together on any other occasion. The tombs seemed to me to have been cut in what
were originally natural caves. The entrance to all of them was *very low,* and
without ornament. The interior was spacious and gloomy in the extreme,
especially that which was said to contain the Sanhedrim. There were between Tombs of
sixty and seventy niches where bodies may have been placed; and from this the San-
number, perhaps, the idea originated that they were the crypts of the seventy hedrim
men of the Great Synagogue. Dr. Wilson seems to have heard of these tombs,
but he confounds them with those of the judges, which are a mile or more to
the north-west.

On the general subject of *willies* and sacred tombs, have you ever thought of Sacred
the interpretation put upon them by our Lord? In Luke we read, " Woe unto tombs.
you! for ye build the sepulchres of the prophets, and your fathers killed
them. Truly ye bear witness that ye allow the deeds of your fathers: for they
indeed killed them, and ye build their sepulchres."[1] *How? why?* might not
the Pharisees have replied, that, by honouring their remains and their memory,
they condemned their murderers?

---

[1] Luke xi. 47, 48.

41

PART
III.

Allusion of
our Lord.

The greatest sin of Israel and of the world *was*, and *is*, apostasy from the true God and his worship by idolatry; and the most prevalent mode of this apostasy is sacrilegious reverence for dead men's tombs and bones. This is the most prevalent superstition in the great empire of China, and in Western Asia, Jews, Moslems, Metáwelies, Druses, Nesairiyeh, Ismailiyeh, Kurds, Yezedy, Gipsies, and all sects of Christians, are addicted to it. Every village has its saints' tombs—every hill top is crowned with the white dome of some neby or prophet. Thither all resort to garnish the sepulchres, burn incense and consecrated candles, fulfil vows, make offerings, and pray. So fanatical are they in their zeal, that they would tear any man to pieces who should put dishonour upon these sacred shrines. Enter that at Hebron, for example, and they would instantly sacrifice you to their fury. Now, it was for rebuking this and other kinds of idolatry that " the fathers killed the prophets;" and those who built their tombs would, in like manner, kill any one who condemned *their* idolatrous reverence for these very sepulchres. Thus the Pharisees, by the very act of building those tombs of the prophets, and honouring them as they did, showed plainly that they were actuated by the same spirit that led their fathers to kill them; and, to make this matter self-evident, they very soon proceeded to crucify the *Lord* of the prophets because of his faithful rebukes. Nor has this spirit changed in the least during the subsequent eighteen hundred years. *Now, here* in Jerusalem, should the Saviour re-appear, and condemn with the same severity our modern Pharisees, *they would kill him upon his own reputed tomb.* I say this not with a faltering *perhaps*, but with a painful certainty. Alas! how many thousands of God's people have been slaughtered because of their earnest and steadfast protest against pilgrimages, idolatrous worship of saints, tombs, bones, images, and pictures! And whenever I see people particularly zealous in building, repairing, or serving these shrines, I know them to be the ones who allow the deeds of those who killed the prophets, and who would do the same under like circumstances. If you doubt, and are willing to become a martyr, make the experiment to-morrow in this very city. You may blaspheme the Godhead, through all the divine persons, offices, and attributes, in safety; but insult these dead men's shrines, and woe be to you !

Touch of a
tomb pol-
luting.

It was probably that he might render apostasy into this insane idolatry impossible to a faithful Jew, that Moses made the mere touching of a grave, or even of a bone, contamination. The person thus polluted could not enter his tent, or unite in any religious services. He was unclean seven days, and was obliged to go through a tedious and expensive process of purification. And, still more, if the person would not purify himself, he was to be cut off from the congregation and destroyed. Strange, that even this stern law was not sufficient to restrain the Jews from worshipping dead men's graves.

VALLEY OF HINNOM—TOPHET.

This valley commences north-west of the Jaffa Gate, above the Upper Pool of Valley of Gihon. Descending eastward to the immediate vicinity of the gate, it turns Hinnom. south, and the bed of it is occupied by the Lower Pool of Gihon. Below this it bends round to the east, having the cliffs of Zion on the north, and the Hill of Evil Counsel on the south. It is here that Hinnom properly begins, and it terminates at Beer 'Ayub, where it joins the valley of Jehoshaphat. The cliffs on the south side especially abound in ancient tombs, and it was this part that was called Tophet. Here the dead carcasses of beasts, and every offal and abomina- Tophet. tion, were cast, and left to be either devoured by that worm that never died, or consumed by that fire that was never quenched. Hinnom was condemned to this infamous service, perhaps, because in it, when Israel fell into idolatry, they offered their children in sacrifice to Baal. Jeremiah has an extended reference to this place and its horrid sacrifices: "Because they have forsaken me, and have estranged this place, and have burned incense in it unto other gods, whom neither they nor their fathers have known, nor the kings of Judah, and have filled this place with the blood of innocents; they have built also the high places of Baal, to burn their sons in the fire—burnt-offerings unto Baal, which I commanded not, nor spake it, neither came it into my mind: therefore, behold, the days come, saith the Lord, that this place shall no more be called Tophet, nor The valley of the son of Hinnom, but The valley of slaughter."[1] This denunciation was doubtless fulfilled when Nebuchadnezzar sacked and destroyed Jerusalem; and more emphatically by Titus and "his men of war." Josephus says that when Titus saw, from a distance, these valleys below Jerusalem heaped full of dead bodies, he was so horrified at the sight that he raised his hands, and called Heaven to witness that he was not responsible for this terrific slaughter.

Jeremiah was commanded to *break* the potter's "*bottle*" or *jar* in the pre- Breaking sence of the ancients of the people and the priests, after he had denounced a jar. these terrible judgments upon them in the valley of Tophet.[2] The people of this country have the same custom of breaking a jar when they wish to express their utmost detestation of any one. They come behind or near him, and smash the jar to atoms, thus imprecating upon him and his a like hopeless ruin.

The cruel sacrifices of children in this valley are frequently referred to by Sacrifices Jeremiah. They were made to "pass through the fire unto Moloch;"[3] from to Moloch which it appears that Baal and Moloch were names for one and the same deity. The victims were placed on the red-hot hands of the idol, and their agonizing shrieks were drowned by cymbals and the shouts of the frenzied worshippers. Milton thus sings indignant at these "abominations:"—

> "Moloch, horrid king, besmeared with blood
> Of human sacrifice, and parents' tears,

---

[1] Jer. xix. 1–12.   [2] Jer. xix. 10.   [3] Jer. vii. 31; xix. 5; and xxxii. 35.

Though for the noise of drums and timbrels loud
Their children's cries unheard, that passed through fire
To his grim idol—in the pleasant vale of Hinnom, Tophet thence,
And black Gehenna called, the type of Hell."

The place seems to have become infamous for idolatry at an early age. Isaiah speaks of it metonymically by the name Tophet, for the place where Sennacherib's army was to be consumed by the breath of the Lord: " For Tophet is ordained of old; yea, for the king it is prepared; he hath made it deep and large: the pile thereof is fire and much wood; the breath of the Lord, like a stream of brimstone, doth kindle it."[1]   Under its original name of Hinnom, Grecised into Gehenna, it is used in the New Testament as synonymous with, or as a type of hell.   The idea seems to be borrowed from the above passages, and from the scenes which were witnessed in this valley.   The language of our Saviour, as given by Mark,[2] is copied almost *verbatim* from Isaiah.[3]

*Valley of
Hinnom a
type of
hell.*

As I move about among these sacred localities, an inquiry of this sort is constantly arising, With what amount of reverence should a pious mind regard them ?

*Respect
due to
sacred
places.*

I prefer to use the word *respect*.   There is nothing now in or about Jerusalem that can justly claim from me any religious reverence whatever.   This subject is one of much importance, and needs to be placed in a clear light and upon a proper basis, for the number of visitors of all ages who resort hither is rapidly multiplying, and I notice an increasing disposition among many Protestants to glide into the same sort of reverential deportment in presence of these localities that Roman Catholics and Orientals generally manifest.   This should be arrested, not by treating with profane levity such places and scenes, but by acquiring correct views in regard to them, and the manner in which we may derive both pleasure and profit from visiting them, while at the same time we escape this dangerous bias toward idolatrous reverence.

There are two or three *distinctions* to be made, fundamental and broad enough to reach every case of the kind that can come before the pious mind. The first is, that in the Mosaic economy, which multiplied holy places and instruments, it was not the place or the thing itself that was regarded and treated as holy.   Moses, for example, was commanded to put off his shoes before the burning bush, not that it was any more holy than any other bush in the desert of Sinai.   The reverence was simply and solely to the infinite and uncreated Being who for the moment dwelt in it in a peculiar manner.   So the ark, with the mercy-seat, and the apartments in the Tabernacle and Temple where it was placed, were holy, for no other reason than that God, who is ever to be approached with fear and reverence, there made his special abode.   The " bush," without the Presence, differed in nothing from any other; and so of the Holy of Holies in the Temple, and of every other place on this earth. When the divine presence is withdrawn, all religious reverence before the place

*The divine
presence
the object
of re-
verence.*

---

[1] Isa. xxx. 33.   [2] Mark ix. 44-48.   [3] Isa. lxvi. 24.

or thing must cease of course. There is nothing, therefore, about the Temple area, or the so-called Sepulchre of Christ Jesus, that can now receive any other worship than that which is purely idolatrous. The prophets and apostles always acted upon this principle. To mention but one of a hundred instances, the disciples of our Lord, when they hurried to ascertain the truth of the report about the resurrection, manifested not the slightest reverence for the tomb. Peter ran right into it without stopping to take off his shoes, as you must now do before the fictitious sepulchre in the church, and this, too, though he knew with absolute certainty that his Lord had been there, and had but just left the place. The same is true in the case of the women; none of them seem to have dreamed that the rock-tomb merited any reverence when the Lord himself was gone. Nor do we again hear a whisper about this tomb throughout the entire New Testament history. There is no evidence that any one of them ever revisited it.

The second great principle in regard to these shrines is, that no religious reverence to *human beings* or to *angelic spirits* was ever tolerated, nor to any place or thing that represented them. We cannot, therefore, participate in any such rites or ceremonies without enacting a piece of naked idolatry, every way, and in all ages and places, extremely offensive to God. This sweeps into one general and undistinguished category of condemnation the entire catalogue of shrines, and tombs, and caverns sacred to dead men.

The third grand fact bearing upon this subject is, that God, in his providence, has so ordered matters that not one of all these shrines can show any just title to the honours claimed for them. The bush is gone, the tabernacle has vanished, not one stone of the Holy of Holies remains, and doubt and uncertainty absolutely impenetrable rests on every sacred locality, and upon everything connected with them. And in view of the sad and ruinous perversions to which their very shadows give rise, I am thankful that there is not a single tomb of saints, nor instrument employed in manifesting miraculous power, nor a sacred shrine, whose identity can be ascertained.

You have given only a negative answer to my inquiry, and, after all, I feel that the whole truth has not been stated.

Certainly not. To discuss the matter of sacred sites and scenes in detail would require a volume, and I have no disposition to enter the arena of such earnest controversy. The proper use to be made of these things can be laid down in a few words. We should so conduct our visits as to confirm faith and deepen the impressions which the Bible narratives of what here took place in former ages are intended to produce; and for this the materials are abundant and satisfactory.

CHAPTER XLII.

EXCURSION TO BETHLEHEM.

Valley of Rephaim.	Was Jesus born in a cave?
Convent of Elijah.	Flocks—Reapers.
Tomb of Rachel.	Boaz and Ruth—Customs.
Ramah—Bethlehem.	Tomb of Jerome.

May 10th.

WELL, how have you enjoyed your excursion to the City of David ?

It was perfectly delightful. Having sent our horses to the Jaffa Gate, we looked in upon the ceremonies which were being enacted in the Church of the Holy Sepulchre. Wearying very soon with what we could not understand, we mounted and set off for Bethlehem. Rising out of the valley of Gihon at the point, I presume, where the boundary-line between Judah and Benjamin passed from the valley of Hinnom into the plain of Rephaim, we stopped a while to allow our guide time to point out the precise spot where the Philistines had their camp when David "fetched a compass, and came upon them over against the mulberry-trees." [1] The plain itself is stony and uneven, and declines rapidly toward the west. In an hour from the gate of the city we reached the Convent of Elijah. Of course, the tradition that the prophet rested at that place in his flight from the wicked Jezebel has no foundation in authentic history, and in itself the establishment merits no particular attention. From there we passed round to the south-west, and came in fifteen minutes to the Tomb of Rachel. This is a plain Saracenic mausoleum, having no claims to antiquity in its present form, but deeply interesting in sacred associations; for, by the singular consent of all authorities in such questions, it marks the actual site of her grave. Such a spot must ever be regarded with that sort of respect and tender emotion which are accorded to deep sorrow. The first mention of it occurs in the 35th chapter of Genesis, where Rachel, as her soul was departing, for she died, named her new-born babe Ben-oni, son of sorrow. "And Jacob set a pillar upon her grave : that is the pillar of Rachel's grave unto this day." [2] Reference is again made to this matter in the 48th chapter : "As for me, when I came from Padan, Rachel died by me in the land of Canaan, in the way, when yet there was but a little way to come unto Ephrath; and I buried her there in the way of Ephrath : the same is Bethlehem " [3] This is the narrative; but it is more than mere history, for the event occurred, and the record was made, to symbolize a greater sorrow that was to occur at Ephrath nearly two thousand years after, in connection with the birth at Bethlehem of that

(marginal notes: Valley of Rephaim. Convent of Elijah. Tomb of Rachel.)

---

[1] 2 Sam. v. 22–25.　　　[2] Gen. xxxv. 18–20.　　　[3] Gen. xlviii. 7

Man of Sorrows in whom every important event in Hebrew history received its CHAPTER final and complete significance. XLII.

Not four hundred yards from Rachel's Tomb the guide showed us a heap of old rubbish, which he said was called Ramah. This appeared to me like a Ramah. modern invention, originating in a desire of these very accommodating people to gratify the solicitude of Biblical antiquarians. One thing, however, is certain, that *if* there was such a name attached to any site in that vicinity, all obscurity would at once vanish in regard to that much controverted reference to *a* Ramah in the second chapter of Matthew:[1] "In Rama was there a voice heard, lamentation, and weeping, and great mourning; Rachel weeping for her children, and would not be comforted, because they are not."

Whether this locality is in fact the one that existed in the time of Herod is, of course, highly problematical; but not, as I think, the fact that there was such a place in that vicinity when Herod slew the infants in and about Bethlehem. I cannot believe that either of the present well-known Ramahs could be meant. They were too far off, and separated from Bethlehem and from Rachel's Tomb by other villages, and intervening mountains and wadies. The place in question must have been contiguous to Bethlehem, was subject to the same calamity, and, being near Rachel's Tomb, the poetic accommodation of Jeremiah was natural and beautiful.[2] Of course it *is* accommodation. The prophet himself had no thought of Herod and the slaughter of the infants. That such a small hamlet, a dependence of Bethlehem (and all important towns have now such dependent *mezr'ahs*), should have perished, is not strange. The name Ramah, in some of its forms, is applied to *any* place seated on a hill. There are scores of Rams, Ramahs, Ram-allahs, etc., all over the country, and here there may have been one of them, somewhere near Rachel's Tomb.

Bethlehem itself shows to great advantage across the valley from Mar Elias. Beth-We, of course, looked at the sacred localities pointed out, but without much lehem. satisfaction. The so-called Cave of the Nativity is quite as much transformed and mystified as the Holy Sepulchre. This is to be the more regretted just in proportion to the greater probability that it may really have some connection with the advent of our Lord.[3]

It is not impossible, to say the least, that the apartment in which our Saviour was born was in fact a cave. I have seen many such, consisting of one or more rooms, in front of, and including a cavern, where the cattle were kept. It is my impression that the birth actually took place in an ordinary Birth of house of some common peasant, and that the babe was laid in one of the Jesus. mangers, such as are still found in the dwellings of the farmers in this region. That house may have stood where the convent does now, and some sort of cave, either natural or made by digging the earth away for building and for the roofs of houses, *may* have been directly below, or even included within its court. Thus all the demands of the tradition would be met, without resorting

[1] Matt. ii. 18.   [2] Jer. xxxi. 15.   [3] Matt. ii. 5, 6.

PART IV. to the suspicious circumstance of a cave. This locating of so many Biblical scenes and transactions in caves has stumbled the faith of thinking and impartial men, and it is to be regretted that we cannot separate this tradition concerning the birth-place of Jesus from such doubtful associations. The tradition itself can be traced almost up to the death of the apostle John, and Was Jesus it appears never to have been entirely lost. Justin Martyr, who was born in born in a Nablûs, and educated in this country, though he suffered martyrdom in Rome, cave? says expressly that Jesus was born in a grotto at Bethlehem. He, of course, did not invent, but merely referred to a tradition already established. This carries up the matter very high indeed, nor is there anything to contradict his testimony in subsequent ages. It must be confessed, however, that Matthew does not much favour the idea of a grotto. He says of the magi that "when they came into the *house*, they saw the young child, with Mary his mother, and fell down and worshipped him." But a truce to dry criticism. The point in dispute is too insignificant to rob us of the delightful reflections and hallowed emotions which the sight of Bethlehem is calculated to awaken. The glorious Redeemer of our lost world was truly born there, according to prophecy and promise. On the neighbouring plain were the "shepherds abiding in the field, and keeping watch over their flock by night, when lo! the angel of the Lord came upon them, and the glory of the Lord shone round about them; Glory of and they were sore afraid. And the angel said unto them, Fear not: for, the Na- behold, I bring you good tidings of great joy, which shall be to all people. For tivity. unto you is born this day, in the city of David, a Saviour, which is Christ the Lord. And suddenly there was with the angel a multitude of the heavenly host praising God, and saying, Glory to God in the highest, and on earth peace, good-will toward men!"[1] Thus was announced and celebrated the most astonishing event that ever occurred in the universe—and it took place at Bethlehem.

History of We need not follow minutely the history of Bethlehem. Though mentioned Beth- by Jacob, it remained for many ages small and unimportant, as I suppose, for lehem. the name does not appear in the list of villages assigned to Judah by Joshua, nor do we meet with it again until the 17th chapter of Judges, where it is stated that the young Levite, who subsequently became the first idolatrous priest in Micah's house of gods, and afterward the head of that grand religious apostasy which had its seat in Dan, was of Bethlehem-judah. This is not much to the honour of the place. And the next event in her story is even less creditable, for the terrible catastrophe which befell the tribe of Benjamin was directly connected with a woman of bad character from Bethlehem, as we read in the 19th chapter of Judges. In these narratives *Judah* is added to the name, to distinguish it from another Bethlehem in Zebulun, west of Nazareth. It is not until the time of Boaz and Ruth that anything pleasant occurs in the history of Bethlehem, but after that it rose to great celebrity as the

---

[1] Luke ii. 8–14

birth-place of David; and, finally, it was rendered for ever illustrious by the advent there of David's greater son and Lord. Still, it never became large, and never will, for there is a fatal lack of water, and of certain other natural advantages, necessary to create and sustain a great city. The present number of inhabitants is not far from four thousand, and nearly all of them belong to the Greek Church. There was formerly a Moslem quarter, which Ibrahim Pasha destroyed after the great rebellion in 1834; but even this terrible vengeance failed to quell the turbulent spirit of the people. They are ever distinguished in the great feasts at Jerusalem by their fierce and lawless manners, and if any row occurs they are sure to have a hand in it. It is asserted in this country that there is something in the water of certain places which renders the people sturdy, hard, and fearless; and it is curious enough that people of this character have ever been connected with Bethlehem. David and his family, his mightiest captains, Joab and others, came from it, and they were fierce, terrible men. Had the water which David so longed for[1] any influence in compacting such bones and sinews, and hardening such spirits? Perhaps we can find another influence. They were noted shepherds, even to the time when the angel announced the birth of the Saviour. This occupation, in such a region, contributes greatly to educate just that sort of men. The position of Bethlehem is admirably adapted to call out those elements of character, and train them to the utmost perfection. Seated on the summit-level of the hill-country of Judah, with deep gorges descending east to the Dead Sea, and west to the plains of Philistia, the shepherds of Bethlehem had to contend not only with bears and lions, whose dens were in those wild wadies, but also with human enemies—the Philistines on the west, and Arab robbers on the east. They would, therefore, from childhood, be accustomed to bear fatigue, hunger, heat and cold, both by night and by day, and also to brave every kind of danger, and fight with every kind of antagonist. Thus the youthful David learned to sling stones when he led his father's flocks over the hills, and thus was he prepared to conquer Goliath;[2] and so, too, by defending his charge against bears and lions,[3] he learned to face lion-like men in war, and to conquer them.

I saw many flocks of sheep and goats on these same hills to-day, and was vividly reminded of those passages in Bible history in which the flocks and the shepherds of Bethlehem figure with so much interest, as in David's youth and at the birth of Jesus. I was struck by and equally delighted with another sight on the plains of Bethlehem. The reapers were in the fields cutting barley, and after every company were women and children gleaning, just as Ruth did when Boaz came to look at his labourers.[4]

Yes; and in the evening you might see some poor woman or maiden, that had been permitted to glean on her own account, sitting by the road side, and

Marginal notes: CHAPTER XLII. Character of the people. Shepherds. Their training. Flocks. Reapers.

---

[1] 2 Sam. xxiii. 15, 16.   [2] 1 Sam. xvii. 49.
[3] 1 Sam. xvii. 34.   [4] Ruth ii. 5–7.

beating out with a stick or a stone what she had gathered, as Ruth did.[1] I have often watched this process in various parts of the country. That entire scene of Boaz and Ruth might be enacted at the present day by the dwellers in Bethlehem with but trifling omissions and variations. The salutations that passed between the proprietor and the labourers[2] are no exaggeration of modern politeness. " The Lord be with you" is merely the " Allah m'akum " of ordinary parlance ; and so, too, the response, "The Lord bless thee." Again, it is implied that there was a considerable company of reapers, and that the reaping season was prolonged for a considerable time; for it is added that Ruth continued to glean until the end of barley harvest and of wheat harvest,[3] which are quite distinct, occur in the order here stated, and are

protracted through several weeks. It is further intimated by the tenor of the story, that the reapers were apt to be rude in their deportment toward defenceless females, and hence Boaz commanded them to behave respectfully to Ruth; and he told her, also, not to fear, for he had taken care that she should not be insulted. Such precautions are not out of place at this day. The reapers are gathered from all parts of the country, and largely from the ruder class, and, living far from home, throw off all restraint, and give free license to their tongues, if nothing more. The meals, too, are quite in keeping—the

dipping her morsel in the vinegar, and the parched corn.[4] Harvest is the time for parched corn—not what we lads in Ohio meant by the words. It is made thus : a quantity of the best ears, not too ripe, are plucked with the stalks attached. These are tied into small parcels, a blazing fire is kindled with dry grass and thorn bushes, and the corn-heads are held in it until the chaff is mostly burned off. The grain is thus sufficiently roasted to be eaten, and it is a favourite article all over the country. When travelling in harvest time, my muleteers have very often thus prepared parched corn in the evenings after the tent has been pitched. Nor is the gathering of these green ears for parching ever regarded as stealing. After it has been roasted, it is rubbed out in the hand and eaten as there is occasion. This parched corn is often referred to in the Bible. So, also, I have often seen my muleteers, as we passed along the wheat fields, pluck off ears, rub them in their hands, and eat the grains, unroasted, just as the apostles are said to have done.[5] This also is allowable. The Pharisees did not object to the thing itself, only to the time when it was done. They said it was not lawful to do this on the Sabbath day. It was work forbidden by those who, through their traditions, had made man for the Sabbath, not the Sabbath for man.

We have on various occasions seen the summer threshing-floors in the open country, and the owners sleeping at them to prevent stealing, just as the wealthy Boaz did when Ruth came unto him.[6] Though it is not allowable that women in general should sleep at these floors, and to do so would produce

---

[1] Ruth ii. 17.   [2] Ruth ii. 4.   [3] Ruth ii. 23.   [4] Ruth ii. 14.
[5] Matt. xii. 1, 2; Mark ii. 23; Luke vi. 1, 2.   [6] Ruth iii. 2–7.

the same unfavourable impression which Boaz apprehended, yet it is not un-usual for husband, wife, and all the family to encamp at the *baiders* (threshing-floors), and remain until the harvest is over. These family groups, however, do not render it proper for single females to be found there at night, and it is a fact that doubtful characters do actually come about them sufficiently often to keep suspicion alive, and there was doubtless the very same occasion for watchfulness three thousand years ago here at Bethlehem.

Boaz measured six measures of barley and put it into Ruth's *veil.*[1] It would appear from this that barley was used for bread in those days, and also that the veil must have been very different from the light article now used by the women.

Barley and the veil.

Barley is, in fact, very often eaten by the poor in Palestine; and as to the veil, you have only to look at those still worn by the fellahin to understand what kind of article is referred to in this story. It is merely a square piece of cotton cloth, and I have often seen it used for just such service as that to which Ruth applied hers.

In view of the impropriety of women resorting to the *baiders* at night, how did Boaz reach the conclusion expressed by him: "All the city of my people doth know that thou art a virtuous woman?"

Boaz, no doubt, knew her general character, and knew also that in the present instance she acted in accordance with the advice of her mother-in-law, who had taught her that she not only had a right to claim Boaz for her husband, but that she was precluded by the law of God from forming any other reputable connection. Boaz also remembered that he was old, and she young and attractive, and, though from the heathen Moabites, yet she preferred to walk in the sober path of honest married life rather than to associate with the young and the gay, by whom, it is intimated, she had been tempted. He was therefore fully justified in ascribing to this very act an honourable and virtuous principle, notwithstanding the *apparent* violation of modesty and propriety. And in this he judged correctly, for such was the fact. Ruth manifested true modesty and virtue, therefore, by claiming that to which she was entitled, and to which, in truth, she was bound by the law of God. That she applied to the wrong person was through the mistake of her mother-in-law.

Is there anything in modern customs among the Arabs to illustrate the singular act of pulling off the man's shoe who refused to marry his brother's widow?

Pulling off the shoe.

This matter is passed over very mildly here in Ruth, for it appears now to have become common to omit the harsher features of the law as laid down in Deut. xxv. 7–10, where the details are rough enough certainly. When a man publicly refuses, "in the gate of the city," to take his brother's wife, "then she shall come to him in the presence of the elders, and loose his shoe from off his foot, and spit in his face, and shall answer and say, So shall it be done

---

[1] Ruth iii. 15.

PART IV.

unto that man that will not build up his brother's house. And his name shall be called in Israel, The house of him that hath his shoe loosed." Perhaps in the case of Ruth all these offensive actions were omitted, possibly in consideration of the facts, that the man in question was not Ruth's husband's brother ; that she was an alien and a foreigner ; that he could not fulfil the law without injuring his own family; that there was another, the next in kin, who was more than willing to take his place ; and also that Ruth wished to avoid any unnecessary publicity in the transaction. So much of the law, therefore, only was observed as was necessary to confirm the transfer of the rights to Boaz.

Arab proverb—the slipper.

In regard to modern customs, there is a proverb among the Arabs which may possibly owe its origin to this law of Moses. When an Arab divorces his wife, he says of her, "She was my *babûj* (slipper), and I cast her off." In both the law and the proverb the *babûj* represents the woman and her matrimonial rights and claims. It is one thing, however, for a man to kick off his slipper in disgust, and quite another to have it plucked off in scorn and contempt by the insulted lady, especially if she should spit in his face, and fasten upon him in Israel the nickname, Beit Khabûtz hanaal, " the house of him whose shoe is loosed." In any event, the comparing of woman to a slipper is not very complimentary to the sex, but it is eminently Arabic, and it is a deplorable fact that all her matrimonial rights can be kicked off, like a worn-out *babûj*, at the caprice of her heartless lord and tyrant.

But you must allow me to complete my visit and return home. I examined with much interest the great church, which is certainly ancient and is really worth seeing ; and the paintings in various parts of it, which *are not*.

Tomb of Jerome.

But did you not enter the Tomb of Jerome, and his study, where he spent so many years in translating the Bible ?

Most certainly I did, and was deeply impressed by the visit. I suppose that these may be genuine, as also the last resting-place of the two ladies, his companions and patrons. These are all beneath the premises which belong to the Latin monks, and it is no more than justice to add that they manifested more decorum and solemnity in their deportment than do the Greeks and Armenians. After completing the circuit of *Holy Places*, and refreshing ourselves at the restaurant, kept by a talkative Greek, we took a long circuit eastward to see the surrounding country, and then returned hither across those plains where the shepherds watched their flocks on that night when the Redeemer of the world was born.

CHAPTER XLIII.

JERUSALEM AND NEIGHBOURHOOD.

May 11*th*. In my walks about Zion to-day I was taken to see the village or quarter assigned to the lepers, lying along the wall directly east of Zion Gate. I was unprepared for the visit, and was made positively sick by the loathsome spectacle.

You could not be more surprised and startled than I was on my first intro- Lepers' duction to this awful disease. Sauntering down the Jaffa road, on my quarter. approach to the Holy City, in a kind of dreamy maze, with, as I remember, scarcely one distinct idea in my head, I was startled out of my reverie by the sudden apparition of a crowd of beggars, "sans eyes, sans nose, sans hair, sans everything." They held up toward me their handless arms, unearthly sounds gurgled through throats without palates—in a word, I was horrified. Having never seen a leper, nor had my attention turned to the subject (for a quarter of a century ago Jerusalem and its marvels were not so well understood as they are now), I at first knew not what to make of it. I subsequently visited their habitations, as you have done to-day, and have made many inquiries into their history. It appears that these unfortunate beings have been perpetuated about Jerusalem from the remotest antiquity. One of my first thoughts on visiting their dens of corruption and death was, that the government should separate them, and thus, in a few years, extinguish the race and the plague together ; and I still think that a wise, steady, and vigilant sanitary system might eventually eradicate this fearful malady. But it will not be so easily or expeditiously accomplished as I then thought. It is not confined to Jerusalem, for I have met with it in different and distant parts of the country. And what is particularly discouraging is, that fresh cases appear from time to time, in which it *seems* to arise spontaneously, without hereditary or any other possible connection with those previously diseased. This fact, however, has not yet been fully established. Law of the

It is evident that Moses, in his very stringent regulations respecting this leper.

plague and its unhappy victims, had in view its extinction, or at least restriction within the narrowest possible limits. Those who were merely suspected were shut up, and if the disease declared itself the individual was immediately removed out of the camp, and not only he, but everything he touched, was declared unclean. For all practical purposes the same laws prevail to this day. The lepers, when not obliged to live outside the city, have got a separate abode assigned to them, and they are shunned as unclean and dangerous. No healthy person will touch them, eat with them, or use any of their clothes or utensils,—and with good reason. The leper was required by Moses to stand apart, and give warning by crying, "Unclean! unclean!" Thus the ten men that met our Saviour stood afar off, and lifted up their voice of entreaty. They still do the same substantially, and, even in their begging, never attempt to touch you. Among tent-dwelling Arabs the leper is literally put out of the camp.

Stories of Tacitus about leprosy and the Jews.
Tacitus has some strange stories about the leprosy and the Jews. When he comes to speak of the Jewish war in the time of Vespasian, he takes occasion to give an account of the origin of this people, in which there are almost as many fables as sentences. He then goes on to say that "one thing is certain. The Jews, when in Egypt, were all afflicted with leprosy, and from them it spread to the Egyptians. When the king, Bochorus, inquired of Jupiter Ammon how his kingdom could be freed from this calamity, he was informed that it could be effected only by expelling the whole multitude of the Jews, as they were a race detested by the gods. He accordingly drove them all forth into the desert, where one Moses met them, and succeeded in bringing them all into obedience to himself," with a great deal more of such nonsense. He accounts for the rejection of swine's flesh among the Jews by the fable that the leprosy was caught from swine.[1] This much, I think, can be safely inferred from a careful study of the 13th and 14th chapters of Leviticus, that the Hebrews were actually afflicted with the awful curse of leprosy beyond all modern example—leprosy of many kinds: in their persons: "leprosy in garments"—in the warp and in the woof—leprosy in the skins of animals—leprosy in the mortar, and even in the stones of their houses,—phenomena not only unknown, but utterly unintelligible at this day. It is probable that some obscure traditions of these things, which were afloat in the world, furnished the materials out of which the fancy of the historian worked up his malignant libel on the Hebrew nation.

Have you any explanation of this very obscure subject, and especially in reference to leprosy in garments and walls of houses? This is one of many inquiries I wished to have answered during my visit to this country.

Leprosy in stones and garments.
I have no light to shed upon it. For many years I have sought in every possible way to get at the mystery, but neither learned critics or physicians, foreign or native, nor books, ancient or modern, have thrown any light upon

---

[1] Tacitus, Ann., book v. chap. iv.

it. I have suspected that this disease, which, like the anthropophagous CHAPTER ghouls of the Arabs, leisurely eats up its victims in one long remorseless meal, XLIII. is, or is caused by, living and self-propagating animalculæ; and thus I can conceive it possible that those animalculæ might fasten on a wall, especially if the cement were mixed with sizing, as is now done, or other gelatinous or animal glues. Still, the most cursory reference to the best of our recent medical works suffices to show how little is known about the whole subject of contagion, and its propagation by fomites. One finds in them abundant and incontestable instances of the propagation of more than one terrible constitutional malady, in the most inexplicable manner, by garments, leather, wood, and other things, the *materies morbi* meantime eluding the most persevering and vigilant search, aided by every appliance of modern science, chemical or optical. This much, however, about leprosy is certain, that there are different kinds of it, and that fresh cases are constantly occurring in this country. What originates it, and how it is propagated, are points enveloped in profound darkness.

But though we cannot comprehend the leprosy nor cleanse the leper, there are many things to be learned from this mysterious disease. It has ever been Leprosy a regarded as a direct punishment from God, and absolutely incurable, except divine by the same divine power that sent it. God alone could cure the leprosy. It judgment was so understood by Naaman the Syrian, who came from Damascus to Samaria to be cured by Elisha; and when "his flesh came again as the flesh of a little child," he said, "Behold, now I know that there is no God in all the earth but in Israel."[1] It is a curious fact that this hideous disease still cleaves to Damascus, the city of Naaman, for there is a mild kind there which is sometimes cured, or apparently cured, even at this day. I have met with cases, however, where the cure is only temporary, and perhaps it is so in every instance.

There is nothing in the entire range of human phenomena which illustrates so impressively the divine power of the Redeemer, and the nature and extent of his work of mercy on man's behalf, as this leprosy. There The disare many most striking analogies between it and that more deadly leprosy ease. of sin which has involved our whole race in one common ruin. It is feared as contagious; it is certainly and inevitably hereditary; it is loathsome and polluting; its victim is shunned by all as unclean; it is most deceitful in its action. New-born children of leprous parents are often as pretty and as healthy in appearance as any, but by-and-by its presence and working become visible in some of the signs described in the 13th chapter of Leviticus. The "scab" comes on by degrees in different parts of the body; the hair falls from the head and eyebrows; the nails loosen, decay, and drop off; joint after joint of the fingers and toes shrink up, and slowly fall away. The gums are absorbed, and the teeth disappear. The nose, the eyes, the tongue, and

---

[1] 2 Kings v. 14, 15.

PART
IV.

the palate are slowly consumed, and, finally, the wretched victim sinks into the earth and disappears, while medicine has no power to stay the ravages of this fell disease, or even to mitigate sensibly its tortures.

The type.

Who can fail to find in all this a most affecting type of man's moral leprosy ? Like it, this too is hereditary, with an awfully infallible certainty. As surely as we have inherited it from our fathers do we transmit it to our children. None escape. The infant so lively, with its cherub smile and innocent prattle, has imbibed the fatal poison. There are those, I know, who, as they gaze on the soft, clear heaven of infancy's laughing eye, reject with horror the thought that even here "the leprosy lies deep within." So any one might think and say who looked upon a beautiful babe in the arms of its leprous mother, in that little community near Zion's Gate. But, alas ! give but time enough, and the physical malady manifests its presence, and does its work of death. And so in the antitype. If left unchecked by power divine, the leprosy of sin will eat into the very texture of the soul, and consume everything lovely and pure in human character, until the smiling babe become a Nero, a Cæsar Borgia, a bloody Robespierre, or the traitor Iscariot. These were all once smiling babes.

The cure.

Again : leprosy of the body none but God can cure, as is implied in the strong protestation of the king of Israel when Naaman came to him : " *Am I God, to kill and make alive,* that this man doth send unto me to recover a man of his leprosy ?" So, also, there is only one Physician in the universe who can cleanse the soul from the leprosy of sin. Again : medicines of man's device are of no avail, but with Him none are needed. He said to the ten who stood afar off, and lifted up their voices and cried, " Jesus, master, have mercy on us !" " Go show yourselves to the priests ;" and as they went they were cleansed. And with the same divine power he says to many a moral leper, " Go in peace, thy sins be forgiven thee ;" and it happens unto them according to their faith. To my mind there is no conceivable manifestation of divine power more triumphantly confirmatory of Christ's divinity than the cleansing of a leper with a word. When looking at these handless, eyeless, tongueless wrecks of humanity, the unbelieving question starts unbidden, Is it possible that they can be restored ? Yes, it is more than possible. It has been accomplished again and again by the mere volition of Him who spake and it was done. And He who can cleanse the leper can raise the dead, and can also forgive sins and save the soul. I ask no other evidence of the fact.

Pools and
fountains.

I devoted this day to the pools and fountains of Jerusalem. The first one examined was that of Hezekiah, within the city, and just south of the great Greek convent. It is nearly two hundred and fifty feet long, and one hundred and fifty wide,—an immense reservoir, capable of holding water sufficient

Pool of
Hezekiah.

for half the city. My guide called it Birket Hammam, and said that the water was used chiefly for baths. From a terrace near the north-west corner there is a beautiful view of the city, the domes of the Holy Sepulchre, the Mosque of Omar, and of the Church of the Ascension on the top of Olivet.

After looking at this as much as its importance merits, I went out at the CHAPTER Jaffa Gate, and to the Upper Gihon, as I choose to call it, though its name is XLIII. Birket Mammilla among the Arabs. The water is brought from it by a small aqueduct into the city, and supplies the pool of Hezekiah.

This Upper Gihon is about one hundred and fifty rods west of the city, near Upper the head of the shallow valley, and is about three hundred feet long, two Gihon. hundred wide, and twenty deep. From its situation and appearance, it may be of any age which our peculiar theories of the topography of the city demand. There is now no water in it.

The Lower Pool—Birket es Sultan—is in the same valley, south of the Jaffa Lower Gate. It is about six hundred feet long, two hundred and fifty broad, and Gihon. forty deep,—a cistern of prodigious capacity. The aqueduct from the Pools of Solomon passed along west of it, round the north end, then down the east side, and so round Zion to the Temple. At some former time a pipe led the water from the aqueduct to an artificial fountain on the top of the south wall of the pool, where it emptied into troughs made of old sarcophagi. From this pool the valley of Hinnom descends rapidly eastward to Beer 'Ayub—Well of Job, (or of Nehemiah)—below the junction of Hinnom and Jehoshaphat.

I also examined with much interest the Pool of Siloam and the Fountain of the Virgin, and looked into the tunnel which connects them ; but my antiquarian zeal would require to be largely stimulated before I could repeat the exploit of Dr. Robinson and Dr. Smith.

POOL OF SILOAM.

There are several other pools which I merely looked at in passing round the city; but as the identity of all of them with pools mentioned in the Bible is controverted, I could not manage to get up any very great amount of enthusiasm in regard to them. That of Siloam seems to be about fifty Pool of feet long, twenty deep, and as many in width, though the sides are so Siloam. broken down that it is not easy to take correct measurements. It lies

PART
IV.

in the mouth of the Tyropean, and the water runs from it, under a rock precipice, across the road to some gardens in the valley of Jehoshaphat. It is a small rill which is soon exhausted among beds of radishes and cucumbers.

Fountain
of the Vir-
gin.

The Fountain of the Virgin is about four hundred paces up the valley from Siloam, and I descended to it by twenty-seven steps. I made no new discoveries, however, and have nothing to add to the elaborate discussions in regard to it and to all the other pools and fountains of the city which I have been reading in Robinson and Williams. I looked in upon the vast chasm or fosse on the north side of the Temple area, which I hear called Birket Israîl, and see on the maps written Bethesda. There is a considerable pool also outside St. Stephen's Gate, which my guide called Birket sitti Myriam. By this time I was thoroughly tired, and returned home to rest, and to enjoy this delightful view of the Holy City.

Water
supply of
Jerusa-
lem

I fully sympathize with your lack of interest, but still the questions about the waters of Jerusalem are of considerable importance. The main dependence for a constant and convenient supply is, and always has been, I suppose, the domestic cisterns. Every house has one or more; so has every church, mosque, convent, castle, and bath. Many of these are well kept, and the water is cool, sweet, and free from worms. The house I first rented in Jerusalem had three cisterns; that of Mr. Lanneau, my missionary associate, had four, and two of his were very large.

Antiquity
of cisterns.

No fact in relation to this country is better attested than the extreme antiquity of cisterns, and nothing about old sites has so much surprised me as the immense number of them. Often, where every trace of buildings has disappeared, the whole site is perforated with these under-ground reservoirs. Neither Beer 'Ayub, nor the Fountain of Mary, nor any of these vast pools, nor the aqueduct from beyond Bethlehem, would be much needed except for the Temple service, and during the grand convocation of the tribes in their annual festivals. Jerusalem was so abundantly supplied with water that no inconvenience from this source was experienced even during the many and long sieges which the city sustained. The people perished from famine, not from thirst. It is surprising, and not a little perplexing to a visitor who is obliged to carry a "bottle" of water with him in his excursions round the environs, to learn that there was once such an abundance of water *outside*, that

Fountains.

king Hezekiah had to summon all the strength of Israel to aid in stopping the *fountains:* "So there was gathered much people together, who stopped all the fountains, and *the brook that ran* [or overflowed] *through the midst of the land,* saying, Why should the kings of Assyria come, and find much water ?" [1] After suffering from intolerable thirst in many rambles around the Holy City, I read with wonder of "much water!" "many fountains!" "a brook overflowing through the midst!" Strange expressions these when applied to this topography. Hezekiah and his "much people" stopped them up so effectu-

---

[1] 2 Chron. xxxii. 3, 4.

ally that they could never be found again, even by the Jews themselves.
This will not appear extravagant if we take into account the calamities by
which Jerusalem was utterly overthrown, and lay in ruins for seventy years ;
and also that, when the remnant returned from distant Babylon few and
feeble, they were in no condition to search for these fountains, and, in fact,
had no particular need of them.

In regard to these pools, whether immediately around the city or those
beyond Bethlehem, there is no difficulty in assigning to them any age which
history requires. Cisterns that can sustain a thousand years of comparative
neglect would last many thousand when in use and properly repaired. So
far, therefore, as the works themselves are concerned, they may date back to
the age of Solomon ; and, if speculation and inference were of avail in such
questions, we might suppose that, when Solomon was building his magnificent
Temple, and adapting his capital to be the centre of the whole Hebrew race,
he would not fail to make ample provision for the indispensable article of
water. He therefore may have constructed the pools beyond Bethlehem, and
built the aqueduct which brought a supply to the Temple sufficient for the
ablutions and other services of that great sanctuary. And as the prodigious
assemblies at the national feasts would require a large quantity of water in
different quarters, and of easy access, he made those pools on the west, and
others of smaller size distributed in and about the city, for the greater convenience of the pilgrims. We find in these conditions an adequate emergency
and a suitable occasion for the construction of these reservoirs,—a great want,
a king wealthy, and wise, and given to building, and a time of peace. It
must be remembered that we are speaking of works quite unique and extraordinary. No other city in this part of the world had anything like these
cisterns, and the supposition that most of them were made by Solomon and his
immediate successors is not extravagant. The only serious objection that occurs
to me is found in the passage already quoted. If there were " many fountains, a brook running through the midst of the land, and *much* water," there
would have been no occasion, up to the time of Hezekiah, to resort to such
expensive contrivances as these pools. After these fountains had been
stopped up, however, and the supply outside the city thus cut off, artificial
means would become indispensable. It is quite possible, therefore, that most
of these " pools" have been constructed since the return from Babylon. And
if those beyond Bethlehem were made by Solomon, and are referred to in
Ecclesiastes,[1] yet the *aqueduct* connecting them with the Temple may have
been built after the "captivity." Solomon himself intimates that his pools
were not designed to supply Jerusalem, but to irrigate his gardens and
forests.

These pools about Jerusalem are now empty, and as thirsty as the disappointed pilgrim who resorts to them. How do you account for this?

[1] Eccles. ii. 6.

PART IV.

Pools now empty.

Certainly not by the assumption that less water falls now than formerly. These mountains are deluged with rains in winter such as we rarely experience in America, and yet I never saw water running into any of the pools, or down any of those valleys, except just while it was literally pouring from the clouds. On occasions of this kind muddy streams rush down Jehoshaphat and Hinnom with great violence. The water, however, quickly sinks beneath the accumulated rubbish, and finds its way to the Dead Sea without re-appearing on the surface. No doubt a far greater quantity of winter rains was made to flow into the cisterns anciently than now, and they may have been filled in part by streams from living fountains which are now lost. Traditions of such streams are still kept alive among the inhabitants, and they seem to be countenanced by the passage from Second Chronicles. The main cause of the present deficiency is, that the cisterns are not now kept in good condition. It would be quite possible to fill them all during winter if they were made water-tight, and suitable care were taken to conduct into them the rain-water from the rocks and fields above. This whole subject is one of much interest, but there must be more exploration and excavation than has hitherto been possible before all the problems connected with it can be solved. What did you make out of Beer 'Ayub?

I found it in the bed of the Kidron, just below the junction of Hinnom and Jehoshaphat, and five hundred and fifty feet below the top of Zion by the aneroid. Do you suppose that this is the En-rogel of Joshua?[1]

Beer 'Ayub— En-rogel?

There is no reason to doubt it. In the 18th chapter and 16th verse, where the south line of Benjamin's lot is drawn, the situation of En-rogel at the bottom of Hinnom, south of Jebusi, or Jerusalem, is clearly indicated. It was near this well that Jonathan and Ahimaaz lay hid during the rebellion of Absalom, in order to collect and send news to David ; and afterward Adonijah slew sheep, and oxen, and fat cattle by En-rogel, when he conspired to seize the kingdom. The celebrated Joab was with him, and by this act forfeited his life; and if the well was called Beer Yoab instead of 'Ayub, as some have maintained, we might find the origin of the name possibly in this last act of Joab's political career. As matters stand, we cannot discover why, or on what occasion, the name En-rogel was changed into 'Ayub, or into Nehemiah, or into that of the Well of Fire—by all which titles it has been distinguished. The patriarch Job could have no connection with it, and that Nehemiah recovered the sacred fire from this well, after his return from Babylon, is a mere fable. In itself it is a singular work of ancient enterprise. The shaft, sunk through the solid rock in the bed of the Kidron, is one hundred and twenty-five feet deep. The idea of digging such a well at that precise spot may have been suggested by the fact, that, after very great rains, water sometimes rises nearly to the top, and then flows out into the valley below, a strong brook capable of driving a mill. This, however, soon ceases, and the water in the

Its history.

----

[1] Josh. xv. 7.

well subsides to less than half its depth. From that point a stream seems to CHAPTER XLIII. run constantly across it, and pass down the valley under the rock. This appearance of the water below may have first suggested the plan of sinking a shaft higher up and near the city wall, that there might be access to it in times of invasion. The water is pure and entirely sweet,—quite different from that of Siloam, which proves that there is no connection between them. I have seen the water gushing out like a mill-stream, some fifteen rods south of the well; and then the whole valley was alive with people bathing in it, and indulging in every species of hilarity. Thus it was in the time of David, and most likely the quantity and duration of the flow were much greater then than now. "The stone of Zoheleth, which is by En-rogel," was therefore a Stone of Zoheleth. most suitable spot for Adonijah at which to slay sheep, and oxen, and fat cattle, make a great feast, and complete his conspiracy; for the people were accustomed to assemble there on festive occasions, and multitudes might find themselves entrapped into the rebellion ere they were aware of it. In this connection, it may be remarked that Gihon, *down* to which Solomon was immediately conducted, by order of David, to be anointed king, was probably on the other side of the city. David would certainly not send him into the midst of the conspiracy. It is evident, however, from 1 Kings i. 40–42, that Gihon was so near En-rogel that Adonijah and his company could hear the rejoicing of the people that were with Solomon; and this incidentally confirms the correctness of the sites of Gihon as now received, on the west and northwest of the city.

The whole vicinity of En-rogel, and of Siloam too, including the slopes of Poetry—Milton. Zion and Ophel, are now the very last resort for any muse, either heavenly or earthly. Milton's famous invocation,—

> "If Sion's hill
> Delight thee more, and Siloa's brook, that flowed
> Fast by the oracle of God, I thence
> Invoke thine aid to my adventurous song,"—

would never have been written if the poet had encountered there the sights and scents which disgusted me this morning.

It will do very well for a poet "smit with the love of sacred song" to accommodate Zion with—

> "Flowery brooks beneath,
> That wash thy hallowed feet, and warbling flow."

Milton, however, never visited this country, and withal was blind; but I have Disenchantment. seen the Kidron in ancient maps expanded into a broad river, and enlivened with boats and *lateen* sails! Where the geographer fables, the poet surely may dream.

Mr. Williams amuses himself with the contradictory accounts of historians and travellers in regard to the taste of this water. Josephus says it is sweet, Taste of the water one calls it bitter, another tasteless. Dr. Robinson makes it sweetish and

PART
IV.

slightly brackish ; and he is right, according to my experience. I never could endure it—always thinking that it smelled and tasted of the bath. I have little doubt but that it is mingled, to say the least, with water used for Moslem ablutions and bathings in the great mosques of Omar and El Aksa.

You think, then, that there is a connection between this fountain and the wells, subterranean cisterns, etc., beneath the southern part of the Temple area ?

I do not doubt it, and have always suspected that the irregular fluctuations in the quantity of water are occasioned, in part at least, by the draining into the channel at different times the water from these hidden reservoirs. I suppose it was so in ancient days, and this well-known phenomenon may have suggested to Ezekiel that striking allegory of the mystic river whose small beginnings he saw flowing down from under the altar of God.[1] The machinery of some of Ezekiel's visions was strange and complex—

Ezekiel's
river.

"Wheels within wheels, with living creatures wedded."

Others, again, were remarkably simple, and, withal, rich in beautiful imagery and suggestive drapery. Of this kind is this river, which the man with the line in his hand showed to the prophet. There were things very peculiar and significant in its origin, accidents, and attributes.

Its source.—" Behold, waters issued out from under the threshold of the house, came down from under, at the south side of the *altar*."

Its course.—It flowed toward the east country, into the desert, and entered the east, that is, the Dead Sea. There is no other in that direction ; and water issuing from the " south side of the altar " must, by a topographical necessity, flow down the valley of Jehoshaphat, along the bed of the Kidron eastward into the desert, and thus into the Dead Sea by Wady en Nâr.

Its rapid increase.—A mere rill at the beginning, it was to the ancles at the end of the first thousand cubits, to the knees at the second, the loins at the third, and at the fourth thousand " it was a river to swim in, that could not be passed over."

Imagery
of Eze-
kiel's
vision.

Its effects.—" Everything shall live whither the river cometh." On either bank grow " all manner of trees for meat, whose leaf shall not fade, neither shall the fruit thereof be consumed." What a contrast to the present banks of the Kidron—a horrid wilderness, blasted by the curse of God, with nothing to relieve its frightful desolation ! But where this river from under the sanctuary comes, the desert blossoms, the banks are shaded with trees, and vocal with music of birds. And more wonderful still,—the river "being brought forth into the sea, the waters thereof shall be healed." Now, this Sea of Sodom is so intolerably bitter, that although the Jordan, the Arnon, and many other streams have been pouring into it their vast contributions of sweet water for thousands of years, it continues as nauseous and deadly as ever. Nothing

[1] Ezek. xlvii. 1-12.

lives in it ; neither fish, nor reptiles, nor even animalculæ can abide its desperate malignity. But these waters from the sanctuary heal it. When they come thither the shores are robed in green, its bosom teems with all manner of fish, and fishermen stand thick on every rock "from En-gedi even unto En-eglaim. They shall be to spread forth nets, for the fish shall be as those of the great sea, exceeding many."

This beautiful allegory was doubtless not thrown into the Bible merely to amuse us. What is your explanation ?

There are good men, and learned in the Scriptures, who interpret it literally, and maintain that a mighty physical miracle is here predicted. But we find in it only a spiritual allegory, which foreshadows miracles of mercy in store for the whole world far more stupendous. That God will cause such a river of actual water to flow down from Mount Moriah, to gladden the Desert of Judea and heal the Sea of Sodom, I do not believe. There is another desert, however, which he will surely heal—the desert of sin, the sea of spiritual death. Explanation of the allegory.

I discover in this richest of allegories a most comprehensive and delightful exhibition of the scheme of redemption, from its beginning to its final and glorious consummation. There is good gospel, and much sound and even profound theology in it. Every incident is suggestive, every allusion instructs. The waters flowed out from under the *altar*—intimating, not darkly, that the stream of divine mercy, the river of life, has its source in *sacrifice* and *death*. Until justice is satisfied by the atoning sacrifice of the Lamb of God *upon the altar*, the waters of life cannot flow forth from beneath it. The altar.

There can be little doubt but that the prophet borrowed the drapery of his allegory from the physical features of the Temple area, and that of the country east and south-east of it. Though the waters first appeared issuing *from under the altar*, yet we need not suppose that the fountain-head was there, but further back, under the Holy of Holies, beneath the ark and mercy-seat, where abode the Shekinah of God's presence, intimating that the true fountain-head of the river of life is in the heart of infinite love, but, on its way out and down to ruined man, it must pass *under the altar of divine justice*. There is, therefore, no other place in the universe whence these emblematic waters could flow forth so appropriately as under the altar.

Again, this river was small at first, but increased rapidly as it flowed onward ; and thus it has been with the river of life. It was a mere rill from Adam to Noah—the waters were to the ancles. From the Deluge to Moses it grew broader and deeper—the waters were unto the knees, and patriarchs with their flocks reposed in green pastures along the verdant banks. From Moses the lawgiver to David the sweet singer, it rolled onward, ever gathering breadth and power, and its shady groves became vocal with psalms and hymns to the God of salvation. And thus it continued to swell, and expand, and deepen, by the addition of many a rill of prophecy and promise, until He who is the true Fountain came, sending forth a mighty river of unfathomable depth, which cannot be passed over—a river to swim in ; all the world may bathe in it and The river

PART
IV.

be cleansed—may drink of it and thirst no more; and ever since the Advent it has rolled onward further and further into the desert; and thus it will continue until its most distant borders shall blossom, and the great dead sea of sin shall be swallowed up of life. The divine allegory foreshadows the millennium in its amplest acceptation.

The transformation.

From the physical topography of the allegory, the waters could only descend into the vale of the Kidron, and run eastward toward the Dead Sea, a region of hopeless desolation. What it was twenty-five centuries ago to the eye of the prophet, it is now to the weary traveller. But when Ezekiel's river came thither, there was life—luxurious, joyous life. Delightful transformation! Now there is another desert whose sterility is more stern and stubborn than this of Judea, and nothing lives in all that dreary land until it is healed and vivified by the waters which issue out of the sanctuary of God. But wherever these salutary streams come, there spring up the plants of righteousness blooming like Eden, and loaded with the fruits of Paradise. A thousand such deserts have already blossomed, and other thousands are beginning to bloom; and, though these deserts are wide as the world, this river, by its very constitution, is adapted to reach and heal them all. The natural streams from the mountains of Arabia and Africa dwindle and fade away in her thirsty Saharas, but this grows broader and deeper the further it penetrates the desert. Thank God, it will reach earth's remotest wilderness, and enter at length and vivify the great sea of death itself.

The Dead Sea.

This sea figures largely in the allegory, and well it may. The whole world affords no other type of human apostasy so appropriate, so significant. Think of it. There it lies in its sulphureous sepulchre, thirteen hundred feet below the ocean, steaming up like a huge caldron of smouldering bitumen and brimstone. Neither rain from heaven, nor mountain torrents, nor Jordan's flood, nor all combined, can change its character of utter death. Fit symbol of that great dead sea of depravity and corruption which nothing human can heal! Science and art, education and philosophy, legislation and superstition, may pour their combined contributions into it for ever, but they cannot heal—cannot even dilute its malignity; but the *supernatural* streams of divine mercy from the sanctuary can and will. Let the world-wide desert rejoice. These waters are rolling onward, will surely reach its utmost borders, and clothe its sterile wastes with beauty and life.

Where are those miry and marshy places, mentioned in the 11th verse, which could not be healed, and what may they signify?

Salt marshes.

They are along the southern shore of the lake, at the base of Usdum and the thick strata of rock salt which there bound the plain. It is interesting to notice how accurate the prophet is in all his topographical allusions. The existence of these salt marshes has but recently been revealed to the world by modern exploration, but Ezekiel was acquainted with them twenty-three centuries ago. If you wish to attach significance to every item in the drapery of the allegory, these strata of rock salt, with their incurable marshes, may represent that fundamental corruption of man's nature which will remain even in CHAPTER millennial peace and purity. The waters from the sanctuary do not heal these XLIII. marshes, *because they do not come to them.* Wherever the waters come there is life, but they were never intended to reach up to these rock-salt sources of bitterness and death. And so in the spiritual antitype ; the river of divine mercy is not designed to reach to and remove the corrupt nature of man. In the full splendour of millennial glory the *fountains* will still be impure, and the ever-descending streams would quickly flood the world with death, did not these waters from the sanctuary continue evermore to flow over and renew them to spiritual life. With the prophet's marvellous telescope I delight to look down the verdant vista of this mystic river, and out upon our world's glorious future. No other glass discloses such enchanting prospects. Nor are they mere "dissolving views," fair but fading. More than meets the eye lies deep concealed, and brighter days than fancy paints shall surely dawn on earth's long and dismal night.

In our ride to-day we passed up Wady Gihon, west of the city, crossed over Convent a rocky ridge, and descended into a valley which comes down south from the of the Cross. Jaffa road, our first object being a visit to the Convent of the Cross. This is a large establishment, pleasantly situated, and with surroundings which suggest the idea that its finances must be in a flourishing condition. The monks were very polite, and one of them showed us the place where the tree grew from which the cross was made ! Whether true or not, let others discuss ; but one thing is certain,—this great convent, with all its revenues, has grown up out of that hole in the ground in which the tree is said to have stood.

The good Padre Francesco expresses doubts about this tradition, perhaps because the place is in the hands of the Greeks, for whom he cherishes the utmost abhorrence. He, however, says that if the belief in the fact serves to awaken devout thoughts, it is not to be condemned. Maundrell sums up its title to our reverence somewhat after the manner of the famous house that Jack built : " It is because here is the earth that nourished the root, that bore the tree, that yielded the timber, that made the cross ;" and he adds, rather profanely, " Under the high altar you are shown a hole in the ground where the stump of the tree stood, and it meets with not a few visitants, so much verier stocks than itself as to fall down and worship it."

Leaving this convent, which the natives call El Mûsŭllabeh, we went on 'Ain nearly an hour further to 'Ain Karîm, the village of Zacharias and Elisabeth, Karîm. and of course the birth-place of John the Baptist and Forerunner. In the convent they point out the precise spot where the babe was born. It is beneath the chapel, which is a handsome and neatly-arranged affair of its kind. Our padre labours hard to explain how it could possibly come to pass that the Baptist should be *born in two places*—beneath the rich altar within the convent, and in the grotto at least a quarter of a mile from it, where a convent was also erected, over the house of Elisabeth. It is not very important how we dispose of this difficulty. Elisabeth may possibly have divided the time of

PART
IV.

'Ain Ka-
rîm—
Fountain
of the Vir-
gin.

that important occasion between the two, in order to multiply the number of sacred places, and thereby increase the piety of future generations!

Did you see the Fountain of the Virgin, for which name our padre is again puzzled to find a plausible reason? He thinks it scarcely probable that the Virgin would have been allowed to go to such a distance from Elisabeth's house to fetch water. She might have occasionally frequented it, however, and from that circumstance her name came to be applied to it; but it required a very resolute and robust faith to tear out by the roots the sycamore-trees of scepticism which kept springing up in this gentleman's heart during his excursion to "St. John's in the mountains." He toiled up the rocky hills south-west of 'Ain Karîm for more than an hour, to visit the grotto where John dwelt in the wilderness, and practised those austerities which we read of in the third chapter of Matthew. The whole thing, wilderness, grotto, and all, did not correspond to his preconceived notions; but these, as in duty bound, he magnanimously surrendered to grey-haired Tradition. Did you go out into that desert?

Birth-
place of
John.

Time did not permit. My programme included Kuriet el 'Aineb, and I therefore made the stay at the Convent of St. John very brief. But, before leaving it, let me ask seriously whether there is any good reason to doubt or to disturb this ancient tradition as to the main fact. Why may not this be the village of Zacharias, to which Mary came in haste to salute her cousin Elisabeth?

I know no decisive reason against it. 'Ain Karîm is certainly in the hill-country of Judea,[1] though not perhaps exactly in that part of it in which, a priori, we should expect to find Elisabeth. When I visited it many years ago, I had no doubt as to the tradition, nor is there any obvious reason why the home of the Baptist should be lost, any more than the site of Bethlehem, or Bethany, or Nazareth, or Cana. The village was probably small, as no name is mentioned; perhaps it was not a village at all. But John became very celebrated in his day. Our Lord himself testifies of him that there had not risen a greater prophet than he. It is, however, not likely that he was born in either of the grottoes which tradition selected as suitable sites for convents, but in some humble habitation which has long since disappeared. Thither came Mary with that salutation which made the unborn Baptist leap for joy; and Elisabeth herself, filled with the Holy Ghost, spoke out with a loud voice, and said, "Blessed art thou among women, and blessed is the fruit of thy womb." And Mary responded in that noble magnificat, "My soul doth magnify the Lord, and my spirit hath rejoiced in God my Saviour."[2] Who can doubt but that these two inspired cousins—the highly favoured among women—spent the three subsequent months of Mary's visit in holy and elevated devotion and communion of spirit, speaking of the instant performance of those wonderful things which had been told them from the Lord. Truly

[1] Luke i. 39.   [2] Luke i. 46.

these sacred associations must ever clothe with richest interest the vale and CHAPTER
hill sides of 'Ain Karîm.   XLIII.

Do you suppose that the ordinary food of the Baptist was really locusts and
wild honey ?[1]

After he had retired to the wilderness to seek preparation for his divine mis- John's
sion, no doubt it was.   Nor is there any great difficulty about it, for we know food.
from Leviticus xi. 22 that it was lawful for Jews to eat this insect.   I do not
suppose, however, that the desert was that rocky hill south-west of 'Ain
Karîm, covered with corn, vines, and olive-trees, as Maundrell says.   John
probably retired much further from the busy haunts of men, into those barren
parts which produce none of these luxuries, and where the wandering Arabs
to this day feed on locusts.   The monks during the dark ages perhaps thought
this incredible, and therefore planted *locust-trees* near John's grotto in the
desert, as Maundrell informs us.   The kharûb is also found in the same region,
and the name of "St. John's bread" has been given to the gelatinous pods of
this tree by pious pilgrims, anxious to rescue the Baptist from the imputation of
feeding on locusts.

There are two or three other places of interest in this region, at least to pil- Sites.
grims and antiquarians.   The *well* (?) at which Philip baptized the eunuch,
tradition has located in the wady south of 'Ain Karîm.   This is doubtless a
mistake.   Again, Mr. Williams believes that he has found the ancient Bether in
Wady Beitîr, which comes down from the south, and unites with Wady el Werd.
The position will agree well enough with all that is known about the situation
of this last stronghold of the Jews.   Eusebius says that it was an impregnable
fortress not far from Jerusalem.

There the rebel Messiah Barchochobas, in the reign of Hadrian, held out Bether.
for a long time against the furious assaults of the Roman army.   The place,
however, was at last stormed, and the slaughter was so dreadful that the brook
below it ran blood all the way to the sea, according to the tradition of the
rabbis.   No calamity, except the destruction of Jerusalem by Titus, was so
fatal to the Jews as the sacking of Bether.   Eighty thousand of this devoted
race fell by the sword in battle, besides a vast number who perished by famine,
pestilence, and other calamities.

The only place in the canonical books where the mountains of Bether are
mentioned is in the Song of Songs : "Turn, my beloved, and be thou like a
roe or a young hart upon the mountains of Bether."[2]   The allusion is natural
enough, for I myself have seen beautiful roes leaping upon those mountains,
skipping upon the hills.[3]

They are certainly better adapted to them than to horses, as I can testify.
That whole region is rough and rocky in the extreme, especially along the path
from 'Ain Karîm to Soba, and thence to Kuriet el 'Aineb.   Soba is in ruins, Soba.
destroyed by order of Ibrahim Pasha in 1834 ; but its position is naturally very

[1] Matt. iii. 4.   [2] Song ii. 17.   [3] Song ii. 8.

PART
IV.

strong, and the whole conical summit was surrounded by a wall. It was long the stronghold of the robber family of Abu Goosh, as I was informed by my companions.

When I first came to Jerusalem it was occupied by one of that famous family, to the no small terror of the pilgrims. You are aware that erring tradition located Modin, the city and cemetery of the Maccabean family, at Soba; but this cannot be correct, as that place was at or near the foot of the mountains, not far from Lydd. Dr. Robinson identifies Soba with Ramathaim-zophim, and his elaborate argument makes the idea at least plausible. The same remark may be made in regard to Kirjath-jearim, or Kirjath-baal, or Baalah, for all these names belong to the same place. Kuriet el 'Aineb may represent that city, but the evidence is not perfectly conclusive. The frequent mention of this point in defining the borders of Judah and Benjamin render it certain that it must have been in this neighbourhood. Monkish, or rather ecclesiastical tradition, makes it the birth-place of Jeremiah, and many writers only mention it under this name; and it is certainly possible that the prophet may have resided there, though he was born at Anathoth. Convents and churches were early erected at this St. Jeremiah, and I suppose the traces of them are to be found on the hills north and north-west of the present village, where are many tombs in the live rock. The only ancient edifice in it is the ruined church, which strikes one with surprise. Its age and origin are uncertain, though it was probably built by the Crusaders.

If this was Kirjath-jearim, the ark must have had a rough road from there to the city. The house of Abinadab appears not to have been in Yarim itself, but on the hill north-west of it. In 1 Samuel vii. 1, our version has it *hill*, but in 2 Samuel vi. 3, 4, the Hebrew word Gibeah is retained, as if it were a separate village. It is not likely, however, that there was a town adjoining Yarim, with the identical name of another place not far off to the north, and I suppose that the house of Abinadab, where the ark abode, was on the *hill* above, not at a village called Gibeah. Such an arrangement would be the most convenient and satisfactory to the congregation which assembled from all parts to worship before the ark. The hill was probably called *Gibeah*, by way of eminence, after the ark had been brought there, and thus our translators may have indicated the exact truth by translating it *hill* when it is first mentioned, and *Gibeah* twenty years afterwards, when David and all Israel went to remove the ark to Jerusalem. There is no obvious reason at present why it should be called *Yarim—rocky forests*. There are *waars*, however, on every side almost, and some very impracticable ones north and south-west of it.

The first long descent from the village toward Jerusalem is not steep, and a good road could easily be made. Indeed, the traces of an ancient way are visible in several places, and an arch belonging to a Roman bridge below Deir Yesîn is still quite perfect. The names Kŭstŭl and Kulonia along this line suggest the idea of Roman colonies, and somewhere in their neighbourhood, I

Modin.

Soba.

Kuriet el 'Aineb.

Kirjath-jearim.

Roman traces.

have little doubt, we are to find or fix the locality of that Emmaus to which the two disciples were proceeding when the Lord joined them.[1] Kuriet el 'Aineb itself would be the proper distance from Jerusalem, and being on the road to Jaffa, and on the dividing ridge between the plain and the mountains, the Roman emperor might have deemed it an advantageous post for a colony made up of his disbanded soldiers, who could keep in check the surrounding country. Certain it is that in these later ages the occupants of this place have controlled the whole adjacent region, and for many a generation exercised their lawless tyranny upon helpless pilgrims.

It took just three hours' moderate riding from Kuriet el 'Aineb to Jerusalem: first, a long descent into Wady Hanîna, which passes between it and Soba; then a similar ascent, succeeded by a very steep pass, and a very slippery path down to Kulonia. At this place are some heavy foundations of church, convent, or castle, by the road side, which may be of almost any age; and also gardens of fruit-trees, irrigated by a fountain of excellent water. Kulonia is on a hill north of the road, and appears in a fair way to become a ruin itself before long. The path then winds up a valley, and stretches over a dreary waste of bare rocks until within a mile of the city, when the view opens upon its naked ramparts and the mysterious regions toward the Dead Sea. *Road to Jerusalem.*

These rides about Jerusalem reveal to the weary traveller the extreme ruggedness of this territory. It could never have been a corn-growing region, but is admirably adapted to the olive, the fig, the vine, the pomegranate, and other fruit-trees. Such a country, in a high state of cultivation, is incomparably more beautiful and picturesque than those tame, flat plains where grain is the crop. The neighbourhood of Jerusalem, when thus clothed with orchards and vineyards, must have shown one of the most agreeable panoramas the eye of man ever beheld. Nor are we to imagine, that because it did not grow wheat, its productions were of little importance. The olive is a more valuable crop, acre for acre, than any kind of grain, more so even than silk. Josephus, therefore, was not mistaken when he represented the country about Jerusalem as more fruitful than other parts of Palestine. Restore to it the proper cultivation, and it would again hold the same relative superiority. *Ruggedness of the district.* *Its fertility.*

In what sense can the mountains about Jerusalem be regarded as her defence, according to the allusion in the psalm: "As the mountains are round about Jerusalem, so the Lord is round about his people?"[2]

Certainly not by their height. None of the surrounding hills, not even Olivet, has any relative elevation above the north-western corner of the city itself. But Jerusalem is situated in the centre of a mountainous region, whose valleys have drawn around it in all directions a perfect net-work of deep ravines, the perpendicular walls of which constitute a very efficient system of defence. The *ravines* on three sides of the Holy City might be made a very important protection, and doubtless were, in the days of the Psalmist; but the

---

[1] Luke xxiv. 13.   [2] Ps. cxxv. 2.

mountains whose rugged ramparts and impracticable passes secured the tranquillity of Zion were at a distance.

NEBY SAMWIL—GIBEON.

This has been a very exciting and instructive excursion, including Neby Samwîl and the territory of the Gibeonites, who so cleverly outwitted Joshua and the elders, and negotiated a treaty of peace with them. I was forcibly reminded of one item in the sentence of condemnation pronounced upon them for their cunning deception—that they should be hewers of wood[1]—by long files of women and children carrying on their heads heavy bundles of wood. It seemed to be hard work, especially to the young girls.

The Gibeonites.

It is the severest kind of drudgery, and my compassion has often been enlisted in behalf of the poor women and children, who daily bring loads of wood to Jerusalem from these very mountains of the Gibeonites. To carry water, also, is very laborious and fatiguing. The fountains are far off, in deep wadies with steep banks, and a thousand times have I seen the feeble and the young staggering up long and weary ways with large jars of water on their heads. It is the work of slaves, and of the very poor, whose condition is still worse. Among the pathetic lamentations of Jeremiah there is nothing more affecting than this : "They took the young men to grind, and the children fell under the wood."[2] Grinding at the hand-mill is a low, menial work, assigned to *female slaves*, and therefore utterly humiliating to the young men of Israel. And the delicate children of Zion falling under loads of hard, rough wood, along the mountain paths ! Alas ! "for these things I weep : mine eye, mine eye runneth down with water, because the comforter that should relieve my soul is far from me ; my children are desolate, because the enemy prevailed."

Hewers of wood and drawers of water.

But to our excursion. Passing into Wady Beit Hanina, west of the Tombs of the Judges, by a very rocky path, we climbed the long mountain to Neby Samwîl, making this distance in little over two hours. The prospect from the neby is very extensive and grand. Dr. Robinson identifies it with Mizpeh, but an old tradition makes it the Ramah of Samuel, and hence its present name. I shall not attempt to decide, and my companions from Jerusalem are equally in doubt. No better place, certainly, could be selected for a mizpeh, or watch-tower, but then no place would be more naturally called *Ram*, or *Ramah*, or some other compound of that favourite title of high hills.

Neby Samwîl.

After looking at the prospect from the top of the mosque (once a Christian church), we descended northward into the deep valley which lies between Neby Samwîl and El Jîb,—the Gibeon of the Bible. This village is situated on an isolated and rocky hill of moderate elevation, with plains, valleys, and higher

El Jîb.

---

[1] Josh. iv. 21.　　　　　[2] Lam. v. 13.　　　　　[3] Lam. i. 16.

mountains all around it. Remains of ancient buildings, tombs, and quarries indicate a large and important city, though it is now a miserable hamlet, occupied by a few hundred sour and stupid Moslem peasants. We of course drank of the famous fountain, deep under the perpendicular rock in the vale to the south-east of the village.

Those old Gibeonites did indeed " work wilily" with Joshua. Nothing could be better calculated to deceive than their devices. I have often thought that their ambassadors, as described in the narrative, furnish one of the finest groups imaginable for a painter; with their old sacks on their poor asses; their wine-bottles of goat-skin, patched and shrivelled up in the sun, old, rent, and bound up; old shoes and clouted upon their feet; old garments, ragged and bedraggled, with bread dry and mouldy—the very picture of an over-travelled and wearied caravan from a great distance. It is impossible to transfer to paper the ludicrous appearance of such a company. No wonder that, having tasted their mouldy victuals, and looked upon their soiled and travel-worn costume, Joshua and the elders were deceived, especially as they did not wait to ask counsel at the mouth of the Lord.[1]

Devices of the Gibeonites.

This El Jîb was " a great city; as one of the royal cities, greater than Ai, and all the men thereof were mighty." Their treaty, therefore, with Israel very naturally struck terror into their neighbours, and hence that combination of kings against them which brought up Joshua in all haste to their relief. It must have been somewhere in those open plains east of Jîb that the great battle took place, and the memorable rout and flight of the Canaanitish host down Wady Yalo (Ajalon), when Joshua said, in the sight of Israel, " Sun, stand thou still upon Gibeon; and thou, Moon, in the valley of Ajalon,"[2]—an event fit to immortalize any site on earth !

Greatness of Gibeon.

Jîb is well supplied with water, not only by the fountain you mentioned, but in the wet season there is also a considerable pond in the plain below the village. It was probably on this account, in part at least, that the Tabernacle was established there for many years; and in part, I suppose, because the plains around Jîb afforded suitable camping-ground for the vast multitudes who came thither to keep the great feasts of the Lord.

The Tabernacle at Gibeon.

The existence of this little lake, I suppose, is referred to in Joshua xviii. 14, in drawing the north-west border of Benjamin from near Beth-horon to Kirjath-jearim. Thus it reads : " And the border was drawn from thence, and compassed the *corner of the sea southward,* from the hill that lieth before Beth-horon southward." It has always appeared to me impossible that the line should have made a grand sweep from Beth-horon, without an intervening point, clear down to the sea, and back again to Kirjath-jearim. But if we suppose that this little lake near El Jîb is the *yam,* or sea, in this passage, all difficulty vanishes. This explanation is confirmed, as I think, by two other passages. In Jeremiah xli. 12 we read, " Then they took all the men, and

Waters of Gibeon.

PART IV.

went to fight with Ishmael the son of Nethaniah, and found him by the *great waters* that are in Gibeon." And in 2 Sam. ii. 13 it is stated that "Joab the son of Zeruiah, and the servants of David, went out, and met together [with Abner's army] by the pool of Gibeon, and they sat down, the one on the one side of the pool, and the other on the other side of the pool." It is clear that this *pool*, which separated the two companies, must have been a pond or small lake. The Hebrew sometimes has that meaning, and the identical word in Arabic is now applied to Lakes Hûleh and Tiberias, and even to the Dead Sea. I suppose, therefore, that this was actually the *sea* at the corner of which the border of Benjamin passed, and thus a curious obscurity is cleared away from the face of our good old Bible.

Beit Ur.

From El Jîb the road to Beth-horon, now called Beit Ur, winds round the head of the great Wady Yalo, the Ajalon where the moon stood still. The village of Beit Ur occupies a conical hill just at the top of the ascent from Beth-horon the lower, which is one hour below it toward the north-west. Both these places abound in marks of antiquity, and were celebrated, particularly in the wars of the Maccabees. The ascent between them is very rocky, and along it were fought by those leaders of Israel some of their bloody battles with the great armies of the kings of Antioch.

Wady Sûleyman.

The profound Wady Sûleyman, which passes on the north of Gibeon, may have derived its name from the fact, that Solomon was in the habit of going to Gibeon to sacrifice before the Tabernacle, which was there until after he had completed the Temple. "That was the great high place: a thousand burnt-offerings did Solomon offer upon that altar."[1] There the Lord appeared unto him in a dream by night, and God said, "Ask what I shall give thee." His petition was for wisdom. And the speech pleased the Lord, that Solomon had asked this thing; and because he neither asked for long life, nor for riches, nor for the life of his enemies, therefore he gave him not only a wise and understanding heart, so that there was none like him, neither before nor after, but also added what he had not asked, both riches and honour. Alas! that such a glorious beginning should have ended in foul disgrace and apostasy! Solomon loved many strange women, and when he was old his wives turned away his heart after other gods, Moloch, the abomination of the children of Ammon, and Chemosh, the abomination of Moab,[2] whose temples he reared—

> "On that opprobrious hill
> Right against the temple of God—
> Audacious neighbourhood."

After lunching at the fountain of Gibeon, we struck over the country to the east, sometimes without any road, and always along most rocky paths, leaving Ramah on our left, and also Jîb'a, the ancient *Gibeah*, which we could see

Anathoth.

from different points, and descended to "poor Anathoth," the city of Jere-

---

[1] 1 Kings iii. 4.   [2] 1 Kings xi. 1-8.

CHAPTER
XLIII.

miah. There is no reason to question the identity, and I am always pleased to find certainty when I am groping about among these ancient ruins. The prospect east and south-east toward the Dead Sea and the Lower Jordan is one of the most dreary that my eye ever rested on, and again and again it reminded me of the author of "Lamentations," who gazed upon it with tearful eyes two thousand five hundred years ago. 'Anātā is a small, half-ruined hamlet, but was once much larger, and appears to have had a wall around it, a few fragments of which are still to be seen. It took us just one hour to reach our cottage from the hill above the village. Several wadies along the path run down to the valley of the Jordan, and the road sometimes keeps round the head of them, and at others passes through them. I did not note their names.

All those places which you passed without visiting are mentioned in the Sennacherib's approach. 10th chapter of Isaiah, with several others to the north of them. The prophet is describing the approach of Sennacherib's army: "He is come to Aiath, he has passed to Migron; at Michmash he has laid up his carriages: they have gone over the passage:' they have taken up their lodging at Geba; Ramah is afraid; Gibeah of Saul is fled. Lift up thy voice, O daughter of Gallim; cause it to be heard unto Laish, O poor Anathoth."[1] Thus one can follow, step by step, the invading host of Assyria, until they reach "poor Anathoth," and shake their hand against the mount of the daughter of Zion, from Nob, which was at the north end of this Mount of Olives.

No neighbourhood in Palestine is more crowded with interesting Biblical Biblical sites. associations than this over which you have passed so hastily. I should like to spend a day wandering over the rough hills between Er Ram, Gibeah, Michmash, Rimmon, Bethel, and Beer. Perhaps we might stumble upon the site of Ai, which Joshua's curse has hidden from all the world; for he "burned Ai, and made it a heap for ever, even a desolation unto this day."[2] It must be somewhere between Michmash and Rimmon, a region greatly cut up with gorges and ravines; and as I passed from Beit-în toward Michmash, I could easily understand how Joshua's ambush of five thousand men could lie hid between Ai and Bethel.[3] Some of our Jerusalem friends identify Ai with a conspicuous mound which I saw from a distance. It bears now no other name than Tell, which you may translate "heap;" and as for "desolation," it remains complete unto this day. No doubt traces still remain, could we but find them, of that great heap of stones which Joshua raised over the carcass of Ai's hapless king.[4]

May 14*th.* Is it not remarkable that there is no allusion to the common Barn-door fowl. barn-door fowl in the Old Testament, and that in the New they are only mentioned in connection with Jerusalem? In Matthew Christ thus addresses this wicked city: "O Jerusalem, Jerusalem, thou that killest the prophets, and stonest them which are sent unto thee, how often would I have gathered thy children together, even as a hen gathereth her chickens under her wings, and

---

[1] Isa. x. 28–32.   [2] Josh. viii. 3.   [3] Josh. viii. 12.   [4] Josh. viii. 29.

43

ye would not!"[1] Matthew,[2] Mark,[3] and Luke[4] refer to the crowing of the cock when Peter denied his Lord; and Mark mentions cock-crowing as one of the watches of the night in connection with Christ's prophecy concerning the destruction of Jerusalem.[5]

I have often thought of this remarkable silence in regard to one of man's most common associates and greatest comforts, especially in this country. The peasants, not to say citizens in general, would scarcely know how to live without fowls. Their eggs, and they themselves, answer the place of meat for most of their meals. They swarm round every door, share in the food of their possessors, are at home among the children in every room, roost over head at night, and, with their ceaseless crowing, are the town-clock and the morning bell to call up the sleepers at early dawn. If they were thus common among the ancient Hebrews, it seems strange that they should never have been mentioned.

Cock-
crowing.
Is not the cock-crowing a very indefinite division of time? I have noticed throughout our wanderings that they seem to crow all night long.

That is true, particularly in bright warm nights; and what is curious, too, I have heard a single cock crow so often and continue so long that I gave over counting from mere weariness. It is, however, while the dawn is struggling into day that the whole band of chanticleers blow their shrill clarions with the greatest energy and emulation. It seems to be an objection to the sign given to Peter, that a thousand cocks in Jerusalem might crow at any hour. For him, however, it was sufficient that in the house of Caiaphas there was but one which gave forth its significant note in immediate response to his cruel and cowardly denial of his Lord, and it answered the purpose intended perfectly. Peter heard, and then "went out and wept bitterly." We must not be very severe upon the Armenians for attempting to preserve the identical spot where this incident occurred, since the Evangelists record the fact with so much particularity.

---

[1] Matt. xxiii. 37. [2] Matt. xxvi. 34. [3] Mark xiv. 30.
[4] Luke xxii. 34. [5] Mark xiii. 35.

CHAPTER XLIV.

JERUSALEM—SACRED PLACES.

Sacred shrines.
The Holy Sepulchre.
"Navel of the Earth."
Holy fire.
A house in Jerusalem.
The virtuous woman—Customs.
Jews of Jerusalem.
Instrumental music.
Mosque of Omar—El Aksa.

Jews' wailing-place.
Remains of ancient arch.
Ancient oriental cities.
Size of ancient Jerusalem.
Jerusalem during festivals.
Siege by Titus.
Modern history.
Bethany—Bethphage.
Sacred scenes on Olivet.

WHEN you were laying down rules for visiting these sacred localities with Sacred shrines. safety and advantage, I felt and remarked that the whole truth had not been stated, and I now resume the subject in connection with my visit to the Holy Sepulchre, and inquire whether it is not possible that we carry our disgust at what is doubtful and puerile much further than is necessary or profitable. For example, do not the purest and best feelings of our nature prompt us to preserve and protect from desecration such sites as this of the Holy Sepulchre? And then, again, look at another aspect of the matter. Suppose that on our arrival here we inquired for the tombs of prophets and kings who rendered this place so illustrious, and were answered by the people that they knew nothing about them; that they had never heard of such men as David and Solomon; that there were neither tradition nor memento of their ever having lived and reigned in this city. "Strangers from a distance, like you, come to us with these stories, but neither we nor our fathers ever heard of them, nor is there any locality in our vicinity that has now, or ever had, any such associations connected with it."

And if our most diligent inquiries proved fruitless—there really were no Reverence Calvary at Jerusalem, no Garden of Gethsemane, no Bethlehem, no Olivet, no due to sacred Bethany—would we not, upon opening our New Testaments, look into each sites. other's face with perplexity and blank dismay? On the other hand, what is it now that gives such supreme gratification to our visit at Jerusalem? Is it not these very names, clinging to these sacred sites and scenes with invincible tenacity, through wars and destructions absolutely without parallel, and repeated down long centuries of most dismal darkness and confusion worse confounded? And because, in the death-struggle to hold fast these sacred land-marks, ignorant men or crafty priests have perverted them to selfish purposes, or pushed becoming reverence and love over into sinful superstition, are we therefore to scout the whole thing, and scowl upon these cherished sites, and upon those who have cherished them, as though they were guilty of the sin of witchcraft? I more than admit that nothing can justify idolatry; but is even a little too much reverence in such a case as odious to Him in whose honour it is manifested as cold contempt or proud neglect?

One more of my many thoughts and reflections to-day :—If these sacred sites were to be preserved at all, how was this to be done? Leave the stable and the manger just as they were on the night of the advent, you reply; and so Calvary, and the garden, and the sepulchre. Certainly this would have been more satisfactory, but then it would have required a succession of the most stupendous miracles from that day to this. War, earthquake, fire, and fierce fanaticism have driven by turns their ploughshares of destruction through all these scenes, and to preserve them exactly *where* and *as* they were became impossible; and when kings and princes sought to restore and preserve them, they did it in accordance with the sentiments of the age. Hence arose over and around these sites the splendid basilica and the spacious convent. We may regret their bad taste, we condemn their superstitions, we must abhor their frauds, but we cannot wisely refuse the confirmation of our faith and hope which their faulty zeal has furnished.

The Holy
Sepulchre.
This train of reflection has, as I said, been suggested by a visit to the Holy Sepulchre. I have come to regard that as by far the most interesting half acre on the face of the earth. Nor is this appreciation materially affected by the doubts which hang over the questions of identity and genuineness. Around that spot, whether it be or be not the real tomb, have clustered the hopes and affections of the great Christian world for sixteen centuries at least, and with all but a few learned men it is still the accepted representative and *locale* of events of such transcendent magnitude as cast all others into the category of mere vanities. The reputed sepulchre of the Son of God is no place for soulless criticism, calm, cold, and hard as the rock itself.

Your imagination, I perceive, has been quite captivated, and yet I do not believe you have explored half the wonders of that wondrous temple. Did you see the altar of Melchizedek? No! Nor that on which Isaac was sacrificed—nor the chapel of St. John—nor of the angels—nor the marble chair on which St. Helena sat—nor the chapel of the division of garments—nor the sweating pillar—nor the *navel* of the world—nor the place where Mary Magdalene stood —nor the chapel of Adam—nor the rent in the rock whence his skull leaped out—nor the altar of the penitent thief—nor—

You may cut short your categories; I saw none of these things, probably because I asked not for them.

Possibly the "scourge" of modern scepticism has whipped them all out of this temple; no very wonderful achievement, for, as credulity brought them in, unbelief can cast them out. But you should not have undertaken to go the round of these "pilgrim stations" without some courageous champion for their integrity by your side. Here, for example, are three smart volumes of Padre Francesco Cassini, an Italian monk of the Minori Riformati. They are the

Cassini's
work.

very latest thing of the kind, hot from the press at Genoa this very year, and
dedicated to Ferdinand Second of Naples, better known by the sobriquet of
Bomba,—a real curiosity in their way, lively, full of *wit*, *Metastasio*, and the
Bible, three things remarkable in a brother of the Riformati. His countless
quotations from the Bible are, however, all in good old canonical Latin, and
therefore harmless to the general reader. It is refreshing to follow a gentleman
and a scholar who treads fearlessly among all these crumbling traditions of the
Dark Ages. He would have been an admirable guide for you.

I prefer my own way, and my own thoughts were my best companions.
There were but few people present, and but little noise, and the impression
produced was solemn and very sad. Though there may not be one thing there
that had any actual connection with the passion of our Saviour, yet they have
long represented the various scenes of that mysterious and awful, yet joyful transaction, and I gave myself up to reverent, devout meditation and humble prayer.

You have been fortunate. My introduction to this church was totally
different, and the first impressions most unhappy. It was on the 6th of April, First visit
1833. I arrived from Ramleh much fatigued, but, as an important ceremony
was going forward in the church, I hastened thither at once. The whole vast
edifice was crowded with pilgrims from all parts of the world, and it was with
difficulty that I followed my companion into the rotunda. There a priest who
knew us came up, and, after inquiring about the news of the day, asked if we
would be conducted into the interior of the Greek chapel, where the religious
services were going on, and then, summoning a Turkish *cawass*, we began to
move in that direction. To my amazement and alarm, the cawass began to A human
beat the crowd over the head, when down they crouched to the floor, and we pavement
walked over their prostrate bodies! There was no help for it; those behind,
rising up, thrust us forward. After proceeding some distance, we paused to
take breath where the crowd was more dense and obstinate than usual, and I
was seriously informed that this was the exact *navel* of the earth, and these
obstinate pilgrims were bowing and kissing it. Finally we reached the altar Navel of
at the east end without any serious injury to the living causeway which we had the earth
traversed, and I had time to look about me. The scene throughout had all
the interest of entire novelty. I was young, and fresh from America, and was
seized with an almost irrepressible propensity to laugh. The noise was deafening, and there was not the slightest approximation to devotion visible, or even
possible, so far as I could judge; while the attitudes, costumes, gestures, and
sounds which met the eye and stunned the ear were infinitely strange and
ludicrous. Such splendour, too, I had never seen. By the aid of numerous
lamps the whole church seemed to flash and blaze in burning gold. I stood
near the altar, which was covered with gold cloth, and decorated with censers,
golden candlesticks, and splendid crucifixes. A bench of bishops and priests
filled the entire space within the railing, and two monks were waving, or, more
accurately, swinging their censers before them. The " cloud of incense " rose
wreathing and circling to the upper dome, diffusing on all sides a strong aro-

matic odour. After some delay, the whole priesthood of those denominations which then united in this ceremony were assembled, properly robed and fumigated, and, with lighted candle in either hand, stood ready for the grand feat of the day. In single file, seventy priests and bishops, in long robes of gold and silver texture, marched out into the body of the church with solemn pomp. Turkish officers went before, beating the heads of the crowd, who bowed down as they had done for us. Slowly the gorgeous procession worked its way along the north side, singing, with nasal twang and stentorian lungs, harsh harmony in barbarous Greek. In a few minutes they returned, laid aside their robes, extinguished their tapers, and the multitude dispersed, greatly enlightened by —a vast number of wax candles, and edified by a devout manifestation of splendid canonicals. Our friend, in his robes and with candles lighted, inquired in the careless tones of ordinary conversation concerning our journey, the roads, Ibrahim Pasha, and the war that was then going on with the Sultan; while the people in the body of the church were laughing, talking, praying, shouting, or quarrelling, as suited their convenience. The noise was perfectly astounding to American ears. I would have taken the whole affair for a city auction, or the exhibition of a travelling show, rather than an assembly engaged in the worship of God. Such was *my* introduction to the Holy Sepulchre; and I have never been able to banish from my mind the first unhappy impressions, nor can I visit the church with either pleasure or profit.

I am thankful that I have no such associations to disturb and disgust. I entered the open court from Palmer Street, which there runs east and west. This court is paved with the common flag-stone of Jerusalem, and I judged it to be about ninety feet long and seventy wide. Certain parts of the church seem to be ancient,—that is, of the Greek Empire anterior to the Crusades. The two ample doorways are elaborately ornamented with the architectural devices common on all temples and churches of that era. The whole, however, is much dilapidated, and disfigured with additions and patch-work of every conceivable degree of barbarism. The campanile on the west of the court must have been an imposing tower when perfect.

It is said to have been five storeys high, and richly ornamented, but there remain now only the two lower, with the ruins of the third. The under storey is the chapel of St. John, south of it is that of Mary Magdalene, and adjoining this is the Chapel of St. James. These are now ordinary churches.

Having entered by the great door, only one of whose large leaves was open, I came upon the " stone of unction," with its colossal wax candles. Turning westward along the aisle, and then north, I entered the grand rotunda between
two huge square columns. This is striking and impressive. I estimated the height of the dome to be about one hundred feet, and the circular opening at the top, for light, to be about fifteen feet in diameter. This dome is sadly out of repair, and the rain must descend in torrents over the whole south-western part of the rotunda.

Its covering of lead has been torn off by the winds, and a contest between the rival races of monks for the privilege of making the repairs keeps it in this ruinous condition.

Of course, "the Sepulchre" was the object which most attracted my attention, and I had as good an opportunity to examine it as could be desired. Externally it looks very much like a small marble house. All the world knows that it is twenty-six feet long and about eighteen broad, and, I should think, something more than twenty feet high. It stands quite alone, directly under the aperture in the centre of the dome. I went into the Chapel of the Angel by its low door, saw the stone on which the angel sat; crept into the proper sepulchre room, and looked at the raised, altar-like recess on the north side, whose fine *marble* slab is said to cover the real rock couch where the body of our Lord was laid. I did not measure these rooms, nor count the silver lamps which crowd the little apartment overhead. A thousand pilgrims have counted and measured, and given very various results.

As to the lamps, they seem really to vary in number from time to time. There are at least forty of them now, and I do not well see how there can be any more suspended from the roof. The Chapel of the Angel is admitted to be artificial, but it is stoutly maintained by all who venerate the place that the small anterior room is a genuine rock tomb, merely *cased* in marble. The ecclesiastical tradition is, that Constantine's architect caused the rock to be cut away all round this tomb, so as to leave it standing alone, beneath the church raised over it. This is certainly possible, but if it could be proved it would settle nothing as to the identity of this sepulchre with that of Joseph of Arimathea. I could not tell whether it was native rock or artificial masonry, nor do I care which it is, or whether it is partly natural and partly artificial.

After standing a long time in front of this affecting tomb, I sauntered off into the Greek Church. It is a gorgeous affair, blazing with gold quite up to the dome. It is a sort of cruciform structure, with the high altar at the east end, and broad transepts at the west. I judged it to be about one hundred feet from west to east, and nearly the same from north to south. The only other places that I cared to visit were the Chapel of St. Helena, to which I descended eastward from the grand circular aisle by thirty steps. It is a half-subterranean church, nearly fifty feet square. There are various altars and sacred places in it connected with the "invention" of the cross, which, however, actually took place in a real cave, to which one descends still further eastward by twelve steps. In this cave the pious Helena (so the Church tells us) was rewarded for her long travel and labour by finding the *three* crosses, the *nails*, the crown of thorns, etc. After examining the place sufficiently, I returned along the south-eastern aisle, and ascended *Calvary* by a flight of eighteen steps; there looked at the three holes in which the crosses are said to have stood; but this seems to me the most bungling arrangement in the whole "invention." The three holes are too close together, and there is an

PART
IV.

air of desperate improbability about the entire contrivance that cannot be over-come. Besides, it is notorious that a large part of this Golgotha is an *arti-ficial vault*, with rooms underneath.

Multitude of objects.

I see you are yet less than half a pilgrim. Your faith is not sufficiently robust to cast into the sea the dark mountains of scepticism over which it stumbles. You must summon to your aid the courageous maxim of Padre Francesco,—" that it is better to believe too much than too little." With this brave maxim he valiantly assaults all impertinent improbabilities, and stead-fastly stares them out of countenance. I myself have been a much more per-severing *pilligrino* than you. Why, there are some seventy "stations" within and connected with this vast and confused mass of buildings, all of which I have had the resolution to visit, and most of them many times. It is no light achievement, to be done up in an hour. The whole pile of edifices connected together is three hundred and fifty feet long, from Joseph's sepulchre, within the aisle on the west of the rotunda, down to the extremity of the Chapel of the "Invention" on the east; and it is not less than two hundred and eighty feet from the south wall of St. James's Chapel to the north side of the apart-ments belonging to the Latins. Within this vast enclosure there seems to be no end to aisles, windows, stairways, vaults, tombs, dark recesses, chapels, oratories, altars, concealed relics, and other holy "inventions." Verily, nothing is too hard for stout-hearted Credulity. She has not only removed mountains, but wrought *impossibilities* of transposition and aggregation. At her bidding, rocks and caves, and distant localities gathered from all quarters into this temple, as the wild beasts came to the ark; and, having got them in, it is very difficult to get them safely out, however offensive their presence may be to the eye of modern research.

Reality of the Se-pulchre?

I have very little of this wonder-working credulity in my composition, but your raillery (scarcely becoming on such a subject) cannot rob the place of all its sacred titles and honours. It is not *certain* that the main claims to respect and affection are mere "inventions." Though some may fancy that they have completely exploded the whole series of traditions which have clustered around the spot for so many centuries, they are egregiously mistaken. That battle is not over yet. Many, perhaps most of even Protestant critics, either maintain the reality of the Sepulchre, or, at least, are doubtful; while all the rest of the Christian world, with one voice and one heart, as stoutly and earnestly defend it now against the assaults of sceptics as the knights and militant monks of yore did against the Saracens. The difficulty of the defence is immeasurably augmented by this herd of impertinent and intolerable intruders, that have no right to be there, but still victory is not yet declared in favour of the assailants.

Fourteen "sta-tions."

After leaving the church and examining some curious old buildings a little to the south-west of the court, I returned by the Via Dolorosa, stopping for a moment at each of the "stations" along its crooked line. This whole street, with all its sacred points and places, I give up at once. The buildings are modern, and no plausible evidence can be produced for the identity of any one CHAPTER XLIV. of the "stations."

You should have had our friend P. Cassini with you, who would have stoutly contended for the integrity of the whole *fourteen*. According to him, however, this street is intolerably long. He says that the Via Dolorosa for the human race began in Eden when Adam was condemned to eat his bread in the sweat of his brow, and all men travelling along it from that day to this have had their "stations" of sorrow and of suffering!

To return now to your original inquiries. I am free to confess that it is Shocking utterly impossible for me to regard the Church of the Holy Sepulchre, and its scenes. incredible congregation of sacred sites, with complacency; nor could you, if you had been a spectator of the scenes which I have witnessed there, not once, but often. I will not shock your sensibilities with details of the buf- Holy Fire. foonery and the profane orgies performed by the Greeks around the tomb on the day of the Holy Fire. I doubt whether there is anything more disgraceful to be witnessed in any heathen temple. Nor are the ceremonies of the Latin monks on the night of the Crucifixion a whit less distressing and offensive. The whole scene, in all its parts, is enacted before a strong guard of Turkish troops, stationed all around to keep the actors in this dismal tragedy from being assaulted by the rival players in the Greek *comedia*—a precaution absolutely necessary and not always successful. Furious and bloody riots have occurred several times since I have been in the country, and many travellers mentioned similar battles between the monks in former years. I was here in 1834, when several hundred pilgrims were crushed to death on the day of the Holy Fire.

Now I am devoutly thankful that no amount of learning or research can establish the remotest connection between any act of our Saviour and any one of these so-called holy places. And I seem to find, in this uncertainty which hangs over every sacred locality, the indications of a watchful Providence in beautiful accordance with many similar interpositions to save God's people from idolatry. The grave of Melchizedek, the typical priest—of Joseph, the Conceal- rejected of his brethren and sold—of Moses, the lawgiver and deliverer—of ment of tombs in- Joshua, the captain and leader into the land of promise—of David, the shep- tentional. herd and king—of John the Baptist and Forerunner—and of Mary, the mother whom all nations shall call blessed—the tombs of all these have been irrecoverably concealed: and the same watchful care has hid for ever the instruments of the Saviour's passion; the exact spot where he was crucified, buried, and whence he rose again to life; and also the place from which he ascended into heaven. I would have it thus. And certainly, since God has concealed the *realities*, we have no need of these fictitious sites to confirm our faith. We are surrounded by witnesses, and these mountains, and valleys, and ruins, that cannot be effaced or corrupted. They are now spread out before our eyes. *There* was the Temple, type of the Saviour. *Beyond* it was Zion, symbol of the Church of God. *Here* lies the whole scene of our Lord's last

PART
IV.

actions, teaching, and passion. *There* he instituted the Supper. *Below* us is the garden of agony and betrayal. The palace of Pilate was on that hill above it, where he was examined, was scourged, buffeted, robed in mock purple, and crowned with thorns. Along that rocky way he bore his cross; there he was nailed to it, was lifted up, was reviled, was given gall and vinegar to drink, and when all was finished he bowed his head and died. Then the sun refused to shine, and darkness fell on all the land; the earth quaked, the rocks rent, and the graves were opened. There was the new tomb in the garden of Joseph of Arimathea. Thither the angel came down and rolled the stone from the door, while the Lord of life burst the bars of death, and rose triumphant o'er the grave. All those things—

> "Which kings and prophets waited for,
> But died without the sight,"

did actually take place here. These eyes gaze up to the same heaven which opened to receive him ascending to his Father's right hand. The great atoning sacrifice of the Lamb of God, and every item of it, was offered up here, on this unquestioned platform of the Holy City. This is all I care for, all that mere topography can offer. If sure, to the fraction of a foot, in regard to the sepulchre, I could no more worship it than I could worship the boat in which he sailed over Gennesaret, or the ass upon which he rode into Jerusalem, and hence I have no need of any of these "inventions;" and since they are perverted to an idolatry worse than the burning of incense to the brazen serpent, I would have them all removed out of sight, that He who is a spirit may be worshipped, even at Jerusalem, in spirit and in truth.

House in Jerusalem.

My cicerone took me to his house this morning, and I was pleased to be introduced to the interior of a native Christian family on Mount Zion. There was an ease and a cordiality in the reception which surprised as much as it delighted me, and a grace displayed by the ladies in presenting sherbet, sweetmeats, coffee, and argelehs, which would have attracted the admiration of any society in the world. They showed me over their house, and explained the various contrivances which excited my curiosity. Nothing can be further from our notions in regard to the fixtures necessary for the comfort of a family; yet some things are pretty, and all are adapted, I suppose, to the country, and the actual state of civilization. The reception-hall, with its heavy vault above, matted pavement, and low divan ranged round three sides of the apart-

Tesselated pavement.

ment, was cheerful and inviting; and the floor of an inner room was beautiful, with its tesselated pavement of various-coloured marble drawn in many elegant and complicated patterns. The Arab artists exhibit great skill in this kind of work, and, indeed, one rarely sees prettier pavements in any country.

One reason of their success in mosaics of both stone and wood is, that this art has always been in demand in the East. Tesselated pavements are found beneath the rubbish of all ancient cities, and, beyond a doubt, our Lord and his apostles often reclined upon them at meat. The "large upper room" where he celebrated his last Passover and instituted the "Supper" may have CHAPTER XLIV. been finished in this style.

Tesselated pavement is seen in greatest abundance and highest perfection in Damascus, around their delightful fountains and in their magnificent *lewans*. The Damascenes also take great pride in having their window-shutters made after patterns even more intricate than those of the pavement. Having no glass, their ambition is to show window-blinds as elaborate and attractive as possible. I have counted more than two hundred bits of polished walnut wood in the shutter of a small window. Window shutters.

I saw a woman sitting at the door of her hut on Zion, spinning woollen yarn with a spindle, while another near her was twirling nimbly the ancient distaff, and I felt some curiosity to know whether in other things they resembled king Lemuel's good wife, according to the "prophecy that his mother taught him." Spinning.

There are such even now in this country, and in this city, where the prophecy was uttered. They are scarce, however, and their price is above rubies.[1] The very first item in the catalogue of good qualities is the rarest of all: "The heart of her husband doth safely trust in her."[2] The husband, in nine cases out of every ten, does not feel very confident that "she will do him good and not evil," and therefore he sets a jealous watch over her, and places every valuable article under lock and key. His heart trusts more in hired guards and iron locks than in his wife. This is mainly owing to two things,— bad education and the want of love; both grievous sins against her, and committed by her lord and tyrant. She is kept in ignorance, and is married off without regard to the affections of her heart; and how can it be expected that the husband can safely trust in a wife thus trained and thus obtained? The virtuous woman.

There are numerous allusions to the domestic habits of Orientals in this "prophecy" of Lemuel's mother which are worth noticing: "She seeketh wool and flax, and worketh diligently with her hands."[3] In Sidon, at this day, a majority of the women are thus working in raw silk and cotton instead of wool and flax. Many of them actually support the family in this way, and, by selling the produce of their labour to the merchants, "bring their food from afar." A leading Moslem told me that nearly every family in Sidon was thus carried through the past scarce and very dear winter.

"She riseth while it is yet night," and "her candle goeth not out by night."[4] The industrious of this country are very early risers. Long before day they are up and about their work; but, what is especially remarked, they never allow their lamp to go out by night. This, however, is not always a sign of industry. The very poorest keep a light burning all night, more from timidity or from habit than from anything else. Early rising.

"She girdeth her loins with strength, and delivereth girdles to the merchant.[5] The use of the girdle is universal, under the impression that it Girdles.

[1] Prov. xxxi. 10. [2] Prov. xxxi. 11. [3] Prov. xxxi. 13.
[4] Prov. xxxi. 15, 18. [5] Prov. xxxi. 17, 24.

greatly contributes to the strength of the loins, around which it is twisted tightly in many a circling fold. Being always in demand, it is an important article of domestic manufacture. And again, scarlet, and purple, and tapestry, and embroidery, mentioned in verses 21, 22, are still the favourite colours and patterns of Oriental taste. The husband of such a faithful and industrious wife is known in the *gates*, where he sitteth among the *elders* of the land. What the *Bourse* is in Paris and the Exchange in London, the open spaces about the gates of the city were to the Orientals, and still are in many parts of the East. There the elders congregate to talk over the news of the day, the state of the market, and the affairs of their particular community. The husband of such a wife is distinguished among his compeers by a costume clean, whole, and handsome, and a countenance contented and happy. " Her children, also, call her blessed ; and her husband he praiseth her," [1]—a most happy exception ; for children in this country too often treat their mother with contempt, and the haughty husband says *ajellak*—" my woman"—when he has occasion to speak of his wife.

Grass on the house-tops.

Isaiah says that because God had brought it to pass that Sennacherib should " lay waste defenced cities, therefore the inhabitants were dismayed, . . . and became as grass on the house-tops, . . . blasted before it be grown up;" [2] and this morning I saw a striking illustration of this most expressive figure. To obtain a good view of the Tyropean, my guide took me to the top of a house on the brow of Zion, and the grass which had grown over the roof during the rainy season was now entirely withered and perfectly dry.

When I first came to reside in Jerusalem, in 1834, my house was connected with an ancient church, the roof of which was covered with a thick growth of grass. This being in the way of a man employed to repair my house, he actually set fire to it and burned it off; and I have seen others do the same thing without the slightest hesitation. Nor is there any danger ; for it would require a large expense for fuel sufficient to burn the present city of Jerusalem. Our translators have unnecessarily supplied the word *corn*, and thus confused the idea and diluted the force of this passage from Isaiah. Corn does frequently wither away, but the reference here, I suppose, is to that grass on the house-tops which David says " withereth afore it groweth up ; wherewith the mower filleth not his hand, nor he that bindeth sheaves his bosom. Neither do they which go by say, The blessing of the Lord be upon you : we bless you in the name of the Lord." [3] The latter expressions are most refreshingly Arabic. Nothing is more natural than for them, when passing by a fruit-tree or corn-field loaded with a rich crop, to exclaim, *Barak Allah !*—" God bless you !" we bless you in the name of the Lord !

A syna-gogue.

Expressing a desire to visit a synagogue, my obliging cicerone took me to a large one which was crowded with worshippers. The room had nothing in or about it like any other place of worship I ever entered, and the congregation was in

---

[1] Prov. xxxi. 28.   [2] Isa. xxxvii. 26, 27.   [3] Ps. cxxix. 6–8.

character and keeping with the place. I never saw such an assemblage of old, CHAPTER XLIV.
pale, and woe-begone countenances. There is something inexpressibly sad in
the features, deportment, and costume of these children of Abraham, as they
grope about the ruins of their once joyous city.

This is partly owing to the fact that many of them have been great sinners Jews of Jerusalem.
elsewhere, and have come up here from all countries whither the Lord hath
driven them, to purge away their guilt by abstinence, mortification, and devotion; then to die, and be buried as near the Holy City as possible. This also
accounts for the ever-increasing multitude of their graves, which are gradually
covering the side of Olivet. The Jews come to Jerusalem to die, and a community gathered for that specific purpose will not be particularly gay, nor very
careful about appearances.

The behaviour of the worshippers was very peculiar and somewhat ridicu- Behaviour at worship.
lous. The men, with broad-brimmed hats, and whatever other head-dress they
possessed, were reading or muttering prayers; and while doing so they twisted,
and jerked, and wriggled about incessantly, and at times with great vehemence,
that "all their bones should praise the Lord," as one of them explained the
matter to me. When they began what was understood to be singing, it was
the most outrageous concert of harsh nasal sounds I ever heard. It was
Hebrew, too; but if David thus "praised the Lord," I should never have
thought of calling him "the *sweet* singer of Israel."

And yet, I presume, it was very much after this style that he and all his Nasal twang in singing.
band of trained musicians did actually celebrate the praises of the Most High.
You hear the same nasal twang and grating gutturals in the singing of every
denomination throughout the East. The Orientals know nothing of harmony,
and cannot appreciate it when heard; but they are often spell-bound, or wrought
up to transports of ecstasy, by this very music which has tortured your nerves.
It is useless to quarrel about tastes in this matter. I have never known song
more truly effective than among these Orientals; and no doubt the Temple
service, performed by those trained for it, stirred the deepest fountains of feeling in the vast assemblies of Israel gathered at Jerusalem on their great feasts.
They had also instrumental music, which these have not; and David himself
was a most skilful performer.

I made that remark to my guide, and he immediately offered to take me to Instru-mental music.
a coffee-shop where I should hear a grand concert of instrumental musicians.
Thinking it would be a pleasant remembrance to carry away from the Holy
City, I went, and was not disappointed. Seated on a raised platform at one
end of the room were half a dozen performers, discoursing strange music from
curious instruments, interspersed occasionally with wild bursts of song, which
seemed to electrify the smoking, coffee-sipping congregation. They had a
violin, two or three kinds of flutes, and a tambourine. One man sat by himself, and played a large harp lying upon his lap.

That is called a kânûn; and an expert performer, with a voice not too sharp,
often makes very respectable music with it.

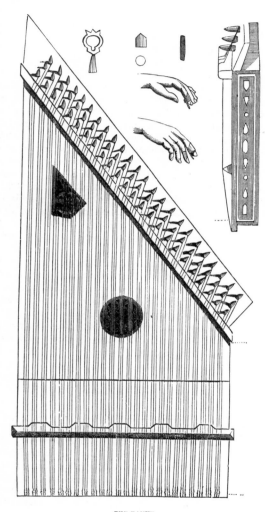

THE KANUN.

KANUN, AND MODE OF PLAYING IT.

There was one with a droll but merry countenance, who told stories and per- Instru-
petrated jokes, to the infinite amusement of the audience, and now and then he mental music.

KAMANJEH, AND PERFORMER ON IT.

played with spasmodic jerks and ludicrous grimaces upon an instrument called kamanjeh.   There were also players on the guitar, and one of them had a very large instrument of this kind, over whose chords his nimble fingers swept, at times, like magic.   The notes are much louder than those of an Italian guitar.

MODE OF PLAYING THE 'OOD.

The Greeks, and especially the Albanians, manage this 'ood with the greatest skill.   They have a small kind, which they take with them in their extemporaneous pic-nics, and on the shady bank of some murmuring brook they will sit by the hour and sing to its soft and silvery note.

Music of the country. But the most popular of all music in this country are the derbekkeh, the tambourine or deff, and the nŭkkairat or kettle-drum, with cymbals, casta-nets, and the clapping of hands.   At weddings, birth-days, and all other festal

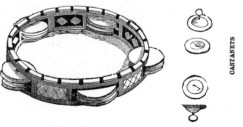

DEFF—TAMBOURINE.

CASTANETS

MOSQUE OF OMAR.

gatherings, this is their chief entertainment; and they will beat the derbek- CHAPTER
keh, thrum the deff, rattle the castanets, and clap their hands in concert, XLIV.
without weariness or intermission, until long after midnight.

I attempted to look into the Temple area this morning, at the pool inside of Temple
St. Stephen's Gate, but was rudely ordered away by some loungers within. area.
This is the only instance in which I have been insulted during my walks about
Jerusalem.

The Moslems have become suddenly very fanatical in regard to this holy Mosque of
Harem, owing in part to the injudicious behaviour of travellers. In company Omar.
with a large party I was taken in by the British consul, and the old sheikh of
the Harem treated us with great respect, showing everything about the Mosque
without reserve, and allowing us afterward to ramble as we pleased in the
vaults below, and over the area above, without any surveillance whatever.

We entered by a small rude door near the north-west corner of the area, and
walked in our ordinary shoes to the raised *stoa* upon which the Mosque
of Omar stands. Here we put on red morocco shoes, purchased from the
bazaars for the purpose, and kept them on until we left the Mosque of El
Aksa.

The first thing that struck me within the enclosure of the Harem was its The
great size. It contains about thirty-five acres more or less; for, owing to irre- Harem, or
gularities in its outline and boundaries, it is not possible to arrive at entire Omar.
accuracy. It is about 1500 feet on the east side, 1600 on the west, 1000 on
the north, and 900 on the south end. This large enclosure undoubtedly takes
in, on the north, the whole area of the Castle of Antonia. I noticed that the
rock on the north-west corner had been cut away, leaving a perpendicular face,
in some parts at least twenty feet high.

The surface is not a perfect level, but declines in various directions. From
the entrance we walked over smooth bare rock, descending rapidly toward the
south-east, then rose over green sward to the foot of the stoa, which may be
elevated about twelve feet at the north end. There is also a large descent
southward from the Mosque of Omar to El Aksa, and on the east side there is
quite a depression at the Golden Gate.

The stoa is not paved with marble, as has been often stated, but with slabs The build
of the ordinary flagging-stone of this country. We have admirable drawings ing.
of the Mosque of Omar and its surroundings, and from them one obtains a
good idea of the whole affair. The pen-pictures are immensely over-drawn, and
the coloured views are glaring exaggerations. Externally, at the base, the
edifice is an octagon of about one hundred and seventy feet diameter, each of
the eight sides being sixty-seven feet long. There are four doors at the opposite
cardinal points. The dome is sustained by four great piers, and has twelve
arches, which rest on columns. There are also many other columns with
arches which mark off the inner aisles. But you can study the details of this
curious edifice in the works of Williams, Catherwood, Bartlett, Fergusson, and
many others, if you have a desire to do so. Dr. Richardson's account of what

PART
IV.

he saw within the Harem is also worth reading. We found nearly everything mentioned by him, and very much as he describes them.

The Rock.

The beauty of the interior of the Mosque is greatly marred by numberless contrivances for illuminating the edifice, and by railings and galleries which seem to answer no particular end that I could discover. The greatest curiosity is certainly the immense stone from which the name, Es Sakhrah (the Rock), is derived. It is a mass of native rock, the sole remnant of the top of the ridge of Moriah, some sixty feet long by fifty-five wide, and ten or twelve feet high on the lower side. All the rest of the ridge was cut away when levelling off the platform for the Temple and its courts. No tool of iron has left its mark upon this Sakhrah, and I please myself with the idea that it was the basis on which the altar of sacrifice was arranged. Nor am I convinced by the reasoning of those who hold that the Temple was a small edifice erected further to the south. It is not yet *proved* that the substructions by which the area in that direction has been extended are not of an age long posterior to Solomon, and therefore, on any scale of measurement, it must remain a matter of uncertainty just how far northward the Temple stood. Hence I do not quarrel with the tradition that the Mosque of Omar is on the site of that sacred sanctuary ; and if this be so, the *Sakhrah* may well mark the exact spot of the altar. Beneath the south-east end of it is a cavern, the bottom of which is covered with the usual flooring of the country. Stamp upon it, and you discover that there is a well or shaft below; and the sheikh of the Harem told me that this shaft terminated in a horizontal passage leading southward from some place further back under the edifice, and that water descended along it. May not the blood and the ashes from the altar have originally been cast into this pit, and thence washed down into the valley of the Tyropean or of the Kidron, quite beyond the precincts of the holy house ? Those who now speak of *fountains* in the enclosure must mean merely places where water is obtained from cisterns below the stoa. The curb-stones of these openings are deeply worn by the ropes of those who have drawn from these enormous reservoirs during many hundred years.

El Aksa.

El Aksa was undoubtedly a Christian church, and probably the one built by Justinian. In converting it into a mosque, but little alteration was necessary, and hence we have the columns very much as they were in the original building. There is a close resemblance to the interior of the church at Bethlehem. The vaults beneath are very remarkable, but whether any of the huge limestone columns, with their architectural peculiarities, were of Solomonic times, I will not attempt to decide. It is my opinion, however, that there is nothing absurd in ascribing arches and columns to that age, for they were both employed in architecture long anterior to it.

Instead of attempting to describe these vaults, columns, gateways, and mysterious passages, I must direct you to the works of others, and to the numerous drawings of artists. I ran about, half wild with excitement, until I

Vaults.

was quite exhausted. The main vaults now accessible are beneath the south-

eastern corner of the area. The piers which sustain the most eastern group
are arranged in lines running from south to north, parallel to the outside wall
of the Harem. There are fifteen rows, at very unequal distances, ranging
from about six to twenty-three feet apart. And so also the length of the lines
is very different. Those which extend furthest northward may reach two
hundred feet, while the shortest terminate at the solid rock in less than forty

VAULTS UNDER EL AKSA.

feet. The piers are built of blocks about four feet square more or less, rudely
bevelled, and laid up somewhat carelessly. This group of piers and vaults is
succeeded by another further west, similar to it, but less every way, and they
extend to the substructions beneath El Aksa. No one can examine them for
an hour without being convinced that the pillars are made out of older ruins,
and that the vaults spread over them are comparatively modern. There are
many remains, however, extremely ancient, particularly near the south-east
corner. The roof has fallen through in several places, and we descended to
the vaults from one of these openings. The time will come when these interesting remains, in a most remarkable locality, will be fully cleared of
rubbish, and thoroughly explored by scientific architects, and then we shall
know what revelations they have to disclose. The description of these will
take volumes, and, moreover, they will be very dry to all but artists and
minute critics. I looked at the various traditional sites, Moslem and Christian,
sat down on Solomon's throne and Mohammed's judgment-seat, and stood on
the top of the Golden Gate for an hour, looking at this most suggestive spot
and its surroundings. Olivet is beautiful, even in its present desolation; and
the area itself, with its mosques, minarets, oratories, columns, cypress, kharûb,
olive, and other trees, form a tableau which will never be forgotten.

PART
IV.

Nehemiah speaks of bringing *sheaves* into Jerusalem : [1] is it not singular that the people should carry their grain into the city to thresh it ?

Carrying
sheaves.

It would be strange with us, because our citizens are not husbandmen. In the East, however, the farmers all live in villages and towns, and *go forth* to cultivate the surrounding country. It is not unusual, therefore, for them to bring their harvest home to thresh it ; and thus we find that Araunah the Jebusite had his threshing-floor on the present site of the Temple in the days of David.[2] The farmers brought their grain within the walls of Jerusalem at the time of Nehemiah to secure it against robbers, for the country was then in an unsettled and unsafe condition ; and I do not suppose that he rebuked them for adopting this precaution, but because they did the work on the *Sabbath*. They made the disturbed state of the country an excuse for violating the law of God, which was clear and emphatic on this very point : " In earing time and harvest thou shalt rest." [3] These people, as thousands still do, set aside this command, and maintained that during harvest and the vintage they must work on the Sabbath day—so they treaded their wine-presses, gathered grapes and figs, and brought in sheaves on that day. If Nehemiah were here now, he would be grieved with precisely the same violations, and might also find men of Tyre who *bring fish*, and all manner of ware, to sell on the Sabbath ; [4] nor would he be able to break up these practices, and free Jerusalem from that sin on account of which God brought all this evil upon this city.[5]

Jews'
Wailing-
place.

No traveller thinks of leaving Jerusalem without paying a visit to the Wailing-place of the Jews in the Tyropean, at the base of the wall which supports the west side of the Temple area. Those stones, no doubt, formed part of the foundations of the holy house, placed there certainly not later than the time of Herod, perhaps long before. They are, however, not very large, and here, as everywhere else about Jerusalem, either the stones have been broken and *ensmalled,* or the measure used by Josephus was much shorter than has been assumed, or he greatly exaggerated. The latter is true, at any rate. There is not a specimen in any part of the Temple area, or about the Castle of David, which even approaches the size of those which he repeatedly affirms were placed in these towers and walls. Still, those at the Place of Wailing are large enough for all the purposes of strength and durability.

Antiquity
of the cus-
tom

No sight meets the eye in Jerusalem more sadly suggestive than this wailing of the Jews over the ruins of their Temple. It is a very old custom, and in past ages they have paid immense sums to their oppressors for the miserable satisfaction of kissing the stones and pouring out lamentations at the foot of their ancient sanctuary. With trembling lips and tearful eyes they sing, " Be not wroth very sore, O Lord, neither remember iniquity for ever : behold, see, we beseech thee, we are all thy people. Thy holy cities are a wilderness, Zion is a wilderness, Jerusalem a desolation. Our holy and our beautiful house,

---

[1] Neh. xiii. 15.   [2] 2 Sam. xxiv. 16, 18.   [3] Exod xxxiv. 21.
[4] Neh. xiii. 16.   [5] Neh. xiii. 18.

where our fathers praised thee, is burned up with fire: and all our pleasant CHAPTER
XLIV. things are laid waste." [1]

South of this Wailing-place are the great stones of the arch which Dr. Arch of Robinson identified as part of the bridge on which Titus stood in order to hold bridge a parley with the Jews in the Temple. One of these stones is twenty-five between
Zion and feet long, another a little more than twenty, and the whole width of the bridge Moriah. was about fifty-one feet, while its length across the Tyropean to the perpendicular face of Zion could not have been less than three hundred and fifty. Of course there must have been several piers and arches. The whole causeway is supposed to have formed a magnificent passage from Zion to the south porch of the Temple. The identification, history, and object of this gigantic work have in our day furnished an arena of debate and strife almost as noisy

SPRING OF THE GREAT ARCH.

and earnest as when the Temple was sacked and burned by the Romans. It is subsiding now, and we shall do nothing to renew it. In consequence of a vast growth of cactus in that neighbourhood, and the closing of the blind paths

[1] Isa. lxiv. 9-11.

which formerly led to it, one cannot reach the spot without much trouble, and few travellers now visit it.

Looking down upon the city this morning, and comparing the area with that of other great capitals, the question how Jerusalem could have accommodated the vast multitudes that resided in or resorted to her continually, occurred to my mind with unwonted emphasis.

It has perplexed many before you, but the problem has been embarrassed by extreme assumptions. We are not required to find room for more than 200,000 *regular* inhabitants at Jerusalem in her highest prosperity and largest expansion. As to the 2,565,000 assembled at the Passover in the time when Cestius was governor, or the 1,200,000 shut in by Titus and his army, they were not citizens, but strangers. Josephus has given us an elaborate and minute topographical description of the city, from which, if no mistake has crept into his numbers, it is certain that the area within the walls did not much exceed one mile square. Other statements give larger dimensions, but we shall adhere to the thirty-three furlongs of Josephus for the entire circuit of the walls. Allowing for the Temple, there could not have remained more than the above superficies for dwellings, markets, offices, shops, streets, pools, and all other purposes and demands of a great city. Reasoning from these data, and from the statistics of *modern European* cities, Mr. Fergusson, in his ingenious but reckless critique, reduces the population to a very low figure indeed, and scouts the numbers of Josephus with utter contempt. But there are many circumstances overlooked or overleaped by Mr. Fergusson which must be carefully considered and allowed for if we would arrive at even an approximation to the truth. I do not believe his basis of calculation, that no modern European city has more than 25,000 inhabitants to the square mile. But admitting this extreme statement, it does not follow, because modern cities have only this number, that therefore Oriental cities in olden times had no more! We must remember that those ancient cities were built within walls; that gardens, parks, and open spaces were excluded, and the entire area occupied with buildings; that the streets were narrow, and covered over with houses; that stores, shops, markets, etc., were small, and had dwellings in the rear and above them; that the houses were several storeys high; that Orientals have even now but little furniture, and can and do crowd into very small apartments—an entire family in one room—many families in a single house; that the topography of Jerusalem, broken into valleys, is favourable to the erection of houses having many storeys, as in certain parts of Edinburgh, for example; and, finally, that the pressure of a constant necessity would lead both the government and the people to make provision to receive within the walls the largest possible number. These things considered, it will not appear unreasonable to allow for ancient Jerusalem twice as many rooms on the *ground floor* as can be found in a mile square of any modern European city, and *double* the number of people, on an average, to each room. This would give 100,000 inhabitants upon Mr. Fergusson's own data. But there were doubtless two if not three storeys to the

houses, and upper storeys have more rooms and larger available space than the
lower, and so always accommodate much the greater number of people. This at
once furnishes accommodation for at least 200,000 inhabitants, and no impartial person who has opportunity to examine modern Oriental cities, or to
observe how densely the poor Jews can and do pack themselves away in the
most wretched hovels, will deem these calculations extravagant. But we are
prepared to lay aside all speculations and theories, and take Jerusalem *as she
now is* for the basis of calculation. I have seen *more than twenty-five thousand
people in the present city*, nor was it overcrowded. Then it must be remembered
that the whole of Bezetha, and a large part of Acra, is uninhabited; the space
taken up by the Mosque of Omar is much larger than was that of the Temple;
the parts about Bab el Mugharabeh and the south-east end of Zion are either
ploughed fields or overrun with cactus; the entire western face of Zion is
occupied by the gardens of the Armenian Convent; the space south of Calvary
is vacant; convents, churches, and mosques take up much room; and, finally,
that even in those parts occupied by dwellings, the houses are low, small, badly
contrived, and many of them in ruins. All these things taken into account,
we can readily admit that, if the whole area were covered over with high houses,
economically built, a hundred thousand inhabitants could find homes *within
the present walls*. It only remains to state that the southern half of Zion, all
of Ophel, and the broad expansion of the lower Tyropean, is *without* the walls
on the south; and so, also, on the north, is the entire space enclosed by the
third wall, about which Josephus speaks in such glowing terms. Take in the
whole, cover it with habitations as it once was, and I hesitate not to say that
two hundred thousand inhabitants could dwell comfortably " within thy walls,
O Jerusalem." Should any one think differently, I will not argue the point
with him. We are not obliged to assume so high a figure, for neither the
Bible, nor Josephus, nor any other old author, gives such a number for the
actual resident population of the Holy City.

How the vast multitudes at the great feasts could be accommodated may easily
be explained. Let us take even the astounding statistics of Josephus himself,
and suppose that the two millions and a half who partook of the Passover at
the time of Cestius was neither an exaggeration nor an exception, it is by no
means certain that one-fifth of this multitude sat down to the Paschal Supper
within the walls. The Jews originally were dwellers in tents. It is certain
that in some parts of the country they did not abandon this custom, at least
not until after many generations. The proverb, " To your tents, O Israel ! "
was not a mere Oriental metaphor; and the tribes, when they assembled at
small places, such as Gilgal and Shiloh, *must* have come up with their tents,
or, at least, prepared to sleep out-doors. Nor is even this last supposition
absurd. The feasts occurred in the warm, non-rainy months, and throughout
all the southern part of Palestine the people at this season do not hesitate
to sleep in the open air, under trees, vines, or even in open gardens. Now
not only two, but half a dozen millions of people could find room to eat

and sleep on the mountains which are "round about Jerusalem." At such times, no doubt, every garden was thrown open, and every available spot occupied. We may gather this much from two incidents in the history of our Lord. When he drew near the city, and sent two disciples to prepare the Passover, they were to say to the man whom they should meet bearing a pitcher, " *Where is the guest-chamber ?*" [1] implying the existence of such apartments, and the custom of allowing the use of them as a matter of course. Again, after supper our Lord went out into a garden in Olivet.[2] Neither he nor his disciples owned a garden there, but the matter thus mentioned clearly implies that such gardens were on these occasions left open for all who needed them.

Appearance of Jerusalem during festivals.
I have often tried to realize the appearance of these profound valleys and high hills around Jerusalem during the great feasts. Covered with olive-groves, fruit-orchards, and vineyards, beneath whose friendly bowers many a happy family and neighbourhood group assembled, rising rank over rank to the very top of the mountains, I marvel that no artist has thought of reproducing this scene. Innumerable thousands gathered to the Passover, with happy children, busy servants, festooned victims, and all the joyful host, in picturesque costumes, hastening hither and thither, as business, or pleasure, or worship prompted, furnishing all the elements for the most magnificent and impressive panorama the world has ever beheld. It might require the lifetime of the artist, but he who should realize the idea would need to execute no other work.

Arrangement of the tribes
These hills, and valleys, and mounts lie all around the Holy City, as if on purpose for such convocations. The artist might arrange the tribes, with their ensigns and standards, round about Jerusalem, as they were commanded to pitch their tents about the Tabernacle in the wilderness. Judah would then occupy this Mount of Olives; for that tribe, with Issachar and Zebulun, encamped on the east side, toward the rising of the sun. Reuben, Simeon, and Gad, with their standards, pitched on the south. On the west were Ephraim, Manasseh, and Benjamin; and on the north, Dan, and Asher, and Naphtali.[3] Thus they continued to pitch and march for forty years. Now, it is not improbable that when the Tabernacle was in Gilgal and in Shiloh this same order was preserved, and, as far as circumstances permitted, it might have been kept up even after the Temple at Jerusalem took the place of the Tabernacle. Without some well-arranged system, there would be endless confusion in such vast assemblies. Each tribe, therefore, had its proper station on these noble hills. Every important city may also have had its appropriate quarter, every village its terrace, every family its shady tree or sheltered arbour. Fancy now, if you can, this great city, thus surrounded by all Israel, assembled here to worship; the glorious Temple towering up on Moriah like a pyramid of snow; the smoke of victims and the clouds of incense ascending up to heaven

---

[1] Mark xiv. 12–17.　　　　[2] John xviii. 1.　　　　[3] Numbers ii. 18.

from morning to night; while Temple, court, hall, street, valley, and hill side CHAPTER XLIV. echo and re-echo with the songs of Zion from millions of devout and joyful worshippers of the living God. Who would not join the sons of Korah in their triumphal psalm: "Great is the Lord, and greatly to be praised in the city of our God, in the mountain of his holiness. Beautiful for situation, the joy of the whole earth, is Mount Zion, the city of the great King. God is known in her palaces for a refuge. Walk about Zion, and go round about her: tell the towers thereof. Mark ye well her bulwarks, consider her palaces; that ye may tell it to the generation following. Let Zion rejoice, let the daughters of Israel be glad; for this God is our God for ever and ever: he will be our guide even unto death."[1]

Josephus, near the close of his Wars, gives the following rapid sketch of the Josephus' history of Jerusalem:[2] "He who first built it was a potent man among the of Jerusalem. Canaanites, and is in our tongue called the Righteous King, for such he really lem. was; on which account he was the first priest of God, and first built a temple, and called the city Jerusalem, which was formerly called Salem. However, David, the king of the Jews, ejected the Canaanites, and settled his own people therein. It was demolished entirely by the Babylonians four hundred and seventy-seven years and six months after him. And from king David, who was the first of the Jews who reigned therein, to this destruction under Titus, were one thousand one hundred and seventy-nine years; but from its first building till this last destruction were two thousand one hundred and seventy-seven years. It had been many times besieged and taken—first by David, then by Shishak, king of Egypt; afterward by Nebuchadnezzar, then by Antiochus; after him by Pompey, then by Sosius, then by Herod, and finally by Titus, in the second year of the reign of Vespasian, on the eighth day of the month Gorpieus"—September. He closes the sad story with this affecting remark: "Yet hath not its great antiquity, nor its vast riches, nor the diffusion of its nation over all the habitable earth, nor the greatness of the veneration paid to it on a religious account, been sufficient to preserve it from being destroyed."

How much importance do you attach to the statement of Jerome, that the Salem of Melchizedek was near Beisan?

Not enough to disturb my settled belief that he was mistaken. I follow Melchizedek. Josephus, and am convinced that his account coincides with the Bible; dek. but the old tradition that Melchizedek was no other than Shem is a vast improvement on the Jewish historian. Such an origin for the city of the great King is so gratifying that one is reluctant to carry research into the cold region of critical scepticism. Let us therefore believe, if we can, that here the son of Noah founded the City of Peace, reigned in righteousness, and was priest of the most high God. Perhaps it was near his very altar that Abraham, in a figure, offered up Isaac—type of that other sacrifice,

---

[1] Ps. xlviii.   [2] Wars vi. 10.

when an infinitely greater Father offered his only-begotten Son on this same mountain.

From Abraham's sacrificial visit to the conquest under Joshua there is nothing said about Jerusalem. At that time it bore the name of Jebus, and appears to have been already a very strong place. Though the king of it was slain in the great battle of Gibeon,[1] the city did not fall into the conqueror's hands, nor was it until the reign of David that the Jebusites were finally subdued. Having taken the stronghold, he transferred the seat of government at once from Hebron to Zion, and ever afterward Jerusalem appears as the capital of the Jewish commonwealth, and the centre of the Hebrew faith and worship.

Siege of Jerusalem by Titus.

The siege of Jerusalem occupied Titus four months and twenty-five days— from April 11th, A.D. 70, to the 7th of September. After this destruction we hear but little of Jerusalem until the reign of Hadrian. No doubt it was speedily occupied by both Jews and Christians, and I am disposed to credit Eusebius, who supposes that the city was not wholly destroyed by Titus. Indeed such a thing is scarcely to be imagined. There were, doubtless, multitudes of the lower vaulted rooms uninjured, and in these, when slightly repaired, a considerable population could reside, and no doubt did. Indeed, it soon acquired somewhat the proportion of a city and the character of a fortress, for when the Jews rebelled against Hadrian, about A.D. 132, it was able to make a prolonged resistance. Having destroyed it, Hadrian built a new town, which he called Ælia, and for several generations afterward Jerusalem was only spoken of under this heathen name. Constantine restored its ancient name, and greatly enriched and adorned it with splendid churches and other edifices. Henceforward it became the grand centre of pilgrimages from all parts of the Christian world, and such it has continued to be down to the present hour.

Modern history.

Jerusalem during the last fourteen centuries has suffered terrible calamities and undergone many important changes. It was taken by the Persians under Chosroes II., with vast slaughter. The Basilica of the Holy Sepulchre was burned, and the city sacked and pillaged, about the year 614; and in 636 it was permanently wrested from the Christians by the Khalif Omar. From this event to the appearance of the Crusaders before her walls, about the first of June 1099, the history of the city is almost a blank. There were, however, frequent contests between the Moslem rulers of Egypt and of Syria for its possession, and it suffered many calamities from its peculiar position and character, being sacred to Mohammedan, Christian, and Jew.

The Franks kept possession of it less than one hundred years, for it was given up to Saladin in 1187, and from that day to this it has remained in the hands of the Mohammedans. Saracen and Osmanly in succession have held it, and the flag of the Turk still floats over the Tower of David. Such is a

---

[1] Josh. x.

BETHANY.

rapid survey of the long history of Jerusalem. If it had existed 2177 years when overthrown by Titus, its whole age is now about 3964 years. Spreading over almost the entire historic period of the human race, it has shared largely in that history—*and the end is not yet !*

It took half an hour to walk over Olivet to Bethany this morning, and the distance from the city, therefore, must be about two miles. This agrees with what John says: "Now Bethany was nigh unto Jerusalem, about fifteen fur-longs off." [1] The village is small, and appears never to have been large, but it is pleasantly situated near the south-eastern base of the mount, and has many fine trees about and above it. We, of course, looked at the remains of those old edifices which may have been built in the age of Constantine, and repaired or changed to a convent in the time of the Crusades. By the dim light of a taper we also descended very cautiously, by twenty-five slippery steps, to the reputed sepulchre of Lazarus, or El Azariyeh, as both tomb and village are now called. But I have no description of it to give, and no questions about it to ask. It is a wretched cavern, every way unsatisfactory, and almost dis-gusting.

I have never been so painfully impressed as to-day with the importance of the advice, not to allow mere topographical controversies to rob one of the delightful and precious influences which these sacred scenes ought to afford. We not only disputed about the tomb of Lazarus, but fell into an earnest dis-cussion in regard to other matters equally indifferent—as whether Bethphage (of which no one now knows anything) was east or west of Bethany, according to the directions of our Lord to the two disciples in reference to the ass, or whether it might not have been on the north or south of the village. Then came the grand question about the true site of the "Ascension," whether in this church at Et Tûr, or on the spur of Olivet, which lies over against Bethany to the north ; and thus we walked through scenes suggestive of the most glorious anticipations to the Christian, with scarcely a single profitable reflec-tion. Indeed, we came out of the Church of the Ascension with feelings of utter disgust.

You have certainly fallen into a serious mistake. Olivet, including Geth-semane on the west, and Bethany on the east of it, has witnessed the most affecting and the most stupendous scenes in the history of our blessed Redeemer. It was in connection with this mount that the God-man—the divine Logos—chose to reveal more of his *human* nature than anywhere else on the earth. How often, after the fatigues and temptations of the day in this wicked and captious city, did he retire in the evening to Bethany to enjoy the hospitality and affectionate sympathy of Lazarus and his pious family ! There he laid aside the awful character of prophet and teacher divine, to rest his hard-tried energies in the gentle amenities of social life ; and such was the freedom of intercourse between these chosen friends, that Martha could even

[1] John xi. 18,

PART
IV.

come to him with her little domestic troubles. Alas! how many Marthas there are, careful and troubled about many things; and how few Marys, anxious to sit at Jesus' feet and hear his word! As excuse for this Martha, we should remember that she was the responsible house-keeper, and that they belonged to the class of society in which the women of the family performed the household work with their own hands, and hence it was perfectly natural that she should claim the assistance of her younger sister. What a touching exhibition of lowliness and divine condescension does this reveal! He who is Lord of the universe selects, of choice, the humble poor for his dearest friends and most intimate associates! "He whom thou lovest is sick," was the only message sent by the sorrowing sisters. Most honourable distinction! He whom angels adored, and from heaven to earth hastened to serve, lavishes his richest love upon a poor man called Lazarus! The Son of God groaned in spirit at the sorrow of Mary and Martha. He *wept* over the grave of his friend. He did more. He asked of the Eternal Father, and received power to raise him from the grave, and, standing at the head of that dark cave, he cried with a loud voice, "Lazarus, come forth!" Wonderful voice! It startled the dull ear of Death, and the inexorable Grave heard, and gave up his prey. Here on Olivet the Christian learns to sing the song of victory over the king of terrors: "O Grave, where is thy victory? O Death, where is thy sting?" No wonder that much people of the Jews came six days after, not for Jesus' sake only, but that they might see Lazarus also, whom he had raised from the dead; nor that on the next day they should take branches of palm-trees and go forth to meet Jesus, crying, "Hosanna! blessed is the King of Israel that cometh in the name of the Lord!"[1]

Conde-
scension
of Jesus.

Again: it was on this mount, with the city and Temple in view, that our Lord sat down, and in private answered those three pregnant inquiries of the anxious disciples: *When shall it come to pass that there shall not be left one stone of the Temple upon another? What shall be the sign of thy coming?* and the sign *of the end of the world?*[2] And in response there fell from his sacred lips those wonderful revelations recorded in the 24th and 25th chapters of Matthew. It was from this same mount, also, that the compassionate Jesus beheld the city and wept over it, saying, "If thou hadst known, even thou, at least in this thy day, the things which belong unto thy peace! but now they are hid from thine eyes."[3]

Sacred
scenes on
Olivet.

It was also unto Olivet that he retired to pray on that doleful night when "his sweat became as it were great drops of blood falling down to the ground."[4] Here he was betrayed with a kiss; was surrounded by soldiers with lanterns, and torches, and swords; was rudely seized, bound with cords as a malefactor, and led away to Caiaphas.

And, finally, this favoured mount witnessed the glorious out-come and

---

[1] John xii. 1, 9, 12, 13.   [2] Matt. xxiv. 3.
[3] Luke xix. 42.   [4] Luke xxii. 44.

consummation of this mystery of sorrow and suffering. It had been watered CHAPTER
by his tears, had drunk his bloody sweat, and it must also behold his trium- XLIV.
phant and glorious ascension to the right hand of the Majesty on high. The
Olivet first heard the grand commission to the Church: "Go YE INTO ALL THE Ascension
WORLD, AND PREACH THE GOSPEL TO EVERY CREATURE." He had led out his
disciples as far as to Bethany, and, having thus spoken, "he lifted up his
hands, and blessed them; and it came to pass that while he blessed them, he
was parted from them, and carried up into heaven."[1] Men of Galilee! favoured
of God above all the race, I would, oh! I would have been of your company
on that triumphant morning,—with you to look steadfastly toward heaven as
he went up, and with you to worship; or, better still, I would have been
among the heavenly host that—

> "Thronged his chariot-wheels,
> And bore him to his throne;
> Then swept their golden harps, and sung,
> "The glorious work is done!'"

---

[1] Luke xxiv. 50, 51.

INDEX OF NAMES AND SUBJECTS.

EXPLANATIONS OF TERMS AND CONTRACTIONS USED.

'Ain, Hebrew En, Fountain.
Beit, Hebrew Beth, House.
Deir, Convent.
Jebel, Mountain.
Jisr, Bridge.
Khan, Caravansary.
Kul'aet, Castle.
Mazar, Shrine.

Merj, Plain.
Nahr, River.
Neb'a, large Fountain.
Neby, Prophet.
Scr. all., Scripture allusions to.
Tell, Mound, Hill.
Vill., Village.
Wady or W., Valley and Brook.

Gether, land of, 251.

Gethsemane, garden of, described, 634.

Ghawaraneh, Arabs of the Hûleh, 255.

Ghazziyeh, vill., 140.

Ghor Beisan, extent and fertility of, 454; Scripture sites in, 456.

Ghufr en N'aamy, khan, 58.

Ghujar, Nusairîyeh, vill., 164, 226.

Giants, scr. all. to, 586; Rabbinical and Arab stories about, 586, 587.

Gibeon and Gibeonites, their doom, 668, 669; great waters at, and incidents connected with, 669, 670.

Gideon threshing in a vineyard, 448; overthrows the Midianites, 449, 550.

Gihon, 641; pools of, 655.

Gilboa, mountain, rain and dew on, 452; range of, 462.

Gilgal, Jiljulia, 524, 612, 613.

Glass, discovery of, 313; manufactured at Hebron, 584, 585.

Gnats and fleas at Tiberias, 411, 412.

Goats, wild, 603.

Golden gate, 629.

Goliath's battle with David, 567.

Gourd of Jonah, 69, 70.

Grass on house-tops, scr. all. to, 682.

Gulgal, possibly the wild artichoke, 563, 564.

Hadathy, vill., 443.

Halhul, vill., 600.

Hamath, entrance of, 233, 238; water-wheels of, 518.

Hamathites, 164.

Hammath of Naphtali (Emmaus), 395–399.

Hand-mills, women grinding at, scr. all. to, 526, 527.

Hands, washing of, 128.

Harbours, Phoenician, want of, 100.

Harothieh, Harosheth of the Gentiles, identification discussed, 436, 438, 479.

Hart, 171.

Harvest, among thorns, 348; scene in Philistia, 543.

Hasbany, river, Upper Jordan, 214.

Hauran, country of, 365.

Hawk, migration of, scr. all. to, 326.

Hazor, city, destroyed by Joshua, 215, 216; site of, 285.

Heber the Kenite, 272; on plain of Esdraelon, 437, 438.

Hebrews, increase of, in Egypt, 595, 596.

Hebron, first view of, 577; houses, population, pools, vineyards of, 582, 583; glass factory at, 584, 585; antiquity and history of, 585; not visited by our Saviour, 585; Lower Pool of, 596, 597; houses and watch-towers in vineyards of, 597, 598; Scripture sites in neighbourhood of, 600, 601.

Hens, not mentioned in Old Testament, 671.

Hermon, seen from Sarepto, 159; view of,

from plain of Tyre, 177; seen from Dead Sea, 611.

Herodium, Frank mountain, Jebel Fureidîs, 607.

Hero-worship, 328.

Hibbariyeh, temple at, Greek inscription,232.

Hidden treasure at Sidon, 134, 137; at Safed, 272; existence of, accounted for, 136; infatuation of seekers for, 135.

High places, scr. all. to, 141, 142.

Hind, 171.

Hinnom, valley of, idolatrous worship in, 641; sacrifice of children in, 641, 642.

Hiram, extent of his kingdom, 189; tomb of, 196.

Hittites, 162.

Hivites, 164.

Hobah, ancient city, 215.

Holy fire in Church of the Sepulchre, 679.

Holy Land, physical features of, typical, 340, 341.

Holy Sepulchre, Church of, 673–678; sacred shrines within it, 674; scenes enacted in it, 675, 676; description of the edifice, 676, 677; of the "sepulchre," 677; of Calvary, 677, 678; not site of the crucifixion, 678, 679; holy fire in, 679.

Honey in forest-trees and in carcass of a lion, 566.

Hoopoe, Hedhood, 76, 77.

Horned ladies, tantour, 73.

Horns, scr. all. to, 74.

Hot springs at Emmaus, 395; are hot springs mentioned in the Bible? 396.

House on the city wall, 97, 98; windows of, 97, 98; summer and winter houses, 309; Arab, construction of the roof described, 358, 359; built with untempered mortar, 390, 391.

Household furniture, 126–128; suitable to the character of Oriental life, 127.

House-top, proclamation from, 41, 42; scr. all. to, 41, 43.

Hul, land of, 251.

Hula, wady and village, 212.

Huleh, marsh and plain, 214; battle-ground of Abraham, 214, 215; ditto of Joshua, 215; ditto of the Danites, 216; ditto of Joab against Sheba, 216, 217; beauty of the plain, 225.

Huleh, lake of, 259; wild fowls on, 260, 261.

Humsin, column and ruins, 307.

Hunin, castle, 218; a night at, 221, 222.

Huttin, vill., horns of, 423; great hedges of cactus, 424; legends of, 424; Saladin's victory at, 424.

Hyssop, 112.

Idolatry, prevalent sin of all Oriental sects, 640.

Ijon, plain and city, 222, 223.

INDEX OF SCRIPTURE TEXTS ILLUSTRATED.